The Keyboard Music of
J. S. Bach

The Keyboard Music of J. S. Bach

DAVID SCHULENBERG

SCHIRMER BOOKS
An Imprint of Macmillan Publishing Company
NEW YORK

Maxwell Macmillan Canada
TORONTO

Maxwell Macmillan International
NEW YORK   OXFORD   SINGAPORE   SYDNEY

Schirmer Books   Maxwell Macmillan Canada, Inc.
Macmillan Publishing Company   1200 Eglinton Avenue East, Suite 200
866 Third Avenue, New York, N.Y. 10022   Don Mills, Ontario M3C 3NL

Macmillan, Inc., is part of the Maxwell Communication Group of Companies.

Library of Congress Catalog Card Number: 91-39348

PRINTED IN THE UNITED STATES OF AMERICA

printing number
1   2   3   4   5   6   7   8   9   10

LIBRARY OF CONGRESS CATALOGING-IN-PUBLICATION DATA
Schulenberg, David.
     The keyboard music of J. S. Bach / David Schulenberg.
        p.   cm.
     Includes bibliographical references (p.   ).
     Includes index.
     ISBN 0-02-873275-8 (alk. paper)
     1. Bach, Johann Sebastian, 1685-1750 Keyboard music. 2. Keyboard
  instrument music—Analysis, appreciation.   I. Title.
MT145.B14S415   1992
786'.092—dc20   91-39348
                                                                    CIP
                                                                     MN

The paper used in this publication meets the minimum requirements of American
National Standard for Information Sciences—Permanence of Paper for Printed Library
Materials. ANSI Z39.48-1984. ⊚™

To Gail

Contents

Preface

This book is intended to serve as a guide to and commentary on Bach's keyboard music. It is meant above all for the student, teacher, listener, or scholar seeking information, analysis, and criticism about individual works. While it may serve as a reference book, it can also be read from cover to cover or chapter by chapter, as one wishes—preferably with score, instrument, or recording at hand.

The vast expansion of information on the subject has made it impossible to gather in one volume anything but a small and inevitably personal selection of information and views. The only previous guides to Bach's complete keyboard output are the works listed in the bibliography as Keller (1950) and Bodky (1960), which are now quite out of date and inadequate to the needs of serious students of this music. Thus, the present work is inevitably much larger. Moreover, while not focusing on textual criticism, this book reflects the nature of modern Bach scholarship in its frequent discussion of sources (manuscripts and early prints), readings, and editions. Indeed, one of its purposes is to review and make available to the English-speaking reader the products of recent scholarly work on Bach, much of which is virtually inaccessible to all but specialists.

I have sought to balance the discussions of texts and editions with material of an interpretive nature, including suggestions concerning problems of performance practice. Actually, if recent studies in music have taught us anything, it is that analysis, criticism, and "positivistic" textual research are interrelated with one another and with the actual business of performing and listening to music. The date and readings of a given source may provide clues to both the compositional history of a work and the instrument for which it was written; from this one might proceed to choices about tempo or the interpretation of the work's rhythmic notation—choices that influence the work's expressive character and are therefore crucial to criticism.

The nature of this book limits how deeply one can delve into individual works. But where it seemed important to do so I have presented relatively extensive discussions of individual issues: the compositional history of several movements of the *Well-Tempered Clavier*, the tonal and harmonic structure of the Chromatic Fantasia, the interpretation of dotted rhythms in the B-minor overture, and so forth. I have also attempted to contribute to ongoing debates over such questions as the authenticity and dating of some of the early works attributed to Bach, the nature of and reasons behind his revisions in particular compositions, and the identity of the keyboard instrument for which he composed his "clavier" music. In addition, I have occasionally noted relationships between Bach's music and that of his sons Wilhelm Friedemann and Carl Philipp Emanuel, whose works, once regarded as stylistically quite independent of their father's, can now be viewed as a continuation of the more galant side of Sebastian's multifaceted musical personality. While it has naturally been impossible to discuss every work in depth, I hope that readers will be encouraged to extend the approaches to problems of analysis, textual criticism, and performance practice adopted here to other pieces.

Chapter 1 serves as introduction and explains in greater detail the purpose of the book and how I imagine it being used. It also discusses other vital matters such as the precise extent of the repertory under discussion. Chapters 2 and 3 contain introductory discussions of performance practice and Bach's stylistic development. The remainder of the book consists of commentaries on the individual works, grouped into chapters according to genre and, very approximately, chronology. While the format of individual chapters varies, depending on the nature of the works discussed, each chapter (after the first three) opens with a general introduction to the group of works covered, followed by the commentaries on individual works.

In some chapters the commentaries are prefaced by lists of sources and editions; these, where present, are intended to be representative, not comprehensive. Dates or copyists' names are included in the listings of sources only where these are firmly established in the existing literature. For certain pieces whose texts seemed defective as presented in modern editions, I have offered lists of emendations at the ends of the individual commentaries. These lists are not meant to serve as detailed accounts of variant readings, nor is space available for discussion of the philological and analytical reasoning underlying most of the suggestions. The readings listed are those of the sources, as opposed to the available editions; readings placed in brackets or followed by question marks are my own conjectures.

Several readers of early versions of the book objected to the extensive coverage of the early works, the "lute" works, and the *Art of Fugue*, which are not what one usually thinks of when one hears the expresion "Bach keyboard music." But these are vital parts of the portion of Bach's *œuvre* that was composed with keyboard performance in mind. They are not to be left out simply because the nineteenth- and early twentieth-century performing tradition neglected them or mistakenly assigned them to other instruments. The continuing neglect of these pieces, at least by keyboard players, is due in part to the undeniable problems of text, style, and performance practice that they raise. All the more reason, however, to consider them here, in the hope that they will once again become widely accepted as parts of Bach's keyboard repertory.

As in any scholarly work, I have tried to make it clear whether I am presenting my own views, those of others, or generally acknowledged facts. But the literature on Bach is so vast that to cite every relevant work at every point would have been impractical. The citations concentrate on recent writings, and I have often stated without citation older findings that have passed into general currency as well as observations about the works that would occur to anyone who studied them closely. I apologize to those whose ideas I have borrowed without citation and acknowledge here my great debt to the many who have preceded me.

While I have consulted all the readily available published facsimiles of early musical sources (manuscripts and early prints), as well as microfilms of many others, I have relied heavily on the commentaries of various editions for information about titles, contents, and readings. Where I have not cited a source for such information, it should be understood as coming from one of several standard sources: a critical edition (usually one of the two collected editions of Bach's works), the Schmieder thematic catalogue, or Kast's catalogue of the Berlin Bach manuscripts. In suggesting readings for certain early works I have also consulted the lists of variants in Robert Hill's 1987 dissertation. A number of scholars have kindly provided information from forthcoming publications and editions. But inevitably I will have overlooked some material. New sources and new readings are continually being discovered and reevaluated; a salutary example occurred during the final stages of preparing this volume, when a supposedly fragmentary source for one work was found to be complete (see Chapter 10 on BWV 895). At this writing the keyboard volume of the *Bach-Compendium* (BC) has not been published; it can be expected to supplement the present discussions of sources.

The writer of a volume such as this incurs numerous debts. Portions of the book were read prior to publication by Russell Stinson, Robert Marshall, Joshua Rifkin, Howard Schott, Christoph Wolff, and several other known and anonymous readers, to each of whom I am most grateful. I also owe thanks for useful information, fascinating ideas, suggestions, and comments offered in conversation and correspondence by Joshua Rifkin, Peter Wollny, Howard Schott, Laurence Dreyfus, Michael Marissen, E. Eugene Helm, Rachel Wade, David Kopp, Peter Kirwin, Robert Mealy, Peter Watchorn, and many others. While writing I was honored by and I remain grateful for fellowships from the Andrew Mellon Foundation (held at New York University) and the American Council of Learned Societies. I also received invaluable support and encouragement from many friends, several of whom were generous enough to place their instruments at my disposal for practice and study when no others were available to me. Above all I thank Gail Glintenkamp for her unceasing understanding and patience.

A Note on Musical Examples, Bar Numbers, and Pitch Names

Unless otherwise indicated, bar numbers and readings are those of the most recent scholarly edition named in the commentary on the work in question. In citations of bar numbers, small letters (e.g., 5a, 27b) indicate the first and second halves of measures, respectively. Large letters (5A, 27B) refer to first and second endings. Bar numbers for two or more parallel passages are often given in the form "bars 63–65 || 56–58," where the sign || means "are parallel to" or "are closely based upon."

The examples have been checked, where possible, against original sources (or, rather, films and facsimiles thereof). They are, however, for illustration only and do not pretend to present critically edited texts. In many cases the notation has been altered in the interest of legibility, economy of space, or clarification of the point illustrated.

Pitches are named using the Helmholtz system, which is descended from the German keyboard tablature occasionally used by Bach. Middle C is c'; the notes below and above it are b and d', respectively. The pitches an octave lower are B, c, d; an octave higher, b', c", d". Notes below C (two octaves below c') are designated by double letters (AA, BB).

The Keyboard Music of
J. S. Bach

1

Bach's Keyboard Music: An Introduction

Bach's keyboard works form one of the oldest and most important repertories of Western compositions that have remained in active use since their conception. Although his church music passed into oblivion soon after his death, his keyboard works continued to be highly valued and assiduously studied, at first by a relatively small circle of students and admirers, but in ever-widening circles that now encompass virtually everyone who has ever played or listened to Western art music.

The fact that Bach's music—some of it, at least—has always been in the repertory of performers hardly means that its performance and interpretation represent a uniform or unbroken tradition. Every generation has had its own image of Bach's music and of Bach himself. The image presented in this book has been shaped by modern Bach scholarship and colored by modern Bach performance. Since 1950, Bach studies have been one of the richest and most active spheres of musicological activity, producing a new edition of his works as well as discoveries that have overturned previously held convictions about their dating, their manner of performance, and their relationship to other eighteenth-century music and culture in general. Performers, drawing on this scholarship and on the work of instrument builders, on researches into historical performing practice, and on practical experience, have revealed new aspects of the works and revised the ways in which both their sound and their expressive content are understood.

The remainder of this chapter—as well as the two following—provides introductory matter likely to be especially useful to those who are not professional Bach specialists. Otherwise, what is offered here is, to use the apt term employed in Peter Williams's magisterial survey of the organ works (1980–84), a commentary on the keyboard works. The commentary, which begins in Chapter 4, includes what seemed at the time of writing the most essential historical background as well as other appropriate material about the editions of each work, the literature on it, and the work itself. But the literature on Bach is so voluminous and the music itself so

1

rich and multifaceted that any survey is bound to consist of a fairly subjective selection of facts and observations. Still, the aim has been to present the findings of recent scholarship while balancing textual and source-critical discussions with notes on problems of analysis, performance practice, and other interpretive matters. The works in each chapter are roughly contemporary with one another and belong to the same or closely related genres; for example, Chapters 4–7 deal with early works (suites, fugues, toccatas, etc.), Chapters 10–12 with the *Well-Tempered Clavier* and works leading up to it, Chapters 13–15 with the mature suites and partitas. As in any *catalogue raisonné*, the reader is invited to skip forward to discussions of whichever pieces are of the greatest interest.

The Repertory

The boundaries of the subject covered in this book have been the object of considerable debate. Here, "keyboard music" means those compositions for a single keyboard instrument that lack a full-fledged pedal part and do not fall into any of the genres that imply the use of the organ, such as the *pedaliter* chorale prelude. Roughly 200 of Bach's pieces meet this definition, falling into three general categories: (1) suites, partitas, and similar works; (2) preludes and fugues, including pieces under such titles as fantasia, toccata, and sinfonia; and (3) a miscellaneous group containing variation sets, sonatas, a concerto, and transcriptions of works originally composed for other instruments.

Unfortunately, while Bach's intentions regarding the instrumentation of his ensemble works were usually very precise—far more precise than is sometimes thought—he was reluctant to indicate any precise medium for most of the music discussed here. The works have long been regarded as being for the "clavier," but the meaning of that term has changed with time. During Bach's lifetime it was probably a generic term for any musical keyboard; after his death it acquired the more specific meaning of "clavichord" and, in the nineteenth century, of "piano." Today, although pianists everywhere play some of this music, the works are generally regarded as having been meant for the harpsichord. Robert Marshall (1986) has argued, however, that, while some of this repertory really was conceived for the harpsichord, much of it was not. Thus, he has proposed a division between works for harpsichord—essentially, group 1 in the list above—and generic "clavier" works, which contain most of the remaining pieces. This proposal, although it has not yet found general acceptance, has the substantial merit of corresponding with Bach's own intentions insofar as they can be discovered from explicit indications of medium in the authoritative sources. That many of the proposed "clavier" works were, in practice if not in principle, composed for the harpsichord and not for some generic clavier will be argued in Chapter 2 and in the discussions of the individual pieces. Nevertheless, the term "keyboard music" has been adopted here, despite possible objections, as the best English expression that can be applied to the repertory in question without making questionable assumptions about the intended medium.

The keyboard music, so understood, forms one of the four main divisions of

Bach's output, the others being the organ works, the works for instrumental ensemble, and the sacred and secular vocal music. The distinction now made between organists and harpsichordists, and thus between organ music and "keyboard" music, might have surprised Bach and some of his students, who appear to have been equally at home on both instruments.[1] Nevertheless, the distinction between organ and "keyboard" music is a real one, based on differences in style and genre that are usually (though not always) clearly drawn. Moreover, the keyboard works have a somewhat exceptional place in Bach's œuvre, for they were the one part of it that was not written in direct fulfillment of any of Bach's official duties.

If we discount his school years and a brief early stint as a "lackey" (Lacquey) at Weimar, Bach began his professional career as an organist, serving in the cities of Arnstadt (1703–7) and Mühlhausen (1708) and in the ducal court of Weimar (1708–14). He was then promoted to Concertmeister at Weimar and later served as Capellmeister to the Prince of Cöthen (1717–23). From there he went to Leipzig, where he remained Director musices (director of church music) and Cantor of the St. Thomas school for the rest of his life. In each of these posts Bach was expected to produce music to order. Thus, at Weimar and Leipzig he provided new church cantatas on a regular basis, at least for portions of his tenure there.[2] Many of the instrumental works appear to have been written at Cöthen; some probably date from Weimar, others from Leipzig, but all were probably composed for specific performances, including concerts by the Leipzig Collegium Musicum, which Bach directed from 1729 to 1737 and again from 1739 to 1741. Bach probably composed much of his organ music on a similar occasional basis; many, perhaps most, of these works date from the Weimar years and earlier, although a significant number were revised at Leipzig.

Keyboard pieces, however, seem to have flowed from Bach's hands in substantial numbers throughout his career. This is likely to reflect a continual association with the harpsichord, an instrument with which Bach must have been engaged throughout his life with the same intensity as with the organ, if not more so. While he was officially employed as a keyboard player—that is, organist—only at Arnstadt, Mühlhausen, and Weimar, titles could be misleading. Whatever his formal designation during a briefly held position at Weimar in 1703, when Bach came to Arnstadt he was regarded there as Weimar court organist.[3] In addition to playing organ he may well have participated, especially during the main Weimar period (1708–17), in rehearsals and performances in which he accompanied and perhaps directed ensembles from the harpsichord. This he certainly did at Cöthen and Leipzig, in secular works like the Brandenburg Concerti and cantatas composed for the Collegium Musicum, and perhaps in sacred works as well.[4] Indeed, the only contemporary report of a church performance mentions Bach playing harpsichord—that is, directing the ensemble while improvising a basso continuo realization—in the Trauerode (BWV 198) of 1727.[5]

There is little evidence for Bach's having performed any solo harpsichord music as a part of his public or official roles; solo harpsichord playing in public would probably have been confined to the occasional keyboard concerto. The organ was the only keyboard instrument with a tradition of use in public recitals, and thus the keyboard music considered in this book must have been composed largely for private practice and study. But Bach would have had occasion to play solo keyboard pieces, presumably on the harpsichord, before small audiences in less formal situations and possibly for his aristocratic patrons at Weimar and Cöthen.[6] Moreover, because of the inconveniences that would have attended organ practice—bellows had to be pumped, and churches were unheated—the harpsichord must have played a major role in Bach's teaching as well as in his own early study of keyboard playing. We know that Bach played keyboard pieces now and then for his students at Leipzig; presumably these performances were on the harpsichord, although other instruments are not out of the question.[7]

Sources

Only a fraction of Bach's keyboard pieces were published during his lifetime. Most, even the few that appeared in print, circulated mainly in manuscripts, the majority of which appear to have been copied by students during the course of their studies.[8] While Bach's own scores survive for some of the most important works, autographs are lacking for many others and for almost all of the earlier music. Early works, in particular, are sometimes preserved in but a single manuscript copy, and this has naturally led to disputes over the authenticity of certain pieces. Even where autographs do survive, they are generally fair copies or revision scores, not first drafts, making it difficult to establish when works were originally composed.[9] Still, it is fascinating to reconstruct the process of correction and revision that is clearly visible in some of the autographs; even where no autograph survives it is often possible to trace the course of Bach's revisions for a piece by comparing the readings of copies made from different versions of his own score.

Although sources are not the primary focus of this book, any critical examination of certain pieces must consider their authenticity, date, text, and compositional history—that is, Bach's successive revisions. All these subjects are closely intertwined with the study of the sources themselves, which need not be viewed as a necessary evil or an avoidable exercise in "positivistic" musicology. The sources open a window onto the working habits and even the personalities of their writers and copyists, most of whom were professional keyboard players like Bach. Apart from the inherent value in establishing the correct reading of a disputed passage, or in following Bach's own thought as he corrected details of counterpoint or reorganized whole sets of pieces, the sources offer insights into how Bach's music spread beyond his own circle: who copied what, how widely individual pieces were disseminated, and how those outside Bach's circle understood or misunderstood his intentions.[10]

Both manuscripts and prints of Bach's works have been the subjects of intensive study, and modern Bach scholarship has gone to extraordinary lengths to identify the handwriting, paper, and other aspects of the manuscripts. Even the gradual changes undergone by handwriting over time have been carefully studied, not only for Bach himself but for many of the copyists. Through this has come a slow but steady improvement in our understanding of when certain pieces were written and what revisions, if any, they underwent. Nevertheless, the sheer number of keyboard pieces and of manuscripts containing them has contributed to their being the last of the four large groups of Bach's works to be studied in this manner, and many questions remain open and perhaps unanswerable.

The manuscripts range from single sheets of paper inscribed with a few lines of music to massive volumes comprising once-separate manuscripts that have been bound together. They may be in the hand of Bach himself (autographs) or in the hand of someone else (copies). The greatest concentration of Bach manuscripts is in Berlin, but there are major collections in other European cities (Leipzig, Dresden, Göttingen, Vienna, Brussels), and important sources can be found in London, New Haven, Washington, D.C., and even Tokyo.[11] Among the copyists are students or associates of Bach who were important musical figures in their own right. Others have yet to be identified by name, although the distinctive features of their handwriting have been recognized; these include Anonymous 5, Anonymous 303, and several others who have become as familiar as the named copyists to two generations of Bach scholars. Usually the most important manuscripts are autographs or contemporary copies by members of Bach's immediate circle, but for some works the only surviving manuscripts were made by peripheral figures of the later eighteenth and early nineteenth centuries. A few copyists were responsible for assembling large manuscript compilations, and as these will be referred to in many of the individual commentaries they are briefly described at the end of this chapter.

The printed sources that interest us are primarily those which Bach himself published (or prepared for publication), beginning in 1726 with the Partitas and ending with the posthumously issued *Art of Fugue*. These were the only substantial publications of Bach's keyboard music in the eighteenth century, although editions of previously unpublished works began to appear in profusion at the very beginning of the nineteenth century. Music printing and publishing in the first half of the eighteenth century were very different from today or even in the later eighteenth century; how this bears on our understanding of the music will become clear in the relevant discussions (Chapters 15–18).

Catalogues and Editions

Since 1950 the thematic catalogue by Wolfgang Schmieder (SWV) has been the basic reference source, listing Bach's works as well as providing dates, bibliographic entries, and much other useful information. Although recently revised, Schmieder's work will probably be supplanted in time by the *Bach-Compendium* (BC) of Hans-Joachim Schulze and Christoph Wolff. But Schmieder's catalogue numbers ("BWV" numbers) are likely to remain the standard way of referring to both authentic and inauthentic works that have been attributed to Bach. The BWV numbers are not chronological; compositions are listed by medium, beginning with vocal works, then music for organ, music for "clavier," and finally works for other instruments and for instrumental ensemble.[12] Within each of these four groups are subdivisions for the various genres. Ordering within the subdivisions follows no obvious principle, although at times it seems to reflect the arrangement of pieces in the old Bachgesamtausgabe (BG).

That edition, produced between 1850 and 1900 by the German Bach Society

(Bach-Gesellschaft), was one of the first and most successful scholarly editions of a composer's complete works. Although many pieces, including much of the keyboard music, had already appeared in good editions, for most works the BG set a high standard of accuracy and scholarship, and it remained the basis for most subsequent editions of Bach's music published in the first half of the twentieth century. It remains indispensible for Bach scholars. But the New Bach Edition (Neue Bach-Ausgabe, or NBA), in progress since the 1950s, represents the findings of modern Bach research, and its texts are in general superior to those of the BG. This is especially true for the keyboard works, and publishers who continue to put out editions and reprints based on the BG or other nineteenth-century editions do musicians a grave disservice.

Unfortunately, at this writing the NBA is incomplete and likely to remain so for some time to come. For works not yet issued in the NBA, players and students must often make do with various so-called Urtext editions that cannot be particularly recommended. It cannot be too strongly emphasized that an edition that adds fingerings or indications of dynamics, articulation, or ornamentation, even if carried out according to the latest theories on "authentic" performance, is no "original text" (Urtext). Implicit in such markings are many interpretive decisions that all too readily insinuate themselves into a player's interpretation. For example, the fingerings in modern editions are usually based on the late nineteenth-century principle of maintaining as smooth a legato as possible. The manual contortions sometimes needed to ensure legato can lead in turn to questionable decisions about tempo or registration. Even the harpsichordist who owns a perfect new instrument and follows the latest word on historically informed performance practice will find that confronting Bach's music on its own terms is impossible if a faulty text or an editor's fingerings are in the way.

Some Major Manuscript Sources for the Early Works

The Andreas Bach Book (ABB) and the Möller Manuscript (MM) are the earliest of the major Bach sources.[13] Compiled by Bach's older brother and teacher, Johann Christoph of Ohrdruf, both are known by the names of later owners. The long-debated identity of the principal copyist of these manuscripts was established by Schulze (1984a, 52–56); Hill (1987) is a detailed study. Hill identified some of the subsidiary copyists and showed that MM is probably the earlier of the two, copied while Bach was at Arnstadt; ABB corresponds more or less with the beginning of the Weimar period.

Both manuscripts contain a repertory of "free" pieces for both organ and harpsichord—suites, preludes and fugues, sonatas, transcriptions of French and German orchestral music—but almost no chorale pieces. The contents include many of Bach's most important early works, several in his own hand. Most of the copies are accurate, although some contain ornaments added later.

DSB P 801, P 802, and P 803 form a complex of manuscripts related to Johann

Gottfried Walther, the Weimar organist and composer who was a friend and relative of Bach. P 801 and P 802 include copies not only by Walther but by his student Johann Tobias Krebs, who also studied with Bach. So did Krebs's son Johann Ludwig, whose hand appears in P 803. P 802 contains chiefly chorale settings, but P 801 and P 803 include important copies of Bach keyboard works as well as harpsichord works by Dieupart and other French composers and transcriptions of orchestral music. The dates of the copies have not been positively determined, but the Bach works appear mostly in early versions that presumably date from Weimar, in generally accurate copies.[14]

SPK P 804, unrelated to the previous group, comprises fifty-seven separate fascicles, each originally an independent manuscript. Known in the nineteenth century as the "Kellner miscellaney," it belonged to Johann Peter Kellner, an organist, composer, and apparently an acquaintance if not an actual student of Bach, whose works he began copying in about 1725. Stinson (1989a) is a comprehensive study of this and several other Kellner manuscripts.[15]

Among Kellner's Bach copies are the sole sources for many pieces and the earliest known sources for others. Not all of the Bach works were copied from scores obtained from Bach himself, and Kellner's tendency to add ornaments and make other changes has raised questions about his dependability. Especially serious is the question of the reliability of his attributions, especially where Kellner merely provided a title for a copy in another hand. Some pieces were even left anonymous but have been generally accepted as Bach's.[16] The traditional attributions are accepted here, but it remains curious that Kellner should have copied or collected pieces that Bach's own students and sons apparently ignored during the same period.

The *Mempell-Preller* collection consists of separate manuscripts in several libraries; these manuscripts originally belonged to Johann Nicolaus Mempell, cantor from 1740 at Apolda near Weimar, and Johann Gottlieb Preller, apparently his pupil and later cantor at Dortmund. The two most important manuscripts are LEm mss. 7 and 8; the most complete discussion of the collection is in Schulze (1984a, 67–87). Of the two main copyists (other hands are present as well), Mempell is usually the more reliable. It has been proposed that he studied with Kellner, but this has not been positively established, and it is uncertain how Mempell obtained the works by Bach. Despite its relatively late date and sometimes inaccurate texts, the collection is the sole source for a number of works, including several of Bach's earliest compositions; here, too, attribution is a problem that must be dealt with on a piece-by-piece basis.

2

Some Performance
Questions

It is no longer possible to discuss Bach's keyboard music without considering how it was originally performed and how it was meant to be performed. Unfortunately, performance practice in the repertory as a whole is far too large a topic to be discussed adequately in any one book, let alone a single chapter. Selected questions will be raised in the discussions of individual pieces. Certain general problems recur so often in Bach's keyboard music, however, that it seems advisable to mention them briefly and suggest possible solutions before considering the works themselves.

The present discussion is necessarily abbreviated and does not include detailed explanations for the conclusions reached. It is directed more toward nonharpsichordists than to those already well versed in eighteenth-century performing practice, and it is intended to give pianists and players of other modern instruments an idea of how harpsichordists approach certain practical aspects of Bach interpretation. It would be inappropriate for the author, himself a harpsichordist, to offer more than a few technical suggestions for pianists, but they and others are invited to incorporate any insights gained here into their own approach to Bach.[1]

One general comment, however, might be offered. Beginning students today are frequently expected to deal with certain Bach keyboard pieces in a stylistic vacuum. That is, they are expected not only to master the music's considerable technical difficulties but also to gain some interpretive insight into it without ever having heard adequate performances of works by Bach's forerunners and contemporaries—composers such as Corelli, Couperin, or Telemann, who in many cases provided somewhat simpler models for Bach's own works. Bach's own students certainly had access to such music—indeed, they evidently studied it before graduating to his own works (see Appendix B)—and they were, of course, surrounded by "authentic" performances of eighteenth-century music. Teachers today can hardly provide the latter. But at the very least they owe it to their students to gain some familiarity themselves with recent, stylish performances of the music from which Bach himself learned.

"Authenticity"

In recent years the most fundamental controversy in performance practice has revolved around the concept of authenticity.[2] The word itself has been so frequently misused and misunderstood that it is now generally avoided by serious students of historical performance practice. In practice the expressions "authentic" and "historically accurate" have come to mean performance on "original" instruments, but no reputable performer or scholar today claims that merely using an old instrument (or a supposed copy thereof), or even playing it according to the latest ideas about historical performing practice, assures fidelity to the score or to the composer's intentions. Indeed, few players are so naive as to suppose that it is possible to discover and reproduce Bach's (or anyone else's) precise intentions concerning the performance of a particular work, especially when it is unclear that he even had a specific intention about something as fundamental as the medium of the "clavier" works.

Still, the concept of authenticity is perhaps worth saving (as argued in Schulenberg 1990 and Schulenberg 1991), not only in the sense of following an authentic text—that is, the score as the composer left it—but of interpreting it according to the conventions of the time, as best we can understand them. Authenticity in this sense seems fairly noncontroversial, especially when applied to such mundane things as the realization of ornament signs or the interpretation of rhythmic notation. Temperatures rise when "authentic" interpretation begins to affect not only the actual sounds but the expressive character of the music. That expression is central to the debate is clear from a notorious exchange over the dotting of the French overture. The differences between the participants ultimately came down to the fact that what seemed majestic to one listener sounded jerky and awkward to another.[3]

One might suppose that it would be better to play such pieces in a way that conveyed "majesty" to twentieth-century listeners, even if this meant ignoring certain eighteenth-century conventions. But Bach's (or Mattheson's, or Telemann's) majesty is not the same as that of Beethoven or Verdi or Copland. Besides, musical compositions, or at least those of a master composer like Bach, do not exist in order to express simple affects like majesty. They are complex, integrated musical organisms in which sonority, rhythm, ornamentation, and other aspects of performance practice are as much a part of the musical fabric as the written notes. No one would purposely ignore the tempo or the dynamic markings in a Debussy piece. Yet one still hears (and teachers still teach) Bach's keyboard pieces played as if well-understood conventions regarding ornaments, rhythm, and other matters could be disregarded. For instance, tempos for dance movements that can be easily established from other sources (even though Bach did not explicitly mark them) are frequently disregarded. This will not affect the structure of the music—and the structures of many of Bach's works, especially the fugues, are profound and beautiful in their own right. But structure is not the whole story, and some of the expressive character of the works will have been lost or misstated. Indeed, it is probably through such manifestly inauthentic performances that Bach's music is still often thought, wrongly, to be abstract or even mathematical in nature, or else invariably religious (just as Mozart is still sometimes thought to be always melancholic).

What sort of performance of a Bach work might be considered authentic is as much a philosophical as a practical question. But, whatever one's point of view, anyone studying or performing the works needs to consider both the instruments and the practices that Bach would have taken for granted in composing them. Much remains, and will always remain, uncertain. Yet scholars and players have reached an impressive degree of agreement on many questions, notwithstanding some well-publicized (and, by and large, welcome) challenges to what at any given point has been the received wisdom. Perhaps the best way—especially for nonspecialists—to stay informed about changing views of performance practice is simply to listen routinely to a broad selection of current recordings of "early" music—instrumental and vocal as well as keyboard.

Instruments

The keyboard instruments dating from Bach's time are not standardized; each of the main categories (organ, harpsichord, clavichord, fortepiano) contains many varieties. Harpsichords, for example, include distinct Italian and French types, and among the latter are both single- and double-manual instruments. German harpsichord makers borrowed elements of both French and Italian models; some also built experimental instruments possessing three manuals or unusual combinations of stops, as well as hybrids such as the lute-harpsichord (*Lautenwerk*). Yet, despite the great differences between, say, a north-German Baroque organ and an Italian harpsichord, the two share with all contemporary instruments certain basic characteristics that distinguish them from their "modern" counterparts. Besides their limited dynamic capabilities and the absence of anything resembling a damper pedal, eighteenth-century organs, clavichords, harpsichords, and even early fortepianos are all characterized by the distinct timbres of the different registers of the keyboard. When properly regulated they possess light but very efficient actions, and this, together with the well-defined attack and release on each note, gives the practiced player precise control over articulation and ornaments. In addition, individual tones on the older stringed keyboard instruments seem to take a bit longer to achieve full resonance than on the modern piano, but they fade much more quickly, a fact having important implications for tempo, among other things. Most notes also seem richer in upper overtones than on modern instruments, so that attacks are clearer and inner voices can be heard even through a complex contrapuntal texture.

Hence, early keyboard instruments all speak the same language, permitting a common approach to articulation, ornamentation, fingering, and other aspects of technique and style. Indeed, the principles governing articulation and ornamentation seem to be essentially the same in all the media used by Bach (as Butt 1990, 140, concludes), so that it was possible for him to transfer pieces such as his solo concertos from violin to either organ or harpsichord. Even if, as some suppose, certain of Bach's keyboard pieces constitute "demonstration counterpoint" meant for an abstract "clavier," they presuppose the general qualities of an eighteenth-century instrument, not a twentieth-century one.[4]

Although we possess a list of the instruments that Bach owned at his death, it fails to indicate much beyond the relative size and value of each.[5] Earlier documents, including one relating to Bach's acquisition of a harpsichord for the Prince of Cöthen in 1719 (see Germann 1985), also provide less information than one would like. Hence, precisely what types of instruments Bach owned or employed in playing his solo keyboard music remains a matter of conjecture, and efforts to connect particular compositions with particular instruments must be regarded as speculative. In view of his interest in instrument building and in innovative combinations of sounds,[6] one may assume that Bach took an interest in unusual instruments. But there is little evidence that he ever composed pieces specifically for unusual instruments, save for a few organ pieces and several works possibly intended for the lute-harpsichord.[7]

The sources for the keyboard music rarely give an explicit indication of instrument, more often using ambiguous terms such as *Clavier* or *manualiter*. Even though Bach must have realized that certain pieces would suit one instrument better than another, he evidently accepted the custom of composing in a manner that made most music readily transferrable from one keyboard to another. Like most early eighteenth-century composers, he rarely wrote music limiting players to the use of a particular type of instrument, and the occasional dynamic markings (implying use of a two-manual instrument) can usually be disregarded without grave loss to the musical effect. Even the simple pedal parts found in some early pieces, like a few sustained bass tones elsewhere that seem to call for organ pedals, do not rule out the use of other instruments.[8]

Nevertheless, Bach's suites, like the French pieces on which they were modeled, were certainly meant for harpsichords of one sort or another. The French explicitly demanded the harpsichord in their titles for such works (calling them, e.g., *pièces de clavecin*), as did Bach himself in the first, second, and fourth parts of the *Clavierübung*. By extension, pieces whose style or texture resembles that of the suites, such as the F-major prelude in Part 2 of the *Well-Tempered Clavier* (WTC), might be assigned to the harpsichord. Even the *Art of Fugue*, that most abstract of keyboard works—and it is, without question, keyboard music—contains idiomatic harpsichord writing, including various types of broken-chord figuration and accompaniments (the so-called *style brisé*). The same is true of the *manualiter* toccatas, much of the WTC, and many other works whose medium remains somewhat ambiguous.

Of course, some of the keyboard works contain passages in sustained style for which the organ or the modern piano may seem more suitable than the harpsichord. Yet, even in a quasi-vocal piece in *stile antico* like the E-major fugue of WTC2, the clear articulations of the harpsichord contribute greatly to phrasing and to the crisp delineation of individual motivic gestures. In addition, the harpsichord's ninute variations in the breaking of chords, which may range from a ̣̣̣̣̣̣̣ous striking of all notes to a distinct arpeggiation, provides a means for ̣̣̣ading each verticality. One argument against the use of the harpsichord in such pieces, its relatively weak sustaining power, largely evaporates when the music is played at the relatively quick pace implied by its *alla breve* notation. The same applies to the clavichord, which, although rarely heard today in Bach, must be considered a possibility in certain pieces, especially in light of Agricola's remark that Bach used the instrument in playing transcriptions of the music for unaccompanied strings (see Chapter 16). Nevertheless, Forkel's reference to the clavichord as Bach's favorite instrument appears to have been the result of a misunderstanding.[9] Bach's frequent chromatic progressions and his use of "remote" keys like F$^\sharp$ or E$^\flat$ minor would have made many pieces awkward if not impossible to play on the fretted (*gebunden*) clavichords of the early eighteenth century.

All this merely proves that the harpsichord is a *suitable* medium for the keyboard pieces—not necessarily the optimal or the intended one. Few of the compositions that were already regarded in the second half of the eighteenth century as "clavier" pieces can be considered the exclusive domain of harpsichordists.[10] Clavichord and fortepiano remain possibilities, and Marshall (1986) makes a strong case for the organ in certain works. No doubt Bach was well aware of the capabilities of all these instruments and could use each of them to bring out certain aspects of any piece. But this is merely to say that a good performer makes the most of any performance situation. It remains necessary to consider the question of best medium carefully for every work, in conjunction with the piece's date and sources, its genre, and its internal musical characteristics.

In this writer's judgment a good harpsichord or other eighteenth-century type of instrument will always be preferable to the piano, other things being equal. But Bach's music will continue to be played on the piano, and pianists will continue to make contributions to its interpretation. In principle the piano can do almost everything the harpsichord (and clavichord) can do. Yet ornaments that can be played crisply and with little effort on a properly regulated harpsichord seem heavier and require stronger fingers on the piano. Chords—especially the swiftly arpeggiated chords used so frequently in harpsichord playing—practically voice themselves on "original" instruments, while pianists must carefully weigh each note.

The greatest problems in playing Bach on the piano, however, are probably not those arising from the instrument per se but from inappropriate habits and mental conditioning carried over from other repertories—for example, the *horror vacui* inculcated in many players at an early age through the insistence on legato pedaling in nineteenth- and twentieth-century music. Such pedaling, and the concomitant disregard of slurs in eighteenth-century music—which imply some degree of non-legato after the slur and on all unslurred notes—discourages the pianist from using the finely honed silences that are one of the harpsichordist's most valuable resources. Some pianists would argue that use of the damper pedal is essential to the true nature of the instrument. But legato pedaling—like the continuous vibrato of modern string playing—is an innovation of the mid- or late nineteenth century, and its appropriateness in Mozart, Beethoven, and even Chopin is open to question, let alone in Bach. An articulate, unpedaled approach to the modern piano need not be dry or percussive, but it does require placing a certain amount of weight on each note and paying the same attention to each attack *and* each release as a good organist or harpsichordist does.

Doing so makes good musical sense; it is not simply to imitate the older, non-dynamic instruments. Indeed, pianists certainly ought to use dynamic accents on appoggiaturas and suspensions, and there is no reason not to increase and decrease volume to reflect the rise and fall of melodic lines. Such attention to "light and shade," as Quantz and others referred to it, was normal in eighteenth-century performance in other media. Still, too much reliance on the unique resources of the piano to shape or "bring out" certain aspects of the music—inner voices, for example—risks producing a mannered effect. Harpsichordists shape upper lines as well as basses and inner voices through the same means: careful attention to artic-ulation and judicious use of ornaments, arpeggiation, and rhythmic nuance. Pi-anists have more means at their disposal, but in attempting to rectify the "limitations" of Bach's instruments they should be careful not to gild the lily.

Temperament and Registration

Keyboard temperament has been a much-studied problem, particularly in relation to the author of the *Well-Tempered Clavier*.[11] Already in Bach's day, temperament was a favorite subject of debate for both theorists and practitioners, including organ builders and players. Since even some of Bach's earliest keyboard music employs distant keys and enharmonic equivalents, he is likely throughout his life to have been familiar with fairly sophisticated tuning systems, including more or less equal temperament (precisely equal temperament being unattainable in the absence of electronic tuning devices). But there survive no unambiguous accounts as to how Bach tuned his instruments, and it is entirely possible that he used different systems at different times and for different types of music. By selective citation of individual pieces one can adduce "evidence" that Bach used one sort of tuning or another, but this amounts to little more than an expression of personal preference, and assertions such as that in Lindley (1990, 180) that "the tuning theorist whom Bach most respected was J. G. Neidhart" cannot be verified.

Nevertheless, Bach's concern with "pure" temperament is documented by his rejection of the system adopted by the organ builder Gottfried Silbermann.[12] In-deed, any system that produces very sharp Pythagorean thirds or other noticeably out-of-tune intervals—as in temperaments described by Werckmeister and Kirnberger—seems inappropriate for Bach's music. Proponents of unequal temper-ament point to the shadings that such systems can give to certain keys and that in some instances produce a pleasing variation of sonority as one passes between distantly related tonalities. But Bach's own transposition of several pieces by half-step (among them the B-Minor *Ouverture* BWV 831) makes it doubtful that he linked the choice of key with a work's expressive character or other musical qual-ities. Rather, it had to do with tonal relationships between separate pieces within a set and perhaps with practical matters of keyboard technique. This would seem to favor the case for equal temperament; so too does the fact that at Leipzig the organs were pitched a whole-step above the other instruments, making the organ a trans-posing instrument.

Still, it would have been possible to tune an organ in an unequal temperament whose central (most pure) key was B♭, not C. Moreover, Bach, like other practical musicians, probably tuned his instruments according to pragmatic recipes depen-dent on ear and personal taste. The resulting temperaments could well have con-tained subtle shadings of certain keys, as in the more refined temperaments described by sophisticated theorists such as Neidhart, and there seems no harm in using one of these.

Registration is the art of selecting an effective and practical combination of ranks—sets of strings or pipes—for a piece. Even in organ music, where registration obviously is a topic of considerable importance, it probably receives more attention than it warrants. Organ registration in Bach's day must have been governed not by subjective determinations of "affect" but by conventions that determined, within more or less clearly defined limits, the range of choices available for each genre.[13] The same was surely true in harpsichord music as well, where the range of choices is of course far more restricted. Notwithstanding the fascination that builders, players, and listeners have always felt for inventive sound colors, novelties in this sphere wear off quickly and in any case would not have been available on most types of harpsichord in use during Bach's lifetime. For this reason, and because they tend to distract attention from more substantial musical qualities, most harpsichordists today avoid the colorful registrations that were once fashionable. Hence, it may be necessary to remind players that some German instrument makers of Bach's time did construct instruments with unusual stops, such as "lute" and sixteen-foot ranks, and that in a few pieces, such as the Goldberg Variations, Bach would certainly have expected the player to take full advantage of the capabilities of any given instrument.[14] Moreover, in two pieces that do call for two manuals, the Italian Concerto and the B-Minor *Ouverture*, the changes of manual are occasionally quite tricky, suggesting that Bach was willing to tolerate technical awkwardness for the sake of variety in sound.[15]

Nevertheless, it proves extremely difficult to introduce changes of manual or registration in the course of other pieces without doing violence to their architec-ture.[16] In Bach's contrapuntal textures, lines often cross between the hands, which in such cases should presumably play on the same manual. Moreover, all voices do not always "breathe" simultaneously between phrases; the soprano may pause while the alto is in the middle of a gesture, making it impossible to jump between manuals at that point. In concertolike pieces (such as the preludes of English Suites Nos. 2–6) the contrast between "tutti" and "solo" may be clear at first but grow ambig-uous later in a movement, making rather arbitrary the assignment of a given passage or line to the loud or the soft manual. Adding an extra rank or two for a closing section may provide a momentary dramatic effect, but it is likely to upset the symmetry that so often governs a piece's overall structure and thus may seem vulgar to a careful listener. Hence, to insist on an austere approach to registration is not to rely on the doubtful "aesthetic convention" that "a composition should embody only one affect";[17] it is a way of being faithful to the music itself. Both "authenticity" and musicality urge a conservative approach to registration, and the interpreter's ingenuity is best exercised in other domains.

Articulation and Rhythm

Two such domains are articulation and rhythm.[18] Eighteenth-century keyboard articulation tended more toward nonlegato than did nineteenth- and twentieth-century playing,[19] and modern harpsichordists have arrived at a consensus about certain desirable aspects of articulation in Bach's keyboard music. Chief among these is the placement of minuscule articulations (silences) before accented notes, creating in effect an agogic accent on the latter; another is the use of short slurs on certain frequently occurring figures—for example, between an appoggiatura and the following note. By placing articulations before most accented beats, the metrical structure of each bar is clearly defined. This does not mean that every beat receives equal emphasis; on the contrary, while eighteenth-century musicians were not as obsessed as some modern ones seem to be with the alternation of strong and weak beats, it is clear that beats within each bar could be distinguished by subtle gradations in both duration and dynamic level. The underlying principles are inherent in eighteenth-century treatises on string and wind performance and in Bach's own writing of slurs, which nearly always begin on accented beats and rarely extend for more than four notes.[20] Each slur marks a small, indivisible motivic unit usually consisting of the arpeggiation of a single harmony or the embellishment of one note (e.g., through an appoggiatura).

This function of the slur, recognized as early as 1925 by Schenker (1925–30, 1:43–60, especially 54), should probably take precedence over "phrase marks" that one might be inclined to add as a result of motivic analysis (as illustrated in Williams 1983, 334–39; 1990, 37–39). Motives or figures that cross the barline or straddle more than one harmony need not be slurred in order to retain their integrity; indeed, many motives are defined by a specific *combination* of slurred and unslurred notes (e.g., groupings of sixteenths in patterns of 1 + 3 or 3 + 1). In such a combination the little articulations or silences preceding and following the slur do not break up the gesture but become a part of it. By the same token, slurring into a beat is not the only way to join upbeat to downbeat in a single gesture; indeed, detached upbeats are clearly the rule in the music of Bach and probably all Baroque composers. Most figures, however, can be correctly articulated in more than one way; Bach himself sometimes placed signs ambiguously or indicated different slurs for the same passage (see Butt 1990, 122–30; 136–39).

The relatively few fingerings known to stem from Bach himself add little to the picture. As has also been observed in other repertories (see the illustrations in Lindley 1990), the precise manner of holding the hands and pressing the keys has more effect on articulation than do fingering patterns. The latter do suggest that some notes that modern players might take great pains to connect should actually be played nonlegato (see Chapter 10 on the Applicatio BWV 994). The same evidence confirms the convention of using nonlegato for unslurred notes.

But a uniform nonlegato is as out of place in most eighteenth-century music as is a uniform legato. Wind and string treatises make it clear that, for the unslurred notes of a melody, players employed a variety of articulations ranging from true staccato to tenuto tones that are still distinctly separated from one another. While there is no documentary evidence for extending the subtle distinctions in articulation made by eighteenth-century wind players to keyboard instruments, the latter are technically well suited for it. Thus, modern harpsichordists follow the suggestions of writers such as the flutist Quantz (1752), who offered specific articulation patterns for a large number of motivic gestures, the articulation depending upon the rhythm and melodic intervals of the line. The variety of figuration in most Bach works inevitably leads to great variety in articulation patterns. Hence, it is potentially misleading to characterize melodic lines in Bach's keyboard music simply as legato or nonlegato. Moreover, assumptions about the "natural articulations" (Williams 1985c, 336) appropriate to certain figures should perhaps be resisted; in particular, it seems doubtful that in Bach "all chromatic lines are by nature smooth," a possibility raised by Williams (1984–84, 3:210). To judge from wind and string sources, the opposite is usually true in early eighteenth-century music, including Bach's, where chromatic motion is usually in large note-values (unslurred) that need to be clearly articulated.

Articulation cannot be discussed separately from rhythm, since, as modern players of historical instruments have shown, agogics and slurs function together. To produce an accent, the little silence preceding an accented note can be "stretched," as can the note itself. For this to occur without doing violence to the coherence of the larger gesture and phrase requires that rhythmic freedom be applied primarily to small note-values within the beat, the latter remaining fairly steady. The result is a true tempo rubato rather than the manipulation of the beat or tempo itself, which is probably more characteristic of nineteenth-century practice. Of course, relaxation of the tempo at cadences can be heard in most good performances of eighteenth-century music. But the nature of the ritard differs from that employed in Romantic practice. Bach usually maintains a piece's prevalent rhythmic pattern right up to the last bar-line, and thus ritards in his music are best begun late. Even in the final bar of a piece one must not lose track of the beat; otherwise the written-out arpeggiations so common in final bars (especially in dance movements) are likely to seem superfluous or dragged out. As in all notational matters, Bach was generally quite precise in indicating the value of final notes, and the fermata at the end of a piece merely confirmed for the copyist that the end had been reached. The fermata is unlikely to have had any bearing on the actual duration of the last note, which probably should not be stretched much beyond its written value.

This is not to argue for the dull, metronomic playing that can arise from a literal reading of Baroque notation, which of course lacks the expression marks of later music. Certain clues in the music itself point to considerable freedom within the beat. Small note-values often fail to add up properly, implying quick, partially indeterminate performance; ornaments, leaps in melodic lines, and (in string music) bowings (i.e., slurs) often force the taking of additional time on or immediately after notes that fall on strong beats.[21] The beat itself—that is, the note-value on which the pulse should fall—is nearly always indicated in Bach's music by the time-signature; theorists associated specific time-signatures with given ranges of tempo, and while there is considerable room for leeway in these prescriptions, it is clear that, as a rule, one ought not subdivide the notated beat. In other words, pieces notated *alla breve* should be counted in half-notes, and even in heavily embellished adagios and sarabandes one should not count eighths or sixteenths. Doing so causes the written-out embellishment to lose the character of passionate improvisation that it was presumably meant to imitate. In French-style pieces, including most suite movements, one must assume that the rhythmic patterns underlying the various dances were meant to be heard clearly. Some of these patterns, especially the shifting hemiolas of the courante, can be difficult to grasp in Bach's own settings and are best studied first in the simpler examples by Dieupart and others from whose music Bach himself learned them.

Whether or not Bach employed *notes inégales* has raised some controversy. No contemporary German writer seems to have described the practice, but Bach must have had opportunities to hear Frenchmen performing their own music, and he can hardly have been unaware of this or other widely recognized rhythmic conventions. Over-dotting, another of these, has sometimes been confused with inequality, but the two apply to different types of pieces and involve differing notation and performing practice. While inequality can be used in almost any French dance, over-dotting seems largely confined to overtures, where, as a general rule, all notes following a dot can be shortened to the value of a sixteenth, resulting in a crisp and energetic movement. Much of the controversy regarding dotting in Bach has been a needless product of misapprehensions concerning tempo and articulation. The apparent distinction between "literal" interpretation and over-dotting largely disappears when overtures are performed with sufficient speed—they are almost never marked "slow" and are often notated *alla breve*—and when clear articulations are placed both before and after the dotted notes.[22] To be sure, notational details in a number of overtures and similar pieces may point against automatically "double-dotting" quarter-notes.[23] But there are no clear indications anywhere for systematically double-dotting smaller values, although the dots on some eighths might be lengthened in the course of the usual rhythmic freedom described previously.[24]

One technique not usually associated with articulation and rhythm but in fact intimately related to it, at least on the harpsichord, is the breaking of chords. Although no treatise seems to say so, modern harpsichordists often take it for granted that all chords should be broken to some degree, if only to prevent the impression of a harsh or clunky accent on every chord. This rule, like the one requiring agogic accents on every strong beat, should probably not be universally applied. But there can be no question that the ability to "spread" chords is a crucial element in the harpsichordist's vocabulary, making it possible, by varying the precise speed of the arpeggiation, to soften or accentuate individual verticalities and to give chords (especially accented chords containing many notes) a little extra time. Such arpeggiation should probably begin on the beat; starting before the beat, like slurring into a downbeat, weakens the pulse.[25] Like other aspects of articulation, Bach rarely dictates this sort of arpeggiation; the ornament sign signifying a broken chord seems to have been written only where it seemed absolutely essential, perhaps implying a slower, that is, more perceptible, breaking than usual.

Ornaments and Embellishment

The arpeggio and other ornaments must, by Bach's day, have been thoroughly familiar to most keyboard players, although this was not necessarily true of the signs used to indicate them. Indeed, the ornament tables found in many sources are less likely to have served as instructions in how to play the ornaments than as explanations for each composer's particular system of ornament signs. Bach's system is derived from that of D'Anglebert (see the discussion in Chapter 10), and despite arguments to the contrary, the best guide to their realization is probably C. P. E. Bach's *Versuch* (1753–62), at least in Bach's later keyboard works.[26] Even where C. P. E. Bach's guidelines lead to parallel fifths or other apparent errors, they need not be disregarded. "Forbidden" parallels crop up occasionally in Sebastian's music, and those arising from ornaments are positively objectionable only when they become blatantly obvious, as may occur with the long appoggiatura.[27]

In general, Emanuel (and presumably Sebastian) Bach's approach to ornaments was close to that of Couperin and other French writers of the early eighteenth century. This dictates caution in departing from such familiar rules as those governing the performance of trills—on the beat, starting from above—and the length of appoggiaturas. In the case of appoggiaturas, however, it is necessary to remember the distinction (not indicated notationally) between long and short appoggiaturas. Only long appoggiaturas take half the value of the main note—two-thirds that of a dotted note—and this type seems to be rare if not absent in Bach's earlier works. Some short appoggiaturas, especially those of the type known as the *tierce coulée* (which fills a descending third at the end of a phrase), were sometimes played before the beat, at least in French music.[28] But C. P. E. Bach's vehement rejection of this manner of performance cannot be dismissed, especially as one of his examples is practically a quotation from the aria of the Goldberg Variations.[29]

One practice that Sebastian clearly adopted from Couperin and other Frenchmen was the indication of all necessary ornament signs, at least in the final versions of the English and French Suites and in the published keyboard works. Unfortunately, many signs were drawn hastily or unclearly in the sources and therefore are subject to varying interpretations.[30] Even Bach's own students and the engravers of his printed works, who presumably worked under his direction, seem to have sometimes confused the various types of trill, as variants in the French Suites (e.g., the sarabande of Suite No. 6) and ambiguous signs in the Partitas suggest. Morever, many ornament signs were added only at a relatively late stage of revision, and signs are sometimes lacking at points where ornaments surely belong (as in certain cadential formulas). Bach used a few signs in more than one way; conversely, the same ornament (e.g., a trill with termination) may be notated in several different ways.

Hence, Bach's own approach to ornamentation—both its notation and its realization—may have changed in the course of his career. The absence of signs does not mean the absence of ornaments, and every ornament probably need not be played precisely as marked. But when adding ornaments one must be careful not to overdo it, as some performers did even in the eighteenth century, to judge from some sources with nonautograph ornament signs.[31]

Stereotyped ornaments are distinct from *embellishments*, which we may define as any sort of melodic elaboration more complex than the simple stylized varieties that can be indicated by signs.[32] To add embellishment is to introduce genuine variations, a hazardous venture unless one improvises as well as Bach composed. Bach is famous for having written out the embellishment that other composers left to be improvised, an observation first made in Scheibe's famous attack on Bach's style. But, as Birnbaum noted in his reply (BD 2:304 [item 409]/BR, 246), a similar objection could be made to the French composers whose works Bach imitated. Outside the French style, Germans like Telemann and Pisendel and Italians like Vivaldi sometimes indicated both ornaments and embellishments with great precision.[33] No keyboard piece by Bach cries out for embellishment in the same way as do certain adagios by, say, Corelli, and unless one is convinced that one can really add something to what Bach has written, it seems pointlessly self-indulgent to add or, for that matter, subtract anything except a few simple ornaments.

3

Bach's Style and Its Development in the Keyboard Works

Bach's music was the product of a mingling of ideas and influences from current and earlier German, French, and Italian traditions, which he integrated into a personal style that developed over a period of half a century. It was once customary to regard this style as a conservative one; now it has become clear that the style incorporates many "progressive" traits (as argued, in particular, in Marshall 1976a). Still, all composers of Bach's generation were conservative in the sense that their works were usually composed within established genres. Genre governed not only medium and function but also determined the form, length, texture, and other aspects of a work. Hence, for Bach, as for any Baroque composer, it can be misleading to speak of a single style; he cultivated various styles, each appropriate to the genre within which he was working at any given time.

Like most composers of his time, Bach took the works of esteemed contemporaries as his models, learning from them the types of rhythm, melody, and texture appropriate to the genres in which he worked. While the music of Vivaldi, Telemann, and other contemporaries can seem simple when compared to Bach's, this should not obscure the fact that, throughout his life, Bach was eager to learn and adopt whatever was of value in the current music of Italy, France, and Germany. Bach was never isolated musically, even though portions of his career (especially at the beginning) were spent in relatively provincial locations. Hence his stylistic development and choice of style in various genres reflects those of European (and especially German) music at large.

Nevertheless, it is possible to speak of certain personal tendencies in Bach's mature keyboard works. For instance, it was characteristic of Bach that, while in principle retaining the conventions of each genre (such as the use of binary-form movements with dance titles to form a suite), he transformed most of the genres in which he worked by expanding the traditional formal structures and admitting technical and stylistic features borrowed from other genres. Thus, while Bach throughout his life gave the appearance of remaining attached to the genres prevalent during his youth—in particular, the suite and several types of preludes and fugues—few pieces follow any one model.

For example, the dances of the English Suites, while adhering to the traditional rhythms and general character of their French models, incorporate invertible imitative counterpoint—a traditional device, to be sure, but not one traditionally associated with the suite. Although suites were associated with the French style, five of the six English Suites open with a large prelude in the manner of a concerto—that is, in Italian style. Some of the composers whose influence might be detected in these suites were, at the time of composition, already quite old, while others, among them Vivaldi (especially through his concertos), were very new, at least to German musicians like Bach. Indeed, here, as in many of Bach's works, the synthesis of old and new is a fundamental element of the style.

Partly for this reason, it is problematical to read political or sociological metaphors into Bach's mingling of styles and genres (as in McClary 1987, 44). Not all dotted pieces are "French," nor is every "impetuous" piece Italian, and in neither case can one be sure one understands all the connotations that national styles or their mixture had for Bach and his contemporaries. It is possible, for example, that Bach's early "French" overtures reflect opera sinfonias heard at Hamburg, not the music of francophile German courts, thus associating such music (in Bach's mind) not with Louis XIV but with the bourgeois elite of the free Hanseatic city.

This is not to deny that Bach's music has been used in the service of various ideologies. The historian Hans-Georg Gadamer, perhaps seeing in it a corrective to recent German history, regarded Bach's achievement as "the creation of a world of order which requires no Romantic inspiration or sentimental humanization."[1] Dreyfus (1980, 2), noting a more ominous aspect of earlier German Bach interpretation, pointed to the appropriation of Bach himself as a bearer of the virtues of "industry, sobriety and religiosity," and the use of his "severe counterpoint" as a metaphor for an authoritarian social "order," with potential implications for performance practice.[2] In fact, since his own day Bach's adherence to contrapuntal textures has been taken as a fundamental trait of his music and as a mark of his personal conservatism. But it might be best to avoid such politically charged terms as "conservative" and "progressive" in analyzing Bach's style. The view of Bach as an old-fashioned contrapuntist goes back to a cliché of eighteenth-century writing on music: the habitual distinction drawn between strict (*gebunden*) contrapuntal style, derived from Renaissance polyphony in four or more parts, and free or *galant* composition in which melody and bass are the only consistently maintained voices.[3] Bach certainly paid more attention to strict counterpoint than did most of his contemporaries. But this does not necessarily ally him with any particular earlier composers—let alone an ideology—since, except when he was employing the *stile antico* (the Baroque version of Renaissance counterpoint), Bach's counterpoint is fundamentally different from that of his predecessors.

First, the motivic material of Bach's contrapuntal works usually incorporates figures from current style. Froberger had already used fugal imitation in his gigues, and later seventeenth-century composers considerably extended the motivic and expressive vocabulary of fugue. Bach's fugues go even further, incorporating violinistic figuration, declamatory motives reminiscent of recitative, and virtually every other type of writing available in the nonfugal music of the early eighteenth century. In addition, the individual parts move with unparalleled melodic freedom and rhythmic independence; this contrasts with the texture of many seventeenth-century works, especially those in more than three voices, in which the parts tend to move in stepwise intervals, often outlining diatonic triads. Moreover, with earlier composers the bass is often static, and chromaticism is reserved for pieces in which a special expressive effect is desired. With Bach, however, any part may move through dissonant intervals (chromatic half-steps, tritones, diminished sevenths), and even in relatively lighthearted pieces there may be more chromaticism and more frequent passing dissonances than would previously have been expected except in music meant to be highly expressive.

The complexity of Bach's counterpoint led some of his contemporaries to regard his music as turgid and incomprehensible—that is, more concerned with its own technique than with conveying a clear "affect" or expressive character. Perhaps there was some truth in this, although it is also likely that some of Bach's critics were unable to follow his more complex arguments. Yet even the most complex, dissonant voice-leading is firmly controlled by the principles of tonal harmony. Modern students of Bach usually understand his progressions in terms of chord symbols standing for harmonic functions. Bach himself might have explained his more complex passages as being governed by or derived from simpler progressions through the principle of "composition by variation" described below.[4]

As essential as it is in Bach's keyboard music, counterpoint is hardly the only important element. Indeed, his stylistic development is perhaps more easily traced through other musical elements, such as his adoption of contemporary French and Italian genres, rhythms, and melodic formulas, or his use of structural patterns such as ritornello form and (a neglected topic) types of sonata forms. Unfortunately, problems in dating individual works make it difficult to trace Bach's development accurately. Moreover, developments within any given genre tended to follow a logic unique to that genre; fugues, for example, do not always show developments parallel to those found in preludes or dance movements. Most of the best-known works date from relatively late in Bach's life; partly for this reason, Bach's music is often discussed as if it showed little stylistic development at all. One hears of "the Bach fugue" or "the Bach chorale," the implication being that the style did not change to any appreciable extent in the course of his lifetime. Bach himself contributed to the impression through his manner of revising older works. For example, his thorough reworking of the melodic lines in the organ fugue in G minor (BWV 535/2), a very early composition, brings it significantly closer in style to much later pieces, at least insofar as the melodic surface is concerned.[5] It is possible that many other works were significantly revised, but the absence of a large number of sources from the early period makes it difficult to reconstruct Bach's early development.

The Early Keyboard Works

A quick survey of the keyboard works can nonetheless give some idea of the development of Bach's style (or styles). No surviving music can be securely placed earlier than Bach's Arnstadt period, but the latter (1703–7) presumably saw the creation of most of the early suites, fugues, and other compositions discussed in detail in Chapters 4–6 and perhaps the toccatas as well (considered in Chapter 7). Many chorale settings that also probably date from this period lack pedal parts and thus could be considered "keyboard" pieces, but only a few of these—especially individual movements from the chorale *partite* (variations)—seem suited to the harpsichord or clavichord. The rest, like the big *pedaliter* preludes and fugues, must be regarded as organ pieces.[6]

The suites are the least complex of the early works, though not necessarily the earliest. They are comparable with suites by Bach's older German contemporaries, such as Pachelbel, Reinken, and Böhm, who were themselves indebted to Froberger and to the French *clavecinistes* of the seventeenth century. But two of the suites open with overtures in orchestral style, showing that from very early on Bach was concerned with adapting up-to-date orchestral styles and genres to the keyboard.[7] The early suites also reveal Bach's mastery of French *brisé* notation, of the various dance rhythms, and, above all, of the distinction between the idiom of the harpsichord (or perhaps the clavichord) and that of the organ—something that is not always apparent in the keyboard pieces of other German composers, such as Kuhnau.[8]

The early sonatas, toccatas, preludes and fugues, and like works are all close to the German organ tradition; indeed, they might have been intended primarily for organ. Like the ensemble sonatas of the seventeenth century, of which they are the keyboard counterparts, they often consist of loosely connected sections too brief to be considered self-contained movements. Each such work, however, usually includes at least one lengthy fugal section that could have stood on its own and perhaps did at an early stage in the work's history; in at least one instance the fugue is in fact transmitted separately. By the same token, some of the fugues surviving as separate pieces might have been envisioned as sections of larger compositions.

Some of these fugues might have been composed as part of Bach's self-instruction in composition, which was described many years after his death in a letter by his son Carl Philipp Emanuel.[9] Other aspects of Bach's early work as a composer can be gleaned from the repertory preserved in ABB and MM, the two large manuscript compilations of Bach's older brother Johann Christoph. For example, one of Bach's early preludes and fugues for organ, BWV 531 in C, opens with a virtuoso pedal solo similar to that at the beginning of the work by Böhm in the same key.[10] Several of Bach's *manualiter* toccatas (including the one in C minor, which appears in ABB) have similar passages in their opening sections. While the Bach works may not have been modeled on any specific pieces by other composers, the latter obviously represent the type of music that Bach was emulating—and at times already surpassing—in his early years.

This is certainly true in the case of the famous Capriccio BWV 992, which seems to have taken its inspiration from the Biblical Sonatas of Kuhnau, several of which were copied in ABB. Not only the programmatic rubrics of the Bach work but much of its motivic material recalls the sonatas of the earlier composer, to whose position Bach eventually succeeded at Leipzig. A close relationship with earlier pieces can also be assumed in the case of the early Praeludium et Partita BWV 833 (preserved in MM), which represents a special type of suite sometimes referred to as a "variation-suite." In such a work the courante (and often additional movements as well) is composed as a variation on the first dance movement, the allemande.[11] Reinken and Buxtehude, among others, wrote such suites, probably drawing on earlier models by Frescobaldi and Froberger; one suite given anonymously in MM employs variation technique in all four movements.[12] Bach later made keyboard arrangements of portions of two of Reinken's variation-suites (see Chapter 6); moreover, an allemande and courante from a variation-suite by one Richter were included in the *Clavier-Büchlein vor Wilhelm Friedemann Bach*.

"Composition by Variation"

The importance of the variation-suite lies not in the form itself, which Bach used only in BWV 833, but in the underlying compositional thought and technique. The latter is worth a brief digression. In the type of variation-suite under consideration here, it is not the melody but an underlying harmonic progression and phrasing-scheme that are varied. This principle lies at the basis of the composition treatise of Friedrich Erhardt Niedt, published in 1706 as the successor volume to his treatise on figured bass realization and illustrated by a variation-suite. Although his works were published at Hamburg, Niedt himself was born in Jena, where he evidently studied with Johann Nicolaus Bach; this fact has led to speculation that Niedt's teachings represent a "Bach family tradition" (Heimann 1973, 131; see also Niedt 1989, xiii).

Neither this, nor the fact that manuscript extracts from one of Niedt's volumes bear a title and corrections in the hand of a Bach associate, answers all questions about Bach's own musical education or his later teaching. But the "instruction . . . designed for an organist" that Bach apparently received as a child from his brother Johann Christoph must have included not only figured bass realization but also score notation, which was championed by Niedt at a time when many organists still relied on tablature.[13] We know too that later in life Bach himself started his students out with figured bass realization, entirely avoiding species counterpoint. In this approach to composition, melodic material was understood as the embellishment of underlying harmonic progressions, or, to be more precise, a variation of simple three- or four-part counterpoint that could be represented by figured bass (as it was in Niedt's treatise). Hence composition was in essence nothing more than a very elaborate variety of figured bass realization, a concept that Bach and his own pupils probably put to use in their teaching as well as in improvisation and composition.[14]

In addition to implying a reliance on what might be called "composition by variation" in the creation of melodic material, the variation-suite in effect presupposes a tonal conception of musical form. Form, although not a major concern in treatises of the seventeenth and early eighteenth centuries, would eventually be described (e.g., in Marpurg 1756) in terms of a series of phrases, each beginning with the statement of a distinctive theme and proceeding to a cadence, generally after a modulation to a new key. This view of form is already implicit in Niedt's plan for each movement of his suite, since the underlying ground bass falls into what has been called "three-phrase binary" form (Rosen 1988, 18–21), one of the most common plans for Bach's own dance movements and sonata-form preludes.

Weimar

That Bach ever thought of composition in precisely the terms just described cannot be proved. In any case, not all of Bach's music could have been conceived through "variation." Fugal works, or at least those fugues that emphasize rigorous contrapuntal technique, often employ relatively unembellished part-writing and sometimes comprise a series of more or less self-contained sections progressively introducing more advanced fugal devices (inversion, stretto, augmentation). In such pieces each section tends to remain close to the tonic rather than articulating one step in a rounded series of modulations to different keys. While such pieces are fairly rare in Bach's output, they occur at all stages in his career. The early period, however, is particularly rich in works whose form seems additive rather than rounded or symmetrical. This is hardly surprising, since the principle of organizing musical form according to a closed series of modulations was still a new idea at the beginning of the eighteenth century.

The adoption of such forms for works in most genres was one of the principal accomplishments of Bach's Weimar years. This was also apparently the period in which Bach can be said to have come into his own as a composer; while there are many distinctive earlier pieces, it is not always possible for us to recognize their style as Bach's. That Bach from the beginning had been straining to expand the vocabulary of the traditional genres can be seen in such audacious early experiments as the chromatic passage in the G-Minor *Ouverture* BWV 822 or the overextended fugue (called a Capriccio) in E, BWV 993.[15] But despite the very confident handling of voice-leading and keyboard idiom in most passages, these pieces often retain a certain clumsiness. Bach had not yet learned the technique of tonal planning described above, and the longer pieces seem to ramble. Moreover, the effort to combine sophisticated counterpoint with imitations of orchestral and even vocal style sometimes came into conflict with the requirement of writing notes playable by a single performer at the keyboard.

Bach gradually overcame these difficulties, and while it is impossible to say precisely where or when, the crucial developments seem to have taken place between the end of the Arnstadt years, around 1707, and the middle of the Weimar period, around 1713.[16] The toccatas, although counted above among the early works, actually represent a point well on the way toward somewhat more mature works that seem to belong to the later Weimar years, in particular a number of large preludes and fugues. The latter, discussed in Chapter 9, are roughly comparable with the examples for organ from the same period.[17]

The most important development of this period is probably the assimilation of the Venetian concerto style into Bach's work in other genres. The process probably had begun by the time (around 1713) when Bach carried out the concerto transcriptions discussed in Chapter 8; Forkel attached great importance to the transcriptions and to Vivaldi's influence on Bach, perhaps reflecting a Bach family tradition (see Forkel 1802, 24/BR, 317). Forkel seems to point less to the virtuoso figuration and other superficial aspects of Vivaldi's solo concertos than to structural features: disciplined motivic work, closed modulatory schemes, and other aspects of eighteenth-century style that indeed seem to enter Bach's work as regular elements at about this time. Only now, for instance, do the fugues as a rule follow large-scale modulatory schemes instead of additive or permutational designs. Improvisatory postludes disappear, and episodes emerge as clearly distinct from the expository passages, often resembling the solo sections of a concerto in their reduction of the texture to two voices.[18]

The fruits of Bach's Italian studies can be seen not only in the quasi-ritornello forms of certain preludes and fugues, and in the soloistic figuration of many episodes, but also in a distinctive type of embellished adagio. This too is prefigured in what are probably somewhat earlier works (e.g., the Reinken arrangements BWV 965–66), but it achieves its mature form around 1714, in several of the Weimar cantatas and one or two movements from the concerto transcriptions. Italian style is also present in movements from the English Suites, which have traditionally been dated to Cöthen but are now thought to have been composed, at least in part, at Weimar (see Chapter 13). These suites adopt the Venetian concerto style in five of their six preludes. But, as suites, their basic style is of course French, and they seem to reflect Bach's study of fairly recent French music, including works by Grigny and Dieupart copied at Weimar.[19] Direct imitations of Froberger or Kuhnau are now rare, and instead the dance movements show a highly idiomatic use of melodic and rhythmic formulas reminiscent of current French music. These ideas, however, are worked out in imitative counterpoint, previously rare in keyboard suites except in the gigues of Froberger, Reinken, and other Germans.

Cöthen and Leipzig

The English Suites are probably the earliest group of keyboard pieces that Bach himself assembled into a collection; the toccatas, concertos, and other groups of earlier pieces do not occur as complete sets in any early source. While the English Suites may already have been complete when Bach left Weimar in 1717, his revision and organization of his keyboard pieces into sets seems to have begun in earnest at Cöthen in connection with the pedagogic needs of his own growing family. For example, the *Clavier-Büchlein* (Little Keyboard Book) of Wilhelm Friedemann Bach and the first of the two books for Anna Magdalena Bach were begun at Cöthen.[20] These sources contain the earliest copies of the Inventions and

Sinfonias, of some of the French Suites, and of movements from the first part of the *Well-Tempered Clavier* (WTC1), also compiled at Cöthen. At least some of this music, however, as well as various other small preludes and fugues never incorporated into the famous sets, must have been composed prior to being entered into the famous Cöthen manuscripts; certain movements in WTC1 and even a few in WTC2 (which was assembled much later) seem fairly archaic. Nevertheless, these works are generally distinct in style from those mentioned previously and, if composed at Weimar, must date from the later part of Bach's tenure there.

The French Suites were almost certainly begun at Cöthen, and they were completed only at Leipzig. They represent a considerable development of style beyond that of the English Suites—a development continued in the Partitas, which constituted Bach's first keyboard publication, appearing in installments between 1726 and 1731. The six Partitas collectively formed the first part of the *Clavierübung*, which was followed in 1735 by a second volume consisting of the Italian Concerto and French *Ouverture*. Both the concerto and the dances of the suites and Partitas largely abandoned the invertible counterpoint that figures so prominently in the English Suites. Moreover, elements of what is now called galant style had since Cöthen been becoming increasingly apparent in all of Bach's work, even in fugal movements. The most obvious of these elements are "sigh" figures and singing melodies accompanied in parallel thirds or sixths, which, while they can be found in works from Weimar and earlier, are now met more frequently.

To a contemporary the mere presence of suites of dances in Bach's keyboard publications might have signaled his adoption of galant style—that is, the fashionable, homophonic modern idiom. Considered in this manner, almost any piece that was not deliberately archaic might qualify as "galant." But the term remains meaningful insofar as it suggests a deliberate lightening of touch or a direct appeal to popular taste, such as Bach clearly undertook in the *Clavierübung*. This did not, however, mean abandoning the distinctive elements of his style. The music retains a strong contrapuntal component, and many movements combine contrapuntal texture and chromatic harmony with the galant idiom, which, as Bach showed, could be expressive as well as elegant.

That "galant" works could be expressive may seem surprising today, since in modern usage the term generally describes music in which the expressive effects are mild if not frankly trivial. But in eighteenth-century parlance the term "galant" was as appropriate to the *empfindsamer Stil* of Bach's sons Friedemann and Emanuel as to the less demanding music of, say, Quantz or Heinichen. Indeed, the most attractive feature of the galant style for Bach's contemporaries was perhaps its ability to suggest easily understood expressive quantities in what was judged to be a natural manner. Bach obviously did not share the disfavor in which some writers, such as Scheibe, held the old polyphonic forms. But there can be no mistaking the adoption in his later keyboard works of the expressive language of galant music, especially as represented by new types of melody and ornament, such as the long appoggiatura.

Besides growing increasingly galant, the three sets of suites—the English, the French, and the Partitas—reflect other ongoing developments in eighteenth-century style. For example, the individual binary-form dance movements grow longer, in some cases becoming indistinguishable in proportions and style from sonata movements of the period.[21] The same process becomes evident when the preludes of Parts 1 and 2 of the *Well-Tempered Clavier* are compared. At the same time, however, or at any rate after 1735 or so, Bach developed an intense interest in the strict contrapuntal genres of canon and of fugue in *stile antico*. The *stile antico* is evident in several fugues of WTC2 (completed around 1742), the two ricercars from the *Musical Offering* (1747), and the *Art of Fugue* (published posthumously in 1751). Canon plays an important role in the last two publications and also in the Goldberg Variations, usually regarded as the final installment of the *Clavierübung* (1741). Yet, all four late keyboard collections temper the "research" into archaic polyphonic forms with elements of galant style; they also incorporate a considerable amount of pure keyboard virtuosity. Hence, even in works that seem to have been intended as models of contrapuntal rigor, Bach retained his stylistic eclecticism and the conception of the keyboard player as a brilliant soloist. And the purposes of the music, insofar as we can judge, remained those of earlier works: models of composition and improvisation as well as instruments of expression.

4

The Early Suites

Bach's earliest keyboard pieces are often charming, sometimes earnestly rhetorical, and occasionally quite inventive. But they have remained fairly obscure to all but specialists, in part because they are quite different from the pieces that everyone studies. None of the early suites, sonatas, preludes, fugues, and other works were ever, so far as we know, gathered into an ordered collection like the WTC or the *Clavierübung*. Some of the pieces belong to stylistic traditions that are unfamiliar even to many harpsichordists. One seeks in vain in most of them for unmistakable hints of Bach's later style or greatness; at most, one senses a certain audacity, as in the chromatic modulations of the G-Minor *Ouverture*. Nevertheless, these pieces do share small touches—favorite motivic ideas, characteristic cadential formulas— with Bach's early work in other genres, making it clear that we are dealing with a distinct musical personality, if not the familiar Bach of Cöthen or Leipzig.

These pieces must already have been fairly obscure by the time Bach reached Leipzig; they tend to survive only in early or peripheral sources or in manuscripts written by collectors like Kellner who seem actively to have sought out unusual or early pieces. Bach himself might not have kept copies of all of these pieces, and with few exceptions he seems not to have revised them or made them available to his students after his departure from Weimar. It is possible to attach only rough dates and a relative chronology to the pieces discussed here and in Chapters 5 and 6. But it is safe to say that most if not all were drafted before Bach arrived in Weimar. If Bach ever used any of them in his teaching, they were later replaced by others; whether Bach wrote them for that purpose, for his own performance, or as exercises in composition is impossible to say since we know nothing of the circumstances under which they were written. We begin with the suites, not because they are necessarily the earliest but because they are the least complicated of the early pieces. Simplicity is no firm guide to chronology; nevertheless, the five relatively simple suites considered first in this chapter are probably among Bach's earliest surviving works.

Although the term "suite" is used here for all seven works, the latter bear various titles in the sources: *Suite, Partita, Ouverture*. That the first two titles were essentially synonymous is clear from the fact that one work (BWV 832) appears as both a *Suite* and a *Partie* in different manuscripts. Moreover, each of the two *ouvertures*, BWV 820 and 822, could have been described more precisely as "overture with suite," the last word referring to the series of movements that follow the overture proper. The diverse titles for what is essentially the same type of work are probably due to the fact that the idea of an ordered set of short keyboard pieces was relatively new in the years just after 1700. The terminology remained unstable throughout Bach's lifetime, as his own varying titles show (*Suite, Prélude avec la suite, Partita*). The word *ouverture*, however, clearly connoted a piece in orchestral style, if not an actual transcription, and of Bach's *ouvertures* only the Fourth Partita includes the allemande-courante pair that usually opens a harpsichord suite. For this reason the French word *ouverture* is used here for a suite in orchestral style, the English word "overture" for the opening movement of such a work.

We know from the successive versions of some of Bach's later suites that movements could be added to or subtracted from such works. Thus, his suites are not closed cycles but open sets of pieces in the same key, arranged in a certain order; the latter was determined chiefly by convention, not personal choice. That musicians around 1700 were beginning to think of groups of dances as having a definite form is suggested by the "better order" (*meilleur ordre*) in which Froberger's keyboard pieces were arranged in a posthumous edition (Amsterdam, ca. 1697). But only where the movements are linked thematically or harmonically, as in the variation-suite, is there a concrete cyclic element. It is probably best to view other suites as loose assemblages of pieces sharing a common key and (perhaps) similar proportions and character. Especially in his early years, Bach, in composing harpsichord pieces, may have set out to write not suites but individual movements that could be grouped together at a later date; this might explain the presence of only two movements of the *Partie* BWV 832 in its earliest source.

It seems appropriate to open this survey of Bach's keyboard music with the two *ouvertures*. The F-major work (BWV 820) is perhaps the earlier of the two, smaller in scale and somewhat simpler in texture and in technique. Either piece might be a transcription; the one in G minor (BWV 822) is even designated a transcription in NBA V/10.[1] ABB and MM, the two manuscript collections compiled by Bach's older brother, contain transcriptions of orchestral music by Lully and others. Similar transcriptions had previously been published among the *Pièces de clavecin* (Paris, 1689) of D'Anglebert, whose music is not represented in ABB or MM but whose influence is felt in many works in both manuscripts.[2] But no orchestral model for either of Bach's early *ouvertures* has been found, and there is no reason Bach could not have written such pieces as original keyboard works, perhaps after having heard opera overtures of this type at Hamburg. Handel, who arrived in Hamburg in 1703 (probably after Bach was already installed in Arnstadt), wrote comparable works, including two early keyboard suites that only later were adapted as orchestral works.[3]

Ouverture in F, BWV 820

Sole independent source: ABB (No. 13). *Editions*: BG 36; NBA V/10; Dadelsen (1975).

This *ouverture*, or suite in orchestral style, is typical of the genre in being heavily weighted toward the overture, which is followed by four dances: entrée, minuet (alternating with trio), bourrée, and gigue. The opening gestures of the overture and of the entrée have similar contours, as do those of the minuet and trio, but this is not enough to make this a variation-suite (there is no common harmonic ground).

The work occurs early in ABB, within a group of pieces in French genres that include an *ouverture* by Telemann and Böhm's Suite in D (the one in overture style). At least some of these pieces, including the *partie* by Pestel that immediately precedes BWV 820, might be transcriptions—perhaps even transcriptions by Bach.[4] That BWV 820 might be a transcription as well is suggested by the thin, predominantly two- and three-part textures of all but one movement (the trio). Such a texture could have been the result of copying only the outer parts of a work for four- or five-part ensemble. Where inner voices are present, they are not always completely satisfactory; for example, in bar 12 of the overture the third (e') of the first chord is omitted. Sometimes an inner voice enters and then drops out for no good reason; in such cases the voice might have been a somewhat arbitrary late addition. (See, for instance, bars 14–15 of the minuet.) Yet these are insufficient grounds for concluding that the piece is not an original—or for filling out the harmony with additional inner voices (as suggested in NBA V/10, KB, 63). As in countless other eighteenth-century harpsichord pieces, the harmony is usually sufficient as it stands and will sound full enough on a reasonably resonant instrument.

Even if BWV 820 is indeed a transcription, its model might have been the work of a francophile German composer, not a Frenchman. That the composer was Bach himself, and that the work is original, becomes more plausible the more closely one studies it. Both subject and countersubject in the fugal portion of the first movement employ short repeated motives of a type common in German keyboard fugues, including Bach's own early ones. Also reminiscent of other early works attributed to Bach are the weak harmonic implications of the fugue subject; even when combined with its countersubject, the passage merely oscillates between III^6 and I^6 (bars 18–21). Bach evidently had not yet learned the importance of composing fugue subjects that by themselves imply a strong harmonic progression. In addition, the closing phrase of the fugue, with its four bars of tonic prolongation and chopped-off final chord, is entirely within the German organ tradition. In organ music the cutting short of the last chord (which surely requires no rallentando) might have been meant to exploit the natural reverberation of the final sonority throughout the church; here one must settle for the after-ring of the strings of the harpsichord.[5]

Williams (1989, 187) describes the fugue subject as "a slurred (*legato*) theme, with the ornaments beginning on the main note." The ornament signs are not necessarily original, however, and if realized in what was the normal manner by 1700—that is, starting on the upper note, as shown in the tables in ABB and MM—the ornaments may imply a more thoughtful character than the "fleeting, scurrying quality" that Williams finds here. While the fugue has been criticized for the disproportionate lengths of its sections (NBA V/10, KB, 60), it is actually one of Bach's most satisfactory early fugues, if also one of the least ambitious. Like most fugues composed around 1700, it still lacks real modulations. Despite brief excursions to related keys (C, B♭, G minor), it quickly returns to the tonic after each of them. Nor is contrapuntal work a major concern; although there are four entries in the initial exposition, the fugue is essentially in three voices, often reduced to two. Its strength lies not in its counterpoint, however, but in the intense motivic development of the ideas in the subject and countersubject. Particularly notable is the reprise (as the fugue nears its end) of a passage from the initial exposition; this serves as a sort of recapitulation (bar 89). While it would not do to stress anticipations of sonata form in such a piece, the reprise is preceded by a skillful retransition in which the two hands both have running sixteenths—a type of texture very common in the episodes of Bach's early fugues, here serving as the climax of the entire movement.

An *entrée* is a dance, usually in binary form, that resembles the dotted portion of an overture; indeed the overture of the Pestel suite in ABB is labeled *Entre* (*sic*) despite the inclusion of a fugal section in triple time. While adopting the traditional pompous character, the entrée in BWV 820 includes an expressive turn toward the minor in the closing phrase.[6] And while the movement shares the general features of an overture, the eighth-notes in the manuscript are not dotted except in bar 26, suggesting that one should not play them dotted elsewhere. But it remains possible that some sort of rhythmic inequality was applied to eighths throughout the movement, even to the point of having an effect identical to dotting.

The three-bar phrasing of the minuet can be traced to French examples (e.g., one from D'Anglebert's *Pièces de clavecin* that follows an entrée arranged from Lully's *Triomphe de l'amour*). The trio is a different sort of movement, in three parts that one can imagine scored for two oboes and bassoon. It seems to require a somewhat slower tempo than the minuet if its rather intricate counterpoint is to be fully heard.

Bourrée and gigue are both straightforward little dances, although the bourrée contains an expressive touch characteristic of Bach's early style: a slurred "sigh" motive that droops downward through a fifth instead of a half-step (bar 7). The gigue is almost a *moto perpetuo*, similar to but more restrained than the one in Handel's early D-Minor Suite HWV 437.

As in most of Bach's early keyboard works, the text is not without problems. Some arise because the youthful composer (or the copyist) left vague certain points that Bach would spell out more clearly in later works. Thus, the repeats in the minuet and trio lead to discontinuities in the bass line when played as written; presumably one was expected to improvise appropriate alterations. In each of the last three movements the repetition of the opening section was indicated by a Da Capo, but one should also probably repeat the portion of the movement following the double bar, leading to the form AABABA.[7] The ornament signs given in both BG and NBA are in the manuscript but are not necessarily Bach's; those in the dotted portion of the overture seem stylistically appropriate, and since some ornaments are absolutely essential in a piece of this type, these might as well be played.

Emendations (see Preface). *Overture*, 2, r.h., appog.: f′; no accidental beneath ornament sign. 4, r.h., 1st chord, add sign for downward arpeggio; l.h., 3d note, orn.: trill. 7, 2d orn.: trill. *Entrée*, 18–19, no ♯ on c′, f″. 24, no accidentals (flat is later addition in manuscript). *Minuet*, 1 (2d time), l.h., first 2 notes F, c? 8, r.h., last note, a″? 9, l.h. rhythm quarter, half? *Trio*, 8 (2d time), l.h., last 3 notes a, g, f? 24 (1st time), like 8?

Ouverture in G Minor BWV 822

Sole source: LEm ms. 8 (unidentified copyist, dated 1743). *Edition*: NBA V/10.

Bach's other early *ouverture* was unknown to the editors of the BG and bears in the NBA the label "probably an arrangement of a foreign composition." Its style is more confident than that of BWV 820, and several movements, including the opening dotted passage, contain as convincing an imitation of orchestral style as any of Handel's early suites. Yet, like BWV 820, the suite bears the hallmarks of the young Bach and seems no more—perhaps somewhat less—likely to be a transcription. The fugue is highly economical in its use of motivic material and contains a remarkable modulating excursion. The following movements include an aria with written-out Italianate embellishment and two minuets consisting entirely of invertible counterpoint; neither type of movement is likely to have originated in an orchestral work. An awkward passage near the end of the overture (bars 142–43) has been cited in support of an orchestral origin (NBA V/10, KB, 84) but is perhaps just a clumsy bit of four-part writing, as in later works of Bach.[8] Several passages in the last movement (a gigue) involve repeated notes that might be thought unsuited to the keyboard but only at a tempo that is probably faster than appropriate for this variety of gigue. Because the chromatic modulations in the first movement seem to point squarely to Bach, it has even been suggested that he interpolated this passage into an existing piece (NBA V/10, KB, 80), but there is no way to prove this.

Small parallels between this work and the *Ouverture* in F, insignificant in themselves but suggestive when taken together, support a common authorship. As in BWV 820, the opening part of the overture closes on a dominant pedal, while the fugal section is highly sequential; several passages use the same sixteenth-note motive as BWV 820.[9] There is again a sort of reprise near the end of the fugue (bars 104ff.), although this now precedes a short passage in which the outer parts both move in sixteenths (bars 118ff.). The gigue, while employing a different sort of rhythm, is again in Da Capo form.

On the other hand, the dotted portion of the overture abandons the simple imitative counterpoint of BWV 820 for a more brilliant orchestral texture characterized by flying *tirate* (quick scales). The fugue, longer and even more insistent in its repetitions of the principal motive, contains some substantial modulations, with decisive cadences to III (bar 38), V of v (bar 55), and VI (bar 90)—the sort of clearly articulated tonal design that would be taken for granted in later works. Preceding the cadence to VI is the extraordinary chromatic passage, which works its way downward through the circle of fifths from D minor to G^b major (bars 55–57) and from there back up to E^b. Unfortunately, the modulations into and out of the distant flat areas are carried out a bit mechanically, as if Bach had just discovered the circle of fifths and was eager to make use of it. Curiously, one sequence employed in the chromatic passage (bars 68–74) recurs later (bars 94–102) with altered accidentals, resulting in a completely different modulation (to G minor instead of G^b). This may be ingenious, but because the modulations in the chromatic passage occur so quickly the fugue as a whole has a slightly madcap quality. Nevertheless, it reveals a fascination with distant modulations; moreover, the most distant tonal excursion occurs in the center rather than near the end, as in some of Bach's other early fugues.

The aria is at least as inventive as the overture and might even be considered the high point of the suite.[10] It is in binary form, with a second "half" somewhat shorter than the first. Despite its brevity the aria is fairly sophisticated; for example, the two-part texture of bar 11 (Example 4.1.) implies deeper voice-leading worthy of the

EXAMPLE 4.1.   *Ouverture* in G Minor BWV 822, aria, bars
    10b–14

mature Bach (especially as emended here). The movement also contains some highly rhetorical writing: the leap of a ninth up to the insistent A♭s in bar 11 and the fourfold repetition of another motivic gesture in bars 14–15, each statement of the motive articulated by rests. The rhetorical "figure" involved in the latter passage—that is, the obstinate or expressive iteration of a note or a simple motive—is fairly common in earlier German keyboard music and can be traced to Frescobaldi.[11] But Bach uses it in conjunction with a tonal scheme whose crux is the fermata on the unexpected chord on the downbeat of bar 13; the rhetoric plays an essential role in the modulation from the subdominant back to G minor.

The *gavotte en rondeau*—that is, a gavotte in simple rondo form—might have been modeled after D'Anglebert's piece of the same title. But Bach concentrates on developing a smaller number of motives than is usually the case with his French predecessor; one of the motives, the sigh introduced in bar 2b, also plays an important role in the following movement, which lacks a title in the source. The NBA calls it a bourrée (perhaps on the model of the *bourrée anglaise* in the partita for unaccompanied flute BWV 1013), but it is closer to a rigaudon. In any case the movement shows harmonic invention recalling that of the overture and aria. A diminished chord plays a prominent role in the opening theme, and the closing phrase includes a quirky Neapolitan harmony. The latter is something that Bach is unlikely to have learned from the French, even though it is part of what was probably meant to be a written-out *petite reprise*—a common device in the French *pièce de clavecin* but also employed in music by Corelli and other Italians.[12]

The invertible two-part counterpoint of the first two minuets resembles that of the canonic minuets of later eighteenth-century composers, including Haydn and C. P. E. Bach. The idea was probably suggested by the canonic dances occasionally encountered in the French harpsichord repertory. The two-part writing and the crossing of voices in minuet 2 suggest that the parts are best played on different (equal) manuals.

In minuet 3 both bass and treble use motivic material related to that of the first two minuets. But this movement is a weak effort, with banal if not faulty melodic writing and voice-leading.[13] Although the manuscript omits a Da Capo indication at the end, minuet 1 presumably should be repeated after this one, so that the three minuets form a rondeau, anticipating the minuet of the First Brandenburg Concerto with its three trios. In such cases it is unclear whether or not repeats should be taken in the "Da Capos" of the first minuet, as Zaslaw (1989, 501–4) argues was the case in Viennese Classical symphonies. The numbered endings in Couperin's rondeaus indicate that the rondeau theme was repeated only the first time.

The suite ends with a French gigue, a type characterized by dotted rhythms and rarely employing imitation. This movement, too, seems weak, lacking the rhythmic subtlety of D'Anglebert's gigues of the same type; the second half falls into routine sequences (bars 8b–11a, 14–18) that seem foreign to the French style emulated here.

Although the source is neatly copied, it contains many apparent errors; emendations are suggested below.

Overture, 136, last 2 beats, 3 voices only, middle voice d', c'? 144, chord, bass c, not d? *Aria*, 5, bass, g, f, g, f, g, a? 6, bass, 2d note, a? 11, treble, notes 9–11, c, d, e♭'? 14, r.h., 1st note, g'? 16, r.h., 5th note, g'? *Bourrée*, 19, treble as in bar 1? tenor b♭, d' (quarters)? See also Note 12. *Minuet 3*, 15, r.h., note 2, add *accent* as in bar 7?

Praeludium et Partita del Tuono Terzo BWV 833

Sole source: MM (No. 44; Johann Christoph Bach). *Editions*: NBA V/10; Dadelsen (1975).

Like the *Ouverture* in G Minor, this little suite was unknown to the editors of the BG, and when it appeared some commentators were reluctant to accept it into the Bach canon. The curious Latin/Italian title perhaps provided grounds for this, as did the work's preservation in only one source. But the identification of the copyist as Bach's older brother has dispelled any serious doubt. Less pretentious than the *ouvertures*, BWV 833 is nevertheless fairly ambitious for its time and follows what seems to be an original plan, if it was indeed conceived as a unity.[14] Although the word *partita* often means "variation," as in the works of Frescobaldi, Kuhnau used a similar title (*Partie*) for his suites.[15] Perhaps it was from Kuhnau also that Bach borrowed the idea of prefacing his suite with a prelude (here called *Präludium*) in a rather reserved imitative style resembling that of some seventeenth-century German consort music.

The suite as a whole has a roughly symmetrical design, the two outer movements (praeludium and air) framing the dances, which Hill (1985, 252) sees as forming two pairs. This is certainly true of the allemande and courante, thanks to their common harmonic ground; the sarabande and its double constitute a pair in a somewhat different sense. The dances are more energetic than the rather restrained outer movements; even the allemande is characterized by repeated notes and leaping motives, while the double of the sarabande is an allegro somewhat reminiscent of seventeenth-century violin writing.[16]

The prelude is marked andante, which at this date should probably be taken literally ("going," "walking"), as a warning against a slow tempo. The imitations, though simple, are handled skillfully, but the most distant modulations perhaps occur too late, an expressive move toward C minor taking place just four bars from the end.

The courante is notated in $\frac{3}{4}$ (the time-signature is just "3" in MM) but is really in what we would call $\frac{6}{4}$. As in many courantes, the bar-lines signify beats rather than measures;[17] two measures here correspond to one in the allemande. Although the two movements share some motivic material, their main common point is the harmonic ground, a notable feature of which is the use of the minor mode in the closing phrase of the first half (as in the entrée of BWV 820). At one point the courante departs from the ground, two bars (29–30) being inserted. But because several other bars of the model are compressed, the length remains the same as in the allemande: twenty bars of $\frac{6}{4}$.[18]

The sarabande, with its cadences on the third beat of every fourth bar, is of a type more common in the seventeenth than the eighteenth century. There is hardly any sign of the accented second beat usually taken to be typical of the dance, and while only the double is marked allegro, the sarabande itself perhaps should have the lively character of many seventeenth-century examples. Indeed, the tempo mark of the double may reflect not a real change in tempo but merely that smaller note-values prevail here (sixteenths in place of eighths). These probably should not be taken too quickly; the counterpoint is fairly intricate, and the lines would lose clarity and grace at too lively a tempo.

The most original movement of the suite is the final air, an imitation-aria whose ritornellos even employ figured bass notation, hence resembling those of a late seventeenth-century continuo aria. As a translation of a vocal idiom to the keyboard, the movement resembles the *Lamento* of BWV 992 and points forward to the recitative section of the Chromatic Fantasia. Quasi-vocal writing is also evident in certain "rhetorical" details: the pauses in the opening theme, which is broken up into small "speaking" motives, and the motives themselves, short descending gestures whose contour and sequential treatment recur in other early works like the Sonata in D (BWV 963) and the opening movement of the cantata *Aus der Tiefen* (BWV 131). The air seems to share some of the melancholy character of those works and despite the allegro marking seems best if not rushed. As in Bach's later titles, the use of French as opposed to Italian may be significant; this movement (unlike the aria of BWV 822) lacks Italianate embellishment, and it is more a rondeau than a Da Capo form, the "Dal Segno" indication at the end signifying only a repetition of the opening ritornello.[19]

By Bach's later standards the movement goes too far in imitating the vocal idiom; the figured bass notation makes it unclear precisely what sort of realization the composer had in mind. Since the bass has the melody in the ritornellos, the right hand should probably add a fairly discreet accompaniment, without elaborate counterpoint. In general, two added parts probably suffice, perhaps to be amplified at cadences and elsewhere, as in the suggested realization (Example 4.2). Should this accompaniment be played on the quieter upper manual (if available)? And should the harmonic filling-in continue after the end of the ritornello, in the "solo"

EXAMPLE 4.2.   Praeludium et Partita in F, BWV 833, air,
bars 1–21, with suggested inner voices (parentheses indicate
later additions in MM)

passages? Some such filling-in seems necessary (see Example 4.2); on the other hand, the entries of the upper part occasionally overlap the ends of the ritornellos (e.g., in bar 20), making it impractical to divide accompaniment and melody (or ritornello and "solo") between manuals.

Textual problems are few. In the prelude, an added d' on the downbeat of bar 14 would allow the soprano to enter with the first note of the subject (compare bar 19). A natural can be placed before the B (-flat) in bar 4 of the allemande on the basis of the parallel harmonic structure of the courante. In the courante, some trills on ascending notes are better played as mordents or left out: in bars 5 (on b♭'), 33 (on a'), 35, and 36. On the other hand, the mordent signs in Example 4.2 might be better realized as trills, if played at all.

Partie in A, BWV 832

Chief sources: MM (No. 38, Johann Christoph Bach; title: Suite; allemande and air only); Gb, Sammlung Scholz (without title); B Br II 4093 (formerly Fétis 2960; title: Partie). Editions: BG 42; NBA V/10; Dadelsen (1975).

The authenticity of this little suite was once rejected on stylistic grounds, and as recently as 1984 it was listed in a thematic catalogue of the works of Telemann.[20] But the sources listed above independently attribute it to Bach.[21] MM, while giving only the first two movements, also adds a few ornaments and a few obvious mistakes, but its attribution to Bach can hardly be doubted.[22]

Whatever the original title—a point on which the sources disagree—all five movements seem plausible products of the young Bach, despite their stylistic heterogeneity. Actually, the one odd movement is the second, the Aire pour les Trompettes. The title might have been borrowed from the Air de Trompette in a group of pieces (ABB, No. 38) arranged from the opera Alcide by Marais and Louis de Lully; Eichberg (NBA V/10, KB, 71) notes a fleeting motivic resemblance. But the French piece is a real trumpet tune; like the one by Purcell called the Cebell (Z. T678) it is in duple time and its melody is playable on the natural (valveless) instrument. That is hardly the case here. Indeed, the music has little in common with Baroque trumpet writing, and the title might refer to the organ stop known as the trompette. If so, however, that would suggest playing the melody on a separate solo manual, which again is impractical. In any case, trumpets are not the only brass instruments alluded to; bar 21 contains the octaves of the posthorn, the instrument referred to in two movements of the Capriccio BWV 992 (see Chapter 6).[23]

Despite some fleeting motivic parallelisms (noted by Hill 1985, 253) and the use of similar cadential formulas in different movements, this is not a variation-suite. But the plans of the first two movements do have some points in common; both are in the usual binary form, and both reach somewhat exotic keys midway through the second half: C♯ minor in the allemande, F♯ minor in the air. The sarabande also contains some notable harmonic progressions, passing from a chord of the mediant (C♯ minor) to that of the Neapolitan (B♭) in the space of just six bars (9–14); the Neapolitan appears as part of another expressive excursis in the minor mode.

The simple two-part writing in both bourrée and gigue may have contributed to the assignment of the suite to Telemann, but it is also characteristic of Bach's later bourrées, and we have already seen it in BWV 820. On the other hand, the easy arpeggiations of the left hand in the gigue are uncharacteristic of Bach's later music. But they are more than an Alberti-style accompaniment, for the bass is the lower voice in a two-part texture that is inverted after the double bar.

Suite in B♭, BWV 821

Sole source: SPK P 804/24. *Edition*: BG 42.

The Suite in B♭ is one of many works published in the BG as Bach's but banished to a projected supplementary volume in the NBA. On a stylistic basis this little suite is no less plausible than the others considered in this chapter. But it has the misfortune of being preserved only in a copy of uncertain provenance that found its way into the Kellner miscellaney (P 804). Recent discoveries strengthen the assignment to Bach: Several of the early chorales attributed to Bach in the "Neumeister" manuscript at Yale (LM 4708) show parallels with the last movement. Various other details also suggest Bach; for example, the first half of the allemande swerves toward the Neapolitan (in bar 8) in a manner reminiscent of the untitled dance in BWV 822, and there are a number of melodic formulas commonly met in Bach's early pieces.[24]

The overall form—three dance movements framed by a prelude and an *echo*—resembles that of BWV 833. The prelude is again imitative but livelier and limited to three voices except at the end, hence resembling a trio-sonata. A few passages, especially some parallel sixths in running sixteenths (bars 10, 13), are hard to play, but they are fully justified by the logic of the voice-leading and hardly speak against Bach's authorship.[25]

In texture the allemande closely resembles the prelude and comes close to quoting it (compare bar 16 with bar 11 of the prelude). This is only one of several connections between movements. As in BWV 832, the allemande and courante, although not forming a variation pair, are related by their unusual harmonic designs. The first half of each ends in a minor key, that of the allemande in the relative minor (vi), of the courante in the mediant (iii). The right-hand solo over a pedal-point at the opening of the courante forms a continuation of the passage for right hand alone at the end of the allemande; it also recalls courantes in two of Handel's suites (HWV 430, 439), but this is no doubt fortuitous.

The sarabande is of an altogether different type from that of BWV 832 or 833. Rhythmically and melodically it is more in the French mold (e.g., in the cadential formula in bars 15–16), but the imitative opening is unusual. This opening shares a certain delicate pathos with other early Bach works, thanks to two unexpected arrivals on G-minor triads (bars 4, 7). The cadence to F *minor* in bar 16 could be another expressive touch, but the flats in that bar may merely be a mistaken extension of those in the preceding bar; it would be more in keeping with the French gesture imitated here to return to F major for the cadence itself.[26]

The concluding *echo* opens with a motive similar to that of the sarabande. Echo movements in suites are a rarity, but they had been common in German and Dutch organ music since the early Baroque. The device, best known to harpsichordists from the echo movement in the B-Minor *Ouverture* BWV 831, also occurs in the last of the *partite* (variations) on *O Gott du frommer Gott!* (BWV 767), which contains a passage very similar to bars 41ff. here. Echoes also occur in one of the "Neumeister" chorales (*Ich hab' mein' Sach'* BWV 1113).

The "Neumeister" chorales also furnish a parallel for the coda of the echo movement, which is notated as a melody with figured bass under the rubrics *adagio* and *Tutti*. This has led to the suggestion that the *echo* is an arrangement of a lost orchestral work (see NBA V/10, KB, 48). But, as Stinson (1989a, 123) notes, the closing passage bears a remarkable resemblance to the conclusion of the setting of *Alle Menschen müssen sterben* BWV 1117, which is in the same key and bears the same adagio marking.[27] Realizing the figured bass in this passage is less a problem than in BWV 833 and 992, as a simple chordal texture with full harmonies in both hands is clearly what is intended and is easily improvised.

The movement itself is in the form of a rondeau. In the source, the repetition of the initial section after bar 18 is indicated by a Dal Segno—implying that a further Dal Segno (not marked) should be taken before the coda. That, however, might be more repetition than the rather slender musical content can bear. Forte and piano measures alternate regularly up to bar 36; by then the novelty of the echo effects will have worn off. Yet the movement was planned with some care. The first *couplet* (bars 9–18) moves to G minor and D minor, the keys reached at the double bars of the allemande and courante, respectively. The second *couplet* (bars 27–39) moves toward "flatter" tonalities, E♭ and then F minor, on the way passing through a few compelling chromatic progressions; this is the high point of the entire suite, not unworthy of Bach. The coda is unrelated to the rest of the movement, but like the codas of some of the early fugues, serves to bring the suite to a grand ending.

Emendations to the text as given in BG: *Allemande*, 17, r.h., last three notes: f″-d″-e♭″? *Sarabande*, 15–16, natural, not flat, after the first a″? *Echo*: the only figures in P 804 are 7 (bar 45, on g) and $\frac{7}{5}$ (bar 48, on g).

Suite in F Minor BWV 823

Sole source: P 804/45 (Kellner). *Editions*: BG 36 (appendix); NBA V/10; Dadelsen (1975).

This suite has been thought inauthentic and in the BG was designated "Fragment of a Suite." Kellner's copy ends with the customary *Fine*, indicating that he thought it was complete, but his lapses as a copyist in other works have led scholars to question his attribution here.

Indeed, it is not entirely obvious that "the style of all three movements confirms the ascription to J. S. Bach" (Eichberg, in NBA, V/10, KB, 65). If Bach's, the suite must be somewhat later than those previously discussed; Dadelsen's suggestion (1975, 133) that it stems "from the middle of Bach's Weimar period, before 1715" would be plausible. But the style differs considerably from that of the mature suites, and there are still a few gaucheries: the low rumbling accompaniment through much of the sarabande and the implicit parallel octaves in a recurring passage of the gigue (bars 24–31, 44–51). Moreover, the sequence of movements is odd: prelude, sarabande, gigue. Kellner might have omitted some movements, but the internal forms of the first two movements are also exceptional. The prelude is a "rondeau with three couplets," as Eichberg puts it, while the sarabande is in Da Capo form, which is found in other early dances by Bach, but not sarabandes. In addition, the prelude is a sort of chaconne, for the *couplets* form a series of variations upon a bass; the A section of the sarabande is likewise constructed over a descending tetrachord in the bass.

Is the style that of Bach? The forms of the first two movements hardly speak against him. The embellished melodic line of the sarabande includes formulas reminiscent of many authentic works, and it can be played on a separate manual, as in the sarabandes of three of the French Suites (presumably later works). The writing in the third couplet of the prelude—sequences composed of running figuration in both hands—resembles that found in many of Bach's early keyboard works. In short, until a conflicting attribution is found, Bach does seem the most likely composer.

Emendations: *Prelude*, 1, 5, etc.: ornament: *Schleifer* (slide), not appoggiatura. 9: ornament: inverted turn with natural. *Sarabande*: title includes the words *en rondeau*. 2, 10, 12, 18, 22: appoggiaturas are written as 8ths, not 16ths. 3, 5, 19, small values (16ths, 32ds) are slurred. 6, l.h., c′ is half-note without dot.

Suite in E Minor for Lute BWV 996

Sources: DSB P 801 (Walther); copy by Heinrich Nicolaus Gerber; B Br II 4093 (= Fétis 2960). *Editions* BG 45; NBA V/10.

Most if not all of Bach's lute music was played on keyboard instruments in the eighteenth century, and there is good reason for thinking that Bach himself had the keyboard in mind for such pieces, at least as an alternative medium. The works survive more in keyboard than in lute sources; two copies of BWV 996 are in the hands of organists—one a colleague, one a student, of Bach—while the third source gives the piece in a keyboard version transposed to A minor.[28] In Walther's copy somebody has added an indication that the piece is for the lute-harpsichord, but the handwriting is unidentified and the entry is probably just a plausible conjecture.

The lute and its repertory had exerted a profound influence on harpsichord music in the seventeenth century, but in Bach's music the inspiration flows from his keyboard style to the lute works.[29] While Bach knew lutenists at Leipzig and owned a lute at his death, he did not necessarily play the instrument with any facility and seems to have written the pieces in score rather than in lute tablature, leaving the transcription to others. He himself must have played the works at the keyboard, and thus it is not surprising that most of the lute works contain slurs and sustained notes, many of which would be routine in keyboard writing but can hardly be made audible on the lute.

Nevertheless, BWV 996 is a true lute work. It lies entirely within the instrument's range, which is lower and smaller (restricted to three octaves) than usual in Bach's keyboard music. Many passages contain figuration more suited to the lute than to the keyboard, and the inner voices and even the bass are often broken up in a way that would not be necessary in a keyboard work. On the keyboard one might sustain certain notes longer than written, even add a few chord tones or alter the register of an occasional bass note. But any further adaptation is likely to do violence to Bach's harmony and voice-leading, which, as in the unaccompanied violin and cello music, is entirely self-sufficient.

The E-Minor Suite is clearly the earliest of the surviving lute pieces, although its relatively mature style implies that it is somewhat later than the suites considered above. The prelude, as in English Suite No. 6, is actually a self-contained prelude and fugue, but the fugue is relatively short, and the initial section resembles that of some of the toccatas and other early works. The initial flourish on the tonic chord—a standard device in preludes and improvisations[30]—bears the indication *Passaggio*. Term and gesture both recur at the beginning of the Prelude and Fugue in G Minor BWV 535a for organ. Despite its brevity, the fugue achieves considerable intensity as the texture builds to four real parts in bars 46–54 and again in the closing bars.

Bach's assimilation of the French style in the first two dances is flawless, apart from a prosaic sequence in the allemande (beginning in the middle of bar 13). The sarabande is as compelling as any from Bach's later suites, already revealing what was to be his characteristic mixture of French and Italian styles. The latter is evident in the melodic embellishment, which is of far greater sophistication than in the ornamented slow movements of the earlier suites. As in BWV 820, the last two dances, a bourrée and a gigue, seem less close to French models. Indeed, the gigue is very much sui generis; it is not strictly fugal, nor is it really a gigue at all, but simply a freely contrapuntal movement in binary form.

5

The Early Fugues

Bach's name is inseparably associated with fugue. When or how Bach came to recognize his special talent for fugal writing is impossible to say, but C. P. E. Bach's testimony that his father studied fugue on his own suggests that it took place during his years at Arnstadt (1703–7).[1] By the time he reached Weimar in 1708, Bach was a master of various types of fugal writing—not only in those keyboard pieces actually called fugues, of which only a few survive from that date, but in the fugal sections of larger keyboard pieces and vocal works.

Fugue is essentially a texture, not a form or genre. Any composition could employ *fuga*, that is, imitation, but before Bach's time few pieces were designated fugues as such. We have already seen a few fugues serving as parts of the suites considered in Chapter 4, and there will be more in the sonatas, fantasias, toccatas, and other works discussed in Chapters 6 and 7. It is possible that the self-contained pieces considered in this chapter were composed in emulation of the ricercars, fantasias, and other fugal works by Sweelinck, Frescobaldi, Froberger, and other composers.[2] But while some of Bach's early fugues (BWV 896, 949) contain exhaustive contrapuntal workings-out of their subjects, only the Canzona BWV 588 adopts the *stile antico*, the quasi-Renaissance manner generally employed in the learned fugal compositions of seventeenth-century composers. None contains more than a suggestion of the intense chromaticism associated with the *stile antico* in certain Baroque works (e.g., Froberger's capricci) and in some of Bach's own late works (see Wolff 1968). On the other hand, the more idiomatic keyboard style of Bach's early fugues would have allowed them to serve as sections of larger works in which fugue as such was not the main concern: *praeludia*, toccatas, and sonatas.

Thus the Fugue in B♭ on a theme by Reinken (BWV 954) might have been destined for a complete transcription of one of Reinken's chamber sonatas, like BWV 965. Several other early fugues conclude with free *pedaliter* codas such as occur at the ends of Bach's, Buxtehude's, and other composers' *praeludia*, where the coda balances a free section at the beginning of the piece. In the absence of a separate prelude or prelude-like section, players might even have felt obliged to improvise one, and in several instances Bach is known to have brought together a prelude and a fugue composed separately. Copyists sometimes took the matter into their own hands, without the composer's authorization, as appears to have been the case with the B-Minor Fugue BWV 951 (discussed below), which in some sources is preceded by a prelude in the same key (BWV 923).

One aspect of the early fugues that has drawn frequent attention is the use of borrowed subjects and other material. Bach borrowed thematic material not only from Reinken but from Corelli, Albinoni, and other Italian composers.[3] How Bach selected his models and why he wrote these pieces is unknown. They were not necessarily study pieces, since, with the exception of BWV 946, they are relatively mature in style. Moreover, they are new compositions, not transcriptions, sharing only the subject and sometimes a few additional motivic ideas with their models, from which they depart in fundamental matters of style and form. Perhaps these pieces contained an element of personal homage; probably too Bach was eager to show what he could do with subjects whose potential had hardly been exhausted by the works in which he found them. It is also possible that these fugues reflect a tradition of virtuoso improvisation on existing subjects. With the exception of BWV 946 and BWV 955 these are large display pieces, and among them are some of the most impressive of Bach's early fugues.

The presence of simple pedal parts in several closing passages raises the question of medium. In two cases (BWV 949 and 950) the pedal is limited chiefly to holding a few pedal-points that can be dropped without any significant loss. Another (BWV 955) requires only minimal participation of the pedal, at a few points where tenor and bass are momentarily separated by wide intervals. While at least some of these pieces were probably intended originally for the organ, the absence of thorough-going pedal parts distinguishes them from "organ fugues" as such. The subjects are not limited to motives playable on the pedals, and the bass is as lively as the other voices. The absence of a true pedal part means that the large structure cannot be articulated by climactic pedal statements of the subject (e.g., at the end), as is often the case in organ fugues. But these "clavier" fugues form a distinct category, and harpsichordists are probably justified in adapting the closing passages to make them playable on instruments without pedals.

Another question arising in these pieces is that of authenticity. Like the suites, these early fugues are preserved in manuscripts of greatly varying dependability. Recent discoveries have clarified the authorship and even the genre of one piece (BWV 957), but for several others the attribution depends upon stylistic consider-ations. All the pieces treated in this chapter, if not surely by Bach, have at least good prospects for being his. BWV 957, 533a, and 588 are also certainly Bach's, but because they raise special questions of setting and genre they are considered out of chronological sequence at the end of the chapter.

The earliest fugues may have survived only by accident or because collectors regarded them as curiosities. Bach cannot have used them in his teaching except during the earliest period. Still, BWV 951 and possibly several others exist in more than one authentic version, showing that Bach found them worth saving and revising either for teaching or for his own performing.

Chronology and Style

As with attribution, the determination of chronology depends largely on style. While the counterpoint of these works is often strong and imaginative, it does not always measure up to Bach's later standards. Passages in four parts are rare—in four-part fugues the first voice usually drops out at the entry of the fourth—and clumsy parallelisms, harsh passing dissonances, and excessively wide spacings (exceeding an octave within either hand) sometimes arise. Presumably this is due not so much to weak contrapuntal technique per se as to inexperience in the difficult art of writing meaningful counterpoint playable without pedals on a keyboard instrument. Indeed, what attracted Bach to fugue in the first place may have been not contrapuntal artifice but the particular sorts of drama attainable only in fugue: the gradual accumulation of sonority during the initial exposition and the climaxes achieved through strategically placed entries of the subject later on (as in a final bass entry). Eventually he also discovered how to incorporate into his fugues something resembling the concerto's dramatic alternation between tutti and soloist. The result was the type of design that alternates between "tutti" expositions and soloistic episodes; examples of this already occur among the early fugues, although without the rounded modulating scheme of the mature Venetian concerto.

Bach's interest in the dramatic aspects of fugue might explain his avoidance in the early fugues not only of the *stile antico* but also of the somewhat mechanical permutational schemes used in some of Reinken's works (see the discussion of BWV 954 below). To be sure, among the surviving early fugues are one or two that focus on contrapuntal work. But even these avoid the abstract subjects of the old ricercar, preferring dancelike or rhetorical themes. Such subjects sometimes led to problems, however, as the pauses and repeated motivic gestures of some of the more "rhetorical" subjects (like that of the fugue in BWV 533a) are not particularly suited to complex counterpoint. Idiomatic keyboard writing in the subjects of some other fugues caused comparable problems; the wide leaps in the subject of the closing fugue of BWV 992 make for a lively theme (and are perfectly playable by themselves) but produce awkward spacings and voice-crossings when combined with other parts. Subjects (or countersubjects, as in the G-Minor Toccata) containing octave leaps are more easily maintained in *pedaliter* works—there is a notable example in Buxtehude's E-Minor Praeludium for organ (BuxWV 142)—and Bach must have gradually learned what sorts of subjects are appropriate to a given setting and a given type of fugue.

While Bach's approach to keyboard counterpoint matured, his sense of form changed. The Capriccio BWV 993, one of several early fugues that stress virtuoso keyboard writing, has an improvisatory structure: Expositions combine the subject with continually changing counter-material, and each episode likewise introduces new material. BWV 946, while concerned more with strict counterpoint than with keyboard display, is also improvisatory in the sense that the order of the entries follows no obvious plan. Later fugues generally have more cogent structures that seem to reflect some acquaintance with the rounded modulatory designs and clearly articulated ritornello structures of the Venetian concerto. The two versions of the Fugue in B Minor after Albinoni show Bach's progress very clearly. The earlier (BWV 951a) is a patchwork, while the later (BWV 951) is conceived more as a large formal unity, even containing hints of the recapitulatory structure found in most concerto movements and in many of Bach's later fugues.

The term "recapitulation" is used here not in the sense familiar from the study of Classical sonata form but to refer to any transposed restatement of episodic material.[4] The rarity of long episodes in Bach's earliest fugues makes recapitulation in this sense irrelevant there. But as fugues began to incorporate long episodes, often in concerto style, recapitulation became an essential device. It made possible a sense of order lacking in those rambling early fugues (e.g., BWV 993) that give the impression of having been improvisatorily extended. Such works obey an earlier, more literally baroque, aesthetic that placed a high value on variety and the absence of pattern. This aesthetic, though congenial to a composer still under the sway of the seventeenth-century *stylus fantasticus*, was at odds with the incipient classicism that can be perceived in, for example, the sonatas by Albinoni that supplied several of Bach's subjects. By the time of the final version of BWV 951 Bach had apparently accepted the need for more predictable formal patterns.

BWV 951 in its final form might date from the very end of the Weimar years. But most of these fugues clearly predate the works discussed in Chapters 7 and 8. Except for BWV 951, the early fugues cannot be counted among Bach's great works. But they show that Bach posed difficult compositional challenges for himself and that on the whole he met those challenges successfully.

Prelude and Fugue in A, BWV 896

Chief Sources: MM (No. 34; Johann Christoph Bach); SPK P 804/3 (Mey; fugue only). *Editions*: BG 36 (fugue only); BJ 9 (1912) (Wolffheim; prelude only).

Although this piece is furnished with a short prelude in the copy by Bach's older brother, the prelude is lacking in the other, later copy from which the BG edition was made, and at this writing the two pieces still have not appeared together in a critical edition.[5] This is a pity; the fugue is attractive and, for its time, ambitious, while the prelude, though too short to stand on its own, goes well with the fugue. Neither movement calls for pedals; suggestions of *brisé* or *luthé* style in the prelude together with the dancelike character of the fugue (in a giguelike $\frac{6}{8}$) make both suitable for the harpsichord. Christoph Bach's title *Praeludium ex A*[#] seems to refer only to the prelude, and while it might have been meant to apply to both movements taken together, the frequent omission of work-titles in MM (as in other manuscripts) makes it unlikely that the two movements were conceived as a unified *praeludium*.[6]

The prelude is like nothing else in the Bach canon, although Hill (1987, 435–36) notes parallels with "a type of keyboard aria" cultivated by earlier German composers; the same rhythmic texture occurs in the eighth of Buxtehude's *partite* on La Capricciosa (BuxWV 250). The continuous dotting of the upper part has nothing to do with the French overture but may instead be a sort of written-out inequality, well suited to the flowing melodic line. The piece consists of just two phrases of six bars each, both ending with wistful cadences ending on the weak part of the bar.

The second cadence is repeated in a written-out *petite reprise* (bars 11–12 are a varied repetition of 9–10).

The fugue has a vivacious giguelike subject, yet it looks forward to certain of Bach's later fugues in its systematic exploration of strettos and inversions using a single subject. The initial exposition—in four real parts—leads to paired stretto entries by the lower and upper voices, respectively (bars 24bff.). A second exposition, opening with an entry in the dominant, begins precisely at the midpoint (bar 34) and includes the one entry of the subject in a minor key, a stretto entrance in B minor (tenor, bar 35). Thus the modulation, while ephemeral, is sensibly placed just after the center of the piece. In this sort of fugue, however, the drama lies more in contrapuntal work than in modulation, and the final exposition combines *rectus* and *inversus* versions of the subject in stretto (bar 48ff.) and in a pair of simultaneous entries (bar 56). This is, in simple form, precisely the sort of design that Bach would use in many later fugues that were meant to demonstrate the artifices of counterpoint—for example, the fugue in B♭ minor in WTC2.

The inspiration for this type of fugue might have come from Reinken's fugal gigues, which offered a model for strict contrapuntal writing outside the *stile antico*. But unlike Reinken's gigues, BWV 896 offsets rigorous expository passages with episodes. The latter, although short and restrained, are just distinct enough in style to set the expository sections in relief. The episodes, curiously enough, suggest another possible model, the dance movements in Kuhnau's Biblical Sonatas, which the fugue seems to quote at several points.[7]

The edition of the fugue in the BG, based as it is only on a later and inferior source, contains some erroneous editorial emendations. The copy in MM is not faultless either. Emendations: 12–13, l.h., tie f♯ and a. 18, sop., 2d half of bar, dotted quarter-rest (not d″); ten., 5th note, d♯″. 36, alto, 4th note, d″; bass, last note, d♯? 40, ten., 2d half of bar, dotted quarter-rest (not b)? 41, ten., 1st note, a (not e′). 47, alto, 4th note, d′ (not d″). 54, bass, 4th note, A (not A♯). 66, bass, 1st half of bar, quarter-note, 8th-rest.

Fugue in A, BWV 949

Chief sources: ABB (No. 19; Johann Christoph Bach); SPK P 804/37 (Mey). *Editions*: BG 36; Dadelsen and Rönnau (1970).

BWV 949 is another fugue in A, preserved like BWV 896 in copies by Johann Christoph Bach and from the Kellner circle.[8] The use of A major in both fugues may be only a coincidence, but since BWV 949 is another contrapuntally organized fugue it is possible that Bach associated rigorous contrapuntal writing with the use of what was at the time a fairly adventurous key on the distant "sharp" side of C.[9]

Hill (1987, 447) considers BWV 896 "probably a considerably earlier composition than BWV 949." But the pieces have much in common. As in BWV 896, the subject of BWV 949 moves by step after an initial "repercussive" motive, and the few episodes are brief and restrained. The present subject is more square, without strong dance implications, but the writing gradually grows more exuberant, with hints of violin style in the episodic passages. Figuration emerges triumphant over contrapuntal work in a short *pedaliter* coda. Elsewhere as well BWV 949 seems the more adventurous of the two pieces. Only BWV 949 modulates to F# minor, even introducing the subject—in inversion—in that key (bar 35). Indeed, Bach seems to have had something of an obsession with F# minor in this piece, altering two entries of the subject chromatically in order to permit modulations to the relative minor (bars 22, 61). To be sure, the repeated moves to F# minor become somewhat monotonous, and there is no tonal design underlying the piece as a whole. The large design turns instead on the introduction of the inversion just short of the midpoint (bar 35). But the introduction of the inversion does coincide with the least ephemeral of the modulations to F# minor, the only one marked by a strong cadence in that key (bar 41).

The fugue must be one of the earliest of Bach's to have a regular countersubject—two countersubjects, actually. But perhaps more important than the presence of countersubjects is the fact that there is very little motivic material anywhere that is not directly related to the subject or the first countersubject. Unfortunately, this single-mindedness, like that governing key relations, is not to the piece's advantage. It winds up nearly repeating itself several times—the second of the two altered entries in the relative minor is almost a reprise of the first one—and the repetitions do not fall into any rational recapitulatory pattern as in some later fugues.

Hence, this may be a somewhat less successful piece than BWV 896. Both works, it must be said, suffer from occasionally rough passing dissonances, although the seconds and fourths that arise from the melodic logic of the individual lines are barely noticeable at a sufficiently lively tempo. The problem here is that the subject is essentially an ascending pentachord, and rather too many expository passages consist of little more than parallel or contrary movement within the triad outlined by the subject. Such polyphony is easy to write and occurs frequently not only in Bach's early works but throughout the earlier Baroque. It leads to a proliferation of sequential progressions over stepwise bass lines and to more frequent doublings of the third of the triad than would be tolerated in Bach's later works (see bars 62 and 64). Moreover, the tolerance for parallel octaves and fifths on successive strong beats suggests that Bach—like most composers before 1700—still had his eyes firmly on the musical surface, paying little attention to voice-leading at deeper levels.[10]

The coda calls for four pedal notes, and this fact together with the break in the texture at the diminished chord in bar 80 sharply articulates the coda from the rest of the piece. Nevertheless, the *pedaliter* close seems a natural extension of the main body of the fugue, thanks to the use of related motivic material. Harpsichordists can omit the pedal notes, which form inessential octave doublings with other voices.[11]

Existing editions of BWV 949 contain some questionable editorial emendations, but as the manuscripts appear to be faulty some changes are probably justified. Further emendations: 19 and 67, sop., 3d note, g♮'?

Capriccio in E, BWV 993

Chief sources: SPK P 804/7 (Kellner); SPK P 1087 (Preller); B Br 4093 (Fétis 2960; in F); SPK P 409 (in F). *Editions*: BG 36; NBA V/10.

Bach wrote two very different early works entitled *Capriccio*: the present one and BWV 992 (see Chapter 6). Both are connected in some way to one of his brothers;

otherwise they have little in common. Kellner's copy of BWV 993 bears the subtitle *in honorem Johann Christoph Bachii*, to which several later copies add *Ohrdruf*, presumably to identify the dedicatee rather than the place of composition. It is curious that the piece is found in neither MM nor ABB. This cannot be because BWV 993 is particularly late; its style is probably roughly contemporary with that of BWV 896 and BWV 949. Perhaps Sebastian gave his older brother a special dedication copy too precious to have been kept in the larger collections. Christoph lived until 1721; whatever the reason for Sebastian's writing a piece in his honor, there is no question of *honorem* meaning the same as *memoriam*.

The word *capriccio* also raises questions. In MM and ABB it is attached to a number of diverse compositions and may have meant nothing more than a free, otherwise unclassifiable piece. BWV 993 is a fugue, but an exceptionally long one containing lengthy episodes in violin style; in this it resembles the first of two ambitious but rather clumsy capricci in ABB (Nos. 10 and 44) attributed, somewhat doubtfully, to "Polaroli."[12] Bach's piece is much more accomplished, touching upon an unusual variety of tonalities and figuration and extending longer than any other single movement in Bach's early keyboard works—120 long bars, not counting the brief *pedaliter* coda. It is tempting to suppose that the work was intended as a summing up of everything that Bach had learned through his first twenty years or so, with a grateful bow to his older brother. But while the Capriccio makes somewhat greater demands on the player than the works previously considered here, and explores the remote keys of $D^{\sharp}$ minor and $G^{\sharp}$ minor, it avoids the relatively sophisticated counterpoint displayed in works like BWV 896 or 949. In its rambling episodic structure it resembles two long fugues attributed to W. H. Pachelbel; Bach's older brother was a student of Johann Pachelbel, and perhaps such pieces were characteristic of fugal improvisation in the Pachelbel school.

Veracini, in his unpublished treatise *Il trionfo della pratica musicale*, gave a definition for *capriccio concertato* that perhaps applies to this type of fugue (see J. W. Hill 1979, 269). But while the design of BWV 993 somewhat resembles that of a concerto movement, an equally compelling analogy might be made to the rondeau. There is only one regular exposition, at the beginning, after which the entries of the subject alternate with often lengthy sequential episodes. These episodes form the real substance of the work. Some employ violinistic arpeggiation of the sort found in BWV 947 (considered next), but most of the material seems closer in inspiration to north Germany than to Italy.

The rondolike structure does not preclude some of the more effective design elements found in Bach's other early fugues. The most remote key, $D^{\sharp}$ minor, is reached at about the middle of the piece (bar 61), and there is some sense of accumulating tension in two of the last three episodes (bars 81b–89a, 92–97), thanks to the massive chords accompanying the figuration in the right hand. The last two statements of the subject are presented in four parts, accompanied by three sustained voices; this sounds quite grand after the rather nervous passage-work in two and three parts. Yet, despite the variety of figuration and the sure command of counterpoint, modulation, and keyboard idiom, the piece is perhaps too long to hold interest. The structure remains episodic, and the flurry of thirty-seconds in the coda is almost as irrelevant to the rest of the work as the solemn closing passage of BWV 946. The pedal notes here, incidentally, cannot be left out and (on the harpsichord) must be taken with the left hand, although this makes the figuration barely playable. Two entries of the subject in the body of the piece are also marked for pedal, but these indications appear to be a copyist's additions, and harpsichordists can disregard them.[13]

Fugue in A Minor BWV 947

Source: Edition by Griepenkerl (Leipzig, 1847). *Modern editions*: BG 36; Dadelsen and Rönnau (1970).

The authenticity of BWV 947 is somewhat questionable, as the manuscripts in which it was preserved are lost and it is known only from nineteenth-century editions.[14] Although a real fugue, it is more homophonic than any of the others examined in this chapter. There is a regular countersubject, but the last few statements of the subject are accompanied simply by chords, and the episodes throughout are composed largely of figuration with equally simple accompaniment. These episodes depend to an unusual degree on sequences and formulaic passage-work; they alternate with expository passages somewhat more regularly than in the most dependably attributed early Bach fugues, producing a design particularly reminiscent of the concerto.

Since a somewhat similar design occurs in the Capriccio BWV 993 and other early works, the form alone does not rule out Bach's authorship. Indeed, the subject and the style are both quite close to those of the opening movement of the organ Fantasia in G, BWV 571. But that work's authenticity is also open to question, despite a somewhat more dependable source situation.[15] In both cases, however, it may be wrong to see the somewhat simplistic style as a point against Bach's authorship. These pieces may simply be early attempts to write a type of fugue drawing on the newer types of Italian ensemble music. The imitation of concerto style (if that is what it is) in BWV 947 and 571 is far from exact; violinistic figuration and ritornello style have been filtered through the traditions of the German keyboard fugue. If the composer was indeed Bach, he is likely to have written both pieces considerably earlier than 1713, since the Vivaldi transcriptions probably dating from around that year are technically far more sophisticated.

Fugue in B♭ (after Erselius?) BWV 955

Earlier version: *Sources*: SPK P 247/2 (in G); SPK P 595/9 (Ringk, in B♭). *Edition*: BG 42, appendix (in B♭).

Later version: *Sources*: SPK P 804/17 (title by Kellner); SPK P 425/2 (Kellner circle). *Editions*: BG 42; Dadelsen and Rönnau (1970).

The obscure Johann Christoph Erselius owes his small share of immortality to Bach, or rather to the unidentified person who wrote the words *di Erselio* at the head of one copy of the present fugue.[16] Erselius became organist at Freiberg Cathedral in 1731; Agricola praised him in 1768 as "one of Germany's strongest [*bravsten*] players" (Adlung 1768, 1:229). While he had previously been a musician at the

Dresden court (Flade 1953, 128n.), these dates suggest that Erselius belonged to the generation following Bach. Thus, Erselius seems unlikely to have furnished the latter with the model for the present composition. Moreover, while the G-major version bearing Erselius's name has been regarded as the original (e.g., in the NG work-list), it contains a few errors implying that the copyist himself made the transposition, perhaps to permit the use of pedal for the entries in bars 27 and 48, which would otherwise pass above middle C, the highest note on many Baroque pedalboards. [17]

Hence, there is reason to question the title *Fuge von J. C. Erselius* under which the G-major version of the fugue appeared in the appendix of BG 42. While it is clearly an early version of the piece otherwise attributed to Bach, the differences between the two are not very significant. In the later version some of the melodic material is lightly embellished, and the bass is transposed up an octave in one passage to eliminate an unduly wide spacing. [18] At any rate, this is a strong piece with a clearly articulated form, and it seems possible that Bach was responsible for both versions, although there must remain some question about Bach's involvement in either. [19]

The opening exposition calls to mind the a capella fugues of middle and late Baroque choral music, and its conventional subject and countersubject are practically ready-made for invertible counterpoint and sequential development. For this reason it remains possible that at least the opening *fuga*—that is, the exposition (to the downbeat of bar 24)—was taken from a (vocal?) work by Erselius or an older Dresden composer. Only with the first episode (bar 24), which introduces a new motive, is instrumental style firmly in evidence, and it is in the episodes that one most feels the presence of Bach. The new episodic motive is not in itself particularly memorable. But it is the basis of most of the subsequent episodes, undergoing a somewhat different development in each one. In each episode the repetitions of the motive, separated by "rhetorical" rests, relate it to the "sigh" figures found regularly in Bach's early works; so too does the half-step present in the motive when it appears in G minor in the final episode (bars 69–70a).

The piece seems equally suited to organ and harpsichord. The later version retains some awkwardly wide spacings (bars 48, 78–79), and this might be taken as a point against Bach's authorship. But neither version requires an independent pedal part, and the earlier version should probably not be distinguished as an organ work (as in NG, work-list). The text of the later version seems dependable, save for various ornaments and appoggiaturas that give the piece a mannered quality and might have been added by a copyist.

Fugue in B♭ on a Theme by Reinken, BWV 954

Sole source: SPK P 804/14. *Editions*: BG 42; Dadelsen and Rönnau (1970).

BWV 954 is preserved in a single copy by an unidentified copyist who failed to indicate the composer. Yet its style, together with the existence of two other fugues by Bach on Reinken's themes (in the sonatas BWV 965 and 966), strongly implies Bach's authorship. [20] Keller (1949) described these as "large keyboard fugues in concerto style [*grosse konzertarte Klavierfugen*]," and while the analogy to concerto style and form is far from exact, all three fugues transfer the thematic material of Reinken's seventeenth-century consort fugues to a new type of piece influenced by Venetian instrumental style. Moreover, Bach abandoned the rigid permutational structures of Reinken's originals for more flexible designs that include at least one long episode in each case.

The theme of BWV 954 is from the second of the ensemble sonatas in Reinken's *Hortus musicus* of 1687.[21] Of the three fugues, the present one seems the earliest (a conclusion previously reached by Siegele 1975, 19). Its tonal design is relatively simple, there are occasional unmotivated breaks in the sixteenth-note pulsation, and like the fugue of BWV 966 it does not go beyond the three-part texture of Reinken's original. On the other hand, BWV 954 makes the greatest number of changes in Reinken's subject, which, as in the two other fugues, is virtually the only material taken from the model. BWV 954 is, moreover, perhaps the most immediately gratifying of all the early fugues to play and the most successful in reconciling the impulses of the keyboard virtuoso and the contrapuntist.

The subject, originally for violin, is rendered more brilliant (at least on the keyboard) by Bach's elimination of most of the repeated notes found in the original, except for those in the opening motive (Example 5.1). This subject, as

EXAMPLE 5.1.   Fugue subjects from (a) Reinken, *Hortus musicus*, Sonata 2 (basso continuo omitted), and (b) Fugue in B♭ after Reinken BWV 954

emended by Bach, provides the motivic material for most of the subsequent passage-work; there is only a single extended episode containing figuration not directly derived from the subject (bars 71b–80). Indeed, perhaps the most impressive technical advance that this fugue makes over the earlier ones lies in the fluent but never unimaginative figuration, especially that occurring in the bass. Instead of the stolid bass lines in halves or quarters found in many earlier fugues (and in Reinken's original), the bass here almost always moves in small note-values. This reflects Bach's adoption of the motoric pulse of the Venetian sonata and concerto style and his abandonment of the declamatory or rhetorical manner of his own earlier works. Only in a few spots, for example the brief series of "sighs" and chromatic harmony in bar 41, does Bach seem unable to resist a momentary return to the rhetoric of his earlier style, which now sounds out of place. While there are still some poorly hidden consecutives (e.g., in bar 11), the structure of BWV 954 has a firm tonal basis, organized according to a symmetrical design that places an entry of the subject in the subdominant at the center (bar 47) and statements in minor keys (G and C, respectively) on either side of it (bars 37, 54). The style is brilliant throughout, but the most striking figuration—scales descending through three octaves (c''' to B^b)—is reserved for accompanying the return of the opening motive in the tonic, a dramatic moment that follows the last episode (bars 71b–80).

Perhaps the surest sign of Bach's mastery of the new style is his ability to bring the fugue to a convincing conclusion. There is no thematically irrelevant coda, nor does the music simply stop after the final bass entry (as in BWV 533a). Instead, a short extension of the final entrance of the subject (bass, bar 90) leads naturally and unpretentiously to the final cadence, without any break in the rhythmic texture.

Fugue in C on a Theme by Albinoni, BWV 946

Chief sources: LEm Go.S.11 (F. W. Rust); LEm ms. 1 (J. A. G. Wechmar); edition by Griepenkerl (Leipzig, 1847). *Modern editions*: BG 36; Dadelsen and Rönnau (1970).

The little Fugue in C is one of three Bach fugues on themes from Albinoni's Opus 1, a set of trio-sonatas published in 1694.[22] BWV 946 seems somewhat earlier in style than the two other "Albinoni" fugues, BWV 950 and 951. Unlike them it was not immediately recognized as deriving from another work, since Bach transposed the subject, which no source identifies as Albinoni's.[23]

Albinoni's fugues, including those cited in BWV 946 and 950, are notable for sometimes restating or recapitulating previously heard passages, though without falling into the mechanical designs of Reinken's permutation fugues. While Bach seems not to have been prepared to include recapitulations in BWV 946 and 950, a brief passage is recapitulated in the final version of BWV 951. The model for BWV 946 was one of Albinoni's simpler fugues, the closing presto of Op. 1, No. 12, and while the syncopations in the subject might have formed the basis for strettos and expressive dissonances, their treatment by Albinoni seems more playful than learned. Bach, however, evidently set out to write a serious four-part fugue echoing the seventeenth-century ricercar. Four-part writing is limited to the opening and closing expositions, but the mild chromaticism creeping in at several points (e.g., bar 15) is reminiscent of Frescobaldi or Froberger. The absence of extended four-part writing and the confinement of the subject to entries on the tonic and dominant suggests an early date, perhaps even earlier than BWV 896 and 949. There are no real episodes, and the piece ends with a short *pedaliter* passage quite unrelated to the fugue proper. Since the pedal notes here are essential, harpsichordists will have to adapt the passage by transposing some of the bass notes up an octave.

Fugue in A on a Theme by Albinoni, BWV 950

Chief sources: SPK P 804/51 (Kellner); SPK P 595/3 (Ringk). *Editions*: BG 36; Dadelsen and Rönnau (1970).

BWV 950 is a successful example of the type of fugue essayed in the Capriccio BWV 993. Entries of the subject in the tonic and dominant alternate with extended episodes that continually introduce new material, and the fugue ends with a free *pedaliter* coda. The episodes are almost always in two parts and often imitate Venetian violin writing (appropriately enough, considering the source of the subject).[24] Unlike BWV 946, which contains no exact echoes of Albinoni's original apart from the subject, here the soprano continues to follow the first violin line for another bar after the second voice has entered. While Bach, unlike Albinoni, does not use this line as a regular countersubject, he does make two further quotations from the model; both citations provide motivic ideas that recur in several episodes.[25] Albinoni restricts the entries of the subject to the tonic and dominant; Bach includes entries in C$^\sharp$ and F$^\sharp$ minor in an exposition at the center of the fugue (bars 48b–59a).

The closing passage reverts to Germanic keyboard figuration; harpsichordists can let go of the two pedal notes (after initially striking them) with little loss. The fugue as a whole perhaps runs on a bit too long, like BWV 993. But one should not overlook Bach's attempt to use stretto for dramatic effect in bars 75–77, where a descending series of partial entries heralds the last full statement but one (bass, bar 78). The effort to dramatize an important moment toward the end of the fugue is less successful than in BWV 954, but it involves the same type of quasi-orchestral writing, at a similarly climactic moment.

The version in G copied by Kellner is probably his own, as various other alterations suggest. Particularly suspicious are the trivialization of Bach's athletic bass line in bars 16–17 (given as the main text in the BG and editions based upon it) and a variant in the bass of bar 70 that results in parallel fifths.[26]

Fugue in B Minor on a Theme by Albinoni, BWV 951

Earlier version (BWV 951a): *Chief sources*: LEm Rudorff 16 (Mey); LEm Poelitz 9 (with alternate ending); LEm Poelitz 27 (C. F. Penzel, dated Leipzig, 1753). *Editions*: BG 36 (appendix); Dadelsen and Rönnau (1970).

Later version: *Chief sources*: DSB P 801 (Walther); LEm ms. 8 (Preller); SPK AmB 606. *Editions*: BG 36, Dadelsen and Rönnau (1970).

The third "Albinoni" fugue may have been first composed at about the same time as BWV 950.[27] BWV 951a, the earlier version, is archaic in its use of old-fashioned cadence formulas, "obstinate" figures (at bars 51, 54–55, 78), and occasionally awkward counterpoint and jerky rhythms. But at some point Bach recognized that he had accomplished something special with this fugue, and he revised it thoroughly. Only one other early fugue is known to have undergone an overhaul as radical as that of BWV 951; this was the organ fugue in D, BWV 532/2. In both works the effect was to change a fairly old-fashioned fugue into one that is much closer to the fugues in concerto style considered in Chapter 9.

Especially in its revised form, BWV 951 is important for several reasons. First, it is designated a harpsichord piece in two copies, making it one of the earliest *manualiter* works to bear a reasonably dependable indication of this type.[28] Second, it seems to have been recognized, with justice, as the greatest of Bach's early *manualiter* fugues. It was widely copied, and variant readings in some of the later manuscripts suggest that Bach might have been revising it into the Leipzig period. Remarkably, several manuscripts contain both BWV 951 and 951a, indicating that some musicians were aware of and took an interest in Bach's revisions.[29] Several late copies attach the prelude BWV 923 (discussed in Chapter 10); there is no evidence that the pairing stems from Bach, but it implies that the piece was still played and admired well after his death.[30] In addition, BWV 951 is one of Bach's earliest surviving pieces in B minor, a key in which he would write some of his most profound later works. Only two other early works (not counting chorale settings) are in this key; one of them, the organ fugue on a subject by Corelli BWV 579, bears an obvious relationship to BWV 951.[31] The subjects of the two fugues closely resemble each other, and the trio-sonatas from which the subjects were taken are nearly contemporary.[32]

Yet the differences between the two fugues probably outweigh the similarities. The "Corelli" Fugue is, like its model, a double fugue, or rather a "simple" fugue in which the opening statement of the subject is already accompanied by the countersubject (which is never presented in an exposition of its own). As one might expect, the expository passages in BWV 579 are rich in the chains of suspensions made famous by Corelli. These recur in other pieces from more or less the same period, among them the "Reinken" Fugue in B♭ BWV 954, but not in BWV 951. In addition, there is a strong sense of concerto style in the "Corelli" Fugue, which contains three distinct "solo" episodes, the last featuring the pedal.[33] Both BWV 951 and the Albinoni fugue on which it is based are graver, more austere works, and while there is episodic passage-work in both early and late versions of BWV 951, in neither version does the figuration represent more than a brief easing of tension. Despite the key of B minor, there is little chromaticism in Bach's "Corelli" Fugue. But BWV 951 shares with its model a saturated chromatic harmonic texture; the subject contains a descent in eighth-notes through the chromatic hexachord, and the fugue accordingly tends toward a heavy harmonic rhythm in which every eighth bears a change in harmony.

As in BWV 950, Bach quotes directly from Albinoni's original at several points beyond the subject itself. One quotation consists of a prominent alternation between tonic and dominant chords that would otherwise be inexplicable (Example 5.2). Bach does not merely quote, the idea is used, as in the original, to mark a formal articulation between a cadence to the dominant and an entrance of the subject in the tonic. Also borrowed is an ascending chromatic hexachord—the inversion of the motive used in the subject—heard in the closing phrases of both pieces (Example 5.3). Both borrowings were somewhat obscured in the later version of BWV 951. The bass of the tonic/dominant alternation (Example 5.2b) was turned into sixteenth-note arpeggiation, eliminating the reference to the subject found at the corresponding point in the earlier version. And at the close, instead of merely repeating the chromatic motive in the upper voice, Bach worked it into a sort of three-part stretto.[34]

EXAMPLE 5.2.   (a) Albinoni, Trio-Sonata in B Minor Op. 1,
   No. 8, second movement, bars 29–30; (b) Bach, Fugue in B
   Minor BWV 951a, bars 59–60

The form of the work remains close in conception to that of BWV 993 and 950. While the episodes are based on motives from the subject (especially the chromatic hexachord), both BWV 951a and 951 return to the tonic after each significant tonal excursion. Perhaps the early version manages to produce some sense of accumulating tension toward the end; if so, this is a product of the un-broken sixteenth-note motion in bars 70–80, containing both the final episode and the penultimate entry of the subject. But it is difficult to avoid the conclusion that the chief appeal of BWV 951a lies in the rhetoric of its details, not in any large-scale drama.

The revised version might be explained as Bach's effort to bring a favorite early work into line with the structural principles that govern the later Weimar works. At the surface level, the rhythm was smoothed out, and unfashionable varieties of figuration and cadence formulas were eliminated. The revised version also reveals Bach's reduced tolerance of hidden fifths; those originally occurring in bars 20–21 were eliminated. Yet, despite the lengthening of many passages and the insertion of several entirely new ones, it was not possible for Bach to alter the fundamental design of the work. The inserted passages fall within the last third of the piece, starting in bar 68 (a few bars after the quotation from Albinoni's fugue at bar 61b). The new section includes a modulation to G (bar 86), a key absent from the BWV 951a and lending a welcome relief here from the predominantly minor tonalities. But Bach also added a new entry of the subject in the tonic (bar 78), hence reinforcing the rondeaulike character of the original design.

Nevertheless, the new modulation to G, or III of IV, complements an earlier move to A—that is, III of V (bar 50b). Hence, the revised version has a symmetry lacking in the more improvisatory older plan. Bach makes the symmetry of the later plan explicit by also inserting a brief recapitulation. Only three bars are involved, but the restatement of a striking prolongation of the Neapolitan from earlier in the piece is sufficient to tie the two ends of the piece together.[35]

EXAMPLE 5.3.   (a) Albinoni, Trio-Sonata in B Minor Op. 1, No. 8, second movement, bars 33–36; (b) Bach, Fugue in B Minor BWV 951a, bars 84–87

Fugue in G (*Machs mit mir, Gott, nach deiner Güt*), BWV 957

Chief sources: US NHy LM 4708 (the "Neumeister" codex; facsimile in Wolff 1985c); Schelble Gleichauf collection (lost; source for BG). *Editions*: BG 42; Wolff (1985b).

    The authenticity of BWV 957, long questioned, was confirmed by its discovery in a group of early chorale settings by Bach and others in the Yale manuscript that has come to be known after its original owner (and possibly copyist) J. G. Neumeister.[36] The piece had previously been regarded as a fugue, although a rather odd one; no one had suspected that the subject was based on a chorale, for it embellishes the opening phrase of the chorale melody beyond all recognition.

    As a chorale fughetta BWV 957 would appear not to be a keyboard work as defined here. But the Yale copy gives a distinct version, probably a revision of that edited in the BG. Not only does the Yale version add a "simple" four-part setting of the chorale at the end, but many passages in the fugue proper are substantially rewritten. Among other things, the poorly hidden octaves in bars 16–17 are replaced by somewhat more tolerably disguised parallel fifths. Since the earlier version was evidently transmitted simply as a fugue, it may well have been regarded as suitable for any keyboard instrument, as indeed it is.[37]

BWV 957 is not, however, a proper fugue as we now understand the term. The first two entries of the subject are both in the tonic, and a third voice is present even before the third entry of the subject. The final entry is a partial one in the subdominant, and what passes for counterpoint is really just arpeggiated figuration. These features make more sense when the piece's true identity is known; in any case BWV 957 remains a viable little prelude and undoubtedly one of Bach's very earliest surviving pieces.

Neither of the sources on which existing editions are based gives a good text. Emendations for BG version: 15, ten., omit editor's e'; read d' for b on 3d beat? For Yale version (as given in Wolff 1985b): 14, alto, 6th note, read f#'' for d'? 20, ten., notes 5–6, add tie, i.e., read as d' quarter? 21, sop., 3d note from end, a'', not b''. 24, omit naturals; bass, 7th note, a, not g; alto, ten., last chord, g'/b' not e'/g'.

Prelude and Fugue in E Minor BWV 533a

Sole source: LEm ms. 7 (Preller). *Edition*: NBA IV/6.

BWV 533a is a *manualiter* version of the "Little" E-Minor Prelude and Fugue BWV 533 for organ, whose earnest rhetoric has won it a place in the hearts of organists. Like many of Bach's early organ works, BWV 533 shows signs of having once existed in either a *manualiter* version or one lacking a fully independent pedal part.[38] But it is far from certain that BWV 533a is an authentic early version.

Preller, the copyist of the only source, does not inspire confidence; he transmitted overembellished versions of several pieces, including the Canzona BWV 588 discussed below.[39] Naturally one wonders if Preller was himself responsible for these and for a few brief passages in BWV 533a that are absent from or present in simpler form in BWV 533.[40] On the other hand, BWV 533a lacks the written-out trills and tremolos of BWV 533, regarded there as a "unifying motif" by Williams (1980–84, 1:67). Such ornaments might well have been left out in Bach's own original version, and any written-out embellishments present in BWV 533a but not in BWV 533 could be explained by assuming that both extant versions stem from a lost original.

In any case, even if it is an authentic *manualiter* version, BWV 533a poses problems on stringed keyboard instruments. In particular, the syncopated bass and later treble lines in the prelude (bars 13–19), as well as the concluding bass entry in the fugue (bar 33), require the sustaining capability of the organ to be heard clearly against the massed chords of the other voices. The piece is nevertheless worth examining as a good example of the young Bach's keyboard rhetoric. The prelude contains several examples of insistent or "obstinate" repeating figures (bars 6b–8, 20ff.), and the fugue subject is famous for its eloquent two-note motives sharply chiseled by rests. The prelude has a free improvisatory shape—Williams (1980–84, 1:67) notes the resemblance to the *passaggio* that opens the Suite BWV 996—while the fugue has a compact symmetry bisected by the little episode in two voices (bars 15–18). There is no pretentious coda; the piece stops short after the final bass entry, having said all that it needs to say.

Canzona in D Minor BWV 588

Chief sources: MM (Johann Christoph Bach; fragment, last 16 bars only); SPK P 204 (Schwenke, 1781); lost copy by Kittel (basis for BG); LEm ms. 7 (Preller, ?spurious ornamented version). *Editions* BG 38, NBA IV/7.

BWV 588, like BWV 533, is generally known as an organ piece, and while it probably cannot be played entirely satisfactorily without pedals, its genre and texture require that it be mentioned here as a "clavier" work. It is of great interest as the purest example of *stile antico* among Bach's early keyboard works. Title, subject, and texture all place it in "the common Italianate tradition of Froberger, Kerll, and others" (Williams 1980–84, 2:184), that is, the German tradition of strict contrapuntal keyboard pieces modeled after Frescobaldi's fantasias, ricercars, and canzoni. Indeed, Bach appears to have taken the subject from the *Canzon dopo la Pistola* (Canzona after the Epistle) in Frescobaldi's organ mass for the Blessed Virgin. The latter forms part of the *Fiori musicali* (Rome, 1635), of which Bach owned a copy dated 1714 (NBA IV/7, KB). Such pieces never have independent pedal parts, and the assignment of the bass line of BWV 588 to the pedals in most modern editions (but not the NBA) is inauthentic. Pedals are needed only for three chords that would otherwise require the left hand to span a tenth, and in a *manualiter* performance one might, if necessary, simply take the bass up an octave at these points.[41] Harpsichordists might be tempted to use the overornamented version given in the appendix of NBA IV/7, but it appears only in the copy by Preller, whose lack of dependability and taste has already been noted.

The work, like many seventeenth-century keyboard canzoni, consists in essence of two four-part fugues, the first in duple time, the second in triple time and using appropriately altered versions of both subject and countersubject. The work's presence in MM implies a fairly early date, probably before Bach's arrival in Weimar. But it is a surprisingly mature and assured piece, notable in particular for the confident handling of the chromatic countersubject, whose promise of adventurous modulation is perhaps realized in the second section. The latter wanders as far as E minor (bars 132–34), then swiftly but gracefully moves to the subdominant. Other than this not a great deal stands out as unusual save for the cadences at the end of each section, which, as Williams (1980–84, 1:274) notes, are somewhat "more dramatic" than in Bach's models. This was perhaps Bach's way of asserting his individuality at the end of what is otherwise a clear demonstration of his mastery of an archaic style traditionally associated with the study of counterpoint. He would not return to the *stile antico* in such pure form until his last works, above all in the *Art of Fugue*.

6

Miscellaneous Early Works

The fantasias, sonatas, and other remaining pieces from Bach's early years vary greatly in length and style. They must have been written at various points throughout Bach's early period (roughly 1703–13), but, as usual, precise dates are hard to come by. The seven *manualiter* toccatas belong to this group as well, but because they form a distinct set of pieces in a relatively mature style, they are treated separately in Chapter 7.

The toccatas and most of the pieces treated here are related to the seventeenth-century ensemble sonata, which they resemble in being composed of several linked sections, usually including at least one fugue. There is not, however, any standard order to these sections, many of which are too short or transitory to be considered self-contained movements. Nor do the individual sections employ the formal schemes familiar from later works, such as ritornello form, although several of the nonfugal sections have a vaguely rondolike structure.

Besides these sonatalike pieces the young Bach also cultivated the variation, a form in which he subsequently showed little interest until the end of his career. With one exception, however, the early variation sets with firm attributions are on chorale tunes. Only a few of the individual variations (*partite*) require pedals, but they are rarely as idiomatic to stringed keyboard instruments as are some of Böhm's or Buxtehude's *manualiter* chorale settings. For this reason the chorale *partite* will not receive further consideration here.

Praeludium in C Minor BWV 921

Sources: ABB (No. 32; mainly Johann Christoph Bach, last three bars autograph); LEm ms. 7; SPK P 222 (Johann Christoph Schmidt, 1713). *Edition*: BG 36.

Obviously a very early effort, BWV 921 is a good example of the "unruly virtuoso and improvisatory elements in Bach's early works" (Wolff 1983a, 120), some of which he may have come to regret later.[1] Although designated a *praeludium* in ABB, BWV 921 has little to do with any of Bach's other preludes apart from its dependence on arpeggios and other chordal figuration.[2] Indeed it is almost a catalogue (though hardly a comprehensive one) of the ways in which simple progressions might be elaborated while improvising at the keyboard. There are five brief sections in four different meters; the central section is the longest, consisting in part of variations over a very simple ground bass. There is no obvious rhyme or reason to the order of the sections or to the rather limited modulations, except that the last and presumably climactic section is marked *prestissimo* and calls for a simple pedal part. As in the coda of BWV 993, which likewise divides a single line of melodic figuration between the two hands, the pedal notes can be taken by the left hand. This, however, makes it difficult to achieve the incisive articulation obtained when the notes of the upper line are divided between the two hands. Bach entered the notation dictating this effect in what is otherwise his brother's copy (facsimile in Schulze 1984a, plate 5). Despite the pedal part, which implies that BWV 921 was conceived for the organ, the *arpeggiando* chords (so marked) at opening and close seem more idiomatic for a stringed keyboard instrument. Perhaps for this reason the pedal notes are absent from the copy in P 222.

As silly as the piece may appear, if played with fire it perhaps provides a taste of how the youthful Bach indulged himself and his first audiences. Its authenticity has been questioned, as the style is obviously immature and the copy in ABB lacks an attribution. But the autograph entry of the last three bars argues for its authenticity. The following piece in the manuscript is also in Bach's hand, though in tablature; it is a fantasia in C minor (BWV Anh. 205) for which BWV 921 might have been meant to serve as prelude (as suggested by Hill 1987, 357–58). But the difference in notation weighs against this. The fantasia (which cannot be accepted as Bach's without reservation) is reminiscent of the archaic type of chorale fantasia that resembles a sixteenth-century motet. While no chorale tune has been discovered in it, it seems unsuitable to the harpsichord; it is, however, playable without pedals.[3]

Praeludium in A Minor BWV 922

Chief sources: DSB P 803 (J. T. Krebs; title: *Fantasia*); LEm ms. 8 (with fingerings). *Editions*: BG 36; Dadelsen and Rönnau (1970).

BWV 922 is somewhat more recognizable than BWV 921 as Bach's, though it cannot be much later; some of the figuration in the first section resembles that of the C minor work.[4] Although its authenticity has also been questioned—it is listed as "doubtful" in the NG work-list—the piece is remarkable both for its dogged repetitions of a few motivic formulas and for the remote keys reached in the middle section. There is an impressive coda in the improvisatory, recitativelike style also found in the transition sections of the toccatas; an expressive Neapolitan harmony is prolonged in a manner reminiscent of a passage in the "Little" E-minor prelude.[5] The more dependable of the two copyists, J. T. Krebs, was one of Bach's Weimar students, and his copy in P 803 immediately precedes that of the early version of the Chromatic Fantasia and Fugue. While the two pieces are very different, Krebs labeled BWV 922 as a fantasia and wrote *Fuga* at the beginning of the middle section (bars 34ff.).

The flurry of harmonically inspired figuration at the opening has an almost demonic intensity. As in most such pieces, none of the material of this initial section comes back exactly. But there is a suggestion of an echo in the closing section, which contains somewhat similar chordal figuration (bars 87–92) as well as a prominent Neapolitan, recalling the one in the first section (bar 29).

What Krebs called the fugue consists essentially of more chordal figuration. The "subject," though introduced in the customary imitative manner, is little more than an arpeggio; the motive is heard twice in almost every one of the section's fifty-three bars. This would rapidly grow tedious were it not for the adventurous modulations, which reach $F^{\sharp}$ minor (and hint at $G^{\sharp}$ minor) in the first half, then turn toward the "flat" keys D minor and G minor in the second half. The second half (bars 58ff.) modulates somewhat less remotely than the first, but it achieves a certain intensification through two deceptive cadences (bars 66 and 68), each of which lands squarely on a dissonance. In addition, massed chords as in BWV 993 increase the general level of sound near the end (bars 83–86). Despite its impressive architecture, the section needs to be performed with delicate timing and subtle distinctions in the articulation and breaking of the chords, something more achievable on harpsichord than on organ; otherwise it may sound mechanical.

Fantasia duobus subiectis in G Minor BWV 917

Chief sources: MM (No. 52; Johann Christoph Bach); LEm ms. 7 (Preller, with fingerings and ornaments). *Editions*: BG 36; Dadelsen and Rönnau (1970).

The Latin title of BWV 917 calls attention to its serious, almost academic concern with invertible counterpoint, which prevails except in the brief opening flourish and an even briefer one at the end. Yet those flourishes, brief as they are, place the little piece within the format of a toccata or an old-fashioned praeludium. Thanks to the work's transparent texture (mainly in three parts), it remains lively and attractive even as it sets forth systematically all six permutations of the three subjects, giving the effect not of a counterpoint exercise but of a Corellian piece of chamber music.

The title mentions only two "subjects," but as Hill (1987, 423) explains, the word *subjectum* must refer to what we would call a countersubject, as in the organ fugue BWV 574, which is entitled *Thema legranzianum . . . cum subjecto* (Theme by Legrenzi . . . with a Subject) in Johann Christoph Bach's copy.[6] The implication, then, is that BWV 917 also uses a borrowed "theme," although it is unclear which of the three ideas this might be: perhaps the descending chromatic tetrachord first heard in the alto, although the suspension motive in the bass is equally conventional (compare the countersubject of BWV 955). Against these two slower ideas Bach sets a running figure. Despite its brevity the piece seems too polished to be a student work. The skillful rhythmic differentiation of the thematic ideas recurs in other Bach works—for example, the fantasia in A minor (BWV 904/1), a mature composition also combining an ostinatolike descending theme with a running figure.

Sonata in D, BWV 963

Sole source: SPK P 804/10 (Mempell). *Editions*: BG 36; NBA V/10; Dadelsen (1975).

Neither BWV 963 nor the much shorter BWV 967 (discussed below) has much in common with the type of keyboard sonata that became common later in the eighteenth century. The term as applied to BWV 963 is virtually synonymous with "toccata," save for the absence of an improvisatory opening section, and indeed the overall plan resembles that of the D-Major Toccata BWV 912. The second of the three main sections is in a contrasting minor key, and there are dramatic modulating transitions connecting the larger sections. In each work the last two of the main sections are fugues of contrasting types; the central movement here is a motetlike fugue in B minor, the last a lively if not comic D-major fugue in gigue rhythm.

The work begins with a section reminiscent of some of Buxtehude's instrumental movements and other German consort music of the late seventeenth century. Similar instrumental music provided models for Kuhnau's keyboard music, published in several collections and undoubtedly known to Bach.[7] This first section employs some of the same little descending motives found in other early Bach keyboard works, and the short phrases divided between the hands recall antiphonal exchanges in several early vocal works, especially the opening chorus of the cantata BWV 131.[8] Like BWV 967, the movement resembles a ritornello or rondeau form, and despite the Italian title (*sonata*) there are frequent hints of French style (e.g., the falling thirds in the metrically weak phrase-endings in bars 4, 30, etc.). The movement anticipates the key of the middle section by moving rather early to B minor (bar 28); the prominence given this and related keys (rather than the dominant) reinforces the somewhat elegiac character that might be discerned in some of the repeated descending figures.

The transition between the rather gentle opening movement and the first fugue opens dramatically with a sudden F#-major chord and a pair of animated flourishes. This sudden change of texture on a remote harmony is a rhetorical effect, imitating the use of surprising chords (often third-related) at important junctures in vocal works from Monteverdi onward.[9] The effect is strengthened by the apparent use of pedal notes, called for only at this point (and thus somewhat questionable; see below).

The first fugue works out its "repercussive" subject quite skillfully, though without any real episodes to relieve the general tone of severity. The following transition passage consists largely of arpeggiated chords, like certain bridge passages in works by Reinken and Böhm. The close-spaced tempo markings at the end of this passage (presto, adagio, allegro) probably indicate fairly restrained rhythmic nuances, not real tempo changes; the motive used in the bar marked allegro is the same as in the bar marked presto, but with half the written values.[10]

The title of the last movement relates it to an old tradition in Italian and German keyboard fugues; *Thema all' Imitatio Gallina Cuccu* presumably means something like "Theme in imitation of the chicken and the cuckoo."[11] Bird-calls are found as fugue subjects in keyboard music at least as early as 1624, when Frescobaldi published a *Capriccio sopra il Cucco*, and similar pieces were written throughout the later seventeenth century.[12] This fugue combines *two* traditional motives—in the subject and second countersubject, respectively—but as in other bird-song fugues there probably is no deeper programmatic significance. The main subject represents the hen (*gallina*), imitating her clucking through the repercussive motive heard at the outset. This is an arresting idea, but the theme as a whole makes a poor fugue subject; like some of Bach's other early fugue subjects (e.g., in the overture of BWV 820), it fails to imply a compelling harmonic progression, instead tracing a progression from I to ii and back to I again. Hence, this and many subsequent passages are condemned to oscillate between two weakly related harmonies, and despite its charm, the fugue must be judged one of the more disappointing in Bach's early works. While the simplicity of the counterpoint is excusable in a light concluding movement, there are also some inept joins in the structure; several entries of the subject are intended to effect phrase elisions (e.g., at bars 47, 54, 72) but instead seem patched in clumsily.

The sole source is carelessly written; the many errors include some apparent lacunae. The conjectures given in the BG for bar 10 in the first section and bars 5–7 of the first bridge are retained in the NBA. The first of these makes sense, but the pedal-point on A suggested in the first bridge may be unnecessary. Moreover, it is suspicious that the pedal notes in this section can be transposed up an octave or omitted without difficulty, suggesting that the bass originally lay an octave higher and was transferred to the pedals by a copyist.

Emendations to NBA: *1st section:* 16, add # on g'? 51, omit d♯'? 53, omit g'? 79, read g' for a'? 82, add ♮ on c"? 85, last two chords, a'/c♯''', b'/d"? 99, omit b'. *1st bridge,* read all bass notes an octave higher, omit editorial A in 5–7? *1st fugue,* 11, bass, last note, read e♯ for g? (BG has g♯). 13–14, tie d"-d". 32. alto, read c♯'', d' (=BG) for a, c♯'? *2d bridge,* 4, r.h. as in bar 3? 5, ten., 3d beat, f♯''? 9, 1st chord, alto, g', not a'? 4th chord, f♯'' (=BG), not g'? *2d fugue,* 43, ten., 3d note, a (=BG), not b?

Sonata in A Minor BWV 967

Sources: MM (No. 33); SPK P 804/27 (Kellner); Stuttgart, Württemburgische Landesbibliothek, Cod. II, 288 (Lorenz Sichart). *Editions*: BG 45/1; Dadelsen (1975).

Though possibly a fragment, this one-movement piece could have been considered a complete sonata at a time when the word was often used to refer to a single instrumental movement at the beginning of a larger work (as in Bach's early cantata BWV 182). The sketchy notation of several passages written in two parts (with figured bass) has led to the suggestion that this is an "arrangement of [the] first movement of [an] anonymous chamber sonata" (NG work-list). But the fully written-out passages are idiomatically conceived for the keyboard and show no signs of being arrangements. The sources contain errors and other details suggesting that they derive from a hastily or illegibly written autograph, and it may be that what we have here is a piece that Bach left in a partly finished state.[13]

The first two phrases of BWV 967 suggest, respectively, (1) a fully scored ritornello followed by (2) a solo passage notated in two parts with figured bass. But the "ritornello" is never again heard in complete form, and its main thematic idea, which is built out of repeated "sigh" motives reminiscent of other early Bach melodies, is later combined with running figuration that would seem to be more appropriate for "solo" than "tutti" scoring. Hence, despite the superficial resemblance to ritornello form, the sonata has as yet little to do with the Venetian concerto style. The episodic design is closer to that of the Capriccio in E (BWV 993) and other early fugues, and, like them, it generally returns to the tonic after each modúlation. The same design is found in two or three of the free (nonfugal) movements of the toccatas, which might even have originated as separate little "sonatas" of this sort.

While the style is early, this is not the work of a beginner, and had it been fully notated its sophistication would be more evident. The running figuration, at first placed discreetly in the bass as accompaniment to the half-step motive (bar 14), gradually attains greater prominence. It reaches the top of Bach's keyboard near the end, in a climactic passage accompanied by fully notated chords (bar 61). There is a brief flurry of thirty-seconds at the very end, but this is not really a coda, just a cadenzalike elaboration of the final phrase.

The realization of the passages employing figured bass raises the same problems as in the air of BWV 822. But while the latter uses figured bass as part of the imitation of a vocal genre, here it might have been part of Bach's precompositional sketching, never intended for the finished work. There are in fact only a few figures, but the need to fill in the harmony seems clear; bars 6ff. are notated in just two parts, but when the passage is repeated with the two lines exchanged between the hands (bars 46ff.) the right hand has three-part chords. These chords imply that the realization of the figures should be simple, limited to the addition of one or two easily managed inner voices in chordal style.

The texts of both editions are heavily emended, and neither takes into account readings from all sources, but it would be pointless to suggest emendations here in the absence of a thorough critical evaluation of the sources.

Capriccio sopra la lontananza del suo fratello dilettissimo
BWV 992

Chief sources: MM (No. 35; Johann Christoph Bach); SPK P 595 (Ringk; final fugue only); B Br II 4093 (Fétis 2960). Editions: BG 36; NBA V/10; Dadelsen (1975).

Bach's most famous early work, BWV 992 was evidently modeled upon Kuhnau's Biblical Sonatas (Leipzig, 1700), with which it shares the use of programmatic rubrics for each section. The work is supposed to have been written upon the departure of Bach's brother Johann Jacob to join the retinue of Charles XII of Sweden. In the brief family history compiled by Sebastian in 1735, Jacob's departure is set in the year 1704; but Sebastian mistakenly gave 1704 as the year of his own arrival in Arnstadt, so there is some doubt as to the year of the event that the piece is supposed to represent.[14] For that matter, the word lontananza more properly means "distance" or "separation," not "departure," and the piece could have been written well after the event. The words del . . . fratello ("de il fratro" in MM) are equally open to interpretation; Hill (1987, 125n.) suggests that they might refer to any close male friend. It is even conceivable that the words refer not to Jacob but to Sebastian himself, who was separated from his older brother Christoph during his trips to Lüneburg and Lübeck. Buxtehude's lost *Castrum doloris* (BuxWV 134), which Bach heard during his Lübeck visit, also contained an instrumental lament (noted by Wolff 1991b, 402). But Bach is supposed to have gone to Lübeck on foot, and the departure depicted here is by post-coach. That fact plus the possible reference to military trumpets in the subject of the last movement strengthens the traditional interpretation. Hill (1987, 126) dates the copy in MM to "circa 1705," and a date of composition in either 1703 or 1704 would fit the style and the known facts.

For all its charm, the work is somewhat overrated and perhaps misunderstood. The title *Capriccio* cannot indicate capriciousness in the modern sense; nevertheless, one must wonder if the work really is to be taken entirely seriously. The chromaticism of the central *Lamento* seems overdone; must we assume that this, as well as the programmatic rubrics attached to each movement, was intended in the same earnest, humorless spirit as Kuhnau's Biblical Sonatas? If so, the somewhat flippant tone of the last two movements—the *Aria del Postiglione* and *Fuga all'imitatione della posta*—seems out of place. One writer (Vendrix 1989, 201) has noted the work's combination of "Traurigkeit und Humor," and it seems possible that both might even be present in a single movement, especially the *Lamento*. To be sure, the irony of an overwrought lament might have escaped the young Bach. But in any case the movement seems drenched with symbols, not with tears. To use Scheibe's language of two decades later, it is a baroque display of learned musical metaphors, not an immediate expression of feeling, and perhaps for this reason it never seems quite convincing even in a good performance.[15]

The opening movement represents, according to its subtitle, the efforts of Jacob's friends to talk him out of making his journey.[16] But there is unlikely to be any programmatic significance in the large number of what are here called "obstinate" repetitions of one motive in the final phrase (bars 14–15). This would be reading too much into a common stylistic mannerism of Bach's—one that he would have found in Albinoni, whose Opus 1 includes a somewhat similar passage in the same key.[17] The following section, a little fugue, is supposed to represent (according to its programmatic heading) "various misfortunes [*Casuum*] that might occur to him [Jacob?] in foreign countries." But it is more convincing as an expression of grief than of physical danger, thanks to the motetlike style (as in the corresponding section of BWV 963) and the generous use of tritones and other dissonances. The pattern of entries is one of the more mechanical in Bach's keyboard fugues; an impression of stiffness is avoided, however, by the unusual modulating scheme, which begins and ends in different keys (G minor and F minor, respectively). Bach accomplishes the downward journey through the circle of fifths by putting the fugal answers in the subdominant, an unusual but not unique procedure (it occurs also in the opening exposition of the organ fugue in C, BWV 531).

It is no accident that the *Lamento* (subtitled "the friends' general lament") is in F minor, a rare key in the early eighteenth century and certainly not one that would have been expected within a work in B♭ major. The tempo is *adagissimo*; the rare superlative, indicating the movement's special significance, also occurs in the long arpeggiando bridge of the D-Minor Toccata in some sources. The lament is the centerpiece of the present work, and it marks the farthest remove, in both tonality and character, from the outer movements. It is an ostinato movement, built upon twelve statments of a four-bar bass line that is varied along with the upper parts. Three phrases for bass alone (the first, seventh, and last) serve somewhat like ritornellos; the first two of these are figured, and some harmonic filling-in seems necessary elsewhere as well. Indeed, the reference in the title to *general* lamentation implies a rather heavy, full-voiced realization, with both hands striking as many tones of each harmony as they can. In addition, some sort of additional motion seems called for in bars 13–15, in order to avoid a rhythmic hiatus on the down-beats, although this could be provided by ornamenting the melody (Example 6.1).

EXAMPLE 6.1.   *Capriccio sopra la lontananza*, BWV 992,
   third movement: a possible realization for bars 13–15

"Since they see that it cannot be otherwise," the friends bid their adieus in a short adagio transition, which, if unconvincing as program music, is no worse than much of Kuhnau's. The actual departure is depicted in the following two movements in rather breezy fashion. The *Aria di Postiglione* is little more than a jolly tune,[18] yet, even here, Bach introduces a measure of contrapuntal elaboration by freely invert-ing the counterpoint after the double bar, as he did in the little gigue of BWV 832.[19]

As in BWV 963, the closing fugue combines two distinct motives. The subject suggests trumpets, while the downward leap of the posthorn (referred to in the title of the movement) is heard in the countersubject.[20] Unfortunately, such motives again produce subjects ill-suited to idiomatic keyboard fugue-writing. The posthorn motive itself is used to brilliant effect, especially in a climactic group of sequences near the end (bars 42–48) in which the motive becomes the basis for flying figu-ration in both hands. But the same passage leads the fugue into its most distant tonal excursion (D minor) just ten bars before the end, and the return to B♭ is not entirely convincing. There is no coda—perhaps Bach could think of none that would fit the program—but the last three bars are a variation of the same harmonic formula elaborated in the closing passages of the echo movement of BWV 821 and the "Neumeister" chorale prelude BWV 1117.

Sonata in A Minor after Reinken BWV 965

Sources: DSB P 803 (Walther); SPK P 804/20 (Kellner); PL LZu Spitta Ms. 1752/3. *Editions*: BG 42; Dadelsen (1975).

Reinken's *Hortus musicus* (Musical Garden), published at Hamburg in 1687, was a set of thirty pieces for four-part chamber ensemble (two violins, viola da gamba, and harpsichord).[21] The pieces are divided into six groups, each consisting of a "sonata" followed by a four-movement suite (allemande, courante, sarabande, gigue) in the same key. Each "sonata" consists of an adagio, a fugue, and a free postlude. The fugues are of the permutational type, that of the first sonata systematically presenting all possible combinations of subject and countersubject in such a manner that each voice states each theme four times in the tonic and four times on the dominant.[22] The postludes of the first two sonatas each consist of a brief adagio for the full ensemble followed by a solo for the first violin; the solo is then repeated by the gamba, although this repetition is omitted in Bach's arrangements. The dances are often linked by thematic resemblances, and in three cases the allemande and courante form a strict variation pair like those of BWV 833 and Reinken's own keyboard suites.

The importance of Bach's transcriptions was recognized by Keller (1949), who drew particular attention to the fugues. While employing Reinken's thematic material, the fugues are essentially new compositions; BWV 954, based on the subject of the second fugue in *Hortus musicus*, was discussed in Chapter 5. Keller placed the fugues toward the end of a series that concludes with the Chromatic fugue (BWV 903/2), which he put around 1720. Keller's relative chronology seems basically sound, even if he may have been wrong to assume that all of the Italian-influenced fugues (BWV 949–51, 954, and 965–66) postdate those of the toccatas. Less sound is the absolute dating, especially if the large fugues were already composed by the time Bach left Weimar. Wolff (1986a, 110–12) dates the arrangements to "the period of Bach's general encounter with Reinken" and "self-study in counterpoint." But while Bach's familiarity with Reinken and the *Hortus musicus* can presumably be traced to Bach's student years, his departure from the repetitive permutational schemes of Reinken's fugues implies a certain distance in both time and place from Bach's first exposure to the works. The fugal movements—including the gigue of BWV 965—show a more sophisticated compositional technique than either the contrapuntally oriented fugues (BWV 896, 947) or the more virtuosic ones (BWV 950, 951a) of the early years. The written-out embellishment of the preludes is also mature in style, closer to the Vivaldi-inspired adagios of the Weimar cantatas and concertos than to the air in the *Ouverture* BWV 822. Some awkward writing—for example, the left hand must span a tenth in the gigue of BWV 965— implies that these pieces preceded the great preludes and fugues discussed in Chapter 9, but they may not have come long before them.

It is impossible to say what led Bach to arrange the pieces, which were already somewhat old-fashioned even before he arrived at Weimar in 1708. Perhaps Bach's arrangements stem from an effort to preserve and at the same time to refashion works that he had admired in his youth. But the existence of the arrangements does not necessarily indicate any particular influence of Reinken on Bach. A conscious rejection of Reinken's style might even be seen in Bach's substitution of his own fugal technique for Reinken's rigid schema, as well as in the suggestions of modern Italian violin style that can be heard in the figuration of the fugues and the written-out embellishment of the preludes. If Reinken's pieces enjoyed special fame or popularity, this might have been due as much to his personal fame and prestige as to the works' musical qualities. For the melodies and the harmony seem conventional, and the writing for the strings is not always idiomatic; many passages betray the origin of the material in keyboard style (Example 6.2).[23]

EXAMPLE 6.2.   Reinken: Courante No. 1 from *Hortus musicus*, bars 21–22

Bach apparently arranged only the first of Reinken's five-movement sets in its entirety. BWV 965, the resulting work, is called a sonata, although Reinken evidently applied that word only to the opening movement. Except in the fugal sections, Bach's method of adaptation was essentially one of variation—the same process by which Reinken himself had composed the courante of this set, using the same harmonic ground as the allemande. While embellishing the outer parts, Bach's transcription generally preserves the salient voice-leading of the three original parts.[24] The middle line, however, is often dropped an octave or incorporated into an idiomatic left-hand accompaniment that serves as a realization of Reinken's figured bass. Bach's procedure yields generally idiomatic, effective keyboard writing; yet the arrangement is not an unqualified success.

For example, in the opening adagio Bach adds a layer of Italianate embellishment to Reinken's relatively simple violin and gamba lines. No doubt this is how anyone would have treated the piece circa 1710. But by then Reinken's work was more than twenty years old, and Bach could be accused of embellishing it excessively and in a stylistically inappropriate manner. At one point Bach's embellishments fill the eloquent silences of Reinken's original (bar 12, second and fourth beats). Moreover, certain embellishments (e.g., in bars 8–9) are treated as motives and exchanged imitatively between different voices. In this manner Bach rationalizes what would otherwise be an arbitrary, improvisatory process. Yet, by incorporating some of the embellishments into an imitative contrapuntal structure, Bach deprives them of their fire and spontaneity.

The dances likewise seem overworked in spots, as if Bach was trying too hard to add counterpoint or embellish the bass wherever the opportunity arose. To be sure, Reinken's originals lack the sophisticated rhythm of a French *pièce de clavecin*, and the old-fashioned bass lines are often stodgy, moving slowly by step even in climactic passages. In the allemande of BWV 966 Bach left one such bass line untouched (bars 15–17). But in BWV 965 a similar passage has been reworked so that it resembles those episodes in Bach's early fugues in which each hand has running sixteenths (Example 6.3).

EXAMPLE 6.3.　(a) Reinken, Allemande No. 1 from *Hortus musicus*, and (b) Sonata in A Minor after Reinken BWV 965, allemande, bars 24–25

Regardless of any problems in the dance movements, the fugue is one of the most important of Bach's early *manualiter* efforts. As in the two other "Reinken" fugues, Bach omits the continuo line that originally accompanied the initial entries of the subject. But Bach's countersubject is a very free variation of Reinken's, although it is not maintained in the rigorous permutational manner of the original. Bach does place the next three entries of the subject in the same bars as in the original, but not in the same voices. For instance, the bass entry in bar 13 corresponds to the second entry for the first violin, marking the beginning of Reinken's second exposition. But from that point onward Bach's music is completely new. A fifth entry (bar 20) brings the opening exposition to a close, and thereafter each entry of the subject leads to a soloistic episode, more or less in concerto style but invariably based on material from the subject. The successive episodic passages grow in length, and the most substantial, in bars 57–70, is also perhaps the most up to date in style, at one point suggesting a parallel with Bach's Concerto for two violins BWV 1043.[25]

In the gigue, although Bach kept little of the original apart from its subject, he retained its basic design: The two halves of the movement are exactly equal in length, the second half using the inversion of the subject. Also as in the original, the two halves contain an equal number of entries of the subject, which appears twice in each part. Unfortunately, Bach's addition of a fourth voice to Reinken's three led to a texture that is unusually dense for a gigue. Given the uniform eighth-note motion of the subject—which resembles the subjects in Reinken's keyboard gigues—it might have been impossible to avoid all heaviness, regardless of the setting. But Bach, like Reinken, avoids entries on any degree except I and V. The counterpoint, moreover, often consists of parallel thirds or simple contrary motion; again, Reinken's subject is no help here, but the writing is not as imaginative as in the fugue in the opening movement.

The edition in BG 42 contains substantial errors and arbitrary alterations, notably in *fugue*, 55–56. Dadelson (1975) contains two errors: In *gigue*, 16, sop., notes 1–2, read a', b', not c", d"; 55, 3d beat, alto and bass, G♮, not G♯.

Both editions emend *fugue*, 38, sop., note 10, to a, not f♯ (to avoid a cross-relation). Further suggested emendations: *gigue*, 8, sop., 1st note c" (tied over barline), not b'? 41, alto, ♭, not g? In bar 54, if one cannot manage the tenths in the left hand, read ten., a (quarter), not b, c' (eighths).

Neither edition had access to the copy now in PL LZu, which, although of uncertain provenance, is clearly of eighteenth-century origin and suggests solutions for several textual problems (it also contains what appears to be an early version of *fugue*, 5). In the allemande and the courante, the editions insert first and second endings as well as conjectural repeat signs (e.g., before the first full bar of the allemande). But PL LZu gives the last three notes of *courante*, 22 (bar 22B in the editions) as sixteenths, not eighths, implying that these notes are to be played rapidly after the end of the first half (i.e., after the last note of bar 22A in the editions). Other emendations from PL LZu: *courante*, 12, sop., note 4, omit sharp; 18, 3d beat, sop., two sixteenths, eighth (not eighth, two sixteenths); 19, sop., e", not c". *Gigue*, 50, sop., note 2, f♯''', not f♮'''.

Sonata in C, BWV 966

Chief sources: DSB P 803 (Walther); SPK P 804/33 (Kellner). *Editions*: BG 42; Dadelsen (1975).

BWV 966 is an adaptation of the "sonata" and allemande from the third set of pieces in Reinken's *Hortus musicus*. Evidently, Bach chose not to transcribe the three remaining dances, but this does not make BWV 966 a fragment, since in the original print the pieces are not grouped explicitly into suites.[26] The method of adaptation here is exactly as in BWV 965, but the style is simpler, particularly in the fugue, which is in three voices, as opposed to four. Of the three "Reinken" fugues, this one seems to come closest to true concerto style in its rounded tonal design and its regular alternation between expositions and episodes. Moreover, as in BWV 955, a distinct thematic idea recurs in four of the five "solo" episodes. The episodic motive, first heard in bar 16, is nearly identical to a figure that serves the same function in the "Dorian" toccata BWV 538/1.

The assimilation of Venetian concerto style is by no means complete, however. As in BWV 954, the subject and thus the fugue as a whole are pervaded by the running sixteenths employed in many concerto movements. But the pulsation in sixteenths is interrupted briefly at a few seemingly random points (e.g., bars 8, 50, and 64). The counterpoint is not perfect; bars 7–8 contain empty octaves on the even-numbered beats, and there are parallel octaves in bar 9. The last bar of the fugue is filled out with an archaic formula that seems misplaced here (compare the close of BWV 949). But despite such occasional awkwardnesses it is clear that Bach was well on the way to incorporating the Venetian concerto style into his own.

Aria Variata in A Minor BWV 989

Chief sources: ABB (No. 38; Johann Christoph Bach; title: *Aria. Variata. all Man. Italiana*); DSB P 801 (Johann Tobias Krebs: . . . *all'manual-Italiana*); SPK P 804/21 (Kellner: . . . *all Imitatione Ittalian* [*sic*]). *Editions* BG 36; NBA V/10; Dadelsen (1975).

The Aria variata is, apart from the chorale partitas, the only assuredly authentic variation work of the early years (the doubtful variation set BWV 990 is discussed in Appendix A). Like the chorale works, it opens with a chordal setting of the theme. But the theme in this instance may be by Bach; the chromaticism and the leaps of bars 3 and 7 seem unlikely to have occurred in a popular tune. And while fragments of the opening melody recur in embellished form at points in the variations, it is really the theme's compelling harmonies that form the basis for the variations, not the melody (as in the chorale variations). The word *aria* is thus to be understood here in the same manner as in the Goldberg Variations and other encyclopedic Baroque variation sets: a short binary form that defines the harmony and phrasing but not the melodic contour of each variation.

Although in some respects close to the chorale partitas, BWV 989 differs from them in the largely two-part writing of the variations—above all in the climactic ninth variation, where both voices contain the running sixteenths that characterize the more virtuosic of the early *manualiter* fugues. Similar figuration marks the final variation in two works from Pachelbel's *Hexachordum Apollonis*, a collection of "arias" with variations that might have provided models for BWV 989. The writing here, however, is very assured and seems roughly contemporary with the Capriccio BWV 993, rather than with the earliest fugues and other works. But the technique remains archaic in some respects—for example, the insistent use of *figure corte* and other simple motives (as in variation 1) in a way reminiscent of seventeenth-century variation sets, like those of Sweelinck and Scheidt.[27] Moreover, the rhetoric of some variations is also old-fashioned, with "obstinate" repetitions occurring (perhaps a bit too predictably) in bar 7 of both variations 2 and 3. Varying the registration for each variation helps and is perfectly appropriate (see Chapter 2). One might also vary the tempo, although the tempo markings given in the BG are to be disregarded as inauthentic and stylistically inappropriate (e.g., *Largo* in variation 1).

The work raises difficult questions of text and setting. It exists in two distinct versions, Krebs and Kellner giving what may be an adaptation meant to avoid low AA.[28] Moreover, Krebs and Kellner diverge from each other in the theme, giving different versions, both distinct from the version of ABB.[29] All three versions contain wide stretches in the lower staff that would seem to call for either pedals or some special type of keyboard, and indeed the title as given in ABB and P 801 has been taken as evidence that the piece was written for a special "Italian manual."[30] The odd bass formulas in the closing bars of variation 1 (as given in ABB) surely imply some unusual sort of keyboard, but the wide intervals between tenor and bass in the theme would remain unplayable on a keyboard equipped with an ordinary short octave, whether or not it supplied the low AA. Since the latter note appears in a few other early works (BWV 806a, 903a), it seems that Bach—or his older brother—had access to some special keyboard instrument during the Weimar years; this piece might have been written expressly for it.

Williams (1980–84, 3:195) suggests that in such cases the notated music is to be taken as an "ideal" that the player is to amend in order to play "as best he can." Odd variants in the sources suggest that, as in BWV 820 and 967, Bach's own score left some details unclear.[31] Some of the ornaments in the theme as given in ABB may not be Bach's; the short diagonal lines in bars 5–6 should probably be interpreted as *séparés*, indicating a measured breaking of the two-note chords (Example 6.4).[32]

EXAMPLE 6.4.   Aria variata BWV 989, aria, bar 5

7

The Manualiter
Toccatas

The seven *manualiter* toccatas mark the culmination of Bach's early work for keyboard instruments without pedals. They also form the earliest group of "clavier" pieces known by a collective title, but unlike the English Suites, WTC, and various other collections they do not appear to have been organized into a set by Bach himself. While individual works from the group are preserved in over two dozen eighteenth-century manuscripts, only one source contains more than three of them,[1] and the number of copies preserving individual pieces varies widely. This suggests that while certain toccatas may have become fairly well known during Bach's lifetime, others remained relatively obscure. Two of the toccatas existed in separate manuscript copies by Heinrich Nicolaus Gerber, one of Bach's students from the early Leipzig years. But apart from this there is little evidence that Bach used the pieces in his teaching or normally made them available to his students. Indeed, there may have been a tradition in the Bach circle, perhaps traceable to Sebastian himself, of considering the toccatas as belonging with his early experiments; Forkel (1802, 57; BR, 343) mentioned them only in passing among Bach's "youthful efforts" (*Jugendübungen*).

A *manualiter* toccata by Reinken (copied in ABB) perhaps comes closest among the works of Bach's predecessors to his own pieces of this type. To be sure, like the sonatas and other pieces considered in Chapter 6, the toccatas bear a family resemblance to the *praeludium* and other quasi-improvisational genres cultivated by German organists during the seventeenth and early eighteenth centuries. But while the *praeludium* seems to have been evolving toward a well-defined two-movement form—the one we refer to as the "prelude and fugue"—for Bach the word *toccata* continued to refer to a piece comprising various types of sections, not all of them capable of standing as self-sufficient movements. Those sections that could stand alone, especially the fugues, might have originated as separate pieces that were later gathered together to form toccatas. The only direct evidence for this occurs in the

E-Minor Toccata (see below). But if the toccatas were assembled out of a diverse group of existing pieces, it would explain their heterogeneous structures as well as the rough joins between sections in certain works (e.g., following the first fugue in the F#-Minor Toccata).

Even if the toccatas were assembled out of separate pieces, they remain strong works, each with its own distinctive design. Each toccata closes with a fugue, and all but one opens with an improvisatory prelude. Otherwise there is a great deal of variety. Three of the toccatas include extensive sections or movements not in the tonic; in one of these, the Toccata in D, the modulatory bridges are particularly dramatic. Here, and to a lesser degree in the connecting passages of the other toccatas, one senses a kinship with recitative: Melodic lines are fragmented by rests and chromatic motion, and short declamatory motives alternate with sudden bursts of figuration and tremolos. It is, however, all too easy to suppose that recitative served as a model for keyboard writing; this has been suggested for toccatas by composers as early as Frescobaldi. Few if any of the melodic and harmonic formulas used in real recitative are borrowed here. But the fact that Bach incorporated actual instrumental recitative into one later work (the Chromatic Fantasia) perhaps strengthens the possibility that he had the vocal genre in mind in other keyboard pieces, including these.

Although the toccatas as a group seem later than the pieces discussed in Chapters 4–6, again there are few firm guidelines for dating them. The early version of the D-Major Toccata is preserved in MM and might therefore be dated to around 1707; three other toccatas (including the one in G) appear in ABB and might therefore be a bit later. Attempts have been made to establish a relative chronology for the seven works, based on style, keyboard compass, and other considerations, but none is completely convincing. For example, the apparent imitation of concerto style in the G-Major Toccata could place the work around 1713–14, "when Bach seems to have been preoccupied with the Italian concerto form" (Marshall 1986, 228–29). But the concertolike elements are superficial, and the sources provide no evidence for what would be a relatively late date for a work of this sort. The most one can say for sure is that the seven works were probably all completed before the end of Bach's Weimar period and might have been first drafted before his arrival there.

Both the D-Major Toccata (BWV 912) and the one in D minor (BWV 913) survive in distinct early versions, raising the possibility that Bach only revised these works during his Weimar years, perhaps at about the same time as his revisions of BWV 951, 532, and other early works. The revision of the two toccatas did not affect the large structure of either work, but it did include the insertion of brief passages as well as additional melodic embellishment, alteration of the figuration, and refinements of the voice-leading. It is conceivable that the written-out embellishment in the slow sections was intended to make the work more idiomatic to the harpsichord (as opposed to the organ), for the unadorned four-part writing of the adagio in the early version of BWV 913 seems rather lame on the harpsichord. But it is possible that Bach never intended the work to be performed in that form and merely wrote out embellishments at a later date for the benefit of students (as suggested by Stauffer 1980, 170–71).

At least two other toccatas also show signs of having been revised, or at least of having been assembled from preexisting material composed at different times. The two adagios of the G-Minor Toccata contain written-out embellishment in Bach's mature style, implying a relatively late date, but the fugue is archaic and occasionally awkward in both its counterpoint and its demands on the player. The fugue in the E-Minor Toccata appears to derive from a work by an unidentified Italian composer and, moreover, is preserved in an early version as a separate piece, without the remaining movements of the toccata.

The choice of instrument is again a problematical issue. Marshall (1986, 229–30) speculated that each of the *manualiter* toccatas forms a complement to a member of the *pedaliter* series. But the pieces do not pair off very satisfactorily, and even if the pairs were part of Bach's plan they do not shed much light on the question of medium.[2] Nor does the avoidance of certain notes (d''', C$^\sharp$) in individual toccatas, since those notes were absent from many harpsichords and clavichords as well as organs. What is clear is that the toccatas, especially the opening passages, contain many passages in organ style. These include long bass solos (e.g., in the C-Minor Toccata) that can never be entirely convincing on a stringed keyboard instrument lacking the impressive mixtures and other stops that can strengthen a solo voice on an organ. Yet Bach often imitated other instruments in his harpsichord music (e.g., the Italian Concerto). As difficult as it may be to distinguish real organ music from an imitation composed for harpsichord, it seems significant that none of the toccatas employs the wide spacings or the sustained pedal-points that would make organ performance clearly preferable.

Even if the organ was the medium of choice when the works were first composed, it may not have been by the time the revisions had been carried out. In addition to the evidence of the added embellishments, there is the fact that Gerber's copy of the G-Major Toccata calls expressly for *clavecin*. Also pointing to the harpsichord are the passages in arpeggiando style—two bridge passages in the works in D minor and F$^\sharp$ minor as well as the adagio of the E-Minor Toccata, which at points resembles a French unmeasured prelude. Another passage to bear in mind is the opening of the G-Major Toccata, whose numerous octave doublings—like those in the Sonata BWV 967—would be superfluous on the organ. Marshall (1986, 235–36) raised the question of why Bach would have written "such virtuosic and manifestly 'public' display pieces" for harpsichord, but the same question could be asked about the preludes of the English Suites and other pieces indubitably for harpsichord.

The toccatas present difficult problems for editors, but at this writing the relevant NBA volume has not appeared and no edition can be particularly recommended. The most complete listing of variant readings for BWV 912–16 is probably that in BG 36, from which one can reconstruct the early versions. But BWV 910 and BWV 911 were published in BG 3, which lacks an adequate critical apparatus. Unfortunately, more recent editions, such as that of Rudolf Steglich (Munich: Henle, 1962), do not provide an accurate evaluation of the sources or a complete accounting of variant readings, and the texts consequently contain numerous questionable details (too numerous for emendations to be suggested here). Bar numbers in the following are taken, not without some misgivings, from Steglich's edition, which counts bars in a single continuous series for each toccata.[3]

Toccata in F# Minor BWV 910

Chief sources: ABB (No. 20; Johann Christoph Bach); DSB P 801 (Walther); SPK P 804/47; LEm ms. 8 (Preller); SPK P 419 (Kittel); SPK P 597/4 (Hering); SPK P 287/9 (Anonymous 300); B Br II 4093 (Fétis 2960); A Sd MN 104.

The toccatas in F# minor, C minor, and G fall close to one another in ABB, where they rank among the most important of the pieces that Bach evidently gave to his older brother.[4] The chronology of the toccatas is not established and Bach himself is not known to have ordered them in any way; thus we may as well start with the work most commonly encountered in the sources. As the selection of sources listed above shows, the work was indeed widely distributed. Any of the *manualiter* toccatas would have given keyboard players who lacked an advanced pedal technique the opportunity to play a virtuoso work in a style that seemed similar to that of the Weimar masterworks for organ. But BWV 910, through its exotic key and the presence of two fugues—one of them on a chromatic subject (the descending hexachord)—might have seemed especially attractive to serious musicians.

Schmieder, perhaps in view of the impressive proportions, the "difficult" key, and the capable handling of chromaticism, at first (1950) proposed a relatively late date for this work (and for the Toccata in C Minor). But the suggestion of a Cöthen origin seems impossible, if only in light of the work's inclusion in ABB and P 801. While it might be a little later than some of the other toccatas, it relies on the same archaic formal principles as do Bach's earlier multisectional works, only carried out at greater length. And therein lies a problem for all the toccatas, but especially the three longest ones—those in D minor, C minor, and F# minor. Even in the masterfully extended passage-work of the opening prelude, there is in all three works a possibility of excess. This is particularly true in the arpeggiando passage connecting the two fugues of BWV 910, where the same figure is used twenty-one times to set forth a not especially compelling series of harmonies (see Example 7.1). Individually, the two fugues are not especially long, and both show signs of tonal planning, as in the move to the relative major shortly after the center of the second fugue. Yet the second fugue makes no other moves to a major key, and there is but one such modulation (also to A) in the first fugue. Hence, the work as a whole has the same monochrome quality as the "Albinoni" Fugue BWV 951 and other early minor-key works.

In this light, it is unclear whether the piece is helped or hindered by the similarity between the chromatic subject of the final fugue and that of the adagio that follows the opening prelude. The adagio is one of several slow imitative passages in the toccatas comparable to the motetlike first fugue in the Sonata BWV 963 or the Capriccio BWV 992. The present adagio is the most chromatic and the most heavily embellished of the three. Many of the ornaments and embellishments might be later additions, as in the corresponding movement in the D-Minor Toccata. While they greatly intensify an already expressive movement, they probably should not be allowed to weigh down the tempo exessively or to obscure the underlying rhythm, which seems to be that of a sarabande.

The tempo marking of the first fugue—*Presto e staccato*—is probably best interpreted as meaning "fast and separated," the last word referring to the eighth-notes of the subject. Both *presto* and *staccato* are common in the Italian concerto repertory, where *presto* seems to have been hardly distinguishable from the modern *allegro* as an all-purpose term for a quick movement. *Staccato* seems to imply articulate but not necessarily abrupt playing, like the similar term *spiccato*, used in the first movement of the oboe concerto by Alessandro Marcello that Bach transcribed as BWV 974. The combination of the two terms might imply a somewhat more vehement manner of performance than would otherwise be the case—a bit faster and a bit more emphatically articulated. But one should probably avoid an exaggerated accentuation of each eighth as well as an overly rapid tempo that would turn the fugue into a blur.

Indeed, the fugue derives much of its energy not from the tempo but from the character of its subject, which is shorter and simpler than in many of Bach's early fugues. The counterpoint too is fluent but simple, often consisting of little more than parallel thirds or sixths that accompany the most striking feature of the subject, the descending staccato scale in eighth-notes. The episodes—at bars 57, 67, and 80b—use a common motivic idea, an old-fashioned figure in sixteenths that is combined contrapuntally with fragments of the scale motive in the third episode. The combination is, as usual, felt as an intensification, an effect that is perhaps heightened here by its coinciding with a sequence that momentarily shifts the meter to $\frac{3}{4}$ (bars 83–86). A few bars later the subject enters in the most remote tonality reached in the course of the fugue (D$^\sharp$ minor, bar 88b). But despite these efforts to produce a sense of accumulating dramatic tension, the fugue perhaps runs on for too long without letting up. The problem, if it is one, is not solved by increasing the tempo; it might even be alleviated by adopting a tempo slow enough to permit an occasional expressive rhythmic nuance.

The arpeggiando bridge that follows may also be too long. But there is no point in trying to hurry through its measured modulations, which lack any clear direction until the bass begins a stepwise ascent half-way through (Example 7.1).

EXAMPLE 7.1. Toccata in F$^\sharp$ Minor BWV 910: underlying bass line of bars 108–31

The closing fugue is the climax of the work, not because it is more brilliant than the first fugue but, on the contrary, because it is more expressive. In addition, it employs four instead of three voices, at least from bar 155 onward. Although notated in ⁶⁄₈, its rhythm is that of the chaconne, which in Baroque examples may or may not have a ground bass but which normally opens on the second beat of a triple bar. Bach might have derived the idea of a fugue in chaconne rhythm from Keiser, several of whose Hamburg opera overtures include similar sections.[5] The present fugue has not only the rhythm but the refined grandeur and pathos of the greatest French chaconnes; the subject begins on the second eighth of the bar and makes its chromatic steps on the second note of each group of three eighths.

The use of chaconne rhythm naturally calls to mind Bach's chaconnes from the Weimar period: the first chorus from the cantata *Weinen, Klagen, Sorgen, Zagen* BWV 12, later used in the B-Minor Mass, and the great organ Passacaglia BWV 582, which concludes in a fugue. There is also a closing chaconne chorus in Cantata No. 150, whose status is uncertain but which might be an early work.[6] The ground bass of the movement from BWV 12 is practically identical to the subject of the present fugue, whose second countersubject also appears in the cantata.[7] Cantata No. 12 was first performed April 22, 1714; the chromatic density of the toccata has been taken as a sign of a late date (e.g., by Marshall 1986, 228), and, whether or not this is true, the rich detail of its chromatic voice-leading makes the final fugue one of the most impressive single movements in the toccatas.

Toccata in C Minor BWV 911

Chief sources: ABB (No. 25; Johann Christoph Bach); LEm ms. 8 (Preller); B Br II 4093 (Fétis 2960); SPK P 204 (Schwenke); SPK P 320 (Gebhardi).

Both its BWV number and its position in many editions seem to suggest that the Toccata in C Minor is a companion to the one in F♯ minor. But there is no reason to consider them related in any particular way, and the C-Minor Toccata follows a very different plan: After a prelude and another motetlike adagio comes a single very long fugue. The toccata shows some of the best aspects of Bach's early style—emphatic musical rhetoric, economical and intensive use of thematic material, inventive keyboard scoring. Yet some of these very traits seem to work against the piece, and the fugue in particular perhaps develops too limited a range of ideas for too long.

One problem for the fugue is its rather ponderous rhetoric. The opening figure in the subject is immediately repeated after a short rest, a familiar rhetorical gesture. But the figure that is repeated is itself somewhat repetitious, containing two downward arpeggiations of the C-minor triad, and in the course of the fugue it is likely to grow tiresome.

Another rhetorical device might be perceived in the "obstinate" repetitions of several motives in one passage (bars 138–40), perhaps employed to point out the fact that the passage connects the only two entries of the subject in major keys. But the absence of striking contrasts of key, texture, or motive elsewhere makes the fugue rather colorless, despite some imaginative figuration. For example, bar 69 introduces a countersubject that begins in the soprano and then migrates into the tenor, in the process crossing the subject and spanning more than three octaves (c''' to G). The registral play resembles that previously noted in the fugues BWV 949 and 954. Related effects occur in bars 115b–117a, where the countersubject is divided between soprano and bass, and in bars 130b–132a, where the two opening gestures of the subject itself are similarly divided between two voices (and registers).

Unfortunately, these efforts are undercut by the monotonous rhythm and a diffuse form. Like the Capriccio in E (BWV 993), the fugue makes some gestures toward concerto style in the use of distinct "solo" episodes and an almost constant pulsation in small note-values (sixteenths). But the sixteenths cannot flow as quickly as in more up-to-date Italianate pieces (e.g., the fugue of BWV 944), and a slower tempo seems necessary to accommodate the *figura corta* (sixteenth plus two thirty-seconds) first heard at bar 82b.

The motive is introduced in an improvisatory passage placed about a third of the way into the movement, following a cadence in the tonic. This is an odd place for a cadenza, and one wonders if the piece did not originally end here, the "cadenza" taking the place of a free coda that was altered to permit a continuation of the fugue after a cadence on the dominant (bar 85). It is only beyond this point that expositions alternate with long concertolike episodes (bars 109–15a, 127–33a, 147–52a, 157b–62a), the episodes making increasing use of *figure corte*, presumably in an effort toward a gradual enlivening of the motion. But the piece is at best a partial success.

Toccata in D, BWV 912

Early version (BWV 912a): *Sources*: MM (No. 28; Johann Christoph Bach); SPK P 804/50. (For readings, see Preface and Appendix of BG 36, and Lohmann 1968–79, vol. 3.)

Later version: *Chief sources*: LEm ms. 8 (incomplete); SPK P 286/13; SPK P 289/14; LEm Go.S.309.

Perhaps the most successful of the toccatas is the one in D, not on the strength of any single section but because of its uniquely effective overall design, which has at the center a fugue in the fairly remote key of F$^\sharp$ minor. The general plan is similar to that of the Sonata in D (BWV 963), but the toccata, apart from being composed on a larger scale, adds a free allegro after the opening section. Similarities between the toccata and the organ prelude and fugue in the same key (BWV 532) have also been noted (e.g., by Wolff 1983a, 148). Not only do both works open with comparable figuration, but they share an unusual emphasis on the mediant (F$^\sharp$ minor) and on remote "sharp" keys in general. [8]

The allegro is, like the corresponding section in the G-Minor Toccata, a rondolike movement that might have been inspired by the allegros of Italian solo concertos, inasmuch as some of the episodes make use of arpeggiated figuration. But both the main theme and the "solo" figuration are treated in imitation (or rather are exchanged between treble and bass), and the style closely resembles that of other early Bach keyboard works, especially the Sonata BWV 967. The allegro provides the first hints of the toccata's special preoccupation with "sharp" minor keys, modulating several times to F$^\sharp$ minor but never remaining there for long.

The decisive move occurs in the first of two adagio transitions, when two sudden descending scales interrupt the recitativelike writing (bar 75). The first fugue, which follows, is unexpectedly quiet and understated for a piece in F⁺ minor, and despite considerable chromaticism it has little in common with the fugues in the same key in BWV 910. Like the "Corelli" fugue for organ BWV 579, it announces subject and first countersubject jointly at the beginning. Actually, there are two countersubjects, which combine with the subject in five of the six possible permutations. The subject enters only six times in all, but the fugue is neatly articulated into three expositions. These alternate with two short episodes (at bars 89 and 100, respectively), giving the fugue a pleasant symmetry.

In the sources the second transition passage (bars 111b–26) bears only the indication *con discrezione*, and it seems at first only a free extension of the fugue.[9] But it is clearly a distinct section, returning to the free style of the first adagio and even employing the same tremolo ornament at one point (bar 114). Like the first adagio it eventually bursts into figuration; indeed, of the two bridges it is the more dramatic, returning to D major by a circuitous path through E minor and including short cadenzas elaborating the chords of C (VI of ii) and E minor (ii). By dwelling on these indirectly related harmonies the cadenzas heighten the sense of suspense, even mystery; the device is one that Bach would exploit further in the Chromatic Fantasia. The cadenzas are already present in the early version, suggesting that they were part of Bach's original conception of the passage.

The toccata closes with what is in principle a fugue, though governed more by harmony than by counterpoint; the subject is little more than an oscillation between two thirds (d'–f⁺' and c⁺'–e') suggesting tonic and dominant, respectively. The harmonic basis of the counterpoint is reminiscent of the "fugue" in the youthful Praeludium BWV 922. So too is the almost demonic affect that arises from the perpetual motion in triplet sixteenths, although the figuration has parallels in numerous other pieces (e.g., Buxtehude's C-Major Fugue BuxWV 174 = No. 26 in ABB). Several harmonic progressions are somewhat unusual for the period; particularly striking is the sudden shift from a major key to the parallel minor, which occurs three times: in E (bar 201), C⁺ (bar 220), and finally the tonic (bar 261). In addition, the toccata's obsession with distant "sharp" keys resurfaces in the last third of the fugue. This section opens with a statement of the subject in the bass—without accompaniment—in C⁺ minor (v of iii) at bar 220. Shortly afterward (bar 227) the fugue reaches the most remote key of the entire toccata, G⁺ minor, then gradually dissolves into harmonically inspired figuration. The passage culminates in a flurry of thirty-seconds (present only in the revised version), which in a later work would doubtless have led straight into the final cadence. But the toccata ends—somewhat disappointingly—by reverting briefly to adagio style for an old-fashioned cadence in full harmony.

The early version (BWV 912a) already possesses the salient features of the later one.[10] BWV 912a uses ties to indicate the holding down of the chord-tones in the arpeggios of the opening passage, and this has led to the suggestion that BWV 912a was intended for organ.[11] But the omission of ties in the later version may be a notational variant of no practical significance. By the same token, only the later version has the tremolos written out in the adagios. But both versions have them in the opening section, and MM indicates them in the first adagio through the abbreviations *trem* (bar 68) and *tr* (bars 69 and 70).[12] The tremolos, incidentally, produce a striking effect but must have seemed gauche to the mature Bach, who never used them; hence, even the revised version must be fairly early.

Toccata in D Minor BWV 913

Chief sources: print (Leipzig: Hoffmeister und Kühnel, 1801; early readings); LEm ms. 8 (Preller); DS Mus. ms. 65; SPK P 281; B Br II 4093 (Fétis 2960); SPK P 499 (Michel?).

The D-Minor Toccata is perhaps the most popular of the seven, thanks to its relatively transparent textures, which make it somewhat easier to play than the others. This might also explain why the work appears in some sources as *Toccata prima . . . manualiter*; the numbering does not necessarily stem from Bach. BWV 913 was, however, the first of the toccatas to reach print, although the 1801 edition gave an early version. This is not entirely surprising, as the publisher Kühnel at one point owned MM and may have possessed other Bach manuscripts as well (Schulze 1984a, 39–41).[13] While the toccata occurs in neither MM nor ABB, it reportedly bore a dedication to Bach's "most dear brother" Christoph in a lost manuscript.[14] Thus, like the Capriccio BWV 993, which was similarly dedicated "in honor" of the Ohrdruf Bach, BWV 913 might have been presented to him in a special fair-copy autograph.

The design is similar to that of the Toccata in F♯ Minor, even to the point of including a long passage of apreggiando figuration in the second adagio. But the present work avoids the chromaticism of the F♯-Minor Toccata, and its fugues are characterized by smooth sequences, many of them incorporating Corelliesque chains of suspensions. Hence, the style is somewhat closer to the new Italian sonata and concerto, although this does not necessarily have any bearing on its date. The introduction alludes to the *pedaliter* prelude and fugue with its bass solos and the pedal-points of bars 8–11. It also includes a bar of figuration virtually identical to one in the Aria variata, but Bach carefully avoids the wide spacings found between bass and tenor in that work.[15]

Only a short rest separates the introduction from a passage in four-part motet style (bar 15b), corresponding with the adagio found at this point in several other toccatas. There is no imitative subject as such, but the passage is held together by its steady descending sequences, suspensions, and "sigh" figures, all favorite expressive devices in Bach's early works.

The following section, referred to here as a fugue, is labeled in the sources as *Presto* or *Thema*. The latter term presumably refers to the subject and seems to imply that it was borrowed from another piece; perhaps this explains the similarity between this subject and that of the second fugue. Both subjects incorporate the conventional suspension motive previously seen in the "Erselius" Fugue BWV 955. Neither is a fugue in the usual sense, however. This section, instead of opening with the normal fugal imitation at the dominant, begins like an invention with the *thema* imitated in the tonic. The final section opens with a version of the same *thema* combined with a countersubject; the two ideas are immediately repeated in inverted counterpoint, a procedure also employed in some of the inventions.

Both sections have the rondolike structure of many other early fugues. One might complain of the somewhat facile sequences, especially in the second fugue. But these occur in other early works as well, such as the organ fugue in G minor BWV 578 and the *manualiter* fugue in A minor BWV 947, and in each case the sequences seem part of a successful emulation of Italian violin style. The present fugue reverts to a more rhetorical German style in its coda, which opens with "obstinate" repetitions of a motive reminiscent of sevententh-century organ music (bars 111ff.). The final fugue also flirts with the idea of a free close, falling (like the fugue of BWV 965) into arpeggiated figuration unrelated to the theme as it approaches the end (bar 271). But the subject returns, and the fugue ends with one of the most successful (and exciting) closing phrases in any of Bach's earlier *manualiter* works, based on an ascending sequence that Bach might have taken from the first allemande of Reinken's *Hortus musicus* (Example 7.2).[16] The toccata con-

EXAMPLE 7.2.   Toccata in D Minor BWV 913, bars 291–93;
  (a) early version; (b) later version

cludes with an echo; the last two bars lack a dynamic indication, but the piano marking implied here could be found in comparable ending phrases in Corelli's Opera 5 and 6.

As in BWV 912, the early version differs above all in the less embellished form of the first adagio. The later version also includes numerous small alterations of detail in the two fugues, the first of which has an extra two-bar phrase (bars 50–51).

Toccata in E Minor BWV 914

Chief sources: copy by Gerber (see Wiemer 1987); DS Mus. ms. 64; B Br II 4093 (Fétis 2960); SPK P 213/3 (partly by J. C. Westphal).

Perhaps because of its understated opening, which lacks the *passaggi* present in the other toccatas, BWV 914 is preserved complete in a relatively small number of sources and was evidently little known even in the eighteenth century. Yet next to BWV 912 it is perhaps the most satisfying of the seven compositions, if not the most ambitious or virtuosic. The biggest movement is the concluding fugue, which is preceded by a short introduction, a fugal allegro, and a rhapsodic adagio; several copies give the fugue alone.

The low tessitura and light texture of the introduction lead one to wonder if it was originally for lute, although the initial four-note gesture could equally well be a pedal solo. The following section resembles the motetlike adagios of several other toccatas, but here it is labeled *Un poco Allegro* and accordingly lacks the florid embellishment of the other movements. It is a fine little double fugue, although it perhaps ends a bit abruptly just after the final entry (in the bass). One subject opens with an expressive rising half step; both subjects contain suspension motives, which are further developed in the brief episodes.

In Gerber's copy the adagio bears the additional title *Praeludium*, which leads Wiemer (1987, 31) to suggest that this, together with the fugue, once formed an independent piece. Indeed, this section differs in style from the adagios occupying analogous positions in the other toccatas, for nearly every harmony is composed out through a series of figures amounting almost to a small cadenza. While seemingly a free improvisation, the greater part of the adagio is built upon a simple linear bass line (Example 7.3), a device that recurs in later pieces (e.g., the pre-

EXAMPLE 7.3.　Toccata in E Minor BWV 914: underlying bass line of bars 42–62

lude in E minor from WTC1). Eventually the writing coalesces into more regular figuration, still harmonic in inspiration but using a propulsive figure found also in BWV 922.[17]

The brilliant closing fugue in three parts has become one of the more mysterious pieces in the Bach canon with the discovery in a Naples manuscript of an anonymous fugue, large portions of which are nearly identical to the present one. The Naples manuscript contains a "blanket" attribution to Benedetto Marcello, but, as Selfridge-Field (1990, 327) observes, the subject of the fugue is "not characteristic of Marcello's keyboard music."[18] Bach's borrowings in other Italian-inspired fugues (BWV 579, 949–51, etc.) are limited mainly to the subjects. Here, however, opening and closing expositions are transparently derived from the analogous sections of the fugue in the Italian manuscript; two central expository passages also appear to derive from the anonymous piece (Example 7.4).[19]

If, as appears likely, Bach borrowed directly and liberally from the anonymous piece, he nevertheless made characteristic alterations. The chief motive in the

EXAMPLE 7.4.   (a) Fugue in E Minor, from Naples, Biblioteca
del Conservatorio, Ms. 5327, fols. 46v–49r, bars 1–4 and
47–48; (b) Toccata in E Minor BWV 914, bars 71–74 and
125–27

subject of the Naples fugue is a literal imitation of violinistic string-crossing (bariolage). The corresponding motive in Bach's subject is more clavieristic and flows
a little less easily because of the implied passing dissonances (escape tones). Everywhere, in fact, Bach's fugue has somewhat more refined and, at the same time,
more complex readings, as in the interpolation of rests to avoid the barely audible
parallel octaves in Example 7.4. Still, in the passages common to the two fugues,
the voices accompanying the subject remain somewhat perfunctory. That Bach was
fully responsible only for the episodes is suggested by the fact that these are distinctly
richer in harmonic implications than the expository passages, even though the first
episode (bars bars 90b–94) uses a motive taken directly from Italian violin style (and
from bar 2 of the subject). In any case it is easy to see why Bach might have wished
to substitute his own episode at this point, in place of the long central episode in the
Naples fugue. The latter has at this point a simplistic sequence involving repeated
hand-crossing, a technique that Bach never incorporated into a fugue except in the
fragmentary BWV 906/2.

   While the full history of the toccata's text remains to be elucidated, it seems clear
that it underwent several revisions. One manuscript (P 213) originally gave the
fugue alone, in a version that ended five bars earlier, just after the final entry of the
subject in the bass.[20] The coda present in the familiar version ends with a passage
in the arpeggiando style of the adagio, which would have been particularly appropriate in an intermediate version of the Toccata consisting only of the "praeludium"
(adagio) and the fugue.[21]

Toccata in G Minor BWV 915

Chief sources: SPK P 1082 (Preller); B Br II 4093 (Fétis 2960).

   Despite its lively allegro and two expressively embellished adagios, the G-Minor
Toccata seems always to have been less popular than the others, perhaps because of
its long fugue, which is extremely awkward to play. The only surviving eighteenth-
century manuscripts are relatively late and inaccurate; Preller even left out a bar of
the subject at the opening of the fugue, an error perpetuated in some modern
editions.

   The plan of this work centers on two main sections, an allegro (in $B^\flat$) and a
closing fugue. In addition, the opening flourish recurs at the very end, giving the
toccata a cyclic form very rare if not unique in works of this type. The actual
amount of material that returns is very little, and probably not too much should be
made of it. But the gesture is a striking one, since it includes a deceptive cadence
to a big IV^6_4 chord. This cadence has a further echo at the end of the second adagio
(bar 75), which reinforces the cyclic unity in the toccata.

   As in BWV 910 the first adagio resembles a sarabande, but it is shorter, consisting
essentially of just a few elaborated progressions, several of them repeated sequen-
tially. Thus, the progression 2:V^6_2, I is repeated in D minor (bars 8–9), C minor
(10–11), G minor (12), and F (13–14), the last time with a deceptive resolution to
the same chord that serves as part of the toccata's unifying idea.

   The allegro, like that of the Toccata in D, seems inspired by Italian style, coming somewhat closer to true concerto form thanks to the clearer imitation of solo/tutti contrasts, which is accomplished through variations in texture and, if the indications are authentic, dynamic level. Yet the underlying texture is, as in BWV 912, invertible two-part counterpoint, and here the more important of the two subjects is the one stated at the outset in the bass. Moreover, unlike most ritornello forms the allegro proceeds mainly in short one- and two-bar fragments. Such construction is, however, also found in some of Bach's early arias—for example, the soprano aria of BWV 150 (if authentic), with which this seems to share some thematic material.

Since the allegro is in B$^\flat$, it is actually a lengthy digression within the plan of the toccata as a whole. Indeed, the allegro ends by returning (via another deceptive cadence) to the dominant chord of G minor that preceded it. For this reason, and because of the common tempo mark and meter ($\frac{3}{2}$), the second adagio is in a sense a continuation of the first one, even though it lacks the latter's sarabande meter, substituting a more declamatory rhythm characterized by repeated chords in the lower voices.

The fugue, alone of those in the toccatas, has pretensions to being of the contrapuntal type. It is in four parts, with a regular countersubject, and both subject and countersubject are used in inversion (at bar 99). The subject contains an ascending sequence, and this, when combined with the driving triplets of the countersubject, gives the effect of a crescendo that generates considerable excitement in the first exposition.[22] But the remainder of the fugue fails to sustain that excitement consistently. The gigue rhythm, although maintained steadily for 111 bars, is not in itself dull; Bach would write many equally long works in homogeneous rhythmic textures. But, as in the gigue of BWV 965, the inversion of the subject and the permutations of the contrapuntal texture, even the occasional episodes, do not provide sufficient variety.

Still, unlike the fugue of the C-Minor Toccata, which likewise seems too long, this one possesses an impressive design, with strong evidence of tonal planning. While the danger of monotony is just as great here, there is a momentary softening of the texture into parallel thirds at bar 153. The passage is comparable with bars 139–41 in the C-minor work; both passages represent a brief homophonic respite from the prevailing counterpoint, and each marks its piece's only move to major keys. Here Bach handles the modulation more effectively, turning immediately afterward to F minor in a passage that recovers some of the urgency of the opening exposition.[23]

Toccata in G, BWV 916

Chief sources ABB (No. 27; partly Johann Christoph Bach); copy attributed to Gerber, lost; B Br II 4093 (Fétis 2960); LEm ms. 7 (Preller, embellished version of adagio); DSB P 803 (signed "J. Willweber").

The three-movement form of the G-Major Toccata distinguishes it from the others, and already in the lost Gerber copy it was called *Concerto seu Toccata pour le Clavecin* (Concerto or Toccata for Harpsichord). Bach's obituary listed only six, not seven, "clavier" toccatas (BD 3:86 [item 666]/BR, 221), and one wonders if this was the work overlooked by its authors. As in the so-called Toccata, Adagio, and Fugue for organ BWV 564, the plan does bear a general resemblance to that of an

Italian concerto. But even if Bach was consciously borrowing an Italian form, he filled it with detail belonging to the German keyboard tradition and, as in the other toccatas, reserved the weightiest movement (the fugue) for last. Use of the harpsichord, as indicated by Gerber, seems entirely appropriate, but as in the other toccatas there is nothing clearly ruling out the organ.[24]

In the opening allegro, the heavily scored initial phrase serves somewhat like a ritornello, alternating with "solo" passages and articulating a cogent tonal design. Klein (1970, 36) and later Zehnder (1991, 48) have noted the close formal parallelism between this movement and the first movement of the organ toccata BWV 564 (following the initial fourishes); Zehnder speaks in both cases of "concerto form with short ritornellos" (*Konzertform mit Kurz-Ritornellen*). Yet the phraseology is not that of a concerto; the short-winded phrases and the opening flourish on the tonic triad belong rather to the traditional toccata or *praeludium*. Unlike the corresponding section of BWV 564, the present movement even backtracks once to the tonic (at bar 15), although not repeatedly as do the allegros of the toccatas in D and G minor. But this movement remains closer in conception to passages in the other toccatas than to a genuine concerto movement.

The adagio also has much in common with the corresponding passages in the other toccatas, adopting their freely imitative style, with very restrained melodic embellishment. Actually, a few bars pass before the movement settles into its motetlike style; the second phrase (bar 60) begins like an embellished repetition of the first one, and only with the alto entry (upbeat to bar 61) does Bach decide upon the *thema* that is to be the basis for the rest of the movement. Perhaps this reflects some compositional changes that had involved the opening bars, which might have been added to connect the allegro with the remainder of the adagio, if and when the toccata was compiled from previously existing movements.

In any case, the embellishments in the fourth, fifth, and sixth bars of the adagio might have been the products of revision. A few further ornaments—not necessarily authentic—appear as later additions in the copy in ABB, while Preller's copy includes a substantial layer of additional embellishment (a portion is reproduced in Schulze 1979a, 54). Preller's embellishments, which may well be his own, are stylistically eclectic and very unlikely to be by Bach. They presumably give some idea of how a provincial organist on the fringes of the Bach circle played this music, but it is unlikely that they represent his own taste or practice.

The fugue is in three parts. While its subject includes the skipping rhythm of a French gigue, it also contains running sixteenths that bring it close to the type of gigue found in the suite BWV 996. The impressive design is built around expositions in minor keys one-third and two-thirds of the way through, at bars 114 (E minor) and 142 (A minor). Yet, as in the other toccatas, the counterpoint is occasionally awkward to play, and there may be insufficient variety; Bach, having found that the opening of the subject makes a fine stretto, introduces similar strettos in three of the four main episodes (bars 96, 112, and 149). Moreover, the last exposition opens (bar 154) with two incomplete stretto entries, and the final phrase opens with yet another stretto (bar 173b). But Bach wears his learning lightly; the piece concludes with scales cascading down to G, followed by an abrupt silence (Example 7.5).

EXAMPLE 7.5.   Toccata in G, BWV 916, bars 173b–77

Such endings are not unknown in German organ music. Composers and copyists are unlikely to have filled out the final bar with rests unless the notation meant what it says. Hence, players should probably resist the temptation to lengthen the final note or to end with an unnecessary allargando.[25]

8

The Concerto Transcriptions

Sometime around 1713–14, Bach is thought to have made keyboard versions of some twenty concertos by various composers. The originals were mostly by Italian (or, more precisely, Venetian) composers, including Vivaldi and Benedetto Marcello. But they also included at least one work by Telemann and three by the talented young Prince of Weimar, Johann Ernst. The composers of three works are unknown. Five arrangements are for organ, with pedal; sixteen or seventeen are *manualiter* and are generally assumed to be for harpsichord. Two concertos exist in both *manualiter* and *pedaliter* versions.

Many of these arrangements are significant keyboard pieces in their own right and for that reason alone would merit careful consideration here. As a group they have been considered important documents for Bach's musical development. While this is open to qualification—we have already seen numerous Italian influences in earlier works—the arrangements do seem to represent a crucial step toward Bach's mature style, which emerges in works probably dating from the following years at Weimar.[1]

In his biography of Bach, Forkel explained that it had been by studying and transcribing the concertos of Vivaldi that Bach had managed to put aside the crudeness of his early style and learned to compose in a manner that went beyond superficial digital display: He learned "to think musically." In his discussion, Forkel reveals himself to have been seriously misinformed on several matters, and the source of his information on this point is unknown.[2] But it is likely to have come from either Friedemann or Emanuel Bach, and thus it may reflect Sebastian's own view (as stated in his later years) of how he gained an understanding of a style that had swept Europe, and especially Germany, in the first and second decades of the eighteenth century through its vitality, expressive power, and sheer novelty.

Schulze (1984a, 146ff.) has shown that Bach's opportunities for studying and playing the works of Vivaldi and others probably broadened considerably in 1713, when Prince Johann Ernst of Sachsen-Weimar returned from university studies in Utrecht.[3] Thanks in part to the Prince, Weimar seems to have acquired a reputation as a center of concerto performance. A letter written in 1713 by Bach's student Philipp David Kräuter mentions the opportunity of hearing both French and Italian music there and that this would be useful for learning how to compose "concertos and overtures" (see Schulze 1984a, 157). At the time, many German musicians and their patrons were buying prints and manuscript copies of the new Italian music; in addition, Weimar exchanged music with other German courts (Schulze 1984a, 165–67), and Bach's arrangements presumably drew on the resulting fund of music. Certainly, despite his official role as organist, Bach was involved in the performance of secular music; in his letter of resignation to the Mühlhausen authorities he had referred to himself as a member of both the ducal *Hoffcapell* (*sic*) and the *Cammermusic*.[4]

It is unknown whether the transcriptions were really meant for Bach's private study (as Forkel implied) or as virtuoso display pieces. Bach is unlikely to have had a need to study works by the teenaged Prince, no matter how talented; on the other hand, by 1717 concertos were being played as organ solos during recitals at Amsterdam (see Schulze 1984a, 155–56), and the practice might have been fairly widespread.[5] In addition to Bach, Walther and Scheibe are also known to have transcribed Italian concertos.[6] But some of Bach's *manualiter* concertos are little more than unembellished keyboard reductions, and these, at least, might have been made for study purposes. Concertos were normally disseminated in parts, not scores, and as the number of real voices in such works was rarely greater than four and often reduced to two or three, a student would have found it convenient to score the outer parts onto just two staves. In the process, of course, the melodic lines could have been embellished or otherwise altered for more convenient performance at the keyboard. But Bach could surely have improvised an idiomatic keyboard version from just the original outer parts. The apparently unfinished form of some of the arrangements could be due to these having been left in a more or less preliminary state, while the more elaborate transcriptions might have been the products of revisions carried out later, perhaps for the benefit of students.

The sources for the *manualiter* concertos are, as for most of the earlier works, relatively late and few in number, and the absence of concordances and even attributions for several raises questions of authenticity.[7] Moreover, it is unclear whether Bach himself put the pieces into any order. The numbering adopted here is that of Schmieder, who followed that in BG 42, at this writing still the only readily available edition. For the first eleven concertos Naumann's order is that of the most important source, a copy by Bach's Eisenach cousin, Johann Bernhard Bach.[8] With the exception of Concerto No. 11, and possibly also Concerto No. 6, the arrangements copied by Bernhard Bach were of Italian works. It is conceivable that their sequence was determined by Sebastian himself; the volume opens with a splendid D-major work of Vivaldi, while weaker, or at least more problematical, pieces fall toward the end. A few movements in the transcriptions falling toward the back of the book (e.g., the second adagio of Concerto No. 10) remain incompletely adapted for keyboard performance, and this is also the case with several of the transcriptions not included in P 280. Otherwise, however, it is difficult to discern any pattern in the ordering of the works.

Forkel's discussion of the transcriptions and their influence on Bach emphasizes their importance as a source of "ideas," that is, thematic material (motives) and figuration. Moreover, in adapting to the keyboard Italian virtuoso "ideas" originally written for the violin, Bach might well have discovered new ways of writing for keyboard instruments—discoveries that would have proved useful when he later arranged his own violin concertos for organ and harpsichord.[9] But Bach must also have gained important lessons in musical form as well. At the largest level, he would have gained an appreciation for the infinite possibilities inherent in what we now call ritornello form, and he would have learned how to give large movements a rational, symmetrical architecture articulating a reasoned tonal structure—in contrast to the somewhat arbitrary, rondolike patterns of his own earlier works. Just as important, he would have realized that simple repetition and regular periodic phrasing, far from being marks of banality—as they would have seemed within the *stylus fantasticus* of many older keyboard works— were essential elements in the new style, whose rational architecture depended upon recurring themes and a hierarchy of small structural units defined in large part by their repetition, either literal or in sequence. Indeed, Bach would have had to recognize the usefulness of formulaic sequential and cadential writing for the articulation of large forms. He might also have found in several of these works impressive examples of the principle of recapitulation. Several movements are in early versions of sonata form—that is, expanded binary rather than ritornello forms, with recapitulations in the modern sense. But the term "recapitulation" will, as in the discussions of fugue, be applied here to any transposed restatement of a substantial portion of a piece, excluding the ritornello (which, like a fugal subject, is constantly "recapitulated").

Bach's method of transcription ranged from verbatim reduction—transcription in the more literal, restricted sense of the word—to wholesale rewriting that included the embellishment of treble, bass, and even inner voices, as in the Reinken arrangements. Indeed, Bach's arrangements are in general more elaborate than the plainer and possibly earlier ones of Walther, whose choice of models (perhaps dictated by what was available to him) was also much weaker.[10] While some unidiomatic passages remain, in most of the concertos Bach rescored passages that were not suitable to a keyboard instrument and enriched the texture with additional counterpoint and imitation. In a number of cases, the transcription is transposed to a different key from the original, usually in order to bring the highest notes of the violin parts down into the four-octave range used in most of Bach's keyboard works of the period (C–c''').

It is at first surprising that Bach tended to add embellishment more frequently in the bass than in the upper part. But in quick movements the solo violin part could receive only occasional elaboration. The simple basses of the originals were more readily embellished, a procedure that, in the solo passages, brought the bass closer in style to the upper part, yielding two relatively equal voices. The result was also more elegant than the chordal filler that would otherwise have had to substitute for the continuo realization of the orignal. In slow movements, of course, tradition dictated an embellished melodic line, but Bach was sparing in his elaboration. While he did write out embellishments in several slow movements, others were left largely as he found them, in several instances because they were already heavily embellished; the embellishments in the slow movements of Concertos Nos. 1, 2, and 7 are Vivaldi's own.

The transcriptions present few special problems of performance practice. One recurring question, however, concerns the repeated notes and chords that are a common feature of Italian orchestral style in both quick and slow movements; examples occur in Concertos Nos. 3, 4, 7, and 11. Bach makes no effort to disguise these or to adapt them to the keyboard idiom, even though a series of four or six repeated chords in a slow movement poses something of an interpretive challenge on any keyboard instrument, while the rapidly repeated sixteenth-note chords in several allegros can present a technical challenge, depending on the tempo and the nature of the keyboard action.[11] Repeated notes in Bach's own instrumental music sometimes bear slurs, indicating the technique known as "bow vibrato" or "slurred tremolo"—that is, a pulsation of the note without re-articulating it, a sort of measured shimmer.[12] Although it is possible that string players would have used this technique in several of the slow movements containing repeated chords, these chords are not placed under slurs in any of the originals, or in the transcriptions. On the contrary, in both original and transcription the slow movement of Concerto No. 7 calls explicitly for staccato chords. Hence, it would appear that one has little choice but to play such chords cleanly, with crisp articulation. Overinterpretation, for example in the form of imaginatively varied arpeggiation for each repeated chord, would probably impede the forward motion and fail to convey the intended orchestral effect, which simply does not translate particularly well to the keyboard.

Marshall (1986) seems to have been the first to question the traditional division of the *manualiter* and *pedaliter* transcriptions between harpsichord and organ, respectively. Walther's arrangements, including three without pedal, are explicitly for the organ; on the other hand, a "relatively early" Darmstadt copy of Concerto No. 3 has a title specifying "Clavessin" (mentioned in Schulze 1984a, 168). As usual, internal evidence is inconclusive. A few long sustained notes might sound more clearly on the organ,[13] and some passages would be less awkward to play if a few notes were taken on the (organ) pedals.[14] But other passages might be less effective on keyboard instruments other than the harpsichord,[15] and several of the transcriptions exceed the four-octave range of Bach's organ music.[16] Bach seems to have intentionally avoided high d''' in two other cases, raising the possibility that the transcriptions were made for varying instruments and purposes.[17]

Whatever the instrument, the use of two manuals may seem an obvious necessity, not only in order to reflect the tutti/solo distinctions of the originals but to facilitate performance in several passages where voices cross. But the sharp distinction in sound between ritornello and episode, now taken for granted in the ensemble concerto, would have been far less marked in the performances of Bach's day and is not present at all in many movements. Only a few dynamic markings occur in the sources, and in Concerto No. 5 these are for echoes *within* the opening ritornello (played in Vivaldi's original entirely by the tutti). Similar echoes also occur in the compositions transcribed as Concertos Nos. 4 and 7, but their arrangements lack all dynamic indications.[18] While appropriate changes of manual can be managed in some of the pieces—and the slow movements of Concertos Nos. 2 and 11 can be played with melody and accompaniment on different keyboards— Bach's elaboration of the bass or treble line often leaves no convenient place for changing keyboards between "tutti" and "solo." In such instances, both must be played on one manual, any desired variation in sound being written into the notes themselves.[19] The criss-crossing scales at the end of Concerto No. 2 are virtually unplayable on a single keyboard, yet dividing them between manuals raises questions: Where does one begin divided performance, and what registration can be used on each manual to prevent one voice from overshadowing the other? Presumably, both lines should be equally loud, yet on most harpsichords divided manuals require light or unequal registration, and even on the organ precisely equal registration is difficult to attain. Evidently, a dazzling virtuoso climax was intended here, and the scales are just barely playable on a single keyboard through the use of old-fashioned fingering (without thumbs), one hand being held well above the other (Example 8.1).[20]

EXAMPLE 8.1.   Concerto No. 2 in G, BWV 973, third
movement, bars 55b–60

Concertos after Vivaldi

Only six of the *manualiter* concertos (and possibly a seventh, BWV 977) are actually based on works by Vivaldi (see Table 8–1). But he remains the composer most frequently represented in the *manualiter* transcriptions. Bach arranged four other works by Vivaldi, three in *pedaliter* settings for organ and one in the concerto for four harpsichords (BWV 1065). Of these ten works after Vivaldi, six are based on originals that appeared in Vivaldi's Op. 3 (Amsterdam, 1711). The remaining four also appeared in print (in either Op. 4 or Op. 7), but Bach knew three of them in distinct prepublication versions that he must have obtained in manuscript copies.

Vivaldi's Opera 4 and 7 were published as sets of five part-books each. They contain works now identified as "solo" concertos, that is, works for one *violino principale* plus four-part string ensemble (and continuo). Opus 3, on the other hand, was issued in eight part-books—four violins, two violas, and two bass parts. In neither type of work were any of the parts necessarily meant to be doubled. All of the music is chamber music, and the scoring in Opus 3 varies between that of a "solo" concerto and what is now usually called a concerto grosso. The resulting freedom and variety of texture was surely one of the great attractions of this set for Bach and his contemporaries, but it is not something that can be readily conveyed in a solo keyboard transcription. Perhaps for this reason the concertos from Opus 3 selected for *manualiter* transcription are of the "solo" type, in which only one of the violins has a soloistic part. Still, players should bear the original scoring in mind; a passage scored for all four violin parts, as in the opening tutti of the last movement of Concerto No. 1, was quite possibly intended for just four players, not a large modern string section.

TABLE 8–1. Concertos after Vivaldi

Transcription			Original				Sources
No.	BWV	key	R.	Op./No.	M.	key	(of transcription)
1	972	D	230	3/9	414	D	P 280, P 804/55 (3d mvt. in-complete
2	973	G	299	7/8	449	G	P 280, P 804/54 (without 3d mvt.), Poel. 29
4	975	g	316a	4/6*	(123)	?g	P 280
5	976	C	265	3/12	417	E	P 280, P 804/15 (lacks 2d mvt.)
7	978	F	310	3/3	408	G	P 280
9	980	G	381	4/1*	514	B♭	P 280

*alternate version
R = number in Ryom catalogue (Ryom 1986)
M = volume number in *Le opere di Antonio Vivaldi*, ed. G. F. Malipiero et al. (Rome, 1947–72)
P 280 and P 804 are in SPK; Poel. 29 is in LEm

Concerto No. 1 in D, BWV 972

The full D-major chords and forthright dotted rhythms of the opening passage make this a suitable work to start off the series, whether or not Bach actually intended it for that purpose. Nevertheless, the opening allegro confounds modern expectations of what a Vivaldi concerto movement should be like. It is barely recognizable as a ritornello form; indeed, the opening tutti is hardly a ritornello at all (the opening three-and-a-half bars never come back), and apart from a short excursion to the relative minor the entire movement remains in the tonic. Still, the movement serves as a demonstration of how much Vivaldi could accomplish in a series of short phrases confined to a few harmonies. The music seems simple, yet it maintains considerable tension through judicious use of dominant prolongations as well as varied figuration and scoring. While Bach did not follow this model in his own concertos, there is an echo of one phrase from this movement in the prelude of the Fourth English Suite, which comes as close as any of Bach's original keyboard works to concerto style.[21]

Although the bass has been varied or rewritten at many points, Bach hardly altered the top line at all. The only significant embellishment is the substitution of figuration in thirty-seconds for sixteenths in the central solo of the last movement (bars 58ff.). In the slow movement the written-out embellishment is taken verbatim from the original, even though the figuration is much more repetitive than what Bach used in his own decorated adagios.

Concerto No. 2 in G, BWV 973

Of the four Vivaldi works that Bach transcribed from sources other than Opus 3, only this one follows the same version as the later print. Particularly striking here is Bach's embellishment of the slow movement, which is a model of its type and should be carefully considered by anyone who envisages adding their own embellishments to other movements. Bach wisely avoids filling in the rests in Vivaldi's violin line (bars 2, 9, 11, etc.); these rests articulate a beautifully asymmetrical phrase structure. The diminished chord in bar 14, where treble and bass come to rest together on a long note for the first time, is marked by only a mordent; a more elaborate embellishment at this point would have ruined the eloquent effect of the pause on a dissonant harmony. Similar restraint marks the closing phrase of the movement (from bar 19); flourishes occur on the beats preceding cadential formulas, not on the cadences themselves—that would be anticlimactic—and the final chord is again elaborated by a bare mordent.

Bach also added inner voices to the original two-part texture, which was scored for solo violin accompanied by unison violins and violas (without basso continuo). In the transcription, melody and accompaniment can be played on separate manuals, as in the slow movement of the much later Italian Concerto. That the same is possible here can hardly be an accident, and it facilitates several passages where melody and accompaniment cross (bars 16–17, 18).

The other movements remain closer to the original, and the embellishments in the first movement are mostly Vivaldi's own. These include the variation of the ritornello theme at the first entrance of the soloist (bar 22), the further variation of the theme in the second solo passage (bar 46), and the soloist's variation of the second phrase of the ritornello just before the end (bar 117). But in both allegros Bach made additions to the rushing scale figures in the closing phrases; in each case Bach added a second scale moving in contrary motion. Hence, the criss-crossing scales at the end of the last movement (shown in Example 8.1) are a heightened version of what happens at the end of the first. Bach also chose to eliminate a series of dramatic rests in the last movement, where a series of striking staccato chords became homogenized through the addition of running sixteenths (Example 8.2).

EXAMPLE 8.2.   (a) Vivaldi: Concerto in G, R. 299

(b) Concerto No. 2 in G, BWV 973, third movement, bars 43–44a

Yet Vivaldi's lesson was not lost on Bach, and in the closing passages of Concertos Nos. 5 and 7 he retained the idea of a dramatic interruption of the "motoric" pulsation in small values. He later imitated the idea at the end of the Fourth Brandenburg Concerto (third movement, bar 229).

Concerto No. 4 in G Minor BWV 975

The first two movements of this arrangement correspond closely with the version in Vivaldi's Opus 4 (Amsterdam, ca. 1714). But the last movement is completely different, and the slow movement also shows important variants.

One has to agree with Vivaldi that the later version is better. Moreover, although it is fully worked out, Bach's transcription inevitably fails to reflect the original scoring of the opening ritornello, whose opening phrase (bars 1–8) was first repeated piano by the tutti, then followed by a forte passage for the soloist accompanied by the ripieno (bars 17–23a).[22] It would not be impossible to play the piano phrase (bars 9–16) on a softer manual. But there are no dynamic markings in the transcription, and it would be difficult, not to mention distracting, to make all the leaps between manuals necessary to reflect the rapid alternations between forte and piano in the original at bars 73bff.

In the slow movement, Bach again embellished the melody, and he inserted a new chromatic element into the bass as well. While not adding any inner voices, he provided an effective realization of the basso continuo by transforming the lower voice into a sort of Alberti bass that implied inner voices as well (Example 8.3).

EXAMPLE 8.3.   (a) Vivaldi: Concerto in G Minor, R. 316a, and (b) Concerto No. 4 in G Minor BWV 975, second movement, bars 1–3a

Slurs in bars 7–8 suggest that the chord tones should be held out, but if they are authentic one wonders why the slurs are not present from the beginning. The first ritornello, in A minor (bars 9–10), enters awkwardly following a half-cadence to an A-major chord; this passage is understandably absent from the published version of the concerto, and the remaining ritornelli were rewritten.

What is presumably the original final movement (transcribed here) is in binary form. The print substituted a through-composed movement, as is also the case in the work transcribed as Concerto No. 9.[23] Although some composers continued to use binary form for the quick movements of their concertos, Vivaldi (like Bach) seems to have come to regard such a form as unsuitable in a genre that was becoming increasingly defined by the contrast between solo and tutti. Here (but not in Concerto No. 9) Bach elaborated the binary form by providing written-out repetitions in which the bass is varied.[24]

Concerto No. 5 in C, BWV 976

This was originally the work that closed Vivaldi's Opus 3. It is one of the longest and most brilliant concertos of the set, and the dotted rhythms in the closing phrase brought the collection to a ringing finish. Bach left them intact and did not fill in the rests with figuration as he did in Concerto No. 2. Elsewhere, however, Bach was oddly inconsistent in the degree to which he elaborated the original. The largo is not much more than a literal reduction. But both treble and bass are considerably varied in the last movement, and the figuration in the upper part in bars 64–79 is Bach's own realization of an arpeggiando passage originally notated as three-part chords.

Kellner's copy (in P 804) omits the largo as well as part of the last solo passage of the closing movement (bars 106–10). Perhaps Kellner felt that the movement contained one too many long diatonic sequences. But despite their formulaic quality the sequences seem correctly calculated to add to, rather than diminish, the accumulating dramatic tension in the passages preceding the final tutti reentrance.

Concerto No. 7 in F, BWV 978

The third of the works transcribed from Vivaldi's Opus 3 is an "easy" Baroque concerto that many violinists encounter at an early stage in their training, probably never recognizing the impact that its clear, concise architecture and inventive scoring may have had on Bach. Curiously, the one weakness in both outer movements lies in the manner in which, having modulated through several foreign keys, they reestablish the tonic. Each does so through sequential statements of the ritornello theme in A minor, C, and (in the first movement) F.[25] The problem is that F major is never sufficiently tonicized; it sounds like the subdominant of C, not the tonic of the entire movement. If this was a miscalculation, however, Bach evidently was not troubled by it.

Bach's substantive alterations are in the bass line, including the imitation of the violin figure at the opening of the first movement (the original lacks the imitation). The second movement, which Bach transcribes quite literally, is a largo. The tempo mark is perhaps to be interpreted literally ("broad"); if so, a relatively quick pace may be most likely to achieve the desired effect. This will give the soloist's arpeggiations some virtuosic fire and will make believable the combination of arpeggiation and staccato on the chords of the tutti.

Concerto No. 9 in G, BWV 980

Bernhard Bach's copy of Concerto No. 9 correctly identifies it as a version of the work that opens Vivaldi's Opus 4.[26] But the first movement of the published concerto is, from bar 28, different from the version transcribed here, and the second and third movements are entirely new. In the early version of the concerto the overwhelming weight, as in Concerto No. 4, falls on the first movement. This alone is no fault, but the motivic material is dull, and Vivaldi himself seems to have felt the movement lacking, for in the published version he introduced some needed variety in the figuration, rewriting the last two solo passages (here, bars 63–68 and 71–76). It is possible that Vivaldi's scoring brings the limited thematic material of the earlier version to life, but the movement does not transfer well to the keyboard. The ritornello, for example, involves close imitations at the unison between the two violin parts; Bach attempts to adapt this to the keyboard idiom, transposing the second violin part an octave lower, but the result is a pale reflection of the original (Example 8.4). For a more inspired imitation of the Vivaldi model one might look

EXAMPLE 8.4.   (a) Vivaldi: Concerto in B♭, R. 381

(b) Concerto No. 9 in G, BWV 980, first movement, bars 1–2

to the first movement of the Sixth Brandenburg Concerto, whose opening is somewhat similar.

The last movement is a sonata form like that at the end of Concerto No. 4. Indeed, the opening themes of the two movements are practically the same, despite the difference in mode,[27] and the present arrangement uses the embellished bass line found in the varied reprises of Concerto No. 4.

Concerto No. 6 in C, BWV 977

Sources: SPK P 280 (Johann Bernhard Bach, 1715–30); SPK P 804/56 (Mey).

The original of Concerto No. 6 has not been found among Vivaldi's known works. The copy by Mey bears the title *Concerto in C♮ di Vivaldi accomadato sul Clavicembalo di Giov. Seb. Bach*, and while Mey's title may be faulty, the work is strongly Italianate in style—more so than the two other transcriptions of unidentified works (Concertos Nos. 12 and 15), which might have been German imitations of the Venetian style.[28] National style is, however, hard to judge at a distance approaching three centuries. Schering's guesses (1902–3, 242) about Concertos Nos. 8 (German) and 16 (Italian) proved wrong, and thus his suggestions of an

Italian origin for Concerto No. 6 and a German origin for Concertos Nos. 12 and 15 are adopted here with a certain amount of circumspection.

The original key of Concerto No. 6 is likely to have been D, since the Fs in the opening ritornello could not have been played on violins.[29] The plan is as much that of a sinfonia (or overture) as of a concerto. The first movement is a full-fledged, if compact, ritornello form, but the adagio is short—only nine bars, ending in a half-cadence. Nevertheless, the first seven bars are worked out imitatively in four parts, rare in the Italian concerto but perhaps an aspect of the original that had caught Bach's attention. Like Concertos Nos. 4 and 9, the work ends with a short dance in binary form, here labeled explicitly a *giga*.

It seems possible that a second solo violin or a solo cello joined the principal violin in the solo sections of the first movement (e.g., bars 27–32). But the accompaniment of the melody in parallel tenths and sixths in those passages could just as easily have belonged to the ripieni or been added by Bach. No clear tutti/solo contrasts at all are implied in the last two movements, but this would not be unusual in an early concerto; the same is true in the last movement of Concerto No. 4 and apparently also in Concerto No. 10.

Whatever its origin, this is one of the more attractive and idiomatic of the transcriptions. The outer movements contain some effective keyboard writing, in particular a series of descending sevenths in the left hand (first movement, bar 16) that look bizarre on paper—and cannot have been present in the original—but seem perfectly natural in performance.[30] The adagio is perhaps less effective, for its dense four-part writing seems a little studied, like the somewhat overembellished opening of the C-Major Sonata after Reinken BWV 966. The gigue makes a little excursion to the minor at the end of each half. This might have been inspired by Corelli's C-major violin sonata (Op. 5, No. 3, last movement), which is practically quoted in bars 32b–33. Unfortunately, the preceding phrase appears to have been garbled in both sources, and one must do a little composing for the passage to make any sense (Example 8.5). Even then it seems unsatisfactory; perhaps Bach's own score contained corrections at this point, and one might even delete the whole phrase, skipping from bar 30a to 32b.[31]

EXAMPLE 8.5.   Concerto No. 6 in C, BWV 977, third movement, bars 30–32

Concertos after "Marcello" and Torelli

Benedetto Marcello was the better known and by far the more prolific of two Venetian nobles who were brothers and composers. But despite the fact that he was thirteen years younger than Alessandro—from whom he was, moreover, estranged for much of his career (see Selfridge-Field 1990, 4–6)—the two concertos transcribed by Bach are similar in many respects (see Table 8–2). Both are serious, well-crafted pieces; in addition to showing similarities in their motivic material, the quick movements of the two concertos reveal symmetrical architectures involving extensive use of recapitulation that must have impressed Bach. Particularly notable are the final movements, sonata-form allegros resembling the last movements of Concertos Nos. 4, 6, and 9 but longer and more serious in tone than those dance-like pieces. Bach and Walther may have had no idea that the two concertos were not by the same composer; the manuscripts omit the first name, and Benedetto's older brother is not mentioned in the brief entry in Walther (1732), as noted by Hanks (1972, 214).

TABLE 8–2.   Concertos after Marcello: Sources

Transcription			Original			Sources (of Transcription)
No.	BWV	key	Composer	Op./No.	key	
3	974	d	Alessandro	—	c (d)	P 280, P 804/4, DS ms. 66
10	981	c	Benedetto	1/2	e	P 280, DSB P 801 (Walther), B Br XY 25.448 (J. A. Scheibe), LEm ms. 8

Concerto No. 3 in D Minor BWV 974

This is an arrangement of an oboe concerto ascribed to Alessandro Marcello in an anthology entitled *Concerti a cinque* (Concertos in Five Parts, i.e., "solo" concertos), containing works by various composers and published at Amsterdam around 1716. The concerto became known earlier in this century under the name of Benedetto Marcello, in a somewhat embellished C-minor version preserved in a German manuscript.[32]

Bach's setting evidently depended on yet another version transmitted in manuscript, as the first movement lacks six bars that, in the other versions, in effect constitute the beginning of a recapitulation in the tonic (following bar 44a). Hence, the movement is in a concise sonata form; indeed, it is so concise, and so restrained in style, that it has more the character of a sonata than a concerto movement in the usual sense. In the middle of the movement, however, Bach rewrote one passage that became a climactic demonstration of how to achieve a crescendo on the harpsichord (Example 8.6).

EXAMPLE 8.6.   (a) Alessandro Marcello, oboe concerto

(b) J. S. Bach, Concerto No. 3 in D Minor BWV 974, first movement, bars 34b–35

Nothing so dramatic happens in the last two movements, although Bach considerably embellished the adagio. In the Kellner collection (P 804) the last movement is followed (despite a *Finis* indication) by a three-bar fragment in an unidentified hand. The latter has been described as a "modulating transition" (NBA V/5, KB), but it may be an unrelated fragment. The passage, merely a crude series of cadences in G, leads to a rather clumsy fugue in the same key. This is labeled as a gigue, without attribution.[33] It certainly has nothing to do with either Bach or Marcello; Stinson (1989a, 132) also rules out the possibility that it might have been by Kellner. The subject bears a family resemblance to that of the gigue in a Suite in F (BWV Anh. 80) bearing a very doubtful attribution to Bach (see Appendix A).

Concerto No. 10 in C Minor BWV 981

The concerto by Benedetto Marcello was one of a set of twelve *concerti a cinque* published at Venice in 1708. The original solo part (*violino principale*) is lost, and Bach's transcription is thus a primary source for the work, although soloistic writing appears to have been confined to the first two movements.[34] The transcription may have enjoyed some popularity, for it also occurs in copies by Walther and J. A. Scheibe.[35]

The concerto is in the four-movement form today associated with the *sonata da chiesa*. The first movement, an adagio, opens with dotted rhythms that might, as in several concertos by Corelli, refer to the French overture (despite the time signature of $\frac{3}{4}$). But solo figuration evidently replaced this in the second half (from bar 20). Bach is likely to have taken this figuration unchanged from the original, as it contains repeated notes more apt for the violin than for the keyboard, and in the original key it would not have descended lower than a^b.

The ritornello theme of the first allegro was evidently stated imitatively in each of the three violin parts, the bass (and viola?) remaining silent until bar 8b. Yet the movement comes close to being a true sonata form, inasmuch as the material that originally leads to a cadence in the dominant (bars 21b–29a) is restated at the end in the tonic (bars 37–45a). The closing movement is even closer to genuine sonata form, longer and with more extensive recapitulation than the corresponding movement of Alessandro's work. The entire second half (from the double bar onward) consists of previously heard material transposed upward or downward by a fifth; only the phrase in bars 16–22 is never restated.

Unfortunately, these schematic repetitions can become tiresome in a solo keyboard performance, and there is little opportunity for adding embellishments in the repeats. Moreover, despite having extensively reworked the first two movements, Bach left the tutti passages of the third movement in a verbatim reduction that seems to cry out for further adaptation, calling not only for embellishment, but for the elimination of some awkward spacings. But however unsatisfactory the arrangement remains in its existing form, it would appear to make possible a reliable reconstruction of the lost solo part of the original.

Concerto No. 8 in B Minor BWV 979

Arrangement of: Torelli, Violin Concerto in D minor. *Source*: SPK P 280 (Johann Bernhard Bach, 1715–30).

Torelli was the most important member of the first generation of composers of concertos, and if the work transcribed here is really his then it may well be the earliest of the pieces arranged by Bach.[36] Zehnder (1991) argues for a stronger influence by Torelli on Bach than has previously been recognized, but the only tangible evidence for the hypothesis appears to be that furnished by this arrangement. Like many seventeenth-century ensemble sonatas, the original work consists of mostly short, linked sections, and it might have reminded Bach of his own toccatas and early preludes and fugues. There is an introductory section consisting mainly of passage-work, as well as two slow transitions in arpeggiando style. The two largest movements, both allegros, are each constructed in highly regular fashion around four statements of a ritornelo theme. Unfortunately, both large and small sections tend to rely on a limited variety of arpeggiate motives used in fairly ordinary sequences. Played by a virtuoso string band the piece might have made a strong impression, but on the keyboard it seems colorless and not entirely idiomatic (as in the repeated notes in the ritornello of the last movement).

Concertos on German Models

Of the seven remaining works, five are known to be arrangements of German compositions (see Table 8–3). The appearance of Telemann among the composers of the originals should elicit no surprise, for by 1713 he had established himself as the leading German composer of his generation, having held positions at the courts at Erfurt and Eisenach, among others. He also had connections with the court of Weimar, dedicating his first publication (six violin sonatas, 1715) to Prince Johann Ernst, whose own Opus 1 (six concertos) appeared posthumously in 1718 with Telemann as editor. In addition, Telemann stood as godfather to Sebastian's son Carl Philipp Emanuel in 1714, and Bach must have had considerable admiration for the slightly older composer, whose early works—at least those sonatas and concertos available in modern editions—show an imaginative personal version of current Italian style.

Telemann's early concertos are somewhat more compact and more economical in their use of motivic material than the better-known works by Vivaldi. Phrases tend to be shorter and virtuosity is somewhat restrained. Similar qualities also characterize the other works considered below. While these lack the spaciousness and verve of Vivaldi's concertos, at its best the style produces music of considerable eloquence.

It seems possible that the young Prince of Weimar modeled his own concertos more closely on Telemann's than on any Italian imports, to judge from the examples available in print. But Johann Ernst is likely to have known at least the Italian concertos transcribed by Bach and by Walther, who dedicated his *Praecepta* to the Prince on the latter's twelfth birthday in 1708. Walther's elementary textbook contains little of direct relevance to concertos or indeed to any of the newer French and Italian genres. But presumably the Prince gained oral instruction concerning the concerto from Walther as well as from Telemann and Bach.[37] Not unexpectedly, Johann Ernst's inexperience reveals itself in the brevity and inconclusiveness of several movements, although the unusual plans of several movements and perhaps

TABLE 8–3.   Concertos on German Models: Sources

| Transcription | | | Original | | | Sources |
No.	BWV	key	Composer	Op./No.	key	(of transcription)
14	985	g	Telemann	—/—	g	P 804/28 (Mey)
11	982	B♭	J. Ernst	1/1	B♭	P 280
16	987	d	J. Ernst	1/4	d	P 804/34 (Mey)
13	984	C	J. Ernst	—/—	?C	P 804/52 (Ringk), Poel. 29, LEm ms. 8
—	592a	G	J. Ernst	—/—	G	Poel. 29
12	983	g	?	?	?	P 804/35 (Mey), Poel. 29
15	986	G	?	?	?	P 804/46 (Mey)

even of whole concertos (see Concerto No. 11 below) reveal originality. Indeed, the music is superior to some of the minor works that Walther transcribed, and there are frequent attractive details of melody and scoring. The Prince's early death, preceded by a long illness, may have made him something of a romantic figure to his contemporaries. But there is no evidence to support Schering's suggestion that Bach's arrangements of the Prince's works might have been intended as private, posthumous homage.[38]

Concerto No. 14 in G Minor BWV 985

Easily underestimated because of its brevity and restraint, Telemann's concerto is a very fine work, and it received careful attention from Bach. Bach followed an early form of the concerto; a later version has an extended solo passage after bar 44 of the last movement.[39] Like the Marcello and Torelli concertos, Telemann's has in its quick movements a logical, clearly articulated design that must have appealed to Bach. Another reason for Bach's interest in the work would have been the spare rhetoric of the adagio, whose high point is a series of chromatic modulations passing quickly, via several deceptive arrivals and surprising dissonances, from G minor through B$^\flat$ to the tonic C minor (bars 9–14). The imitative ritornello of the last movement recalls that of the first allegro in Concerto No. 10; an even closer parallel can be found in a trio-sonata by Albinoni published in the set from which Bach himself borrowed three fugue subjects.[40] Bach may have borrowed from the present concerto as well; the closing flourish of the first movement reappears at the end of the sonata in the same key for viola da gamba (BWV 1029).[41]

Bach's substantive changes are confined to restrained embellishment of the bass and occasional alteration of figures not idiomatic to the keyboard (e.g., third movement, bars 15–16a). The adagio is an almost exact copy of the original, which is scored for soloist and continuo only.[42] As a result, it may seem a little bare. But it is not clear if the player should attempt to "improve" it, through ornamentation or harmonic filler. Even the empty tritone between bass and treble in bar 9 (second beat) might stand. This is the sort of well-placed harmonic surprise that Telemann often places at a strategic location in a movement; in a keyboard setting it might be more effective as is, without added notes.

Concerto No. 11 in B$^\flat$, BWV 982

This first concerto from Johann Ernst's Opus 1 is something of a hodgepodge, perhaps assembled from heterogeneous fragments. The first movement is a very competent ritornello form reminiscent of Telemann, but the last movement suffers from a too-late return to the tonic just seven bars from the end, an error that Bach himself committed in some early fugues. The second and third movements are for solo violin and continuo alone; they form an adagio-allegro pair in the foreign key of G minor, and the second movement seems to open in the middle of a phrase.[43] Bach may have edited the Prince's composition or worked from memory, for (as in BWV 984 and 592a) the transcription lacks several bars found in the original; a few others are added. In any case he probably worked from a prepublication version, as a manuscript copy of the original concerto (in ROu) eliminates the ripieno in bars 41–57 of the last movement, leaving a duet for two solo violins—a scoring apparently imitated in Bach's arrangement (the viola part is ignored).

In the adagio the opening and closing passages (marked piano) were originally scored for continuo alone, so that Bach's version represents a written-out continuo realization; it is fairly elaborate, in four real parts. The solo line is marked forte perhaps to indicate that it is to be played on a separate manual.

Concerto No. 16 in D Minor BWV 987

Like the concerto by Torelli, this work consists of relatively short, linked movements. But here the first brief passage is an expressive grave (*Adagio e staccato* in the original)—a very different, perhaps more Germanic, call to attention than that of Concerto No. 8, although a model for the present alternation of grave and presto sections could be found in various Italian works (e.g., Corelli's Op. 5, No. 1). Johann Ernst marks the quick passages *piano e presto*, but the word *piano* is probably just a way of indicating a solo passage, and Bach leaves no opportunity for changing manuals. The longest section is the central allegro, whose chaconnelike harmonic ground resembles the *Follia* bass (as Schering noted, 1903–4, 569), while the staccato triadic theme perhaps imitates that of the third movement of Vivaldi's "Grosso Mogul" Concerto R. 208a.[44] The last movement, a short vivace, has some points in common with the prelude of Bach's Third English Suite.[45]

Concerto No. 13 in C, BWV 984

The model for this transcription is lost, but Johann Ernst's authorship is established by the title in ms. 8 and in the two sources of the organ version BWV 595. BWV 595 gives only the first movement, in a somewhat longer version that one would assume to be later than that of BWV 984 were it not for some redundancies and awkward modulations.[46] The somewhat more varied figuration of the *manualiter* version suggests that it in fact is the later one, perhaps representing Bach's own abbreviation of the original.

In both versions the first movement is the most Vivaldiesque of the Prince's concerto movements transcribed by Bach. The keyboard transcription is attractive and carefully worked out; unfortunately, the last two movements are marred by prosaic sequences for which Bach's embellishments can do little.

Concerto in G, BWV 592a

The frequently overlooked BWV 592a was included in BG 42 only in an appendix of "Doubtful Compositions," even though the editor regarded it as a variant "probably by Bach himself" (BG 42:xxxiii) of the organ arrangement BWV 592. The two transcriptions stem from an unpublished work of Johann Ernst, and while the *manualiter* version appears to have been based on the *pedaliter* one, it is a thorough reworking and not merely a simplification of the organ arrangement. The lateness of the source and the fact that the copyist remains at this writing unidentified raise questions about Bach's involvement in BWV 592a. While the manuscript contains three other transcriptions generally accepted as Bach's, at least one of these is also slightly suspect (Concerto No. 12, anonymous in the only other copy). Certain details in BWV 592a are stylistically doubtful—for example, the inclusion of the note c' in Example 8.7b, bar 3 (i.e., the substitution of a $^6_5$-chord for a 6-chord) in order to avoid parallel octaves between the two parts. Still, the arrangement is a good one, and it departs from the model at the same point as does Bach's organ transcription.

The concerto itself evidently enjoyed some popularity, and the *manualiter* arrangement is worth rescuing from obscurity. The somewhat greater embellishment of the upper line in the *manualiter* version again suggests that it is the later of the two keyboard versions. Both discreetly revise one phrase (first movement, bars 60–65), which becomes a bar longer than in the original. But many imaginative touches, such as the switch to triplets for the solo passages of the first movement, are the Prince's own, and his distinctive scoring of the last movement forced considerable rewriting in both transcriptions (Example 8.7). The movement—the original and both transcriptions—seems artless, but it is so good-natured and so cleverly transcribed that it ought to be heard more often, if only as an encore piece.

Concerto No. 12 in G Minor BWV 983

Concerto No. 12 is a fiery and imaginative work, given in a thoroughly idiomatic keyboard version. One might suspect that the original was an early work by Bach himself. But there are some prosaic sequences in the outer movements, both of which suffer from weak, redundant modulating schemes that never move very far beyond the tonic and the relative major. The opening theme of the first movement somewhat resembles that of a weaker work by Luigi Mancia, transcribed by Walther. But the polyphonic texture of the very expressive adagio and the echoes in the concluding presto perhaps suggest a German composer.[47] The attribution of the arrangement is a bit weak, but the style, especially the scrupulous voice-leading in the four-part ritornellos of the first two movements, contains nothing foreign to the other arrangements.

Concerto No. 15 in G, BWV 986

This is a charming work, more compact than Concerto No. 12 and thus perhaps even more likely to be based on a German original. The "speaking" repeated notes in the adagio recall those in the grave of Concerto No. 16, the model of which is by Johann Ernst. But this work is free of the occasional weak modulations and sequences noted in the Prince's other concertos, and it might instead be by a master composer such as Telemann, as Schering (1902–3, 242) suggested. Perhaps this concerto even furnished the model for the work that Bach arranged as BWV 592/592a; as in that work, triplets are introduced in what appears to be the initial solo of the first movement (bar 8b). In addition, the figuration of a brilliant (tutti?) sequence in bars 33ff. bears a resemblance, in Bach's arrangement, to the opening of the last movement of BWV 592a. The last move-

EXAMPLE 8.7 (a) Johann Ernst von Sachsen-Weimar,
Concerto in G, (b) J. S. Bach, Concerto in G, BWV 592,
and (c) Concerto in G, BWV 592a, third movement, bars
1–4

ment, although the shortest of all the binary final movements in these concertos, is nevertheless a complete sonata form. It opens on the second quarter of a bar of $\frac{12}{8}$ in order that the final chord should fall on a downbeat, reflecting a concern for correct musical prosody also expressed in German writings of the period (see, e.g., Mattheson 1739, 147).

9

The Virtuoso Fugues

The concerto arrangements discussed in the previous chapter seem to be closely related to the preludes of the English Suites (discussed in Chapter 13) and to five large fugues, each paired with a prelude or fantasia. All five are important and impressive works in virtuoso style; among them is Bach's single best-known keyboard piece outside the great collections, the Chromatic Fantasia and Fugue BWV 903. Dating is, as always, problematical; the position taken here is that, with the exception of BWV 906, the pieces probably originated toward the end of Bach's Weimar period (1714–17). But arguments for later dates—for example, placing BWV 903 at Cöthen (Stauffer 1989) or BWV 894 in the Leipzig period (Stinson 1989b) on the basis of notational evidence or patterns of manuscript transmission—cannot be dismissed. Evidence of this sort, however, establishes only a *terminus post quem non*, that is, an upper limit for the date of the earliest surviving version of a piece. Large display pieces like the Chromatic Fantasia might, however, at first have been withheld from circulation, serving as Bach's private repertory for performance on special occasions. Eventually, however, these pieces—above all the Chromatic Fantasia and Fugue—circulated relatively widely and, unlike Bach's earlier keyboard works, remained in use long after they had been composed. There is evidence that they were copied by Bach's students and that Bach himself revised them at Cöthen or Leipzig, in one or two cases bringing together separately composed preludes and fugues; the later datings proposed for some of these pieces might then apply to the revised versions.

Whatever their dates, these works are distinct in style, dimensions, and form from both the early works considered in Chapters 4–7 and the contents of the WTC. Opening movements as well as fugues are large in scope and adopt many formal elements of the concerto—ritornello form in the first movements of BWV 894 and 904, extensive "solo" episodes in the fugues of BWV 903 and 944—and always within a rounded modulating scheme. In this the present works are distinct from both the rambling, episodic movements of the toccatas and other early works and from the preludes and fugues of the WTC, which lack true ritornello forms and tend to be more restrained in dimensions and level of virtuosity. To some degree these pieces are the *manualiter* equivalents of the great preludes and fugues for organ. The latter also appear to date mostly from Weimar, and, while some were later revised and widely circulated, they were never brought together into a named collection. Although the *manualiter* pieces are also, of course, playable on the organ, only in BWV 904 is the style arguably as appropriate to organ as to harpsichord. Moreover, at least one movement in each of the five preludes and fugues is explicitly assigned to the harpsichord in one or more sources. Hence, with the possible exception of BWV 904, it seems safe to refer to these as virtuoso *harpsichord* pieces.

This raises the problem of the purpose of the pieces. One can speculate about private or semipublic performances at Weimar, Cöthen, and elsewhere, and it is even possible that Bach was often called upon to play solos such as these during court concerts. But his solos there might have been extemporizations rather than compositions; the famous accounts of Bach's solo performances (the contest with Marchand, the Hamburg audition, and the Potsdam performance that led to the *Musical Offering*) all mention improvisations, not prepared compositions. Still, one suspects that in preparing for the 1717 "clavier" contest with Marchand (who never showed up), Bach would have brought a few compositions along.[1] The Chromatic Fantasia or the A-minor fugue BWV 894/2 might well represent the sort of music played at such an event, whether improvised or composed. These two pieces seem to be idealized examples of two types of improvisation that Bach was no doubt able to carry off with equal ease: the free fantasia, with its open form and wide-ranging modulations, and the virtuoso fugue worked out in relatively simple counterpoint and with a good deal of arpeggiated passage-work. Such pieces might have been what C. P. E. Bach had in mind when he told Forkel (BD 3:289 [item 803]/BR, 278) that his father, while usually composing away from the keyboard, in certain compositions "took the material from improvisations on the clavier."

Fantasia and Fugue in A Minor BWV 904

Chief sources: SPK P 320 (Kittel); SPK P 804/25 (Kellner; fantasia only); SPK P 288/11 (Kellner; fugue only); DSB Mus. ms. 30112 (fugue only); SPK P 617 (Anonymous 404; fugue only). *Editions*: BG 36; Dadelsen and Rönnau (1970).

BWV 904 is the most old-fashioned of the three large fantasias and fugues for harpsichord.[2] The word *fantasia* means something different in each; here it may reflect a certain gravity of character that, together with the contrapuntal texture, is shared with a few organ works of the same title (BWV 562, 563, 570).[3] The two movements are preserved separately in the earliest sources, and Stinson (1989b, 455–59) argues that the copyist Kittel, not Bach, may have been "the architect of the pairing." Still, as Stinson (1989b, 460n) notes, the opening thematic material of both movements includes the progression e″, f″, e″. While the importance of this sort of fleeting motivic parallel should not be exaggerated, it helps make the pairing plausible even if it is not original.

Both movements avoid outright virtuoso display and instead emphasize contrapuntal development. The result, especially in the fugue, is some unusually awkward writing. Individual parts are divided oddly between the hands, and voices cross in ways not often encountered in Bach's mature works.[4] Kellner, who copied the two movements separately, designated the fantasia *pro Cembalo*, the fugue *manualiter*. But there is nothing in the fugue specifically pointing to organ; the bass, for example, cannot have been conceived as a pedal part.

Still, the fact that the movements are preserved separately in most early copies supports the idea that they originated separately. Stinson (1989a, 107), arguing for a "post-1725 origin" for the fantasia, points to its "extraordinarily symmetrical design," which closely resembles ritornello form. Equally symmetrical schemes do, however, occur in what are probably Weimar works.[5] In any case the fantasia, while on paper a textbook example of ritornello form, lacks distinctly concertolike material except perhaps in the arpeggiated figuration of the last episode. The "ritornello" is a twelve-bar phrase constructed over a descending chaconnelike bass and repeated at regular intervals in E minor, D minor, and again at the end in the tonic. There are three episodes ("solos"), all making use of a suspension motive related to one in the "ritornello" (compare treble in bars 3–4, alto in 12–13). This idea, together with the contrapuntal texture and the use of *alla breve* meter, suggests the *stile antico*; it also recalls the early little Fantasia BWV 917.

The fugue is in three sections and has two subjects; the central section introduces the second subject (bar 37), while the last section (bar 61) combines the two.[6] The design is an old one, predating Bach, who used it throughout his career; the "Legrenzi" Fugue for organ BWV 574 is probably a somewhat earlier example. Such fugues are particularly effective when there is a strong contrast between the two subjects, as is the case here. The first subject is characterized by rhetorical pauses and repeated gestures, the second by more restrained motion—longer note-values, fewer leaps—and chromaticism.[7] Each outer section closes with a statement of the first subject in the soprano, so that the fugue is as symmetrical in its own way as the fantasia. Indeed, the symmetry here is even more imposing than the more literal one of the fantasia, since the final statement of the subject is extended slightly and combined with the second subject.

Fugue in A Minor BWV 944

Chief sources: ABB (No. 56; mainly Johann Christoph Bach; with fantasia); LEm ms. 8 (Preller). *Editions*: BG 3; Dadelsen and Rönnau (1970).

The fugue BWV 944 is much more a virtuosic display piece than BWV 904, closer to the Italian concerto style although not necessarily any later in date. Indeed, its presence in ABB suggests that it is earlier, although it is probably one of the last entries in that manuscript. There it is preceded by a short fantasia, but most other sources give only the fugue, and it is possible, as Hill (1987, 360) suggests, that "Bach himself suppressed the fantasia." Suppressed, or simply abandoned—for the fantasia consists of only ten bars of not very striking chords, marked *arpeggio*. As such it seems little more than a framework for improvisation or a preliminary sketch, like the series of five-part chords that represents the earliest form of the prelude in C♯ from WTC2. While Bach's finished works occasionally use similar shorthand, the arpeggiation of the first few chords is usually written out in order to suggest how the remainder should be realized. Here Bach offers no such suggestion, and the varying number of voices in the chords makes it impossible to use exactly the same arpeggio pattern for each. For further discussion, see "The Arpeggio Notation in BWV 903" at the end of this chapter.[8]

While the arpeggiando fantasia seems especially suited to the harpsichord, the title in Johann Christoph Bach's copy (*Fantasia in A♭ pour le Clavessin*) does not necessarily extend to the fugue, as Marshall (1986, 230) notes. Nevertheless, the fugue, with its running figuration and clear three-part texture, is eminently suited to the harpsichord; a few sustained bass notes can presumably be restruck if they cease to sound. The subject is often said to be a version of that of the organ fugue in A minor BWV 543/2, and indeed there is a certain family resemblance. Otherwise, however, the pieces are distinct.[9] BWV 944 seems the more mature work, drawing virtually all of its motivic material from the subject and containing a great deal more recapitulation (as defined in Chapter 8). The first and only exposition in a major key (C) falls near the exact center of the piece (bars 93–108) and closes with a passage previously used at the end of the first exposition (bars 27–32). Moreover, virtually all of the last third of the piece (i.e., from bar 122) is patched together out of recapitulated material. Monotony, always a danger in the absence of strong contrasts, is avoided by the ever-inventive writing, in particular a sequence that contains some remarkable chromatic juxtapositions (e.g. A minor: V, I; B♭: V⁷ in bars 62–63). A dominant pedal-point first heard at the end of the second section (bars 117ff.) returns to lead directly into the coda (bars 177ff.). Hence, the latter is not a motivically unrelated improvisation, as in the early works, but a natural extension of the main body of the piece—incidentally, a further distinction from (and advance over) the organ fugue BWV 543/2.

The work's great length and its perpetual motion in sixteenths make it tempting to play the fugue as quickly as possible, as a demonstration of digital dexterity. No doubt it was written partly for just this purpose, and it makes a brilliant display piece. But as in other "motoric" pieces, a tempo that reduces the constant sixteenths to a mechanical blur may be less exciting than a slightly slower speed that permits occasional rhythmic nuances.

Prelude and Fugue in A Minor BWV 894

Chief sources: DSB P 801 (J. T. Krebs, 1715–25); LEm ms. Rudorff 9 (Johann Bernhard Bach); SPK P 804/29 (Kellner, dated 1725); SPK P 1084 (Mempell); SPK AmB 549 (Anonymous 301); US NHy LM 4717b. *Editions*: BG 36; Dadelsen and Rönnau (1970).

BWV 894 is, like BWV 944, in A minor and comes even closer to true concerto style. Hence, it is perhaps no coincidence that Johann Bernhard Bach, who was responsible for the most important manuscript copies of the concerto transcriptions, also made one of the earliest copies of the present work, under the title *Praeludium pro Clavicembalo* (facsimile in Schulze 1984a, 195). Eppstein (1970) has argued that BWV 894 was itself drawn from an actual keyboard concerto, but the sources do not support this, and the internal evidence is inconclusive. Still, as is well known, the material of BWV 894 recurs in the outer movements of the Triple Concerto BWV 1044, which is scored for flute, violin, solo harpsichord, and strings (the same instrumentation as in the Fifth Brandenburg Concerto, with the addition of a second *violino di ripieno*). The extensive differences between BWV 894 and BWV 1044 raise the possibility that both works do go back to some earlier, lost model—while also casting some doubt on Bach's authorship of the orchestral version.[10]

There can, however, be no questioning Bach's authorship of BWV 894. The prelude follows a design remarkably close to that of the opening allegro of the harpsichord concerto in D minor BWV 1052. The latter dates from the 1730s but is probably descended from a much earlier work, now lost, that can be assigned to Weimar (see Breig 1976, 32–33). The formal crux in both movements is a cadenza (or a series of cadenzas) placed just after the midpoint, following a cadence to the subdominant.[11] Moreover, the final ritornello in each movement is prepared by a climactic flurry of passage-work. Yet, despite its clear ritornello structure, the "tutti" and "solo" passages of the prelude cannot be divided between manuals (as suggested in Bodky 1960, 334). Particularly at the center of the movement (bars 53b–63a), where short cadenzas alternate in rapid succession with fragments of the ritornello, it is awkward for the player and ineffective musically to shift to a softer manual for the brilliant soloistic phrases.

The fugue is reminiscent of BWV 944; both are allegros (or rather prestos) in perpetual motion, and the subjects of both compose out essentially the same underlying progression.[12] The two fugues also have comparable formal schemes. The fugue in BWV 894 employs relatively little exact recapitulation, but there is, as in BWV 944, only a single strong move to a major key, which leads to a cadence in C a little more than halfway through.[13] There is also a substantial coda, again based on material from the subject.

The present fugue seems less successful than BWV 944. Both are long, but the slower harmonic rhythm of BWV 944—which often has but a single harmony per bar—counters the effect of the incessant rushing figuration and permits it to achieve considerable breadth. In BWV 894 the harmony changes on almost every dotted eighth, and this can prove wearying. Moreover, while sequences are omnipresent in both pieces, BWV 894 lacks the chromatic progressions that raise certain sequences in BWV 944 out of the ordinary.

Perhaps the most serious problem, however, is simply that the fugue of BWV 894 is too much like the prelude for the two movements to form an effective pair. Bars 2–3 of the subject are a virtual quotation of bar 3 in the prelude, and further parallelisms also occur.[14] One wishes that there were an intervening slow movement—as there is in the concerto version, which inserts an adagio drawn from the organ sonata BWV 527.

Chromatic Fantasia and Fugue in D Minor BWV 903

Early version (BWV 903a): *Sources*: DS Mus. ms. 69; "Rust" copy (lost; signed "J. L. A. Rust, Bernburg 1757"). *Edition*: Schenker (1984; after nineteenth-century Peters ed.).

Intermediate (?) version: *Source*: DSB P 803 (two copies: J. T. Krebs, Samuel Gottlieb Heder).

Later version: *Chief sources*: SPK P 421 (dated Dec. 6, 1730); SPK P 651 (Agricola); SPK

P 275/5 (Müthel; fantasia only); SPK P 887 (Anonymous 300; with fingerings); SPK P 320 (Gebhardi); SPK AmB 548 (Anonymous 414 and Anonymous 401; with fingerings added); SPK P 551 + P 535 (signed "Gebhardt"; fantasia and fugue separately, arpeggios in fantasia written out: see BG 36, preface); SPK P 577 (source of dynamics in BG 36); SPK P 212 (Forkel; basis of his 1803 edition); print, ed. Griepenkerl (1819). *Editions*: BG 36; Dadelsen and Rönnau (1970).

Few of Bach's solo keyboard works have been as admired as the Chromatic Fantasia and Fugue, which, as Forkel noted, is "unique, and never had its like" (1802, 56/BR, 342). Much of the work's mystique derives from its seemingly diametric opposition to everything else that Bach stands for; it is romantic, not baroque, improvisatory rather than strictly architectural. The adjectives apply chiefly to the first movement, which already in the later eighteenth century seems to have been viewed as a precursor of the free fantasia, a genre cultivated especially by C. P. E. Bach.[15] This view continues to be held, not entirely without justification. Chromatic passages comparable to those occurring here are found in other instrumental pieces by Bach, but only in the G-minor organ fantasia BWV 542/1 in such concentration and with so little apparent regard for the usual niceties of modulation. This, together with the piece's rapid changes of character, forms an obvious parallel to the fantasias of C. P. E. (and also W. F.) Bach. A recently identified fantasia by C. P. E. Bach from the 1740s (H. 348, described in Lee 1988) even seems to form a link between BWV 903 and Emanuel's later works, since, like the Chromatic Fantasia, it opens with measured figuration before proceeding to recitativelike writing. Still, whatever influence BWV 903 may have had on later works was probably less than that of actual improvisations that Sebastian's sons would have have heard in their youth.

The large number of sources, many of them late, shows that BWV 903 was widely played and remained influential well after Bach's death. Not surprisingly, it was among the first of Bach's keyboard pieces to be edited (or rather revised) to suit later musical fashions. Griepenkerl's 1819 edition is interesting for the indications of dynamics, articulation, and embellishments that were claimed to stem from Friedemann Bach, who presumably would have played it on the clavichord, at least after 1750 or so.[16] This was followed by the notoriously romanticized piano edition of Hans von Bülow (Berlin, 1859–65, still available in modern reprints) and by the edition in BG 36. The latter, though an improvement over earlier editions, included slurs and dynamics of doubtful authenticity, while Schenker's 1910 edition is, despite its analytic commentary (translated in Schenker 1984), merely that of the BG with arbitrary alterations. Although there have since been important studies of the sources by H. David (1926) and Stauffer (1989), at this writing there is still no real critical edition; Dadelsen gives a satisfactory "Urtext."[17]

As in BWV 904, there are indications that the two movements were originally separate. Some sources give only one movement, and the fantasia—but not the fugue—shows signs of stemming from an autograph that lacked the key-signature of one flat. In addition, the sources show important variants in both movements, particularly in the first half of the fantasia, the earliest version of which (BWV 903a/1) descends to low AA. This may have some implications for dating; the low note appears at the end of a descending arpeggio and perhaps implies the use of a special keyboard, much as in Johann Christoph Bach's version of the Aria variata BWV 989, presumably a Weimar work. But the note might also have been available on the Berlin harpsichord acquired by the Cöthen court during Bach's tenure there. In support of a relatively late (Cöthen) dating, Stauffer (1989) points to some parallels between the figuration here and that in the Fifth Brandenburg Concerto. Yet, while the familiar version of the concerto is dated 1721, it could have been composed earlier at either Weimar or Cöthen.[18] The instrumental recitative in the fantasia seems to have been inspired by a Vivaldi work (see below), and this would support a Weimar date for the fantasia.

The title appears in various ways. Usually it is clear that the adjective "chromatic" applies to the fantasia; P 803, for example, specifies *Fantasie chromatique pour le clavecin*. The fugue has a chromatic subject, but a separate title like the *Fuga cromatica* of P 535 appears to be late, perhaps reflecting an awareness of the *Recercar cromaticho* of Frescobaldi. Marpurg had drawn attention to the latter by citing the subjects of the two pieces side by side in his *Abhandlung von der Fuge* (1753–54, 1:83).

A detailed harmonic analysis of the fantasia, identifying the chord tones in each bar and distinguishing anticipations and suspensions from passing tones, can hardly be given here, although it is essential for an intelligent performance of the piece. In any case, harmonic analysis in the usual sense seems less useful than one carried out in terms that Bach himself might have understood, that is, by extracting the essential bass line (as in Example 9.1) and adding figures. Such analysis reveals, among other things, that the baffling chromatic progressions at several points in the opening section are all elaborations of essentially the same progression. What look like

EXAMPLE 9.1.   Chromatic Fantasia BWV 903/1: bass line sketch for bars 1–49 (open note-heads = tones of primary importance; filled note-heads = tones of secondary importance; slurs and ties connect notes belonging to the same harmony)

augmented-six chords in bars 7, 9, and 11, as well as the apparent C-minor harmony in bar 12, all arise through similar chromatic voice-leading (Example 9.2).

EXAMPLE 9.2. Chromatic Fantasia BWV 903/1: (a) bar 7a, and (b) bar 12, with figured bass sketch

The fantasia as a whole falls into two distinct sections, the first of which moves to the dominant (bar 49), the second returning to the tonic. The first half is essentially an arpeggiando prelude, though the figuration ranges from regular sequences using broken-chord motives to free cadenzas. BWV 903a gives bars 3–20 in an earlier and less striking form while following essentially the same harmonic scheme and bass as the later versions.[19] Up to bar 33 the harmony is rather conventional, save for the chromatic progressions mentioned above. The strange harmonies found in these passages probably should not, however, be dismissed as momentary chromatic dents in a straightforward diatonic framework.[20] The C-minor harmony at bar 12, in particular, constitutes a momentary dislocation into a distant "flat" realm, anticipating the more extensive tonal dislocations that occur further into the fantasia.

These begin in earnest at bar 33, where Bach reverts to the indeterminate arpeggio notation used in the fantasia of BWV 944. In addition, what has been a steady descent in the bass from d' to A (see Example 9.1) now gives way to irregular voice-leading containing diminished fourths and other odd intervals that resist easy reduction to a simpler line.[21] The passage moves from "flat" (G minor, bar 33) to "sharp" (E minor, bar 34) and again to "flat" areas (B♭ minor, bar 38).[22] The only lasting modulation is the one at bar 45 to A minor; this is, of course, the dominant, but by this point the sense of normal harmonic progression has nearly evaporated.

Hence, one is prepared for the violent tonal lurch that launches the following section. The title Recitative for this section is evidently original and evidently applies to the entire remainder of the fantasia. The imitation of recitative is less literal while at the same time more idiomatic to the keyboard than in later examples of instrumental recitative in works by Bach's sons.[23] Sebastian himself seems to have drawn on earlier examples of instrumental recitative rather than imitating the vocal idiom directly. Kuhnau's Biblical Sonatas already contained one or two fairly explicit examples, but a more immediate model may have been the slow movement of Vivaldi's "Grosso Mogul" concerto, which Bach arranged for organ as BWV 594.[24] Vivaldi's violin line is highly embellished—in a distinctly nonvocal manner—but it is accompanied by basso continuo alone, notated as in a normal *recitativo semplice*. Bach, in his organ transcription, realizes the figured bass and rewrites the bass notes and chords as quarters separated by rests, making explicit the "short" accompaniment that was probably Bach's normal way of realizing the type of notation found in Vivaldi's original.[25]

The recitative in the Chromatic Fantasia employs the same explicit short notation, and its chromaticism is more extreme than Vivaldi's, the cadenzalike passages more brilliant. But even the pedal-point at the end of the fantasia has some precedent in the Vivaldi work, which ends with a fairly conventional ascending progression over a dominant pedal (Example 9.3). In the corresponding passage in the

EXAMPLE 9.3.   Vivaldi, Concerto *il grosso Mogul* in C, R. 208, second movement, bars 20b–23

fantasia (bars 75–79), the treble descends chromatically through a full octave over a tonic pedal; the underlying gesture is essentially that of a plagal cadence, marvelously prolonged.[26]

Despite its chromaticism, the harmony at the end of the recitative is reasonably straightforward. Not so the beginning, which seems to cast all normal harmonic logic aside with a sudden move from A to D♭ (bar 50).[27] From there until bar 63, where the music reenters the realm of D minor (on a V of iv chord), the keys tonicized bear no obvious relation to the tonic. Of course, distant and even arbitrary modulations are to be expected in recitative. But one still expects them to make sense, and indeed the modulations here do make more sense than the notation might suggest. The dominant chord tonicizing D♭ in bar 50 is enharmonically equivalent to the one tonicizing C♯ minor in bar 61 (as indicated by the asterisks in Example 9.4), and the intervening passage is essentially a sequence over a descending bass line.[28] Hence, the opening section of the recitative is essentially a digression in C♯ minor—that is, iii of V. The latter, to be sure, represents a very distant

EXAMPLE 9.4.   Chromatic Fantasia BWV 903/1, bars 50–68:
harmonic outline (lowest staff shows bass of bars 50–58 in
enharmonically equivalent notation)

relationship to the tonic D minor. It is likely that Bach's intention was simply to modulate at the center of the fantasia to the most distant key he could think of, just as Emanuel Bach half a century later placed the central sections of two free fantasias a tritone and a half-step from the tonic, respectively.[29]

Did Bach have any specific expressive intent here? Schleuning (1969) has attempted to link the work to the tradition of the seventeenth-century *tombeau*, such as occurs among the works of Froberger and Louis Couperin. But the Vivaldi parallel is more concrete and is supported by Bach's organ arrangement. If the fantasia indeed dates from Weimar, that would rule out the possibility (raised by Wiemer 1988, 165–66) that the work is a lament for Bach's first wife, Maria Barbara, who died in 1720. But in any case the work lacks any clear sign, such as the chaconne bass used in the *Lamento* of BWV 992, that it is indeed a lament.

Less concretely (and more plausibly), it has been suggested that Bach occasionally, as in the Saint Matthew Passion, employed alternations between "sharp" and "flat" keys in order to represent opposing "polarities," such as "light/dark" (see Chafe 1981, 54). But it is difficult to apply the same type of reasoning in the present case, where the recitative does not convey a text. There are polarities here—that is, tonal centers—but to call some "light" and others "dark" would be arbitrary. The most one can say is that through the use of remote modulations the music passes between parallel but virtually unrelated tonal worlds, as Bach had already done in the early G-Minor *Ouverture* BWV 822, and as he would do in the passions on a greatly extended time-scale. Perhaps it is anachronistic to speak here metaphorically of passing "into another world," as in a Nabokov novel. Yet precisely these words (*wie in eine andre Welt*) are applied to a musical modulation in Wilhelm Heinse's 1794 novel *Hildegard von Hohenthal*—a work not entirely unrelated to the proto-Romantic descendents of the Chromatic Fantasia.[30]

The fugue, despite its chromatic subject and virtuoso episodes, is inevitably something of a letdown, although several exceptional features reflect its pairing with so extraordinary a fantasia, among them the unusual, almost bombastic octave doublings of the bass in the final phrase and the protean character of the subject, which is treated with great freedom, appearing in many varied forms. The free treatment of the subject has drawn attention from many commentators, beginning with Marpurg (1753–54, 1:83), who showed that in the answer (bars 9ff.) the original half-step a′, b♭′ (bar 1) is replaced by the third d′, f′.[31] The passing tone e′ in bar 9 is an embellishment, but the point was lost on Bülow, who arbitrarily "corrected" the answer in his edition, eliminating the surprising dissonance (d′/c″) formed when the middle voice enters. In fact, the d′ of the alto (bar 9) is a continuation of the same note struck by the soprano on the preceding downbeat.

If the fugue indeed deserves its epithet "chromatic," it is not because of its subject; Bach wrote other fugues on equally chromatic subjects. Rather, like the fantasia, the fugue moves to tonalities not normally encountered in D minor, here B minor and E minor. Yet the fugue suffers from the absence of major keys. Perhaps the subject is unsuited for use in a major key, but the excursions to unexpectedly "sharp" minor keys do not entirely compensate for the overwhelmingly minor coloration. Still, the fugue has been planned with a clear sense of tonal design, and the modulations to the remote keys of B and E minor are at the center (around bar 83). As in BWV 944, most of the last third of the piece is patched together from recapitulated material; this is no failing, although one might criticize the somewhat pedestrian sequences first announced in bars 118–25 and restated not much farther along (at bar 147).

Fantasia and Fugue in C Minor BWV 906

Chief sources: Autograph of the fantasia in the possession of the Bethlehem Bach Choir, housed at Lehigh University (facsimile: Marshall 1976b); Dl Mus. 2405-T-52, Aut. 3 (autograph of the fantasia, with the fragment of the fugue; facsimile in Schulze 1984b). *Editions*: BG 36 (fugue in appendix); Dadelsen and Rönnau (1970).

The C-Minor Fantasia and Fugue is clearly later than the other pieces considered in this chapter, but because it was never incorporated into a larger set it is most conveniently treated here. The fantasia is indistinguishable in form from "the allegro of a sonata," as Forkel (1802, 56/BR, 342) put it, and is close in style to a few of the more extended preludes in sonata form from WTC2. The fugue survives only as a fragment of what was probably to have been a much longer movement.

The fantasia might have been conceived as an opening movement for the C-Minor Partita, published in 1727 (as Marshall 1976b suggests). The earliest source, the Bethlehem (Pennsylvania) autograph of the fantasia, dates from around 1729, two years later, but it is a fair copy and the original draft could have been written earlier.[32] The Dresden autograph was written around 1738 and might have been destined for WTC2, whose "autograph" is actually a set of separate manuscripts for each prelude and fugue (Marshall 1976b). But the key of C minor was instead represented in WTC2 by a different pair of pieces, although the prelude is also a sonata form and is related motivically to the fugue of BWV 906. Perhaps Bach felt that the virtuoso style of BWV 906 was inappropriate to the WTC; for example, both movements of BWV 906 require hand-crossings. Hand-crossings occur once in WTC2, in the prelude in B♭, but the latter is a gentler and more restrained piece than the present fantasia, even if also a sonata-form movement of ambitious proportions.

The fantasia is in three main sections, the double bar following the first; there is a short retransition (bars 28b–33) prior to the last section (the recapitulation). The title "fantasia" may seem inappropriate for such a movement, but there is a fantasia by Friedemann Bach in the same form (F. 14 in C), and it is conceivable that Sebastian wrote the present work expressly for his eldest son, who was a noted virtuoso and might have been the original owner of the Dresden autograph. Hand-crossing seems to have enjoyed a modest vogue in the Bach household during the 1720s and 1730s; it occurs in the First Partita (published 1726) and in Emanuel Bach's first published work, the Minuet H. 1.5 (W. 111) of 1731. The technique naturally calls to mind the sonatas of Domenico Scarlatti, but Rameau is another possible influence.[33] Hand-crossings also occur in the anonymous fugue that Bach may have reworked as the last movement of the E-Minor Toccata BWV 914. In any case, by the time of the C-minor fantasia, hand-crossings are unlikely to have been a novelty to a virtuoso such as Bach. They are incorporated into the symmetrical architecture of the piece, crossings by the left hand over the right in the first section being balanced by crossings of the right over the left in the second.

By the late 1730s, Bach's sons—at least Emanuel—were composing full-fledged keyboard sonatas in galant style.[34] The fantasia's affinity to such pieces is evident not only in its clearly articulated sonata form but in the triplets, the periodic phrasing, and the leisurely underlying quarter-note pulse. But Sebastian's hand is recognizable above all in the contrapuntal texture—limited to two or three essential parts, but these engaging in frequent imitation—and in the somewhat quirky chromaticism, especially in the final phrase.

Although an attractive and extremely effective work in performance, the fantasia has a slightly manic character due to the packing of so many virtuoso gestures into a simple, compact structure. The first section ("exposition") consists of two equal periods—2 × (4 + 4) bars—while the third ("recapitulation") is a simple period ($3\frac{1}{2} + 4\frac{1}{2}$ bars). Hence, no matter how deliberate the tempo, extraordinary gestures like the dissonant chromatic sequence in the closing phrase (bars 37b–38) may seem to fly by quickly without receiving sufficient emphasis. On the other hand, a certain deemphasis of the expressive role normally accorded chromatic lines in Bach's music seems appropriate here. Most of the chromatic lines, above all the quick chromatic scales moving in contrary motion just before the return (bar 38), are sweeping gestures in which the individual chromatic steps lack the weight normally accorded them in Baroque music. While not quite ornamental, as in Mozart—each chromatic step retains at least a vestige of harmonic significance—the long chromatic lines in small note-values might even receive slurs, like the similar figure in the augmentation canon of the Art of Fugue (bar 29).

It is curious that, except perhaps at the cadences, the only substantial interruption in the flow of the triplets occurs early, in bar 8.[35] There the repeated sixteenths in the left hand should probably be interpreted literally (without "assimilation" to the prevailing triplets); the passage is made more effective by prolonging the initial (upper) note of the trill. This will emphasize the expressive cross-relation (f♯/f′), which was to become a favorite mannerism in the *empfindsam* style of Emanuel Bach (Example 9.5). Assimilation is more plausible in bars 21–23, where the

EXAMPLE 9.5.   Fantasia in C Minor BWV 906/1: (a) bar 8; (b) bar 21

thirty-seconds might be altered to triplets.[36] It may be, however, that Bach wrote out the mordents only to avoid any ambiguity about accidentals and that his thirty-seconds are merely shorthand for a quick ornament.[37]

The fugue, had Bach finished it, would have been a remarkable addition to the repertory, not only because of its hand-crossings (the only substantial ones in a Bach fugue) but because of the elaborate chromaticism and permutational counterpoint of the opening section. In fact, Bach may have completed the work in some form, for the entry in the Dresden autograph seems to start as a fair copy. But certain details underwent changes, probably as Bach was copying. Thus, in bars 34–35, Bach altered one of the two new themes introduced at that point, showing that by this point he was revising, perhaps even composing as he wrote. The hand-crossings begin in bar 38, and Bach broke off work on the manuscript after reaching the downbeat of bar 48.

Curiously, this is not the only fragmentary fugue attached to a fantasia in C minor. The autograph containing the organ fantasia BWV 562/1 also includes twenty-seven bars of a five-part fugue, but the latter probably dates from the 1740s, and the copy was almost certainly completed on a page now lost. In the case of

BWV 906, Bach might have had doubts about the propriety of introducing hand-crossing into a fugue, or he might have concluded that the stylistic disparity between the opening section and that on which he was now working was too great. Forkel already noted the change of character that occurs at bar 25, questioning Bach's authorship of the remainder of the fragment (Forkel 1802, 56/BR, 342). Indeed, bars 25–33 could almost be by Friedemann Bach. These bars constitute a sort of free coda, bringing the initial section to a close in the tonic (bar 33). But neither this coda nor the section that follows has any significant motivic connection to the opening section. Nor can the subject be combined contrapuntally with the new themes introduced at bar 34.

It is generally assumed that the fugue was to be in Da Capo form, like a number of large virtuoso fugues for other instruments.[38] But there is no fermata (signifying a *Fine*) at the end of the first section, and it is unclear whether one would place it at the middle of bar 33 or on the downbeat of bar 34; neither choice makes for an entirely satisfactory final cadence. It seems obvious that, having introduced new material at bar 34, Bach would have developed it at length in episodes alternating with entries of the principal subject; indeed, the latter enters just as the fragment breaks off (bar 46). Hence, the suggestion given in several editions to repeat bars 3–33 following the downbeat of bar 48 (at the end of the fragment) must be understood only as a provisional stopgap.[39] Edward T. Cone (1974) has offered a more extensive completion that emphasizes contrapuntal development of the chromatic subject; another approach is illustrated in Example 9.6.[40]

EXAMPLE 9.6.   Fugue in C Minor BWV 906/2, bars 48ff. (suggested completion)

EXAMPLE 9.6. (continued)

EXAMPLE 9.6. (continued)

EXAMPLE 9.6.   (continued)

Dal Segno
(bar 5)

The Arpeggio Notation in BWV 903

The incompletely notated *arpeggio* passages in the fantasia are the most extensive in any of Bach's frequently performed keyboard works. Since Bach provided a written-out breaking of the first chord, there is presumably no question of playing anything more elaborate, and would-be improvisers and composers should probably resist the temptation to compete with Bach (as Liszt did in his realization of the short arpeggiando fantasia in BWV 944). The written-out arpeggiation in bar 27a suggests that all of Bach's half-note chords should simply be broken once upward and once downward. But the number of notes in the chords varies, and several chords include passing quarter-notes in one part or another.

Several sources extend the written-out arpeggiation beyond bar 27a, and, while probably not taken from Bach's autograph, they provide reasonable solutions to several problems posed by Bach's incomplete notation, perhaps reflecting his own manner of performance. These sources indicate that passing tones (such as c′ in bar 33) were incorporated into the descending part of the arpeggio. They suggest further that one should omit the notes of the left hand from the descending part of the arpeggio when the left hand must move to another register for the following chord (Example 9.7a).[41] One may further speculate that chords notated as whole-notes (such as the one that opens BWV 944) can be broken twice, and that it is permissible to end a phrase with an upward arpeggio (e.g., in bar 42; Example 9.7b).[42]

EXAMPLE 9.7.   (a) Chromatic fantasia BWV 903/1, bar 33, with realization of arpeggios from SPK P 551 (as reported in BG 36)

(b) Fantasia in A minor BWV 944/1, last two bars

10

The Clavier-Büchlein vor Wilhelm Friedemann Bach *and Related Works*

Bach came to Cöthen late in 1717 and remained there until the spring of 1723. Since at Cöthen he was not employed as a church musician, he evidently concentrated on the production of secular music, and some of his most important collections of instrumental music, such as the Brandenburg Concertos and the Sonatas and Partitas for solo violin, were assembled if not actually composed during this period. Bach's Cöthen autographs survive not only for those two sets of pieces but also for two important collections of keyboard music: the first part of the *Well-Tempered Clavier* (WTC1), and the Inventions and Sinfonias. In addition, the Cöthen years saw the commencement of two other important musical documents: the little keyboard books (*Clavierbüchlein*) for Wilhelm Friedemann and Anna Magdalena Bach.

The autographs of WTC1 and of the Inventions and Sinfonias are fair copies that were probably meant to serve as the basis for further copies by Bach's students. The two little keyboard books, on the other hand, were apparently intended as family albums for use in domestic music teaching and recreation. Anna Magdalena's book—actually the first of two manuscripts bearing her name—is the earliest source for the French Suites and is discussed in Chapter 14 (with additional material in Appendix B). Friedemann's book (hereafter, CB) contains a selection of pedagogic pieces, including early versions of the Inventions and Sinfonias as well as some of the preludes of WTC1.[1]

Friedemann's book was begun (according to the title-page) on January 22, 1720, two months after Friedemann's ninth birthday. The pages of the book were only gradually filled with music, the majority of the entries being made probably from 1721 to early 1723. While some of the pieces entered by Sebastian into the volume appear to be first drafts, others are fair or revision copies. Still others are in Friedemann's hand, among them copies of several works by composers other than Sebastian Bach. Hence, the book may have drawn on a stock of pieces that Bach had already assembled for use in teaching. Sebastian's pieces may not all have been composed specifically for Friedemann, although Bach's growing family must have provided an impetus not only toward collecting easy pieces by other composers but toward creating new teaching material as well.

Bach might have already composed a considerable number of teaching pieces by the time he left Weimar, where he had already been active as a teacher. There he had put together the first of the major keyboard collections, the *Orgelbüchlein* (Little Organ Book), a set of chorale preludes. Perhaps the title of Friedemann's book (Little "Clavier" Book) was meant to complement that of the organ volume, whose title was added to the manuscript only at Cöthen.[2] While most of the pieces in CB were soon incorporated into WTC1 or into the fair copy of the Inventions and Sinfonias, others were left outside the great collections. The same is true of a number of preludes, fugues, and other compositions not found in CB that might have belonged to Bach's larger repertory of teaching pieces. This chapter will consider pieces from the latter group alongside the better-known ones in CB.

The instrument for which all of these "clavier" pieces were intended is, as usual, uncertain. Marshall (1986, 234) suggests that the clavichord is the "most likely candidate" for the "avowedly preparatory compositions" with which Bach evidently commenced his sons' musical instruction. Indeed, there can be little doubt that for a while later in the century the clavichord become "the traditional 'practice' instrument," at least in Germany. But Couperin, writing evidently for Parisian amateurs, assumed that beginners would be taught on a lightly quilled harpsichord (Couperin 1717). While conditions in Germany might have been different, one would expect suitably regulated harpsichords to have been available from the beginning in a family of professional musicians such as Bach's. The word *clavier* did not, in 1720, imply the clavichord, and CB contains two movements from a suite by J. C. Richter specifically for the "clavecin" (i.e., harpsichord). That indication cannot have been intended to distinguish Richter's work from the others, since there are two other suites (CB 47–48, by Telemann and Stölzel, respectively) whose brilliant style is equally suited to the harpsichord, even though the titles of these pieces do not mention any instrument.[3] Bach himself added a movement (the trio BWV 929) to the Stölzel suite. To be sure, this piece, like the preludes, fugues, and the rest, is playable on the clavichord. Yet the arpeggiated chords of some pieces (BWV 846a/1 = CB 14, BWV 848/1 = CB 21), the lively violinistic figuration of others (BWV 779 = CB 35, BWV 796 = CB 53), and the contrapuntal textures of the inventions and sinfonias seem in general more effective on the harpsichord.

Friedemann's book seems to have been planned to contain five main divisions:

1. tables illustrating clefs, the names of the notes, and an *Explication* of ornament signs and their meanings

2. a group of simple pieces, opening with a demonstration of keyboard fingering and including several preludes and two chorales (CB 1–13)
3. a further group of eleven preludes, later included in WTC1 (CB 14–24)
4. the fifteen two-part Inventions, here termed *Praeambula* (CB 32–46)
5. the fifteen Sinfonias, today often called three-part inventions but here designated *Fantasias* (CB 49–[63])

While the above plan suggests that the book was meant to serve as a graded course in keyboard instruction, the compositions were not simply copied from beginning to end. Blank pages were originally left at various points, and these were later filled, not always according to the plan sketched above. Thus, the suite by Richter (CB 25) was one of several items copied by Friedemann in the gap between the third and fourth groups of pieces. Several pieces falling within the second group are also in Friedemann's hand and may be early compositional essays of his own. Sebastian himself added a three-part fugue (BWV 953 = CB 31) just before group 4. The seemingly illogical placement of this last work is no more readily explained than the fragmentary state of several other pieces, such as the chorale prelude *Jesu meine Freude* (BWV 753 = CB 5), which Sebastian broke off after reaching the end of a page in group 2. One suggestion is that Sebastian left this as a fragment to impress upon the young Friedemann the necessity of properly planning one's music-writing in order to conserve space and avoid awkward page-turns (NBA V/5, KB, 67f.; see also Herz 1984, 96). But a complete score might have been thought unnecessary if Friedemann had already learned the piece by rote or if the fragment had been meant to be completed improvisatorily by the student; in either case, there would have been no need to finish the copy.

Only four pieces in CB bear attributions, and only one attribution (for the trio BWV 929 = CB 48/5) is to Bach. There is little reason to doubt Bach's authorship of the many pieces that he himself wrote into the book, especially when these show his own revisions and corrections, as do the Inventions and Sinfonias. But at least two pieces copied by Friedemann Bach seem to be his own works. In several other pieces, as well as a few little preludes preserved only in Kellner's copies, the style appears to be that of Sebastian Bach, and his authorship seems never to have been seriously questioned. Yet the pieces are too short and simple for their authenticity to be guaranteed on the basis of style alone. The absence of independent concordances with attributions makes it conceivable that some were the work of others, perhaps Friedemann or other Bach students.[4]

Tables of Notes and Ornaments

The opening material—illustrations of clefs, notes, and letter-names for pitches—was a traditional element in instructional books. A more modern feature, borrowed from French keyboard music, was the ornament table. Such ornament tables cannot have been meant to explain how to play ornaments—something that musicians would have learned through oral tradition—but rather to indicate which signs were used by a particular composer for each ornament. An ornament table thus served much the same function as the tables of notes, teaching the student the names and the manner of notating things with which he or she was already well acquainted through aural experience.

Ornament tables are necessarily schematic. Even Bach's table employs rhythmically ungrammatical notation for a few things that could not, in any case, be precisely notated. Hence, any attempt to puzzle out the performance of his ornaments through a literal interpretation of such a table is destined for failure. The table in CB presents Bach's own rationalized and simplified adaptation of ornament tables such as those published in the books of pieces by D'Anglebert and Dieupart. D'Anglebert's table appears to have served, directly or indirectly, as the basis for the tables in the older manuscripts MM and ABB,[5] but Bach's table is considerably shorter, omitting signs not encountered in his own scores.

Several of Bach's departures from French ornament tradition are worth noting. First, most of the ornaments' names are different, and Bach's mixture of French, Italian, and German may reflect his own synthesis of several distinct performing traditions. For example, the ornament that Bach calls the *accent* is roughly equivalent to the type of appoggiatura called a *port de voix* by D'Anglebert and other French musicians. Yet, as Couperin makes clear, the French *port de voix* was actually a gesture incorporating not only the appoggiatura itself but the notes preceding and following it. With Bach, as with D'Anglebert, the appoggiatura is signified by a comma or hook preceding the note to which it applies; the sign resembles a small letter "c" and is therefore sometimes referred to as a "c-appoggiatura" (Example 10.1).

EXAMPLE 10.1.   (a) D'Anglebert, *Pièces de clavecin: Cheute ou port de voix en montant*; (b) CB: *accent steigend*

Unlike his French contemporaries, Sebastian places the sign for the *accent* on the actual line or space representing the ornamental tone, not on that of the main note. Moreover, the sign is often accompanied by a slur, and as the slur and the comma look alike, notes graced by such an *accent* often appear to be preceded by a pair of slurs or hooks.[6] An appoggiatura indicated in this manner is presumably identical to one notated as a small eighth-note (or other value). But in neither case can one assume that the length of the appoggiatura is governed by the rules later given by C. P. E. Bach (1753–62, i.2.2.11). Emanuel's rules govern only the long type of appoggiatura, which he terms the "variable" appoggiatura (*veränderlicher Vorschlag*). Most appoggiaturas in French harpsichord music seem to be of the short or "invariable" type, and the same is likely to be true in Bach's own works in French style.[7]

Another important distinction lies in Bach's treatment of the turn and its relatives. The sources transmit a confusing terminology for these ornaments. But the apparent inconsistencies in the terminology of the French ornament tables may be due to their use of highly abbreviated labels that were easily misunderstood, especially by foreigners. Thus D'Anglebert's expression for a simple turn standing alone ("sans tremblement") is evidently *Cadence.*[8] The precise meaning of his expression *Double cadence* is less clear, but it can be understood as referring to the pair of turns that precedes the trill (*tremblement*) in the common cadential formula shown in Example 10.2c.

Bach probably used the word *Cadence* in the same sense as D'Anglebert. But Bach apparently applied the expression *Doppelt-cadence* somewhat illogically to a trill preceded by a single turn—that is, to the ornament that comprises only the second half of D'Anglebert's cadential formula (Example 10.2). The result was a

EXAMPLE 10.2.   (a) D'Anglebert: [*cadence*] *sans tremblement;*
(b) CB: *cadence;* (c) D'Anglebert: *double cadence* [*avec tremblement*]; (d) CB: *Doppelt-cadence*

long trill that begins with a turn played on the beat. C. P. E. Bach later referred to this ornament as the "trill from below" or the "trill from above," depending on the direction from which the prefix begins.[9]

More important than the labeling of the ornaments is their relationship to the musical text. Are they a part of it or are they an inessential addition, "ornaments" in a literal sense? While ornamentation was in certain contexts (e.g., cadential trills) clearly a mandatory element of performance practice, Bach, like most of his contemporaries, probably thought of the ornament *signs* as unnecessary—at least until he began to prepare works like those in CB for study by his pupils. His early works rarely use the signs illustrated in the CB, and early copies of the Inventions and other works show substantial differences in ornamentation. This implies that despite his scrupulous notation of complex melodic embellishment in adagios and other movements in the Italian style, Bach did not originally regard the signs for *accents,* mordents, trills, and turns as fixed elements in the text. Those ornament signs that do occur in the earlier sources might have been given to students as suggestions—not prescriptions—for proper ornamentation. Bach, however, was a systematic musician and teacher, and what were originally offered as suggestions might have gradually become prescriptions; in the course of teaching the same elementary principles to two generations of students, advice regarding the interpretation of ornament signs might have been reduced to easily memorized rules. This, together with shifts in musical style (Bach's own and that of European music in general), might have led by the 1730s or 1740s to the "hardening" and "rigidity" of ornamentation practice that Neumann (1978, 39) attributes only to the generation of C. P. E. Bach. Perhaps Friedemann's clavier book marked the beginning of the process.

Preludes and Related Pieces

The short pieces in group 2 probably were not Friedemann's first exercises at the keyboard. That function might have been served by simple minuets and other dances learned by rote (as Couperin suggests). This would explain the relatively sophisticated nature of even the first short pieces in the CB, which demand as much care and thought in performance as the best French *pièces de clavecin*.

Applicatio BWV 994 (CB 1)

The Applicatio might be viewed as a continuation of the introductory matter preceding it. The term is perhaps not a title but a label: "Fingering," demonstrated in a little piece of eight bars in which virtually every note bears a fingering numeral. [10] The piece bears a striking similarity to a *Prelude oder Applicatio* that opens a somewhat earlier German keyboard book (see NBA V/5, KB, 74). The first bar is almost identical in the two pieces, as is the archaic fingering used for scale passages. But in these Sebastian makes 1, 3, and 5 the "good" (accented) fingers of the right as well as the left hand; this might have seemed a more modern approach than that taken in the other work. Still, the use of the old "paired" fingerings (3-4-3-4 and 1-2-1-2) would contradict what is often thought to have been Emanuel's claim that his father invented modern thumb-under fingering (C. P. E. Bach 1753–62, i.1.7). Emanuel, however, merely indicated that his father had expanded the use of the thumb, especially in "difficult" tonalities, and Emanuel himself still gives old-fashioned paired fingerings as alternatives in the simpler keys. In fact "paired" fingerings remain necessary in Bach's music for the occasional scale passage that must be played by the outer fingers of one hand while holding down an inner voice with the thumb (e.g., in the A-minor fugue of WTC1, bar 42), and a player who practices these fingerings will find that many other passages are facilitated as well. Indeed, as Faulkner (1984, 22) shows, some such scale fingering appears to have remained the norm for W. F. Bach and perhaps other members of the Bach circle, at least in keys involving few accidentals.

Efforts to connect such fingerings with particular schemes of rhythm or articulation are now generally dismissed, since, with practice, one can learn to play most passages in Bach as smoothly as one wishes, using either "modern" or "paired" fingering. [11] Moreover, neither the Applicatio nor the other fully fingered piece (the prelude BWV 930) is long or complex enough to provide fingerings for more than a handful of commonly occurring types of figures, and these contain few surprises. Bach's fingerings do imply articulate or nonlegato performance in certain contexts, as in the direction to repeat the same finger for successive different notes (in bar 4). Several passages in BWV 930 likewise imply that strong articulations were tolerated, if not encouraged, before strong beats and ornaments.[12] In addition, it is clear from the Applicatio that Bach required his students to train the weaker fourth and fifth fingers for use in playing ornaments and that he occasionally called for unusual stretches between the outer fingers of either hand. A few of the stretches demanded here may seem rather wide for a boy of ten. But perhaps the young Friedemann already had the unusually long fingers visible in the reputed portrait by Friedrich Georg Weitsch (see Wolff 1983a, 241) or was taught on an instrument with unusually narrow keys. But even if the keys were no narrower than on a modern piano, a light action and a shallow key-dip would have made chords like that in bar 4 comparatively easy to play.

Despite its brevity the piece seems to show Bach's imprint. Unlike the anonymous prelude from which it might have been derived, it falls into a symmetrical binary form. As in many of Bach's larger binary forms, the second half opens with an inversion of the opening motive, which is treated in quasi-imitation in both sections.

Chorale Preludes

Although the chorale prelude as a genre is more closely associated with the organ, the two examples in CB (*Wer nur den lieben Gott lässt walten* BWV 691 [CB 3] and *Jesu, meine Freude* BWV 753 [CB 5]) are, like some of Böhm's chorale *partite*, at least equally suited to the harpsichord or clavichord. The same is true of the chorale *Jesus, meine Zuversicht* BWV 728 in the first *Clavier-Büchlein* for Anna Magdalena Bach. These pieces represent the *manualiter* version of what Breig (1990a, 260–61) has termed the "monodic" organ chorale, in which a decorated chorale melody is accompanied by lower voices that can be played on a different (softer) manual. Organists must have routinely improvised such pieces, which occur among the works not only of Bach and Böhm but many others, especially Buxtehude. The style of the decoration derives partly from the older German tradition, partly from that of the Italian adagio; Bach, like his predecessors, also includes French ornaments. Some of the more tortuous figures, as well as the occasional chromatic voice-leading in the lower parts, recall expressive slow movements in his concertos and sonatas, which no doubt drew on the same store of improvisational formulas. As noted earlier, BWV 753 is a fragment; a continuation is suggested in Example 10.3.

Chorale settings of this sort must have played a regular part in Bach's teaching regimen. BWV 691 occurs in a second copy in Anna Magdalena's second *Clavier-Büchlein*, and it is also known in a spurious version (BWV 691a) in which ritornellos are added at the beginning and end and between phrases.[13] BWV 691a might be the work of a Bach pupil; indeed, another such arrangement, BWV Anh. 73, is attributed in one source (LEm R 25) to C. P. E. Bach. While the attribution is questionable,[14] the existence of such arrangements suggests that short chorale preludes sometimes served as the basis for more extended composition exercises or improvisations. The same process, carried out on a larger scale, produced the chorale fantasia *Vor deinen Thron tret' ich* BWV 668 as well as the Triple Concerto BWV 1044.[15]

EXAMPLE 10.3. *Jesu, meine Freude* BWV 753, bars 9ff.
(suggested completion)

Little Preludes

The little preludes in group 2 were apparently drawn from a larger repertory of such pieces. A few others appear in the gap between groups 3 and 4, and other sources contain additional preludes. The surviving repertory is shown in Table 10–1, which lists the pieces roughly in order of increasing complexity; this does not, of course, necessarily correspond with the order of composition.[16] The titles vary in the sources; CB uses *Praeambulum* and *Praeludium* for different pieces, but the two terms seem to be entirely equivalent.

While Bach was certainly responsible for the ordering of the pieces in groups 3, 4, and 5—that is, the preludes of WTC1 and the Inventions and Sinfonias—he may never have put all of the little preludes listed here into any particular order. Unlike the pieces in the three other groups, the selection of pieces appearing as group 2 in the CB does not form an integrated set. Nevertheless, later sources and printed editions do sometimes put selections from the repertory into various arrangements, some of which have become traditional. The collection known as the "Twelve Little Preludes" draws on pieces in both the CB and in Kellner's manuscript collection (P 804). One of the "Twelve" (BWV 999) is actually a lute piece, and another (BWV 929) is not a prelude but the movement added to the suite by Stölzel.[17] Another set, known as the "Six Little Preludes," first appears as a group in several late eighteenth-century copies.[18]

The four preludes BWV 939–42, found with BWV 927 in the "Kellner miscellaney," are on the whole closer than the others to what one might regard as real improvisations tossed off with little forethought. The two shortest, BWV 939 in C and BWV 940 in D minor, open with what seem to be improvisatory variations on conventional formulas, that of BWV 939 strongly recalling the first prelude of WTC2. But in all four preludes the opening motive is imitated in the bass, and the

TABLE 10–1.   Little Preludes and Related Pieces

BWV	Key	Chief Sources	Copyist	BG	NBA	Remark
939	C	P 804/53	anonymous mem-	36:119	[V/9]	No. 2 of the "12"
940	d	P 804/53	ber of Kellner	36:123	[V/9]	No. 6 of the "12"
941	e	P 804/53	circle, 1726–27	36:123	[V/9]	No. 7 of the "12"
942	a	P 804/53		36:127	[V/9]	No. 12 of the "12"
927	F	CB 8	WFB, 1722–23/ 25–26	36:124	V/5	No. 8 of the "12"
		P 804/53	Kellner circle, 1726–27			
924	C	CB 2	JSB, 1720	36:118	V/5	No. 1 of the "12"
924a	C	CB 26	WFB, ca. 1726	36:221	V/5	"Variant" of BWV 924
926	d	CB 4	JSB, 1720–21	36:122	V/5	No. 5 of the "12"
928	F	CB 10	JSB, 1720–21	36:124	V/5	No. 9 of the "12"
930	g	CB 9	JSB, 1720–21	36:126	V/5	No. 11 of the "12"
925	D	CB 27	WFB, ca. 1726	36:121	V/5	No. 4 of the "12"
932	e	CB 28	WFB, ca. 1726	36:238	V/5	fragment
931	a	CB 29	WFB, ca. 1726	36:237	V/5	not by JSB?
943	C	P 804/2	Mey, by 1727	36:134	[V/9]	
933	C	various	various	36:128	[V/9]	No. 1 of the "6"
934	c	various	various	36:128	[V/9]	No. 2 of the "6"
935	d	various	various	36:130	[V/9]	No. 3 of the "6"
936	D	various	various	36:131	[V/9]	No. 4 of the "6"
937	E	various	various	36:132	[V/9]	No. 5 of the "6"
938	e	various	various	36:138	[V/9]	No. 6 of the "6"
999	c	P 804/19	Kellner, after 1727	36:119	V/10	No. 3 of the "12"

form hinges on a modulation to the dominant, articulated by some sort of elided cadence at the exact center. Hence, even these simple exercises offered students a demonstration of imitative texture within a tonal design.

BWV 941 and 942 resemble short versions of the Inventions, already composed when the copies in P 804 were made. Following a central cadence to the relative major (bar 11), the Prelude in E Minor BWV 941 moves on to a sort of stretto involving simple invertible counterpoint. The Prelude in A Minor BWV 942 opens like a fugue with imitation at the dominant and after the midpoint (bar 9) introduces a quasi-inversion of the subject. The sole source for BWV 942 contains an obvious error in bar 9; an emendation is suggested in Example 10.4.[19]

One other very brief prelude appears in both CB and in Kellner's collection. The Prelude in F, BWV 927 (CB 8) does not modulate at all, but right at the center (the

EXAMPLE 10.4.   Prelude in A Minor BWV 942, bars 8–10
(with suggested emendation for bar 9, left hand)

middle of bar 8) there is a weak cadence to the tonic and a momentary change of texture. Friedemann's copy of this piece, incidentally, is the only fragment in the entire volume that he later completed, adding the last seven bars some three years after he had copied the beginning of the piece.[20] Sebastian possibly left the piece in a somewhat sketchy form, for the surviving sources show differing types of notational shorthand (as well as some corrections) in bar 14 (Example 10.5).

EXAMPLE 10.5.   Prelude in F, BWV 927, bar 14 (right hand):
(a) reading of CB; (b) reading of SPK P 804/53; (c)
suggested interpretation

The first prelude in CB, BWV 924 in C, recalls some of the illustrations of how to "vary" a bass line in Niedt's *Musicalische Handleitung*. Friedemann later wrote out a similar prelude, BWV 924a, sometimes described as a "variant" of BWV 924. It is more than that, however, since the harmonic schemes of the two pieces diverge after bar 1. The general plans, however, are similar, and a pedal-point on the dominant—with a bass in leaping octaves as in BWV 939—is the eventual goal in both pieces. Since BWV 924a is in Friedemann's hand, one wonders if he, rather than Sebastian, was the composer. But the copy shows no compositional revisions, and there is no reason Sebastian could not have written an alternate realization of the scheme used in BWV 924.

The second prelude in CB, BWV 926 in D minor, is an expanded version of the same general design.[21] The score, in Sebastian's hand, is apparently a first draft showing several layers of corrections at one point. Bar 41 (six bars from the end) originally contained a dramatic cessation of surface motion, as in several of the Vivaldi concertos. In its final form, however it extends the passage-work of the preceding bars onward to the first bass note of bar 45 (Example 10.6).[22]

EXAMPLE 10.6.   Prelude in D Minor BWV 926, bars 43–45, showing successive versions of the bass

The Prelude in G Minor BWV 930 is, like the Applicatio, a binary form with most of the fingerings marked. It is, however, a larger piece, and the second "half" falls into two subdivisions. The bass has been left largely unfingered in the last four bars, leaving it unclear how Bach dealt with the movement of the bass from dominant to tonic in the final cadence. Probably successive fifth fingers were used, producing a strong articulation of the final tonic note; this is how Emanuel Bach fingers such progressions in his *Probestücke* of 1753. (Example 10.7.)

The Prelude in D, BWV 925 is more heavily scored, its texture (in from three to five parts) recalling the writing in some of the preludes of the English Suites. Despite its brevity and the absence of any substantial modulations, it closes with a rather pretentious four-bar tonic pedal. Since the copy is again in Friedemann's hand, a few corrections and odd notational details in the coda (over a tonic pedal) raise the possibility that he himself composed the piece. A fermata on the downbeat of bar 15, where the coda begins, implies that this passage was absent in some earlier version. But neither the coda nor the rest of the piece has much in common with Friedemann's known works.

Two further preludes, BWV 928 in F and BWV 932 in E minor, are on a larger scale than those discussed so far. The Prelude in F could almost be the ritornello for a large concerto-style movement like the prelude of the English Suite in the same key (BWV 809). Both pieces open with the solo statement of a running subject and continue in lively orchestral style. While lacking a Da Capo of the opening section, BWV 928 does have a strongly marked return (bar 20) and a miniature recapitulation section (bars 22–24).

The Prelude in E Minor BWV 932 is close in style to some of the Sinfonias—for example, BWV 790 in D minor, whose principal subject opens with the same motive. Unfortunately, Friedemann copied only the first page of BWV 932, which remains a fragment. Since the fragment is a fair copy, it almost certainly stems from a score by Sebastian; despite a few corrections it contains no signs of having been Friedemann's own work. The fragment is close in its opening harmonic and con-

EXAMPLE 10.7.   (a) Prelude in G Minor BWV 930, bars 39–42

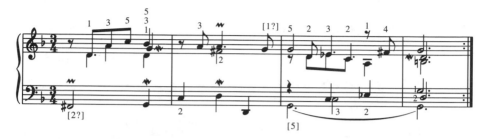

(b) C. P. E. Bach, *Probestück* in C, H. 70/3 (W. 63/1/3), bars 16–18A

trapuntal scheme to the little Prelude in E Minor BWV 941. But the breadth of the fragment suggests that it was to have been a more extended work comparable in scope to BWV 928. It reaches the dominant only after eight long bars, and the blank page that follows would have allowed space for at least one further modulation (to G or A minor) before returning to the tonic. Perhaps it was even longer, and Friedemann broke off the copy when he realized he lacked space for it, thereby depriving us of a very attractive work. Example 10.8 gives a hypothetical completion based on the assumption that only one page is missing.

The little Prelude in A Minor BWV 931 seems less likely to be entirely by Sebastian. It does not closely resemble any of Sebastian's preludes, nor is there any imitation or substantial motivic work of any kind. This gives a clue to the piece's real identity. The bass line is far more coherent than the upper voices and opens with a formula employed in the last movements of the chamber sonatas BWV 1021 and 1038. These sonatas share a common bass line and seem to have been employed in the teaching of "composition as variation" (see Schulenberg 1982); perhaps BWV 931 was the product of a similar exercise set out by Sebastian and realized by Friedemann Bach.[23]

Against this hypothesis must be weighed the fact that the copy of BWV 931, in Friedemann's hand, employs several French ornament signs not included in the table at the beginning of the CB. Among them is the comma or hook after the note to indicate either a mordent (*pincé*), as in bar 1, or a turn at the end of a trill (*tremblement et pincé*), as in bar 2. Friedemann also places strokes through the stems of several chords, presumably to indicate arpeggiation, perhaps with an or-

EXAMPLE 10.8.   Prelude in E Minor BWV 932, bars 11ff.
(suggested completion)

namental *acciaccatura* or *coulé* (passing note) in the two-note chords. He also seems to misplace the signs for *accents* or *ports de voix*, setting them even with or above the main note. The departures from his father's practice raise the possibility that Friedemann was copying from some foreign source.

The manuscript collection P 804 contains an additional prelude in C (BWV 943) copied by Mey, apparently an associate of Kellner. BWV 943 is actually a short imitative fantasia in three parts, hence comparable to the Sinfonias. But the middle voice is distinctly unequal to the outer ones, only the latter participating fully in the contrapuntal work. Despite the simplified texture there remains some awkward part-writing (especially in bars 26–27 and 50). Nevertheless, the piece has the rational design we expect in Bach's mature works, reaching a cadence in the dominant at almost the exact center (bar 28) and immediately afterward introducing the subject in inversion. The motivic material and the general character might have been suggested by the prelude in G from Fischer's *Ariadne musica*, a work from which Bach drew in the WTC. The prelude might be paired—purely for the convenience of the modern player, as there are no documentary grounds for doing so—with the little Fugue in C, BWV 953.

The "Six Little Preludes" BWV 933–38 are not found in CB or any other early source, but they do occur in several independent copies stemming from later associates of Bach or his sons.[24] Whether or not the set was assembled by Bach himself, it presumably drew from the same repertory of miscellaneous pieces mentioned earlier. Unlike the inauthentic set of Twelve Little Preludes, these form a coherent collection based on ascending keys (C, C minor, D minor, D, E, E minor). All six preludes are in binary form, with central double bars, and the material is more "composed," less improvisatory, than in most of the preludes discussed thus far.

Nevertheless, there are significant variations in style among the six, perhaps reflecting different dates of composition. Nos. 1 and 4 (BWV 933 and 936) might be relatively late, No. 1 because of its galant parallel thirds and "sigh" motives, No. 4 because it extends upward to e''', a note rarely used by Bach.[25] No. 4 is also the one prelude from the group to use trio-sonata texture; this, together with its opening subject, recalls variation 2 from the Goldberg set. One passage (bars 29–32), however, also recalls the gavotte of the Sixth English Suite (BWV 811), a much earlier work. In No. 2 (BWV 934) the first eight bars follow a harmonic scheme closely parallel to that of the courante in the French Suite in the same key (BWV 813); the prelude and the courante are also similar in texture and character. The three remaining preludes, Nos. 3, 5, and 6 (BWV 935, 937, and 938), all involve two-part imitative counterpoint and thus bear comparison with the Inventions, especially the one in E (BWV 777), also in binary form.

There remains the lute prelude BWV 999. Like most of Bach's lute music it is equally playable on keyboard; Kellner, who made the sole copy, was an organist otherwise not known to have been interested in lute music.[26] More problematical is the fact that the piece, which opens in C minor, ends in G. Kellner uses a key signature of two flats, but it could have been used for either key.[27] Kellner writes the final chord (on G, with "Picardy" third) as a quarter-note, implying that the piece is not over at that point and that a subsequent section in C minor might have followed. Bach in fact wrote another prelude (BWV 872a/1) consisting of a fugato preceded by an arpeggiando section ending on the dominant; BWV 872a/1 was eventually incorporated into the second part of the WTC as the prelude in C♯.[28] Perhaps Bach intended to use the lute prelude in a similar way; either he never completed it, or Kellner omitted the continuation.

Suites, Dances, and Other Pieces

Two stylistically tentative allemandes (BWV 836–37) entered early in the CB are likely to be Friedemann's own compositions. One (BWV 837) is a fragment, but since both are given in fair copies they are likely to have been completed prior to being copied here. Friedemann's stylistic models were furnished not by Sebastian Bach but rather by composers like Telemann and the two other German composers represented in the CB. The inclusion of their music shows that Bach was not averse to, and rather welcomed, his sons' study of fashionable galant keyboard music; further evidence for this can be found in the 1725 *Clavier-Büchlein* for Anna Magdalena Bach (see Appendix B).

Telemann's three-movement suite (CB 47) lacks an attribution and was accordingly listed as BWV 824. Bach might have seemed a likely composer, as the gigue has a fugal subject resembling that of the Fourth French Suite (BWV 815), while a recurring passage on a dominant pedal-point (e.g., bars 21–28) calls to mind the pastorale in Part 2 of Bach's Christmas Oratorio (BWV 248). But the attribution in another source to Telemann makes better stylistic sense (despite the reservations expressed by Rose 1968, 219). The *Partia* [sic] by Stölzel (CB 48) is a much duller work, save for the *Menuet Trio* (BWV 929) that Bach added at the end. Sebastian probably did not check his son's copying of the other movements, for the text of the bourrée appears to have been garbled; Friedemann may have telescoped two similar bars into one (Example 10.9).

EXAMPLE 10.9.   Stölzel, *Partia* in G Minor, bourrée, bars 9ff., with suggested emendation

The allemande and courante by Richter (CB 25) form a variation pair, like that in Bach's Praeludium et Partita BWV 833 but in a much more galant style. Friedemann failed to complete his copy of either movement, but the parallelisms between the two halves of each binary movement make them easy to reconstruct. A Johann Christian Richter (1700–85) became court organist at Dresden in 1727; despite his youth, he is perhaps a more likely candidate than the Dresden oboist of the same name, who lived from 1689 to 1744.

Minuets BWV 841–43

The three minuets (CB 11–13) were copied at the end of group 2 by father and son jointly. Although the pieces might have been some sort of collaboration between the two,[29] Sebastian's revisions in the second minuet are typical of those he applied to his own compositions. Plath, noting the low tessitura of BWV 843, suggested that it was transposed downward from C in order to form a "cycle" with the other two (NBA V/5, KB, 82). Indeed, the pieces form a little suite, the three movements increasing in musical and technical sophistication.

The first minuet—the simplest in style and entirely in Friedemann's hand— recurs in Anna Magdalena's first *Clavier-Büchlein* of 1722, where it might have been intended to complete the French Suite in the same key (BWV 816). But it is the third of the pieces that is by far the most interesting musically, no longer a true minuet but rather an example of a type of cantabile movement that Bach seems to have perfected during the later Weimar years or at Cöthen. Other examples, both in G, are the prelude BWV 902/1 and the sarabande of the Fifth French Suite.

Fugue in C, BWV 953; Fugue in C, BWV 952

Bach wrote three similar fugues in C, all short, all in three voices, with material consisting largely of running passage-work. One of these, BWV 953, occurs in CB (No. 31) in what appears to be a composing draft. Another, very similar to BWV 953, is BWV 952, which is known only from a few eighteenth-century copies.[30] Evidently, neither fugue seemed quite substantial enough to be incorporated into the WTC. Yet, when Bach assembled Part 2 of the WTC, the piece selected as the first fugue in the volume was a third fugue in C whose original form (BWV 870a/2) is similar in style and dimensions to BWV 952 and 953.

The uncertain provenance of its sources presumably accounts for the listing of BWV 952 as "doubtful" in the work-list in NB. But it is remarkably similar to BWV 953 in structure; both, for example, reach a cadence in E minor in bar 23. BWV 952 also contains two short, complementary pedal-points (at bars 13 and 22b), symmetrically placed on either side of an important arrival that marks the midpoint of the piece (bar 16). Pedal-points help to articulate the tonal design in several Weimar fugues (e.g., BWV 944, 951), and if this is indeed a Weimar tendency then BWV 952 might be somewhat earlier than BWV 953.

Prelude in C Minor BWV 919

Source: SPK P 1229 (Preller). *Edition*: BG 36.

Three two-part pieces in C minor are, like BWV 952, orphans whose legitimacy has been questioned. The simplest is the prelude BWV 919 (called a *Fantasie* in BG 36), which in form and material recalls the Prelude in F, BWV 928. Like the latter, BWV 919 seems a short essay on motivic ideas similar to those in the prelude of the Fourth English Suite. But BWV 919 lacks that work's references to concerto style and is really a two-part invention; indeed, like some of the Inventions, it contains a couple of voice-crossings (bar 18) that make performance on two manuals appropriate. As in the Invention in C Minor (BWV 773 = CB 46), there is a brief Da Capo of the opening exposition (at bar 23). But BWV 919 lacks that work's rigorous canonic design; instead, at a rather late point in the form (bar 15), it introduces a second subject that is not, however, ever combined with the principal one.

Hence, there is good reason for questioning Bach's authorship of the piece, which is attributed to "Bernhardt Bach" in the only surviving copy.[31] There were several Bernhard Bachs, the best known being the composer Johann Bernhard of Eisenach and Erfurt, to whom Schulze assigns the piece (1984a, 80–81). But it seems conceivable that the copyist Preller could have had another composer in mind, either the Ohrdruf Bach of the same name (1700–43) or Sebastian's son Johann Gottfried Bernhard, who, like Preller, studied at the university in Jena.[32] BWV 919 seems too close to Sebastian's style to be by the Eisenach/Erfurt composer, suggesting that it is at least a student's imitation and that "the matter of authorship must remain open," as Stinson (1989a, 129) puts it.

Fugue (Fughetta) in C Minor BWV 961

Chief sources: SPK P 804/1; SPK P 542; LEu M. pr. Ms. 20[i]. *Editions*: BG 36; Dehnhard (1973).

The little Fugue or Fughetta BWV 961 is more surely Bach's, though difficult to place chronologically. Unlike BWV 919, it is a true two-part fugue, though a rather loosely constructed one, lacking any full statements of the subject in the second of its three sections (bars 11–17). It is preserved alongside the Inventions and Sinfonias in one source, P 542, which is interesting for bearing an inscription that indicates that it was prepared for Beethoven's patron Karl Lichnowsky during the latter's studies at Göttingen, where Forkel taught from 1772.

Fantaisie sur un Rondeau BWV 918

Chief sources: LEu M. pr. Ms. 20[i]; SPK P 319. *Edition*: BG 36; Dadelsen and Rönnau (1970).

The most interesting of the three C-minor pieces mentioned above is the "Fantasia upon a Rondo" BWV 918. Although the somewhat shaky source situation is again cause for some concern, BWV 918 would seem to be one of the more imaginative of Bach's smaller works. While it could never be a crowd-pleaser, it is a fascinating demonstration of how a popular galant genre could be turned into a contrapuntal fantasia. In two equal parts throughout, it can be played as a duet on two matched keyboards.

The title implies that Bach based the piece on an existing rondeau, presumably by borrowing the theme of a French *pièce de clavecin* in rondo form. The rhythm at the opening, which consists of an upbeat of five eighth-notes in $\frac{3}{4}$ meter, is indeed very French,[33] but otherwise the quirky little theme seems more characteristic of

Bach than anyone else. Hence, there may not have been any model, and the present title may be incorrect. Yet the piece remains a sort of rondeau, the main theme returning three times in the tonic: at bars 28, 80, and at the end (bar 120). Between these refrains come polyphonic *couplets* in which motivic ideas more or less closely related to the theme are worked out in two-part imitative counterpoint. But the distinction between theme and *couplet* becomes somewhat blurred when fragments of the theme are treated in inverted counterpoint during the *couplets* (as at bar 36) and later when the second restatement of the theme is expanded through the canonic treatment of its first two phrases.[34]

Preludes and Fugues (Fughettas) in D Minor, E Minor, F, and G, BWV 899–902

Chief sources: SPK P 1089 (Vogler, 1727–31); SPK Mus. ms. 10490 (Michel); SPK P 804/38 (Kellner; lacks BWV 899/1, has BWV 902a in place of BWV 902/1). *Editions*: BG 36 (BWV 902a in appendix); Dadelsen and Rönnau (1970; BWV 901 and 902/1 only); Dehnhard (1973; lacks BWV 901).

While the little fugues discussed above seem to have remained isolated pieces, another group of short fugues with preludes includes several that were eventually revised and incorporated into WTC2. Only the pieces not incorporated into WTC2 are discussed here; for the others, see in Chapter 12 the discussions of the preludes and fugues in C, C♯, D minor, G, and A♭, some of which were originally in other keys.

Although the original dates of the pieces are uncertain, it is possible that they were composed as a set, perhaps at Weimar or Cöthen prior to Bach's conceiving the idea of a collection of large preludes and fugues in all twenty-four keys. They can be arranged into a series beginning on C and rising to G, or, if one includes BWV 895 (discussed below), to A. This is, however, somewhat speculative, as no one manuscript contains the entire series, and they have apparently never been edited as a single set.[35]

The Prelude and Fughetta in D Minor BWV 899 is most notable for the fugue subject, which is composed of the simplest imaginable four-note motive. The subject behaves like a harmonically neutral cantus firmus; the major event of the fugue is a demonstration of invertible counterpoint at the twelfth, a point that is brought home by the wide separation of the outer voices in bars 33–40.[36] The prelude, a serious little piece, much of which is constructed over pedal-points, perhaps overwhelms the fughetta, being composed in four parts. The counterpoint is sometimes more notational than real, however; like the Prelude in C belonging to the same group (BWV 870a/1, later incorporated into WTC2), the movement contains elements of both imitative polyphony and the *style brisé*.

The Prelude and Fugue in E Minor BWV 900 is perhaps the most impressive of the group. The prelude is a concise mixture of harmonically inspired melodic writing and imitative counterpoint, reminiscent in this respect of the allemande from the English Suite in the same key. It differs in introducing the inversion of the subject right at the start, in the first imitative entry (bar 2), and in the somewhat surprising outbreak of scale figuration in thirty-seconds at the end of each of the three sections—all this in a piece of eighteen bars! The fugue, on the other hand, is the longest in the group. Its subject is of the old-fashioned rhetorical type, punctuated by silences that are filled in by running figuration in the countersubject. The counterpoint is rough in spots, but no more so than in, say, the "Chromatic" fugue (BWV 903/2), with which this fugue shares what appear to be signs of a Weimar dating: the sequential praseology of the subject; long passages in two voices, often setting figuration in sixteenths against "walking" eighths; and a flashy final cadence that immediately follows a statement of the subject in the soprano (here embellished).

The Prelude and Fughetta in F, BWV 901, while not as imposing as BWV 900, is technically perhaps the most perfect of the group, notwithstanding the fact that Bach later found that he could double the length of the fugue when he adapted it (transposed to A^b) for WTC2. The prelude falls into a simple three-phrase form, like that of BWV 900, but it is not so strictly imitative. The fugue, the only one of the group in four parts, is in a style not far removed from late-Baroque vocal polyphony. The subject opens with a motive found in many Baroque choral fugues,[37] while the countersubject is another conventional (though very different) idea, the descending chromatic hexachord. The four voices are used together only in the last phrase, and it seems possible that Bach originally wrote the piece in three parts; this might explain the lacuna in the tenor in the penultimate measure.

The fughetta in G, BWV 902/2—also later incorporated into WTC2—seems originally to have been paired with the little Prelude BWV 902a, which is found only in Kellner's copy. This prelude is akin in dimensions and general character to one in D minor (BWV 875a) that Bach later expanded and used in WTC2. But by the time Bach was assembling WTC2 in the late 1730s, he had apparently replaced the original prelude in G with a new one that is now listed as BWV 902/1. Actually, the shorter prelude, BWV 902a, makes a more suitable companion to the fughetta, which is equally short. Both end with a stroke of wit, the fugue with a sudden burst of figuration, the prelude with a sudden *interruption* of the prevailing figuration (as in the Vivaldi concerto in the same key arranged as BWV 973).

The longer G-major prelude, BWV 902/1, is the more memorable one, indeed one of the best examples of the cantabile type of movement referred to earlier. Like the somewhat similar E-major prelude of WTC2, it is in binary form, with two repeated halves of equal lengths. Nevertheless, it is a true sonata form, the second half containing a medial cadence to E minor (bar 36) as well as a distinct retransition and a real recapitulation section (from bar 41). The quietly expressive character at the opening deepens considerably in the closing phrase of each half, where the music touches on the minor mode.

The enormous disparity in length and style between this prelude and the fughetta in G probably accounts for Bach's having written yet a third prelude for use with the revised version of the fugue in WTC2. But the new prelude remains in binary form and opens, like BWV 902/1, over a tonic pedal-point. Curiously, Bach abandoned a similar movement in the same key (the cantabile of BWV 1019a) when he put together the familiar set of six sonatas for harpsichord and violin. It seems unlikely that Bach rejected these cantabile movements per se, but in each case Bach's strong sense of stylistic propriety evidently led him to eliminate a splendid piece from a collection to which it seemed not to belong.

Prelude and Fugue in A Minor BWV 895

Chief sources: SPK P 804/9; US NHy LM 4982 (J. C. Bach [1673–1727]). *Editions*: BG 36; Dehnhard (1973).

Although Dehnhard (1973, vi) suggests linking this pair with the group just discussed, its sources are unrelated to theirs and it seems earlier and somewhat weaker in style. The prelude is reminiscent of the *passaggio* that opens the lute suite in E minor BWV 996, and it lacks any contrapuntal or tonal design of the sort found in even the simplest of the "Little" preludes. The fugue subject is dull and the counterpoint unadventurous, although the *brisé* writing used in some passages is not in itself a weakness; it represents an effort to incorporate idiomatic harpsichord textures into fugue, something accomplished much more successfully, however, in the fugue in G, BWV 902/2. The present fugue lacks episodes and closes with a free coda, a sign of an early date.

Not surprisingly, doubts have been raised about the piece's authenticity (as in the NG work-list). But these are answered by the copy at Yale, which gives the work in a text superior to, if perhaps slightly earlier than, that of the better-known copy from the Kellner circle.[38] In the Yale manuscript, copied by a distant cousin of Sebastian who also copied the Inventions (in LM 4983), the piece is followed immediately by instructions on how to tune and string harpsichords and clavichords.[39] While there is no reason to think that these instructions were copied from an exemplar in Sebastian's possession, they do, together with the repertory of the manuscript as a whole—a collection of small preludes and fugues (and similar pieces), organized by key—reveal a concern with the same musical issues that led to Bach's *Well-Tempered Clavier*.

Emendations to the text in BG 36: *Praeludium*, 2, r.h., slur b, c', d', *tr* on g$^{\sharp}$, last note g$^{\sharp}$ not a. 3, ten., last beat, 8th, two 16ths. 4, sop., second note f″, not e″. 6, beat 3, alto, 16th-rest followed by [dotted]? 8th; ten., 8th, two 16ths. 10, beat 2, fingering in LM 4982: 5 4 3 2 1 2 1 2; beat 3, first five notes for l.h., last three for r.h.; beat 4, first three notes for r.h., last five for l.h. 12–13, ten., bass, no ties. 12, beat 2, add a' (quarter [tied to dotted quarter?]). *Fugue*: 8, sop., last note d$^{\flat}$″. 9, alto, first note b', not e'. 11, first note, sop., e″ (8th, followed by rests); alto, g$^{\sharp}$″ (without double stem). 14, beat 3, bass, g$^{\sharp}$, b, c', d' (16ths). 15, bass, last three notes, f', d', b. 20, beat 3, ten., a (quarter, tied); c', b, a in alto. 27, ten., first note c', not f. 31, beat 3, add alto e' (quarter). 32, first chord, sop., b, alto, g$^{\sharp}$.

Prelude in B Minor BWV 923

Chief sources: SPK P 401 (Anonymous 5; fragment); SPK P 648 (with BWV 951). *Editions*: BG 42; Dadelsen and Rönnau (1970).

BWV 923 was probably not composed as a teaching piece, but because of its association with the WTC in one source it may be discussed here. Actually, the fragment in P 401 is a late addition at the end of that manuscript; other copies attach the prelude to the "Albinoni" Fugue in the same key (BWV 951), probably without Bach's authorization.

The prelude is intriguing because the only other thing like it in Bach's output is the Chromatic Fantasia (BWV 903/1). Indeed the two pieces share several passages or, rather, distinctive harmonic progressions within a series of arpeggiando chords.[40] In general, however, the progressions here are less compelling than in BWV 903, and the present piece is probably unfinished. For, after a striking opening, it dissolves into a very long series of arpeggiando chords, most likely a shorthand form of notation that Bach would have spelled out had he ever revised the piece. There does exist a later version (BWV 923a), but it is a clearly spurious adaptation (see Appendix A).

The arpeggiando passage raises textual as well as interpretive questions. In particular, the final modulation back to the tonic seems too hasty and too late to be completely successful. Yet the prelude remains worth playing for the remarkable free improvisation in the opening half and as the only suitable companion piece for BWV 951.

Pastorale BWV 590

Chief sources: SPK P 287/6 (Kellner); SPK P 277 (Anonymous 401). *Editions*: BG 38; NBA IV/7.

Although the Pastorale as it stands is an organ work, only one of the four movements requires pedal, and it might well have been concatenated from movements composed separately. Indeed, its apparent character as a pastiche has led to frequent questions about its authenticity, but the attribution appears to be sound. Galant elements and various aspects of the notation in the earliest sources lead Stinson (1989b, 460–61) to accept arguments for a "Leipzig origin," but there are many parallels to earlier works. The first movement recalls the pastoralelike preludes in E from WTC1 and in A from the First English Suite; bars 5–6 strongly recall the corresponding measures in the G-major prelude of WTC1. The last movement seems almost a parody of the closing allegro of the Sixth Brandenburg Concerto. Chafe (1991, 81), pointing to the somewhat unusual tonal design traced by the four movements (F–a, C, c–F, F), concludes: "Undoubtedly his [Bach's] intent was for the minor and major dominants to represent a contained dualism dealing with the meaning of the incarnation." But while the unique structure of the work may invite speculation about its "meaning" (and about its compositional history), the somewhat ambiguous authorship and genre dictate caution in any assertions about the composer's expressive intentions.

Harpsichordists cannot play the Pastorale in its present form, since the four movements are clearly intended to be played in unbroken succession.[41] The first movement requires pedals, and the third movement closes with a modulating transition to the fourth. In any case the third movement may be better served by a properly registered organ; it somewhat resembles the aria "Unerforschlich ist die Weise" with obbligato organ in Cantata No. 188. The second and fourth movements, on the other hand, might have originated as separate harpsichord pieces not unlike those composing the "Six Little Preludes." The second movement, in a compact sonata form, is another example of the cantabile type. The fourth movement, in binary form, could have served as the gigue of a suite (cf. Stinson 1989b, 461).

Air with Variations in C Minor BWV 991

Source: DSB P 224 (autograph). *Edition:*NBA V/4.

Bach's composing score in the 1722 *Clavier-Büchlein* for Anna Magdalena is the sole source for this apparently unfinished piece. The fragment consists of a rather ornate sixteen-bar melody in binary form, for which Bach wrote the bass for the first nine-and-a-half bars only. In addition, the upper line has been written out for one variation and for the first eleven-and-a-half bars of another. The whole piece was subsequently crossed out (not necessarily by Bach). The text, as edited in NBA V/4, contains evident errors (bars 3, 8A), and the simple, gavottelike melody given as the first variation would seem more likely to have been the original theme, perhaps borrowed from another composer. The four blank staves that follow in the manuscript imply that Bach intended to compose at least one more variation. But what he did write is not very promising, and his failure to complete the piece does not seem to have deprived us of anything very significant.

The Inventions and Sinfonias

Most of the items in group 2 of the CB were apparently meant to serve as preliminaries to those in group 3, the eleven preludes later incorporated into WTC1. Discussion of these preludes is reserved for Chapter 11. The next group of pieces, the Inventions, represents a further advance in complexity and technical difficulty, leading to the final group, the Sinfonias. Of course, the order of the pieces in the book need not reflect the order in which the pieces were composed. But the Inventions and Sinfonias were all entered into the CB at about the same time, many in what appear to be Bach's composing drafts. Within each of the two groups there are similarities of style, dimensions, and overall conception that, notwithstanding certain exceptions, support the idea that all originated during the same brief period of concentrated work. Moreover, one gains the impression that these pieces are later than most of the isolated preludes and fugues discussed above (e.g., BWV 943 or 952); they are more assured, free of even the occasional awkward detail in voice-leading or structure. In addition, many of the pieces seem to reflect Bach's acceptance of galant elements—"sigh" figures, expressive "singing" melodies—into his keyboard polyphony. This is not to say that the pieces are easy to play; the Sinfonias are often difficult, more difficult in fact than many pieces in the WTC. But the combination of learned and popular elements has certainly helped these pieces win their place in the canon of pedagogic works still taught to keyboard players.

It is presumed that the CB originally included all fifteen Inventions and all fifteen Sinfonias, each under the titles *Praeambulum* and *Fantasia* respectively. The last two leaves of music have been lost, and with them presumably the last sinfonia and half of another. Except for a few inventions copied by Friedemann, all are in

Sebastian's hand. Several appear to be fair copies, but the remainder are either composing scores or revision copies.[42] Within a few months of their entry into the CB, Sebastian recopied all thirty pieces, lightly revising them in the process.

Franklin (1989b, 259) points out that the choice of fifteen tonalities corresponds with the idea of "a group of fifteen primary keys" found in both Mattheson and Niedt. In CB the order of keys is slightly different for the two sets of pieces, but in both cases it involves an ascent upwards from C major (C, D minor, E minor, etc.), followed by a descent back to C minor (E minor, E^b, D, C minor). The later autograph (DSB P 610) substitutes the familiar simple ascent (C, C minor, D, D minor), which has the distinct advantage of making it easier to find a given piece in the book.[43] The later autograph also gives the pieces their now-familiar titles. As in the *Orgelbüchlein*, Bach also added a general title expressing his pedagogic intentions for the work as a whole. Like Bach's other fair copies, P 610 eventually acquired new corrections and revisions, but these never became as extensive or numerous as the ones visible in the CB. Two students, Heinrich Nicolaus Gerber and an unidentified student known to Bach scholars as Anonymous 5, made copies that include additional ornamentation possibly stemming from Bach, who himself entered ornaments into Gerber's copy of Sinfonia No. 5 (see below).

The significance of the pieces' original order has been noted by Derr (1981), who even discerned a grouping of the original praeambula into "triptychs"—that is, groups of three that are distinguished by various details of form and compositional technique. The basis of some of Derr's groupings, such as the supposed need for two manuals in performing pieces of the third "triptych" (starting with the one in B minor), is debatable. But inasmuch as the order of the works in CB may well correspond with their apparent order of composition, it is not surprising to find certain common features in adjacent members of the set: conjunct motion in the themes of Praeambula 1–3, disjunct motion in 4–6, longer subjects, possessing distinct countersubjects, in 7–9.

Both sets were frequently copied by members of the Bach circle. Forkel (1802, 38/BR, 328) explained that the Inventions (as well as the "Six Little Preludes") had been drafted "during the hours of teaching" as substitutes for the tedious finger exercises that Bach supposedly gave beginning students prior to their study of "his own greater compositions." The report that Bach had subjected his students to mechanical five-finger exercises, while happily accepted by modern proponents of a similar approach to keyboard pedagogy, seems suspicious and might have been conditioned by the apparent fascination of some early Romantics with technical studies. But other aspects of Forkel's account are supported by E. L. Gerber (son of the Bach student H. N. Gerber), who reported that Bach's students worked on the Inventions before continuing to the suites.[44] In Bach's Leipzig period, many of his students must have made their own copies of the Inventions and Sinfonias at the beginning of their studies. Indeed, H. N. Gerber's copy survives (in NL DHgm); it is dated 1725 and includes additions in Bach's hand in Sinfonia No. 5, perhaps added in the course of a lesson. The pieces would have served as both exercises in performance and models for composition; the deep impression that they made on Bach's students can be seen in Friedemann's and Emanuel's keyboard sonatas, which include movements written in imitation of both inventions and sinfonias.[45]

Bach's general title (in P 610) makes clear the work's pedagogic function, opening with the words (in large letters) "Candid Instruction."[46] The long title is worth considering in some detail, as Bach evidently chose his words with care. He addresses the work to both *Liebhabern* and *Lehrbegierigen*: lovers of music as well as those eager for instruction. The latter—that is, his students—would not have been beginners, since they would already have studied simpler pieces while also, in all likelihood, having had several years' experience as choristers. Thus, the teaching of Bach's peculiar style of keyboard polyphony would not have started out in the stylistic vacuum mentioned in Chapter 2, as is all too often the case today.

According to the remainder of the title, both the two- and the three-part pieces are meant to teach *inventio*, which here refers not to a type of piece but rather the invention of motivic material. The *inventiones* in question are not only to be of interest in their own right but will be "developed," an expression also employed in the general title of the *Orgelbüchlein*. In modern German, Bach's term (*Durchführung*) can refer both to the working-out of motives (as in a Classical sonata form) and to the exposition of a fugue subject. For Bach, however, the word appears to have meant nothing more than "worked out polyphonically." The same word also appears in the title of the *Orgelbüchlein*, where it is used in reference to chorale melodies. Since here the term is applied to "good inventions," the term *inventiones* must have had as its fundamental meaning the thematic material rather than the pieces themselves.[47]

Bach adds that the pieces are meant "above all" (*am allermeisten*) to serve for teaching a "singing" (*cantabile*) manner of performance and as a preview of *Composition*, which probably means what we would call counterpoint.[48] It is hard to know what to make of the term *cantabile*. When employed by an instrumentalist the term obviously cannot be taken literally, and its interpretation seems unavoidably subjective. Walther gives two definitions for a "cantabile" composition; one is simply the common sense of possessing a "fine melody," while the other, evidently referring to a capella polyphony, signifies that every part is capable of being sung. Butt (1990, 11–15) notes the possible relationship between "cantabile" and the clear articulation of words in singing. But Bach's notion of cantabile style was evidently broad enough to include both the sighing half-steps of Sinfonia No. 9 and the rapid arpeggios of Invention No. 10 and Sinfonia No. 15. Hence, the use of the word in Bach's title cannot imply the predominance of legato articulation or "expressive" dynamic nuances, though it may remind us that hardly anything in the pieces goes beyond what was considered suitable for the voice in the early eighteenth century.

The original title *Praeambulum* for each of the inventions must have reflected their similarity to other, probably earlier, imitative preludes like BWV 930 (CB 9). The selection of the title *Fantasia* for the three-part pieces might have been a fairly arbitrary way of distinguishing them from the ones in two parts. While we have previously seen one rather rigorously contrapuntal fantasia in three parts (BWV 917), the same title could mean many other things (as in BWV 903 and 904). Much has been made of Bach's use of the rhetorical term *inventio* for the revised versions of the two-part pieces. But while he obviously thought carefully enough about the titles to change them, it is not clear why he did so or why he applied a different term (*sinfonia*) to the three-part pieces.[49] Although the terms may not have been previously used as titles for keyboard pieces, both had been indeed been used previously in musical titles, and this ought to discourage efforts to draw elaborate parallels between Bach's Inventions and Baroque exercises in rhetoric. Bach knew, for example, the *Invenzioni da camera* (Op. 10, Bologna, 1712) for violin and continuo of Francesco Antonio Bonporti, which he appears to have used at just this time in the teaching of figured bass.[50] In 1720 the word *sinfonia* could still, of course, apply to any piece for instrumental ensemble, especially a movement within a larger vocal work, such as the overture.

Perhaps Bach's decision to substitute new titles reflected his realization that here he had created two essentially new genres of keyboard music. Unlike most earlier preludes, the Inventions are true keyboard duettos, somewhat resembling older fughetti but differing in their technical preoccupations.[51] Here invertible counterpoint is of greater importance than imitation per se, and thus the opening passages usually involve imitation at the octave (or voice-exchange) rather than at the fifth. Instructional two-part imitative pieces by earlier composers rarely contain real modulations; most of the Inventions, however, fall into sophisticated yet compact modulating schemes comparable to those of Bach's larger fugal works. The thematic material is generally lively, the subjects very concise; thus, the Inventions have a modern, galant character, although only the one in B minor (BWV 786) has a texture clearly imitating that of a solo sonata for, say, violin and continuo.[52]

The modern habit of referring to the Sinfonias as "three-part inventions" goes back at least to Forkel.[53] But Bach's distinction is worth maintaining, since the two sets of pieces differ in substantial ways. The subjects of the Sinfonias are generally longer than those of the Inventions, and the texture more closely resembles that of contemporary ensemble music—specifically, the fugal or imitative type of movement found in trio-sonatas, where the bass accompanies the initial entry of the subject, which is invariably placed in one of the two upper voices; every one of the Sinfonias begins in this manner. As in the fugal movements of Bach's own trio-sonatas, the bass usually has the third entry of the subject. But, except in the sinfonias in D (BWV 789) and F minor (BWV 795), there is no permutational counterpoint. The bass, moreover, is usually distinct in material and style from the upper voices except when stating the subject. Indeed, in one sinfonia (BWV 791 in E♭) the bass never shares in the main motivic material, while another (BWV 797 in G minor) is not really imitative at all, although the main motive does appear in all three voices at different points in the opening phrase.

The Inventions and Sinfonias are widely available in generally dependable editions, including that in NBA V/3 (or its "practical" offprint). The NBA is to be preferred over other editions, especially for students, as it presents a clean text unencumbered by anachronistic fingerings and arbitrary suggestions for ornamentation. Unfortunately, at this writing the only thorough textual commentary remains that of Landshoff (1933). The edition by Ratz and Füssl includes a list (in English) of the principal variants and presents in a separate section the "ornamented versions" of several of the sinfonias (from the copies by Gerber and Anonymous 5). A separate discussion of ornamentation included in the volume is uninformed by current understanding of eighteenth-century instruments or performance practice, but Ratz's analytical essay will be helpful to students in need of a bar-by-bar commentary.[54]

The Inventions

A detailed analysis seems unnecessary here, and these remarks will be confined to a few points about selected pieces from each set. As in any of Bach's collections, the general uniformity within each group of pieces may cause us to overlook the occasional odd member. Among the Inventions, No. 2 in C minor is for the most part a strict canon, while No. 6 in E is in binary or rather sonata form (henceforth, the numbering of the pieces is that of the final version, not CB). The last invention, in B minor, is slightly foreign in character, perhaps because the treble enjoys somewhat greater prominence over the bass than in the others. Still, with one or two exceptions, the fifteen pieces are related not only by the obvious emphasis on two-part counterpoint but by a common approach to formal design.

The basic structural principles are similar to those of Bach's larger works but realized on a smaller scale; a single phrase here may correspond to an entire section in a larger prelude, fugue, or concerto movement. For example, an opening phrase generally leads to a cadence in the dominant (or relative major), at which point the initial bar or two is recapitulated in inverted counterpoint. As a result, in Nos. 1 (C) and 13 (A minor) the opening phrase is analogous to the first half—that is, the portion preceding the double bar—of a dance movement or sonata form. The next phrase corresponds to the beginning of the middle ("development") section, and after a third formal articulation the piece has delineated a miniature three-part (or an expanded three-phrase) form. In No. 6 (E) the expansion of each phrase into a period and the insertion of an actual double bar leads to a genuine sonata form. Not every piece follows precisely this plan; in Invention No. 9 (F minor) the first decisive cadence is delayed until the midpoint (bar 17), giving it a binary design, while No. 2 (C minor) is, as already noted, for the most part a strict canon. But the canonic pattern is broken in order to articulate two crucial moments: an arrival on the dominant (bar 11) and the return to the tonic (bar 23), the latter coinciding with a restatement of the theme in its original form. While this return comes very near the end (as it also does in No. 9), in other inventions the final section more closely resembles a true sonata-form recapitulation, inasmuch as the return marks the beginning of a section long enough to balance the first one (Nos. 3 in D, 6 in E, 13 in A minor).

Although a few of the Inventions possess nearly exact binary or ternary proportions (1:1 or 1:1:1), it is unlikely that these should be ascribed to a preliminary plotting out of the work according to a geometric or numerological pattern. Bach possessed a fine sense of musical proportion—one fine enough, however, to recognize that numerically precise proportions could lead to musically unsatisfying results. Thus, in two cases, Inventions Nos. 7 (E minor) and 13 (A minor), Bach broke the nearly exact threefold symmetries of the original versions by expanding the third section. The early versions (CB 34 and 37), both twenty-one bars long, are each clearly divided in three by internal cadences (to III and v, respectively). They lack a clear-cut return, and a return is still absent in the revised version of the E-Minor Invention. But, by adding at bar 18 a restatement of the opening bar in the A-Minor Invention, Bach put it into sonata form, and the phrase in bars 14–17 (expanded from bars 14–16 in the original) became a genuine retransition. The assimilation to later sonata forms is probably fortuitous; had Bach had any special preference for this form he might have revised at least a few of the other inventions in a similar way. But it is clear that tonal design took precedence over measure-counting and other superficial concerns.

Except in Nos. 7 and 13, the versions of the later autograph differ from those of CB only in details. The most extensive revision is that seen at the end of Invention No. 11 (G minor), which is in effect half a bar longer in the final version.[55] Substantial changes are visible, however, within the composing scores of the CB. While in no case did these involve the large structure—Bach seems to have had a clear design in his head even while writing the most hastily drafted composing score—in several instances he later changed the main thematic material. Thus, after writing the score of the C-Minor Invention (CB 46), Bach went back and altered the subject, probably in order to avoid an open fifth in bar 3 and elsewhere (see Example 10.11).[56] In this piece the subject occurs only six times, and always in the same canonic context, so the change had little effect on the counterpoint elsewhere.

Not so in Invention No. 11 (G minor), where Bach changed the subject, only afterward adding the countersubject, which does not fit the original subject (Example 10.10). Most of these alterations must have occurred during the writing out

EXAMPLE 10.10.   Invention in G Minor BWV 782, bars 1–2:
   (a) original version (without bass); (b) final version

(i.e., composing) of the piece in CB. But the initial gesture of the treble probably remained unchanged until after the piece was finished. By then the original form of the opening motive (containing the mordentlike figure g', f'', g') had been worked into the counterpoint of bars 5 and 12, where it remains in the later version as an echo of Bach's first thoughts.[57]

Since the Inventions will always be the first introduction to Baroque keyboard style for many players, a few words on special performance problems are not out of place here. In No. 2 (C minor) the short trills of the countersubject consistently create parallel octaves with the subject (Example 10.11). This has led to suggestions

EXAMPLE 10.11.   Invention in C Minor BWV 773, bar 3

orig.: c'

that one should start these trills from the main note (as in Neumann 1978, 316). But it is just as logical to conclude that Bach took no notice of "forbidden" parallels involving ornamental tones.[58] Bach tolerated more obvious parallelisms in certain contexts,[59] and the present ones will go unnoticed unless the upper tone is excessively prolonged. Normally, of course, the upper note of a trill is a dissonant appoggiatura bearing an implicit accent. But a quick trill creates the impression of an accent even when, as in the present case, it is the main note and not the ornamental one that is dissonant. Both notes are consonant in bars 15, 16, and 26 (second trill). Yet the effect of the short upper-note trill will be perceived on piano and clavichord as well as on harpsichord and is even preserved if weak fingers or a sluggish action force one to abbreviate the trill to a single quick appoggiatura, as allowed by C. P. E. Bach.[60]

Regardless of how one plays the trills, unisons between the parts will cause the hands to collide in bar 13. One could play on two manuals, provided the manuals are evenly matched. But Bach writes unisons in other pieces where two-manual performance is impossible, and the hand-crossing effects of Sinfonia No. 15 (see below) were evidently meant to be played on a single manual. Hence, it would be wrong, here or elsewhere, to insist on dividing the parts between two keyboards for the sake of a few momentary unisons or voice-crossings.

Slurs pose editorial problems, and therefore questions of interpretation, in Inventions Nos. 3 (D) and 9 (F minor). Bach added the slurs only when making the fair copies in P 610. As is often the case, Bach's slurs are hastily and somewhat imprecisely drawn. But precisely because he did not take care to place them over well-defined groups of two or three notes, the slurs are likely to have been meant to apply to long groups of four, six, even eight sixteenths.[61] Such long slurs are, of course, unusual. They do not, however, signify a continuous or unbroken legato, for articulations must still fall before and after each slur. Even in these cases the notes beneath each slur represent but a single harmony (except in bar 4 of Invention No. 9). Each slurred figure should presumably receive a single rhythmic impetus or, to put it another way, be played as a single graceful gesture. This will mean playing the D-Major Invention "in one," since the slurred groups of six sixteenths fill the bars of $\frac{3}{8}$ time and will each constitute a single long beat.

Written-out ornaments and embellishments in several copies of the Inventions (and Sinfonias) suggest that one of the uses for these pieces was instruction in ornamentation. Gerber's copy of the B-Minor Invention has a flourish in the final bar that is absent from all other copies. The flourish seems to create parallel fifths with the bass, but such is presumably not a flaw in an embellishment, and the rhythm is probably to be interpreted freely. Bach himself added embellishments to each entry of the subject in the fair copy of Invention No. 1 (C), producing the triplet version BWV 772a (Example 10.12). But the systematic filling-in of just

EXAMPLE 10.12.   Invention in C, bar 1: (a) BWV 772; (b)
      BWV 772a

about every melodic third ruins the light and graceful theme. The best that can be said for the alteration is that it provides a lesson in motivic consistency and perhaps in the playing of "two against three," though only in bars 13–14 are triplets and duplets sounded simultaneously.

The Sinfonias

The Sinfonias are less familiar to most players than the Inventions, as they are too difficult for beginners and consequently are less often studied. But, for those who love the combination of galant melody and lively counterpoint found in a good eighteenth-century trio-sonata, nothing in the *manualiter* repertory comes closer. The Sinfonias are more like true fugues than are the Inventions. This is evident not only in the more frequent imitations at the fifth but also in the formal designs, which in several cases (Nos. 3 in D, 4 in D minor, 8 in F, etc.) resemble those of Bach's fugues, with distinct episodes and recapitulated episodal passages. This does not rule out the use of sonatalike structures; indeed, one lesson taught here (and repeated in WTC1) is that the two- and three-part forms characteristic of sonata form are thoroughly compatible with fugue. Still, these pieces are neither sonatas nor fugues but, like the Inventions, examples of a distinct genre that in individual cases may resemble fugue or sonata more or less closely. While the presence of three voices theoretically allows for complex inversional counterpoint, true countersubjects appear in only a few works. Two of the Sinfonias (Nos. 5 in E$^\flat$ and 11 in G minor), as noted earlier, largely abandon imitative counterpoint in favor of idiomatic keyboard writing, and only Sinfonia No. 3 (D) systematically presents all six permutations of its subject and two countersubjects, each possible combination appearing once.

Bach took as much trouble over the less complex sinfonias as he did in the more rigorously fugal ones. Indeed, the composing score of Sinfonia No. 5 (CB 61) contains particularly numerous alterations, and most of the ornament signs were added only later as revisions to the fair-copy autograph (P 610).[62] These late revisions also included the small note-values that appear in modern editions as ordinary thirty-seconds but that were originally inserted as *petites notes* after the dotted eighths and rests in bars 9, 10, and elsewhere. Hence, a mathematically exact subdivision of the beat is probably inappropriate for these dotted figures.

The embellishments are not the only aspect of Sinfonia No. 5 to present interpretive problems. Despite the dotted rhythms, the piece has nothing to do with an overture; it is, rather, related to a type of sarabande in three voices that appears in several of Bach's suites (e.g., the G-Major Partita). The sarabande rhythm does not necessarily imply a slow tempo, but finding a suitable pace is not easy. It is probably best to judge the tempo from the original version (CB 61), since even in the final, embellished version the ornamentation probably ought not hold back the tempo. As in the sarabandes of this type, the numerous appoggiaturas are perhaps best understood as short French *coulés* and *ports de voix* (*accents*); the piece loses its dance-like swing if these are performed as long ("variable") Berlin appoggiaturas. On the other hand, the appoggiaturas probably ought not be so short as to be crushed against the main tone, like a modern "grace" note, nor should they precede the beat. In either case the effect of a gentle momentary dissonance would be lost. Careful attention to these and other ornaments will deepen the expressive character of the piece, whose moderately elegiac tone is due in part to the early move to the subdominant (bar 3). This modulation, incidentally, makes possible the wonderfully effortless return to the tonic at the end of the piece. The middle section (bars 13–29) ends in the subdominant, but the recapitulation of the opening phrase follows immediately (bars 30ff.), the harmony of bar 1 being touchingly reinterpreted as V of IV before the tonic is fully reestablished.

Very different in character is the brilliant final sinfonia in B minor, which also raises some performance questions. Though nominally in three parts, it is confined to two voices for much of the time and has as its most noticeable feature a recurring flurry of thirty-seconds. Their penultimate appearance (bars 26–28), which constitutes the climax of the piece, involves a particularly difficult sort of hand-crossing. As in the Concerto BWV 973, raising the wrists and straightening out the fingers may make it possible to play the passage on a single manual. Friedemann Bach must have practiced the piece carefully, for his Fantasia in C (F. 14) contains similar writing.

The B-Minor Sinfonia is not the only one in which three-part counterpoint is partly a notational pretense. Several passages originally notated in two parts in Sinfonia No. 2 (C minor) were later rewritten to create the appearance of three. But, like the Prelude in C, BWV 943, this piece rarely operates in more than two real parts. Sinfonia No. 2 was (presumably) the last piece in CB, and one wonders if, as he approached the end of the series in its original form, Bach drew on a previously (and not very strictly) composed piece to complete the set.[63]

Of the more rigorously contrapuntal sinfonias, No. 9 in F minor is perhaps the most often discussed, on account of the rhetorical pauses in its subject and the chromatic voice-leading of the two countersubjects. The subject itself contains a transposition of the B-A-C-H motive (A♭, G, B♭, A), and the bass in the first two bars originally (in CB) included an apparent quotation of the jagged four-note subject of the C♯-minor fugue of WTC1.[64] In the final version Bach placed slurs over the three-note motives in the theme. But copies by two of Bach's students (Gerber and Anonymous 5) also give a slide (*Schleifer*); the ornament forces a break in the slur but is perhaps necessary on the harpsichord if one is to give the effect of an expressive surge to the higher second note (Example 10.13).

EXAMPLE 10.13.   Sinfonia in F Minor BWV 795, bars 1–3a, with ornaments from DSB P 219 and from copy by H. N. Gerber

The F-minor piece has the most schematic design of any of the Sinfonias, foreshadowing the fugue in F♯ of WTC2. Much of the first half (bars 9–19), which modulates to A♭ and C minor, is later recapitulated with the upper voices exchanged (bars 22–32). Since the restatement is transposed a fifth lower, it takes the piece deep into "flat" territory, the most remote point being reached with the e♭♭' in bar 25—that is, the flat second degree (Neapolitan) of D♭.[65] The considerable amount of near-literal restatement creates a danger of monotony, but the four entrances of the subject in major keys introduce just enough of a change in color to save Bach's design. The change is so subtle, however, that two apparent emendations by Forkel, who may have "corrected" two bars to bring them into conformity with others, are enough to make the entire piece seem monochromatic for the unsuspecting user of older editions.[66] To be sure, the piece's prevailing color is very dark, established at the outset by harsh appoggiaturas and dissonant melodic intervals. The underlying progressions are perfectly conventional, but they are rarely spelled out in full, and odd intervals like the bare augmented fifth on the downbeat of bar 8 are "explained" only as the bar unfolds.

The special character of the F-Minor Sinfonia seems to invite speculative interpretation, and Chafe (1991, 43–51), after first making the most of the piece's potential for numerological interpretation—the "primary thematic material" appears in twenty-one bars, "episodic material" in fourteen, and so forth—finds that "the dynamic here is highly suggestive of Lutheran dogma regarding the efficacy of human works and achievements." But, as in the Pastorale BWV 590, interpretation along such lines seems arbitrary; not every chromatic piece, not even one with a highly schematic design or employing variations of the B-A-C-H motive, requires an "allegorical" explanation. The expressive essence of the music lies in the tension between the almost geometrical regularity of the formal design and the bold dissonance and tortuous melody at the level of detail.

Such boldness is, of course, a hallmark of Bach's style, something to which his students would have grown accustomed early on. They must also have rapidly grown used to the apparent awkwardness of his keyboard writing. If the B-Minor Sinfonia presents some of the worst of this, Sinfonia No. 14 (B$^\flat$) is not far behind. While Sinfonia No. 14 is relatively strict, its technical difficulties do not stem from schoolbook rigor in the counterpoint, for it treats the subject more freely than do any of the other contrapuntally oriented sinfonias. The subject is treated with particular freedom in two pseudo-strettos that occupy most of the last third of the piece (bars 17b–22, which constitute the climax). Difficulties arise for the player because Bach was unwilling to permit considerations of keyboard technique to dictate the voice-leading.

Yet Bach did make concessions to the exigencies of keyboard playing in bar 3, where both autographs show a tie joining tones that belong to two different voices; this illustrates a principle later codified by Emanuel Bach.[67] Another point of notation and performance practice is to be observed in Sinfonia No. 13 (A minor), whose short bars of $\frac{3}{8}$ time are grouped in CB (but not P 610) into pairs. Full bar-lines occur only after each pair of bars, which we might term a "double measure." Hence, as in several other similarly notated pieces (e.g., the first passepied of the English Suite in E minor), the true meter is evidently compound. Perhaps notation in normal $\frac{6}{8}$ time would have implied too fast a tempo; Sinfonia No. 13 contains some complicated rhythms involving thirty-seconds (see bar 36) that would seem rushed if taken too quickly. Hence, the use of double measures may signify a restrained tempo, but one in which each bar (of $\frac{3}{8}$) is still counted "in one."

11

The Well-Tempered Clavier, *Part 1*

The *Well-Tempered Clavier* (WTC) is probably Bach's most famous if not most widely played work. This was already true during the half-century following his death; dozens of manuscript copies survive from that period, and the publication of three editions at the beginning of the nineteenth century was one of the first manifestations of the so-called Bach Revival.[1] No doubt the work's novel organization and its usefulness as a sort of textbook in composition and keyboard performance furthered its popularity at a time when manuals on fugue and other theoretical writings on music were being issued with increasing frequency. Bach's personal fame as a keyboard player as well as that of his students must also have encouraged the work's dissemination; other Bach keyboard works remained available, but the WTC may have seemed a sort of official compendium of examples by a recognized keyboard player of unparalleled ability and a master of the arcane art of strict counterpoint.

Of course the WTC is much more than a compendium of contrapuntal devices, a role belonging more properly to the *Art of Fugue*. And, as useful as both the preludes and the fugues may be as exercises for students, their importance (and their real usefulness in teaching) lies in the richness and variety of their musical content. For the WTC is a diverse set of keyboard pieces united only by their descent from the old multisectional praeludium, now composed of two distinct movements. Within this format Bach was free to write in virtually any of the keyboard forms and styles available to him: dances, virtuoso improvisations, quasi-vocal pieces in *stile antico*, even sonata movements. Especially in WTC1, the prelude is often shorter and less substantial than the fugue, but even in Part 1 the relationship between the two movements is sometimes reversed, with the prelude equal to or larger than the fugue. Even when short, the prelude remains a self-contained composition; eleven of the preludes appeared separately in the *Clavier-Büchlein vor William Friedemann Bach* (CB).

It has become customary to stress the "educational" and "private" character of the WTC (Rosen 1990, 50), in contrast to the "public" character of the preludes and fugues for organ. Many movements indeed lack an outwardly virtuoso character, evoking instead the ricercars and fantasias of seventeenth-century composers like Frescobaldi and Froberger, or recalling the simple keyboard fugues—some with preludes—found in earlier teaching collections. But the WTC contains numerous virtuoso elements, and the implied distinction between "private" and "public" styles in Bach's keyboard output is far from clear. If the requirement of organ pedals is taken as an indication of "public" intention, then this intention already characterizes the *Ariadne musica neo-organoedum* of J. C. F. Fischer.[2] Though most of the twenty preludes and fugues in Fischer's collection have simple pedal parts, in other respects the work might have furnished a direct model for the WTC. Bach apparently borrowed at least two subjects from Fischer, but since Fischer himself might have borrowed, one cannot be sure that he was Bach's source.[3] In any case the plan of Fischer's work is likely to have influenced Bach, who may have taken from it the original ordering scheme for the WTC. Fischer placed each minor key (except for C) prior to the corresponding major key, and a similar arrangement was used for three of the pairs of preludes and fugues in an early copy of WTC1.[4]

Musically the WTC differs greatly from Fischer's collection and other comparable sets. The didactic function of those works is emphasized by the brevity of the individual pieces and the simplicity of the fugue subjects, which often resemble the themes (sometimes chant-derived) of the short *fughetti* and versets employed in liturgical organ playing.[5] The individual movements of the WTC possess far greater dimensions, and while Bach avoids an ostentatiously virtuoso style—there are no movements directly modeled after the concerto—he also avoids a condescending didactic tone.

Another distinction between the WTC and its models is the sheer diversity of the individual pieces in Bach's work. Though no doubt deliberately intended, the diversity may also reflect the history of the work, which may have grown out of a heterogeneous repertory of teaching pieces composed over a certain period of time. A few movements in Part 1, notably the A-minor fugue, have often been observed to be archaic in style and awkwardly written in some passages, and thus likely to have been composed relatively early, perhaps at Weimar. The entire work clearly went through several stages of revision both before and after Bach wrote out the famous autograph of Part 1 (DSB P 415), which bears the date 1722.[6] While 1722 is, therefore, usually given as the date of WTC1, the collection must have existed for some time previously, if not as an integral work, then as a group of separate preludes and fugues. This was certainly the case with Part 2, for which Bach probably never prepared an integral fair-copy manuscript (see Chapter 12).

Bach's compilation of WTC1 was evidently part of the same ongoing pedagogic project that included the assembly of the *Orgelbüchlein* at Weimar and the composition and fair copy of the Inventions and Sinfonias at Cöthen. As in those works, Bach prepared an explanatory title-page:

> The Well-Tempered Keyboard [*Clavier*], or Preludes and Fugues through all tones and semitones, including those with a major third or Ut-Re-Mi as well as those with a minor third or Re-Mi-Fa. For the profit and use of musical youth desiring instruction, and especially for the pastime of those who are already skilled in this study, composed and prepared by Johann Sebastian Bach.[7]

Bach's title puts the emphasis on the work's use of all available tonalities. While his way of explaining this now seems unduly verbose, it is likely that the vocabulary of the day did not permit any simpler way of expressing his meaning with complete clarity. Bach had to be quite precise about what he meant by all keys, since earlier collections like Fischer's had excluded certain rarely encountered tonalities (e.g., C♯), which were unusable in many older tuning systems. It may not have been obvious to every musician that such keys even existed; after all, they had been unknown prior to the Baroque. More or less comparable collections of keyboard pieces organized according to mode had been compiled and published, however, from the sixteenth century onward. By Bach's day, while the number of modes had been effectively reduced to two, the number of major and minor keys in frequent use had expanded considerably since the early Baroque, and Bach's inclusion in the WTC of all twenty-four theoretical possibilities was a logical step. Bach's own music modulates to every available key, but outside of the WTC the most "remote" tonic keys used in his keyboard music are those with signatures of four sharps or flats.[8] At Leipzig (and perhaps elsewhere) organists had to contend with more difficult keys, since the organ was treated as a transposing instrument.

Bach was hardly alone in his concern with providing students with examples of music in all keys. Mattheson's *Exemplarische Organisten-Probe*, published in 1719, contained two figured bass exercises in each key. Bach may also have known Gottfried Kirchhoff's *A B C Musical* (now lost), which reportedly contained preludes and fugues in all keys (see Appendix A, under BWV 907–8); Bach presumably met Kirchhoff, who was organist at Halle, during his visit there in 1716. It is often supposed that such collections were made possible by the invention of the "well-tempered" tuning system announced in Bach's title. But the real explanation lies in the increasing use and toleration of "remote" keys in eighteenth-century music, for, as Mark Lindley (1989b, 19ff.) has shown, equal temperament had been known and used for centuries, though more on plucked and bowed strings than on keyboard instruments.

The word *wohltemperierte* seems to have been used mainly in connection with keyboard temperament, referring not to a particular tuning system, such as equal temperament, but to any one that left all tonalities usable. Efforts have been made to prove that the WTC calls for one "well-tempered" system or another, but the arguments tend to rely on dubious "internal evidence" and debatable assumptions.[9] Besides, some of the pieces in Part 2 were transposed from their original keys, and there are indications that this was also the case in Part 1. It seems unlikely that Bach would have done this had he expected transposition to lead to a significantly different sound (due to an "unequal" temperament) or to elicit different affective associations. Still, the pragmatic approach to tuning doubtless taken by Bach probably left subtle distinctions between keys. If so, the scales of "remote" keys like C♯ major and E♭ minor would presumably have had relatively sharp major thirds, so that even the tonic triad and other consonances would have sounded rougher, a little less sonorous, than in more "natural" tonalities.

"Temperament" is not the only word in the title requiring interpretation; *Clavier* is, of course, equally ambiguous. Here the word *Clavier* probably refers not to any particular instrument but to the keyboard itself, tuned in a certain way. Certainly the translation *Well-Tempered Clavichord* is incorrect, at best reflecting usage in the later eighteenth century, when the word often did mean the clavichord specifically.[10] Williams (1983a, 50) finds that some of the more galant pieces in the WTC are suited to the fortepiano; if so, they might be even more suited to the clavichord. But while either instrument—or the modern piano—could be used to shape beautifully the melodic line of, say, the prelude in G$^{\sharp}$ minor of Part 2 or the C$^{\sharp}$-minor preludes of both books, neither clavichord nor fortepiano is particularly suited for clearly articulating inner or lower voices in a contrapuntal texture. In any case, fortepianos and clavichords were not in a very advanced stage of development when WTC1 was assembled; fretted clavichords, for example, would not have been suitable in certain keys.

Thus, the only serious alternative to the harpsichord would, as in the earlier works, have been the organ—provided that the one in town was "well tempered." The pedal parts in Fischer's *Ariadne musica* show that preludes and fugues of an apparently pedagogic nature might have found use during church services or perhaps even in recitals. An early copy of WTC1 (SPK P 401) includes the word *manualiter* in the titles of most of the pieces, and the word has been taken as an indication for organ use (by Marshall 1986)—but it is not found in the autograph. This should not discourage organists from playing certain pieces; the archaic fugue in C$^{\sharp}$ minor of WTC1 goes splendidly on an organ equipped with low C$^{\sharp}$ (rare in Bach's day), and the fugue in E$^{\flat}$ of Book 2 exists in an apparent organ arrangement.[11] But the harpsichord, as Williams (1983a, 51) argues convincingly, remains the only instrument suitable for the work as a whole. A few passages, notably the pedal-point at the end of the A-minor fugue of Part 1, cannot be played and sustained as written without organ pedals, but there are long-held pedal-points in other works surely meant for harpsichord (see Chapter 2, Note 8). In any case, use of organ pedals would not solve all the performance problems posed by this particular piece (see discussion below).

Today pianists may be inclined to agree with Rosen (1990, 50) that theirs is the instrument that "will deliver Bach's original conception to the public most adequately." But this presupposes "public presentation in large halls"—and even pianists rarely play the WTC nowadays in anything larger than a recital hall, where a harpsichord presumably would come closer to Bach's "original conception." Rather than be overly concerned with which instrument is best suited to the music, pianists might, as in other works, emulate the better qualities of harpsichord performance: clean and thoughtfully worked out articulation, expressive (not mechanical) ornamentation, and disciplined rhythmic freedom.

The Styles of the Well-Tempered Clavier

Although the two parts of the WTC were assembled at different times, their heterogeneous content makes it difficult to characterize their style in general terms or to find clear stylistic distinctions between them. By the same token, the efforts that have been made since Forkel (1802, 55/BR, 341–42) to find one book or the other superior or more consistent in quality seem arbitrary. Still, lines can be drawn in the preludes; Part 1 contains only a single prelude in binary form (that is, with a central double bar), while Part 2 contains ten. On the other hand, Part 1 contains a greater number of fugues in four voices—four being the traditional number of voices for a learned keyboard ricercar or canzona—and only Part 1 contains any fugues (two) in five voices. Part 2 seems to contain a greater number of galant movements, but Part 1 already contains several fugues with prominent galant elements—dance rhythms, expressive "sigh" motives, and so forth—and only Part 1 includes a fugue in the minimum number of voices possible (two).

Although Bach apparently experimented with different ordering schemes for the pairs of Part 1, from the outset he must have followed his predecessors by arranging pieces according to tonality, not by the musical characteristics of individual movements. But it is probably not a coincidence that the volume opens with a relatively simple prelude and closes with one of the longest and most profound of the four-part fugues. No such plan is evident in Part 2, however, and in both books even the pairings of movements sometimes seem incongruous. For example, in WTC1 the A-minor fugue seems inordinately long for its prelude, while the prelude in E^b is much longer and its four parts lead to greater contrapuntal elaboration than occurs in the three-part fugue. In Part 2 the prelude in B^b dwarfs its fugue. One can overlook such discrepancies, since the level of musical accomplishment is invariably so high (though some would demur in the case of the A-minor pair). These examples might have arisen when Bach brought together pieces that had been composed separately, as he is known to have done in WTC2. In WTC1 he may also have had to transpose pieces in order to fill in gaps (as he certainly did in Part 2). But in both books close resemblances between pieces in some of the more "remote" keys—in Part 1, the preludes in $C^\sharp$ and $G^\sharp$ minor or the fugues in $C^\sharp$ and $F^\sharp$ major—could reflect their having been composed in rapid succession specifically for inclusion in the WTC.

Attempts have been made to find some classification scheme other than by key in the ninety-six movements of the two books, primarily by grouping the preludes and fugues into various categories. But few of the pieces belong to any one well-defined genre, instead drawing elements from several different ones. Even the basic distinction between prelude and fugue is blurred by two preludes (E^b in WTC1, $C^\sharp$ in WTC2) that are really self-contained preludes with fugues. Many of the simpler preludes of WTC1 open with passage-work composing out a standard harmonic progression, a type of writing probably descended from improvisatory arpeggiando preludes, like the one prefacing the Fugue in A Minor BWV 944. In the WTC the arpeggiation is always written out—the notation is not left in the form of chords to be broken however the player wishes—and the motives used in the arpeggiation may be intensively developed in a later section of the piece. Other preludes depart from the arpeggiando model entirely and instead resemble Bach's inventions or sinfonias; many of the binary preludes of WTC2 are in effect sonata movements.

The fugues are traditionally distinguished by the number of voices. This is less arbitrary than it may seem, as the fugues in four and five parts tend to be more conservative in style than those in two or three. There are exceptions, however: In WTC1 the three-part fugue in D$^\sharp$ minor is very severe and archaic, while the four-part fugues in A$^\flat$ and B are relatively light. Some commentators (e.g., Kunze 1969) have sought to place the fugues into more precisely drawn categories, distinguishing "ricercar" fugues, *fugae patheticae*, *fugae graves*, and other types. The terminology comes from Walther (1732, 265–67), but it seems more descriptive than prescriptive and does not necessarily refer to well-defined or commonly recognized genres of fugue as such.

In any case, Walther's terms describe only the musical surface and have no bearing on the large structure. The fugues of the WTC draw on the full range of structures used in Bach's earlier fugues, excepting only Da Capo and ritornello forms. They also include a surprising number of designs incorporating elements of sonata form. Curiously, while many more preludes in WTC2 than in WTC1 employ some simple variety of sonata form, Part 1 seems to contain a greater number of *fugues* adopting elements of sonata form. One such element is a strongly articulated entrance of the subject in the tonic at the beginning of the final section, which may also contain extensive amounts of recapitulation.[12] Perhaps, by the time Bach compiled Part 2, he had grown more attracted to fugues emphasizing contrapuntal work as such and was less interested in assimilating fugue to a type of formal design that was rapidly becoming the norm in other types of composition. Still, it is helpful to analyze fugues as well as preludes in terms of their tonal designs and recapitulatory patterns. While there are a few fugues in both books whose forms are defined strictly by the use in successive sections of different contrapuntal techniques (inversion, stretto, etc.), these form a small minority. Even in these pieces it would be a mistake to base an analysis solely on the imitative techniques employed or on the alternation (if present) between expositions and episodes; formal design in Bach's fugues goes deeper than that.

Text, Sources, and Editions

Few of Bach's keyboard works have histories as well documented as that of WTC1. While Bach's composing scores are, as usual, lost, several manuscripts give texts predating the fair-copy autograph, and many other copies were made prior to Bach's final revisions. Hence, it is possible to reconstruct in some detail the revisions made in each movement. This had already been done to some degree in the nineteenth century, and Kroll's edition of both parts of the WTC in BG 14 remains a remarkable piece of scholarship.[13] But early editors, including Kroll, were hampered by the unavailability of many sources (e.g., CB) and the confusion of copies with autographs.[14] Most subsequent editions were based on Kroll's, although that of Tovey (1924) remains valuable for its analytic commentary. More than a century passed, however, before the appearance of a modern critical text (Dehnhard 1977–83); Dürr has since edited Part 1 (in NBA V/6.1), and at this writing a new edition by Richard D. P. Jones of Parts 1–2 is forthcoming.

Naturally, both modern editions of WTC1 follow the autograph.[15] But they also give a selection of the earlier readings, and Dürr even includes, in the second section of his volume, the complete text of WTC1 in its earliest known version.[16] The eleven preludes included in the CB represent slightly later versions, and these can be consulted in NBA V/5.[17] Table 11–1 lists some of the most important sources, indicating the version or versions preserved in each.[18]

TABLE 11–1.   WTC1: Stages of Revision and Chief Sources

Stage	Source	Copyist, Date	Comment
α1	Konwitschny ms.	?2d half 18th cent.	Owned by Franz Konwitschny (1901–62); entries by Forkel
α1*	SPK P 212**	Forkel	
α2	CB**	WFB, JSB, 1720–21	Preludes: C c d D e E F
α3	CB**	WFB, JSB, 1720–21	Preludes: C♯ c♯ e♭ f
α3	SPK P 401	Anonymous 5, 1722–23	Later altered to give readings of A1
A1–4	DSB P 415	JSB, 1722, rev. 1732, 1736 or later, 1744	Revisions fall into 3 main layers; dating subject to review
A1*	SPK P 1074	J. G. Walther, ?1730s	Some readings pre-A1
A1	NL DHgm 69 D 14**	Meissner, ca. 1727 or later	Latter portion of composite ms.
A1	US BER	H. N. Gerber et al.	
A2*	DSB P 202	AMB, Agricola (1740), C. H. E. Müller (ca. 1800)	Müller replaced missing portion of original ms.
A2	Hs MB1974	2d half 18th cent.	Includes WTC2 (titles of Parts 1 and 2 exchanged)
A2	LEm Poel. 34	1st half 18th cent.	?autograph entry in prelude in G
A2	NL DHgm 69 D 14**	1st half or mid-18th cent.	Initial portion of composite ms.
A3	LEm Scheibner 6	ca. 1800	
A3*	SPK P 402	Altnikol, 1755	Includes WTC2
A4	DSB AmB 49	Anonymous 403	?owned by Kirnberger
A4	SPK AmB 57/1	Anonymous 402	Analytical entries by Kirnberger

AMB = Anna Magdalena Bach   JSB = Johann Sebastian Bach
WFB = Wilhelm Friedemann Bach
*contains mixed, arbitrary, or erroneous readings
**incomplete

Bach's revisions in WTC1 are interesting not only for their own sake but because they help explain certain oddities in a number of pieces, particularly those preludes that were expanded for the version of the fair-copy autograph.[19] Some of the preludes betray traces of the revision in a sudden change of texture or material at the beginning of the interpolated passages, but the problem, if it is one, is hardly noticeable. Elsewhere Bach's revisions affected only details, but like his revisions in other works, they reveal his continual effort toward perfecting his texts.

Prelude and Fugue in C, BWV 846

The C-major prelude, like the arpeggiando prelude in the same key near the beginning of Friedemann's CB (BWV 924), consists largely of a series of chords broken in a simple and straightforward pattern. While it may be simple, the prelude was not necessarily intended to be delicate, an impression that has perhaps arisen from so many musicians' first encountering this piece at the opening of what they have been taught to call the Well-Tempered "Clavichord." The fugue is a full-textured piece in four parts that calls, on the harpsichord, for a strong registration. There is no reason the prelude cannot be registered in similar fashion and played quickly enough to make the little flourish at the end sound brilliant.

In the earliest version the arpeggiation was not written out. But the care with which Bach indicated each and every note of the figuration in the final version suggests that his notation should be taken at its word. For harpsichordists this implies not holding out any notes beyond their written values, and this in turn leads to a distinct articulation of each harmony. Pianists might consider playing without pedal, since the pedal tends to reduce the figuration to a vapid blur.

Despite its apparent simplicity, the prelude evidently cost Bach some trouble. It exists in at least two distinct versions, the earliest of which was probably once present in CB (where erasures obscure the original reading). Friedemann's copy subsequently underwent alterations by both him and his father, but its text was never brought fully into line with that of the autograph or later copies. Thus, what looks like an intermediate version in CB may actually be only an incompletely updated copy of the early version.[20] In any case the most important revision, not entered into CB, was the extension of the dominant pedal-point in the final version.[21]

Because this type of prelude seems at first to consist of nothing more than a series of broken chords, its phrasing—that is, its form, understood as a series of modulating phrases—tends not to receive due attention. Like most short pieces, the prelude falls into distinct phrases usually ending in cadences, as shown in Table 11–2. While the essential outlines of this form are already evident in the earliest version, the structure is more clearly articulated in the final version. The arrival on the dominant pedal at bar 24 was strengthened by the insertion of bar 23, and the pedal-point itself was lengthened.[22] The final tonic harmony was also extended, forming a short coda (bars 32–35). And two arrivals earlier in the piece (on G and C, respectively) were strengthened by the insertion of bars 11 and 19, which eliminated the elided phrase-endings originally found at those points.

TABLE 11–2. Structure of the C-Major Prelude (WTC1)

Version of . . .	Number of bars in each section						Total
Konwitschny ms.:	4	5	7	3	4	1	24
CB (after correction):	4	7	8	3	4	1	27
P 415:	4	7	8	4	8	4	35
Key or cadence:	C	→	G→	C→	C:V→	I	
Bar number (P 415):	1	4	12	20	24	32	

The insertion of bar 23 introduced what has become a famous ambiguity, since this is the only bar in the main body of the final version that contains a passing tone. The problem is to determine which of the five notes in the bar is the passing tone. If the passing note is c′, then the harmony is to be understood as a diminished chord ($^6_{2+}$); if b, then the harmony is a suspended supertonic (II^6_3), a form of the subdominant (Example 11.1).[23] At the late stage of revision at which Bach added bar 23,

EXAMPLE 11.1.   Prelude in C, BWV 846/1, bars 22–24:
(a) earliest version; (b) final version; (c) analysis of final version

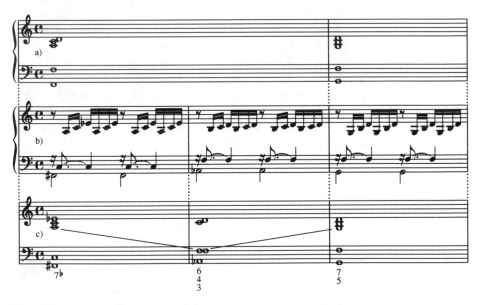

he was probably writing out the arpeggiation of each measure, that is, not leaving the notation in the form of whole-note chords. Thus, Bach himself may never have needed to decide which tone is the passing note, and the ambiguity might have been deliberate (as argued in Cone 1968). The ambiguity is a neat way of sidestepping a problem of voice-leading: In the added bar 23 there is no graceful way to maintain the prevailing five-part texture without introducing a momentary unison doubling (see Example 11.1c). But a five-note chord, without doublings, is necessary if the rhythmic pattern of the arpeggiation is to be maintained.[24]

Bach also revised the fugue, but only after copying it into P 415. The subject originally moved in quarters and eighths, and the dotted rhythm on the third beat is the result of a revision that was extended throughout the fugue.[25] Marpurg still quoted the subject in its original form in his *Abhandlung von der Fuge*,[26] showing the first two entries as an example of a subject that does not leave the tonic (Example 11.2).

EXAMPLE 11.2.   Fugue in C, BWV 846/2, early version, bars 1–4a

The almost pure diatonicism of the opening exposition perhaps reflects the status of C major as a "natural" key (neither "sharp" nor "flat") and seems to borrow from the restrained harmonic style of the *stile antico*. Indeed, the fugue possesses a modal quality, or at least a weakened sense of tonality, inasmuch as the dominant plays a less prominent role in the overall design than does the relative minor. Nowhere does the fugue make a strong arrival on the dominant, the only strong cadences being to the relative minor (at the midpoint) and to the supertonic (bar 19b). Moreover, while not notated *alla breve*, the fugue also recalls certain ricercars of the earlier Baroque in its preoccupation with a particular contrapuntal device—here, stretto, which is used with special intensity after the midpoint (bar 14).

Although not quite as "vocal" in quality as a true *stile antico* fugue, this one raises similar interpretive questions. For example, how detached or legato should one play the subject? The latter somewhat resembles the subjects of Bach's choral fugues on biblical texts; since Bach usually sets such subjects syllabically, articulate rather than legato performance would seem appropriate, at least if one is to maintain the analogy to choral writing (Example 11.3). Tempo might also be judged in vocal

EXAMPLE 11.3.   *Dazu ist erschienen der Sohn Gottes* BWV 40, first movement, bars 29–30 (tenor)

Da - zu   ist   er - schie-nen der Sohn Got   -   tes,

terms, a good pace being one that permits singing the subject (i.e., the alto to the e' on the third beat of bar 2) in one breath. A slow, legato presentation is apt to seem ponderous, and Bach's own alteration of the rhythm might have been calculated to make the subject lighter and the embellishment of the falling half-step (f', e') more graceful. The closing phrase bars 26–27 employs an ascending formula also used in the fugue in G (BWV 860/2) and the organ chorale *Allein Gott in der Höh' sei Ehr'* BWV 663. This does not mean that the fugue has any religious significance but rather that it shares some of the chorale's festive character and should not be interpreted too severely.

Prelude and Fugue in C Minor BWV 847

The second prelude, like the first, is essentially a series of arpeggiations, although the motive used here to compose out each harmony is more complex and more often varied. The minor key, the rushing two-part counterpoint, and the cadenza-like passages in the final section make this a busy piece, but it surely ought to be played with fire and not as an anticipation of twentieth-century (or even nineteenth-century) machinery. As in the C-major prelude, the phrases into which the apparently seamless surface is organized are not hard to discern. Even on the harpsichord certain dynamic effects can be expressed; for example, one can dwell momentarily on the downbeats of bars 6, 8, and 10, thus bringing out the dissonances (2-chords) at these points; each dissonance resolves on the following downbeat. The overall design is similar to that of the previous prelude: an opening four-bar cadence to the tonic, followed by modulations that reach the relative major (bar 14) and later dominant and tonic pedal-points.

Most of the coda (from bar 25), including the cadenzalike passage at bar 28, was the product of Bach's revisions.[27] Cadenzalike passages were also added in at least four other preludes; as in the prelude in E minor, one of the passages here is accompanied by the tempo indication *presto* (at bar 28). Praeludium 15 in Fischer's *Ariadne musica* shows a similar alternation between presto and adagio, which is probably to say between more and less strictly measured passages. Bach's *presto* does not necessarily indicate an acceleration, for he might have expected the arpeggiando passage (bars 25–27) just preceding the tempo mark to be played freely. If so, *presto* here actually means something like *a tempo*, while the word *adagio* in the quasi-cadenza at bar 34 signifies free rhythm more than any particular tempo.[28]

The fugue, if not exactly galant, is in the relatively light style that Bach favored in WTC1 for the three-part fugues, especially in the episodes. There are four of these, and although very short they form clearly articulated, distinct sections; the first episode (bars 9–11) is eventually recapitulated a fifth lower (bars 22–23). The subject enters in the tonic just prior to the last episode with some of the force of a sonata-form return; indeed the passage (bars 20–21) is a restatement of bars 7–8 with the three contrapuntal lines redistributed. Bach must have recognized the structural significance of this entrance, for in the revised version of 1722 he made it more impressive by transposing the bass to the lower octave.[29]

The fugue has been a favorite one for analysts, apparently beginning with Bach himself. Bach himself may have been responsible for the analytical entries in a copy by the student known as Anonymous 5, who has been tentatively identified as the organist Johann Schneider.[30] The entries are limited to indications of key and vertical intervals, using a system of notation that seems to anticipate that later used by Kirnberger in analyzing two other pieces from WTC1.[31] The markings in P 401 include the letter "f" indicating what may have been regarded as the "fundamental" note—that is, the tonic—for each passage. Each additional note in the lowest voice bears a number indicating its interval from the fundamental note, and each note in the upper voices bears a number indicating its interval from the bass (Example 11.4).[32]

EXAMPLE 11.4.   Fugue in C Minor BWV 847/2, bars 7–8, from DSB P 401

Unfortunately, the analysis in P 401 is concerned strictly with the local intervalic context and provides little clue as to how Bach viewed the larger structure of the fugue. Schenker saw the fugue as essentially bipartite, dividing it in half at the cadence to the dominant in bar 17.[33] But the recapitulatory design seems to favor a tripartite interpretation, with divisions at bars 11 and 20. It must be pointed out, however, that the elided phrasing characteristic of fugues—as opposed to dances or sonata forms—tends to make analytical decisions about "bipartite" or "tripartite" form rather arbitrary in the absence of decisive articulations. Bach himself might not have had a distinct plan in mind when he began composing a fugue of the present sort. As noted above, he apparently recognized the importance of the "return" at bar 20b only after writing it, and, notwithstanding the clear plans of some pieces, in others his compositional process may have been improvisatory, a logical, clearly articulated form emerging only in the course of composition. Siegele (1989) has attempted to reconstruct " 'the steps Bach took' in composing the [present] work," but each step in the reconstruction is doubtful, beginning with the initial assumption that Bach planned such things as the order of entries prior to composing. Where we do possess early versions of Bach's fugues, we find that he sometimes added whole sections, as in the fugue in A♭ in WTC2. Even the opening exposition could be a later addition, as in Contrapunctus 10 from the *Art of Fugue*. The symmetrical structure of the present piece may seem to leave little possibility of ever having been fundamentally altered. But it is possible to imagine a hypothetical early version skipping from the downbeat of bar 20 to the middle of bar 26, that is, lacking the recapitulation and ending with the tonic arrival now in the middle of bar 29.

Prelude and Fugue in C♯, BWV 848

The prelude in C♯ again consists largely of arpeggiated figuration. It runs most of its course quite lightly, but at the final cadence (as in several others in WTC1) there appear a few heavy, full-voiced chords. These suggest that, as in the prelude in C, it is wrong to think of the piece as delicate or quiet. On the harpsichord, a full registration may again be in order, the lightness appropriate to the opening sections being achieved through clean articulation—and by not succumbing to the mistaken belief that each note of a broken chord must be sustained beyond its written value. Pianists might again consider holding back on the pedal, although a uniform staccato is bound to sound mechanical; the judicious introduction of short slurs and tenuto notes within the moving lines may well be appropriate.

This prelude was another of those which Bach extended when it was incorporated into the WTC.[34] Unlike the C♯-major prelude in WTC2, this one was not, so far as is known, originally in a simpler key (i.e., C). Its very design seems calculated to force the player into increasingly difficult keys, since the original portion of the piece (through bar 62) consists essentially of sequences moving about the circle of fifths, first upward from C♯ to A♯ minor (bar 31), then downward to F♯ (bar 47). The portion added in the later version (bars 63–98) is a greatly extended prolongation of the original dominant pedal, using a new variety of figuration; without the interpolation the piece falls into four nearly equal sections (these begin at bars 1, 17, 31, and 47).

The fugue is not only one of the liveliest and most galant in WTC1, but it includes one of the most extensive sonata-style recapitulation sections. Indeed, the last page (bars 42–55) consists largely of material, both expository and episodic, drawn with relatively little alteration from the first section (bars 1–11)—that is, the portion of the piece that moves from tonic to dominant, as in a sonata exposition. While it would be misleading to speak of the fugue as being *in* sonata form, the piece gives an impression of neatness and clarity that is in keeping with galant sonata style. For this reason it might be regarded as one of the most modern pieces in the WTC.

Prelude and Fugue in C♯ Minor BWV 849

The C♯-minor pair is one of the great masterpieces of WTC1. The length and seriousness of the prelude—the first example in WTC1 of what might be termed an "arioso" type—match that of the fugue, which is one of the two in five parts.

Despite its arioso melody, the prelude is polyphonic in texture, its design close to that of the inventions. It opens with exchanges of the subject between treble and tenor, and its essentially binary design was originally articulated by a restatement of the subject in the tenor at the beginning of the second half (Example 11.5). The underlying rhythm seems to be that of a siciliano, that is, a slow gigue. But the convolutions of the melodic lines obscure any dance character, and the periodic

EXAMPLE 11.5.   Prelude in C♯ Minor BWV 849/1, early
version (BWV 849a/1), bars 14–15 (corresponding to bars
14–17 of later version)

phrasing of the dance is replaced by long lines that avoid cadences. The coda, a later addition (though already present in the CB), begins with a deceptive cadence (bar 35) that holds off the final cadence for an additional four bars.

The tension inherent in the prelude's long phrases is likely to dissipate if the tempo is too slack; it seems best to maintain a true andante (that is, a "moving" tempo) that permits the underlying dance meter to be felt. Most of the ornaments and appoggiaturas were written down only as revisions to P 415; there is not a single ornament in the copy in the CB. One ornament, the arpeggio sign on a two-note chord in bar 34, may be puzzling; it probably signifies that a passing tone should be inserted. [35]

In the fugue, the form of the subject and the *alla breve* notation recall certain seventeenth-century ricercars, especially one in the same key by Froberger. [36] Ladewig (1991) notes the resemblance between the present fugue subject and that of Frescobaldi's Recercar I (from *Recercari et canzoni franzese* [Rome, 1615]) and finds further parallels between the two works, which can both be described as triple fugues. Bach clearly meant to compose a monumental work connected with the old tradition, and the result stands alongside the organ fugue in F (BWV 540/2) as a worthy predecessor of the second Kyrie of the B-Minor Mass and Bach's other late efforts in *stile antico*. As in the organ fugue, Bach eventually adds (bar 36) a second, livelier idea. But only the main subject is treated strictly. Both the second theme and a third one introduced later (bar 49) are closer to what we would call countersubjects, since they rarely occur except in combination with the original subject. [37] Indeed, while the introduction of the lively first countersubject at bar 36 makes the piece resemble a double fugue, its design from this point onward seems improvisatory, lacking the clear plan typical of Bach's fugues with multiple subjects. There is no modulating design, since the music never leaves the tonic for very long, and because the original subject is also never long absent, it cannot make a dramatic reentrance. A statement in the bass at the very bottom of Bach's *Clavier* (bar 73) may mark a second major divison, giving the piece a tripartite structure overall. But, as in the C-minor fugue, any analytical division into sections seems somewhat arbitrary except at bar 36. Still, the fugue never gives the impression of wandering aimlessly, and the final page achieves particular urgency through the use of stretto combined with some compelling chromatic progressions (bars 94ff.).

Like the introduction of the second subject, the strettos create the impression of rigorous counterpoint. But Bach's notation of the voice-leading in the stretto is ambiguous, and in the autograph it is impossible to trace the path of all five voices through bars 94–100 without positing voice-crossings and rests that Bach failed to make explicit. Evidently, Bach was more concerned here with the dramatic effect of stretto than with rigorous contrapuntal technique as such.[38] Despite its quasi-vocal character, the fugue remains true keyboard music, not an ersatz ensemble piece, even though an instrumental arrangement might "clarify" the voice-leading.[39]

The *antico* character of the fugue is perhaps reinforced by pedal markings in two copies, indicating the use of organ.[40] But many older organs, including the one at Leipzig, lacked the low C$^{\sharp}$ so crucial in bar 73.[41] In any case, organ style does not imply legato, and the diminished fourth in the subject (B$^{\sharp}$-e) might be marked by an especially distinct articulation of both notes. That Bach assumed such perfor-mance is evident from bar 15, where the simultaneous leaps in the three upper parts include the diminished fourth in the subject (here stated by the soprano). Legato would be impossible except with the aid of organ pedals (or, on piano, the damper pedal).

Prelude and Fugue in D, BWV 850

The prelude in D is again of the arpeggiando type, and like the preludes in C and C minor it opens with a variation on a simple cadential formula. But the harmony and the implied voice-leading soon grow quite complex, making it doubtful that this is a five-finger exercise to be tossed off at breakneck speed.

The prelude was heavily revised, and the restatement of the opening bars in the subdominant (bars 20–24) appears only in the later version. From a formal point of view the revisions are the most substantial in any piece of WTC1, since the inter-polation in the subdominant represents the insertion of an entire key area, not merely the extension of a dominant pedal-point. To be sure, as in other preludes the closing dominant pedal (from bar 27) was also extended to include a cadenzalike passage (bars 30b–34), and one should probably understand an implicit adagio at bar 33. In addition, it seems likely that all the chords in the penultimate bar should be arpeggiated, even though the autograph has but a single arpeggio sign, a late addition on the first chord in bar 34. Two other Bach preludes end in a similar manner without any arpeggio signs at all; these are the D-minor prelude of WTC1 and the prelude of the D-minor cello suite (BWV 1008). In each case it seems senseless to end with three or four thuds when broken chords would be more in character with the rest of the piece.

The fugue is a predecessor of Contrapunctus 6 (*in stile francese*) in the *Art of Fugue*. In addition, Bach's appropriation of overture style for a fugue points for-ward to his use of the same style for a chorale chorus in Cantata No. 20, com-posed at Leipzig in 1724 as the opening work in the great cycle of chorale cantatas. The present fugue is a much less pretentious work, despite its incessant dotted rhythms and energetic figures in thirty-seconds. It is also one of the least rigorous fugues in the WTC, abandoning the subject (save for its initial motive) two-thirds of the way through, after the cadence to E minor in bar 17. The absence of fugal rigor hardly weakens the piece musically, however, and it ends with a splendid series of flourishes in thirty-seconds—actually a stretto using the opening motive.

It is unclear exactly how the two rhythmic elements of the subject—the running thirty-seconds and the dotted eighths—are to be coordinated. One might be inclined to double dot each eighth, reducing the following sixteenth to a shorter value. But the episodes (bars 9–10, 17ff.) counsel against this, since there the dotted rhythms are set against steady sixteenths, and there is no reason that a single sixteenth following a dotted eighth in the alto or tenor should be any shorter than one of the continuous sixteenths in the treble. As in most overtures, the inclination to double dot eighth-notes may stem from too slow a tempo; a relatively quick pulse brings the dotted rhythms to life, especially if each dotted note is separated by a small articulation from the following note. It is also helpful to observe that the dotted figures come in pairs—that is, fall on alternating strong and weak beats—and that the flourish of thirty-seconds that opens the subject is an upbeat. Unfortunately, it is difficult to make this clear at the outset, and listeners will probably always hear the initial figure as a downbeat, as in the fugue in A$^\flat$ (discussed below). The ornaments found in some editions on beats 3 and 4 can aid in defining the meter, even though they may not be authentic.

Prelude and Fugue in D Minor BWV 851

The prelude in D minor is again of the arpeggiando type. The bass, which begins as a pedal-point, gradually grows more active and becomes quite expressive by bars 10–11, where it contains a series of "sigh" motives. The annotations in P 401 note the presence of $\frac{4}{2}$-chords on the even-numbered beats of these bars,[42] and the dissonances might be brought out by slurring the "sigh" figures in the bass—for example, the notes a, g and F, E in bar 10. This will be especially effective if the bass elsewhere is somewhat detached.

The early version ends with a chord (D/f$^\sharp$/a/d) on the downbeat of bar 15. The new version grows more contrapuntal in the added coda, introducing a third voice seven bars from the end. Like the "cadenza" in the Fifth Brandenburg Concerto, the coda culminates in a descending series of broken diminished chords, perhaps a favorite improvisatory formula of Bach's (and if so not a dependable index for dating either work).

The fugue seems at first glance to be one of those that systematically and rigorously explore the contrapuntal possibilities of its subject. But in fact its technique involves a rather free, kaleidoscopic permutation of three or four motivic fragments (as noted in Daverio n.d.). Many of the stretto and *inversus* statements are incomplete or inexact, and instead of having a "contrapuntal" design this is one of the clearest examples of a fugue in the binary version of early sonata form. There is a central arrival in the dominant (bar 21), and the phrase that closes the first half returns at the end in the tonic (bars 16–21 || 38–43). The introduction of the subject in stretto just after the central cadence (bar 22) recalls the similar procedure in the fugue in C. But by using the inversion of the subject at this point Bach also alludes to binary-form dances, especially gigues, that invert the subject in the second half, even though the inversion has already been heard once, at bar 14.

Despite its quasi-sonata form and three-voice texture, this is one of the more severe pieces in the WTC, not at all galant in style. The turning motives in subject and countersubject lead to a high level of passing dissonance, since the first note of such figures is generally an appoggiatura, and some sort of turn is present in virtually every bar of the piece. Yet, because the subject is essentially an elaboration of a mere two-chord progression (I, IV; sometimes V, I or V, II), the harmonic character of the fugue as a whole is somewhat static. Moreover, the only lasting modulation is the move to the dominant at the end of the first half.

Such a piece is perhaps most meaningful at a relatively slow tempo, which permits each dissonance to be clearly heard. The rhetorical quality of the subject, with its momentary pause in the second bar, will then also be more deeply felt. Articulation must be particularly precise at a relatively slow tempo, but readings of slurs and dots (as well as ornaments) are unusually problematical here. In the autograph, the slur in the second bar of the subject is almost certainly meant to cover all four sixteenths, but one source specifies a more mannered variety of articulation, with a staccato stroke on the first note and the slur over the next three.

The same source, which Dürr believes could have issued directly from the Bach circle, gives many other unique indications for articulation and trills.[43] These are placed with care and in an internally consistent manner throughout the fugue. Although this version was considered sufficiently plausible for inclusion in NBA V/6.1 (as Appendix 3), the aptness of some of the markings must be questioned. Substituting trills for turns in bars 9–11 is consistent with the subject but makes the passage harder to play; such consistency is suspiciously pedantic.[44] Equally suspicious are the slurs and staccato marks added on the turning figures in bars 4–5. Bach rarely ends a three-note slur on a nonchord tone, but that is the case in bar 5, where slur and dot are added as in bar 4, despite the altered harmonic context of the figure. The same articulation is repeated mechanically on each recurrence of this motive through the remainder of the piece (e.g., three times in bar 17), regardless of the harmony.

Prelude and Fugue in E♭, BWV 852

The pair in E♭ opens with what is perhaps the greatest prelude in the volume and the only one that eclipses its fugue in length and seriousness. This does not mean that the fugue is weak or insignificant, but its function is something like that of a gigue at the end of a suite, a relatively light concluding movement rather than the main event.

The prelude is often thought of as a sort of toccata, as it falls into several distinct sections, including an improvisatory opening. But the form is actually that of a double fugue, and the counterpoint has a richness and assuredness far in advance of that of Bach's *manualiter* toccatas. The opening section, which recalls several of

Fischer's preludes (especially the one in D), leads to an old-fashioned four-part fugato in ricercar style (bar 10). Thus, the first two sections constitute a little self-contained prelude and fughetta, and perhaps at some early stage of its history it was just that, ending around bar 25 (Example 11.6). But the earliest surviving

EXAMPLE 11.6.   Prelude in E$^\flat$, BWV 852, hypothetical early version: final cadence (corresponding to bars 23–25 of later version)

version already presents the piece in essentially its familiar form, save for the absence of bars 3–4.[45] At bar 25 the principal motivic ideas of the two preceding sections are converted into full-fledged fugue subjects (or subject and countersubject), which are now presented simultaneously as in the final section of a double fugue.[46] The two rising fourths in the second subject give it a surging quality that is most completely realized in the final section. Beginning in a low tessitura (bar 49b), the section gradually climbs to the top note on Bach's *Clavier* (bar 59), producing a splendid effect repeated in a number of fugues that likewise climb to a high point shortly before the final reentrance of the bass (cf. the fugue in F minor).

The prelude is not easy to play, and it is difficult to find a single tempo suitable for the two very different opening ideas. But any change of tempo (such as that called for in Keller 1965, 72) damages the piece's coherence and contradicts a remark added—in an unidentified hand—in the autograph at bar 10. The second section, according to this remark, is *not* an *alla breve*, which would imply a quicker tempo as the pulse shifted to the half-note.[47]

The prelude ends following a magnificent cadential passage (bars 64–67) in which the two upper parts ascend in stretto; the soprano here happens to include a quotation of the subject of the C$^\sharp$-minor fugue (bars 66–67). This is no doubt a coincidence; so too the fact that the descending chromatic lines in the coda (D$^\flat$, C, C$^\flat$, B$^\flat$) recur at the end of the fugue (bar 37). Nevertheless, the chromaticism helps join together the two otherwise dissimilar movements.

The fugue, while in three parts, is not all lightness and *galanterie*. The chromatic element enters in the bridge between the last two entries in the first exposition (bars 4b–5). But the essentially witty quality of the fugue is clear from the pause that divides the subject into two halves. Though perhaps descended from the serious "rhetorical" gestures in the subjects of some earlier works (e.g., the fugue of the C-Minor Toccata), this pause seems almost flippant. It is, however, elevated to a dramatic event in the final statement of the subject (bar 34), when the two accompanying voices join the subject in pausing at this point.

The fugue comes remarkably close to Da Capo form, though it lacks the full concerto character of the virtuoso fugues in Da Capo form for organ, lute, and violin, or of the preludes of the English Suites. The central portion of the fugue consists of an exposition in minor keys (bars 17b–22) framed by two episodes. The third section (from bar 26) is, like the first, firmly in the tonic, much of it consisting of untransposed recapitulation (bars 29–35a || 6–12a, with voices exchanged).

Prelude and Fugue in E♭ Minor BWV 853

Like the Prelude and Fugue in C♯ minor, this pair in another "difficult" key immediately declares itself to be one of the more ambitious in WTC1. The prelude is an impressive embellished adagio, while the fugue, although in only three voices, is the first in the volume to systematically apply various contrapuntal techniques to the subject.

Prototypes for the prelude can be found in the slow movements of the Italian concertos transcribed by Bach (see Chapter 8). Nevertheless, the opening harmonic progression is the same one employed in many other preludes (e.g., in C), and the form is binary. Like the prelude in C♯ minor, it was extended by the addition of a coda after a deceptive cadence (bar 29). Friedemann Bach copied the later version, or at least as much as he could fit onto three pages in CB. But the unusual number of corrections suggests that he was reading from a heavily revised autograph, where embellishments might have been sketched without their rhythms being clearly indicated, as in the autograph of Sinfonia No. 5 (in DSB P 610). Indeed, the notation of the last beat of bar 13, containing one of Bach's most characteristic melodic embellishments, remained ungrammatical even after correction in the autograph.[48]

Such notation points to the necessity of improvisatory freedom in the rhythm of the embellishments. But it also counsels against adopting too slow a tempo, for the embellishments cease to be embellishments if the half-note pulse is subdivided with mathematical precision, as is likely to happen when the speed drops below a certain minimum. In both Friedemann's and Sebastian's copies the sixteenths are generally not broken up into groups of four, as in modern editions, but are beamed in units of eight, implying that each group remains a single unbroken gesture. Played with an undivided half-note pulse (and a tempo about double that under which the piece often languishes), the prelude ceases to be merely a dolorous arioso and can achieve real tragic grandeur.

Bach notated the fugue in D♯ minor, perhaps to facilitate transposition from an earlier version in D minor. In the hypothetical D-minor version, the ascending scale in bar 15 would have ascended to c''' instead of faltering on a suspension. The latter would have become necessary only when the transposition took the top note of the scale (c♯'''') above the upper limit of the *Clavier* used in the WTC.[49] The fugue falls into three main sections of almost equal length; these present the subject in its prime form, then in inverted (bar 30) and augmented (bar 61b) forms. Each section is subdivided into ordinary and stretto expositions.

A curious irregularity in the first two strettos proves to be of great formal signifi-cance. Each of these strettos contains an anomalous entry, an incomplete statement of the subject in a sort of quasi-augmentation. The first two of these quasi-augmented entries (bar 24, middle voice; bar 48, treble) anticipate the true aug-mentation of the subject in the last section. Hence, the fugue achieves its culmination when the prime, augmented, and quasi-augmented forms are all com-bined in stretto (bar 77).

The process is a rather abstruse one, unlikely to be sensed by the listener no matter how valiantly the performer attempts to bring it out. In many Bach fugues the introduction of more sophisticated or complex contrapuntal procedures coin-cides with increased chromaticism or rhythmic motion, resulting in a heightening of tension, but that is not the case here. Nor are there any substantial episodes to provide an occasional lightening of the texture. Instead, there is an unalloyed emphasis on rigorous "demonstration counterpoint"—probably to the detriment of the fugue as a piece of music. This is unusual in a mature work of Bach; so too is the very awkward way in which the piece lies under the hands, despite being limited to three voices. Much of Bach's music is difficult to play, but this piece is truly unidiomatic, with inaudible voice-crossings in bars 45–47 and stretches of a ninth or more required in bars 21 and 51.

Such a fugue appeals chiefly to those who can enjoy the details of the counter-point, such as the cross-rhythms that arise in the strettos as the subject enters on different beats in different voices (e.g., bars 24ff.). Such entries are of the type Marpurg called *per arsin et thesin*, that is, with the strong and weak beats displaced in the answer.[50] A pianist can indicate this through stress accents, but even then it seems unlikely that most listeners will get the point. Nor will manipulations of registration on the harpsichord (or organ) make such music more palatable to listeners who are fundamentally uninterested in it. As in other lengthy polyphonic works, the contrapuntal intricacies, especially the entries in augmentation in the last quarter of the piece, are probably clearest to the *Kenner* and least boring to the *Liebhaber* when the piece is played lightly and at a moderately quick pace. But a trill added in P 415 on the eighth-note in bar 74 suggests that by the 1740s (when the addition was made), Bach had a relatively slow tempo in mind; otherwise there is no time for the indicated termination.

Prelude and Fugue in E, BWV 854

The Prelude and Fugue in E is one of the less imposing pairs. The prelude is a concise sonata form (or a large "three-phrase" form), the last section consisting of a recapitulation of the entire first section (bars 15–22a || 1–8a) transposed a fourth upwards. Although the meter and the figuration at the opening suggest a gigue, the pedal-point at the outset—a standard opening gesture for a prelude—is also perhaps a reference to the pastorale. The close in each of the outer sections touches on the minor, including a few somewhat surprising chromatic lines (bars 7b–8a, 21b–22a); these imply a fairly moderate tempo.

The fugue is likewise small in scale and will probably sound clearest at a mod-erate tempo, though the omnipresent running sixteenths seem an invitation to greater speed. Indeed, the fugue is of the same basic type as the little Fugue in C, BWV 953 (in CB), also in three parts and suggesting quick violin writing. One can imagine Bach composing the present fugue (like BWV 953) quickly, almost improvisatorily; he made few subsequent revisions except in the last six bars, where the bass line underwent several changes. Here Bach seems to have aimed originally at a climactic effect with a bass line that made scalar descents first through a fifth (bars 24b) and then through more than a full octave (bar 27). Unfortunately, the stepwise motion in the bass created fifths with the upper parts. These were tolerable, since in each case one of the fifths is diminished, but they had evidently become unacceptable to Bach by the 1730s, when he probably made the alterations in bars 24 and 27 (a change in bar 26b belongs to a later layer of revisions).

The scale originally in bar 27 had had the effect of a broadening of motion in the closing bars; the same effect remains evident in the short series of bass suspensions in bars 25–26. The suspension motive originates in the second countersubject and can be traced through the entire fugue; only at the end, however, does the idea lead to a *chain* of suspensions. The chain remains a short one, containing only two links—four if one counts the subsequent suspensions in the middle voice—but given the small scale of the fugue this is enough to bring the suspension idea to its logical development, hence signaling the end of the piece.[51]

Prelude and Fugue in E Minor BWV 855

Because the E-minor fugue is in only two voices, this pair tends not to be taken as seriously as it deserves. That it ought not be taken lightly is suggested by the considerable expansion of the prelude in the revisions of 1722. The earlier version of the prelude is not only shorter, lacking the coda (bars 23ff.), but it also lacks the familiar arioso melody. In the earlier version the movement is essentially an arpeggiando prelude, comparable to those in D major and D minor although placing the figuration in the left hand. The addition of the melody, with its written-out embellishment, turns the piece into an Italianate adagio and would have been a particularly apt demonstration of "composition by variation" (Example 11.7). Incidentally, Bach's pro-

EXAMPLE 11.7.   Prelude in E Minor BWV 855/1, bars 1–2, (a) early version (BWV 855a/1; bass omitted); and (b) later version

cedure here found an odd—and, for most listeners today, unwelcome—parallel in the once-famous *Ave Maria* by Gounod, who superimposed a "sugary tune," as Fuller Maitland (1925, 1:12) put it, onto the prelude in C.[52]

The coda perhaps serves as a sort of recapitulation, since its first four bars (bars 23–26) repeat the opening bass a fourth higher. But structurally the entire presto section is a vast plagal cadence, and the V–I cadence at the end of the original portion (bars 20–21) can still be viewed as the formal close of the piece. Both original and added sections depend heavily on descending bass lines; disregarding octave transfers, the bass of the first section descends through two and a half octaves (from e in bar 5 to B in bars 19–20). The presto continues where the first section left off, dropping through another two octaves (from a in bar 23 to A and B in bars 40–41).

The presto indication at the beginning of the coda raises the question of tempo. The early version probably cannot proceed at less than a moderate allegro, but the ornate melody of the later version implies a slower tempo in the opening section. Too slow a tempo, however, makes it difficult to sustain the longer notes of the melody even on the modern piano. As in the prelude in D♯ minor, it can also reduce a quite passionate piece to prettiness.

In this connection it is worth noting that the opening section retains from the early version short (eighth-note) chords in the inner voices on the accented beats. These lend the prelude a certain vehemence, an effect that ought not be diminished by holding them out beyond their written values.[53] Despite the presto marking in the coda, a vulgar acceleration through bars 21–22 (as suggested in Keller 1965) ruins the striking effect produced as the bass line sinks against the sustained e″ in the treble; indeed, a modest ritard may be in order in these bars. Unfortunately, the passage is probably not completely realizable on any stringed keyboard instrument; even on the modern piano it requires some imagination to hear the e″ sounding, oboelike, above the descending bass and the chords in the inner voices. It might be helpful to restrike the e″ discreetly on the downbeat of bar 22.

In the fugue, which is a surprisingly dramatic little piece, the prickly chromaticism of the subject implies nonlegato. This does not mean a uniform staccato; the notes that form a descending chromatic line (d‴, d″, c♯‴, etc.) might well be brought out by being held ever so slightly longer than the others.[54] The fugue is not the only two-part one by Bach; we have already seen the C-Minor Fughetta BWV 961, and two of the duetti in the third part of the *Clavierübung* can also be considered true fugues. The present fugue resembles BWV 961 in that the answer constitutes a real modulation to the dominant, not a temporary excursion "on" the dominant. This also happens in the B-Minor Invention, and like that piece the present fugue is in a symmetrical rounded binary form. Indeed, the symmetry here is carried to extraordinary lengths, each half being further subdivided into two similar quarters. The second half (from bar 20) is essentially the same as the first with the parts exchanged and transposed; a minuscule alteration in bar 29 permits the piece to end in the tonic by altering the interval of transposition from a fifth to a fourth.

In the revised version of the fugue the final chord has the value of a mere eighth-note, and its arpeggiation is written out (Example 11.8). This brusque end-

EXAMPLE 11.8.   Fugue in E Minor BWV 855/2, bars 41–42,
with endings from (a) early version (BWV 855a/2) and
(b) later version

ing is more in character with the rest of the piece than is the original chord in dotted halves, and it resonates in particular with the two passages in octaves (bars 19, 38). The latter, while unusual in a fugue, call to mind the rage aria of eighteenth-century opera, which often opens with a ritornello played in unison. That Bach should have included such passages in one of his most geometrically designed movements may be surprising. But through them the fugue fulfills the same eighteenth-century aesthetic requirement as the Da Capo aria: A passionate affect is contained within a rational structure.

Prelude and Fugue in F, BWV 856

The Prelude and Fugue in F is another relatively simple pair. The prelude retains the familiar vestiges of arpeggiando improvisation, among them the harmonic formula used at the opening over a tonic pedal. Bach must have intended the prelude to make a brilliant impression, for in the autograph he specified that most of the long trills, indicated in earlier versions by the abbreviation *tr*, were to be played as *Doppelt-Cadenzen*, that is, trills prefixed by a turn from below or above.[55] No other piece by Bach repeatedly demands this complex ornament, which consequently functions here as a distinct motive—an exceptional role for an ornament in Baroque keyboard music.[56]

In the fugue, Fischer's *Ariadne musica* appears to have provided the outline for the subject and perhaps the countersubject as well (Example 11.9). But Fischer's fugue has the skipping rhythm of a French gigue and, while barred in $\frac{3}{4}$, is effectively in $\frac{6}{4}$ or even $\frac{12}{4}$, since the bars fall regularly into groups of four. Bach smoothed out Fischer's dotted rhythms, halved the note-values, and, by extending the second entry by one measure, threw off the four-square regularity of Fischer's opening bars.

The fugue is bipartite, divided precisely in half by an arrival on V of D minor (bar 36). The second half is very different from the first; the easy-going imitations of the first two expositions, which simply alternate between tonic and dominant, give way to three-part strettos in D minor and then G minor. The subject returns only once more in the tonic (bar 65), and then it is embellished so as to repeat the expressive half-step e♭''', d'' that is so prominent in the G-minor stretto.

EXAMPLE 11.9.   (a) Fischer, *Ariadne musica*, Fuga No. 10,
bars 1–8; (b) J. S. Bach, fugue in F, BWV 856/2, bars 1–9

Prelude and Fugue in F Minor BWV 857

The first half of WTC1 concludes with one of the most imposing pairs. The prelude, whose sonorous texture combines elements of *brisé* and contrapuntal writing, seems quite mature in style, but archaic features in the fugue appear to place it among the earliest movements in either volume.

The prelude resembles the one in C♯ minor in both its essentially bipartite design and Bach's later addition of a coda (bars 16b–21a). The theme is another apparently improvisatory arpeggiation of a conventional progression over a tonic pedal. But it is developed imitatively, as in an invention, and the bass restates it in the relative major at what was originally the halfway point (bar 6b). The theme is to be played over-legato—that is, with consonant tones held out; precisely which ones, and for how long, is indicated by extra stems and ties. Although many of these are absent in the early version, Bach indicated them precisely in the later autograph, as in the C-major prelude. Hence, it is doubtful that one should hold out any additional notes or disregard the written note-values (e.g., through use of the damper pedal); this is likely to render a clear texture opaque. Clarity will also be aided by a steady andante tempo; anything slower may make it difficult to sustain the long lines of the theme. Even then it will probably be necessary to restrike the closing pedal-point once or twice (e.g., on the downbeat of bar 19 and the last quarter of bar 20), regardless of the tempo or instrument used.

The fugue opens with a stern chromatic subject in quarters, to which the countersubject adds *figure corte* that henceforth are heard on practically every beat for the remainder of the piece. A wide leap (more than an octave) in the countersubject leads to occasional voice-crossings, an awkward feature suggesting an early date. Also archaic is the absence of a clear division into expositions and episodes; instead, the fugue consists of individual entries of the subject joined by bridges, which are sometimes quite extensive but never articulated as distinct episodes. The expositions are conceived permutationally, although not all possible combinations of the subject and its three countersubjects are used. The bridges are also constructed in a freely permutational manner, the first two providing the material for all but one of the remaining six. (The exception is the passage in bars 37–40, which draws material from the first countersubject.)

As in the prelude, too slow a tempo may make an already somber piece unbearably dreary. Indeed, the long chromatic notes of the subject may actually be more impressive at a tempo quick enough for the *figure corte* of the countersubject to sound light and fleeting when heard against them. Another interpretive problem is posed by the long note near the end of the subject. As in other fugues with similar subjects (e.g., the one in B minor), a trill seems called for. But there is none in the autograph, and the ornament signs in several other sources may not be authentic.[57] Even if the ornament in the initial statement of the subject is, as Dürr (NBA V/6.1, preface) puts it, "probably an understood performance practice [aufführungspraktische Selbstverständlichkeit]," there is little reason for dutifully attaching the ornament to every statement of the subject. A full trill with termination is impossible to play in some cases (e.g., bar 36). A short trill might, in such instances, help point out the presence of the subject when it appears in an inner voice. But this hardly seems necessary, especially if it detracts from clear performance of the other voices.

Prelude and Fugue in F$^\sharp$, BWV 858

Few preludes and fugues in WTC1 seem as well paired as these two movements, which are both light in texture and character and exceptionally good-natured. The prelude is essentially a two-part invention and is similar in form and material to the Invention in G (which is, presumably, its close contemporary). But in the prelude Bach pays rather less attention to imitative counterpoint as such than to developing the syncopated motive first heard in bar 2. The motive is employed in what is essentially a conventional chain of suspensions, embellished through escape tones and other somewhat irregular passing notes (Example 11.10). The ornamental tones hint at additional voices; for instance, d$^{\sharp\prime\prime\prime}$ on the third beat moves implicitly to c$^{\sharp\prime\prime\prime}$ on the fourth beat. But not everything is spelled out on the surface, and this gives the piece a somewhat elusive character. The prelude was originally two bars shorter; the early version (unknown except through the Konwitschny manuscript) employs a different form of the theme or rather divides it into subject (bar 1) and countersubject (bar 2—see Example 11.10a).[58]

The fugue is similar to the one in C$^\sharp$, suggesting that Bach might have written both at about the same time, perhaps while engaged in filling in the "sharp" part of the scheme of WTC1. Both fugues have vivacious subjects beginning on off-beats,

EXAMPLE 11.10.   Prelude in F#, BWV 858/1, bars 1–3:
(a) early version (BWV 858a/1), upper part; (b) later version;
(c) analysis of upper voice

with even livelier figuration appearing in the first episode. In this case the new figuration (see bar 9, bass) is eventually incorporated into a second countersubject, introduced during the second exposition (bar 12).

Also as in the fugue in C#, sonata-form elements are abundant. But here they delineate a binary rather than a ternary design. The first half ends with a cadence to the dominant (bar 17), and the phrase with which the first half closes is recapitulated at the end of the piece (bars 30–33a), the upper voices being exchanged as usual. This, together with the recapitulation of another episode at the beginning of the second half (bars 18–20 ‖ 8b–10a), gives the fugue a neat, symmetrical quality without its seeming pat or schematic.

The trill on the dotted figure in the subject poses technical as well as interpretive questions. It is a "long" trill, with written-out termination, and it is difficult to imagine the subject without it.[59] Yet the statement of the subject at bar 11b lacks both ornament and termination, presumably because the latter would not only be hard to play here but would clash with the lower parts. In other passages the termination is written out (bars 15, 28), but a long trill is difficult to play and a short trill at the beginning of the note seems sufficient.

Prelude and Fugue in F# Minor BWV 859

The F#-minor pieces seem less closely matched than those in E or F. The first half of the prelude again resembles a fairly lively two-part invention. But the fugue, in four parts, is serious and severe, lacking episodes or passage-work, and permeated with expressive "sigh" motives.

Actually, the prelude changes character in the latter half, and this could be seen as a transition in the direction of the fugue. Shortly after the midpoint (bar 12b) the theme is presented in a somewhat varied, inverted form, and this is accompanied, for the first time in the piece, by short three-part chords (bars 15ff.). One might suspect from the altered character and texture of the passage that it is a later addition, like the interpolations in some of the other preludes, but there is no sign of this. In fact, the chords are a development of the tenor line in the opening bar, and the thickening of the texture in the latter portion of the prelude might have been part of the original conception; it implies a strong registration throughout.

The fugue, although not exactly in *stile antico*, is vocal in inspiration. As in the C-major fugue (likewise in four parts), this implies that the subject should be played in an articulate, "speaking" manner, with well-marked syncopations and cross-rhythms. To a listener the meter will at first be unclear, since the subject moves virtually independently of the barline. But it contains a built-in acceleration—see the diminishing note-values on the suspensions on a, b, and c''—and the meter becomes clear once the answer is combined with the countersubject.

The insistent "sigh" motives of the countersubject perhaps make this an example of what Walther called *fuga pathetica*; this much is already implicit in the melodic chromaticism of the subject itself. But the chromaticism never goes beyond the local raising or lowering of the sixth and seventh degrees of the minor scale, and, despite a high frequency of passing dissonance, in terms of modulation this proves to be one of Bach's least adventurous mature fugues. The subject enters only on tonic and dominant, and although the inversion is introduced after the midpoint (bar 20b) there is only one further *inversus* entry; both inverted entries are buried in the lower voices. The only substantial lightening of the texture occurs in the middle of the second half (bar 28), where tenor and bass briefly drop out and a portion of the first half is repeated in the topmost register (bars 28–31 || 7–10 an octave higher).

The archaic form suggests that this is a relatively early piece. But even if this is true, Bach would certainly have known how to make it more "interesting" had he wished to do so, and its severity was surely intentional. Still, it seems unwise to exaggerate this aspect of the music through an unduly slow tempo. Moreover, performers need to consider carefully just how expressively to play the many "sigh" motives, since undue stress on the first note of each two-note group could weigh down the piece. Even if one adds slurs—as one probably ought to do on the descending "sighs"—they should not be thoughtlessly extended to every apparent two-note grouping. In particular, certain rising whole- or half-steps are not sighs at all but phrase divisions, the first note marking the end of one gesture, the second the beginning of the next (see, e.g., downbeat of bar 5, tenor).

Prelude and Fugue in G, BWV 860

The prelude in G is the last in WTC1 to have been derived from the arpeggiando type and also the last to have survived in a shorter early version. Perhaps this means that Bach for some reason failed to carry out a planned expansion of the preludes beyond this point, as Dürr (1984, 66–67) suggests. But none of the remaining preludes is of the arpeggiando type, and this might mean that they were conceived on a somewhat larger scale from the outset. The four bars later interpolated here (bars 7b–8a and 14b–17a) do not substantially expand the prelude, which remains quite short in relation to the fugue. They do turn two phrases into sequences (bars 6ff. and 14ff.), and they introduce a third, entirely new sequence (bars 16b–17) whose figuration is especially lively, making it the climax of the revised version.[60]

A few collisions between the two parts suggest the use of two manuals (bars 2–3, also bar 7 in the later version). But on most harpsichords this would mean playing each voice on a single eight-foot rank. A more brilliant effect can be achieved by playing on one strongly registered manual and putting up with the occasional inconveniences of Bach's counterpoint.

The fugue has much the same virtuoso character as the prelude. Indeed, it comes closest of all the fugues in the WTC to the concerto-like pieces discussed in Chapter 9. Yet it also has elements of the contrapuntal type of design found in the fugue in $D^\sharp$ minor. The second exposition (bar 20) treats the subject in inversion, and strettos appear in the central third of the piece (bars 38–61a), though none of them is carried out very strictly. As in the fugue in $F^\sharp$, a motive introduced in an episodic passage (bar 10) is eventually combined with the subject, though only once and in inversion, just before the end (bar 80). But the motive, which imitates violinistic bariolage, is used extensively in the episodes, which consequently sound like solos in a concerto.

Prelude and Fugue in G Minor BWV 861

The opening of the G-minor prelude bears a vague resemblance to the type of scoring that Bach used in his Leipzig cantatas when he wanted to imitate the sound of funeral bells.[61] But the funeral bells in question are signified in the cantatas by repeated sixteenth-notes; hence, even if a solemn expression is desired here, it might be a mistake to adopt too slow a tempo. The common-time signature indicates that the pulse falls on the quarter-note, and the figures in sixteenths and thirty-seconds should retain their integrity, that is, not be subdivided, as is likely to occur if the pulse shifts to the eighth-note.[62]

What may appear to be a homophonic texture at the opening is in fact conceived contrapuntally; the three voices of bar 1 each introduce a distinctive rhythmic motive, and these are subsequently treated in a sort of free invertible counterpoint. The simplest of these motives is the long trill in the soprano, which perhaps can begin on the main note, like a *ribatutta*. In any case, by starting the trill slowly, gradually accelerating, and then decelerating, one can achieve an approximation of the singer's *messa di voce*, a swelling followed by a fading of the voice on a long note. This is not easy, especially while the other hand is playing steady sixteenths, but the prelude can serve as a good exercise in this essential element of Baroque keyboard playing.

The fugue subject can be traced to the fugue in $E^\flat$ from Fischer's *Ariadne musica*, which was surely known in the Bach circle. Friedemann Bach also quoted it, somewhat more precisely than in the present case, in his D-Minor Fantasia F. 19 (Example 11.11).[63] Like Fischer, Bach uses a tonal answer, and, as in the Fischer work, the climax of the fugue is a three-part stretto placed just before the close (bars 28ff.). But Bach's fugue also has a regular countersubject as well as an episode (bars 24b–27) in which the motion for once relaxes into flowing sequences prior to the final rigors of the final stretto.

The overall plan is clear, built around arrivals to VI (bar 12) and V of iv (bar 20). But the counterpoint is constantly varied, without any recapitulation, and this, to-gether with the sparing use of real four-part writing, may point to an early date, es-

EXAMPLE 11.11.   Fugue subjects from (a) Fischer, *Ariadne musica*, Fuga No. 5; (b) J. S. Bach: fugue in G Minor BWV 861/1; and (c) W. F. Bach: Fantasia in D Minor, F. 19 (bars 33–35a)

pecially as there are some awkward moments: occasional odd voice-crossings and doublings, and two tenths that the right hand must span in bar 18. In addition, both subject and countersubject contain *figure corte*, and the fugue ends just as the tenor completes the last entry of the subject (another borrowing from Fischer). Unlike many of Bach's early fugues, however, this one is concise, without any padding, and the finely conceived formal plan makes it one of the most satisfying in the WTC.

Prelude and Fugue in A♭, BWV 862

As in the B-Minor Invention, which uses similar material, the opening two bars of the A♭-major prelude could have come from the allegro of a galant violin sonata. So too could the figuration in the modulating passage that begins in bar 9, where the resemblance to violin writing was perhaps even stronger before Bach rewrote the upper voice of bars 9–12, which originally used the same motive as bars 13–15. Like the Invention in B Minor, the prelude is divided in half by a strong cadence near the midpoint (bar 18). But there is also a coda (from bar 35), the latter evidently having been an original part of the prelude, not a later addition as elsewhere in WTC1.

The subject of the fugue is, like that of the prelude, based on leaping eighth-notes. But rather than evoking galant violin music it seems to refer back to the canzonas and ricercars of the seventeenth century.[64] In other respects, however, the fugue is up to date in style, being one of the liveliest of the four-part fugues in the WTC. The one stylistic feature apt to strike modern players and listeners as problematical is the meter. The subject begins on the second beat, but, as in the D-major fugue, it is almost impossible to prevent the first note from sounding like a downbeat. The true placement of the downbeat may not be entirely clear to the listener until the cadence that ends the first exposition (bar 8, first beat). Vigorous stress accents might clarify the meter on the piano or clavichord, but they will seem merely eccentric if the initial gesture continues to be heard (and thought of by the player) as a downbeat. Perhaps the inevitable ambiguity was intentional. Nevertheless, the true meter ought to be clear in the player's mind by bar 3, where prepared dissonances begin to fall on the odd-numbered beats, forming a chain of suspensions.

Prelude and Fugue in G♯ Minor BWV 863

The prelude in G♯ minor, like the one in C♯ minor, combines imitative texture and arioso style in a sicilianolike rhythm. This seems a gentler work, lacking the urgency of the C♯-minor prelude, and perhaps for this reason it lacks a coda. But the prelude is in three real parts throughout, and the second half (from bar 15) even contains a few *inversus* entries of the subject.

The fugue on first hearing seems fairly ordinary, if somewhat archaic, like the fugues in F minor and G minor (which are likewise in four parts). Yet it is actually quite sophisticated, revealing a dry, somewhat abstruse wit. This grows out of the last half of the subject, which is simply the bass line of a standard cadential formula (IV, V, I). The idea is later developed as the bass of several sequential episodes.[65]

In addition, an odd tonal ambiguity in the subject leads to a near reversal of the usual roles of subject and answer. The subject is of the type that is usually said to modulate to the dominant; thus, it requires a tonal answer to avoid a further modulation to V of V. But the answer, theoretically on V, is so altered as to appear to be on IV; every note of the answer except the first is a step lower than one would expect it to be.[66] Hence, while the modulatory plan of the fugue as a whole contains little out of the ordinary, statements of the subjected are often not in the key they seem to be or are subjected to an unexpected modulatory twist. Even the final entry (soprano, bar 37b) is a "real" statement on IV; yet the fugue ends just a few bars later with a perfectly satisfactory full cadence in the tonic.

Prelude and Fugue in A, BWV 864

The Prelude and Fugue in A is among the high points of WTC1, though rarely recognized as such. Perhaps it seems too cheerful or the subject of the fugue is too eccentric to be taken seriously.

The prelude resembles a lively three-part invention. But unlike any of the fifteen sinfonias, it opens with the principal subject (in the soprano) already combined with the two countersubjects (in the lower voices). There are six entries in all, forming three expositions joined by two brief episodes (bars 6b–8a, 14b–17a). In theory the subject could combine with the two countersubjects in all six permutations, but because several permutations lie awkwardly on the keyboard Bach employs only four of them. Despite its fairly schematic design the little piece never sounds studied, and it ends with an exuberant little outburst by the soprano, ascending a two-octave scale.

The fugue, in three voices, is likewise in three symmetrically arranged sections. But these are organized very differently from those of the prelude. The first is a sort of rhythmically perverse gigue, while the second section (bar 23) introduces a running countersubject in sixteenths. The third (bar 42) serves somewhat like a recapitulation of the first.

The initial section is one of Bach's wittiest efforts. The opening gesture of the subject, a lone eighth followed by a long rest, is in effect a caricature of the "rhetorical" pauses in some of Bach's early fugue subjects (e.g., that of the C-Minor Toccata BWV 911). The remainder of the subject is sequential, permitting numerous strettos; the second entry (alto, bar 2) is already a stretto entrance. Moreover, the leaps in the subject give the counterpoint some of the character of Frescobaldi's *Recercar obligo di non mai di grado*, in which stepwise motion is entirely avoided.[67]

Perhaps the most engaging aspect of the subject is its metrical playfulness. The first section is pervaded by syncopations and momentary shifts from $\frac{9}{8}$ to $\frac{2}{4}$ or $\frac{3}{4}$. The three voices are often effectively in different meters; for example, in bar 6 the bass (stating the subject) might be heard in either $\frac{2}{4}$ or $\frac{3}{4}$, while the soprano and alto suggest $\frac{6}{8}$ and $\frac{3}{4}$, respectively (Example 11.12). Other interpretations are possible,

EXAMPLE 11.12.   Fugue in A, BWV 864/2, bars 6–9, with rhythmic analysis

and for this reason performers probably should not "bring out" the interpretation suggested in Example 11.12 to the exclusion of others. The metrical ambiguity is such that the three voices rarely move together to the downbeat; even at the cadence in bar 9, which marks the approximate midpoint of the first section, only treble and bass arrive together.

The introduction of running sixteenths in the second section, following a short bridge (bars 20–22), makes the piece sound like a double fugue. But, as in the fugue in C♯ minor (which is otherwise a very different piece), the running figuration is more a rhythmic motive than a regular countersubject. The sixteenths disappear at the beginning of the last section, only to return at the end as fragments from both preceding sections are recapitulated. The fugue ends, like the sonata-form fugues in D minor and B♭, with a restatement of the closing phrase from the first section. But this is disguised by the addition of a running bass, hence alluding to the second section as well.[68]

Prelude and Fugue in A Minor BWV 865

The A-minor pair is perhaps the most problematical in the WTC. The fugue, much longer than the prelude, has an impressive "contrapuntal" design and contains many attractive details; the closing section is particularly compelling. Yet both movements have a pedantic quality, the prelude because of the repetitious motives used to fill the long bars of $\frac{9}{8}$, the fugue due to the dogged working out of its contrapuntal design. Played with sufficient brilliance, both movements can perhaps achieve considerable power. But there is a danger that both will seem to be composed of empty rhetoric, long-winded and monotonous.

In both movements the main material includes some sort of written-out mordent. In the fugue this takes the form of a simple *figura corta*, but in the prelude the figure is extended to three repercussions (bass, bar 1). The motive recalls the first movement of the First Brandenburg Concerto, which, like the prelude, not only begins but ends with the same figure. This is one of several features suggesting a Weimar origin for both movements, which have long been suspected of being early, although the sources provide no confirmation for this.[69]

The fugue is the longest in the WTC1 (at least in terms of bar-count). It might be viewed as the four-voice counterpart of the rigorously contrapuntal fugue in D♯ minor. But here the *rectus* and *inversus* versions of the subject are introduced in separate expositions (bars 1, 14b) prior to their stretto expositions (bar 27b for the prime form, bar 48 for the inversion). There are no augmented or otherwise varied entries, and, instead of combining different forms of the subject simultaneously, Bach is for the most part satisfied with presenting *rectus* and *inversus* in rapid alternation during the final section (from bar 64b).

The fugue is by no means a dry working out of inversions and strettos. The last section is beautifully conceived, opening with stretto entries for the two lowest parts. It then ascends gradually into the top register for an episode, the second of two (at bar 71). Following two dramatic pauses (bars 80, 82), the fugue culminates in a canonic coda that expands to five parts and, at the very end, nominally to seven. Nevertheless, the rhythmic homogeneity and the absence of lasting or compelling modulations are likely to grow wearying. The somewhat similarly planned fugue in B♭ minor of WTC2 is saved by its more interesting subject and far more sophisticated counterpoint. Here the subject has a simple tertian structure, outlining the ascending line A, C, E, G♯, B, D, which simplifies the task of writing strettos but rules out much variety in harmony (or rhythm, since each note in the underlying line occupies half a bar).

To be sure, the ascending line forming the subject is considerably embellished, and there is a "rhetorical" rest at its center, preceded by the familiar French cadential formula of the falling third. The latter, however, proves to be something of an embarrassment when the subject is turned upside down, for the descending *tierce* seems unidiomatic when inverted; the same is true of the preceding diminished seventh. Still, as Keller (1965, 112) noted, Bach appears to have skipped over several impressive fugues in A minor (those of BWV 944, 965, and 904) in selecting this one for inclusion in WTC1. It surpasses the others in contrapuntal rigor, and when played at a lively tempo and with a light touch—no easy feat—it is perhaps not as ponderous as the above account may indicate.

The closing pedal-point has called for frequent comment. It has been taken as an indication for use of the organ, since it cannot be sustained without pedals (see, e.g., Marshall 1986, 234). But the thick four-part writing and wide gaps between the voices at earlier points remain difficult to negotiate regardless of the instrument used.[70] Since the bass line elsewhere was clearly not intended for organ pedals, it would appear that the ending, at least, is a genuine example of "demonstration counterpoint" that players were not expected to execute precisely as written. Except in the final pedal-point, both movements are as idiomatic to the harpsichord as any other instrument; nonorganists (including pianists) are best advised simply to leave out the low A after bar 84.

Prelude and Fugue in B♭, BWV 866

The pieces in B♭ are understandably among the most popular in the WTC, thanks to their brevity and their lively material. The prelude is the closest thing in the WTC to an improvised free fantasia; it is composed almost entirely of types of figuration also used in the solo passages and cadenzas of Bach's concertos. Preludes by Handel and other contemporaries use similar figures, so Bach presumably drew from the common property of keyboard players. But he may also have drawn specifically from Fischer's *Pièces de clavecin* of 1696, which includes a prelude (No. 6) opening with the same motive as this one and later employing full-voiced chords in dotted rhythm (as in bar 11 here).

Despite its improvisatory style, the prelude falls into two nearly equal halves. Moreover, the rhythm is as precisely notated as in the rest of the WTC, though it must have been meant to be interpreted rather freely, especially in the cadenzalike passages in the second half (i.e., from the downbeat of bar 10). Bach's student Anonymous 5 placed the word *adagio* in his copy (P 401) at bar 11. As in the prelude in C minor this probably implies rhythmic freedom as well as a relaxed but not necessarily very slow tempo.

This freest of preludes leads to one of the most regular of the sonata-like fugues in three voices. There are three expositions separated by two episodes (bars 19–22 and 30–35); the second episode and most of the concluding exposition recapitulate earlier sections.[71] In addition, the fugue has a permutational element, since most entries of the subject are accompanied by both countersubjects.

Prelude and Fugue in B♭ Minor BWV 867

The two pieces in B♭ minor invoke very different types of ensemble music, but they form one of the most impressive and well-matched pairs in WTC1. The prelude is a sort of arioso, but orchestrally conceived; Fuller Maitland (1925, 1:34) was led to compare it with "Passion Music," probably having in mind the opening chorus of the Saint Matthew Passion, which begins with somewhat similar motivic material, also over a tonic pedal-point. It seems appropriate, then, that the fugue, like the other five-part fugue in WTC1 (the C♯-minor), is an evocation of large-scale vocal polyphony in *stile antico*.

The prelude is densely written in up to seven nominal voices, but these make up just three distinct strands. Bass and melody are of course the most prominent, but there is also a two-note rhythmic figure, which, like the short chords in the E-minor prelude, can be thought of as a staccato accompaniment played by strings or winds (Example 11.13). The two-note rhythmic figure is largely confined to the inner

EXAMPLE 11.13.   Prelude in B♭ Minor BWV 867/1, bars 1–2

voices and is prominent only at the beginning of each of the three statements of the theme (bars 1, 7b, and 20). But it contributes greatly to the sense of an inexorable marchlike rhythm, which harpsichordists may wish to mark by detaching the unstressed eighths at the ends of the second and fourth beats and breaking the chords on the following strong beats. In form the prelude is bipartite, divided precisely in half by a cadence to the dominant; in the brief episode at the beginning of the second half the two-note rhythmic figure is transferred to the bass (bars 13–14).

The fugue comes closer than any other in WTC1 to the pure *stile antico*; unlike the fugue in C♯ minor, it has no quick countersubject. Yet it could hardly be mistaken for Renaissance polyphony, and the declamatory subject, with its wide leaps and "rhetorical" pause, belongs to the realm of Bach's own choral writing. Still, the severe style adopted here permits no real episodes; there are only two sequential bridges (bars 6, 42), and even these are canonic, like the episodes in some of the stricter fugues of WTC2 (e.g., in D and B). Canon, moreover, provides the climax of the fugue, which occurs with the five-part stretto near the end (bar 67). Prior to this, at the beginning of the final section, occurs one instance of a contrapuntal device that Bach would employ to climactic effect in several later works; this is the use of simultaneous or paired statements of the subject by two voices in parallel motion (bar 55).

Prelude and Fugue in B, BWV 868

The prelude in B is one of the shorter ones, but it is not lightweight, being composed throughout in three real parts. It broadens to four parts at the end, thus (like the F$^\sharp$-minor prelude) preparing the fugue. There are three brief sections; the three-part texture of the opening is freely inverted at the beginning of the second part (bar 6).

The fugue, although in four voices, is lively and almost galant in character, like the fugue in A$^\flat$. It is, moreover, the only four-part fugue in the volume to have something like the rounded binary form employed in so many of the three-part fugues. Like the D-minor fugue, it reaches the dominant at midpoint (bar 18); an exposition using the inversion of the subject follows. Unfortunately, the inversion does not make for a very attractive melody, for much the same reason as in the A-minor fugue: The downward leap of a fifth in the original version of the subject sounds awkward when inverted. This may be why the inversion is dropped after just two entries. In addition, the fugue suffers from what seems to be rather routine counterpoint, which surrounds the subject with nondescript (and nearly nonstop) running figuration.

Prelude and Fugue in B Minor BWV 869

While the B-major fugue may be a weak effort, the first part of the WTC closes with a masterpiece. B minor was a key that seems to have called forth special efforts from Bach; one thinks immediately of the first Kyrie of the B-Minor Mass and the flute sonata BWV 1030. Those works almost certainly remained to be composed in 1722, but by that date Bach had already written one very fine three-part fugue (BWV 951) in the same key. Perhaps he felt that a four-part fugue was needed to close the volume, although he did not feel that way when he compiled WTC2, which opens and closes with three-part fugues.

Both movements differ in important respects from others in WTC1, suggesting that they may have been the last written. One outward sign of this is that both prelude and fugue have tempo markings—*Andante* and *Largo*, respectively—making them the only pair of movements in either book of the WTC to bear such indications.[72] Moreover, the prelude is the volume's only actual sonata movement—that is, binary form with repeats—although its style and texture derive not from the galant trio-sonata (or from Bach's Sinfonias) but from the older type of trio writing found in Corelli's first four opera. The latter, although all published before 1700, might have still seemed new and up to date at Cöthen in 1722. And while the fugue subject may appear old-fashioned today, it is characterized by expressive "sigh" motives (marked by slurs) and a stark chromaticism that might have seemed radical even for a Bach work. In the autograph, the first page of the fugue bears an unusual number of corrections, suggesting that, as he neared the end of his fair copy, Bach was still undecided about the text of the last movement.[73]

In the prelude, the walking bass and chains of suspensions are only the most obvious borrowings from Corelli. Though longer than most of Corelli's sonata movements, the prelude resembles many of them in its use of a "Phrygian" cadence (in place of a true modulation to the dominant) at the end of the first half. The second half introduces new thematic material, never precisely restating that of the opening.[74] The tempo mark was perhaps meant as an indication of the piece's

Italian style, even though Corelli himself rarely used the word *andante*. For Bach the word would probably have meant literally "walking" or "moving" (not "slow"). Dense chromaticism in the final phrase prevents this from being an *andante allegro*, like several movements by Handel; perhaps it is an example of what Corelli called an *andante largo* in the Concerto Grosso Op. 6, No. 2.

With the chromaticism of the coda, Bach's own style finally comes to the fore, pointing toward the fugue. The latter's *affetuoso* subject is hardly comparable to the archaic subjects of most of the other four-part fugues in WTC1 (e.g., those in F minor and F♯ minor). Key, tempo mark, the half-steps and other expressive intervals in the subject, and the shifting tonality (due in part to the modulating sequence within the subject) all seem premonitions of the first fugue (the first Kyrie) of the B-Minor Mass. Both works achieve impressive dimensions, although the keyboard fugue lacks the clear structure of the one from the Mass. Indeed, this piece possesses few strong formal articulations—the only emphatic cadence is the final one—and, while there may seem to be a great deal of recapitulation, hardly anything is restated literally except for two relatively brief episodes. Yet only in a poor or thoughtless performance does the fugue grow monotonous. There is enough subtle variety of rhythm, texture, and tonality to maintain interest, and when the polyphonic texture clears for a moment just short of the end (bar 73), the brief soprano solo there is no less dramatic than the coda of the A-minor fugue or the improvisatory finales of earlier fugal works.

The material in the more important of the two recurring episodes has been traced to a vocal duet by Francesco Durante (Keller 1965, 128, citing Riemann 1912, 275). But the idea in question is a fairly conventional sequence that any late Baroque composer might have used; the same formula even appears briefly in the prelude (bars 23b–24). The very conventionality of the episode provides some relief from the rigors of the expositions, even though the subject itself makes a curious false entry halfway through the first episode, the first three notes being stated by the alto (bar 19; the effect is repeated when the episode recurs, transposed a fifth lower, in bars 26–29). Perhaps this was the result of a fortunate error made during the composition of the piece; Bach might have begun to bring in the subject, realized that to do so at this point was premature, but left the three notes to stand.[75] The contrived voice-leading in bar 19, with the tenor leaping up by an eleventh to cross over the alto, suggests that Bach indeed made some sort of interpolation or alteration at this point.

A second, unrelated, episode makes two appearances near the center of the fugue (at bars 34 and 41). Indeed, they frame a bass entry that begins at the exact midpoint (bar 38). This is likely to go unnoticed, since the episode develops the first bar of the subject and thus furnishes hardly any contrast to the expository passages. Nevertheless, the second statement of this episode (bar 41) leads to the fugue's one excursion into major keys—D and A, in bars 44–50. By this point, moreover, the rhythm, initially consisting of eighths, has given way to uninterrupted sixteenths. Hence, while the fugue can seem almost formless, the second half possesses greater momentum as well as greater tonal variety than the first, and this presumably drives the music with increased urgency toward its conclusion.

This fugue is second only to the one in A minor in the number of problematical fingerings and voice-crossings, but the difficulties here are surely justified by the special expressive import of the music. A few passages might be slightly modified for the player's convenience; one could, for example, avoid a few awkward repeated notes by introducing discreet ties similar to those allowed by Bach elsewhere.[76] In addition, a few suspensions that are difficult to hold (alto b', a' in bars 36–37) might be released early, especially if they have ceased to sound on one's instrument.

12

The Well-Tempered Clavier, *Part 2*

For as long as two decades there was only one *Well-Tempered Clavier*, the set of twenty-four preludes and fugues whose fair-copy manuscript dated 1722 Bach had assembled at Cöthen. The compilation of a companion volume belongs to a much later stage in Bach's career. But because of its similarities in form and purpose to Part 1 it will be considered at this point rather than among the other late works.

Bach came to Leipzig in 1723. During his first few years there the preparation of new church cantatas (an average of more than one per week) and other duties associated with his new position seemingly would have left little time for the composition of new keyboard music. Yet he also managed to get the Partitas into print (starting in 1726), and not only these but the French Suites and various other keyboard works appear to have been composed or at least revised to their familiar forms during the same period. Whether or not he was also composing new preludes and fugues during the 1720s and 1730s, in those years he revised Part 1 of the WTC at least twice. By the end of the 1730s he had evidently decided to gather together a second such set of pieces.[1]

Bach seems never to have prepared an integral fair-copy autograph for WTC2 as he did for WTC1. Instead, he appears to have left Part 2 as a collection of small manuscripts, each containing one prelude and fugue.[2] Nevertheless, the surviving sources and the tradition of Bach's sons and students leave no question that Bach himself was responsible for the compilation of WTC2 (and for its title). If Bach never prepared a definitive fair copy of WTC2, it would not be surprising. The period around 1740 saw a flurry of contrapuntally oriented keyboard works printed, copied, or drafted: the third part of the *Clavierübung* (published 1739), WTC2 (individual movements revised and/or copied out ca. 1739–42), the Goldberg Variations (published 1741), and the *Art of Fugue* (early version drafted by 1742 or so). WTC2 is the largest and most heterogeneous of these collections, and while the same period also saw revisions to WTC1, Bach cannot have seriously considered

197

publishing either part of the WTC (as, for example, the concluding volume of the *Clavierübung*); it was simply too big and complex. Hence, it made sense for him to leave to others the task of preparing complete manuscripts of WTC2 from his working scores.

In light of the large number of individual movements contained in these collections, Bach presumably would have had to devote a fairly extended period to their composition, as Butler (1990) argues for the third part of the *Clavierübung*, or drawn on older material. If so, then it is conceivable that some movements in WTC2 date in one form or another back to the first few years at Leipzig or earlier, as is true of other works that Bach compiled during his later years, such as the harpsichord concertos and the seventeen great organ chorales. But the few movements of WTC2 that survive in earlier versions cannot be dated with certainty before the mid- or late 1720s, and these were heavily revised. One could hardly guess from the finished version of the fugue in A^b that it was originally only half as long, and in the key of F. Hence, it would be hazardous to attempt to identify, from the final versions alone, other movements that might have been reworked from lost early versions. Still, WTC2, like WTC1, does contain some archaic works, as well as a few seemingly mismatched preludes and fugues and one or two arguably inferior pieces. This suggests that Bach indeed drew some of the individual movements from a heterogeneous group of pieces composed well before the compilation of the volume as a whole.

In general, however, the contents of WTC2 may well be late in origin—that is, after 1735 or so. There are real differences in style, or at least in stylistic tendency, between the two books. The preludes of WTC2 tend to be longer, more nearly matching the fugues in length and weightiness, than their counterparts in WTC1. No fewer than ten preludes in WTC2 are genuine sonata movements, with central double bars, reflecting the fact that by the time WTC2 was assembled, the keyboard sonata had emerged as a major genre; Emanuel and probably Friedemann Bach had already written important examples.[3] Even the preludes lacking central double bars regularly show elements of sonata form, such as a division into two or three main sections, with substantial amounts of recapitulated material in the final section. Bach had evidently distanced himself from the tradition of the prelude as a free, improvisatory piece; only the prelude in $C^\sharp$ is clearly of the arpeggiando type, which is so well represented in WTC1. A few other preludes in WTC2, such as those in C and F, can also be related to this tradition (or to that of the unmeasured prelude), but the broken chords are heavily embellished and the figuration is fitted into a sonata-form mold.

The fugues include fewer four-part pieces than in Part 1, and there are none in five parts (nor in two). But the three-part fugues include some of the longest and most ambitious in the volume, among them two double fugues and one triple fugue. Curiously, fewer of the fugues show the evident borrowings from sonata style found in Part 1. Exact restatements or recapitulations of episodic material occur somewhat less often, and the episodes are more likely to involve short canons or strettos, as in the last two minor-key fugues of WTC1. In a few instances, notably the fugue in D, imitative or permutational polyphony is as pervasive in the episodes as in the expositions. Such writing presumably reflects the interest in pure counterpoint that led Bach to compose the first version of the *Art of Fugue* during or shortly after the compilation of WTC2. Yet Bach was also willing to include the two highly galant fugues in F and in F♯—both of which contain extensive amounts of recapitulation—as well as the dashing little fughetto in G and the fugue in C♯, which is virtually a burlesque of strict counterpoint. The last two pieces were revised for WTC2; thus, during the same period in which he was creating some of his strictest fugues, Bach was bringing some of his freest ones to their final form.

Sources, Versions, Editions

Because there survives no complete autograph for WTC2, its text and its textual history have proved more difficult to establish than for Part 1. At this writing the evaluation of the manuscripts and the determination of Bach's final intentions regarding the text are still in process.[4] The complexity of the endeavor may be judged from Table 12–1, which lists only the most important sources. Kroll's edition in BG 14 was, like his edition of Part 1 (in the same volume), one of the great achievements of nineteenth-century scholarship. But it was done without knowledge of important sources—including the so-called London autograph (see below)—and it is now seriously out of date, as are all subsequent editions based on it. At this writing the only modern critical edition is by Dehnhard (1983), and some of his decisions have been questioned (e.g., by Franklin 1989b, 242).

One reason for the difficulty in establishing the text of the work is that the London autograph is actually, as noted previously, an incomplete set of individual manuscripts, one for each prelude and fugue.[5] A few of the preludes and fugues, moreover, are actually copies in the hand of Bach's second wife, Anna Magdalena. These copies include revisions in Bach's hand, but his final readings for most if not all of the movements occur only in other manuscripts apparently copied from lost composing scores or other autographs. The London set of scores lacks a collective title-page, but the familiar title does appear in several dependable early copies.

The date now usually given for the work, 1738–42 (as in the NG work-list), is actually that of the London autograph. A few movements certainly predate the autograph by a considerable period, including those belonging with the group of little preludes and fughettas (BWV 899–902) discussed in Chapter 10. Two dependable copies of the complete WTC2 have title-pages giving the date 1742, perhaps transcribed from a title-page in a lost autograph; this has led to the supposition that Bach considered the work finished by that date. Later readings are found, however, in a copy by Bach's son-in-law Altnikol (SPK P 430) dated 1744, and there exist still later readings of uncertain date for certain movements. Hence, even though Bach may not have carried out major revisions after 1744, he may never have considered the work finished, instead adding embellishments and refinements of detail to the end of his life.

Attempts have been made to sharpen the chronology of the work by reconstructing the "copying-out process" of the London autograph, which is thought to have occurred in three stages (see Table 12–1). Thus, a division of its component manuscripts into three groups or "layers" has been drawn from the use of the title

TABLE 12–1.   WTC2: Selected Sources

Source	Copyist, date	Comments, including contents if not complete (letters = movements, e.g., "G" = prelude and fugue in G)
Early versions		
SPK P 804, fasc. 5	Kellner, 1726–27	G: early version of fugue (BWV 902/2). Date from Stinson (1989a, 23)
fasc. 38	Kellner, 1727 or later	C: early version (BWV 870a). Date from Stinson (1989a, 24)
SPK P 1089	Vogler, 1729–34	C, d (prelude), G (fugue), A♭ (fugue): early versions (BWV 870a, 875a, 902/2, 901/2 [in F]), with BWV 899–901/1, 902/1. Date from Schulze (1984a, 66–68). BWV 902 added later (Brokaw 1985, 28)
SPK 10490	Michel (2d half 18th cent.)	C, G (fugue), A♭ (fugue): early versions (BWV 870a, 902/2, 901/2 [in F] in cycle including BWV 899–901/1. See Brokaw (1989, 227; 1985, 24–25)
SPK P 563	Michel	C♯ (fugue): early version in C (BWV 872a/2). Sole source (Brokaw 1985, 31)
SPK P 595, fasc. 5	Agricola, ca. 1738–9	c, d (fugues). C♯ (fugue): intermediate version in C (BWV 872b/1). E♭ (fugue, in D). Date from Franklin (1989b, 251)
DSB P 226	AMB, ca. 1739–40 or earlier	C♯ (prelude): early version in C (BWV 872a/1). d: prelude, intermediate version (BWV 875b). Date from Kobayashi (1988, 46)

Surviving autographs and related sources

London, British Library, Add. ms. 35021	AMB, JSB, 1738–42	Separate manuscripts constituting 3 groups (Franklin 1989b). Group 1: c, d, E♭, E, e, F, f♯, G, g, A, a, b. Group 2: C♯, d♯, F♯, g♯, B♭, b♭, B. Group 3: C, A♭. Missing copies (c♯, D, f) would have belonged to group 2. Autograph revisions in all groups
SPK P 416	1738–41	Separate copies, some lost or in other libraries. For copyist, see Franklin (1989b, 278n). Mostly copied from Add. 35021
SPK P 274	JSB, ca. 1743–46	A♭ (fugue, alternate version). Date from Kobayashi (1988; Franklin 1989b, places in late 1730s)

Table 12–1.   (continued)
Copies derived in whole or part from other (lost) autographs

SPK P 430	Altnikol, 1744	Gives later versions than Add. 35021 (and P 274) for most pieces; some earlier readings changed to later ones, corrections by various hands
SPK P 402	Altnikol, 1755	Related to P 430
SPK AmB 57	Anonymous 402	Kirnberger's *Handexemplar*, with his annotations. Includes WTC1. Derives from various sources including Add. 35021
DSB AmB 49	Anonymous 403	Calligraphic copy stemming from AmB 57
"Hering"	?Michel	On location, see Brokaw (1985, 22). Title includes date 1742
Hs MB1974	2 copyists, 1750 or later	Includes WTC1; title-page indicates date 1742

JSB = J. S. Bach
AMB = Anna Magdalena Bach

Praeludium (as opposed to *Prelude*) in what is thought to be the earliest layer.[6] Franklin (1989b, 266; 269–70) points to a tendency for pieces in each layer to have similar dimensions or to employ similar forms and compositional techniques. For example, the first layer contains most of the pieces in the simpler keys, and stylistic features in some of these pieces, such as those in G minor and A (discussed below), also suggest relatively early dates. It is difficult, however, to propose precise dates of composition for any of the pieces, despite the apparent stylistic or technical parallels between, say, the B-major fugue of WTC2 and Contrapunctus 10 from the *Art of Fugue*, which might place both movements around 1740. It is just as easy to draw parallels to works from earlier periods—for example, between the A-major prelude and the prelude of the First English Suite, which is probably a Weimar work.

Since most of Bach's latest revisions do not appear in the London autograph, editors have had to determine which of the various other manuscripts give Bach's latest readings for each piece. Only recently have the decisions been based on anything resembling a clear evaluation of the sources. Fortunately, the differences between versions are rarely as great as in some of the preludes of WTC1. But in virtually every movement there exist many small variants in ornamentation, accidentals, and details of voice-leading.[7]

Prelude and Fugue in C, BWV 870

It is possible that Bach considered opening WTC2 with a relatively simple arpeggiando prelude comparable to that which opened WTC1 (see the discussion of the prelude in C#). But instead he chose an imposing prelude in four strict parts. The decision, together with the subsequent revisions of both movements (see below), seems to indicate Bach's monumental conception of WTC2. The volume opens with a relatively massive piece, like the third part of the *Clavierübung*, and not with a comparatively modest first movement as did WTC1.

To be sure, the polyphonic notation of the prelude to some degree masks a simple arpeggiated texture. Nevertheless, the counterpoint is real enough and includes some striking dissonances and chromatic voice-leading.[8] Both prelude and fugue were originally shorter and, as BWV 870a, evidently formed part of a set of preludes and fughettas dating back to at least 1727.[9] It would appear that, having decided to include the C-major pair in WTC2, Bach found both movements too slight and accordingly lengthened each. The original portion of the prelude was also altered, and the addition of a doubling of the opening pedal-point at the lower octave was another sign that Bach was concerned that the piece should possess sufficient weight to open a collection as ambitious as WTC2 had (or was about to) become. Hence, this is a "big" piece, requiring a full registration, and the thirty-second-notes, added at a still later stage to the figuration over the opening pedal-point and elsewhere, imply a fairly vigorous affect.

The prelude underwent at least three separate revisions in all, and as Bach's alterations show great ingenuity they are worth tracing in detail. This can be done with particular precision, as the London autograph clearly shows the main steps in the revision process (see Table 12–2).

The crucial elements in the expansion are found already in the first group of revisions. In WTC1, the revised preludes were expanded mainly by the addition of a coda. Bach did the same here, adding a closing pedal-point on the tonic to

TABLE 12–2.   Plans of the Prelude in C, Early and Revised Versions

Version	Bars Numbers of Corresponding Sections in each Version					
Early (BWV 870a):	1–12	13–14	—	—	15–16	17
Late (BWV 870):	1–12	13–19 (bridge)	20–28a (recap.)	28b–29	30–31 (final cadence)	32–34 (tonic pedal)
Tonal plan:	C→	d→	F→	g→	C————————	

* = bars 5–14a, a fifth lower

Layer of Revision	Changes Made
1 (initial entry in London autograph)	altered melodic lines and voice-leading (bars 1–14, 30) extension of bridge (bars 15–19) addition of recapitulation (bars 20–29) final chord expanded into pedal point (bars 32–33)
2 (added in London autograph)	replacement of most of bridge (bars 14b–19)
2 (in Altnikol copies)	embellishment: added 32ds (bars 1–4, 6, 9, etc.)

balance the initial one. But more important was the insertion of a new recapitulation section and a bridge passage leading up to it.[10] Bach was dissatisfied with his first draft of the new version, and he eventually replaced most of the bridge, or rather substituted a heavily rewritten version of it (both are transcribed in Brokaw 1989, 235).

The seams do not show. Nevertheless, the prelude remains a singular piece. It was already so in the early version, which obeys the aesthetic of the improvisatory prelude by avoiding exact repetitions, regular phrasing, and sequences. For example, after a weak arrival on the dominant (bar 7) the prelude enters a sequence that would normally have confirmed the modulation just made. But the passage veers off toward the relative minor (A minor) and the supertonic (D minor), never returning to G.[11]

While this might have been disastrous in a sonata-allegro movement, it seems perfectly tenable in the more relaxed ambience of a prelude. Indeed, the most striking aspect of the prelude is its tonal design, which emphasizes minor keys on the "flat" side of the tonic without firmly articulating the dominant. This aspect of the prelude was strengthened in the final version, whose strongest articulations are the cadence to D minor at bar 13 and the arrival in the subdominant at bar 20. The latter marks the beginning of a sonata-style recapitulation—that is, a recapitulation of the type particularly associated with Schubert, in which the opening section is transposed almost verbatim a fifth lower. Normally such a recapitulation leads from the subdominant back to the tonic. But because of the unusual tonal design of the first section, the present recapitulation reaches the somewhat unexpected key of G minor only a few bars before the end.[12] From here it took great ingenuity to modulate swiftly and convincingly back to the tonic. But Bach accomplished the task smoothly, and the return to C major at bar 30 even coincides with a return to the material of the original version.[13]

While the revision of the end of the prelude appears to have gone effortlessly, the bridge in the middle evidently presented problems. Bach's first draft of the bridge had contained some weak voice-leading (e.g., doubled Fs at the end of bar 14). But beyond correcting this Bach also intensified the progression in the passage leading up to the recapitulation. The added chromaticism in bars 18–19, raising the level of tension, automatically produced a corresponding relaxation at the beginning of the recapitulation, which now coincided with a return to diatonicism as well.[14]

The fugue is of the galant type in three parts common in WTC1, although it is perhaps even closer to the little violinistic fugues BWV 952 and 953, also in C. As in the prelude, Bach seems to have drafted the revised version while writing out the London autograph. But here the essential revisions were limited to the addition of a coda (bars 68–83). The coda helps the fugue balance the more heavily scored prelude; the texture thickens to five parts in the last few bars, and a few athletic figures in the left hand (bars 76ff.) reach down to low C, which has not been heard since the opening of the first movement.[15]

Bach also changed the time-signature from C to $\frac{2}{4}$, halving the length of each bar. Similar alterations in the B-minor prelude (see below) and in the Art of Fugue suggest that Bach was concerned during this period with the implications of his rhythmic notation. Unfortunately, it is not at all clear what those implications are.

In this instance the change might imply an increase in speed, pieces in $\frac{2}{4}$ generally being lighter and, presumably, quicker than those in $\frac{4}{4}$. But it might also reflect Bach's realization that the fugue tends to move in one-beat rather than two-beat units. In other words, every beat, rather than every other beat, should receive a certain amount of weight—which might imply a somewhat *slower* tempo. In fact, a slower tempo would seem more in keeping with the grander conception of the piece found in the revised version.

The early versions of both movements appear with very thorough indications of fingering in the copy by J. C. Vogler, a student of Bach and his successor as court organist at Weimar. Vogler's fingerings seem to follow the same general principles as those given by Bach in CB (see the discussions of BWV 994 and 930 in Chapter 10). But the copies date from well after Vogler's studies with Bach, and the choice of fingers does not always seem well thought out, although some of the less likely ones found in modern editions of the pieces are misreadings.[16]

Prelude and Fugue in C Minor BWV 871

The second prelude and fugue belongs to the oldest layer of the London autograph and was in fact copied by Anna Magdalena Bach. It does not appear to have undergone any substantial revisions and thus must have been among the first pieces in the volume to achieve its familiar shape. While the prelude is in binary form, it recalls the inventions in its predominantly two-part writing and the use of voice-exchange at the outset of each half (and elsewhere). The fugue also looks backward, recalling the C-major fugue of WTC1 in certain respects. Subject and countersubject share a restrained character faintly reminiscent of the *stile antico*, and the form is distinctly bipartite, a new contrapuntal technique being introduced after the midpoint, where the subject is presented simultaneously in rhythmic augmentation and in its original values. Almost immediately the inversion appears as well (bar 15), albeit in a fairly free form. Indeed, while strettos play a prominent role from here to the end of the piece, rigorous counterpoint as such is less important than the dramatic effect achieved by the piling up of stretto entries.

The texture is limited to three parts until bar 19, where the bass enters with the subject in augmentation.[17] This might be taken as a sign of an early date, but the organ fugue in C, BWV 547/2 delays the entrance of its last (fifth) voice for similar reasons and until much the same point in the piece—almost exactly two-thirds of the way through.[18]

Obviously, the bass entry in the organ fugue can be made to sound very impressive on an instrument with a strong pedal division. The present fugue might also benefit from organ performance, not only in the first entry of the bass but also in the earlier augmented entry in the tenor (bar 14). But the bass here is not a pedal part; it ascends to d' (bar 21) and has unidiomatic figuration in the coda (bar 26). Moreover, the detached pedal-point in the coda—eighth-notes separated by rests in bars 23–25—is an example of a device that Bach often used in the *absence* of a real pedal part, as at the end of the Chromatic Fantasia. In any case, learned contrapuntal work mingles here with *brisé* writing that seems specially idiomatic to the harpsichord (e.g., bars 9, 11b–13). The final chord even bears an arpeggio sign, suggesting the possibility of a double or triple breaking of the chord (upwards, downwards, and upwards again), not an effect likely to sound very felicitous on the organ.

Prelude and Fugue in C♯, BWV 872

The prelude in C♯, like the prelude in E♭ of WTC1, is a small prelude and fugue in itself. In its earliest known form (BWV 872a/1) it stood on its own, and it is conceivable that either in this form or paired with the Fugue BWV 872a/2 it was to have opened WTC2. Both movements were originally in C, and the arpeggiando character of the first part of the prelude would have made it suitable for this purpose. Instead, however, Bach transposed the two pieces to C♯ and brought them together in considerably revised versions.

None of the arpeggiation was written out in the earliest version of the prelude, which is notated (like the early version of the C-major prelude in WTC1) as a series of five-part chords.[19] In the London autograph the chords were resolved into a three-strand texture; as in a few preludes of WTC1, this was perhaps orchestrally conceived. In particular, the repeated eighth-notes forming the middle line might be played as smoothly as possible, in imitation of "bow vibrato" (cf. the lower string parts of the opening movement of Cantata No. 82).

Bach also revised some of the voice-leading in both the opening section and in the little three-part fugato that follows.[20] In the latter Bach added the chromaticism in the inner voice of bars 44–46, which consequently echo the chromaticism at the end of the first section (bars 23–24). Bach also added the *allegro* tempo-mark, but despite this the fugato retains a French quality, thanks to the *port de voix* in the subject.[21] This suggests that the fugato should have the relaxed character of a minuet or passepied, and the sixteenths might even be played slightly *inégales*.

Such a manner of performance would create a welcome contrast with the fugue proper, which opens with an incisive staccato subject. The fugue is one of Bach's wittiest compositions, and unlike the G♯-minor fugue of WTC1 it makes its humor evident to any reasonably attentive listener. The subject should probably be understood as extending to the middle of the second bar, making the opening exposition a stretto. But Bach abandons the latter portion of the subject before the piece is half over (the last full statement begins at bar 15), and the remainder is a sort of fantasia on the triadic motive contained in the first four notes. Hence, it is somewhat academic to describe the piece in the usual fugal terms. All of the expositions are actually strettos, and most (including the first) incorporate *inversus* entries—but the contrapuntal learning displayed here is worn very lightly indeed.

The piece is better understood as a series of brief vignettes, each consisting of no more than a single phrase that introduces one or two new thematic or rhythmic wrinkles, for example, the running idea in sixteenths at bar 8 or the entries *per arsin et thesin* at bar 11. The running figuration grows less inhibited with each phrase, and the piece concludes brilliantly. This plan is already visible, albeit in a shorter and more restrained form, in the earliest version (BWV 872a/2). Like the C-major prelude, the piece was revised three times, almost doubling in length. But in this case the expansion was by way of the extension or outright replacement of four distinct passages (see Table 12–3).[22] Already in the earliest version, each successive

TABLE 12–3.   Fugue in C$^\sharp$, Early and Revised Versions

Version	Corresponding Measures							
Early (BWV 872a):	1–4a	—	4b–6	7–9a	9b	10–17a	17b	18–19
Late (BWV 872):	1–4a	4b–7a	7b–10	11–14a	14b–17	18–25a	25b–31	32–35
Cadences:	C$^\sharp$	G$^\sharp$	C$^\sharp$	a$^\sharp$:V	C$^\sharp$	C$^\sharp$:V	V	I

phrase increases in length and brilliance, so that the fugue, which begins like a rather dry contrapuntal exercise, ends as a virtuoso improvisation. In revising it, Bach must have had contrapuntal elaboration foremost in his mind, even if he was not taking it very seriously; diminished and augmented entries (bars 19 and 25, respectively) are among the interpolations.

Prelude and Fugue in C$^\sharp$ Minor BWV 873

The two movements in C$^\sharp$ minor, though of different types, form a particularly satisfying pair. Both are of fairly ambitious dimensions, worked out strictly in three parts, and each has a clearly articulated structure: The prelude is in a sort of sonata form, while the fugue is a double fugue, the two subjects being introduced separately and then combined. Each movement is also a gigue of one sort or another; the prelude seems akin to the siciliano, while the fugue is a very quick Italian gigue in $\frac{12}{16}$.

In texture the prelude somewhat resembles the Sinfonias. But it is considerably longer than any of them (or any of the comparable preludes of WTC1), and its model is not the Corelliesque trio-sonata but the later and more homophonic type composed by the Graun brothers and C. P. E. Bach. The texture is still in principle contrapuntal. But the phrases are long and one voice tends to dominate the others. Hence, the listener is less conscious of the interweaving of three independent lines than of the cantabile quality of the leading one. For this reason the repetition of the opening theme by the middle voice (bars 7b–11) is heard not as a fugal imitation but as the consequent half of a period, answering the antecedent phrase in which the upper voice has the principal line. The theme is too long to be restated in this manner after the cadence to the dominant (bar 17). But it does return in full in the subdominant at the end of the second section (middle voice, bar 33); this entry serves as a retransition leading into a sort of recapitulation (bar 39).

All three voices are heavily ornamented in an almost *empfindsam* style. Nevertheless, the tempo should probably not be so slow as to obscure the sicilianolike rhythm; there are three, not nine, beats to the measure. The similarity to the Berlin style of C. P. E. Bach and others suggests that some, at least, of the appoggiaturas should be performed as "variable" appoggiaturas taking half the value of the following note. Indeed, certain readings in the Altnikol sources appear to represent a more explicit notation for some of these appoggiaturas (Example 12.1). Unfortu-

EXAMPLE 12.1.   Prelude in C♯ minor BWV 873/2 (upper
staff), bars 16–17; readings of (a) SPK P 416; (b) SPK P 402

nately, the loss of the autograph from the London set compounds the usual difficulty of ascertaining which ornaments Bach actually wrote. The Altnikol sources seem to preserve an independent set of ornaments that sometimes coincide with, sometimes depart from, those in sources closer to the lost London autograph.[23]

The fugue uses the time-signature $\frac{12}{16}$ which Kirnberger took as an indication for a most lively tempo.[24] But the fugue is serious in character, and the first subject is eventually combined with a chromatic second subject that enters in stretto at the beginning of the second half (bar 35). Each half is further subdivided, the first by the *inversus* exposition beginning at bar 24, the second by the first combination of the two subjects at bar 48.[25]

Although this is the sort of structure one expects in an example of "demonstration counterpoint," the piece is (fortunately) a less than exhaustive working out of the various combinations of the two subjects. Nor is it wholly systematic. The final (combined) exposition includes a demonstration of counterpoint invertible at the twelfth, as shown by the entries in bars 48–49 and 55–56. In between, however, lies a single, rather anomalous statement of the first subject alone, in inversion (bars 53–54). Unfortunately, this entry seems awkward, despite the revision of bar 54b, and it seems a weak link in what is otherwise a well-wrought virtuoso harpsichord piece.

Prelude and Fugue in D, BWV 874

The prelude in D is one of the most magnificent pieces in WTC2, thanks in part to its exuberant theme and brilliant figuration, both worked out at length. Moreover, of the four or five preludes of WTC2 in full three-part sonata form (i.e., with a complete recapitulation section), it comes closest in style and dimensions to some of the large sonata movements composed during the 1740s by Emanuel and Friedemann Bach.[26]

Like the first movement of Friedemann's D-Major Sonata (F. 3, published in 1745), the prelude is still conceived contrapuntally—predominantly in three parts. Thus, bars 1–2 are immediately repeated with the upper voices exchanging material, and a large portion of the first section (bars 1–7) is eventually recapitulated with the upper parts exchanged (bars 41–47). Yet the latter is a sign of Bach's holding back from pure sonata style. For the inversion of the contrapuntal texture in the recapitulation is a way of avoiding a literal restatement of opening material.[27] In other respects, too, the recapitulation, while corresponding bar for bar with the first section, is far from an exact restatement. The bass, which at first failed to take up the theme, now has an inverted stretto entrance (bar 43), and in the last half of the recapitulation (from bar 52) the individual lines are varied to produce even greater rhythmic exuberance than before. Thus, the recapitulation becomes a culmination rather than a simple rounding out of the form, as it is in most pre-Classical sonata movements.

The double time-signature ($\mathbf{\mathnot{C}}\frac{12}{8}$) seems to convey special information of some sort, but it is impossible to say exactly what. The sign obviously reflects the presence here of both duple and triple rhythmic figures and cannot be just a chance survival of the quasi-proportional signs still employed, as a vestige of Renaissance rhythmic theory, in some late-Baroque works (e.g., some of Fischer's preludes and fugues). Nor, however, does the sign have any obvious bearing on the question of whether the piece's occasional duplets—pairs of equal eighths—should be interpreted literally or "assimilated" to the predominant triplets.

One cannot reach a decision about the latter issue by examining Bach's counterpoint, for both literal and "assimilated" readings produce parallel fifths at different points in bar 18 (Example 12.2). Evidently Bach overlooked these, regardless of how he played the rhythm. "Assimilation," however, would trivialize the stark contrast between the lively gigue figuration of bar 1 and the softer "sigh" figures of

EXAMPLE 12.2.   Prelude in D, BWV 874/1, bar 18; (a) as notated; (b) with "assimilated" rhythm

bar 2, which are notated as pairs of eighths. Hence, it seems best to play the duplets literally throughout. It is disappointing that bars 18 and 20 are the only ones in which the two meters are combined; for a more extensive exploration of conflicting meters one must look to the twenty-sixth of the Goldberg Variations. The dotted rhythms appearing throughout the present piece (from bar 5) pose less of a problem; there is no reason to think that these are anything other than the usual shorthand for triplet rhythms.[28]

The prelude overshadows the fugue, but the latter is also one of the more important pieces of WTC2. It seems to emulate the *stile antico*, but if so it is more a canzona than a motet or ricercar, and its structure is a modern one based on a regular alternation between expositions and episodes. Moreover, the underlying structure is tonally conceived, the most important articulations being the arrivals to A (bar 20b) and F$^{\sharp}$ minor (bar 27b). Following the cadence to F$^{\sharp}$ minor the fugue returns at once to the tonic, like many early sonata movements. But at this point Bach gives us not a recapitulation but a series of close strettos, the last of which contains entries for all four parts cascading downward from highest to lowest (bar 44b).

The episodes, unlike those in the more galant fugues, are canonic in texture, hence not very different in style from the expositions. Such episodes would seem to make for a very plain piece, especially as they are all based on the same five-note descending figure drawn from the second half of the subject. In the course of the fugue, however, the motive grows from six notes (bar 7) to eight (bar 16), finally culminating in a two-octave descending scale in the bass (bars 38–40)—a remarkable gesture in a piece ostensibly based on the restrained style of antique polyphony.

In fact, while the fugue is notated *alla breve*, the prevailing note-values are quarters and eighths (rather than halves and quarters), and the piece should probably be quite lively in performance. As in other "alla breves," players may fear that a quick tempo makes it impossible to bring out many details of the counterpoint. A slow tempo, however, makes it harder for individual notes to be heard as parts of lines. In a lively tempo the three repeated eighths at the beginning of the subject form an incisive "speaking" motive, and the gesture stands out even in the overlapping stretto entries of the final section.

Prelude and Fugue in D Minor BWV 875

The prelude in D minor is, like those in C and C$^{\sharp}$, a much-revised, relatively early work. The fugue has an angular quality suggesting that it, too, may be relatively early, although no substantially different version of it survives. The two movements may not be among the more important pieces in the WTC, but they share an intense, vociferous quality, due in part to the packing of so much vigorous counterpoint within their rather concise frames.

As in the C-major prelude, Bach's revisions in the prelude can be traced very clearly. From the start, the piece was conceived as a fiery *moto perpetuo*, probably inspired by Vivaldi. The figuration is notably violinistic, particularly in the original version, which lacks the thirty-seconds later added to a few figures (in bars 22, 24, etc.). The revisions enlarged the piece from forty-three to sixty-one bars, but the basic design remained constant: binary form, the theme restated in the dominant at the beginning of the second half (bar 26; see Table 12–4).[29]

TABLE 12–4.   Prelude in D Minor BWV 875

Version	Corresponding Bars											
1. BWV 875a	1–5	—	—	6–14	15–19	—	20–21	—	22–25	26–32	—	33–34
2. Add. 35021, orig. reading	1–5	6–9	10	11–19	20–24	25–28	29–30	—	31–34	35–41	42	43–53
3. Add. 35021, first revision	1–5	6–9	10–16	18–25	26–30	31–34	35–36	37–38	39–42	43–49	50	51–61
Cadences:		d	d	d:V	a	a		(g)	(F)	d:V		d

The fugue subject has a dualistic structure much like that which has been observed in the theme of the *Musical Offering*. The subject opens with triplet-sixteenths moving diatonically, then shifts to plain eighths in chromatic motion. These in turn are later accompanied by the ordinary sixteenths of the countersubject. As a result, the fugue shifts constantly between duple and triple rhythms—far more often than does the D-major prelude. Again, however, it is disappointing that the two rhythms so rarely sound simultaneously—only once, briefly and almost as if by accident (bar 9b). On the other hand, the piece derives a special quality from the unresolved tension between the flowing triplets and the harsh chromatic eighths, whose effects are never reconciled or "integrated," as they might have been through contrapuntal combination (see below on the prelude in F minor). The antithesis might be marked in performance by clear nonlegato articulation of the chromatic steps in the second part of the subject, although these need to be played tenuto in order to achieve their full weight.

The chromaticism in the subject hints at the possibiltiy of serious, rigorous counterpoint to follow, but the fugue is closer in some respects to a virtuoso improvisation than an example of "demonstration counterpoint." It contains a sufficient number of partial strettos, quasi-inversions, and other manipulated entries for Marpurg to have selected this fugue for bar-by-bar analysis in his *Abhandlung von der Fuge* (1753–54, 1:141–43). Yet most of these entries break off well before the complete subject has been stated, and the fugue lacks a clear formal design; fortunately, it is short enough that this is not felt as a significant failing.

Bach is not known to have made many revisions in the fugue. The most significant was the rewriting of the treble in bars 13–14 to avoid a collision with the middle voice on the downbeat of bar 14. Unfortunately, this weakened the stretto entry of the subject on the next beat, which is no longer preceded by a rest.

Prelude and Fugue in E♭, BWV 876

The Prelude and Fugue in E♭ is one of the less closely matched pairs in WTC2, in character if not in dimensions. The prelude is a lightly scored, giguelike piece comparable to the lute prelude in the same key (BWV 998/1, discussed in Chapter 15). The fugue, in four parts, imitates a capella style, although it has no preoccupation with contrapuntal technique as such, nor is it closely connected to the *stile antico*. The differences in style might reflect different dates of composition; in the London autograph the prelude has the appearance of a first draft, while the fugue is virtually a fair copy and is preserved separately in one possibly earlier source.[30]

The prelude resembles the lute piece, which might be contemporary, in key, motivic material, and texture.[31] The designs of the two pieces also have points in common. For example, both wait until the last phrase to bring the opening theme back in the tonic. In addition, both preludes are descended from the arpeggiando type, the underlying harmony occasionally being composed out in a rather allusive manner. Some corrections that Bach probably made while writing out the London autograph made it even more so. For example, simple whole-steps in the bass of bar 34 were altered retrospectively to agree with the bass of bar 37, where Bach had introduced descending sevenths; the leaps became ninths in bar 39. The effect of such leaps—which are not unknown in the melodic lines of Italian Baroque concertos and arias—is to enrich the implied voice-leading, since the top note of a leap usually suggests a distinct line in the underlying polyphony (Example 12.3).

EXAMPLE 12.3.   Prelude in E$^\flat$, BWV 876/1, bars 39–40:
   (a) final version; (b) earlier readings (bass, bars 34–35);
   (c) analysis of bar 34; (d) analysis of bar 39

The fugue has some of the character of Bach's biblical choruses, though it is not as close to the *stile antico* as is the following fugue in E. Nor is it as learned as another quasi-choral fugue, the one in D, for the contrapuntal work as well as the overall form here is far simpler, despite the presence of strettos in the last two expositions. The emphasis is rather on the straightforward working-out of the subject, which is longer and more varied in rhythm than the subjects of the fugues in D and E. The *alla breve* notation implies a vigorous tempo, the leaps and syncopations well marked; one might compare the *turba* chorus "Wir haben ein Gesetz" from the Saint John Passion.

Prelude and Fugue in D♯ Minor BWV 877

Both movements of this pair might, like the D♯-minor fugue of WTC1, originally have been in D minor, the key in which Marpurg (1753–54) quotes the opening of the fugue. But the manuscripts preserve no trace of a version in D minor, even though both movements would probably have been much easier to play (and read) in that key. If it had originally been notated in D minor, the piece could have been easily transposed through the addition of sharps to the original (lost) autograph. The archaic style of the fugue and its similarities to several fugues in WTC1 suggest an early date, but stylistic evidence of this sort is particularly equivocal inasmuch as WTC2 was assembled at a time when Bach was clearly interested in archaic types of fugal composition.

The prelude is a two-part invention in sonata form, like the Invention in E—but on a considerably larger scale. One suspects that many of the figures involving thirty-seconds were the products of revision, as they are in other pieces, but the sources bear this out only in a few passages. As a result, it is possible that the prelude was conceived from the beginning in a relatively restrained tempo. Such a tempo will certainly ease the player's task of getting the notes, but it may also make the listener all too aware of the somewhat schematic design and the unvarying texture.

The key alone would suffice to make the fugue among the least-often played in the WTC. Its appeal is further limited by the dense four-part texture and somewhat diffuse structure. The basic model again lies in a capella style, the subject having the same freedom from the bar-line that characterizes the subject of the F♯-minor fugue in Part 1. Thus, while the fugue is notated in common (rather than cut) time, it is austere and archaic in character; there are few episodes, and, as in Renaissance polyphony, entries of the subject usually overlap cadences in a manner calculated to eliminate obvious articulations. But a half-cadence near the exact center (to V of IV, bar 24) seems to articulate a bipartite form, and the sole episode of the first half (bars 11–14) is recapitulated in the second (bars 35b–40a). The climactic event, as in several four-part fugues of Part 1, is an ascent into the upper register during this second episode; this is answered, as in the F-minor fugue of WTC1, by the final entrance of the subject, a quasi-*pedaliter* entry in the bass (bar 40b).

The piece could end there and conceivably did so in some lost D-minor version; three movements of the *Art of Fugue* originally lacked their codas (see Chapter 18). The present short coda, in which the subject and its inversion are stated simultaneously (bar 43b), seems somewhat out of place, inasmuch as neither the inversion nor any type of paired entry or invertible counterpoint has occurred previously in the piece. Perhaps Bach made a belated discovery of the possibility of combining subject and inversion and wrote it into the piece as an afterthought. That the coda was meant to serve as the culmination of the piece is indicated by the use on the last eighth of the penultimate bar of the rare German sixth in root position ($\#IV_{3}^{7}$).[32]

Prelude and Fugue in E, BWV 878

The E-major prelude is again in binary form, but unlike the previous prelude it is in three voices, and the opening pedal-point and the predominantly gentle character recall the prelude in G, BWV 902/1. This, however, is a more sophisticated piece; the upper parts, for example, are treated in a more genuinely contrapuntal manner, exchanging their material in the second phrase (bar 5). Nevertheless, the figuration is idiomatic to the keyboard, and the two-part notation of the right hand might in some passages originally have been written as a single voice (e.g., bars 18–20).

The London "autograph" is actually in the hand of Anna Magdalena; numerous corrections suggest that she copied it from a nearly illegible composing score that itself contained corrections and revisions. One passage was left uncorrected, even though Sebastian himself copied the last two bars on an extra system added in the lower margin. The first beat of bar 50 was later altered in an unidentified hand, but other sources provide two further readings, and it is difficult to say which, if any, is right.[33]

The fugue is the purest example in the WTC of the *stile antico*, which is signified here not only by the long bars of $\frac{4}{2}$ time but by the use of a traditional subject traceable to chant (see Wolff 1968). Actually, Bach seems to have taken not only the subject but most of the first six bars from the E-major fugue in Fischer's *Ariadne musica*.[34] Bach continued to follow the general outline of the model up to the cadence on the dominant in bar 9 (bar 19 for Fischer, whose bars are half the length of Bach's). By that point Fischer, working on a smaller scale, had already begun using the theme in stretto, a device that Bach saves for the following section (bars 9–16). This is, then, a true example of "demonstration counterpoint," a new device being introduced after each cadence: a new type of stretto (bar 16), varied and diminuted forms of the subject (bars 23, 27), combinations of different forms (bars 30, 35). But cadences are more frequent here than in Bach's models, and the modulations range more widely than in music by either Fischer or the ultimate model, Palestrina. Hence, the piece is not really as old-fashioned as it may seem.

As usual, too slow a tempo fragments the lines, making it difficult to perceive such details as the shape of the penultimate phrase in the treble, which forms a long arch that rises to the highest note in the piece (a″, at bar 38) before descending through more than an octave. The descent continues in the final phrase, which echoes several chorale melodies whose closing phrases have similar outlines. In fact, the descent is derived from the end of the subject, and its extension into a complete scale just before the end is another example of a process observed previously in the fugue in D.

Prelude and Fugue in E Minor BWV 879

The pair in E minor, like the one in D minor, belongs to the earliest layer of the London autograph and shows signs of being relatively early in date of composition as well. The prelude is a long invention somewhat resembling the prelude in D$^\sharp$ minor. But the voices here are somewhat less equal—the bass often moves like an ordinary continuo part, in eighths—and while there is a double bar there is no return. These points alone do not make this a weaker or an earlier piece. But reminiscences of the Inventions (especially the one in D minor) seem to support a relatively early date, and the rather dogged playing out of several not particularly compelling sequences may make the prelude seem rather long. Thus, many players will be grateful for the absence of a first ending for the second half, permitting one to omit the repetition without qualms.

The four long trills in the prelude raise the question of whether the upper note should be sharp or natural. No one in the Bach circle seems to have indicated such things notationally until C. P. E. Bach began to do so some time after 1750. But the evidence suggests that in works by J. S. Bach it is best not to introduce notes from outside the natural scale of the currently tonicized key (as one might do in a work of Mozart or Haydn). Hence, in the first two trills, where the key is B minor, the upper note would be g (not g$^\sharp$) in bar 29, and c$^\sharp{}''$ (not c$'$) in bar 33. This is so despite the cross-relations that will result in bars 30–32 as the treble twice strikes g$^\sharp{}''$ against the bass trill on f$^\sharp$.[35]

The long, rhythmically complex subject of the fugue (mixing triplets, sixteenths, and dotted rhythms) may also point to an early origin, although one need look no further than the three-part mirror contrapunctus in the *Art of Fugue* for a late example of the same type of subject. The present fugue, however, is much freer, and while there is a regular countersubject it is less a line than a texture: The countersubject is sometimes written as arpeggiando figuration in one voice (e.g., at bar 7), sometimes divided between two parts in *brisé* style (bar 13). By the same token, the rhythmic heterogeneity of the subject is more notational than real; the sixteenths are essentially written-out ornaments (turns), and the dotted figures are certainly to be assimilated to the triplets, as in the D-major prelude.

Originally, the fugue ended with a full cadence in bars 70–71, the coda being added only after the completion of the London autograph. The coda includes one full statement of the subject in the tonic (bar 72), thus correcting what is probably a flaw in the original version, in which the last entry of the theme is in the subdominant (bar 60). The original ending was somewhat abrupt but dramatic, and a memory of this perhaps remains in the sudden fermata in bar 70 (which might be understood as applying not to the note on the second beat but to the rest following it). Curiously, the syntax followed here—fermata, then coda—recurs in the three-part mirror fugue and is even repeated within the present coda, a second fermata occurring in bar 83. One is reminded at both points of the cadenzalike passages added in some of the preludes of WTC1. There may be, as in the latter, a subtle change in style at the beginning of the present coda, which seems even freer and more exuberant than the original portion of the fugue; note, for example, the variation of the countersubject in bars 72–73 to include leaps of a tenth. Yet the tempo never really changes; the Kirnberger copies indicate *adagio* at bar 83, but both this and the fermata may mean only a slight relaxation of the tempo.

Prelude and Fugue in F, BWV 880

The spacious F-major prelude has a majestic sweep that contrasts sharply with the somewhat nervous gigue rhythm of its fugue. Yet the two movements are of roughly equal lengths, and they form a very satisfying pair.

Much of the figuration in the prelude seems a rhythmicized version of that found in the French unmeasured preludes of D'Anglebert and other seventeenth-century composers. The figuration is essentially of the arpeggiando type, although this is somewhat obscured by the numerous passing tones in the figuration. Hence, the figuration often functions as pseudo-polyphonic *brisé* writing; nevertheless, as in the somewhat similar prelude in C, the counterpoint is by no means merely notational, and there are often as many as five real voices.

Whether or not it was inspired by the unmeasured prelude, the piece seems best played with a broad, relaxed type of movement in half-notes. The eighths in the first bar are slurred in groups of four, confirming that there are just three pulses in each bar, and even these need not be very strongly articulated, since the harmony generally changes only at the bar-line.[36] The prelude has some sonatalike formal aspects, above all the presence of a recapitulation (in the Classical sense). But it falls into four main sections rather than the usual two or three, and the greater portion of the second section (bars 17–28) simply restates the first twelve bars in the dominant.

The fugue is in the rare meter of $\frac{6}{16}$, which would normally imply a somewhat more rapid tempo than $\frac{6}{8}$ (according to Kirnberger 1771–79, 2/1:119). But the bursts of thirty-seconds appearing shortly before the end require that the tempo not be overly quick. Moreover, the rhythm of the subject is not so straightforward as it seems at first, and a controlled tempo makes it easier to grasp the true metrical shape of the subject as well as the apparent shifts in the placement of the downbeat. The subject begins in the middle of the bar, and if this is heard incorrectly, as a downbeat, the climax of the melody (the f″ in bar 4) will seem to fall on a weak beat. It may help to lengthen the climactic f″ ever so slightly, especially if one also differentiates the articulation of the sixteenth-note figures on strong and weak beats—for example, by detaching the three notes of the upbeat (c″, d″, e″) but slurring f″, e″ on the downbeat of bar 4 (as one would very likely do anyway, considering the gigue rhythm).[37] But some ambiguity may be unavoidable and perhaps even desirable, especially as the downbeat migrates to the middle of the bar at several points in a hemiolic passage that is effectively in $\frac{9}{16}$ (bars 9–14).

The fugue has an unusual structure dominated by a single long episode occupying the portion of the piece where one might have expected a second exposition (bars 29–52). Since the episode is composed largely of strettos and sequences based on a motive from the subject, one might call the long episode a development section, and the subsequent reentrance of the full subject in the tonic (bar 52b) might then be a return. But the "return" is hidden in the inner voice, and the piece's formal proportions are not those of a normal sonata form, since at this point it is little more than halfway over. The subsequent section quickly sinks to the subdominant (bar 58) and dwells for a while in the tonic minor before reaffirming F major with ecstatic figuration (bars 89ff.). Perhaps one or more sections, or at least the thirty-seconds, were additions made in the course of a revision; there is no evidence for this in the sources, but the fugue ends, somewhat unexpectedly, with a recapitulation of the unassuming phrase that closed the first section (bars 94–99a ||24–29a). It is as if Bach wished to maintain the pretense that nothing extraordinary had happened in the course of this most unusual fugue.

Prelude and Fugue in F Minor BWV 881

Another well-matched pair, the F-minor movements are both in three parts, with strong references to galant style. The prelude opens with what is almost a caricature of a galant or *empfindsam* theme, replete with sighs in parallel thirds and sixths. This theme at first alternates with and is later largely replaced by lively figuration. Since, however, motivic elements from the opening later serve as accompaniment to the figuration in sixteenths, one might, following Hofmann (1988, 54), speak here of the eventual "integration" of the two basic ideas. The movement is perhaps a type of sonata form, but the return at bar 56b comes rather late, and it is intensified by melodic variation and a new bass line. Hence, despite the apparently simple periodic phrasing, the form, like that of the D-major prelude, is cumulative rather than symmetrical, and the prelude ends with a surprisingly emphatic variation of the original closing phrase (compare bars 66b–70 with 24b–28a).

As in the F-major fugue, the metrical structure of the thematic material is easily misunderstood. The opening theme begins on an upbeat; hence, the "sigh" motives fall on downbeats and ought to receive an expressive accent or even a little extra time. One might be tempted to shift to a louder manual for the subsequent figuration, but when the two ideas are combined (e.g., at bar 48b) they need to be equally strong. Despite the expressive opening, this is not a light piece, and the dramatic closing gesture—in which the figuration in sixteenths is interrupted by two full chords (bar 70)—seems to call for a sturdy registration on the harpsichord.

The fugue also contains some extraordinary gestures, notably the long prolongation of the dominant that begins with the pedal-point in bars 50–52 and continues, in effect, through bar 64. The passage generates a level of dramatic tension unusual in a Bach fugue. Yet the fugue as a whole, like the prelude, is characterized by unusually symmetrical, periodic phrasing, especially in a sequential episode that appears three times in all (bars 17–24, 33–40, and at the end). The passage serves as a sort of recurring closing phrase that divides the fugue into three main sections, although the last section occupies fully half the piece (actually slightly more), as in the fugue in F.[38]

Prelude and Fugue in F♯, BWV 882

The movements in F♯ again incorporate elements of the galant. The prelude is pervaded by dotted rhythms, but it is in ¾—hence not an overture—and the first three bars present a theme not unsuited to a sarabande, though it gives way to arpeggiated figuration. The latter is not the virtuoso arpeggiation of a concerto; rather, it possesses a certain poise as a result of the accompanying dotted figures in the bass. Except in the last two bars, the prelude is in two voices—one can imagine it scored for flute and continuo—and, while there is no double bar, it is a clearly articulated sonata form, in three spacious sections plus a retransition (bars 45–56).

All of this relates the prelude to the one in C♯ minor. Both movements are also graced with ornaments giving them the slightly mannered quality of the mature galant style. One senses this particularly in the appoggiaturas, including the one in the opening theme, which is, however, an addition not found in the London autograph and other early sources. Despite the galant style, it is less clear than in the C♯-minor prelude that any of the appoggiaturas should follow C. P. E. Bach's rules on length. Only in the cadences in bars 44 and 67 (second beat) does it seem necessary to hold out the appoggiatura as a "long" one—this because a similar appoggiatura is written out as a quarter-note in the final cadence.[39]

The fugue is in three parts and comes even closer than those in F or F minor to the texture of a galant trio-sonata, thanks to the extensive use of "sigh" motives in parallel thirds and sixths during the episodes (e.g., in bars 24b–32a). The subject opens in the middle of the bar, as in a gavotte, and while the opening trill motive is not characteristic of the dance, the periodic phrasing and the placement of "sigh" motives on the downbeats suggest that the piece ought to be played with the gentle gracefulness of an eighteenth-century French gavotte. In keeping with the somewhat formal character of the dance, the fugue has perhaps the most schematic design of any of Bach's three-part fugues, comparable to that of the E-minor fugue of WTC1 and the four duetti.

The fugue is built around three large expositions (at bars 1, 33, and 65) composed according to the permutational principle—that is, using all four of the possible combinations of subject and two countersubjects.[40] These alternate with two lengthy connecting sections (bars 12–32 and 44–64), the second of which is a recapitulation of the first. Each of these sections includes a single statement of the subject (at bars 21 and 53); hence, expository as well as episodic passages are included in the recapitulatory scheme, and the fugue gives the impression of a tidy, almost geometrically worked out, design. Despite this, it avoids the mechanical quality of Reinken's fugues by allowing for some freely composed material (e.g., the eighths in the bass at bar 41b). Moreover, details such as the "sighs" of the countersubject, which are developed in the episodes, lend it an expressive character that would have pleased the most demanding proponents of the galant style.

Prelude and Fugue in F♯ Minor BWV 883

The Prelude and Fugue in F♯ minor enjoys a high reputation. While this is certainly deserved, one wonders how much of the pair's popularity is due to the fact that the first movement is relatively short and the second relatively easy to play for a triple fugue in a "difficult" key. Unlike most of the other movements in such keys, these belong to the earliest layer of the London autograph. This fact, together with the concision of the prelude and the relatively free, unsystematic nature of the fugue (despite its use of three subjects), implies a relatively early date.

The prelude is of the arioso type, and the melody could be played on a separate (louder) manual, although this would tend to obscure the inventionlike imitations in the inner voice at the beginning of each of the three main sections (bars 2, 13, 31). The three-part texture is maintained strictly throughout, even though the voice-leading of the lower parts is occasionally little more than a notational fiction.[41] The structure is that of a concise three-part sonata form, with a distinct retransition phrase (bars 21–29); this distinguishes it from several preludes of similar texture in WTC1 (e.g., in C# minor) whose forms are bipartite.

The prelude alternates frequently between duple and triple rhythms, and while the two never appear simultaneously, one passage raises questions about the interpretation of Bach's notation (Example 12.4). In bars 7–8, Altnikol's copies have

EXAMPLE 12.4.   Prelude in F# minor BWV 883/1, bars 6–8a
(rhythmic notation from SPK P 402 above staves)

triplets in place of the dotted or duplet rhythms of the autograph, suggesting that here, as in a few other pieces, Bach may have used duple notation as a shorthand for certain figures involving triplets.[42] Yet elsewhere (bars 15, 18, 25) the autograph gives what may be revised readings, and it is difficult to understand why, in the tenor of bar 7, Bach would have written a sixteenth and two thirty-seconds in place of simple triplets if he meant the latter. Hence, even if Altnikol's triplet notation is authentic, it is not necessarily later, and Bach may really have meant to sharpen the rhythm of the passage. Of course, the smaller note-values are not necessarily to be interpreted with mathematical precision; presumably, the thirty-seconds can be played freely, like all written-out embellishments.

The fugue is the only full-fledged triple fugue in the WTC. The first subject is serious and declamatory, its syncopations referring to archaic choral style (as in the fugue in D$^{\sharp}$ minor). But the two later subjects are shorter, livelier, and more regular in rhythm; if the first is "vocal," the third is "instrumental," at least as those terms are understood today. The overall rhythmic shape of the fugue is somewhat similar to that of the five-part fugue in C$^{\sharp}$ minor of Part 1, which begins in *stile antico* and grows more fluid with the introduction of the second subject (or countersubject). But the opening section here is not as severely archaic, and the close is much more up to date (though not galant) in style, resembling an allegro in a trio-sonata.

Although the three subjects receive their own expositions, they are not systematically combined until the final section (bar 51).[43] This distinguishes the present piece from the two triple contrapuncti in the *Art of Fugue*, which more thoroughly investigate the contrapuntal potential of their material. But contrapuntal demonstration as such seems less important here than the "integration" of sharply contrasting material (as in the F-minor prelude). The process is characterized above all by a gradual evolution in the nature of the rhythm. The declamatory quality of both the first and the second subjects means that their expositions are composed primarily of short, overlapping gestures in each of the three voices. The third subject, on the other hand, consists of flowing sixteenths that can be extended indefinitely through sequence. In fact, the first subject is also sequential, an elaboration of a conventional chain of suspensions, but this point is largely obscured by the fragmentary nature of the accompanying voices during the first section. Indeed, the sequence implicit in the opening subject becomes explicit only in the last section, where the halting motion of the first subject is subsumed within a texture dominated by the long, effortless lines of the third subject.

Prelude and Fugue in G, BWV 884

The prelude in G is apparently the latest of three associated at different times with the fugue, which originally belonged to the group of pieces from which Bach drew the pair in C and the fugue in A$^{\flat}$. The little prelude BWV 902a might have seemed too short for inclusion in the WTC and too similar to the D-minor prelude to be worth expanding; both are short pieces in $\frac{3}{4}$ time based on concertolike figuration. Bach did expand the fugue slightly, but it remained one of the shortest and liveliest pieces in the WTC. Hence, the arioso prelude BWV 902/1 must also have seemed inappropriate, especially as it resembled the one in E. The prelude eventually included in WTC2 retains a few points in common with each of the earlier ones, but the similarities are so basic as to be possibly fortuitous. As in BWV 902a the material consists of violinistic figuration, but now, as in BWV 902/1, a double bar follows the first section, and each half opens with a short pedal-point as well as an exchange of material between upper and lower parts.

The fugue subject consists of running sixteenths like those in a number of early pieces (e.g., the A-Minor Fugue BWV 944), and, while this cannot serve as a criterion for dating, the rather simple early version (BWV 902/2) could have been written as early as the Weimar period. Its expansion was limited to the interpolation of one passage (bars 53–64) prior to the closing phrase, and the fugue retains its original dashed-off quality.[44] But Bach refined much of the original counterpoint, which consisted of little more than simple chords played against the entries of the subject. He also eliminated the free entrance of a fourth voice in some of the chords, although a fourth voice remains implicit in some of the *brisé* figuration of the final version (e.g., bars 16–19, right hand). The chordal writing in the original, although rare in Bach's surviving fugues, might have reflected a simpler type of counterpoint employed when fugues were improvised, as the continuo figures in the two *partimenti* BWV 907 and 908 suggest (see Appendix A).

While the substitution of figuration for staccato chords may have reflected a preference for greater elegance during the galant 1730s and 1740s, Bach's changes toward the end added fire, or rather humor. The variation of the last two bars produced a downward scale in thirty-seconds, which brings the piece to a surprising and much more dramatic close than the conventional final cadence of the original. But the new ending remains perfectly in character with the rest of the piece; anything but the merest ritard will ruin its effect.

Prelude and Fugue in G Minor BWV 885

While the G-major pair is a delight, the G-minor pieces are among the more forbidding in the WTC. The key in itself poses no special problems, but the complicated polyphony of the fugue would be difficult in any key, and both movements have harsh, angular lines with much passing dissonance. One's impression of the prelude might be somewhat different, however, if it lacked the persistent dotted rhythms and the tempo indication (*Largo*). In that case it would resemble more closely the elaborated arpeggiando type found in the preludes in C and F. In fact there are some indications that both the tempo mark and the dotting were later additions.[45] The revisions, if they occurred, must have preceded the writing of the surviving autograph, which belongs to the earliest layer of the London set. In any case, the dotting is not that of an overture but rather a sort of written-out inequality, evidently to be performed lightly, without emphatic articulation. Persistent overdotting would likely grow wearying and transform the "broad" (*largo*) common time indicated by Bach into a fussy $\frac{8}{8}$.

The fugue is archaic in its rhetorical, repercussive subject and in the often dense contrapuntal texture. At times it is almost as awkward to play as the A-minor fugue of Part 1, which it resembles in its emphasis on "demonstration counterpoint." There are no episodes to offer any relief, unless one counts the passage beginning at bar 75, which is better regarded as a coda. Nevertheless, this fugue can hardly be as early as the older one in A minor, for the counterpoint is more polished and the chief contrapuntal device illustrated is rare in the fugues of WTC1 or in Bach's earlier work; this is the device here termed "paired entries."

Marpurg, and perhaps Bach as well, would have called the movement a double fugue, since there is a regular countersubject. Indeed, the countersubject accompanies every statement of the subject, even in the stretto that opens the fourth and final section (bar 67). "Paired entries" are the topic of the third and last of the three regular expositions (bars 45–66), where, in addition to being accompanied by the countersubject, the subject is doubled in parallel thirds or sixths (Example 12.5).

Paired entries are closely related to invertible counterpoint at the tenth—indeed,

EXAMPLE 12.5.   Fugue in G Minor BWV 885/2, bars 45–47

their presence is a demonstration that the counterpoint between subject and countersubject is invertible at that interval. The relationship between paired entries and invertible counterpoint was evidently familiar to the more learned musicians of the generation or two before Bach, who might have discovered the technique in works by Scheidt or Buxtehude.[46] Yet while invertible counterpoint had long been a favorite topic of writers on fugue, its use at intervals other than the octave is fairly rare even in Bach's late works, appearing as a major concern only in the B-major fugue of WTC2 and in Contrapunctus 10 of the *Art of Fugue*. Paired entries are equally rare, and their appearance here may be another manifestation of Bach's preoccupation with strict counterpoint in the late works; this would suggest that the fugue is not as old as the style may suggest.

The technique of paired entries has a somewhat self-contradictory musical effect. It is impressive intellectually, and it plays an important role in the structure of the piece, since it is reserved for the last regular exposition. Yet it effects a simplification of texture, since it reduces the number of rhythmically independent parts. Thus, when the climactic moment occurs—the simultaneous paired entries of both subject and countersubject at bar 59—the initial effect is of a lightening of the texture and thus a weakening of tension. The impression is reinforced by the sequential character of the subject, so that the passage at first sounds like an episode. But the passage soon turns into one of the most thrilling crescendos in Bach's keyboard music, as both strands of the texture grow more densely interwoven (bars 62–65).

Prelude and Fugue in A♭, BWV 886

To create the pair in A♭, Bach appears to have joined one of the last-written preludes with one of the earliest fugues included in the volume. The autograph of the prelude has been dated to around 1741 (Kobayashi 1988, 46), and the style confirms that it is at least roughly contemporary with another presumably late movement, the prelude in F♯. As in the latter, there is, first of all, a pervasive but evidently fairly gentle dotted rhythm, which is combined with triadic figuration. In addition, the form is an expansive ternary sonata type, again without double bar, although in this case the recapitulation begins in the subdominant (bar 50). The closing phrases of the two preludes are very similar, this one exceeding the other in intensity by moving to the Neapolitan (bar 74); the move is echoed near the end of the fugue (bars 45–46).[47]

The fugue was originally in F major and, together with a prelude in that key (BWV 901/1), was associated with the early versions of the Prelude and Fugue in C (BWV 870a) and the fugue in G (BWV 902/2). Except for its transposition, the original remains largely intact, right up to the final chord on the downbeat of bar 24. Why Bach chose to transpose this particular fugue, abandoning its original prelude, is impossible to say. To judge from the chronology of the London scores, after copying out most of WTC2 Bach was left without a pair of pieces in A♭. He might have turned to BWV 901, intending to expand both movements to adequate dimensions but, finding it possible to do this only for the fugue wrote a new prelude.[48] To the original fugue Bach added twenty-six bars, disguising the seam by adding a fifth entrance of the subject at the end of the second exposition. Thus, one could hardly tell that the point at which the fugue suddenly veers off to F minor (bar 24) was originally the end.

The added section restates a short episode from the first section; bars 27b–31 are derived from bars 10–13a. But elsewhere the new portion of the piece differs significantly from the original. For example, it makes greater use of all four parts; the original was in three voices except in the final phrase, and the appearance of a four-part opening exposition in the revised version remains largely a notational fiction.[49] The modulations in the added bars range much farther than in the original, to as far as E♭ minor (which is not v but ii of IV; see bar 32). These modulations might be seen as more fully realizing the implications of the chromatic countersubject, for the chromaticism in the early version was largely decorative, the subject entering only on the tonic and dominant. While counterpoint as such is not a big issue in either half of the fugue, the added bars include an entry *per arsin et thesin* (bass, bar 37). There is also, as a way of marking the return to the tonic, a varied version of the countersubject that turns it into a chain of suspensions (bar 41). As in the E-minor fugue, the added section includes a fermata and a cadenzalike passage (bars 46b–47), but it ends much as the original did: no free coda, just a final statement of the subject, the texture bolstered by an additional (here, a fifth) voice.

Prelude and Fugue in G♯ Minor BWV 887

If the prelude in G♯ minor had been written a half-step higher or lower, it would surely be one of the more popular pieces in WTC2. For it is a fiery sonata movement far surpassing the one in the related key of D♯ minor in vigor, dimensions, and richness of material. In the opening theme, galant "sighs" in parallel thirds are set against violinistic figuration; the combination is somewhat reminiscent of the F-minor prelude, but here the ideas are combined contrapuntally from the start. Both ideas are extensively developed; it is odd, then, that Bach does nothing with the echo at bar 3, the piano there and the subsequent forte being the only dynamic indications in the WTC.

There is more to question in the following movement, a long and exhaustively worked out double fugue in three voices. As usual, the two subjects are first introduced separately and then combined. The first subject is that of a gigue, but its monotonous rhythm (all eighths) and simplistic sequential phrasing (2 + 2 bars) give it a static quality reminiscent of Reinken's gigue themes, such as the one adopted by Bach in the last movement of the Sonata BWV 965. The second subject is chromatic, hence forming an antithesis with the first subject, as does the corresponding theme in the A-minor fugue BWV 904/2. But the second subject is oddly banal, merely descending from the tonic through a fourth and then climbing back up.

The failings of the subjects are reflected in the fugue as a whole. It is unusually monochromatic for a mature Bach work. Entries of the subject in the first section are limited to tonic and dominant, and the only significant modulation to a major key (E) is very brief and late (at bar 111). An episode in the second section (bars 82–93) moves halfway around the circle of fifths, but like the second subject it winds up where it started, on the tonic. Hence, the fugue compares unfavorably with the other double fugue in three parts, the one in C# minor. One possible explanation is that the present fugue was an early effort, presumably transposed from G minor. Yet the episodes show what seems to be a mark of Bach's later fugues, that is, the disciplined canonic or permutational treatment of motives derived from or similar to the first subject.[50] Moreover, the fugues in related keys (B, C# minor, F# minor) are also on multiple subjects, implying their composition as a group (see Franklin 1989b, 270).

To reduce the risk of monotony it would seem particularly desirable here for harpsichordists to vary the registration of the three sections. Fortunately, those possessing a two-manual instrument can readily play the first section on one keyboard, the second section on the other, and the third section with the two keyboards coupled.[51] Of course, there is no evidence that Bach himself would have changed registration in the middle of a harpsichord fugue, but this is precisely the sort of piece in which it can be done convincingly, and one might even justify the use of manual changes by citing the dynamic indications in the prelude.

Prelude and Fugue in A, BWV 888

From his youth Bach evidently associated the key of A with a certain type of closely worked imitative counterpoint, as witness the early fugues BWV 896/2 and 949. In the WTC, both A-major preludes are three-part sinfonias, as is the prelude of the First English Suite, also in A. The latter is particularly close to the prelude in WTC2, as both pieces are moderately paced gigues in $\frac{12}{8}$ and share many other features besides (for a possible model, see Chapter 13). But like other preludes of WTC2, this one clearly adopts a sort of sonata form. The middle section (bars 9b–16) uses the inversion of the theme, but the prime form returns at the beginning of the retransition (bars 16–19), and the two forms appear in quick alternation at the beginning of the last section, the greatest portion of which is a complete recapitulation of the first section (bars 22–30a are derived from bars 1–9a). The restated material is somewhat disguised; in addition to being transposed down a fifth and having the upper voices exchanged—both normal procedures—the passage introduces a few small alterations that are sufficient to transform one bar, originally planted firmly on the tonic (bar 3), into a wistful glance toward B minor (bar 24).

The fugue is reminiscent of the one in E from Part 1. Both are in three voices, with light, airy figuration. Both are also short, indeed of exactly the same length, although not notably similar in organization. The present fugue is probably best viewed as falling into three expositions. An apparent revision at the beginning of the third section (bar 16) seems to confirm this analysis. The bass entry here is preceded by a rest in some sources, but others make this moment in the piece more impressive through two additional sixteenth-notes (AA, E) on the downbeat.[52] The low AA, which here serves as a particularly emphatic means of articulation, already appears in some early works (including the First English Suite). But as Bach avoided it in WTC1, it probably represents the later reading here. If so, it is a sign that by 1740 or so, when the London autograph was written out, Bach expected this movement to be played on the harpsichord (the note is not found on most organ manuals). Of course, players whose instruments lack the note can simply play the earlier version.

Prelude and Fugue in A Minor BWV 889

Like the A-major pair, the Prelude and Fugue in A minor is short, on paper. But the repeats indicated in the prelude double its length, and the vociferous character of its fugue makes it seem bigger than it really is.

The prelude has a highly symmetrical, mosaiclike construction recalling that of the C-Minor Invention and the E-minor fugue of WTC1, although here built out of units of one bar rather than two. The symmetry is very nearly exact, but Bach as usual breaks it at a crucial point. The double bar divides the piece into two equal halves, the second of which opens as a nearly exact inversion of the first. Each half is further subdivided, and the two divisions of the first half are virtually identical, save for the exchange and transposition of the two voices. But symmetry is replaced by free composition toward the end of the second half, where the established pattern of one-bar units grouped in pairs is interrupted by three unbroken bars in which the right hand has regular sequential figuration (bars 27–29). Within the present context, this is a dramatic event, and as such it prepares the final cadence.

To be sure, the prelude remains something of a mathematical game, but this is a characterization that only the innumerate will find derogatory. The pervasive chromaticism is part of this game, for it seems not the expressive chromaticism of, say, the B-minor fugue in WTC1 but rather the intellectually playful variety found in, for example, the Invention in E. It is related to the speculative or abstract chromaticism of many early Baroque ricercars and similar pieces. This does not mean that the music is to be played without carefully articulating the individual chromatic intervals or expressively dwelling upon certain dissonances. But while Bach clearly did associate chromaticism with both strict counterpoint *and* extreme pathos in some pieces, this does not seem to be one of them. The numerous accidentals, incidentally, occasionally raise textual problems, but the allusive nature of the two-part harmony makes it difficult to settle them by analysis.[53]

The fugue subject opens with the same four-note motive as the choral fugue "And with His Stripes" in *Messiah*. But as the latter was written in 1741, Bach could only have drawn on the same common tradition as did Handel.[54] Nor can the pieces have anything like the same expressive character: Handel's is a strict fugue approaching the *stile antico*, while Bach's is one of the freest in the WTC, and its mercurial style—especially the brusque ending—suggests that it should not be taken too seriously.

The thirty-second-notes in the countersubject might have replaced a motive in staccato eighths similar to that found at the end of the subject. But the flying thirty-seconds form an apt juxtaposition against the four stentorian quarters at the opening of the subject and thus might have been part of the original conception. Indeed, the general acceleration in surface rhythm that can be observed in bars 1–4 begins within the subject itself, whose initial rhythmic motive is repeated (after a pause) in half the original values. The process culminates with the trill first heard in bar 4. The trill functions in this piece as a distinct motive—hence the novel final cadence, in which the cadential trill is in the bass.

Prelude and Fugue in B♭, BWV 890

The prelude in B♭ is the longest and most impressively worked out of the sonata-form preludes of the WTC. Its opening bar might have been suggested by any of several preludes in Fischer's *Ariadne musica*, especially the one in G. But the piece as a whole bears a particular similarity to Bach's own C-minor fantasia (BWV 906/1), another sonata movement with a hand-crossing passage in each half.[55] Compared to the slightly frenetic activity of the C-minor fantasia, the prelude has a more relaxed, flowing movement, even though it is notated in $\frac{12}{16}$, theoretically an indication for rapid motion. While the central section ("development") is of roughly the same length in both pieces, here the outer sections are more expansive. Moreover, both outer sections—not merely the first, as in the preludes in D♯ minor and G♯ minor—contain distinct subdivisions functionally analogous to the first and second areas or theme-groups of Classical sonata form (bars 21, 65). Still, the hand-crossing passage is recapitulated not in the final section but in the central one, and there with the roles of the two hands reversed, as in the fantasia.

Perhaps it is the scalar, as opposed to arpeggiate, quality of much of the figuration that creates the impression of restraint here. Even if the actual tempo ought to be the same as in the fugue in C♯ minor or the one in F—notated in $\frac{12}{16}$ and $\frac{6}{16}$, respectively—the slower harmonic rhythm and the opening pedal-point make this seem more a pastorale than a normal gigue. The hand-crossings do not contradict this impression, for in each case they grow naturally out of the texture of the preceding phrase; they do not open up new registers but represent continuations of the underlying voice-leading (Example 12.6). Indeed, these passages, unlike the corresponding ones in the C-minor fantasia, could be played without hand-crossing, although this would require dividing the running triplets between the two hands.

The fugue is short in relation to the prelude, but it shares the latter's relaxed character, thanks to the slow harmonic rhythm (generally only one harmony per bar). The form is again close to that of a sonata movement, and the phrase that brings the first section to a close in the dominant (bars 29–32) returns at the end in the tonic. Indeed, this little tag, with its bass of repeated notes, is particularly close

EXAMPLE 12.6.   Prelude in B♭, BWV 890/1: (a) bars 12–14; (b) analysis

to homophonic sonata style. It perhaps sounds a little pat, entering a bit too suddenly, like the similar ending in the F-major fugue; but it is graceful and unpretentious.

The London autograph of this piece belongs to the second layer of copies in that source, which mostly give later readings (see Franklin 1989b, 269). Here, however, it appears that Bach subsequently rewrote several passages, including the first countersubject, which originally moved in quarters (Example 12.7). Another revision

EXAMPLE 12.7.   Fugue in B♭, BWV 890/2: (a) bars 5–8; (b) bars 5–6, early version (bass)

throws some light on an odd embellishment of the alto in the closing phrase, for the figuration in the later version is evidently a way of reconciling the original four-note chord with the prevailing three-voice texture (Example 12.8). Actually, Bach renotated the entire phrase, which was conceived in a free if not exactly homophonic texture. The new version makes explicit some of the polyphony latent in the original, although the resulting two-part writing for the right hand is still something of a notational fiction.

EXAMPLE 12.8.   Fugue in B♭, BWV 890/2, bars 87–90;
(a) early version (upper staff); (b) later version

Prelude and Fugue in B♭ Minor BWV 891

The pieces in B♭ minor occupy a position somewhat analogous to that of the B-minor prelude and fugue in WTC1, since they are the last "big" pair of Part 2, perhaps even its crowning point. The prelude, though not as exact an imitation of trio-sonata style as the B-minor prelude of Part 1, is a three-part sinfonia, indeed the longest and most substantial that Bach wrote. The fugue is a mature version of the rigorously contrapuntal yet expressive type that Bach had attempted in the D♯-minor fugue of Part 1.

As in the B-minor pair of Part 1, the prelude is probably an andante in the literal sense of the word, with a "walking" bass in fairly quick eighth-notes. A slow tempo would cause the many suspensions and especially the dominant pedal near the end (bars 73–76) to lose tension. There is a recapitulation (beginning in the subdominant) at bar 55, but the movement lacks a central double bar, and it is closer in form to some of the larger fugues, such as the one in F♯ (also in trio style), than the sonata-form preludes. Thus, expository passages based on the material of the opening bars alternate with canonic episodes, producing something resembling the fugal movements of Bach's trio-sonatas.[56]

The fugue is a large-scale demonstration of stretto and inversion. As in the D♯-minor fugue of WTC1, prime and inverted forms of the subject are introduced in distinct expositions (bars 1, 42) and strettos (bars 27, 67) before being combined (bars 80). The augmented form of the subject is, however, essentially ruled out by the piece's triple meter. Thus, at the very end, Bach instead plays the trump card previously glimpsed in the G-minor fugue: paired entries, here applied to a close canon between *rectus* and *inversus* forms of the subject.

Despite their common focus on "demonstration counterpoint," the effects of the two fugues are completely different, the present one being far richer, both expressively and compositionally. One obvious reason lies in the choice of subject, which here is one of Bach's most distinctive, punctuated by rests into four rhythmically diverse fragments. (The G-minor subject is also distinctive, but its built-in sequence denies it the high tension of stronger fugue subjects like this one.) Staccato marks (added later) over the first two notes reinforce the subject's declamatory quality.

They probably indicate accentuation as well as staccato while also serving as a warning against too languid or lyrical a performance. Two tritones in the subject (bars 2, 4) foreshadow the chromaticism of the countersubject, which is inverted along with the subject in the *inversus* exposition at bar 42. The countersubject plays no part in the strettos; still, Bach (or at least Marpurg) probably considered this a double fugue.

The fugue returns to the tonic at the beginning of all but the last of the major divisions. Yet it is far from monochromatic, reaching G^b major and A^b minor during the *inversus* exposition (bars 42–62). There is even an augmented sixth in bar 59, marking the furthest modulation from the tonic; this occurs in the course of a statement of the inversion in A^b minor. In addition, while the G-minor fugue, like the D^s-minor fugue of WTC1, concentrates almost single-mindedly on the contrapuntal development of the subject, episodes—or, at least, bridges—play an essential role here. While none of the bridges is clearly articulated from the expositions, through their sequential and generally diatonic character they furnish a respite from the expositions, even though they are themselves canonic or permutational. No two episodes use exactly the same material, but three (at bars 31, 77, and 84) are related by their use of hemiola, being effectively in $\frac{4}{4}$ time. This idea perhaps grew out of the strettos, which are at the interval of a half-note, thus producing cross-rhythms against the underlying meter ($\frac{3}{2}$).

Prelude and Fugue in B, BWV 892

Bach seems to have associated strict counterpoint with minor keys. But the fugue in B is a major exception, and with its prelude it forms one of the most important pairs of WTC2, on the same high level as the preceding pair. The two movements composing the B-major pair, unlike those in B^b minor, are of virtually opposite types: The prelude, the freest in WTC2, has a roughly ternary shape whose central section suggests an improvisation in concerto style; the fugue is in *stile antico*, with notable parallels to the *Art of Fugue*.

The first section of the prelude (bars 1–11) does not seem very far from the corresponding passage in the A^b-major prelude of Part 1; either might have served as the opening section of a sonata movement. After reaching the dominant (bar 12), however, the B-major prelude passes through a series of short-lived changes of texture, twice introducing a third voice, then soloistic arpeggiation of the type found in the solo sections of Bach's harpsichord concertos. The reliance on motion in sixteenths is virtually the only factor common throughout the prelude, although the bass at bar 23b has material from the first section. Yet the central passage never seems aimless, and it eventually leads to a fairly normal recapitulatory section. Perhaps the only close parallel to such a form in Bach's works occurs in the last movement of the D-major gamba sonata (BWV 1028), which includes soloistic passages for each of the two players prior to the final section.

One point near the end of the middle section (bar 35) is worth noting, since it recalls a curious moment in the C-minor fantasia. Both passages come to rest on the dominant after eight repeated, dissonant chords in the left hand. The unusually emphatic formula seems less appropriate in the C-minor fantasia than here, where it comes at a major formal articulation.[57]

The following movement deserves to be called a double fugue, even though the second subject, introduced at bar 28, is presented on its own only twice, elsewhere always accompanying the first subject. Butler (1983b, 296–97) suggests that the odd melodic leaps in the subject reflect the early Baroque tradition of the contrapuntal *obligo*, that is, a rule governing some aspect of the counterpoint or voice-leading—in this case, an avoidance of motion by step.[58] If so, however, Bach abandons the *obligo* after the third bar, and despite its angular subject the fugue as a whole has some of the suavest four-part writing in WTC2, in this respect resembling certain movements in the *Art of Fugue*, especially Contrapuncti 4 and 10.

Although Contrapunctus 4 is relatively late, Contrapunctus 10 belongs (with the other double fugue, Contrapunctus 9) to the first layer of the *Art of Fugue*; thus, all three double fugues might have been drafted around 1740. They are concerned with combining the two subjects in particular types of invertible counterpoint, here at both the octave (bar 27) and the twelfth (bars 42–45, 53–58).[59] By changing the time interval separating the two entries of the two subjects, Bach later combines them in a third way (bars 60–63). Even a sharp listener is unlikely to recognize the different types of invertible counterpoint without a score. But each variety of counterpoint places certain constraints on the intervals used in combining the two subjects, and this has some audible effect on the harmony. Fifths, for example, must be avoided in counterpoint at the twelfth, since they produce dissonant fourths upon inversion. It is therefore not surprising that the combination of the two subjects embellishes what is essentially a series of parallel thirds.

One passage stands out for its departure from the general emphasis on "demonstration counterpoint." This is the episode in bars 64–74, which serves as retransition.[60] The episode, which involves only the three upper parts, makes a modest departure from the fugue's prevailing restraint in matters of harmony and rhythm, even introducing sixteenths in the climbing sequence in bars 68–70. Hence, when the bass reenters with a statement of the subject (bar 75), this has the same impressive effect as the concluding entries in the F-minor and B-minor fugues of WTC1 while also serving as a sonata-style return.

Prelude and Fugue in B Minor BWV 893

Although WTC1 closes with one of its most impressive pairs, WTC2 does not. While by no means inferior or disappointing, the two B-minor pieces here are light and a bit quirky. The prelude is of the invention type; indeed, the two voices are as equal to one another as in any of Bach's two-part pieces. For this reason one might wish to play the prelude as a duet, on two manuals. But at the close it grows suddenly demonstrative, even including a few full chords. There are no signs, however, that the closing section was a late addition, even though Bach certainly revised the prelude; the London autograph contains corrections showing that it was probably copied from an earlier version (known from other sources) written in half the present note-values. Bach also added the tempo mark (*allegro*); in addition, one of the Altnikol copies (P 430) places staccato marks on the chords in bar 64. The staccato makes it clear that the outer voices of the two chords, although moving by half-step, do not form slurred appoggiaturas such as appear in the soprano in the previous two bars.

Emanuel Bach presumably knew this prelude. His "Württemberg" sonata in the same key at one point comes to rest on the same diminished chord, graced by the same appoggiatura, as appears under the fermata in bar 57.[61] The sonata dates from 1744 and includes a closing movement in two voices resembling an invention; perhaps these aspects of the sonata were inspired by Emanuel's receiving a copy of WTC2 around this time, as suggested by Franklin (1989b, 276).

The octave leaps in the fugue subject give it a jolly character, but they pose problems of practicability in keyboard writing, as Bach must have known from his experience in earlier works (e.g., the Capriccio BWV 992). Thus, it is surprising that Bach compounded the problem in the second exposition (bars 27ff.), abandoning the first countersubject in favor of a new one composed almost entirely of wide leaps that suggest violinistic string-crossings. This second countersubject accompanies each of the remaining statements of the subject, despite the repeated voice-crossings that result when the two subjects are placed in the same register (bars 57–59). While this would be frowned upon in a school-fugue, it actually serves very well as pure keyboard figuration, and the voice-crossings are more easily seen on paper than heard in performance.

The dissonant appoggiaturas on the final chord are a later addition, absent from the autograph. While they may call to mind the ornament on the final sonority of the Saint Matthew Passion, they probably should not be taken quite as seriously, nor held out for very long, if played at all. For the last phrase (bars 97–100) is a partial stretto based on the first five notes of the subject. The final entry (soprano, bar 99) is embellished; nevertheless, the fugue can be said to close by converting its opening gesture into a final cadence—a clever and witty way of bringing the volume to an end.

13

The English Suites

Bach's Later Suites

Next to the *Well-Tempered Clavier* and the inventions, Bach's best-known keyboard works are the suites that were composed, or at least collected and revised, during the 1720s and early 1730s. The twenty-one works in question include the six English Suites, the six French Suites, and the seven large suites (six partitas and an *ouverture*) published in Parts 1 and 2 of the *Clavierübung*. In addition there are two suites (BWV 818 and 819) that can be considered in conjunction with the French Suites as well as three compositions for lute that resemble suites and were probably played on the lute-harpsichord and other keyboard instruments.

The suite was the early eighteenth-century harpsichord genre par excellence. The preludes, fugues, and other pieces discussed in the last few chapters drew on the traditions of organ music and of abstract or learned "clavier" music, but the suite stemmed directly from the dances and dancelike *pièces de clavecin* written expressly for the harpsichord by French composers of the seventeenth and early eighteenth centuries. Bach's own suites were used for teaching, according to E. L. Gerber (BD 3:476 [item 950]/BR, 264). But while Bach's extended titles for WTC1 and the Inventions stress the works' pedagogic value, the printed title-page for the Partitas indicates that they are for the "spiritual delight" or "refreshment" of amateurs.[1] Nevertheless, Bach must have viewed his suites as lessons in style or, to use the eighteenth-century term, good taste (*le bon goût*)—a concept that, at least within the realm of the keyboard suite, was virtually synonymous with the French style of composition and performance.

In fact, Bach's suites document his own gradual mastery of the French style of the day. At the same time they demonstrate his incorporation of "German" harmony—that is, imitative counterpoint—into the predominantly homophonic tradition of the *pièce de clavecin*. While Bach had begun to do this in the early suites considered in Chapter 4, those pieces would have seemed outmoded by the 1720s. With the exception of the lute suite BWV 996—which could be contemporary with the English Suites—the early suites appear to have been modeled on French or German compositions of the previous generation. The later suites, on the other hand, reflect Bach's knowledge of more recent French harpsichord music—certainly that of Dieupart, whose suites Bach copied at Weimar, and probably works by Couperin as well.[2] Yet in all these works, and particularly in the earlier ones—especially the A-Minor Suite BWV 818 and individual movements from the English Suites—one senses a tension between Bach's impulses as a keyboard virtuoso and contrapuntist, on the one hand, and the niceties of the French *pièce de clavecin* on the other. Moreover, Bach, not content to imitate individual models, tended to mix styles and genres. Thus the preludes of the English Suites are, for the most part, in concerto style. The French *courante* and *gigue*, normally written in $\frac{3}{2}$ and $\frac{6}{4}$, respectively, tend to be replaced by the Italian *corrente* and *giga*, ostensibly dances but often in effect abstract binary-form or even sonata movements in $\frac{3}{4}$ and $\frac{6}{8}$. Italianate embellishment is written out in some of the sarabandes, which come to resemble an ornamented adagio, and imitative technique, usually confined to the gigue (if present at all) in earlier suites, is extended to the other dances, especially allemandes and courantes.

The titles themselves sometimes indicate the prevailing style of each movement, though Bach was inconsistent in using Italian titles for pieces in Italian style.[3] This was perhaps because the essential ethos of the suite as a genre remains French. Even in heavily Italianized movements the basic rhythmic schemes usually derive from the music of French court and theatrical dance, as do many melodic formulas: ornaments above all, but also distinctive cadential gestures like the *tierce coulée*, a formula used in metrically weak phrase endings. Moreover, Bach's suites, like all his mature keyboard works, follow the French tradition of precise notation. At least in the final versions, all necessary ornaments are indicated, and every detail (ties, note-values) of the passages in *style brisé* is made explicit.

Hence, there can be little doubt that German composers were intensely conscious of the imported nature of the suite. But while striving to avoid embarrassing faux pas, some, at least, aimed at creating a distinctive style of their own. This is clear from the prefaces to Kuhnau's published collections of suites, from which Bach borrowed the title *Clavierübung* for his first keyboard publication. Indeed, the choice and ordering of movements in Bach's suites may also have depended more on the examples furnished by Kuhnau, Fischer, and other German composers than on French works. Bourrées, passepieds, and even gigues are by no means as regularly included in French suites as they are in Bach's. Moreover, German examples of the dances tend to avoid—whether intentionally or not is hard to say—the more elusive stylistic characteristics of their models, incorporating more frequent sequences and more extensive thematic parallelism between the two halves of each movement. Hence, the dance movements in German suites, especially the allemandes and courantes, are apt to be more accessible to modern musicians and listeners than their French models, which may seem formless and even irrational. Indeed, the Bach dance movements least likely to appeal to modern taste are those that most closely imitate the discursive style of D'Anglebert or Couperin, like the two courantes of the First English Suite.

Nevertheless, the ability to recognize the dances from their rhythms and melodic shapes, and to infer from the latter the tempo and general character of a given dance movement, would have been taken for granted by any European musician of Bach's generation. It is not possible to give a full account here of the individual dances. In general, however, each is associated with certain patterns of stressed and unaccented beats as well as with more specific features, including particular motives or textures, like the arpeggiando texture associated with the keyboard allemande. Although not every piece designated as a dance possesses all of the features identified with the dance named in the title, most dance movements reflect the geometric character of eighteenth-century choreography in their construction from clearly delineated phrases of four or eight bars each, often arranged in a highly symmetrical binary form. There is usually a double bar at the center, and while few dances are true sonata forms, many are in rounded binary form, that is, with a reprise of the opening phrase in the tonic somewhere near the end of the second half. To be sure, a few dance movements were apparently composed originally for sonatas (see Chapter 15 on Partita No. 6). Their inclusion within a suite might represent a conscious blurring of the distinction between dance and sonata—that is, between the French and Italian styles—also visible in keyboard pieces by Bach's contemporaries, such as Rameau.

The suite as a whole, that is, an ordered series of dances and other movements in the same key, emerged as a distinct genre only during Bach's youth. Indeed, Bach, like Kuhnau, avoided the term in his published works, using instead the word *partita* and specifying on the title-page that each one consisted of "preludes, allemandes, courantes . . . and other gallantries."[4] But despite the title *partita*, which can mean "variation," in none of Bach's later suites do the movements reveal a common theme or other internal unifying features apart from a key and perhaps a vague commonality of style and dimensions. Like other composers, Bach may have regarded his suites as fairly loose collections of individual movements; the adoption of a standard order (allemande, courante, sarabande, gigue) in most manuscript and printed sources does not mean that composers composed suites as such, nor that performers played them.[5]

This seems clear from the manner in which some of Bach's suites grew through the addition of minuets or other movements in later versions. Indeed, some of the suites, like some of the preludes and fugues in WTC2, may have been assembled out of previously existing material, although this can be proved only in the case of the Sixth Partita. By the same token, the grouping of most of Bach's suites into three neat half-dozens can be traced back only to the mid-1720s or so. Bach appears to have juggled several suites into and out of the collection now known as the French Suites, finally arriving at a more or less rational ordering scheme based on tonality, as in the WTC. Such a scheme can also be detected in the Partitas, but not in the English Suites, whose arrangement may reflect either the order of composition or the increasing difficulty and complexity of the individual suites.

Unfortunately, as with most of Bach's keyboard works the loss of autograph material leaves the early history of the suites far from clear. Most of the keyboard suites, together with the orchestral suites and the suites for unaccompanied violin, cello, and flute, have traditionally been dated to Cöthen, but considerations of style and transmission have thrown this into question (see, e.g., Eppstein 1976). Both style and sources imply that the English Suites are the earliest of the keyboard collections, probably dating back to the Weimar period. What appear to be composing scores for portions of the French Suites survive from the Cöthen years, while the Partitas are known only from Leipzig sources. Since composers like Kuhnau and Couperin had previously used their published suites as a means of bringing their music to a wider public, Bach is likely, from a certain point onwards, to have envisioned publishing his own suites. But practical considerations—the absence of a patron or the dim prospects that such long, complex works as the English Suites would find buyers—evidently forced him to postpone publication until 1726, when he began to issue the Partitas. Nevertheless, the two earlier sets, although circulated only in manuscript, seem to represent ideal publications of the sort that Bach would have issued had circumstances permitted.

Publication, real or ideal, did not prevent Bach from revising the suites in the same ways as the WTC. Bach continued to add ornaments and other small revisions even after the works had been widely copied or, in the case of the Partitas, printed. Copyists also must have made their own additions, some perhaps on the basis of oral tradition, including lessons with Bach himself. Since we possess no fair-copy autographs for either the English or French Suites in their final versions, it is particularly difficult to verify individual ornament signs, slurs, and other textual details in these pieces, despite the relatively uniform text of the English Suites as preserved in manuscript copies. The critical editions of these works by Alfred Dürr (NBA V/7–8), while immensely valuable, necessarily leave certain details open to question, and serious students of the music will carefully consider his editorial commentaries; only occasional points can be discussed here.[6] Users of the BG and editions based upon it should be aware that the BG contained two separate editions of the French and English Suites; the first, in BG 13 (reproduced by Dover), was so poor that the works were reedited in BG 45 (see Becker 1953). Both BG editions mix readings from different versions, and for other reasons as well they are completely superseded by that of Dürr.

The English Suites

The English Suites occupy a medium position, in terms of length and virtuosity, between the French Suites and the Partitas. Yet they are probably the earliest of the three collections. Five of the six suites open with preludes in concerto style; these movements have clear affinities not only with the concerto transcriptions but with the large virtuoso preludes and fugues and with the Brandenburg Concertos, all of which may have originated during the Weimar period (see Chapter 9). The dance movements, especially the allemandes and courantes, also suggest an early date, inasmuch as they still reflect the style of older German and French keyboard dances. Several allemandes open with what appear to be rhapsodic improvisations in a manner that can be traced to Froberger. The courantes are all of the French type (in $\frac{3}{2}$ or $\frac{6}{4}$), even when attached to an Italianate walking bass, as in Suite No. 6.

Bach's attempt to incorporate significant imitative counterpoint into these traditional types of keyboard dance movement appears to have had little precedent. There were, however, other types of allemandes and courantes; the allemandes in Dieupart's suites, for example, have a significant contrapuntal element, and this might even explain Bach's interest in them.[7] One consequence of the emphasis on counterpoint, however, was keyboard writing that in many passages might have struck Bach's contemporaries as awkward and unidiomatic. Bach himself must have been aware of certain rough spots—for example, the stuttering repetition of the note b′ in the allemande of Suite No. 2 (bar 2)—but tolerated them, as he did in the WTC and elsewhere, because they were justified by the voice-leading and by the essential strength of the underlying musical thought.

In the later suites counterpoint as such seems less of an issue, and the writing on the whole is more obviously idiomatic to the keyboard. Hence, the French Suites and the Partitas give the impression of being more polished than the English Suites. While this may be only a reflection of the more galant style of the later works, even on their own terms certain individual movements of the English Suites may be less than wholly successful. Some suffer from fairly monotonous rhythmic textures; for example, the gigue of Suite No. 1 perhaps contains too many sequences composed of running sixteenths in both voices—a favorite device, incidentally, in Bach's early fugues and in the concerto transcriptions. At the risk of sounding like Scheibe, one may also complain that, especially in the courantes, the contrapuntal enrichment of the texture does not always compensate for the lack of a really engaging melody. Thus, in the courante of Suite No. 6, what may seem a good idea in the abstract— the combination of French melody and Italian walking bass—proves dull in the realization.

In addition, the English Suites as a group are less homogeneous than the two later sets. The First English Suite differs from the others not only in the style of its prelude—which resembles a sinfonia (three-part invention) rather than a concerto—but in the presence of two courantes (the second one accompanied by two doubles). Its key, A, does not fit into the descending sequence of the others (A minor, G minor, F, E minor, D minor), and it is the only one of the English Suites to survive in a distinct early version (BWV 806a). Of the remaining members of the set, Suite No. 2 seems somewhat simpler in style and sparer in texture than the rest, at least in the outer movements. It would be hazardous, however, to conclude from this that Suites Nos. 1 and 2 are somewhat earlier than the others, if only because all six suites may contain individual movements that were composed at a relatively early date.

It is clear from the sources, however (see Table 13–1), that Suite No. 1 was probably not an original member of the set, whose composition was probably fixed only after 1725.[8] If Bach had any general title for the set, it was probably something straightforward and pragmatic: "suites with preludes" or the like.[9] The familiar designation as "English" suites does not occur in any early source, but it was already known to Forkel, who called the pieces "Six great suites . . . known by the name of the English Suites because the composer made them for an Englishman of rank."[10]

Forkel wrote as if the title was already well known, having previously referred to the "English" suites without further identifying them (Forkel 1802, 28/BR, 320).

TABLE 13–1. English Suites: Chief Early Sources

Ms	Copyist, Date	Contents (Suite Nos.)	Comments
DSB P 803, pp. 265–85	Walther, after 1712	BWV 806a	Sole source for early version of Suite No. 1
SPK P 1072	Anon. 5, ca. 1719–22 and 1724 or later	1–6	Suite No. 1 originally separate, first part earlier than rest. Basis of BG; once considered autograph
HAu 12C 14–17	Gerber, 1725	1, 3, 5–6	Copied from P 1072; some unique (later?) readings. Includes French Suite No. 6, with prelude from WTC1
DSB P 803, pp. 365ff.	J. T. Krebs	2, 6	Copied from Gerber mss.
DSB AmB 489	Anon. 436 + Agricola	1–6	Gives later readings. Agricola made additions, 1738–40. Later entries by Kirnberger
SPK P 419	Kittel + Michel	1–6	Kittel copied Suite No. 1, part of Suite No. 2; made alterations in the rest
Private ownership	C. F. C. Fasch	1–6	

His explanation for the name is as plausible as any; it is entirely possible that at some point Bach prepared, or had prepared, a copy of the work for a visiting Englishman. Certainly there is nothing particularly English about the music itself or the presence of preludes, although the title might be somehow connected to Dieupart's suites, each of which contains a prelude (actually, an overture).[11]

English Suite No. 1 in A, BWV 806

Bach presumably made the A-major suite the first of the "suites with preludes" because of the brevity of its prelude. By then he probably had revised the suite to essentially its familiar form.[12] The early version (BWV 806a), which is preserved only in the copy by Walther, gives a slightly shorter version of the prelude. It also lacks one of the two doubles or variations for the second courante, as well as the second bourrée. Besides adding these movements, the later version shows many small refinements in voice-leading, ornamentation, and articulation, especially in the prelude, the courantes, and the sarabande.[13]

The prelude is not the only movement to differ stylistically from those of the other English Suites. The second courante is not at all imitative, while the sarabande, even in the early version (BWV 806a), is somewhat more heavily embellished than the sarabandes of the other suites. The gigue, though in principle imitative, is relatively simple in style and texture, closer perhaps to the gigues of the French Suites and the E-minor lute suite. Hence, there is some reason to suspect that at least the dance movements of the early version were composed after the remaining English Suites. If so, however, BWV 806 is still closer to them than to most of the later suites. The concern with variation, seen in the two doubles for courante 2, recurs in the *agrémens* and the double attached to the sarabandes of three of the other English Suites.[14] Courante 1 has the same inventionlike imitations as the courantes of Suites Nos. 2, 4, and 5, and the second double for courante 2 combines a French type of courante melody with a walking bass, like the courante of the sixth suite.

The prelude, however, has little in common with the preludes of the other English Suites. It is closer to the A-Major Sinfonia and the two A-major preludes of the WTC, especially that of WTC2, with which it shares its $\frac{12}{8}$ time and the use of a short, half-bar subject, which is later inverted. The two preludes are also similar in structure, although the present prelude lacks the clearly articulated return and recapitulation section found in the other. But the two bars added in the revised version (bars 10, 16b–17a) strengthen the two most crucial internal articulations, the arrivals on the dominant (bar 9b) and the relative minor (bar 16b).

The brief flourish that opens the prelude (and the collection) recalls the one at the beginning of the Fantasia BWV 917, which, like the prelude, continues as a fairly rigorous contrapuntal exercise. The flourish itself is different in the two pieces, but the figure used here recurs in the early organ chorale *Vom Himmel hoch, da komm' ich her* BWV 738. The use of the same improvisational formula suggests that the two pieces are roughly contemporary and perhaps confirms the dating of the prelude to Bach's Weimar years. The imitative subject of the prelude is also found elsewhere; it is close to the themes of two gigues, also in A, by French composers whose music Bach probably knew when he composed the piece. One is the gigue of Dieupart's first suite, which Bach copied; the other appears in the *Pièces de clavecin* (Paris, 1705) of Gaspard Le Roux, from which Walther copied a number of pieces, although not the gigue in question (Example 13.1).[15] The pitches in Bach's theme come somewhat closer to Le Roux's, but the rhythm is more like Dieupart's (as noted by David Fuller in NG 5:473).

Whatever Bach's source, the parallels among the three pieces seem too extensive to have arisen by chance.[16] The parallels suggest that the prelude should be understood as a gigue—and not, for example, as a gentler pastorale. They also have some bearing on the interpretation of the ornament sign first seen at the end of bar 3. The sign appears variously in the sources for the Bach work. Dieupart calls for a trill with termination (concluding turn), a complex ornament that cannot be played cleanly here if the tempo is too quick. The most authoritative Bach sources seem to substitute the even more complicated *Doppel-Cadenz*—actually a *Triller von oben*—although neither the BG nor the NBA gives the ornament sign found in what is supposed to be their principal source.[17] The *Doppel-Cadenz* requires considerable time for proper performance; hence, the prelude is unplayable as written except at a fairly slow tempo. Perhaps some simplification of the ornament is therefore advisable, although a French gigue (such as Dieupart's) need not, in fact, be very fast.

EXAMPLE 13.1.   (a) Dieupart, *Première Suite*, gigue, bars 1–6;
(b) Le Roux, Gigue, bars 0–3; (c) English Suite No. 1 in A,
BWV 806, prelude, bars 3–5 (lower voices omitted in each)

The opening pedal-point and arpeggiando figuration of the allemande place it in the Froberger tradition. Yet, as in the C-major prelude of WTC2, the figuration is not as rhapsodic as it first appears. The texture remains contrapuntal, and there are in principle two (occasionally three) real parts, additional parts appearing where necessary to represent the holding out of tones in the arpeggiated figures. Moreover, the opening thematic material recurs quite literally at several points, in particular in the four-bar closing phrase of each half, where it is reinterpreted as a prolongation of the dominant rather than the tonic. Such repetitions, or those of the bass figure first heard in bars 3b–4a, might be understood as an attempt to impose motivic unity, that is, some sort of order, on the traditional improvisatory model. Yet Bach does nothing to articulate them as events of special importance, and when bars 9–10a are repeated almost verbatim at bar 12 it sounds almost accidental. Only in the second half, where the modulations grow more compelling, does the music have the sort of urgency one generally associates with Bach. Hence, while it cannot be played with quite the same freedom as an unmeasured prelude, the allemande seems to call for a good deal of quasi-improvisatory rhythmic nuance, at least up to the double bar.

Unlike the allemande, both courantes are in the current French style, and they demonstrate Bach's mastery of the sophisticated rhythm of the French dance. The French courante is typically composed of a succession of small gestures, each of which has a different rhythmic shape that can be brought out in performance through subtle effects of timing and articulation. Hemiolas—that is, shifts from $\frac{3}{2}$ to $\frac{6}{4}$—are the most obvious of the dance's characteristic metrical shifts, but in both courantes Bach confines them to the final bar of each half. Elsewhere the metrical play is more subtle. For example, the first phrase of courante 1 (bars 1–5) consists of a series of gestures beginning on the downbeats, or rather on the preceding eighth-note upbeat (Example 13.2). In the following phrase, however, the first

EXAMPLE 13.2.   English Suite No. 1 in A, BWV 806,
  courante 1, bars 0–7, melody only (braces indicate gestures;
  overlapping braces indicate an elision)

gesture begins with c#''' in the middle of bar 5 and ends with the embellished *tierce coulée* on the downbeat of bar 6. The next gesture begins squarely on the second beat (f#'''). Incidentally, the sequence of events in bars 5–6—a *tierce coulée* followed by a new gesture starting on a higher note—is an indication of Bach's readiness to borrow; this common French formula recurs in bars 12 and 16.

Some of the ornament signs raise questions, in particular the slanting line drawn between the two lower voices at several points (Example 13.3).[18] In the sarabande

EXAMPLE 13.3.   English Suite No. 1 in A, courante 1, bar 6
  (left hand), from (a) BWV 806a; (b) BWV 806

the sign seems to mean an acciaccatura, that is, a nonchord tone included in a rapid arpeggiation of the chord, and this is the interpretation adopted by Neumann (1978, 595–96). But as Walther indicated in his *Praecepta*, the same sign can mean a measured breaking of a two-note chord, and indeed Walther wrote out such a breaking in bars 6 and 16 of his copy of the early version.[19] In the later version, a comparison of bars 6–7 with the corresponding measures of the second half (bars 15–16) leads to the same interpretation of the sign. It would seem odd for Bach to have used the less explicit notation only in the later version, but perhaps the notation of BWV 806a was Walther's own "resolution" of shorthand employed in Bach's own score.

Although this is the only Bach suite with two courantes, Couperin and other French composers sometimes provided whole series of courantes in the same key, as Bach in fact does if one counts the two doubles attached to courante 2. As in Couperin's suites, this second courante is, on the whole, rhythmically somewhat simpler than the first and lacks the latter's imitative texture; both features made it more suitable for variation. The term *double* was applied in particular to variations characterized by flowing eighth notes, as is the case here and in the variation of the sarabande in Suite No. 6. Walther omits the first double and reverses the places of double 2 and courante 2, but the latter remains the simplest of the three movements. Perhaps double 2 originated as a revised version of courante 2, and Bach, after some hesitation, decided to include both of them as well as an additional movement (double 1) as illustrations of the technique of variation.[20] This might explain why the first double, which introduces sixteenths into both outer parts, is more brilliant than double 2, which converts the original bass into walking eighths but leaves the melody largely unaltered.

Like double 1, the sarabande is more florid than one would expect in the French style. Not only the written-out embellishment but the long, soaring line of the opening phrase (bars 1–8) is more likely to occur in an Italian adagio than a French sarabande. The full chords and the figuration in thirty-seconds at two points in the second half show that this was conceived as a grand, sonorous movement, probably to be played with considerable fire. As in other movements of this type, the embellishment constitutes an essential part of the melody and inner voice-leading and seems unlikely to have originated as additions to a simpler original. In a few passages, however, Bach later embellished his own embellishments, especially in bar 24, which leads into the return of the opening theme (Example 13.4).[21]

EXAMPLE 13.4.   English Suite No. 1 in A, sarabande, bar 24; from (a) BWV 806a; (b) BWV 806

The two bourrées are longer and more contrapuntal than the bourrées in Bach's earlier suites or in their probable models in suites by Fischer. Both can be played as duets on two keyboards. In the revised version the articulation of bourrée 1 was considerably refined, if Walther's copy of the earlier version (BWV 806a) is to be trusted. While the unvarying two-note slurs of Walther's copy preserve the underlying quarter-note rhythm of the dance more faithfully, the later version uses differing types of slurs to distinguish two-note "sigh" motives from four-note *tierces coulées* and various other figures. Both versions use slurs on repeated notes to imitate "bow vibrato" (bass, bar 30). The technique, which involves pressure on the string to rearticulate the note without any break in the sound, cannot be literally imitated on the harpsichord, but the notation implies that each note is to be held as long as possible before being restruck.[22] In Bach's keyboard music the notation seems to be confined to bass lines and was probably suggested by the use of bow vibrato in continuo parts, as in the opening sonatina of the *Actus tragicus* BWV 106.

The subject of the gigue resembles that of the prelude and, like that of the prelude, is inverted in the second half, though that was common enough in a German gigue. There is a problematical piano marking in the closing phrase of each half. The phrase resembles a *petite reprise*, that is, an extra repetition of the closing phrase, usually indicated by a Dal Segno and played piano. While the phrase in question does not actually repeat the previous one, it is close enough to it that it might have been suggested by written-out echoes in several sonata movements by Corelli (e.g., the *giga* of Op. 5, No. 10, where echoes occur at the ends of both halves). *Piano* is already marked in BWV 806a, so it is apparently an original part of the text. But the sources differ on precisely where the change of dynamic level should take place; on the harpsichord, the change of manual is awkward wherever one takes it, but it is probably best taken on the note following the downbeat in each voice.

English Suite No. 2 in A Minor BWV 807

As noted earlier, the Second English Suite seems relatively simple in texture, its melodic lines more angular and occasionally somewhat more awkward (especially in the first four movements) than those of the last four suites. Yet the two bourrées are as assured as any of Bach's examples of this dance, and the gigue is a successful imitation of the type of Italian *giga* used by Corelli as the closing movement for many of his violin sonatas. Indeed, it so closely resembles a violin sonata movement that it would come as little surprise to find that it was a transcription. As such it forms a particularly appropriate conclusion to a suite that opens with a concertolike prelude.

Since the same type of prelude is also found in Suites Nos. 3–6, it is worth considering in some detail exactly how these preludes are related to an actual concerto allegro. In fact, the preludes of Suites Nos. 2–6 are not in concerto form—that is, ritornello form—as such, although Bach used their Da Capo design in a number of concerto movements as well as in various other types of piece, including a number of fugues.[23] Nor are the themes of these preludes constructed like that of a typical concerto; the prelude of Suite No. 2 opens like an invention, and that of Suite No. 5 is a genuine fugue. All five preludes include arpeggiated passage-work of the sort usually described as "concertolike," but similar figuration was widespread in solo and trio-sonatas and other types of Italian ensemble music, as well as in concertos.

Of course, themes and figuration may be less important in defining a concertolike style than textural and syntactic elements, such as the alternation between full-textured "tutti" passages and lighter "solos." Yet it is difficult to square the Da Capo forms of these preludes with ritornello form in the usual sense. In the A-minor prelude, the A section is fifty-five bars long—approximately as long as the B section and far too long to be understood as a ritornello. The B section introduces a new idea that can be understood as a "solo" and, as it happens, can even be played on a separate, quieter manual (see Example 13.5).[24] Passages employing this new idea alternate with others using the theme of the A section, thus perhaps imitating the syntax of a concerto—but coming equally close to that of a fugue. Indeed, these "solos" are if anything less virtuosic than the "ritornellos"; the B idea is, thanks to its appoggiatura (discussed below), expressive or *affetuoso* in character.[25]

Yet it would be wrong to abandon the traditional view of this movement and others like it as being in concerto style. The problem lies in equating "concerto" with "solo concerto" and in assuming that every concerto movement will be based on alternating ritornellos and solos (corresponding with tutti and solo textures, respectively). This approach to concerto writing emerged as the norm only gradually; it is, for example, only intermittently visible in Bach's Brandenburg Concertos, which these preludes closely resemble. Indeed, apart from the disproportionate length of its A section, the form of this prelude is close to that of the first movement of the Fourth Brandenburg Concerto. In the latter, as in the present prelude, only the B section contains distinctly articulated solo passages or episodes, despite the presence in the A section of substantial amounts of "solo" material. This "solo" material takes the form of violinistic passage-work, used in particular to sustain an extended dominant prolongation (bars 36–46) that generates considerable dramatic tension. Such writing may well be a mark of concerto style, but it is not dependent on the use of ritornello form, and Bach adopted it in other pieces, such as the A-Minor Fugue BWV 944.

Through a curious error in the first BG edition, the hooks or commas used to indicate appoggiaturas in the "solo" material (e.g., bars 56–59) were mistaken for slurs. The editor compounded the error by extending it to what he considered to be parallel passages. The result was a series of two-note slurs from upbeat to downbeat, a common enough type of articulation in Classical or Romantic music but extremely rare in Bach's (Example 13.5). The editor's slur produces an agogic accent on the upbeat, but the whole point of the intended appoggiatura is to repeat the previous note—that is, the note played on the upbeat. The result is an *accent*, an expressive *port de voix* on the following downbeat. The effect is intensified later (in bars 96, 98), where the ornament becomes an acciaccatura within a dissonant chord—incidentally pointing out the close relationship between the two ornaments (Example 13.6).

The allemande, like those of Suites Nos. 3–6, has an inventionlike imitative structure. The bass of bar 2 imitates the treble of bar 1, or, rather, the *brisé* writing first assigned to the right hand is reassigned, with idiomatic adjustments, to the left. The arrival on the dominant is articulated by a repetition of the process, with voices

EXAMPLE 13.5.   English Suite No. 2 in A Minor BWV 807,
prelude, bars 55–57, (a) after BG 13; (b) after NBA V/7

EXAMPLE 13.6.   English Suite No. 2 in A Minor BWV 807,
prelude, bars 95–96

exchanged (bar 6b). The second half of the movement functions similarly, using a free inversion of the subject. Bach's critics would no doubt have found this procedure, in an allemande, to be pedantic, and in this instance they might have been right. The angular treble line at the outset of the second half is, like other such Bach lines, quite expressive and can be played with a certain amount of rhythmic freedom. But it cannot be played so freely when it is transferred to the bass and combined contrapuntally with other lines also moving in sixteenths. Hence, the effort to incorporate the opening melodic material, in itself flexible and expressive, into a densely woven contrapuntal fabric leads to a certain stiffness. Much the same is true in the courante, in which the traditional rhythmic gestures (which Bach used so idiomatically in the courantes of Suite No. 1) tend to be replaced, or rather embellished, by running eighths in both hands.

The sarabande is the first of two in the English Suites for which Bach wrote a separate set of *agrémens* or ornaments. The idea, and even Bach's manner of notating the embellished treble line, seems to have come from Couperin's *Premier Ordre*, in his first book of *Pièces de clavecin* (Paris, 1713). There several pieces are accompanied by an embellished version of the melody, notated as a single line on one staff at the bottom of the page.[26] It is often assumed that Bach (and Couperin) intended the ornamented version of each half to be played just after the plain version—that is, as a varied reprise. But this is far from certain; the ornamented version includes repeat signs and might have been intended as an alternative to the main text, thus serving as an illustration of "composition by variation" (discussed in Chapter 2). Bach did write varied reprises for a movement in one of the Vivaldi transcriptions (BWV 975), but the practice of varying the repeated halves of a binary form may not have become widespread until later in the century, when C. P. E. Bach mentioned it (1753–62, i.3.31). Still, there can be no harm in applying the practice here.

The gigue also raises a question about repetitions. Bach was evidently not shy about repeating movements that he liked, and therefore he provided a second ending for the second half that leads back to the very beginning; there is a third ending with which to conclude. Similar indications occur in dance movements by D'Anglebert.

English Suite No. 3 in G Minor BWV 808

Suite No. 3 is probably the best known of the English Suites, thanks to the oft-anthologized gavotte and musette and the concise, clearly articulated prelude, which comes closer than any of the others to regular ritornello form. One can even see this prelude as Bach's keyboard emulation of the Corellian or Vivaldian concerto grosso, since the "solo" episodes (at bars 33, 99, and 125) are predominantly in three parts—corresponding to two violins and continuo—while the ritornellos are more heavily scored.[27] For this reason, incidentally, it is unnecessary to point out the structure by leaping from one manual to another; phrase elisions at the points of articulation would in any case make this awkward (e.g., on the downbeat of bar 33).

The symmetry of the movement lies not only in the recurrences of the ritornello but in the close parallelism between the first and third "solo" episodes (bars 125–61 correspond with 33–67). But the symmetry is broken by a dramatic retransition passage, perhaps the most original part of the movement (bars 161–80). This retransition is a substitute for the simple pause found at the end of the middle section in most Da Capo forms, including the prelude of Suite No. 2. The three remaining preludes also have retransition passages at this point, but none is as exciting to hear and play or as elegantly conceived as this one, which prolongs the dominant through several bars of passage-work (bars 176–79) before falling with unslackened energy into the opening of the ritornello. The latter is modified to allow a smoother join, and this clearly cost Bach some trouble. One copy preserves traces of an earlier reading (for bars 181–87), while another contains an autograph entry at this point— the only autograph material that survives for the English Suites. Perhaps Bach wrote out the crucial bars because they had become illegible through revisions in his own score.[28]

In the earliest copy the prelude is barred in "double measures" like the A-Minor Sinfonia (see Chapter 10). Indeed, it is effectively in $\frac{6}{8}$, and the chief arrivals fall on the downbeats of odd-numbered bars. So do the dissonant 7- and $\frac{9}{4}$-chords in bars 9–13 of the ritornello—but not those in bars 16–20. The discrepancy, which results from a phrase elision, might have been Bach's reason for abandoning the notation—if indeed he authorized its abandonment in later copies.[29]

The allemande is exceptional in that the main thematic idea appears first in the bass; at any rate it is this theme that is repeated in bars 6 and 7 and inverted after the double bar. This allemande flows more easily than that of Suite No. 2, and Bach's more relaxed stance is evident in an example of parallel octaves that he makes no effort to hide. The parallels arise naturally as the two parts descend in parallel motion to a bare octave $C^{\sharp}$ on the downbeat of bar 11. One can imagine Bach, a slight glint in his eye, pointing out the octaves to his students as things that "offended every beginner in composition, but afterwards soon justified themselves," as Forkel (1802, 27/BR, 320) put it. Bach's refusal to be bound by rules or pedantic consistency is also evident in the pragmatic fingerings that two students, Gerber and Anonymous 5, included in their copies of the piece. While the "4" in bar 15 and in bar 16 seems to reflect the modern type of scale fingering, the "3" in the inversion of the theme (bar 18) implies an older one (Example 13.7).

EXAMPLE 13.7.   English Suite No. 3 in G Minor BWV 808, allemande: (a) bars 15–16a; (b) bars 18–19a

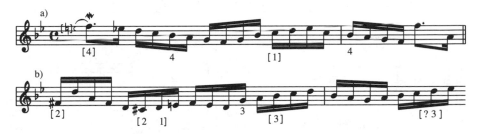

The courante is rhythmically the most complex in the English Suites, rivaling that of the D-Major Partita and going well beyond the subtle metrical shifts normally encountered in French examples of the dance. The most impressive metrical play begins in the treble just after the *tierce coulée* in bar 9, resulting in a passage that is effectively in $\frac{4}{4}$. The bass then introduces its own cross-rhythm with the entrance in the latter part of bar 11 (Example 13.8). The idea returns in the closing phrase of the second half (bars 30–31), where the effective $\frac{4}{4}$ measures of the outer voices coincide, forming a *hemiolia major* (three bars of $\frac{4}{4}$ replacing two of $\frac{3}{2}$).

The sarabande is one of the most original and impressive examples of the dance by any composer, unique both for its opening tonic pedal-point and the enharmonic progressions in the second half. The latter also take place during pedal-points, and this helps give the piece a somewhat mysterious, quasi-romantic quality also found in sections of the Chromatic Fantasia—which might well be a contemporary work. The effect is deepened by the embellishments, which rise to levels of improvisational fire exceeded only in the sarabande of the Sixth Partita. The initial pedal note, which is held for seven bars, must obviously be restruck—perhaps several times—in order to be heard. Frescobaldi permitted this, and Bach must have done so as well in a piece expressly for the harpsichord.[30] In fact, this is neither the first nor the last point in the suite where a literal reading of the notation would seem to require organ pedals.[31] Yet even if the sustained notes are restruck, wide gaps remain between the bass and inner parts (especially in bar 19), suggesting that the piece, like the early versions of the Chromatic Fantasia and the Aria variata, might have been written for an instrument equipped with a short octave or simple pedalboard.

The gavotte is somewhat more sophisticated than students are likely to suspect when they first encounter it. The first half-bar really is an upbeat, as in most gavottes; one group of sources emphasizes this by placing an *accent* in the treble on

EXAMPLE 13.8.   English Suite No. 3 in G Minor BWV 808,
courante, bars 9–12

the first downbeat (b^b′′′). Yet the meter is ambiguous in both the gavotte and its
accompanying musette. In the gavotte, the initial bass note (G) is an octave lower
than the one that appears on the first downbeat, weakening the latter; in the musette
the first bass note is struck on the upbeat and then simply held as a pedal-point.
While the cadences of both movements all fall on downbeats, the gavotte, in
particular, makes significant departures from both the normal rhythm and the
normal phrasing of the dance.

Gavottes normally fall into very regular four-bar phrases, often grouped into
eight-bar periods. Such is perhaps the underlying rhythmic structure here, but if so
both the individual phrases and the overall two-period design have been expanded
by the insertion of additional units. This is shown in Table 13–2, which borrows
from Hugo Riemann's theory of *Vierhebigkeit* (fourfold rhythm), an idea that is
generally discredited but is perhaps applicable here.

Rhythmic irregularities begin with the first phrase after the double bar (bars
8b–14a); the phrase contains two extra bars. The basic gavotte rhythm seems to
disappear entirely after the cadence to D minor (bar 18a); the effect is not unlike that
found in passages by Haydn or Beethoven where the downbeat momentarily slips
onto the wrong part of the bar. Normal gavotte motion is reestablished only with the
restatement of the opening motive at bar 26b, which coincides with the return to the
tonic.

The movement can thus be seen as a concise sonata form; the metrical ambiguity
of the middle section is resolved just as the thematic and tonal design is closed. The
most ambiguous passage, bars 18b–26a, serves as a retransition and gains some
dramatic intensity through the repeated Gs in the bass—a pedal-point on V of

TABLE 13–2. Rhythmic Design of the Gavotte BWV 807/5

	1	2	3	4	5	6	7	8	:∥	9	10	11	12	13	14	15	16	17	18
Actual bar no.:	1	2	3	4	5	6	7	8	:∥	9	10	11	12	13	14	15	16	17	18
No. in 4-bar unit:	1	2	3	4	1	2	3	4	:∥	1	2	3	4	3	4	1	2	3	4
Phrase no.:	1				2				:∥	3						4			
Period no.:	1								:∥	2									
Cadences:				g				B♭								d:V			d

	19	20	21	22	23	24	25	26	27	28	29	30	31	32	33	34	:∥
Actual bar no.:	19	20	21	22	23	24	25	26	27	28	29	30	31	32	33	34	:∥
No. in 4-bar unit:	1	2	3	4	3	4	3	4	1	2	1	2	1	2	3	4	:∥
Phrase no.:	(3)							(4)									:∥
Period no.:	(2)																:∥
Cadences:								g:V							g		

iv—that are further marked by various ornaments.[32] The French gavotte is normally a rather gentle, even delicate dance; thus, the drumlike bass represents a substantial departure from the traditional character of the dance. Perhaps it was inspired by the *tambourin*, a dance that sometimes takes the rhythmic form of a gavotte (as in the example from Rameau's *Pièces de clavecin* of 1724).

The musette also takes its name from an instrument—a small, gentrified sort of bagpipe. Although pieces called musettes often have a gavotte rhythm, that is not always the case, and the title probably includes a programmatic element. Indeed, the sources apparently never designate this movement simply as *Musette* but rather as *Gavotte II*, some copyists adding the qualifier *ou la musette*. As noted earlier, the pedal-point representing the drone bass of the pseudo-Arcadian wind instrument will have to be restruck from time to time, perhaps at the beginning of each four-bar phrase.

The gigue is a true fugue in three parts, both subject and countersubject being inverted in the second half. Despite the promising beginning, there seems to be a dropping off of inspiration in the second half—not a unique instance of this in Bach's gigues, where even he could relax into uninspired sequence writing. The gigue is unusual in returning to the *rectus* form of the subject in the final entry (bass, bar 43). Unfortunately, the closing phrase is preceded by what seems a fairly lame sequential bridge (bars 37b–41a) connecting it with the previous entry.

English Suite No. 4 in F, BWV 809

Suite No. 4 is the only one of the original group of five suites in a major key. This may reflect the fact that Bach generally favored minor keys for his most serious solo music, but the F-Major English Suite is certainly no weaker than the others, even if it is the shortest and perhaps the most popular in style.

The prelude, like that of Suite No. 3, is a brilliant piece containing numerous references to orchestral style. The idea of opening the ritornello with a bar for treble alone might have càme from Vivaldi's Concerto Op. 3, No. 3, arranged by Bach as Concerto No. 7 (BWV 978); the transcription, like the present piece, is in F and has an imitation in the bass in its second measure.[33] Despite the predominantly Italian style, the countersubject (treble, bar 2) is in dotted rhythm and seems borrowed from the French style, especially when played with the ornaments atached to it in some copies. Indeed, the countersubject resembles the one used in the fugal part of the overture to Dieupart's B-Minor Suite; a similar countersubject occurs in the overture of Bach's C-major orchestral suite BWV 1066.[34] Perhaps the most striking parallel to an ensemble work occurs in the "solo" sections, which employ the same motives as the first solo in the allegro of the Fifth Brandenburg Concerto.

The time-signature ¢, found in the earliest copies and also used in the Fifth Brandenburg Concerto, seems to indicate a particularly lively tempo, as does the additional indication *vîtement*. Some late copies place staccato strokes on all of the sixteenth-notes in the initial statement of the theme. This could imply unusually vigorous articulation, but it might have been simply a warning against slurring them or applying rhythmic inequality.[35]

The allemande seems to point toward the one in the G-Major Partita; both are brilliant pieces using both ordinary and triplet sixteenths. But this allemande quickly loses steam; the triplets drop out by the third bar in each half, and although they return there is a subsequent shift to the minor mode in both closing phrases (bars 10b, 22b). It is as if Bach was not quite ready to abandon the traditional expressive style of a German allemande, and as a result the movement alternates uneasily between brilliance and restraint.

The allemande is imitative—the treble of bar 2 becomes the bass of bar 3—and the courante contains comparable imitations at the beginning of each half. Yet while the phrases are somewhat longer than in most French examples, the upper line in the courante is rather too obviously composed of little one-bar fragments, and it cannot be counted among Bach's more successful.

Like the courante, the sarabande is unpretentious and may seem rather plain by comparison with the corresponding movements in the other suites. Indeed, through bar 16 it is, in a sense, a version of the corresponding movement of Suite No. 1 shorn of its *agrémens* but following much the same rhythmic and harmonic plan.[36] Unless the tempo is unduly slow, however, little ornamentation is necessary beyond the breaking of the chords, perhaps with occasional *acciaccature*. Pianists, who might be inclined to see the movement as a quiet chorale like that in the Chopin *Fantaisie*, should remember that the full chords imply strong attacks and a rich sonority on the harpsichord.

Minuets almost by definition are unremarkable in style, and those of the present suite seem to amble along with few complications. Both, however, are longer than usual for the time, and the active bass lines represent, as in the courante, Bach's attempt to invest the dance with some contrapuntal substance.

The gigue seems at first less a fugue than an invention. But if one ignores the bass entrance, which is in the tonic (bar 1b), one discovers a normal three-part fugal exposition. Thereafter, one never hears more than two voices at a time. A stricter working-out, however, might have been fatal to the piece's lively "hunting" character, which is implicit in the fanfare that opens the subject. One gesture, the octave leap, is developed in the second half (bars 30ff.) in a manner recalling the posthorn motive found in several early works. This might have been suggested by the key, the usual one for horns in Bach's music.

A copy once owned by Kirnberger (AmB 489) shows what may have been Kirnberger's own variations for the last two bars in each half. These variations seem unlikely to have been intended for performance. But they might have been sketches or experiments in invertible counterpoint and are of some interest for their possible relationship to Kirnberger's "method for tossing off sonatas."[37]

English Suite No. 5 in E Minor BWV 810

The suite in E minor, like the one in A minor, is somewhat rough around the edges, but after the D-minor suite it is the most ambitious of the set and perhaps the most satisfactory of them all. There are no weak movements, as there seem to be in most of the others; the courante, perhaps the least successful movement in the other suites, is genuinely exciting, while the sarabande represents a new type, galant rather than intensely expressive, but *affetuoso* all the same (as pointed out by Eppstein 1986, 212).

The prelude is a true fugue in Da Capo form—the only example among Bach's harpsichord works, though there are examples for organ, lute, and violin. As in those pieces, the episodes come particularly close to concerto style. The principal episodal idea (bar 40) is clearly violinistic, recalling the first solo in the Fourth Brandenburg Concerto, while another "solo" passage (bars 60–65) bears a striking resemblance to figuration in the last movement of the Third Brandenburg Concerto. The form is an expanded and somewhat clearer version of that used in the prelude of the A-minor suite, the middle section falling into two closely parallel halves (bars 40–73 largely correspond with 82–107).

The allemande has the same earnest fugality as that of Suite No. 2 but is even more severe. Though each contains occasional chords, the parts for the right and left hands can be played on separate keyboards, perhaps the best solution to the voice-crossings in bars 5–6. The thematic material is unusually angular even for Bach and following its inversion in the second half (bass, bar 13) leads to one of the harshest passages in his keyboard music (Example 13.9).[38] While the passage bristles with harsh passing dissonances and nearly simultaneous cross-relations, the contrary motion of the outer voices is quite clear even if the precise voice-leading of the implied inner parts is a matter for debate.

The courante's fiery character is reinforced by the staccato mark on the last note of bar 1. While not present in all sources, the staccato should surely be extended to each parallel passage. The movement's one possible weakness is a slight rhythmic monotony, since it lacks the dance's characteristic rhythmic play. But it makes up for this through its flexibility of texture: Once in each half the two-part counterpoint is relieved by a galant little phrase over a dominant pedal (e.g., bars 6–8).

Galant style is also present in the sarabande, which is in a homophonic three-part texture. The traditional rhythm of the dance is not immediately evident, but in most bars the melodic line changes direction or the bass indicates a change of harmony on the second beat. In the opening bar and elsewhere one might be inclined to slur the eighths in order to form galant "sigh" motives. But certain late

EXAMPLE 13.9.   English Suite No. 5 in E Minor BWV 810, allemande: (a) bars 15–16; (b) analysis

sources place staccato dots over the eighths in bar 1, probably because at later points in the movement the eighths do not always fall into drooping "sighs" (see, e.g., alto of bar 3, all voices in bar 17). The dots, unlike the staccato strokes in the courante (or in the prelude of Suite No. 4), presumably indicate separation, without any accentuation. On the clavichord—an appropriate medium, at least for this movement—they might be executed with what Emanuel Bach refers to as *Tragen der Töne*, a sort of portato.[39] The dots were a later addition in AmB 489 (NBA V/7, KB, 164), perhaps implying the use of the clavichord for this music in the later eighteenth century.

The first passepied is in the form of a rondeau, which was common in contemporary French keyboard dances but rare in Bach's.[40] Musically, a passepied is little more than a minuet with an upbeat, often written in $\frac{3}{8}$; the earliest copy of the present one gives it in double measures, like the prelude of Suite No. 3. The moderate tempo and flowing sixteenths of both passepieds make them good candidates for the use of *notes inégales*, which are especially plausible if the staccato indications in the sarabande and in the prelude of Suite No. 4 are indeed warnings against the use of *notes inégales* there (as Dürr suggests, NBA V/7, KB, 148).

The gigue continues the trend toward increasingly strict fugues; the trend begins in the A-minor suite and reaches its climax in the gigue of Suite No. 6. Here, three real parts are present for most of the time, not only during the opening exposition as in Suite No. 4, and the first half consists of two complete expositions separated by a short episode. The chromatic angularity of the subject is in keeping with the character of the suite, as announced in the subject of the prelude and again in the allemande. Unfortunately, the second half seems to slacken, falling into somewhat routine sequences as in the gigue of Suite No. 3.

English Suite No. 6 in D Minor BWV 811

The last suite is the largest and was surely meant to be the crowning member of the set, though it was not necessarily the last composed. The first indication of its special character is the presence of a separate introductory section in the prelude, which is thus virtually a prelude and fugue in itself. In this it resembles an overture, but the introduction is in arpeggiando style, lacking dotted rhythm. It bears no tempo mark, but it is in the same $\frac{9}{8}$ time as the latter part of the movement and therefore should probably be played at the same tempo (indicated as *allegro* in most copies). Indeed, a substantially slower tempo will make the cadenzalike passage at the center of the introduction (bars 15–18) seem interminable.

The fugue proper is in itself longer than any other prelude in the English Suites; the A section alone contains forty-nine bars. Yet it achieves extraordinary intensity, in part through the mesmerizing quality of its figuration. The effect of a *moto perpetuo* is perhaps emphasized by the presence of a number of "obstinate" figures—passage-work in the right hand that repeatedly arpeggiates the same chord (that is, a treble pedal-point) against a moving bass, as in bars 44–45. The meter is another factor; because of the long bars of $\frac{9}{8}$ time, there is a greater tension than usual between the busy surface figuration and the sustained lines of the underlying voice-leading. The effect is the same as in the A-minor prelude of WTC1 but without the somewhat rhetorical quality of the latter. The subject itself is short and simple, easily developed, and its inversion is introduced early in the A section (bars 49ff.). Indeed, the subject and motives derived from the subject so thoroughly saturate the texture that one may gain the impression that the same material is being constantly recycled. But apart from the Da Capo of the A section, there is relatively little verbatim recapitulation; the B section again falls into two halves (bars 86–112 and 113–43), but they are only roughly parallel with one another. There is also a distinct retransition (bars 143–46), as in Suite No. 3, but it is short and comparatively restrained; the real drama of this movement lies in the long dominant prolongations of the three main sections (e.g., bars 78ff., 131ff.).

The allemande is in much the same vein as that of Suite No. 5. One might note the melodic cross-relation in bar 1, as the treble moves from c♯''' to c♮'''. This is repeated (in a different harmonic context) in bar 5, where the bass restates the opening theme at the dominant (Example 13.10).[41] The last beat of bar 5 is rendered especially surprising by the f' in the inner voice, which leaps by a diminished fourth rather than moving to the expected e'; the f' prepares the diminished seventh in the following bar. The seemingly awkward melodic intervals are essential to the peculiar expressive intensity of the piece, which reaches its climax when the outer voices leap in opposite directions while arpeggiating a diminished chord, near the end of the second half (bar 20).

The courante seems to have been written at a lower level of inspiration. It might have seemed a good idea at the time to combine a French-style melody with a walking bass. But the latter diffuses the energy of the former, evening out its rhythmic irregularities. Perhaps the existing movement stems from an earlier courante with "simple" bass, like double 2 in Suite No. 1; if so, it was a mistake to have discarded it.

The time-signature of the sarabande ($\frac{3}{2}$) may have been intended to signify a slower tempo than usual. But the movement need not lack fire, and this can be attained through a steady tempo, strong registration, and added ornamentation,

EXAMPLE 13.10.   English Suite No. 6 in D Minor BWV 811,
allemande: (a) bar 1; (b) bars 5–6a

including various types of chord-breaking (with and without acciaccaturas). The
tempo is presumably the same as in the following double and thus can be determined from the flowing eighth-notes of the latter. Given a moderate (not slow)
half-note pulse, the double can generate considerable intensity, especially in the
hemiolas—unusual for a sarabande—found near the end (bars 21–22).

In its walking bass, the gavotte resembles one or two examples by Corelli. But
Bach, unlike Corelli, retains the characteristic upbeat of the French dance, at least
on paper.[42] As in the gavotte of Suite No. 3, the phrasing grows irregular after the
double bar, and by bar 14 the dance's normal meter seems to have vanished, even
though the upbeat of two repeated notes remains in the middle voice. The "correct"
meter is restored by the time the theme is restated in the tonic (bar 24b). But the
dance's normal rhythm is brusquely rejected in the final cadence, which seems to
be of a type unprecedented (and quite improper) in a gavotte. Gavotte 2 is, like that
of Suite No. 3, based on a tonic pedal-point. Although only one late source has the
rubric *ou la musette*,[43] the trill in thirds (bars 14b–16a) is surely an imitation of
rustic music-making.

In the gigue the collection's preoccupation with imitation and inversion reaches
its culmination. Large portions of the first half of the movement are inverted almost
verbatim in the second half, leading to mirror writing on a scale exceeded only in
the *Art of Fugue*. The compositional virtuosity is reflected by that required of the
player; the time-signature $\frac{12}{16}$ indicates a rapid tempo, and many of the long trills
must be sustained while a second moving part is played simultaneously with the
same hand.

Bach's precise intentions regarding the ornaments are somewhat unclear, especially on the long pedal notes in the second half. On these notes the NBA consistently places the sign for a long mordent—Couperin's *pincé continu*. But here the
sources show a confusing variety of signs (to judge from the table in NBA V/7, KB,

180). Some of the readings indeed suggest that the trill used in the first half of the gigue is to be inverted into a mordent in the second. But even though the melodic material, and indeed the entire contrapuntal texture, is inverted, it is by no means clear that this should be the case with the ornaments themselves.[44] A mordent is not, in any case, an exact inversion of a Baroque trill, as the latter normally begins on the upper note. One might, however, wish to begin the trills in the first half of the gigue on the main note, both to simplify performance and to avoid the very harsh accented dissonances that would otherwise appear at several spots (bars 11, 20). The trills might be further simplified by converting them to measured figuration of the sort used in variation 28 of the Goldberg Variations; this, however, removes much of their biting brilliance, and there is no indication for it in the sources.

Bach himself did not attempt to make the second half an exact mirror of the first. Instead, he varied the axis over which pitches were inverted to suit his tonal design (see Table 13–3). Hence, the construction of the movement is much less strict than that of the later mirror pieces. Nevertheless, in working out the gigue Bach might have gained insights into the relationships between counterpoint and tonality that would serve him well in his later researches into fugue. For instance, where the first three fugal entries follow the customary tonic-dominant pattern (D minor: i, v, i), those in the second half form a plagal pattern (A minor: i, iv, i). Bach must have remembered this complementary relationship when he wrote the three-part mirror in the *Art of Fugue*, another virtuoso gigue whose two versions show particularly sophisticated complementary tonal schemes (see Chapter 18).[45]

Since the closing passage of the first half could not be inverted to produce an entirely satisfactory final cadence, Bach abandoned the plan after bar 47. The movement ends by combining the two forms of the subject, as in the prelude BWV 900/1 and some fugues of the WTC—a fitting climax to the series of suites in which Bach demonstrated the compatibility of galant dances with strict counterpoint.

TABLE 13–3.   Inversional Structure of the Gigue BWV 811/8

Passage in 2d half	Source passage in 1st half (bar nos.)	Axis of inversion	Voices generated in 2d half by exact inversion
25–31	1–7	$e^{b\prime}$	STB
32–34	8–10	b/c′	B
33–34	9–10	f′	S
35–36	11–12	b/c′	TB (except for tenor a′)
37	13	b/c′	STB (except for tenor a)
38–40	14–16	b/c′	S (except for last three notes of bar 40)
41–43	17–19	$c\prime/c^{\sharp\prime\prime}$	B
44–46	20–21	$c/c^{\sharp\prime\prime}$	STB (except for first and last notes in T; S an octave higher)
47–48a	22–23a	$e\prime\prime/e^{b\prime\prime\prime}$	S

14

The French Suites

The French Suites are the later but smaller pendant to the six English Suites. The autograph score containing portions of French Suites Nos. 1–5 dates from about 1722—the year of the fair copy of WTC1—but the autograph of Suite No. 5 was not completed until some time after Bach's arrival in Leipzig in 1723. The suites cannot have been assembled into the now-familiar set of six until around 1725. By then most of the suites had undergone at least one systematic revision, and it is likely that Bach continued to make at least small changes, as in other works. Closely related to the French Suites are two further suites, BWV 818 and 819, which Bach may for a time have considered including in the collection of "suites without prelude." They are similar enough to the French Suites in style and dimensions to be discussed with them in this chapter.

By contemporary standards the French Suites were not particularly small, and the absence of preludes was hardly unusual. It was the large concerto-style preludes of the English Suites that had been unusual, and the severe imitative writing of the dance movements, especially the allemandes and courantes, had given them an unprecedented contrapuntal density. Nevertheless, the French Suites may have been products of a conscious turn toward a simpler, more popular, more accessible style, perhaps undertaken in connection with the pedagogical program evident in WTC1 and the CB, two other collections assembled at Cöthen. If so, however, the change in style was a gradual one, for the first three French Suites—all in minor keys—are somewhat old-fashioned by comparison with the last three. While none of the allemandes is as severely contrapuntal as those of the English Suites, the courantes of Suites Nos. 1 and 3 are still of the French type (notated in $\frac{3}{2}$), and that of Suite No. 1 has the same imitative texture employed in the English Suites. The sarabande of Suite No. 1 has the plain choralelike appearance of several of the sarabandes in the English Suites, and the gigue of Suite No. 1 follows an archaic French version of the dance in duple time.

Still, none of the French Suites stands apart from the others to the degree that the A-major suite does from the other English Suites. In the French Suites, especially the last four, Bach achieved a suaveness rare in his earlier keyboard music. While the French Suites are not, of course, devoid of counterpoint or virtuoso display, they concentrate—especially in Suites Nos. 4, 5, and 6—on cantabile galant melodies and relatively simple, idiomatic keyboard writing. Perhaps Bach, recognizing that complicated contrapuntal music was not the best means for introducing himself to the public (or, for that matter, to beginning students), aimed at a keyboard style that would be sufficiently idiomatic and galant to make for a saleable publication, without being devoid of musical substance. Indeed, the last three suites, and especially Suite No. 6, are clearly approaching the style of the Partitas, Bach's first actual keyboard publications. While lacking the large dimensions and unabashed virtuosity of that set, many individual movements in the French Suites reveal the same inventive approach to keyboard figuration and the same free treatment of the traditional dance-types that characterize the Partitas. For example, no two of the allemandes or courantes are of quite the same sort, several introducing what appear to be unprecedented types of keyboard writing for these movements.

Bach may never have given the collection a distinctive title. As early as 1762, Marpurg referred to the six works as Bach's "French" suites,[1] possibly reflecting a tradition within the Bach circle. But the title remains as misleading as that given to the English Suites. Indeed, the dance movements of the English Suties are probably somewhat closer to Bach's French models than are those of the French Suites.

Sources, Versions, Editions

The autographs of Suites Nos. 1–5 form the principal part of the first *Clavier-Büchlein vor Anna Magdalena Bach*. This manuscript (DSB P 224), dated 1722, was the first of two that Bach dedicated to his second wife, whom he married at Cöthen late in 1721. The 1722 manuscript is distinct from a second one of the same title presented to Anna Magdalena in 1725 (SPK P 225), which has become well known as the source of many familiar little teaching pieces. Most of these, however, are not by Bach and need not concern us here. Both volumes are edited in integral form in NBA V/4.

The earlier manuscript is often thought to have been a wedding gift from Bach to his new wife. Because the suites make up the bulk of its surviving contents, it has been supposed that the pieces themselves were written for her. A professional singer prior to her marriage, Anna Magdalena is likely to have had some keyboard ability. But while portions of the five suites appear to be fair copies, others are rougher revision autographs, and the manuscript contains Bach's fragmentary composing scores for two other works.[2] It would seem, then, that at some point Bach began to use the manuscript as his own workbook; this might explain why he eventually gave his wife a second Little Keyboard Book.[3]

The textual history of the French Suites following their initial entry in the 1722 book is unusually complicated, with as many as five distinct versions surviving for each piece. As in many works discussed in previous chapters, the revisions included the insertion of ornament signs and other changes of detail. But they also involved the addition and elimination of movements, as well as substantial compositional changes affecting voice-leading and even the length and formal structure of certain movements. Similar revisions took place in BWV 818 and 819.

It is possible that Bach's revisions in these works were no more numerous or substantial than those made in the fugues of WTC1 or in other keyboard pieces for which the composing scores do not happen to survive. Yet it seems remarkable that the apparently simple French Suites should have undergone as many substantive changes as they did. The expansion of the allemande and courante of Suite No. 2, each in several stages, seems to have been a response to what were perceived as real problems in the earlier versions, not merely to a desire for greater length. Likewise, the frequent alteration of melodic lines, inner voices, and basses represents more than embellishment or the refining of small details. In the English Suites, the logic of the counterpoint—of which Bach was already a master—was sufficient to justify unidiomatic, even ungratifying details, just as in Bach's fugues. But the relatively homophonic style of the French Suites, in which technical demands on the player had to be kept fairly light and the norms of the harpsichord idiom more closely observed, may, paradoxically, have posed greater challenges. Evidence of Bach's difficulties can be found in the relatively large number of passages that were revised not once but twice, and not simply by embellishing or intensifying a simpler reading but by improving awkward voice-leading or unidiomatic keyboard writing.[4]

Bach entered his revisions not into the surviving Cöthen autographs prepared for Anna Magdalena but in other scores now lost. Their revised readings must be reconstructed from copies made by students and other members of the Bach circle. These present a complicated picture, and the sequence of alterations—even Bach's final intentions about certain details—cannot always be ascertained with certainty. As in the case of WTC2, there are many manuscripts, not all of them containing the complete set of six suites, and the same manuscript may give later readings for one piece and earlier ones for another.

For this reason each of the following discussions of the individual works is preceded by a summary of its principal sources and versions, as in Chapters 4–7. Most players will no doubt want to use the later versions. But study of the earlier versions is, as always, instructive. It should be borne in mind, however, that the relatively sparse indication of ornaments in the early versions may be illusory. It is likely that in writing them down Bach merely specified, for the benefit of his students, the types of ornaments that a good player would have used anyway.

At this writing there exists no entirely satisfactory edition of the French Suites and BWV 818 and 819. The works, eight in all, have traditionally been edited together and appear thus in the editions discussed below. Nineteenth-century editions, such as those in BG 13 and 45 (both still widely available in reprint), tended to mix readings belonging to different versions. Bischoff usually guessed right about which were the latest readings, and he helpfully reproduced the most important early readings in footnotes. But all such editions are superseded by that of Dürr in NBA V/8, which is based on a far more complete and accurate investigation of the sources. Unfortunately, the format of the NBA edition makes it difficult to compare early and late readings, and users must also note the list of errata included in the KB. An edition by Richard Jones (Associated Board of the Royal Schools of Music,

1985) contains useful, concise accounts—in English—on the principal sources and the history of the text. But there are also many suggestions concerning the realization of ornaments and other points of performance practice that clutter the text and are open to debate. Somewhat less adequate, but presenting a cleaner text, is the edition by Hans-Christian Müller (Vienna, 1983).[5]

As in his edition of WTC1, Dürr presents two distinct versions for each of the French Suites, as well as for BWV 818 and 819. The two versions of the French Suites are designated "A" and "B," but these do not correspond in every case with the very earliest or latest versions. For example, the autograph drafts in the 1722 *Clavier-Büchlein* predate version "A" and were edited separately in NBA V/4.[6] Also given separately, but in an appendix of NBA V/8, are alternate versions of Suites Nos. 3 and 4. Although the NBA designates version "B" as the "later, ornamented" (*verzierte*) version, in Suites Nos. 1–5 the differences between "A" and "B" extend well beyond the more numerous ornament signs of "B" (see, for example, the discussion of the allemande and courante of Suite No. 2). On the other hand, in Suite No. 6 the "A" and "B" texts are virtually identical, raising the question of whether or not distinct versions really exist for this suite, which was the last composed.

Indeed, the actual basis for the distinction between the NBA's "A" and "B" seems to lie in editorial method. Version "A" is based on a single source, a copy by Altnikol of what Dürr believes was a lost autograph fair copy of around 1725 (see NBA V/8, KB, 54). Version "B," on the other hand, combines readings (especially ornament signs) from various sources thought to give later texts. This can lead to an occasional odd discrepancy; in the loure of Suite No. 5, the text for "B" at one point gives an early reading crossed out in the autograph.[7] And since the ornaments given in text "B" have been collected from different sources, they were not necessarily all meant for any one performance, even if all stem from Bach (which is by no means certain).[8] Hence, players probably need not feel obliged to realize every ornament in version "B" exactly as indicated and (as always) should consult the editorial commentary in cases of doubt.

Suite in A Minor BWV 818

Sources: DSB P 418 (Anonymous 5; No. 4 in set); LEm Go.S.9 (Gerber, as No. 2). *Editions*: BG 36; Dadelsen (1975); NBA V/8.

Later version (BWV 818a): *Sources*: LEm ms. 8 (Mempell); SPK P 804/36 (later copy by Mempell). *Editions*: same as for BWV 818 (BG gives BWV 818a in appendix).

The A-minor suite seems to occupy a stylistic position between the English Suites and the First French Suite. But, lacking a prelude, it may for a time have been regarded as part of the later set. Thus, P 418, one of the earliest copies (by the Bach student known as Anonymous 5), presents BWV 818 together with BWV 819 while omitting the later French Suites Nos. 5 and 6. Anonymous 5 later revised his copy to include a number of ornament signs. But he did not add the three movements, including a prelude, that are present in the alternate version BWV 818a. The latter might have represented a short-lived experiment to convert the work into a "suite with prelude"; the movements unique to BWV 818a are discussed separately below, following the discussion of BWV 818.

While firm dates are unavailable for either version, sources and style point to a relatively early origin for BWV 818. It is certainly earlier than the last two French Suites, and it could go back to the time of the English Suites or even earlier. Both allemande and courante are imitative, in the manner of the English Suites, and the sarabande is provided with a double, as in English Suite No. 6. Moreover, the gigue uses a trill motive that seems to have interested Bach in several movements of the English Suites, especially the gigue in A.

Several things cause one to look back farther still, to the period of the early suites treated in Chapter 4, even though the present suite is much more sophisticated than those (with the exception of the lute suite BWV 996). The allemande and the courante are both shorter by at least a few bars than the corresponding movements in virtually all of the other mature keyboard suites. The double of the sarabande is of the same type as that in the Praeludium et Partita BWV 833; that is, it uses running rather than arpeggiando figuration. The gigue has a very simple subject, although it is worked out carefully in three real voices. Although an attractive work, the suite on the whole seems somewhat tentative when placed beside those in the English or French sets. Hence, it is not surprising that Bach apparently abandoned it around 1725, though not without first attempting to bring it up to date in the version BWV 818a.

The allemande opens with what appears to be a quotation from *La Couperin*, the French composer's self-portrait in allemande style. But Bach could have known the latter only if a prepublication manuscript copy had crossed his path (Example 14.1).[9] The revisions to the Bach allemande, in BWV 818a, somewhat refine the

EXAMPLE 14.1.   (a) Suite in A Minor BWV 818, allemande, bars 1–2a; (b) Couperin, *La Couperin*, bars 0–1a

voice-leading; one passage, however (bars 19–20a), contains some clunky sonorities, the result of expanding the original two voices to three.

The courante, with only eight bars in each half, has the concision of many seventeenth-century examples of the dance. For just this reason it may be more successful than some of the longer courantes in the English Suites. Because of the piece's extreme compression, a modulation to the subdominant takes place as late as three bars before the end. But Bach manages a return to the tonic through the unusual progression in bars 14–15, in which one $^6_4$-chord resolves to another. The successful negotiation of this difficult modulation within a compact, highly symmetrical form proves to be one of the somewhat abstruse charms of this suite.

The *Sarabande simple* consists mainly of embellished apreggiation; the same type of sarabande is found in the Fifth Cello Suite and as the double of the sarabande in the Sixth English Suite. In place of arpeggation, the double in the present suite (called *Sarabande double* in the copy by Anonymous 5) substitutes two-part counterpoint. Actually, this counterpoint is implicit in the original sarabande, for the two voices of the double follow the outlines of the original treble and bass and retain from the model the idea of exchanging material after the double bar.

Neither copy of the double explicitly calls for a repetition of the complete second half, indicating only a *petite reprise* of the last four bars. The omission of the larger repeat—that is, of bars 9–24—was probably occasioned by the presence of a *petite reprise*, rare elsewhere in Bach's music. Dürr (NBA V/8, KB, 158) suggests transposing the bass of the first ending (bar 24A) upward by a third in order to connect back to bar 9. But the second ending (bar 24B, without alterations) is perfectly suitable for this purpose.

The gigue has a short, rather prosaic subject. But this made it possible to employ all the artifice of a serious three-part fugue without producing the effect of rhetorical overkill that arises from the long-winded subjects of some of Reinken's fugal gigues. The counterpoint is simple enough to retain its transparency even at the climax of the contrapuntal work, the combination of *rectus* and *inversus* versions of the subject in the latter portion of the second half (bars 33ff.). But strict counterpoint is not really the main issue here. The most striking event—certainly the most dramatic—is the scale that begins at the top of the keyboard in bar 29b and sweeps down to low C by bar 32a after passing through all three voices. Similar gestures occur at crucial moments in a few of the early fugues (e.g., BWV 954, bar 80).

The alternate version, BWV 818a, adds a prelude and a minuet and substitutes a single sarabande for the sarabande and double of BWV 818. Oddities in the prelude have raised suspicions about the authenticity of this version, as has its survival only in two copies by Mempell, a relatively late copyist. But it seems impossible to doubt Bach's responsibility for the two added dance movements or for the revisions in the three movements common to both versions.

Of the two added dances, the minuet is clearly a mature work of Bach, mingling ordinary and triplet sixteenths in an up-to-date galant manner also found in the minuet of the D-Major Partita (published in 1728). Indeed, despite its brevity, the minuet may be the most impressive movement of the entire suite, although its galant singing melody and flexible keyboard idiom (e.g., broken octaves in bar 15) distinguish it from the other movements. Nevertheless, it possesses a strong contrapuntal element, the opening theme being transferred to the bass after the double bar.

The sarabande is no less impressive, and at least one small detail, a chromatic scale fragment in sixteenth-notes (alto, bar 18), points to a late date. While each tone in the chromatic line still has a real harmonic function, this sort of chromaticism verges on the ornamental, and Bach uses it only in a few relatively late works—for example, the C-minor fantasia BWV 906/1. On the other hand, the dotted rhythm in the opening bars is rather old-fashioned; Bach had used it in the sarabande of the early *Partie* BWV 832. But he returned to it in the corresponding movements of Partitas Nos. 1 and 6, so a date around 1725 is hardly out of the question here.[10] In any case, this movement remains a variation of the sarabande of BWV 818. Hence, the sarabande of BWV 818 has, in effect, two doubles, like courante 2 in the First English Suite. Performers of BWV 818 might as well play all three versions of the sarabande, alongside the minuet of BWV 818a.

The first movement, lacking a title in the sources but evidently a prelude, is a different story. Dürr (NBA V/8, KB, 74–75) rightly calls it "primitive" in some respects. The texture seems simplistic for a Bach work of the mid-1720s, and the tempo mark *Fort gai* is likewise unusual. Even odder is the frantic passage-work first heard in bar 15, at which point the broad *alla breve* meter of the opening is effectively replaced by a rather nervous common time (Example 14.2). Some

EXAMPLE 14.2.   Suite in A Minor BWV 818a, prelude:
(a) bars 1–3; (b) bars 15–16

of the voice-leading, including the melodic augmented seconds of both voices in bar 16, is also peculiar. Yet the design of the piece seems satisfactory, resembling the through-composed binary form used in several preludes in WTC1 (e.g., the prelude in A♭). Hence, this movement might have been an old piece that Bach attached to the suite or perhaps a new one sketched quickly in improvisatory fashion. It is, in fact, vaguely similar in conception to the very free praeambulum of Partita No. 5 and thus might constitute another link to the works of the mid- and late 1720s.

Suite in E♭, BWV 819

Chief sources: DSB P 418 (Anonymous 5; No. 6 in set); LEm Go.S.10 (Gerber; as No. 8). *Editions*: BG 36; Dadelsen (1975—allemande only; the remainder of the edition is of BWV 819a); NBA V/8.

Later version (BWV 819a): *Sources*: DSB P 418, with later additions (Anonymous 5); SPK P 420 (Vogler). *Editions*: BG 36, appendix (allemande only); Dadelsen (1975); NBA V/8.

The suite in E♭ comes much closer than BWV 818 to the style of the French Suites. Indeed, while it is natural to think of BWV 818 and 819 as a pair standing between the two well-known groups of six suites, stylistically BWV 819 belongs with the later French Suites (Nos. 4–6). Suite No. 4 is in the same key, and Bach presumably did not wish to include two suites in E♭ within the same set; hence, BWV 819 was dropped. Yet both Anonymous 5 and, later, the Weimar organist Vogler (Bach's ex-student) copied both E♭-major works into their collections of six suites "without prelude"; and at some point Bach prepared a revised version, as he did for the others.

The later version (BWV 819a) substitutes a different allemande, but otherwise the alterations are minor by comparison with those in BWV 818 or some of the French Suites.[11] As in BWV 818, the copies of BWV 819 by Anonymous 5 and Gerber contain additional ornaments. Dadelsen (1975) gives these ornaments in small type; the NBA places them in the main text for BWV 819 but not BWV 819a, which consequently appears in a less ornamented form than does the earlier version.

The original allemande bears a striking similarity to that of French Suite No. 6, both allemandes resembling a sonata movement for flute or violin with continuo. Neither allemande contains much imitative counterpoint as such, but both make use of the same violinistic figure, which is eventually transferred from the upper voice to the bass.[12] Perhaps it was because of these similarities that Bach wrote the new allemande of BWV 819a, in an effort to avoid a duplication and salvage the suite for inclusion in the set of "suites without prelude." The new allemande might well date from the same time as the later version of BWV 818, since, as in the sarabande of BWV 818a, Bach wrote the new movement as an elaborate variation of the older one.

The new allemande demonstrates how sophisticated double counterpoint might emerge from the composing-out of a harmonic skeleton, thus foreshadowing the Goldberg Variations. As in the original allemande, the bass imitates the initial treble line at the distance of a half-bar, and the two parts exchange material at bar 9. But the voice-leading beyond this point is far more chromatic in the new version, and Bach introduces additional contrapuntal tricks as well. Bar 5 was already a mirror inversion of bar 3, a feat made possible because the harmonic progression in bar 5 (I, IV) is the inversion of that appearing in bar 3 (I, V). Later, where two consecutive bars (16–17) of the original allemande presented two different composings-out of the same harmonic progression (F minor: V, I), Bach made the second bar a nearly exact repetition of the first, save for the exchange of material between the two parts in counterpoint at the octave.

Some of the writing, such as the mirror reflection of the two halves of bar 22 (treble only), may seem a bit contrived, but no more so than in the canons of the *Art of Fugue* and some of the other late polyphonic works.[13] Indeed, like the duets of the Goldberg Variations (which employ similar writing), the later allemande can and perhaps should be played on two manuals. The two halves of the new allemande were surely not meant to serve as varied reprises of those in the original one. Vogler's copy lacks the earlier allemande, suggesting that Bach intended it to replace the original one. Anonymous 5, however, inserted the new allemande into his existing copy of BWV 819, and players today would surely be justified in treating it as a double.[14]

The courante, though notated in $\frac{3}{2}$, is largely in compound duple meter ($\frac{6}{4}$), like the courante of Rameau's A-Minor Suite. The beaming of the eighth-notes in the right hand does not always reflect the true meter. Perhaps this is because Bach's own view of the rhythm changed; the only substantial revision in the movement (bar 10) coincides with the one clear shift to triple meter ($\frac{3}{2}$), which the revision was presumably meant to clarify.[15]

The sarabande recalls the Sinfonia in E♭, thanks to its dotted rhythm and trio-sonata texture; the latter was previously seen in English Suite No. 5. The resemblance to the sinfonia is strengthened by the numerous appoggiaturas in the copies of the two pieces, both in the same key, by Gerber and Anonymous 5. As in certain other pieces by Bach, all relatively galant in style (e.g., the F♯-major prelude in WTC2, the sarabande of Partita No. 5), the proper length of the appoggiaturas is open to question. Here, "long" performance would create exposed fifths in bar 10 and harshen the already sharp dissonances in bar 19; hence, the "short" or "invariable" appoggiatura seems best. Throughout the movement, the repeated notes in the bass should perhaps be played as smoothly as possible, in imitation of bow vibrato; a strongly articulated drum bass seems out of the question.

The bourrée is a more athletic version of the dance than occurs in the English Suites, the sturdy quarter-note pulse of the older examples here being broken into exuberant arpeggiated figures. There is, however, an echo of one striking harmonic progression in a bourrée from the older set.[16]

BWV 819 apparently never contained a gigue, and Bach evidently saw no reason to add one when he revised the suite. In fact, it was by no means unusual for a suite to end simply with a minuet or two, as this one does. The pedal-point at the opening of minuet 1 might be a pastoral idea, and perhaps the repetitious melodic writing is meant to remind one of musette players (bars 3–4 contain a variation of bars 1–2). The second minuet is designated *Trio* in the sources and is indeed, like the sarabande, a galant piece in three parts. It is Bach's only keyboard piece outside the WTC in E♭ minor, and one wonders if it was not originally in another key, like the trio of BWV 814a (see below).

French Suite No. 1 in D Minor BWV 812

Earlier readings: *Chief sources*: US Wc (Altnikol); DSB P 224 (autograph fair copy, beginning of allemande and end of gigue lost); DSB P 418 (Anonymous 5; No. 1 in set); DSB P 1221

(Gerber; as No. 1). *Editions*: NBA V/4, first part (after P 224 and P 418); NBA V/8, first part (version "A," after US Wc).

Later readings: *Chief sources*: SPK P 225 (A. M. Bach); SPK P 420 (Vogler). *Editions*: NBA V/4, second part (after P 225); NBA V/8, second part (version "B," including ornaments from P 1221).

Suite No. 1 is somewhat distinct in style from the remaining French Suites, resembling the English Suites in the relatively strict counterpoint of all movements. It is a piece for connoisseurs of Bach's version of French style; even the gigue is relatively severe, and its employment of a pervasive dotted rhythm (in duple time) leaves the suite without any truly quick movement. The suite may well have been composed somewhat earlier than the rest of the collection, since Bach's entry in the 1722 *Clavier-Büchlein* was a fair copy and already contains a few revised readings.[17] Subsequent alterations were limited to refinements of detail and the addition of ornaments.

The opening movement resembles the corresponding movement of the First English Suite in its evocation of the improvisatory allemandes of earlier German composers such as Froberger. As is so often the case in such movements, phrases tend to be held together by scalar descents in the underlying bass line—for example, from d' to d in bars 2–5 and again in bars 5–9. To be sure, the actual bass alternates between static pedal-points, "walking" lines in eighth-notes, and motivic writing in small note-values, including the characteristic French dotted figure on the upbeats to bar 7 and elsewhere (which also occurs in the treble). Hence, some bars languish while others push forward—a feature that might be reflected in performance—the pace quickening, as one would expect, in the approach to each cadence. In this the allemande resembles not only the one in the First English Suite but certain preludes that must date from roughly the same period (e.g., BWV 902/1, BWV 940). A descending scale in sixteenths, introduced without fanfare in bar 10, proves to be a motive of some importance. In bar 18, a related scale in the soprano moves in contrary motion against a scale in the inner part; the two voices land on a tritone on the downbeat of bar 19, which represents the restrained climax of the piece.[18]

The courante is the only one in the French Suites to use the meter traditional for the French version of the dance ($\frac{3}{2}$). It follows a plan similar to that used in the courantes of the English Suites, stating a short *thema* in imitation at the beginning and inverting it in the second half. The opening pedal-point and the striking Neapolitan harmony in the closing phrase (bar 22) are shared with the allemande, but the two movements do not form a variation pair.

The sarabande is in four parts without florid embellishment, as in English Suite No. 4. But the counterpoint here is more dissonant, and the inner parts and bass have more life of their own. The bass even restates the opening treble line at the beginning of the second half, two octaves below the original pitch-level and with the harmony considerably altered.[19] The full chords and the numerous ornaments (found especially in Gerber's copy) imply a somewhat graver tempo than in other sarabandes—probably, however, no slower than the speed now usually considered normal for the dance.

The theme of the first minuet is written in free triple counterpoint, the opening phrase recurring in two further permutations (the only others that are practical on the keyboard). These later statements of the theme contain an ornament indicated by the abbreviation *tr* (bars 9, 21, also in 6); this might be realized as a simple turn and also applied to the alto in bar 1. The second minuet is in Da Capo form; the sources leave it unclear whether the portion after the double bar should be repeated, but it likely should be.[20] Presumably, the first minuet is repeated afterwards, although most sources do not specify this.

The gigue is one of two by Bach in dotted duple time; the other is the gigue of the E-Minor Partita.[21] Overturelike dotted rhythms are common in seventeenth-century gigues, including many by Froberger.[22] There is little evidence for playing such pieces in triple time (as argued in Ferguson 1975, 92–93, and McIntyre 1965). Bach is unlikely to have known the triple-time versions that survive for a few of Froberger's duple-time gigues; on the other hand, he must have known the duple-time gigues in MM and in Book 2 of Kuhnau's *Clavierübung* (*Partie* 1). These, like the present gigue, can be converted to triple time only by positing the existence of all sorts of unlikely notational conventions.[23]

Presumably, the tempo here can be a little quicker than in an overture. Yet the complex rhythm and the numerous ornaments, especially in Gerber's copy, require a fairly moderate pace, despite the *alla breve* notation in the autograph.[24] The incorporation of such a movement in a suite of this date was a striking gesture, perhaps intended to call attention to the movement's strict counterpoint and symmetrical design. There is even a presentiment of a moment in the *Art of Fugue*, composed some twenty years later: An impressive "Phrygian" cadence, with trill in the bass, precedes the combination of the *rectus* and *inversus* forms of the subject at the beginning of the final section (bar 22; cf. Contrapunctus 8, bar 93). Unfortunately, the incessant dotted rhythms threaten to grow monotonous, and the danger may not be entirely alleviated by the dramatic appearance of running sixteenths in the closing phrase of each half (bars 11, 26).

French Suite No. 2 in C Minor BWV 813

Earliest readings: *Sources*: DSB P 224 (fragmentary autograph, minuet copied separately by A. M. Bach); DSB P 418 (Anonymous 5; No. 2 in set). *Edition*: NBA V/4, first part (after P 224 and P 418).

Somewhat later readings: *Sole source*: DSB P 1221 (Gerber; as No. 5).

Intermediate readings: *Chief source*: US Wc (Altnikol). *Edition*: NBA V/8, first part (version "A," with alternate versions of allemande and courante from P 1221).

Later readings: *Chief sources*: SPK P 225 (A. M. Bach, first three movements); SPK P 420 (Vogler, with second minuet BWV 813a). *Edition*: NBA V/4, second part (after P 225 and P 420).

Latest readings: *Sole source*: DSB P 418, revised text (Anonymous 5). *Edition*: NBA V/8, second part (version "B," including minuet BWV 813a).

Although the surviving autograph of Suite No. 2 dates from about the same time as that of Suite No. 1, here Bach was either revising or composing as he wrote. Hence, the suite may be a somewhat later work, and indeed it has more of the galant character that is typical of the remaining works of the set. It adds several new types of movements to those previously found in Bach's keyboard suites: a courante in $\frac{3}{4}$, an ariosolike sarabande, an air (unrelated to the one in the early suite BWV 833), and a skipping gigue in two voices.[25] Despite its relatively simple character, the suite, especially the first two movements, cost Bach considerable trouble; indeed, few works survive in a more extensive array of early and revised readings.

Allemande and courante both exist in multiple versions (see Table 14–1). In each case the earliest known version is divided exactly in half by the double bar; later

TABLE 14–1.   Revisions in French Suite No. 2

Version*	Chief Sources	Edited in	Main distinctions from final version
Allemande			
1	P 418, orig. text	NBA V/8, KB, 92	Bars 12b–13 in simpler form. Lacks bars 14 and 15b–16a. Simpler bass in bars 15a, 16b–18a
2	P 1221	NBA V/8, "A" alt. ending	Simpler bass in bars 15b–18a. Different treble in bar 16a
3	US Wc, P 225, P 420	NBA V/8, "A"	Simpler bass in bars 16–18a
4	P 418, corr. text	NBA V/8, "B"	(= final version)
Courante			
1	P 224; P 418, orig. text	NBA V/4, 1st part	48 bars. In place of bars 38–50: 4 bars using same motivic material as bars 46–49 of final version
2	P 1221	NBA V/8, "A," alt. ending	51 bars. In place of bars 38–50: 7 bars
3	Ed. Forkel	NBA V/8, "A," with variants listed for source Y2	54 bars. In place of bars 38–50: 10 bars
4	US Wc, P 225, P 420	NBA V/4, 2d part; NBA V/8, "A"	Like version 3, with small variants in bars 38–43
5	P 418, corr. text	NBA V/8, "B"	57 bars (= final version)

orig. = original
corr. = corrected (i.e., revised)
*Numbers correspond with *Varianten* as enumerated in NBA V/8, KB, 92–94

versions break the symmetry, inserting new material following a cadence to the subdominant. Indeed, it might have been the rather late placement of this cadence within the binary form that occasioned the revisions. For in neither movement does the original version make such a swift and strong return to the tonic as that noted in the courante of BWV 818. Even in the latest version, however, both movements remain rounded binaries, without a genuine return or recapitulation (as in the revised version of the A-Minor Invention).

The courante closely resembles some of Bach's preludes, especially the "Six" (BWV 933–38), in being essentially a sonata movement, its texture more that of a work for violin and continuo than a *pièce de clavecin*. The revisions here were more extensive than in the allemande, but all five versions retain the idea of returning at the end to a recapitulation of the closing phrase of the first half. Moreover, this closing phrase always follows a climactic ascent to c''', the highest note used in the French Suites. In the original version the ascent to this note was swift and direct, following swiftly upon the cadence to the subdominant (bar 38). In version 2 Bach inserted a new passage just after the cadence, thus postponing and intensifying the eventual climb to c'''. Subsequent versions represent efforts to perfect the inserted passage, versions 3 and 4 no doubt being rejected because of the clumsy leap of a tenth in bar 44.

The sarabande is only slightly closer to its traditional models than is the courante. While there is, in fact, a frequent emphasis on the second beat in either the harmony or the melody, this is essentially a free aria, like the opening movement in the Goldberg Variations. The texture is that of the "monodic" keyboard chorale, a genre represented in all three Little Keyboard Books (see Chapter 10), and thus the sarabande can be played on two manuals, the two accompanying parts being confined to the left hand. The twenty-four bars are no more than in most of Bach's earlier sarabandes, and despite the florid embellishment of the melody the proper tempo may not be any slower than usual. Surely one should play in a clear "three," without subdividing the beats. This will help bring out the underlying sarabande rhythm in bars 3, 7, and elsewhere where the last two beats comprise a florid arpeggiation of a single harmony.

The term *air*, as applied to the fourth movement, is a generic term for a movement that, unlike the preceding one, could not be plausibly identified with any dance. Like the airs occasionally encountered in suites and sonatas by Bach's contemporaries, it is far from cantabile in character, being rather "instrumental" in its running sixteenths and leaping eighths. The opening theme is inverted at the beginning of the second half, where it appears in the treble, and the autograph shows that Bach originally considered having the bass imitate this in the second half of bar 5. He immediately changed his mind, instead giving the theme in its original form to the bass at the return (bar 13). Even here, adjustments were necessary, since the dissonant G on the third beat of the theme does not sit well in the bass; Bach eventually eliminated the dissonance although not the note itself from the bass entry (Example 14.3).[26]

In most copies of the suite there is only one minuet. Even this was absent from Bach's original draft in the 1722 *Clavier-Büchlein*, but a rubric in Sebastian's hand directs the player to the minuet copied by his wife near the end of the volume. A

EXAMPLE 14.3.   French Suite No. 2 in C Minor BWV 813,
air: (a) bar 5, canceled reading of autograph; (b) bar 13

second, little-known minuet (listed separately as BWV 813a) is found in a few later sources, and its addition brought the suite into conformity with Suite No. 1. In fact, both minuets might have been teaching pieces that Bach added to the suite as an afterthought. The NBA gives the slurs for minuet 1 differently in versions "A" and "B," the slurs in version "A" implying fussier and more detailed articulation. Some of the differences, such as the change from three two-note slurs to a single six-note slur in bar 3, seem deliberate. Others, however, might be due only to the careless placement of long slurs meant to cover an entire bar.[27]

The gigue is the only one in the French Suites to employ the dotted figures typical of French examples of the dance. It could have been notated in either $\frac{6}{8}$ or $\frac{12}{8}$, and indeed the autograph—of which only the first twelve bars are extant—contains indications implying that Bach sought to group every four bars into a "higher unity" (NBA V/4, KB, 31). The fact that the piece remained in $\frac{3}{8}$ suggests that Bach wished to suggest a lively *mouvement* with more strongly marked accents. Yet the skipping rhythm is heard almost without a break, and as in the gigue of Suite No. 1 there is a danger here of rhythmic monotony. Running sixteenths, introduced near the end, are clearly intended to hasten the movement toward its conclusion, but they also force one to hold back the tempo at the beginning. Yet a moderate tempo may actually help reduce the danger of monotony arising from the repeated skipping rhythms, since it makes it possible to introduce expressive rhythmic nuances and to make the ornaments more meaningful, for example, by distinguishing a fast mordent used for accent (bars 1, 10) from a slower one used to sustain a long note (bar 12).

French Suite No. 3 in B Minor BWV 814

Earliest readings: *Source*: DSB P 224 (fragmentary autograph; minuets separately). *Edition*: NBA V/4, first part (after P 224 and P 418).

Somewhat later readings: *Chief sources*: US Wc (Altnikol), DSB P 418 (Anonymous 5; No. 3 in set). *Edition*: NBA V/8, first part (version "A," after US Wc).

Intermediate readings: *Source*: DSB P 1221 (Gerber; as No. 4).

Later readings: *Chief sources*: DSB P 418, revised text (Anonymous 5); SPK P 804/49. *Editions*: NBA V/8, second part (version "B").

?Intermediate version (BWV 814a), with alternate second minuet: *Sole source*: SPK P 514 (gigue fragmentary). *Edition*: NBA V/8, appendix.

Suite No. 3 opens with the most delicate of the allemandes in the French Suites but closes with one of the most brilliant gigues. As in Suite No. 2, one senses the influence of galant chamber music, now even in the allemande, which has little to do with older examples of the dance (at least those for keyboard; ensemble examples might be found). The suite exists in at least four distinct versions, but none of the movements underwent changes as substantial as did the allemande and courante of Suite No. 2. Even the substitution of a different second minuet, found in the alternate version BWV 814a, was accompanied by only a few changes in the other movements. The uncertain provenance of the one copy preserving this version, however, places its authenticity in question.[28]

One might imagine the allemande scored for flute and continuo. Because the two parts are so nearly equal, they could be performed on two manuals, perhaps single eight-foot stops, since this is an unusually delicate allemande for Bach. Virtually every beat contains a statement of the opening motive, which consists of an upbeat of three sixteenths moving to a fourth note on the beat, the latter often marked by an *accent* or *port de voix*, as in bar 1 (Example 14.4). Hence, throughout the

EXAMPLE 14.4.   French Suite No. 3 in B Minor BWV 814, allemande, bars 0–2

movement, gestures end on the beat, and even when the accented note is a mere sixteenth it should perhaps be lengthened ever so slightly or followed by a small articulation to separate it from the following gesture. This is fussy by later standards of phrasing and gesture, but it may be appropriate in a movement that comes particularly close to the "speaking" quality of the music of Bach's French contemporaries.

The courante is in $\frac{6}{4}$, except in a few hemiolas (e.g., bar 4), and thus, like the courante in BWV 819, is closer to some later French courantes than to the traditional model. The sarabande, while retaining the imitative texture of the courantes in the English Suites, is another example of the new arioso type seen in Suite No. 2. The melodic writing here is somewhat less intricate, so that the movement flows more broadly, and the bass occasionally replaces the treble as the active melodic voice, in particular when the theme is restated at the beginning of the closing phrase (bars 21–22). For all these reasons, and also because the inner parts occasionally cross between the hands, the movement is probably better played on a single manual.

As in the air of Suite No. 2, Bach found it necessary to revise the passage in which the bass takes the theme. A variant in the treble at this point in BWV 814a seems to represent an attempt to improve the upper part (Example 14.5). Yet the

EXAMPLE 14.5.   French Suite No. 3 in B Minor, sarabande, bars 21–23a: (a) BWV 814, version "A"; (b) BWV 814, version "B"; (c) BWV 814a

reading of BWV 814a is not clearly any better and if authentic might represent a rejected intermediate reading prior to the final reading of version "B."[29]

The next movement, in most sources, is the anglaise, which seems originally to have been called a gavotte despite the absence of the traditional half-bar upbeat.[30] The time-signature "2," also used in gavottes, is equivalent to ¢. The sturdy *mouvement* in quarter-notes and the four-square phrases, many of them cadencing in the middle of the bar, perhaps give the piece some of the rustic flavor supposed to characterize this not very well-defined dance-type.

As in Suite No. 2, the minuets are written separately in the 1722 *Clavier-Büchlein,* and if Bach ever indicated their proper position it was through a rubric written on a page now lost. In most copies the minuets come at the end of the suite, but Altnikol and Gerber placed them between anglaise and gigue, a position corresponding to that of the minuets in Bach's other suites. Minuet 1 received the most extensive revisions of any movement in the suite. A new bass line for the last eight bars was the most prominent change, perhaps a chain reaction set off by a relatively minor alteration of the treble in bars 29 and 31. In the autograph, Bach designated minuet 2 with the heading *Menuet-Trio,* and it is indeed in three parts throughout, resembling the first minuet of Suite No. 1 in its suggestions of triple counterpoint (inverted after the double bar). For minuet 2, BWV 814a substitutes a transposed version of the little trio BWV 929, which Bach had composed for the suite in G minor by Stölzel in CB. It is hard to say why Bach would have substituted the shorter and simpler movement for the original trio, especially as the new trio descends to low BB, a note otherwise not found in the French Suites.[31] Both trios are notated in "3," as opposed to $\frac{3}{4}$; this might imply a slower tempo, which would be appropriate to the more expressive character of both trios.

The gigue, like the allemande, is essentially a binary sonata movement in two voices, showing few signs of the traditional dance rhythm. What seems like new material at the beginning of the second half is actually an embellished variation of the subject. Bars 11–12 and three parallel passages (bars 29–30, 47–48, 61–62) were inserted only after Bach had completed the autograph; this made symmetrical eight-bar phrases (e.g., bars 9–16) out of what had been six-bar ones.

French Suite No. 4 in E$^{\flat}$, BWV 815

Earlier readings: *Chief sources*: DSB P 224 (autograph); US Wc (Altnikol); DSB P 418 (Anonymous 5; No. 6 in set); DSB P 1221 (Gerber; as No. 6). *Editions*: NBA V/4, first part (after P 224), NBA V/8, first part (version "A," after US Wc).

Later readings, including minuet: *Chief sources*: DSB P 418, revised text (Anonymous 5); SPK P 420 (Vogler). *Edition*: NBA V/8, second part (version "B").

Alternate (?intermediate) version (BWV 815a): *Chief sources*: SPK P 289/13 (Michel); US NHy LM 5024 (Rinck). *Edition*: NBA V/8, appendix.

Suite No. 4 may have been composed relatively early, since the autograph begins as a fair copy, implying that the first version had been completed earlier than that of Suites Nos. 2 and 3. Nevertheless, with Suite No. 4 the French Suites move into major keys and take on a more popular style, and parallels with the suites of Froberger, D'Anglebert, and other seventeenth-century composers largely disappear. For example, the allemande is in the arpeggiando style traditionally associated with the genre, but the comparatively regular nature of the arpeggios and of the bass motion recalls Bach's arpeggiando preludes, and the movement lacks the expressive irregularity cultivated in earlier keyboard allemandes. The courante is again a binary-form movement in two voices, this time, however, effectively in $\frac{9}{8}$ (written in $\frac{3}{4}$ with triplet eighths), which is typical for neither the French courante nor the Italian corrente.

The sarabande is more recognizable as such, although its texture has little to do with that of earlier sarabandes. One would hardly have expected the graceful opening gesture of the right hand and the walking bass line accompanying it to change places, yet they do so when the counterpoint is inverted in bar 3 and elsewhere. Like the sarabande, the gavotte is an unusually gentle version of the dance (for Bach), lacking the emphatic upbeat of two quarters and the metrical ambiguities of those in the English Suites. Surely it should be played with the sensitivity appropriate to many French gavottes, which tend to be moderate in tempo and expressive; this is the implication of the two-note slurs placed over the first few drooping "sigh" figures in the later version. The air is almost a variation of the gavotte, containing the same number of bars and even opening in the middle of the bar. There is also a brief, somewhat elegiac minuet, found only in a few later copies and thus absent from many editions, but a worthwhile addition to the suite.[32]

The gigue is a true fugue, though mainly in just two voices, hence resembling the gigue of the Fourth English Suite, to which it is also related by the horn calls in its subject. Actually, the subject is even closer to that of the fugal gigue in the Telemann suite found in the CB. Friedemann's copy of the Telemann piece has been placed around the beginning of 1723, hence precisely the time when Sebastian was copying the present suite into the 1722 *Clavier-Büchlein*. The possibility of Telemann's influence on Bach is obvious; the two pieces even contain similar ornaments, since both subjects were later graced by mordents.[33] Bach made only one substantial revision in the gigue: In bars 35 and 37 the leaps in the main motive were stretched from thirds into tenths, perhaps a reference to the overblowing of brass instruments.

The suite exists in a considerably altered version (BWV 815a) containing a prelude and a second gavotte but no minuet or gigue. The movements that this version shares with the familiar one also contain a few changes, not all of which seem to be improvements.[34] Nevertheless, the relatively good provenance of this version—the copyist Michel worked closely with C. P. E. Bach—as well as its musical worth leaves little doubt about its authenticity. Like BWV 818a, it might represent an experiment of the mid-1720s, although parallels with movements in WTC2 suggest a later date.[35] Performers might well combine movements from both versions.

The prelude opens with a series of chords marked *arpeggio*; this leads to a simple fughetta. Hence, the movement resembles the early version of the C♯-major prelude of WTC2 (BWV 872a/1), although the latter lacks the brief arpeggiando coda found here at the conclusion of the fughetta.[36] Despite the shorthand notation of the arpeggiando passages, the fughetta is fully worked out, the voice-leading precisely notated. There is even a distinct closing phrase (bars 22–24), recapitulated at the end and thus giving the fughetta a through-composed bipartite form.

The second gavotte is also fully worked out, and at much greater length; indeed, it is Bach's longest and most intricate example of the dance. Only its length might have militated against including it in the familiar version of the suite, for it contains some exquisite counterpoint. As in the gavottes of the English Suites, there is a passage in the second half where the meter and phrasing become irregular (bars 36ff.). Normal movement is restored at the return, where the theme is stated by the bass (bar 50b).

French Suite No. 5 in G, BWV 816

Earlier readings: *Chief sources*: DSB P 224 (autograph); US Wc (Altnikol). *Editions*: NBA V/4, first part (after P 224); NBA V/8, first part (version "A," after US Wc).

Later readings: *Chief sources*: DSB P 1221 (Gerber; No. 8 in set); SPK P 420 (Vogler); LEm ms. 8 (Mempell). *Editions*: NBA V/8, second part (version "B").

The suite in G, one of Bach's most elegant harpsichord works, is even more popular in style than the preceding one, since it seems to place somewhat greater priority on singing melody and the idiomatic treatment of the instrument while further reducing the role of imitative counterpoint, except in the courante and gigue. Not surprisingly, it appears to be a somewhat later composition; while Bach sketched out the first few bars of the allemande in the 1722 *Clavier-Büchlein*, he did not complete the score until after coming to Leipzig.[37] Later revisions were very minor, apart from an important variant in the sarabande.

Both allemande and courante make graceful use of violinistic figuration, although it is often confined to the accompaniment in the allemande, leaving the treble with an arioso melody somewhat resembling those in the sarabandes of Suites Nos. 2 and 3. Both movements follow very similar plans, the thirty-two-bar courante having exactly the same structure as the aria of the Goldberg Variations. The courante, however, is in effect a two-part invention, effortlessly incorporating the inversion of the counterpoint after the double bar and of the theme itself in the last phrase (from bar 24).

The sarabande is another example of the arioso type, performable on two manuals. The ornaments are an essential part of the melodic line and (exceptionally) are present in the autograph. The movement appears to be Bach's longest sarabande in terms of bar-count, though probably not in real time, since it lacks the extreme embellishment of some examples and can be played andante or even faster. Bach later varied the final phrase, giving it a somewhat more florid form that soars to high c''' three bars before the end. This gives the sarabande a more satisfactory conclusion than the original version, which reached its peak (b'') in the previous phrase (bar 35).

Harpsichordists may be inclined to over-dot the dotted quarters in the theme of the sarabande (as in bar 1), and there is some support for this in a variant in a late source.[38] Double-dotting of quarters is strongly implied in the sarabande of Partita No. 5, but that is a movement of the trio type with pervasive dotting. In the present arioso sarabande, literal interpretation might seem to accent unduly the passing dissonances in bars 29 and 33 (c/b', B/e''), but these are well within Bach's tolerances for dissonance.

The forthright melodies of the gavotte and bourrée make them favorites with players and audiences, so it is perhaps necessary to point out that neither one is an entirely typical example of either dance. The strongly accented rhythm of the gavotte is rare in French examples; conversely, in the bourrée Bach has softened the dance's vigorous quarter-note pulsation. In fact, the texture of the bourrée seems a simplification of that of the allemande, an arioso melody accompanied by what at first glance appears to be an Alberti bass. A closer parallel to the left-hand part, however, would be the lively cello writing in certain Bach arias.[39]

The loure, mislabeled as bourrée 2 in some sources and editions, is absent from the most authoritative sources of the later version of the suite, and it seems fair to conclude that Bach decided to omit it.[40] It is not one of Bach's strongest efforts, and the modulation back to the tonic in the last phrase is somewhat weak. Still, it is worth playing as one of only two examples of this dance by Bach, the other being in the E-major violin partita BWV 1006 (on the lute version, see Chapter 16). A loure is essentially a slow gigue; Walther speaks of it as being performed "slowly and with gravity," which would be appropriate here.[41] "Slow" need not mean "dragging," and even here it is possible to give the characteristic skipping rhythms a dance-like spring by "over-dotting" the dotted quarter and leaving some space—that is, a small silence—after it and by not dwelling for long on the appoggiaturas. The occasional flourishes in sixteenths appear to have been afterthoughts, and, while they are not exactly the virtuoso embellishments one finds in an Italian adagio, they probably ought to glide smoothly without slowing the basic pulse.[42]

The gigue is the longest in the French Suites, at least on paper; the time-signature $\frac{12}{16}$ implies a very lively tempo. Alongside the gigue of Suite No. 1 it is one of the set's two most fully worked-out fugues, with two expositions in each half. The subject, however, is of a very different sort, built out of repeated violinistic arpeggios suggesting either Vivaldi or country fiddling. The subject leads to the most brilliant keyboard writing in the entire set; the movement is not easy to play, and the second half in particular contains some finger-twisting passages (e.g., bars 34–35, 40–41). Once one has mastered them, it is all too easy to play this as a *moto perpetuo*, but there are plenty of opportunities for expressive rhythmic nuances. One in particular occurs at the dramatic 7-chord on the downbeat of bar 42, where one might pause for a split second before attacking the following cadenzalike passage, which leads to the cadence in the relative minor (bar 44).

At the end of the 1722 *Clavier-Büchlein* stands a minuet in G (BWV 841), which, though previously copied into Wilhelm Fridemann's Little Keyboard Book, has been suggested as a possible candidate for insertion into Suite No. 5. It is, however, the simpler of the two G-major minuets in CB, and no source incorporates it into the suite.

French Suite No. 6 in E, BWV 817

Earlier readings: *Chief source*: US Wc (Altnikol). *Edition*: NBA V/8, first part (version "A").

Later readings: *Chief sources*: DSB P 1221 (Gerber, with prelude BWV 854/1); SPK P 420 (Vogler). *Edition* NBA V/8, second part (version "B").

The Sixth French Suite was almost certainly the last composed, perhaps as late as 1725. The NBA distinguishes two versions, but it would have taken Bach only a few moments to make the few small revisions that set "B" apart from "A."[43] Like the E-Major Partita for unaccompanied violin—in the same key, and likewise closing a set of six—this is the lightest work in the collection. Some of the inner movements—the gavotte, polonaise, and minuet—are remarkably slight for Bach, but the four main movements are certainly imaginative enough.

Gerber's copy opens with the prelude in E from WTCl and thus belongs not with the French Suites but with the "suites with preludes"—that is, the English Suites. If this was Bach's own idea, it might have occurred to him in the course of planning his first keyboard print, the *Clavierübung*, during the year or two that preceded the publication of the First Partita in 1726. Indeed, this suite closely resembles the partita, both being lightly scored, predominantly galant works. Bach might well have written the E-major suite in an attempt to create something that would be palatable to the public and thus suitable for publication. If so, however, he must have decided almost at once that it was too insubstantial even with the addition of the prelude from WTCl and thus added the suite to the collection of "suites without preludes."

As already noted, the allemande closely resembles the corresponding movement of BWV 819. The present allemande is no doubt the superior work, containing greater variety of material and lacking the repetitions of one- and two-bar units that give the allemande of the E^b-major work a somewhat square phrasing.

The courante may be the most lightly and fantastically scored of all of Bach's keyboard dances. A remarkable piece of keyboard writing, it comes close to the concertolike style of the B-major prelude in WTC2. Yet its descent from earlier courantes, particularly that of the preceding suite, is clear, particularly in the inversion of the opening gesture at the beginning of the second half. While the piece may seem a tossed-off improvisation, its note-values are as carefully chosen as always, especially in the bass. Holding notes beyond their written values (e.g., in the arpeggios) will, of course, increase the sonority, but at the risk of weighting down the gossamer filligree.

Unfortunately, the next few movements do not seem to lie at the same level of inspiration, evidently having been conceived as easy, undemanding pieces for not very advanced students. The sarabande is a little too regular in its rhythms and phrasing to be the equal of Bach's more ambitious examples of the dance. It is remarkable, however, for the divergences in the ornaments (and occasionally in the notes) given by Vogler and Gerber, which are conveniently set out on parallel systems in the NBA's version "B." Conceivably, these ornaments are the products of oral, or rather aural, tradition, deriving from the different ways in which Bach himself played the piece for each student.[44] Both ornamented versions are effective, and no one set of ornaments need be regarded as definitive.

The gavotte is another galant version of the dance, as in Suite No. 4, characterized by parallel thirds and sixths and an occasional expressive "sigh" figure. Perhaps the pedal-point in the opening bars also gives it a pastoral quality, although it is no musette. The polonaise is equally galant. Bach wrote only two other examples of this dance, both in orchestral works.[45] But the polonaise—or *polonoise*, as it was then spelled—was popular throughout the eighteenth century, especially as an easy type of keyboard piece, and the 1725 *Clavier-Büchlein* contains several examples by other composers, including (probably) Emanuel Bach. Musically, most eighteenth-century examples resemble minuets, as is the case here; Gerber even calls the movement a "Polish minuet" (*minuet poloinese* [*sic*]). It has little in common with the nineteenth-century version of the dance, apart from the triple meter and the placement of cadences on the second beat.

A few late sources put the minuet after the polonaise, and this is probably the best place for it.[46] The "little minuet," as Gerber called it (*Petit minuet*), is somewhat pallid, constructed like the sarabande in two-bar units that grow rather monotonous. Dürr (NBA V/8, KB, 83) suggests that it could be used as a trio in alternation with the polonaise, but the latter probably is not so remarkable that one would wish to hear it twice.

The bourrée, Bach's last, is also perhaps his most lively, a possible exception being the bourrée of BWV 819, which uses similar motivic material. The gigue, an even more lively piece, opens with imitations at the octave, hence avoiding the traditional fugal answer used in all of the other gigues of the set. The gigue was later the basis for Kirnberger's demonstration of how to compose a "sonata" movement quickly as a variation of an existing piece.[47] Although the method might well have come from Bach himself, Kirnberger's sonata does not speak well for his sensitivity to his teacher's music. His "sonata" is a clumsy pastiche, a far cry from Sebastian's own demonstration of the same process in the allemande of BWV 819a and the sarabandes of BWV 818a.

15

Clavierübung, *Part 1:*
The Six Partitas

Bach's keyboard suites reach their culmination in the six Partitas, in which the experiments carried out in the French Suites—new approaches to the traditional keyboard dances, new types of keyboard texture, and increasing use of galant melody and harmony as opposed to imitative counterpoint—achieved fruition. Partita No. 1 is still close in many respects to the French Suites (especially Suite No. 6). But in general the style of the Partitas seems later than that of the French Suites, and the technical demands on the player are greater. The keyboard range is larger, extended from four octaves to over four-and-a-half (GG to d''' in Partita No. 5). Most of the dances are longer and diverge even farther from the traditional models than in the previous set. Indeed, the preludes, each of which in principle represents a different sort of opening movement (overture, toccata, etc.), are in fact original forms, only the overture of Partita No. 4 closely adhering to the genre that it nominally represents.

The previous chapter has already raised the issue of the relationship between Bach's use of galant style in the keyboard suites and his plans for publishing them. The Partitas were Bach's first keyboard publications, and their content and style were clearly influenced by the circumstances of their publication. Bach had arrived in Leipzig in the late spring of 1723. Three-and-a-half years later he announced publication of the first of what would be six large suites with preludes.[1] These suites, that is, the Partitas, were first issued separately, in more or less annual installments, and then reissued in a collected second edition in 1731. Bach's title for this first collection, *Clavier-Übung*, or "Keyboard Practice," would be extended to three further publications. One of these is for the organ, while the remainder represent Bach's crowning achievement in the genres most closely associated with the harpsichord: suite, variation, and transcription or, rather, quasi-transcriptions of a concerto and an *ouverture* (orchestral suite), respectively.

The entire series is unlikely to have been fully planned or composed by 1726, when Bach began to issue it. On the other hand, Bach would certainly have been thinking long before that date about publishing something. Among his considerations would have been not only the length and complexity of the pieces, which would have influenced the number of potential buyers, but also his own costs as publisher. Like any modern publisher of music (or, for that matter, books on music), he would have been under great pressure to issue something short, easy, and fashionable in tone and content—*galant*, in the language of Bach's time. Yet he must also have felt compelled to issue something worthy of himself and of his reputation as Germany's greatest keyboard player. By 1726, WTC1 and the English Suites might have seemed too long and old-fashioned, but the French Suites may have been too short and, perhaps, too insubstantial.

Hence, it is tempting to suppose that the Partitas were composed at Leipzig expressly for publication. This is by no means impossible; even when one takes into consideration the time and effort that must have been required to see the pieces through the press, writing and publishing one or two partitas each year could not have added greatly to Bach's burdens. Already by March 1725 his production of church cantatas, composed almost weekly during the two years preceding, appears to have slackened, and Bach might well have begun to turn then to revising his existing keyboard works and publishing new ones. In 1726, during the months preceding the publication of Partita No. 1, he composed relatively few new church works, in some cases presenting instead works by his Meiningen cousin Johann Ludwig Bach. He did, however, present a number of new cantatas containing movements with solo organ; conceivably, these helped create interest in Bach's forthcoming publication.[2]

On the other hand, Bach had probably composed at least two of the Partitas before 1726, for the second *Clavier-Büchlein* for Anna Magdalena opens with autograph fair copies—not first drafts—of Partitas Nos. 3 and 6. Morever, Partita No. 2, although not published until 1727, is relatively conservative in style and has a fairly restricted range (BB^b-$d^{b'''}$); hence, it too might have been in existence at least several years earlier.[3] Nothing, however, rules out a Leipzig origin for all of the Partitas. The music is unquestionably more galant than that of the other keyboard suites, with the exception of French Suites Nos. 5 and 6, which were probably completed at Leipzig. Like those suites—and the organ solos in the cantatas of 1726—the Partitas reveal an interest in new keyboard textures and uninhibited keyboard display. This could reflect Bach's knowledge of recent works by Rameau and others, which Bach might have first encountered at Leipzig.[4]

Thus, despite the fact that at Leipzig Bach was occupied with the weekly performance of cantatas and other church music, not to mention the duties associated with his position as Cantor at the Thomasschule, he evidently found the time to revise and publish, and perhaps also to compose, all six Partitas during the period 1725 to 1730. Either because he lacked a patron or because he wished to control every aspect of production, he was his own publisher, overseeing the engraving, printing, and (presumably) sales of each volume himself. It is assumed that the Partitas were initially issued in installments in order to avoid the risks and costs associated with a larger volume. That Bach was eventually able to publish, among other things, four large collections of keyboard music, and was planning a fifth (the

Art of Fugue) when he died, suggests that his enterprise was more successful and his works more highly prized than one might have expected, considering the difficulty and unfashionability of much of the music.

In issuing a collection of keyboard suites, Bach was following the model of Johann Kuhnau, his predecessor at Leipzig, who there published four volumes of keyboard music (two containing suites) between 1689 and 1700. There is even some evidence that Bach originally planned to include seven suites in his collection, as in each of Kuhnau's (see Chapter 16). Kuhnau had called his suites *Parthien*, evidently a German equivalent for the Italian *partita*, which by 1726 perhaps seemed more cosmopolitan. Bach also borrowed his general title *Clavierübung* from Kuhnau's first two volumes. The expression seems to be an equivalent for the Italian *Essercizi* and the English *Lessons*, both used in titles of keyboard publications during the first half of the eighteenth century. While the terms perhaps imply that the music was primarily pedagogic, Bach's full title added that the music was meant to "refresh the spirits of music-lovers."[5] In any case the title reflects the fact that the Partitas, like all solo harpsichord pieces, were intended primarily for private practice and amusement, not public performance.

One might suppose that in published works Bach would have been unable to make the additions and revisions that gradually made their way into his other keyboard works. But the original plates could be and were altered, especially to show new ornaments; many such changes were made for the collected edition of 1731.[6] Moreover, certain exemplars of the print show hand-written corrections, some of which may have been made in Bach's own house prior to sale. What has been regarded as Bach's *Handexemplar* (personal copy) of the 1731 edition contains many further alterations, presumably of a later date, which lead to improved readings.[7]

In addition, Wolff has pointed to the existence of four other altered exemplars, one of which "may have served for performance and instruction in Bach's presence." Two tempo marks added in red ink in this exemplar are of "autograph character," and it is possible that the markings here and in the supposed *Handexemplar* are in the same hand.[8] While earlier editions, including the one in BG 3, ignored the hand-written corrections, NBA V/1 incorporates the revisions from the supposed *Handexemplar* but not those from the other altered exemplars, which are discussed below under Partitas Nos. 2 and 3. For this reason, and because of a number of debatable editorial emendations (some discussed below), the NBA text, while preferable to that of earlier editions, can be recommended only with reservations.[9] The early versions of Partitas Nos. 3 and 6 are edited in NBA V/4 (facsimile in Dadelsen 1988); Wolff (1984) includes a facsimile of the print.

Partita No. 1 in B♭, BWV 825

The opening piece in the *Clavierübung* is not particularly large among Bach's works (e.g., by comparison with the English Suites), and it is relatively light in texture. By the standards of the day, however, its dimensions were ambitious, the technical demands very high. Considering these potential impediments to the work's popular success, Bach must have placed considerable hopes in its novelty. Indeed, those who opened the first installment of the *Clavierübung* in 1726 not knowing Bach's previous music might have been amazed by his treatment of some of the traditional keyboard dances. The allemande opens with fantasia- or concertolike arpeggiation, only later coalescing into more regular writing—the same approach Bach had taken in the courante of French Suite No. 6. The corrente—called here by its Italian title—is in effect a sonata movement in $\frac{9}{8}$, as in French Suite No. 4. The final movement, a giga with hand-crossings, seems to be without precedent.

The praeludium is essentially a sinfonia or three-part invention. Musicians unfamiliar with Bach's Sinfonias might have thought of it as a type of fantasia (Bach's first term for the Sinfonias) and might have been surprised when the theme, accompanied in *brisé* style in bars 1–4a, is imitated at the dominant by the bass, as in a fugue (bars 4bff.). From fairly modest beginnings the movement gradually broadens out, first in register, then in texture, expanding to five nominal voices in the last phrase, whose final chord spans four octaves. At the close the left hand even doubles the bass in octaves; such writing, although less spectacular than hand-crossing, is rare in Bach's earlier works and is characteristic of his free treatment of the keyboard idiom in the Partitas. Not only the magnificent ending but several short pedal-points give the movement a grandeur not encountered in the Sinfonias; the pedal tones (bars 9, 12, 19–20) are not held but rather touched lightly by the left hand, which then leaps to take the inner voice—another special keyboard idiom that Bach had used previously in only a few works, such as the Chromatic Fantasia.

The pedal idea continues in the opening phrase of the allemande, whose arpeggiation (divided between the hands) is far more lively than in traditional examples of the dance. The corrente, longer and more difficult to play than the courante of French Suite No. 4, is not very far in style from the gigue of Partita No. 4. The latter, however, is written in $\frac{9}{16}$, and its melodic gestures are perhaps somewhat simpler, more sweeping; the present corrente thus seems meant to go a bit more deliberately. Brief pedal-points again play a role, notably in a passage that includes three "obstinate" leaps of a major seventh in the bass (bar 43)—perhaps to be interpreted as a deliberately humorous effect.

The sarabande employs written-out embellishment similar to that which Bach gave separately as the *agrémens* for the corresponding movement in English Suite No. 3; the flourish after the double bar is particularly reminiscent of the earlier piece. It might be a useful analytical exercise to reduce the existing melodic embellishment to a simpler version; this makes it easier to see the four-bar phrasing and traditional sarabande meter that lie beneath the florid surface. Embellishment of simple underlying lines is, however, such a basic element in Bach's mature style that there is no reason to assume that the movement ever existed in a substantially simpler form. Nor does it seem wise actually to perform such a reduction, reserving Bach's embellishments for the repetition of each section (as is occasionally done). An instructive analytic device becomes tedious in performance. Besides, why stop at the sarabande? In most movements of this Partita the melodic material seems to depend to an unusual degree on "composition through variation" over simple scalewise descending bass lines. For instance, the first half of the sarabande closes (bars 9–12) over a descending bass also used at several points in the corrente (e.g., bars 18ff.), and one would hardly wish to perform a reduction of the latter.

The minuets are surprisingly simple, perhaps added to give beginners something to play in Bach's first keyboard publication. The first resembles minuet 1 in the Third French Suite; the second is unusual for Bach in its predominantly quarter-note motion and strict four-part harmony, recalling the sarabandes of the English Suites. It is possible that these movements were composed separately, like the minuets incorporated into the French Suites, for they survive in slightly different, probably early versions, in a manuscript collection of pieces for beginners—the only early versions surviving for any movements in the Partitas outside of the autographs for Partitas Nos. 3 and 6.[10]

The giga is unique not only for its hand-crossings but for their use in every bar of the piece, which in conception is closer to an arpeggiando prelude than either a French or an Italian jig. Since the print contains no rubric or preface indicating the use of hand-crossing, Bach must have expected musicians to be already familiar with the technique from other examples. Rameau's second book of *Pièces de clavecin*, published in 1724, is one likely source, for Rameau wrote at some length in the preface of that work about the *batteries* used in one piece (*Les cyclopes*) whose keyboard figuration at times resembles that found here. Perhaps the presence of hand-crossings was intended to disarm Bach's critics—of whom there probably were many by 1726—who found his music overly serious. Certainly Bach plays a joke on the player; one naturally expects the initial high note (f″), to belong to the right hand, but it gradually becomes clear that the piece is more convenient to play if it is the left hand that does the crossing.[11] In the last bar of each half, an emendation in NBA V/1 confuses the division between the hands, which should be as follows: note 1 (left), notes 2–4 (right), notes 5–7 (left).

The movement was evidently known widely; Gluck seems to have based an aria on material from the opening section (see Buelow 1991). In addition, a copy of the giga appears in a nineteenth-century manuscript alongside several other pieces that, like the giga, were evidently thought of as having an etudelike character (see Helm 1989, entry 390.5).

Partita No. 2 in C Minor BWV 826

The Second Partita was announced a little less than a year after the first, on September 19, 1727. Its key and its opening sinfonia declare it to be a more substantial, more serious piece. It also seems somewhat more conventional, containing a relatively traditional allemande and courante as well as a rondeau, a form favored by Couperin and other French composers but treated sparingly by Bach. Yet these movements are conventional only superficially. The sinfonia, whose initial section looks somewhat like the dotted section of a French overture, proceeds in very much its own fashion and without having much to do with the typical Italian overture (*sinfonia*) either. Even the rondeau is a considerably elaborated version of the form, and, instead of a gigue the partita closes with what Bach calls a capriccio, actually a sort of fugue in binary form. Indeed, since there is also a fugue in the opening movement—and the courante, too, is consistently imitative—the partita can be seen as compensating for the absence of fugal writing in the first work of the series.

The short introduction to the sinfonia is in essence the expansion of a single plagal cadence, unrelated to anything that follows except perhaps through the two chords in dotted rhythm at the very end (bars 90–91). The seemingly redundant tempo markings—*Grave adagio*—perhaps were intended to emphasize that this is not an energetic French overture but rather a truly slow, weighty introduction, in which the dark sonority of each massive chord is fully felt. The impression is strengthened by the time-signature: c instead of the ¢ used in the overture of Partita No. 4.

The florid upper line of the andante may resemble that of an adagio, but it is accompanied by a walking bass and contains a number of recurring motives. Hence, except in its closing passage, it lacks the improvisatory qualities of an embellished adagio and should no doubt move somewhat faster. It ends by dissolving into a short written-out cadenza—that is, an ornamented cadence—over which one of the altered exemplars of the 1731 print has had the word *allegro* added (bar 28); this is followed by *adagio* a bar later (bar 29).[12] The markings recall those added in some of the preludes of WTC1, presumably for the benefit of students.

The same exemplar (and another as well) also corrects the ungrammatical rhythmic notation of bar 29. But the latter is unaltered in the *Handexemplar*, implying that Bach, at least for a time, regarded the notation of the print as adequate. No doubt the notation was meant only to suggest the general shape that the free, improvisatory rhythm ought to take.[13] As in other instances of imprecise Baroque notation, there is no reason for editors to "correct" it.

The sinfonia closes with a real fugue—not an invention—in two voices. As in the E-minor fugue of WTC1, also in two voices, the lively figuration is so rich in harmonic implications that the two parts suffice to suggest an orchestral texture. The subject is composed out of a single dominant chord extended over three bars (instead of one as in English Suite No. 6). This is probably one source of the fugue's unusually urgent character, since each statement of the subject serves as a dominant preparation for the following passage rather than serving as a point of repose. The fugue is bipartite, most of the second half (from bar 28) consisting of recapitulation, although the symmetry is not so exact as in the E-minor fugue.

The allemande is also written in two rather severely contrapuntal parts, like the allemande of BWV 819. A few passages echo the toccata of Partita No. 6 (already composed in 1727), but the "sighs" in bars 9 and 10 are softer than those in the toccata, the trill sign being placed on the second note rather than the first, thus indicating a half-trill.[14] The courante is of the French type, in $\frac{3}{2}$, but with an unusually fiery character stemming in part from the melodic embellishment in sixteenths, present in virtually every bar. The meter and the use of imitation recall the courantes of the English Suites, yet rhythm and texture here seem more flexible; in bar 3, for example, the imitative counterpoint momentarily dissolves into an ornamented downward arpeggio.

The printed ornaments in the courante were supplemented with particular enthusiasm in one of the altered exemplars (the one in Washington, designated G 25 in NBA V/1). The *Handexemplar* had already added a mordent in bar 2, and the same ornament perhaps should be added in other statements of the theme as well, including the initial statement in bar 1. But the further ornaments added in the Washington exemplar, given in parentheses in Example 15.1, seem only to com-

EXAMPLE 15.1.   Partita No. 2 in C Minor BWV 826,
courante (ornaments in parentheses from exemplar in US Wc): (a) bars 1–2; (b) bars 12b–13

plicate the lines, making the movement as a whole less vigorous.[15] The inversion of the theme after the double bar raises another question about ornaments, the same one that arose in the gigue of English Suite No. 6. Although the theme is inverted, one cannot assume that the ornaments in the theme should also be inverted. Indeed, the print has mordents in both versions of the theme, and in no exemplar was the sign altered. Yet, at least in bar 13, a trill on g' would not be impossible melodically, and it would avoid the collision between the hands that otherwise occurs on the note f'.

On paper, the sarabande looks similar to the allemande, since both are written largely in two parts moving in sixteenths. But the harmonic rhythm generally accents the second beat, as one would expect in a sarabande. Some of the sixteenths bear carelessly placed slurs, which are interpreted in NBA V/1 as each covering an entire beat (four sixteenths). This is consistent with the piece's gentle, undemonstrative nature, but the more articulate interpretation found in BG 3 (e.g., 1 + 3 in bar 16) cannot be ruled out.

The rondeau (or *Rondeaux*—Bach gives the title in the plural) is an imitative duet, reminding one of the "Fantasia on a Rondo" BWV 918 in the same key. The present movement follows a more normal rondeau design, although the last two statements of the theme are varied (bars 65, 97). Moreover, the theme falls into the customary eight-bar phrases, subdivided into groupings of two bars apiece, although the use of imitation hints at the possibility of the less regular phraseology of fugue. Indeed, in the course of the second *couplet* (bars 48–64) the two-bar "hypermeasures" grow fuzzy, the accented and unaccented bars becoming difficult to distinguish until the return of the theme. Hence, there is a sort of metrical ambiguity or dissonance at the center of the piece, as in the gavottes of English Suites Nos. 3 and 6 (and gavotte 2 of BWV 815a).

The theme itself is built around a sequence of leaping sevenths (bars 3–6). These are derived from a conventional chain of suspensions, although suspensions are not present explicitly until the second *couplet* (Example 15.2). The ornament in the

EXAMPLE 15.2.   Partita No. 2 in C Minor BWV 826,
   rondeau (with implied bass figures and realization): (a) bars
   1–5; (b) bars 49–52

theme, given in bar 1 as a trill, is easier to play when shortened to a turn, and indeed the *Handexemplar* indicates a turn when the theme comes back in bar 33.

In calling the last movement a capriccio Bach might have had his own early Capriccio in E, BWV 993, in mind. That piece had been written "in honor of" his teacher and older brother Johann Christoph, who died in 1721, and this is a fairly strict fugue in three voices, the only irregularity being the presence of all three parts from the outset. Yet it is also one of Bach's more unbuttoned keyboard pieces, and the title might just as easily refer to the wild leaps of a tenth in the subject. These have a parallel in the scherzo movement of a violin sonata in the same key by J. G. Graun (No. 2 in a set published at Merseburg, ca. 1726); W. F. Bach went to study violin with Graun in 1726, but without knowing the precise dates of composition it is impossible to say who influenced whom. The tenths are later developed in the bass in a recurring sequential episode that must be one of Bach's most entertaining passages to play, once one has it under the fingers; Bach obligingly recapitulates it in the second half (bars 81–86 || 11–16). The two halves are exactly equal in length, but they are not exactly symmetrical; as in the gigue of the Third English Suite, the subject returns in its original form (bass, bar 87) after being used in inversion for most of the second half.

Partita No. 3 in A Minor BWV 827

The Third Partita, announced at the same time as the second (September 1727), is lighter in character, or at least seemingly so at the outset. It opens with a fantasia that is essentially a long two-part invention, and later there are two apparently comic movements, a burlesca and a scherzo. Yet these are oddly fiery in character, and the allemande has much in common with the passionate allemande of Partita No. 6, sharing its use of flourishes in thirty-seconds (unusual in an allemande) and ending with a nearly identical final cadence. Perhaps this should not be a surprise, since the early versions of Partitas Nos. 3 and 6 occur side by side in the 1725 *Clavier-Büchlein*. The early version of Partita No. 3 lacks the scherzo; in preparing the work for publication Bach also added two bars at the end of the fantasia (bars 118–19) while revising many other passages, especially in the bass of the first three movements.

The first movement was originally designated *Prélude*. Bach had used the similar title praeambulum for the early versions of the Inventions, so it is curious that the movement wound up with the title originally given to the *three*-part inventions (i.e., the Sinfonias, originally called fantasias). Clearly, none of these titles was very meaningful in itself, although Bach presumably felt that a familiar title such as *fantasia* was preferable to *inventio* in a published work.

While opening very much like some of the Inventions—including the one in the same key—the movement is spun out at greater length. After reaching the dominant at bar 31, the first thirty bars are repeated at the new pitch level, with voices exchanged. This accounts for precisely half the piece (in the published version), and the remainder consists of a retransition (bars 67–78) and a sort of recapitulation (bars 79ff.), although the theme itself does not reappear at the beginning of the latter. The movement may seem a little pale beside the more demonstrative opening movements of the other partitas, and this may account for the relative obscurity of Partita No. 3 as a whole. The quasi-geometric design is less intriguing today than it may have seemed in the eighteenth century, but the movement can be surprisingly expressive if the player chooses to bring out (perhaps through a slur) the mildly dissonant double-appoggiatura in the theme (b', g♯', a' in bar 1). The motive recurs throughout the movement, which therefore need not be played as an unnuanced stream of sixteenths.

The allemande might be thought of as a preliminary study for that of Partita No. 6. The extravagant melodic figuration of both movements reveals them as energetic virtuoso pieces, not to be approached timidly. This in turn implies a vigorous tempo, not one that will shift the pulse from the quarter- to the eighth-note. Even at a fairly brisk tempo, however, listeners are likely to misunderstand the unusual upbeat figure, which lasts the value of a quarter-note. It is liable to sound like a downbeat no matter what the player does, and indeed the differentiation between "strong" and "weak" beats here is sufficiently ambiguous that it may not really matter; cadences invariably fall on the third (not the first) beat of the bar. There is an odd ornament sign in bar 6 on the note g″, given in both BG and NBA as a mordent prefixed by a small half-circle; this probably represents a *port de voix* (appoggiatura) followed by a *pincé* (mordent).[16]

The corrente is the most violinistic example hitherto encountered in Bach's works. One could easily imagine it scored as an actual solo for violin and bass, as was indeed the case with the *Tempo di Gavotta* in Partita No. 6 (see below). As in that movement, Bach made many revisions in the bass but hardly any in the treble, which never descends below g (the lowest string on the violin).

The sarabande is of the trio type, as in the Fifth English Suite and BWV 819. But now virtually nothing remains of the traditional sarabande rhythm or character. Like the allemande (and the corrente) it begins with an unusual upbeat figure, which here recurs as an important motive throughout the movement. An essential element of the motive is the ornament on the second note, whose identity was obscured by the imprecision of Bach's engravers. In many places in the original print the ornament sign looks like a mordent and was so interpreted in BG 3 and other editions. Bach had originally indicated a trill (in the 1725 *Clavier-Büchlein*), and he no doubt wanted this in the print as well. But the print adds a slash at the end of the sign to indicate a closing turn (*Nachschlag*), and the often faulty or ambiguous placement of this slash in the print led to the interpretation of many of the signs as mordents.[17] A contributing factor might have been doubt that so brilliant and complex an ornament as the *Trillo und mordant* (the name given to it in CB) was to be played on the third beat of a sarabande. Clearly, however, this is no ordinary sarabande, and a sturdy trill would not conflict with the piece's almost marchlike character.

Another notational oddity occurs in bar 8, where the print appears to have been corrected after originally omitting the top note of the right-hand chord c″/e″. The autograph has the same two notes separated by a slanting stroke, which evidently led the editor of NBA V/1 to read here two consecutive sixteenths (c″ followed by e″). But the apparent ornament sign found in the autograph is used elsewhere in the Partitas apparently to signify an acciaccatura, and there is no ornament sign at all in the print.

Bach originally called the next movement a minuet (*Menuet*), but the lively figuration is hard to reconcile with that rather calm dance, and it appeared in the print as a *Burlesca*. Perhaps the new title contains some as yet unidentified reference, perhaps it means (as the Italian word can imply) that the piece should be played in an exaggeratedly noble, even mock-heroic manner. The satire, if any, is unlikely to be evident to a modern audience; Bach revised only the title, not the musical text. The original title implies a fairly courtly tempo, which would also allow the rather odd voice-leading in the closing phrase (bars 14–15, 38–39) to sink in. The same is true at the climactic passage in octaves in the second half (bar 32), which one might imagine as a burlesque on the type of octave passage found in the E-minor fugue (WTC1), presumably a more serious piece.

The scherzo was an afterthought, perhaps added when Bach found that there was room in the print for a short piece at the bottom of the last page occupied by the burlesca.[18] The title, which Bach might have taken from a movement in the Bonporti Inventions for violin, recurs in a number of similar pieces by younger members of the Bach circle, especially Friedemann Bach.[19] The title probably refers only to the piece's general character or to its brevity. Conceivably, there is also a reference to the movement's almost crude keyboard texture: staccato chords in the left hand accompanying a violinistic line in the right, the sort of thing that must have arisen when violin sonatas were played as impromptu keyboard solos. Particularly notable is the simultaneous acciaccatura in bar 28 (g#/a), a borrowing from the Italian style of continuo realization, familiar to us from Domenico Scarlatti's sonatas.

The gigue is the one example of the dance in the Partitas that comes close to the traditional German fugal type. Indeed, it looks back specifically to the Reinken sonata in the same key transcribed as BWV 965. As in the gigue of BWV 965, the subject consists of uninterrupted eighth-notes. There are also two regular counter-subjects, at least in the first half, and each half contains two expositions, here separated by an episode. None of these elements is unusual in a Bach gigue. But it seems conceivable that the piece reflects Bach's memory of the older composer, who had praised him at Hamburg in 1720 and who had died in 1722, three years before Bach prepared the surviving autograph of the partita.

As Wolff (1979) showed, three of the altered exemplars of the 1731 print contain substantial changes in the second half of the gigue. These exemplars agree on certain changes in the *inversus* form of the subject but not on all of the resulting "chain-reaction" revisions (Example 15.3).[20] As Wolff noted, the changes seem to

EXAMPLE 15.3.   Partita No. 3 in A Minor BWV 827, gigue (after copy in US Wc): (a) bars 25–26; (b) 39–40; (c) 44–46a

have been motivated by an effort to render the inversion more literal. But it remains inexact, and another purpose for the changes might have been simply to make the inverted form of the subject easier to play by eliminating the need for finger-crossing. Some of the "chain-reaction" alterations led to awkward details in the counterpoint; in two exemplars, thirds became open fifths and tritones in the central episode (Example 15.3b; see asterisks).[21] The final exposition required more extensive changes, and here each of the three exemplars gives a somewhat different version. While these might represent successive revisions by Bach, none of them appears in the supposed *Handexemplar*. Bach's students were certainly not above tinkering with his counterpoint; Kirnberger did so in his "sonata" based on the gigue of French Suite No. 6 and perhaps also in the variations found in his copy of the gigue of English Suite No. 4.[22]

Partita No. 4 in D, BWV 828

The Fourth Partita, whose original title-page was dated 1728, is the most splendid of the Partitas and, with the possible exception of Partita No. 6, the longest. Three or four movements—the overture, courante, gigue, and perhaps the minuet—evoke orchestral style, but the remainder are intimate, highly expressive pieces, above all the allemande, one of the longest and most profound ever written.

The overture is of the same type found in the orchestral suites of Bach and his contemporaries and in chamber works like the Dieupart suites that Bach had copied at Weimar. Such movements are usually regarded as consisting of a slow dotted section followed by a fugue, but many of them can also be viewed as somewhat peculiar sorts of binary form. Often the second half is, as in the present case, a fugue in concerto style having nothing in common with the first half. Yet the tonal structure is that of a binary form, the first half moving to the dominant, and there is no explicit change of tempo at the beginning of the second half, despite the change in meter and character. Thus, a movement of this type may be more unified than is sometimes thought, regardless of whether or not the dotted rhythm returns at the end of the second half. For performers, the more serious interpretive problems in such a piece generally arise in the dotted section, where the complex rhythmic notation and the flurries of *tirate* (runs in thirty-second-notes) can obscure the long lines and essentially simple phrasing of the underlying structure. The dotted section here consists of only three long phrases, and these are the usual ones for a binary suite movement: the opening thematic statement, cadencing in the tonic (bar 5a); a modulating transition (bars 5b–12); and a closing phrase leading to a firm cadence in the dominant (bars 13–18).

Unfortunately, the controversy concerning "over-dotting" in such a movement (see Chapter 2) tends to distract attention from other equally important interpretive issues such as tempo and articulation. The tempo, however, should surely be quick enough for the *tirate* to sound brilliant, as in other pieces with written-out embellishment. Indeed, the time-signature is ¢, as in most French overtures, and while the movement is not an *alla breve* in the usual sense, it can be understood as having only two long beats in each bar. The dotted figures themselves generally consist not of two notes (dotted eighth, sixteenth) but of a three-note upbeat figure (sixteenth, dotted eighth, sixteenth). Hence, most of these figures, including those in the opening bars, move toward, not from, one of the two strong beats of the bar, an effect more likely to be conveyed when the notes (including the dotted notes) are somewhat detached. When this is done successfully there may be little need for over-dotting as such, except on dotted quarter-notes and in the combination of dotted eighth followed by three thirty-seconds (as in bar 7). By the same token, although Bach cannot have intended his rhythmic notation of the *tirate* to be interpreted absolutely literally, the rhythmic freedom taken surely should not be so great as to upset the vertical relationships between contrapuntal parts (e.g., in bar 10, treble g♯‴ should presumably coincide with bass e).

The meter of the fugal section is a somewhat complicated $\frac{9}{8}$ time, the eighths in the opening part of the subject being grouped into anapestic patterns (weak, weak, strong) that reflect the organization of the beats themselves (Example 15.4). As a

EXAMPLE 15.4.   Partita No. 4 in D, BWV 828, overture, bars 18–20

result of this somewhat fussy rhythm the fugue lacks the powerful impetus of the sinfonia in Partita No. 2, even though it is conceived along the same quasi-orchestral lines as the preludes of the English Suites. As in those pieces, however, the imitation of concerto form is far from exact, and the distinction between "tutti" and "solo" sections is less clear than in the B-minor overture in Part 2 of the *Clavierübung*. The lighter texture and the introduction of quieter motivic material at the beginning of the first episode (bars 34–47) indeed suggest a solo passage in a concerto. But the texture remains confined to two voices at the next entrance of the subject (bass, bar 48), expanding to four voices only in the quasi-orchestral passage that leads to the central cadence in B minor (bar 72). This will frustrate attempts to impose on the movement a registration scheme based on alternating fortes and pianos; it shows that Bach conceived the movement as idiomatic keyboard music, not an ersatz orchestral piece.

The first dance movement is arguably Bach's finest allemande, although Froberger or even Couperin might have been hard pressed to identify it as such. The embellished treble line resembles less that of a traditional keyboard allemande than that of the andante in the sinfonia of Partita No. 2, and at certain points—usually when approaching a cadence—the sixteenths and thirty-seconds give way to the galant triplets. Formally, the movement is distinct from most other allemandes in its close approach to ternary sonata form. There is no return, but, after reaching a cadence in B minor in the middle of the second "half" (bar 40), two simple but very beautiful measures of retransition lead to a partial recapitulation that opens in the subdominant (bar 42 || bar 5).

The movement deserves close analysis, which can be attempted here only for the first half. Its unusual character is already apparent in the opening thematic statement (bars 1–4), which accelerates from a plain chord to quietly moving improvisatory figuration. This passage foreshadows the rhythmic shape of the movement as a whole, which gradually gains momentum, reaching thirty-seconds in the closing phrase of each half. The opening phrase, however, comes to rest on f#′, the note on which it began. In the following modulating passage, the treble, having leapt into the higher register, gradually descends from f#‴ (bar 5) to b′ at the beginning of bar 16. Actually, the arrival on b′ is already implicit in bar 13, which marks the beginning of a beautifully prolonged dominant (V of V); the half-step c″-b′, hinted at in bar 12, is finally actualized at bar 16. The dominant continues to be prolonged through the deceptive cadence at bar 18, which is followed by a six-bar closing phrase (expanded to seven bars in the final section). The harmonic progression in bar 18 recurs in the retransition (bars 40–41), where the echo of the earlier passage is almost imperceptible but perhaps contributes to a certain delicate pathos.

Another recurring progression is the half-step c″-b′, whose importance in bars 12–16 was just noted. It is all too easy to find half-steps and declare them to be significant motives. Yet the prominent place of the figure in this movement, and of these two particular pitches, is undeniable. The progression is first heard in bar 2 and returns in various harmonic guises at the movement's most crucial moments, not only in bars 12–16 but in the closing phrase of the first section (bar 23), as the second section approaches its final cadence (note the Neapolitan harmony in bar 37), and in the appoggiatura at the beginning of the third section (bar 42), where the progression occurs twice more (bars 50 and 55). The progression does not merely "unify" the allemande; through its repeated emphasis on a tone outside of the tonic scale (c♮″) it ensures that an expressive tension will be present throughout the course of this very long movement.

While the arioso texture of the allemande suggests performance on two manuals, this is ruled out by the retransition and other passages in which the inner voice crosses between the hands. The voices of the accompaniment (usually two) are as substantial as the top part and can serve as a guide for judging the right tempo. Indeed, if one cannot hear the gradual rise of the tenor in, say, bars 5–6, the tempo may be too slow, preventing the individual gestures in the treble from cohering into larger phrases.[23]

The character of the courante is defined by the jubilant *figure corte* in the opening theme. One does not expect to find such writing in a courante, and although in principle following the French version of the dance, the movement is metrically ambiguous from the start. The opening bar is probably in the indicated $\frac{3}{2}$ time—not $\frac{6}{4}$—the mordent on the penultimate quarter-note (b′) implying a triple division of the bar. The upper line in bars 2–3 is likewise composed of gestures each equal in value to two quarters, implying $\frac{3}{2}$ time. But the bass is clearly moving in $\frac{6}{4}$ time by bar 3, and when a new motivic idea is introduced by the treble in bar 9 it is imitated by alto and tenor at intervals of *five* quarter-notes.

Despite its great vitality, the courante contains a number of written-out examples of the expressive "long" appoggiatura, which would become a favorite mannerism in the Berlin *empfindsamer Stil*, especially when followed by a short trill as it is in bars 8, 11, and 15. The same ornament forms part of the opening theme of the sarabande, which is repeated at the beginning of that movement's two subsequent sections (bars 13, 29).[24] The sarabande theme is the product of a particularly fantastic transformation of the traditional dance-type; the accent on the second beat is clear enough, but the figuration, which juxtaposes a languishing appoggiatura (bar 1) with a sudden arpeggio (bar 2), is unlike that of any other sarabande. The remainder of the movement recalls the allemande in the florid embellishment of the upper part. But the sarabande is a shorter and somewhat lighter piece, even though it is, like the allemande, a complete sonata form with return. The flurries of thirty-seconds, especially the quasi-cadenza in bar 34, may even achieve some brilliance, provided that the tempo does not drag.

The aria preceding the sarabande is not a quasi-vocal piece but, like the air in French Suite No. 4, a short binary form in idiomatic keyboard style. Indeed, the syncopated rhythm at the opening corresponds to what some eighteenth-century writers on keyboard playing referred to as rubato.[25] The presence of a short air or aria before the sarabande in both Partitas Nos. 4 and 6 has led to the suggestion (Louwenaar 1982–83) that the ordering might have been due simply to considerations of pagination in the print—what Rameau, in the preface to his *Nouvelles Suites* (ca. 1729–30), called the "convenience of the engraver." But two gavottes precede the sarabande in the *Ouverture* BWV 831, and in each work the order of the movements is probably just what Bach intended it to be. It is possible, as in the case of the scherzo of Partita No. 3, that Bach composed the aria—as well as the little minuet—to fill what would otherwise have been blank space on their respective pages. But there seems little musical reason for playing the aria after the sarabande, which would place the two shortest movements of the suite side by side.

Still, the placement of the minuet is somewhat problematical, since it is effectively in the same meter as the gigue. The gigue is in $\frac{9}{16}$, the minuet in $\frac{3}{4}$ with numerous triplets; presumably, the gigue should go somewhat faster. Another point of contrast is the alternation between duple and triple rhythms in the minuet. In this respect Bach's notation is certainly to be taken literally; although the dotted rhythms surely ought to be assimilated to simultaneously occurring triplets (as in bar 7), ordinary duplets are clearly meant to stand in audible opposition to the triplets, as in the somewhat similar minuet in the Suite BWV 818a. Bar 15 raises a minor textual question; the last chord contains an unprepared fourth, and perhaps tenor f♯ should be read as e.

Despite its unorthodox meter, each half of the gigue opens in the traditional fugal manner. But Bach was, as ever, exploring new approaches to the old forms. The second half introduces a new subject, against which the original subject is used once as countersubject (bar 55) and then dropped for good, except for the use of its opening motive in the closing phrase.[26] This closing phrase touches briefly on the minor mode, a somewhat curious gesture in so exuberant a gigue but perhaps an echo of the allemande (in which cf. bar 12). Indeed, the subject even contains a prominent c $^{\natural\prime\prime}$, also pointing back to the allemande. Through such echoes the gigue perhaps helps give the partita a unity of feeling rare in a Baroque suite.

Partita No. 5 in G, BWV 829

Partita No. 5 was announced in May 1730, almost two years after Partita No. 4.[27] The new work was shorter than the preceding one, though still a very substantial piece by contemporary standards, with a big opening movement and a particularly impressive fugal gigue. It might have been composed at about the same time as Partita No. 4, for several distinctive passages in the first movement closely resemble the overture and the gigue of the previous suite.[28] Moreover, both gigues follow the unusual scheme of opening the second half with a new subject.

The first movement is designated a praeambulum, the same term Bach had used in the CB for the Inventions as well as for three simple preludes. It seems impossible to find any consistent distinction between a prelude, a praeludium, and a praeambulum, and perhaps the latter term was used here only because the former had already been used for the first movement of Partita No. 1. In fact, the term *fantasia* might have been more appropriate for this improvisatory movement, but Bach had already used it in Partita No. 3. Among the improvisational elements is the alternation between free figuration and two-part counterpoint, recalling the courante of French Suite No. 6 and the allemande of Partita No. 1. But this movement is through-composed, and so the opening passage functions as a sort of ritornello. This is probably another hand-crossing piece, like the gigue of Partita No. 1; the division of notes between the hands, as indicated by the direction of the stems on the notes in bars 5–16, seems to call for the right hand to cross over the left, reaching deep into the bass. Later the left hand gets to leap (bars 73ff.), though without crossing over the right.

The allemande returns to ideas from the allemande of the Fourth English Suite: A short theme containing triplet-sixteenths is developed in two-part imitative counterpoint, then inverted after the double bar. Here Bach avoids a deceleration to ordinary sixteenths after the first phrase, which had put a damper on the enthusiasm of the earlier allemande. But some duple rhythms do occur, and the usual question arises: Which, if any, of the figures written in duple notation are to be interpreted literally? One assumes "assimilation" of the dotted rhythms that occur simultaneously with triplets. But what does one do with the dotted figure in the opening theme (Example 15.5)? Assimilation seems to improve the counterpoint when the theme is transferred to the left hand, producing parallel tenths rather than a dissonance (f$^\sharp$/g$^\prime$) at the end of the third beat of bar 1. Yet the passing dissonance is hardly noticeable, and when, in the last bar of the first half (bar 12), the dotted motive from the theme is set against a duple figure in the tenor, there is no evident need for assimilation. Nor is it clear how one would "assimilate" the figure in bar 25a, a written-out ornament perhaps better interpreted freely than according to any rigid duple *or* triple scheme.[29]

The corrente is another example of the dance that could have served equally well as a prelude or a sonata movement. Three times the treble makes a conspicuous

EXAMPLE 15.5.   Partita No. 5 in G, BWV 829, allemande:
(a) bar 1; (b) bar 12a; (c) bar 25a

climb to d′′′, a note used previously only in the scherzo of Partita No. 3. Bach must have assumed by 1730 that anyone capable of playing the sky-rocketing arpeggio in the closing gesture—whose bass descends to low GG—would have had a keyboard with the necessary range.[30]

The sarabande is of the trio type, with numerous appoggiaturas, some notated as *petites notes*, others written out as regular quarters (Example 15.6). Does this mean that Bach wrote out all of the "long" or "variable" appoggiaturas, and that all of the

EXAMPLE 15.6.   Partita No. 5 in G, BWV 829, sarabande:
(a) bars 0–2; (b) bars 19–22a

petites notes represent appoggiaturas of the "short" ("invariable") type? The written value of the *petites notes* varies, but there is little evidence that such distinctions had any meaning until after Bach's death.[31] Two appoggiaturas (on the note b', bars 20, 22) are indicated by "hooks" or commas, probably not because they are meant to precede the beat, as Neumann (1978, 126) suggests, but because in these instances the main note is approached from below; that is, the appoggiatura in each case is a', not c", which would create parallel fifths in bar 22.[32] The use of the older notation in this instance perhaps strengthens the case for "short" realization.

Actually, the crucial problem in this movement, to be solved before attacking the appoggiaturas, is that of tempo. As in the Sinfonia in E^{b} or the loure of French Suite No. 5, the dotted rhythms and occasional flourishes are lifeless unless the movement is performed at least at a moderate walking pace. This seems to rule out, among other things, "pre-beat" performance of the appoggiaturas; there is simply no time for this, given the dotted rhythms. One presumably should double-dot the quarter-notes; the double-dots in some editions (e.g., BG 3) are not original, however.[33]

The *Tempo di Minuetto* is notated in a cryptic manner that recalls the giga of Partita No. 1. Although the division of notes between the hands does not initially involve hand-crossing, the hands do cross at a few points near the end (beginning in bar 33; see Example 15.7). Bach's distribution of the notes between the hands

EXAMPLE 15.7.   Partita No. 5 in G, BWV 829, *Tempo di Minuetto:* (a) bar 1; (b) bar 33

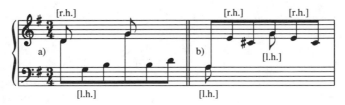

may not have any rhythmic implications, but the melodic contour of the figuration does create a hemiola that persists throughout the piece. This might explain why Bach called the movement *Tempo di Minuetto* rather than a minuet proper; indeed, the passepied that follows has more of the traditional minuet character. Several other hand-crossing pieces from the Bach circle are nevertheless termed minuets; indeed, this movement might have started a small rage in Leipzig for such things.[34] Rameau's 1724 collection provides a possible model in the minuet *Le Lardon*, a *pièce croisée* performed on two manuals. The *Tempo di minuetto* contains no indication for two-manual performance, but it would not be impossible.[35]

The gigue, unlike the one in Partita No. 4, is a full-fledged double fugue, the two subjects being combined in the latter part of the second half (at bar 46). The two subjects complement each other particularly well, since the leaps and rests occur at different points in each, creating an interlocking dialogue. There is also a quieter "sigh" motive, introduced in the episode at bar 14b, that reappears, somewhat unexpectedly, as a parting gesture at the very end.

Partita No. 6 in E Minor BWV 830

The Sixth Partita is the crowning work in the first part of the *Clavierübung* and Bach's greatest suite. The allemande and the sarabande contain some of the most audacious and dramatic embellishment ever written, and the work opens and closes with two of the most ambitious contrapuntal movements in the *Clavierübung*. Hence, it is easy to understand why Bach withheld it from publication until 1730 or 1731, even though it was ready in 1725 for inclusion in the *Clavier-Büchlein* of that year.[36] The autograph is far more heavily corrected than that of Partita No. 3 in the same manuscript, and the printed version shows many additional revisions as well, including the expansion of the opening toccata by the equivalent of three bars. As in Partita No. 3, an entire movement (the air) was added as well.

The toccata has little in common with Bach's earlier pieces of that title, save for the basic plan of a fugue framed by prelude and postlude. As in the early toccatas, prelude and postlude are free, improvisatory passages, but here they have been closely integrated with the central fugue.[37] An important motivic idea from the prelude recurs in the last episode of the fugue (bars 72–81). The fugue, moreover, ends in the dominant, the tonal circle being completed by the postlude. The latter is an abbreviated restatement of the prelude, lacking only the material already recapitulated in the fugue. The entire movement is notated *alla breve* and apparently must be played in a single tempo, although the free cadenzalike passages in the outer sections invite free rhythm.

The fugue subject combines galant "sighs" with "rhetorical" pauses. Indeed, the fugue as a whole, in three voices, resembles some of the more galant three-part fugues of WTC2 in its construction out of fairly regular two- and three-bar phrases, reflecting the sequential character of the subject (cf. the fugues in F minor and F♯ major). But the harmony and voice-leading are dissonant and chromatic; the first note in each "sigh" figure in the subject becomes a dissonant appoggiatura when combined with the countersubject, whose alternation between ascending and descending forms of the melodic minor scale creates a number of melodic cross-relations. Two episodes provide some essential diatonic respite from the chromaticism of the expositions; the second of these, in C (bars 72–75), marks the farthest remove from the tonic.[38] From here, however, there is a swift and inexorable modulation out of the neutral realm of C major toward the "sharp" regions of E minor and B minor, culminating in the return of the prelude in the latter key (bar 89). This is a magnificent moment; that it is in the parallel minor of the dominant, rather than the tonic, might have posed a problem for another composer, but Bach balances the strong arrival in B minor with a dramatic move to the subdominant shortly before concluding (bar 101).

The allemande is a heightened version of that found in Partita No. 3. Both movements, with their pervasive dotted rhythm and virtuoso figuration, bear a certain resemblance to the ritornello of the aria "Komm, süsses Kreuz" in the Saint Matthew Passion.[39] Bach had written at least two earlier allemandes of this sort—in the fifth cello suite and the first violin partita—and perhaps all can be traced back to a type found in French gamba music, such as the first allemande in B minor from Marais's second book of *Pièces de viole* (Paris, 1701). But the scale figures and, in the second half, the arpeggiated *figure corte* (bars 14b-16) make the present allemande a particularly vivid virtuoso piece. Friedemann Bach imitated it in the allemande of his Suite in G Minor (F. 24)—a brilliant work, incidentally, but no match for this.

The corrente forms the perfect pendant for the allemande, even though it was apparently one of two movements taken from an early version of the Sonata in G for violin and obbligato cembalo BWV 1019. Like the movement that replaced it at the center of BWV 1019, the corrente is a large sonata form, comparable to the most ambitious preludes of WTC2. While it opens with the same syncopated *tempo rubato* as the aria of Partita No. 4, the corrente quickly turns into one of the most brilliant movements in the Partitas.

That Bach should have drawn on the violin sonata is not surprising, for the set of six sonatas for violin and cembalo seems to have been assembled during the same period in which Bach was completing the French Suites and planning the Partitas. The Sonata in G is the last in the set and might have been concatenated from several miscellaneous pieces, for Bach subsequently revised it at least twice, substituting and reordering several movements. In the earliest surviving version (BWV 1019a) it had a remarkable cyclic form in five movements, one of them a solo for the harpsichord, another apparently a violin solo accompanied only by unfigured bass, although the loss of the violin part makes unclear the exact form of the movement. The *Cembalo solo* became the corrente of Partita No. 6, while the *Violino solo* was converted into the *Tempo di Gavotta.*[40]

The three versions of the movement show few differences. Only a few notes were altered from the original sonata version, although among these were the first five notes of the theme. Bach also eliminated the notation in "double measures" used in the second version (that is, in the early version of the partita). This alteration was probably due to the phrase elisions that produced a shift in the "downbeat" from the odd- to the even-numbered bars at two points in the second half (compare bars 29–43 and 90–104).

The air, even if it was prompted only by the need to fill a blank page, provides a breathing space between the corrente and the sarabande. It opens like a gavotte, on a half-bar upbeat, as does the otherwise unrelated air in the Fourth French Suite.[41] Virtually every phrase of the little piece is based on some variation of the descending line found in the bass of the opening two bars. This is true even of the closing phrase (bars 24b–28a), which is further varied in a *petite reprise.*[42]

The sarabande combines the majesty of a French *sarabande grave* with the fire of an Italian adagio. The sarabande of Partita No. 1 can be thought of as a preliminary exercise for this one. Both are highly embellished, and both open with a dotted figure, though the latter is now shifted to the upbeat and is later worked into several hemiolas (e.g., in bars 2–3 and in the closing phrase of each section). More important, the embellishment is far more florid than in Partita No. 1—so florid that it obscures the fact that the movement is in a concise sonata form, with a genuine return at bar 29 preceded by a four-bar retransition phrase. That the climactic burst of figuration in bars 28–29 indeed decorates a return is somewhat clearer in the simpler version given in the autograph, which retains the dotted upbeat taken from the beginning of the movement (Example 15.8).[43]

The extraordinary embellishment poses greater interpretive challenges than in any other movement in Bach's keyboard music. As usual, the true form and char-

EXAMPLE 15.8.   Partita No. 6 in E Minor BWV 830,
    sarabande, (a) bars 0–1

(b) Same, bars 28–29 (earlier version from SPK P 225 on upper staves)

acter of the sarabande are likely to be obscured when the tempo is too slow. Excessive rhythmic freedom will have the same effect, although it is clear that the rhythmic notation must be taken with a grain of salt, as in the sinfonia of Partita No. 2 and similar movements. Often the first note in a group of thirty-seconds cannot but be lengthened, as in bar 17, where such a note is ornamented by a mordent.[44] But the underlying beat should probably not be affected by such nuances, even though it will have to be stretched in the cadenzalike passage at the return.

The *Tempo di Gavotta* is another concise sonata form, arranged from an earlier version in the G-Major Violin Sonata. While the movement has little of the traditional gavotte character, the bass does open with the standard gavotte upbeat of two quarters. Elsewhere, however, in incorporating the movement into the partita, Bach heavily revised the bass line.[45] He must also have made substantial revisions in the upper part, at least in bars 23b–26a, where the bass of the violin version cannot be reconciled with the familiar treble line; Example 15.9a includes a reconstruction of the lost violin part.[46] Throughout the movement, the conflicting duple and triple rhythms of the two parts present an obvious performance problem, at least in the surviving version for solo keyboard. Inevitably, there have been arguments for altering the written values, but, as in the allemande of Partita No. 5, "assimilation" seems doubtful except in the case of dotted rhythms set directly against triplets. Presumably, the groups of sixteenths can be interpreted freely.[47]

The gigue is Bach's most profound movement composed under this title. Like the *Tempo di Gavotta*, it has been viewed as a rhythmic conundrum (e.g., by McIntyre 1965, 489), thanks to its dotted rhythms, which are notated under an archaic meter-sign (ϕ) equivalent to $\frac{4}{2}$. As in almost any piece notated in a persistent dotted rhythm, one can alter the written values to produce a more or less convincing version in triple meter, and this would eliminate some of the movement's angularity. But the latter seems to be an essential element of the piece—a rhythmic complement to its thorny chromatic voice-leading.[48] The version of the autograph, where the note-values are half those of the print, looks very much like Froberger's gigues in dotted rhythm or the gigue of French Suite No. 1, where literal interpretation seems best (see Chapter 14). While Bach later doubled the note-values, there is simply no good reason why his notation should not be interpreted literally here as well.

The doubling of the values and the use of an archaic mensural sign were probably meant to associate the piece with the *stile antico* (see Wolff 1968, 45). But the original reason for the doubling of values might have been that the *figure corte*, introduced in bar 9, were an afterthought that Bach began to add only after he had begun writing out the autograph. The *figure corte* in sixteenths and thirty-seconds, unforeseen when the piece had been first drafted, gradually became an important motive, not mere embellishment; thus, it was appropriate for them to be notated in larger values, which would also be more legible.[49]

Apart from the addition of *figure corte*, Bach made no effort to ameliorate the archaic contrapuntal style of the gigue. The subject, leaping through dissonant intervals, recalls passages in Froberger's abstract polyphonic pieces as well as his gigues.[50] The severe character of the counterpoint is reinforced by the absence of

EXAMPLE 15.9.   (a) Sonata in G for cembalo and violin BWV
  1019a, *Violino solo*, bars 23b–27a (reconstruction);
  (b) Partita No. 6 in E Minor BWV 830, *Tempo di Gavotta*,
  bars 23b–27a; (c) same, autograph (SPK P 225), bar 25a;
  (d) autograph, reading prior to correction, bars 26–27a

lasting modulations; the piece never really leaves the tonic, although there are brief,
complementary modulations in the middle of each half—to the dominant in bar
15b, to the subdominant in bar 41b. Indeed, the two halves form a nearly perfect
binary symmetry, which might justify the omission of the repetitions when performing before a sleepy audience. But the second half is slightly longer than the
first, and just before the end, the subject, introduced in inversion after the double
bar, returns in its original form (bar 49). The subject also seems to be alluded to in
the closing phrase; this is clearer in the version of the autograph. Yet Bach failed to
combine the two forms of the fugue simultaneously, as he did at the end of the last
gigue in the English Suites. Perhaps this was because the combination would have

required changing one or two melodic intervals in the inversion, and here, at the close of his collection of *galanteries*, Bach wished nothing to appear that might suggest a departure from contrapuntal rigor. And so the work ends with a strange but compelling movement, as far removed as one could imagine from the gigue of the opening partita.

16

Clavierübung, *Part 2,* *and Other Works*

The success of the Partitas evidently led Bach to continue the series. During the 1730s and early 1740s he brought out three further volumes of "Keyboard Practice" (*Clavierübung*) while also compiling WTC2 and (probably) the first draft of the *Art of Fugue*. These years saw much other musical activity as well, including the preparation of the harpsichord concertos and other ensemble works for the Leipzig Collegium Musicum. Bach appears to have written few keyboard works outside of those included in the great collections, which were gradually taking shape as a consciously organized corpus of carefully selected and revised pieces. He did, probably, compose or revise a few lute pieces that are also playable on the harpsichord; two keyboard arrangements (one fragmentary) also probably date from this period.

Clavierübung, *Part 2*

In 1735, four years after the collected edition of the Partitas, Bach published Part 2 of the *Clavierübung*.[1] The volume contained two works—a concerto and an *ouverture*—representing the two chief orchestral genres of the day. Having taken over the directorship of the Collegium Musicum in 1729, Bach would have been devoting much time and energy to copying parts and directing performances of such works, by composers including Vivaldi and Telemann as well as younger contemporaries like Hasse and the Graun brothers. Despite efforts to reconstruct the repertory of the Collegium, it remains unclear to what extent the works performed by the group might have influenced the two new keyboard pieces. But both pieces, and particularly the concerto, reflect the increasingly galant style of the times.[2] It has even been suggested that "most, if not all, of Bach's [solo] keyboard pieces from at least 1729–1741 . . . were presented at Collegium events" (Wolff 1985a, 169). But no unequivocal evidence for this survives, and one wonders how audiences would have reacted to the playing of long harpsichord "lessons" (*Clavierübungen*) and ersatz orchestral pieces while the rest of the ensemble waited patiently.

The two pieces making up Part 2 were meant, as the title-page declared, to represent the *italiänischen Gusto* and the *französischer Art*, respectively. By 1735 the rivalry between the two national styles had been reduced to a cliché, but it stemmed from real enough distinctions. What the volume really demonstrated, however, was the existence of a German galant style that borrowed from both styles. Even French composers had begun composing in a mixed style, as in Couperin's *Goûts réunis* (Paris, 1724), and Italians like Corelli had been doing so for much longer without making a fuss over it. While Bach's own keyboard works had, from the beginning, blended elements of the two styles in varying proportions, here the French elements can, as in most earlier works, be viewed as predominant, especially in light of Bach's precise indication of ornaments and the requirement of a double-manual harpsichord in both works. Still, the concerto has all the fire and impetuosity traditionally associated with the Italian style, and even the *ouverture* borrows from the same in its fugue, which makes the customary borrowings from concerto style (as in Partita No. 4).

While one would never want to underestimate a work of Bach's, it is possible that the novelty of the two pieces exceeds their intrinsic musical worth. Despite the irresistable vivacity of the concerto, neither piece has quite the splendor of the D-Major Partita or the depth of the Partita in E Minor. The concerto has nevertheless gained deserved popularity among pianists, for whose instrument it is better suited than most of Bach's harpsichord works. On the other hand, the *ouverture* is relatively little known even among harpsichordists, since it is awkward to play and probably too long for most modern recital programs; like the Sixth French Suite it simply contains too many short dances. There are even signs of a certain carelessness in the production of the volume, for the indications for the use of two manuals—one of the special features of the publication, announced on the title-page—appear to have been a late addition and are not always fully integrated into the musical fabric.[3]

These changes of manual are often analogous to the tutti/solo distinctions made in the scoring of a concerto. But, as in an ensemble work, forte does not always correspond with a "tutti" passage (i.e., a ritornello), nor does piano necessarily imply "solo" or "episode." In the first movement of the concerto the episodes are scored mainly for a forte upper line with softer accompaniment in the lower voices. But there is also a piano echo within a ritornello (bars 67–68), and in the last movement both hands have forte passages within "solo" episodes. Occasionally it is unclear whether a passage is a "ritornello" or a "solo," but this occurs in ensemble concertos as well. Indeed, it is probably a mistake to regard either work as a literal adaptation of an orchestral genre or the changes of manual as direct imitations of ensemble scoring. Dreyfus (1985a, 339) argues that even in Bach's ensemble concertos the "solo-tutti distinction" is blurred if not essentially ornamental. The alternations of dynamic level in the keyboard pieces merely lend added weight to alternations of texture and material that are already woven into the fabric and are "not necessary," as Williams (1986–87, 37) puts it; the dynamic contrasts are not essential to the form.

Although prepublication versions of both pieces survive in manuscript, these do not differ greatly from the published versions. Even the transposition of the *ouverture* from C minor to B minor involved fairly small substantive changes. The chief source of the C-minor version, a copy by Anna Magdalena Bach, probably dates from around 1730; hence, the *ouverture* might have been the seventh partita evidently alluded to that year in Bach's newspaper announcement of Partita No. 5.[4] Indeed, the *ouverture* today is sometimes referred to as the Seventh Partita, but Bach did not use that title. Had it appeared as part of the earlier set, its opening movement (an overture) would have duplicated that of Partita No. 4, and its original key, C minor, that of Partita No. 2. By transposing it to B minor Bach was able to continue his series of keyboard publications without repeating any tonalities. Moreover, B minor also formed a tritone with the key of the other new work, the concerto in F, hence symbolizing the distinction between the two styles of the new set's two components.

As in the Partitas, the existence of an authorized early print does not eliminate all questions about the text, and some problems remain in the reading of ornaments and the placement of dynamic markings. Like the Partitas, the new volume underwent alterations before and after printing; indeed, there was a second edition by the end of 1736, and there survives an exemplar (of the first edition) containing handwriting that has been identified as Bach's; this exemplar is therefore regarded as his *Handexemplar*.[5] Readings from the *Handexemplar* are incorporated into the edition in NBA V/2, which, unlike most previous editions, gives the two works together, as they were originally published. As in NBA V/1, errors and omissions in the sources made it necessary to emend dynamics, ornaments, articulation signs, and the beaming of groups of eighths and sixteenths. While most of these emendations involve small details, they occasionally raise issues of substance, some discussed below.[6]

Concerto in F, BWV 971

Part 2 of the *Clavierübung* opens with the Italian Concerto and not, as one might have expected, with the French *Ouverture*. Perhaps Bach wished the shorter and in some respects more up-to-date piece to come first. For the concerto reflects not so much the style of the early Venetian concertos that Bach had transcribed around 1713–14, nor Bach's own orchestral concertos of perhaps a few years later, as it does the later works of Vivaldi and the concertos of Bach's younger German contemporaries like Quantz and the Graun brothers.[7] Indeed, the familiar title "Italian Concerto" is a misnomer, for it is actually a German concerto after the Italian style, a point implicit in Scheibe's extravagant praise of the work as one that "will be imitated all in vain by foreigners."[8] Certain features, such as the periodic phrasing in the ritornello themes in the outer movements and the use of a distinct solo theme in the first movement—a lyrical theme graced by numerous "sigh" figures—are probably more common in concertos of the 1730s than those of twenty years earlier. Likewise, the regular ritornello designs of the outer movements, nowadays so firmly associated with the Vivaldian concerto, are less uniformly present in earlier works than in later ones. Even the slow movement, which was clearly meant to exemplify the Italian style of melodic embellishment, may have a more direct connection with other German compositions containing written-out ornamentation, a feature rare in Italian works.[9]

The first movement lacks a tempo marking but is obviously an allegro. The opening echoes that of a work by Gottlieb Muffat—perhaps an unconscious borrowing, since the movements otherwise have nothing in common, but the similarity is too close to be accidental.[10] The ritornello form of the concerto movement is clear enough, and one can readily imagine the first two episodes (bars 31–52 and 91–103) as solos scored for violin and accompaniment, the latter furnished by upper strings in bars 31–42, basso continuo thereafter. But matters are less simple in the passage that begins with the third, truncated, statement of the ritornello theme (bar 103). Within a few bars the texture has thinned out to two voices, and the material is no longer taken from the ritornello. Yet there has been no decisive articulation following the previous entry of the theme, and the dynamic level remains forte (at least for the right hand; on the dynamic of the bass, see below). Bach has indeed blurred the distinction between ritornello and episode, as he had done previously in the overture to Partita No. 4. In both movements, after a fairly realistic evocation of the orchestral model at the outset, the urge toward free development evidently overcame any desire for maintaining a simple solo/tutti or loud/soft alteration.

The middle movement seems more directly related to Vivaldi, for comparable scoring—a soaring melodic line accompanied by simple lower parts, without ritornellos—can be found in many of his slow movements, as can the simple binary form. Yet, despite the florid embellishment of the upper part, this is not an adagio but an andante, like the second section of the sinfonia in Partita No. 2. A "walking" tempo, with steady motion in the lower voices, can give the embellishment in the upper part some fire and also make it easier to perceive the phrase structure. The first half, for example, consists of a periodic theme (bars 4–7, 8–12) followed by a sequential transition (bars 13–18); after a dominant pedal-point in the relative major (bars 19–25) this leads to a cadence in that key (bars 26–27). The "theme" does not lie in the actual notes of the florid upper part, nor in the melody divested of a few of its embellishments; rather it lies in the underlying progressions.[11] Thus, for example, bars 4–7 are considerably varied when they return (bars 28–31), as is the sequence first heard in bars 13ff. (|| 32ff.).

The last movement was originally also an allegro, changed to a presto in the print. The alteration may have indicated not a change in speed but a recognition of the somewhat more dancelike, less pompous character of the final movement. Its ritornello is shorter and simpler than that of the first movement, and it takes a different approach to the "solos," treating the two hands as equal parts in a duo. The same approach is also evident, to a lesser degree, in the ritornellos, which are more contrapuntal than in the first movement and at one point shift the main line to the left hand (bars 93–96). Formally, the last movement comes somewhat closer than the first to the through-composed sonata form common in galant concertos of the 1740s and afterwards, with a return and subsequent recapitulation section beginning at bar 153.[12]

The sources seem to have omitted a few necessary dynamic markings in the outer movements, but it is not entirely clear where they should be added. A forte should probably be supplied for the left hand at bar 104 of the first movement, as indicated in NBA V/2. Not only does the ritornello theme enter at this point, but in the following passage the left hand is at least the equal of the right, and there is a piano indication later (bar 129). This piano indication is restricted to the left hand in the NBA, but the print clearly assigns both parts to the soft manual.[13] Doubt arises because the texture in bars 129ff is analogous to that in the earlier "solos," in which the right hand remains forte. But the fact that Bach allowed the piano indication to stand in both editions suggests that he did not wish to maintain an exact consistency between what are, after all, only approximately parallel passages.[14]

Nor is it clear that dynamic markings should be inserted at four points in the third movement (bars 127, 141, 155, and 166), as is done in many editions in an effort to ensure that material will be recapitulated on the same manual on which it was first played. Some inconsistency is unavoidable, and despite the emendations in NBA V/2, one passage that originally was divided between two keyboards (bars 38–43) must still be played later on the soft manual (bars 127–37). Considering the prominence of the bass in this movement, it is possible that Bach intended it to remain on the forte manual all the way from bar 92 through 171.

Ouverture in B Minor BWV 831

The B-Minor *Ouverture*, like Bach's two early works of the same type (BWV 820 and 822), is dominated by the opening movement, a large French overture containing powerful dotted sections and a virtuoso fugue in concerto style (or a concertolike section with fugal ritornellos). The proportions of the work, which is heavily weighted toward the front, now seem odd. But in fact the dance movements make up a larger portion of the work than in many contemporary suites and *ouvertures*, and one or two movements, in particular the very expressive sarabande, are more substantial even than the dances in Bach's own orchestral suites. None of the dances contains any changes of manual, but the alternating dynamic levels that represent solo and tutti in the fugue return in the closing *echo* movement, giving the work as a whole a measure of cyclic closure.

The overture, unlike that of Partita No. 4, has a concluding as well as an opening dotted section. It is hard to say why one overture closes with such a section and another does not; in this case it cannot be because of any lack of finality at the end of the fugue. For the fugue is a self-contained section that begins and ends in the tonic, closing with a recapitulation of much of the opening exposition/ritornello (bars 123b–143 || 26b–46). The same is true in the overture of Partita No. 4, and thus the addition here of a final dotted section may have been intended simply to add weight (and length) to the opening movement of the suite. The addition was hardly necessary; the movement is already unusually long, even without the indicated second repeat.

The dotted portions of the overture were the focus of a bruising controversy over the nature of the French overture.[15] Frederick Neumann's argument against the "so-called French style," by which he meant the over-dotting of the dotted sections of an overture, rested in part on the differences between the notation of the present overture in the print and in the manuscript copy by Anna Magdalena Bach. The latter, which gives the early C-minor version (BWV 831a), differs from the print above all in the less heavily dotted notation in the outer sections of the overture.[16]

The question, so far as this movement is concerned, is whether the revisions signified a change in the actual rhythm or merely in its notation (Example 16.1).

EXAMPLE 16.1. *Ouverture* in C Minor BWV 831a, overture, bars 1–3 (rhythms from BWV 831 above and beneath staves)

One might suppose that the two forms of notation were equivalent, the print merely specifying a performance practice taken for granted by the users of the manuscripts. If so, however, Bach must have observed a convention of lengthening not only dotted quarters but also a quarter tied to a sixteenth, and even a single sixteenth followed by three more. This is hard to believe. Yet it seems possible that Bach, while actually altering some of the original rhythms, merely renotated others.[17]

In this view the changes in bars 1 and 2 represent real revisions: A relatively smooth rhythm involving sixteenths is replaced by more vehement motion in thirty-seconds. Even in the original version, however, thirty-seconds eventually appeared just before the double bar (bars 17–20A).[18] While composing the piece, Bach might have viewed the figuration in thirty-seconds as an embellishment, used to intensify the motion toward the cadence at the end of each dotted section. But he later realized that this figuration introduced a certain ambivalence to the piece's rhythmic character and decided that thirty-seconds should prevail almost throughout, sixteenths remaining only in bars 13, 146, 148, and 158. At the same time he specified over-dotting of the dotted quarters by substituting a sixteenth-rest plus a sixteenth-note for the original eighth-note in bar 3 and elsewhere.[19] He also eliminated notational discrepancies of the sort originally found at the end of bar 8, where parallel motion in the outer voices was notated in sixteenths and thirty-seconds, respectively (Example 16.2). Incidentally, the insertion of a rest between the trill and its termination, as in Example 16.2, seems to have been confined to pieces in dotted rhythm and was not a normal element in long trills.[20]

EXAMPLE 16.2.   (a) *Ouverture* in C Minor BWV 831a, overture, bars 8–9a; (b) *Ouverture* in B Minor BWV 831: same

Unfortunately, one effect of the revised rhythm was to make a long piece more homogeneous, and the dotted sections run the risk of monotony, especially if taken too slowly. The fugue is likewise prone to monotony, thanks to its heavy reliance on recapitulation; the three "solo" episodes are all recyclings of the same material, and the outer ritornellos/expositions are essentially identical. The highly schematic structure points toward the great E^b-major prelude (BWV 552/1) in the third part of the *Clavierübung*, but the material here is less compelling and far less varied. The changes of manual, while helping to clarify the ritornello structure, evidently were afterthoughts, and in one passage they require the left hand to leap between keyboards three times in as many bars (bars 91–93). The player hardly needs the added distraction, for this is already the most difficult as well as the one really compelling passage in the fugue. It serves as the third ritornello, although it is based not on the subject but on a new theme derived from the countersubject; the latter enters in four closely spaced statements that mount upward, always forte, through the circle of fifths.[21]

Of the nine dances, the most distinguished are the two slowest ones, the courante and the sarabande. The former is of the French variety, but it opens with an apparently unprecedented idea: a tonic pedal-point that tolls every four beats, thus articulating a hemiola; the idea returns in the last phrase (bars 20–21).[22] It is probably the sarabande, however, that forms the high point of the suite. Like the sarabandes of the English Suites, it is in four strictly maintained parts, but the individual voices have greater rhythmic independence than in the earlier chorale-like sarabandes. The dense counterpoint includes many harsh passing dissonances, and the movement is as difficult to play well as any fugue; it might serve as a touchstone of the harpsichordist's ability to draw out the long lines of the melody (and inner voices) while softening the naturally harsh attacks of the instrument through the breaking of certain chords and the discreet use of over-legato.

The slurs in the sarabande are problematical (Example 16.3). NBA V/2 supplements the text of the original print, perhaps because both editions contained obvious errors. The second (1736) edition eliminated two ties, including a nonsensical one in bars 4–5, and added some slurs, but the length of some of those remaining is inconsistent (compare the treble in bars 1–2 and 5). Probably no slurs should cross the bar-line; those that do so might have been engraved that way by false analogy to the ties, which of course do extend between bars.[23] One might compare with this the slurs in the aria that opens the second half of the Saint Matthew Passion (preserved in autograph), which begins with a similar gesture (Example 16.4).

EXAMPLE 16.3.   *Ouverture* in B Minor BWV 831, sarabande, bars 1–6 (slur cut by single verticle stroke is absent from first [1735] edition; slur cut by double vertical stroke eliminated in second [1736] edition; brackets indicate addition in NBA)

EXAMPLE 16.4.   "Ach, nun ist mein Jesus hin," BWV 244/30, bars 1–4 (violin 1 only)

The smaller dances grouped around the sarabande contain little that is remarkable and do not seem to fall into any purposeful succession, if indeed they were all meant to be played through in order. Even the gigue is a disappointment; it is of the French variety (as one would expect here) and thus employs a constant skipping rhythm that grows somewhat monotonous, despite the presence of a *tirata* motive reminiscent of that used in the overture.

The absence of regular echoes in the last movement may also give cause for disappointment. Even here, where one might have expected some real antiphony, the dynamic marks are essentially ornamental. No full bars are repeated piano, as they are in the echo movement of the suite BWV 821, and thus the dynamic alternations again require some very quick jumps between manuals.[24] It is difficult to avoid the impression that the manual changes are merely an emphatic (and somewhat capricious) way of setting apart certain phrases and gestures in what was originally a binary-form air or sonata movement. Perhaps the embellished echoes of a few very brief gestures refer to the old Baroque tradition of the echo aria, in which only the final word or gesture of a phrase is repeated.[25] Formally, however, the movement is not very different from some of the rounded binary preludes in WTC2; the last return of the theme (tenor, bar 62) is intensified by its combination with new counterpoint, as in the preludes in D major and F minor.

Dreyfus, after criticizing the more literal reflections of concerto style in other movements of the volume, finds in the *echo* the "great Bach concerto" of the set and "the most intensive demonstration of the ritornello principle in the 'Clavierübung'."[26] His discussion offers a reinterpretation of ritornello form that cannot be easily summarized here. Yet it seems possible that the "ritornello functions" that Dreyfus finds in the *echo*, like the concerto elements that have been discovered in the Inventions (Wagner 1979), are nothing more or less than the ordinary elements of eighteenth-century musical syntax, corresponding to those that have been described above in the analyses of the andante of the Italian Concerto or the allemande of Partita No. 4. The most striking feature of the *echo* may in fact be the series of modulations immediately following the double bar, where it takes a sharp turn to the subdominant or "flat" side of the tonic in a kaleidoscopic series of short phrases built from fragments of the theme. Still, the orchestral quality of the theme—which recalls that of the first allegro of the E-major violin concerto BWV 1042—and its recurrence within the first half (prior to the double bar) constitute somewhat stronger parallels to concerto style than are usual in a binary form. This helps make the *echo* an appropriate closing movement for Bach's volume of quasi-orchestral harpsichord solos.

Transcriptions

Sonata in D Minor BWV 964, after Sonata No. 2 in A Minor for Solo Violin BWV 1003; Adagio in G, BWV 968, after Sonata No. 3 in C for Solo Violin BWV 1005, first movement

Sole source: SPK P 218/2 (Altnikol). *Editions*: BG 42, Dadelsen (1975).

Bach's much-reproduced fair-copy autograph of the Sonatas and Partitas for unaccompanied violin (SPK P 967) dates from 1720, but, like WTC1 and other works compiled during the Cöthen period, the violin pieces must actually have been drafted somewhat earlier. As is well known, they belong to a tradition of harmonically self-sufficient works for unaccompanied string instruments. They require no supplementation or accompaniment, but, especially in the absence of string players capable of meeting their considerable technical challenges, they are a repertory waiting to be appropriated by the keyboard and other more conveniently polyphonic instruments, as Brahms, among others, discovered.[27] Bach himself was not immune to this temptation and might well have been playing impromptu keyboard arrangements of them long before these two transcriptions were written down; Adlung commented in 1758 that the works for unaccompanied strings "can be very well played on the clavier,"[28] without mentioning the present transcriptions. As in most of his other keyboard arrangements, Bach transposed both works; the transposition by fifth brought the bass and the inner voices of the original into the bass and tenor registers, respectively, of the keyboard.

The two transcriptions are preserved together in a single manuscript copy by Altnikol, who studied with Bach from 1744 until 1748. Many years later, in a review published in 1775, another Bach student, Agricola, stated that Bach had often played the sonatas and suites for unaccompanied string instruments "on the clavichord," confirming Adlung's report and suggesting a possible medium for the present works.[29] Altnikol's copy gives both title and attribution only for the Sonata BWV 964, and he might have named Bach only as composer of the original work, not as transcriber. Moreover, both arrangements contain some surprises that have been seen as pointing to "the generation of the sons of Bach, especially Wilhelm Friedemann" (Dadelsen 1975). Hence, their authenticity has been questioned (e.g., by Siegele 1975, 88; Eichberg 1975, 39). But the apparent oddities can be found in other works of roughly the same period.

For example, something like the leaping left hand part—practically a ragtime "stride" bass—at the opening of the Adagio BWV 968 occurs several times in the Partitas (e.g., praeambulum of Partita No. 5, bars 73–77). The chromatic scale-fragments in the same movement, and in the adagio of the sonata, have parallels in the Fantasia and Fugue in C Minor BWV 906 and in the keyboard version of the Fourth Brandenburg Concerto.[30] In fact, it would be surprising if anyone but Bach had been responsible for the audacious keyboard writing found in BWV 968, which also deletes a bar from the violin version. Nor does the filling out of the harmony, especially of the inner voices in the fugue (BWV 964, second movement), reveal anything unworthy of Bach. The one disappointment is the last movement of BWV 964, in which the arpeggiando figuration is, for the most part, simply rewritten with indications for division between the hands; only a few bass notes are added. But this very restraint may also point to Bach; the writing is a little thin, but similar textures occur in the lute pieces and in passages in other keyboard works (e.g., the praeambulum of Partita No. 5). Altnikol was one of Bach's more talented students, and, as his son-in-law, inherited part of his music collection; clearly he would have had access to things that were not widely distributed. As no earlier copies survive, it is reasonable to regard these transcriptions as authentic works from the later Leipzig years. While there is no shortage today of performances of the unaccompanied violin works, truly stylish, technically proficient performances are rare. Keyboard players are likely to have an easier time with them, and the unique features of the transcriptions make them valuable works in their own right.

While Bach had added a great deal of embellishment and substantially amplified the harmony in his transcriptions of Reinken's ensemble sonatas (BWV 965–66), that was hardly necessary in BWV 964, since a rich polyphonic texture was already implicit in the original version and the slow movements heavily embellished. Bach did add new counterpoint in the fugue; for example, in one passage (bars 18–19) the added bass forms a brief canon with the original bass line, now placed in the alto. But elsewhere the transcription process was largely confined to the realization of what is implicit in the original, bass tones, inner voices, and suspensions being held out for their full values.

All three of Bach's sonatas for solo violin are *sonate da chiesa* modeled after Corelli's Op. 5, Nos. 1–6, and similar sonatas for violin and continuo. Each opens with an adagio and fugue, followed by another slow movement and an allegro. In BWV 964 the opening adagio is in through-composed binary form, and the recapitulation (which begins in the subdominant at bar 14) is recognizable chiefly from the bass line, the upper parts being considerably varied. The fugue's closest relatives among the keyboard works are the concertolike preludes of English Suites Nos. 5 and 6. Several episodes are composed of idiomatic violin figuration, but there are also episodes of a more contrapuntal nature, some of them using the same chromatic line that serves as countersubject in the fugue in A^b of WTC2.[31] The fugue was evidently known to Mattheson, who expressed his admiration for Bach's ability to draw a long piece from so short a subject.[32] The overall form is somewhat rambling, but it has a roughly bipartite shape, the second half beginning with the introduction of the inversion (bar 125).

In the third movement, an andante in binary form, Bach further embellished one cadenzalike flourish (bar 9) but otherwise left the original essentially unaltered. The allegro is a much larger binary form consisting almost entirely of violinistic figuration. Given the ease of playing the arpeggiated passage-work on the keyboard, one may be tempted to hold out the notes beyond their written durations in order to increase the sonority. Yet Bach seems to have been careful, as always, to indicate exactly the values he intended, and it may be best to add nothing. Nor may it be wise to observe the echo dynamics suggested in the BG at several points; these are present in the violin version but awkward to play on the harpsichord.

Bach seems to have approached the transcription of the third violin sonata (BWV 1005) with greater freedom than the second, as the arrangement of the adagio completely alters the texture and character of the original. Thus, it is a profound disappointment that Bach—or at least the copyist Altnikol—got no further than the first movement, which ends on the dominant. Unfortunately, there are no orphan *manualiter* fugues in G to go with it; one might use it as a sort of "pre-prelude" to the praeambulum of the Fifth Partita, which it somewhat resembles in its inventive keyboard writing.

The adagio opens with an ornamented version of the conventional progression also found at the beginning of the adagio in the oboe concerto by Alessandro Marcello (arranged as BWV 974). But the movement unfolds in a surprising series of harmonies, made all the more remarkable in the keyboard version by the luxuriant scoring. The "stride" bass at the beginning, which pianists may find themselves unable to avoid pedaling, can sound clunky on a harpsichord if played carelessly; perhaps it lies behind the suggestion that the transcription might have been intended for a *Lautenklavier* (Dadelsen 1975), on which the notes (especially the low bass notes) presumably would have rung undamped. Yet a certain dryness at the opening will make all the more effective the arpeggios and chromatic lines added in subsequent phrases, especially if these are played somewhat over-legato. The movement is another through-composed binary form, extended by a modulating coda; the second half begins (bar 15) with a brief reference to the opening. The reference is strengthened in the transcription by the omission of the original bar 17, which contained an odd harmonic surprise that Bach evidently thought better to omit.

The Later Lute Works

At his death Bach owned two lute-harpsichords (*Lautenklaviere*), at least one of which was probably the instrument reportedly built around 1740 at Bach's suggestion.[33] Having had such an instrument built, Bach would surely have made use of it, above all in the lute pieces. These are readily playable on keyboard instruments except in occasional passages; the textures are thin, of course, but, as in the last movement of the Sonata BWV 964—also potentially for lute-harpsichord—it is difficult to add anything meaningful to Bach's texture. The low tessitura of most of the lute pieces helps compensate for the light textures; in the resonant middle and low registers of a good harpsichord one does not miss the absence of fuller harmony. Occasional bass notes must be transposed up an octave to avoid impossible stretches for the left hand, but the resulting discontinuities in the bass line are probably no worse than those Bach allowed himself in his writing for unaccompanied lute, violin, and cello.

Though Bach had acquired a real lute before his death, he did not necessarily have any facility on the instrument, which might have been a recent acquisition (Dreyfus 1987a, 171). The surviving autographs of the lute pieces are written in keyboard score, as are the majority of the copies, whose titles indicate that most copyists were unaware that the piece had ever been intended for lute. Much has been made of the visit of two virtuoso lutenists to Leipzig in 1739,[34] but as Dreyfus (1987a, 171) points out, Bach also knew a number of local lutenists, among them his students J. L. Krebs (who played lute as well as organ) and J. C. Weyrauch, who was responsible for two of the three copies of these works in tablature. The visit of Weiss and Kropffgans may have been remarkable only for having been recorded in a document that happens to survive; none of the three known autographs is quite this late (according to Kobayashi 1988).

It is likely, however, from the relatively late dates of the sources that the pieces considered here originated, or at least were revised, at Leipzig and not earlier. Three of the pieces were arrangements: BWV 995, 1000, and 1006a; the other two, BWV 997 and 998, were substantial new compositions. All presumably sound best on a good lute, well played. But the last movement of BWV 997 might—in light of its wide range (noted in NBA V/10, KB, 144–46)—have been intended specifically for Bach's lute-harpsichord; hence Kohlhase (NBA V/10, KB, 98–100) argues that the lute-harpsichord should be regarded as a distinct medium in its own right, not a mere "ersatz instrument." Still, from Agricola's account one gathers that some of these keyboard instruments could sound very much like one or more of the types of lutes used in Germany at the time. This would have been due not only to the use of gut strings but, apparently, to the absence of dampers and perhaps even to pedals whose function was analogous to that of the extra bass strings of most Baroque lutes. The free after-ring of the undamped strings would have masked the occasional barrenness of the written texture; that such a sonority was admired in the Bach circle is suggested by Emanuel's mention of the beauty of the "undamped register of the fortepiano" in improvised fantasias. [35] Neither the so-called lute-stop (really a mute) found on modern harpsichords nor the true lute-stop (a set of jacks plucking close to the nut) can duplicate the lute-harpsichord or the lute itself very closely. But the music—especially the original works BWV 997 and 998—deserves to be played, and performance on any sort of harpsichord is no worse than on guitar, the usual modern alternative.

Suite in G Minor BWV 995, after Suite No. 5 in C Minor for Solo Cello BWV 1011

Sources: B Br 4085 (= Fétis 2910; autograph in score, 1727–31); LEm Becker III.11.3 (tablature). *Edition*: NBA V/10.

The six suites for solo cello have traditionally been dated to Cöthen, but Eppstein (1976) has argued convincingly that they are Bach's earliest group of instrumental suites, corresponding to the English Suites for keyboard; hence, a Weimar origin is not out of the question. Suite No. 5 is the most French of the group—it opens with a French overture (designated *Prelude* [sic])—and thus was perhaps the most appropriate choice for lute arrangement. It is also the one suite in the set to call for a substantial amount of chordal playing—not, however, in the fugue, whose counterpoint in the original version is entirely implicit, indicated through leaps and arpeggiated figuration within a single melodic line. In the original, Bach directed the player to tune the top string a step lower than normal, from a to g, and notes played on this string were written a tone higher than sounding. This obviously presented problems of legibility for keyboard or lute players attempting a transcription at sight and might have been an additional reason for Bach's having written out a transcription of this particular suite. [36]

Bach's score of BWV 995 includes his note that the work was for a "Monsieur Schouster," possibly a Leipzig book dealer. [37] BWV 995 proper is the version of the autograph; the tablature, by an unidentified copyist, alters many details, presumably to make the piece more idiomatic to the lute. [38] In both versions the fugue retains its very light texture, and only a simple bass is added in the expository passages. Not much more is added elsewhere, although ornaments, especially appoggiaturas, were added in the dance movements, and the dotted rhythms of the allemande were revised much like those in the overture of BWV 831.

Fugue in G Minor BWV 1000, after Sonata No. 1 in G Minor for Solo Violin BWV 1001

Chief source: LEm III.11.4 (Weyrauch; tablature). *Edition*: NBA V/10.

Bach made two transcriptions of the fugue from the first violin sonata, the present one for lute as well as an organ version in D minor (BWV 539/2). Compositional changes in both arrangements make it unlikely that either is by anyone but Bach; among other things, each transcription expands the piece by a total of two bars, although the additions and alterations do not occur in the same places. The organ version is in five voices, with an independent pedal part, but the simplicity of the added voices suggests that this version is relatively early—earlier, for example, than the transcription BWV 964, where the added parts in the fugue make a significant contribution to the counterpoint.

Presumably, then, the present arrangement is later than the one for organ. The harmony is fuller than in the fugue of BWV 995, but it remains sketchy by the standards of keyboard music. Two late copies of the organ version include a *manualiter* prelude, BWV 539/1, but it is in the wrong key for use with the present arrangement of the fugue.

Suite in E, BWV 1006a, after Partita No. 3 for Solo Violin BWV 1006

Chief source: Tokyo, Musashino Music Academy, Littera rara vol. 2-14 (autograph). *Editions*: BG 42, NBA V/10.

By the time Bach copied out the autograph of BWV 1006a he had already arranged the first movement as an organ solo with orchestral accompaniment in Cantata No. 29, performed in 1731.[39] Unfortunately, neither version of the prelude can be easily played on a keyboard instrument lacking pedals. Two hands are needed for some of the figuration involving repeated notes, which were originally intended for performance on alternate strings of the violin (e.g., in bars 13–16). The combination of two-fisted *batteries* with simple pedal writing is reminiscent of the end of the early Praeludium BWV 921; perhaps one of Bach's lute-harpsichords had "pull-down" pedals like the ones apparently built by Johann Nicolaus Bach of Jena (described by Adlung 1768, 2:162).

With a little practice one can play all of the figuration with the right hand, but inevitably the *batteries* lose some of their effect. Still, the effort might be worth it, as the dances of BWV 1006a make reasonably idiomatic *manualiter* pieces. The loure is of particular interest as a more strictly fugal example than the one in the Fifth French Suite, although each half employs a different subject.

Suite in C Minor BWV 997

Chief sources: SPK P 650 (Agricola; title: *Praeludium, Fuge, Sarabande und Gigue fürs Clavier*); LEm III.11.5 (Weyrauch, tablature, lacking fugue, double; title: *Partita al Liuto*). *Editions*: BG 45, NBA V/10.

The rather odd sequence of movements making up BWV 997—prelude and fugue, sarabande, gigue, and double—makes it seem a collection of miscellaneous pieces. But the uniformly mature style points to its having been conceived integrally, and it is perhaps Bach's strongest original lute work. The title "suite" does not occur in the chief sources, and in fact the organization is closer to that of a *sonata da chiesa*. Many copies survive, indicating that the piece was popular; only one source uses lute tablature, most of the rest assigning the work to *Clavier* or *Clavicembalo*.

The keyboard sources give the notes in the top staff an octave above sounding pitch, except in the last movement.[40] The last movement, a double (variation) of the gigue, has too wide a compass to be playable on the lute; indeed, it reaches f''' (bar 8), the only occurrence of this note in Bach's solo keyboard music.[41] This might cast Bach's authorship in doubt, but the double represents a thorough recomposing of the original movement, maintaining only its essential bass and harmonic outlines (as in the allemande of the Suite BWV 819a), and the style is entirely Bach's.

The first two movements, a prelude and fugue, recall earlier concerto-style pairs like BWV 894. But sources and style clearly point to a Leipzig date. The fugue, for example, is a Da Capo form, which Bach used not only in the English Suites and in one of the violin sonatas (BWV 1005) but in the "Wedge" fugue for organ BWV 548/2 and Duet No. 2 in the third part of the *Clavierübung*.[42] While the proportions are similar to those in the preludes of the last two English Suites—the A section is only slightly shorter than the B section—arpeggiated passage-work is confined to the B section, as in the "Wedge." In addition, the B section introduces a varied form of the subject (bar 55), whose oscillating figuration resembles motives used in both the "Wedge" and in the organ prelude BWV 552/1 from the *Clavierübung*.

The opening of the sarabande is known for its resemblance to the theme in the closing chorus of the Saint Matthew Passion, which is in the same key; the two movements also share a galant, or rather *empfindsamer*, style. Two apparent errors in NBA V/10 can be resolved by comparison with Weyrauch's lute tablature.[43] The gigue is also expressive in character, with appoggiaturas playing a prominent role in the motivic material. The opening phrase is composed over much the same bass as the opening of the prelude and of course was "varied" again in the double that follows.[44]

Praeludium, Fugue, and Allegro in E♭, BWV 998

Sole source: Tokyo, Ueno-Gakuen Music Academy (autograph). *Editions* BG 45, NBA V/10.

The customary title for BWV 998 (given above) resembles the familiar name "Toccata, Adagio and Fugue" attached to the organ toccata in C (BWV 564). Bach himself left no title, merely labeling the first movement *Prelude pour la Luth. ò Cembal* [sic]; like BWV 997 the work could be viewed as a sort of church sonata, although lacking a slow movement after the fugue.

The prelude is similar in meter, form, and texture to the prelude in the same key in WTC2, while the fugue opens with a subject reminiscent of the chorale melody *Herr Jesu Christ, wahr'r Mensch und Gott*, the basis of Cantata No. 127 (first performed in 1725). The fugue is in Da Capo form; as in BWV 997, only the B section contains free figuration. This, however, is a somewhat less ambitious movement, perhaps also a less satisfying one, the opening section being marred by a few oddly prosaic passages (bars 7–8, 13–15). The allegro, a large binary form, opens with the same gesture as the gigue of the earlier lute suite BWV 996. It shares that piece's perpetual motion in sixteenths but instead of chromaticism and counterpoint offers galant fluidity and simplicity of texture; perhaps Bach was writing here on commission.

17

Clavierübung, *Parts 3 and 4*

During the 1730s the focus of Bach's keyboard composing appears to have shifted from the suites discussed in the previous three chapters to diverse genres such as variation and canon, in which he had previously worked sporadically if at all. While he continued to revise and occasionally compose more traditional types of pieces—in particular the preludes and fugues of WTC2—the most important new keyboard works of his late years combine canon, strict fugue, and variation in ways previously explored neither by Bach nor anyone else. The chief works in question are the Goldberg Variations, the ricercars from the *Musical Offering*, and the *Art of Fugue*. We may also include in this group Part 3 of the *Clavierübung*, which, although primarily concerned with chorale settings for the organ, includes pieces playable on other keyboard instruments.

The surviving sources for these works date from 1739 and afterwards, but only for the *Musical Offering* can the compositions themselves be dated with any precision. Thus, it is somewhat problematical to speak of these as "late" works, let alone as representatives of a distinctive late style.[1] Even if most of the music was composed after, say, 1735 (as seems likely), the focus on canon and other types of strict counterpoint and the distinctive format of each of the collections as a whole are not really indicative of any particular style as such. Indeed, despite the abstract quality of some of the more strictly contrapuntal pieces from the late period, it would be a mistake to think of the late works in general as growing "inward" or unconcerned with outward effect. Even the *Musical Offering* and the *Art of Fugue* include music as outgoing as anything from Bach's earlier years, proving that Bach in his old age did not quietly retreat into the contemplation of pure counterpoint. Yet there is indeed a recherché quality to some of this music; the allusive harmony, strange melodic lines, and high tolerance for passing dissonance in some pieces (especially certain canons) imply that the composing out of a predetermined contrapuntal design sometimes took precedence over other musical considerations.

One of those considerations was practicality of performance. Indeed, if the *Art of Fugue* and the ricercars from the *Musical Offering* continue to be viewed apart from the rest of Bach's keyboard music, it is due not only to their inner musical qualities—which are not so different from those of certain pieces in the WTC—but to certain practical concerns, which will be considered in due course. Parts 3 and 4 of the *Clavierübung*, although almost equally difficult to play, are less problematical.

Clavierübung, *Part 3*

Part 3 of the *Clavierübung*, published in 1739, retains the dedication to *Liebhabern* (music-lovers) found on the title-pages of the first two volumes but adds "especially for those knowledgeable in such things" (*und besonders denen Kennern von dergleichen Arbeit*). Hence, while not as abstract as the *Musical Offering* and *Art of Fugue*, it may, like those works, have been intended primarily as a token of Bach's learning and skill, for the delight and instruction of sophisticated musicians. If so, it may be considered the first installment in the series of works making up Bach's contribution to the tradition of speculative counterpoint, which extended back to the Renaissance by way of Reinken and other more immediate predecessors.

Outwardly, however, the work is also a practical anthology of pieces composed primarily, if not exclusively, for the organ. Wolff has even suggested that the form of the volume "displays something of the organization of a typically Bachian organ concert" (1986b, 288), although the use of noncircular temperaments would have made the complete list of pieces an ideal rather than a realizable concert program on many instruments (see Wolff 1991b, 417, "Postscript"). The main portion of the volume consists of ten chorale melodies, each presented in a *manualiter* as well as a *pedaliter* setting. The chorales are framed by the two movements of the great *pedaliter* Prelude and Fugue in E♭ BWV 552, the fugue being preceded by four unrelated duetti for manuals only.

Wolff (1986b, 287) and Butler (1990) have argued that the pieces need not all have been written shortly before publication in 1739, as has usually been assumed. Nevertheless, the collection as a whole seems to mark a sharp change in direction from the predominantly galant second volume of the *Clavierübung*. To be sure, the superficial elements of galant style, including the ubiquitous sigh motives, triplets, and "quasi-ostinato bass lines" (stressed by Butler 1990, 17–20), are present in a number of movements. But some of the chorales—for example, the two large Kyries—adopt a rather mysterious neomodal pitch structure, neither fully tonal nor genuinely modal, and they seem purposely to avoid sequences, full cadences, and other ordinary types of formal articulation. Even in movements characterized by galant melodic writing, the presence of canon (as in the *pedaliter* Vater unser BWV 682) or the avoidance of sequence and periodic phrasing (as in the *manualiter* Allein Gott BWV 675) represents a significant departure from galant style as it occurs in, say, the Partitas.

The title-page includes the expression "for the organ" (*vor die Orgel*), but the wording is ambiguous and the phrase might refer only to the chorale settings.[2] There also exists a letter by Bach's secretary, Johann Elias Bach, written just before the work was published, that states somewhat more ambiguously that the "clavier" pieces in the new print are *"chiefly* for organists" (emphasis added).[3] Hence, Bach might have contemplated the performance of some of the music, including the *manualiter* chorales, on the harpsichord or clavichord. But it seems unlikely that any of the music was conceived primarily for stringed keyboard instruments. *Manualiter* pieces mingled with *pedaliter* ones in the collections of organ music that might have served as Bach's models for the volume, such as Grigny's *Premier Livre d'orgue* (Paris, 1699).[4] Even by 1739, not all German organs had pedals, and certainly not all organists had any substantial pedal technique; the *manualiter* chorales in the *Clavierübung* might well have been intended for them. Certainly these settings are of a type different from the "monodic" chorale preludes in CB and elsewhere that Bach probably intended for harpsichord. This is clearest in the absence of *brisé* writing, the restrained use of ornaments, and the frequent use of plain sustained tones even in the top voice.

Among the chorales, the most plausible exceptions to the preceding are the three fughettas. With its lively repercussive subject and dance-like rhythm, the Fughetta on *Diess sind die heil'gen zehn Gebot'* BWV 679 might seem a natural harpsichord piece. Yet the bass must be powerful enough to hold its own when stating the subject against three-part chords in the right hand and rich enough in timbre not to sound empty in several brief passages where it plays alone. Such writing seems to presuppose the sustaining power and registrational possibilities of the organ; it is absent from mature "clavier" works like the WTC. Perhaps somewhat more idiomatic to the harpsichord are the shorter fughettas on *Allein Gott* (BWV 677) and *Wir glauben all'* (BWV 681). The insistent dotting of the latter recalls the gigue of French Suite No. 1; despite its "Dorian" key signature, it is in the pure minor mode (unlike some of the other chorale settings).

The duetti have been regarded as "clavier" pieces since the nineteenth century, but there is nothing in them unidiomatic to the organ. The latter had a long tradition of fugal *bicinia* such as occur among Pachelbel's Magnificat fugues; comparable "free" pieces—duos and trios—also occur in Grigny's *Livre d'orgue.* If, however, the duetti were late additions to the volume, it is possible that they had been initially conceived as "clavier" pieces. Butler (1990, 19–20) dates them to mid-1739, after the engraving of the greater part of the volume had already taken place. While there is no assurance that all four pieces were even composed at the same time, stylistic idiosyncrasies in all four pieces do imply a late date.[5] In each, a straightforward gesture at the beginning of the subject is contradicted later by irregular or otherwise "difficult" writing—unusual chromatic intervals, for example. Thus in Duetto No. 1 the theme opens with a plain scale figure but ends with a series of tortuous, seemingly clumsy gestures (bars 5–6). Duetto No. 2 in F has an almost purely diatonic A section, the subject opening with a broken triad, in quarter-notes, that implies staccato articulation, but the middle section begins with a slurred motive containing an augmented second.

At the outset, all four pieces, and especially Duetti Nos. 1 and 3, resemble large inventions. But the initial imitation is at the dominant, and there are distinct episodes, so that the formal structure of each is that of a fugue of one sort or another. The structures tend toward the geometric and incorporate substantial amounts of recapitulation; Duetto No. 2, which is in Da Capo form, surpasses the two-part fugue in E minor of WTC1 in the complexity and exactness of its symmetry, at least in the B section. Yet these remain playful pieces. Duetto No. 3, for example, introduces a sort of telescoped variation of the subject at the return (bars 28ff.), interpolating a few beats' worth of new material into the rests of the subject so that the latter can be used in a sort of pseudo-stretto.[6] The humor is somewhat abstruse, but this is hardly the work of a contrapuntal pedant or a mystic obsessed with numerical symbolism.

The Goldberg Variations BWV 988

The work popularly known as the Goldberg Variations was published in 1741 under the title "Keyboard Practice, consisting of an aria with diverse variations for the two-manual harpsichord."[7] The work is also generally regarded as Part 4 of the *Clavierübung*, although the title does not make this explicit and, as Marshall (1976a, 342–43) points out, could be interpreted to mean that Bach "intended to separate this work at least to some degree from the preceding parts."[8] Like Parts 1 and 2, it is dedicated simply to music-lovers, without the suggestion of deeper mysteries contained in the title of Part 3—which does not mean that they are not present.

The popular title owes its existence to Forkel's report that Bach had written the work for his student Johann Gottlieb Goldberg, so that the latter could entertain his employer Count Keyserlingk during the Count's frequent sleepless nights (Forkel 1802, 51–52/BR, 339). Elsewhere Forkel (1802, 43/BR, 331) lists Goldberg among Bach's celebrated students, mentioning, however, that Goldberg had no talent for composition. Actually, Goldberg was a good enough composer for one of his trio-sonatas to be misattributed to Sebastian as BWV 1037 (see Dürr 1953). If the variations were really written for Goldberg, he would have been only thirteen or fourteen at the time, but Forkel's story remains credible inasmuch as Goldberg later gained the reputation of a virtuoso. Since Bach was in Dresden in November 1741 as a guest of Keyserlingk, it is also possible, as in the case of the English Suites, that the popular title stems from Bach's presentation of a special copy to a noble connoisseur.[9]

If so, however, the circumstances of the work's actual composition remain obscure. In writing a large set of variations Bach turned to a form that he had not used in a completed keyboard work since the early chorale partitas. But his contemporaries and immediate predecessors had hardly neglected variation form—Corelli, Handel, and Rameau, among others, had published impressive examples. By the 1740s, the variation set seems to have been turning into a simple type of piece primarily pedagogic in nature. Bach, however, evidently envisioned the Goldbergs within a tradition of large, encyclopedic variation sets for keyboard going back to the sixteenth century.[10] The title *Aria* for the opening movement might even have been a reference to the strophic dance-tunes whose basses furnished the models for earlier variation sets, as in Frescobaldi's *partite* on the *Aria di Romanesca*.

Such variation sets served not only as exercises in performance but as demonstrations of compositional technique. In the Renaissance the technique in question had originally been cantus firmus elaboration. But by the seventeenth century the variations generally were being based not on a preexisting melody but on what we would term a harmonic progression, which seems increasingly to have been understood in the same way as the realization of a figured bass line. Indeed, the Goldberg set is built upon a bass line whose first four notes are also the basis of a sarabande on which Johann Christoph Bach (1642–1703) had written a a set of twelve variations.[11] Hence, the Goldberg Variations could have been intended as a demonstration of "composition by variation," serving the same purpose as the doubles for the sarabande of BWV 818 and the allemande of BWV 819a, but on a more massive scale. The Goldbergs show that music belonging to practically any genre, including strict fugue and canon, could emerge as the realization of a single bass line or harmonic progression.[12]

Structure

The large structure of the work, like that of the presumably later organ variations on *Vom Himmel hoch* BWV 769, revolves around canons.[13] These occur in every third movement, alternating with types that can be classified broadly as "duets" and "free" variations. At the end, the initial aria is repeated (see Table 17–1).

TABLE 17–1.   Structure of the Goldberg Variations

Movement	Type	No. of manuals	No. of voices	Mode (m = minor)	Remarks
Aria		1	(3)		
Var. 1	free	1	2		duo; hand-crossings
Var. 2	free	1	3		trio; quasi-canon
Var. 3	canon	1	3		at the unison
Var. 4	free	1	4		
Var. 5	duet	2			
Var. 6	canon	1	3		at the second
Var. 7	free	1 or 2	2		*al tempo di Giga*
Var. 8	duet	2			
Var. 9	canon	1	3		at the third
Var. 10	free	1	4		*Fughetta*
Var. 11	duet	2			
Var. 12	canon	1	3		at the fourth, by contrary motion
Var. 13	free	2	3		embellished andante (sarabande)
Var. 14	duet	2			
Var. 15	canon	1	3	m	at the fifth, by contrary motion
Var. 16	free	1	2–4		overture
Var. 17	duet	2			

TABLE 17–1.   Structure of the Goldberg Variations (*continued*)

Movement	Type	No. of manuals	No. of voices	Mode (m = minor)	Remarks
Var. 21	canon	1	3	m	at the seventh
Var. 22	free	1	4		*Alla breve*
Var. 23	duet	2			
Var. 24	canon	1	3		at the octave
Var. 25	free	2	3	m	embellished adagio
Var. 26	duet	2			juxtaposes $\frac{18}{16}$ and $\frac{3}{4}$ time
Var. 27	canon	1	2		at the ninth
Var. 28	free	2			hand-crossings
Var. 29	free	1 or 2			
Var. 30 Aria	free	1	4		*Quodlibet*

The plan is broadly symmetrical, yet it contains certain anomalies. For example, the basic three-movement pattern of canon, free variation, and duet emerges only with variation 3 and ends with variation 29. The overture, which divides the sequence of thirty variations in half, falls in the middle of one of the threefold groups. Moreover, both canons in contrary motion (variations 12 and 15) occur in the first half, while the three movements in the minor mode (variations 15, 21, and 25) are distributed unevenly, tending to fall toward the end. From such discrepancies, Breig (1975, 254) posited that the first twenty-four variations, which are built around the first eight canons, might constitute the original core of the work. The remaining variations might have been added later, certain movements—in particular the overture (variation 16)—perhaps being substituted for some of the original twenty-four. In any case it seems likely that the Goldbergs, like other Bach collections, grew by increments, the final arrangement emerging only after some experimentation.

The structure as we know it certainly produces effective juxtapositions between individual variations. For example, the overture forms a splendid contrast with the canon in the minor mode that precedes it; this makes the overture seem like a new beginning, as is appropriate at the outset of the second half of the work. But it is less clear whether the work as a whole constitutes a true cycle, with a perceptible large structure, or simply an ideal cycle, as in the ordering of tonalities in the WTC. Perhaps the threefold pattern, like the series of widening intervals of imitation involved in the canons, is a purely constructive device, intellectually satisfying but largely irrelevant to the way in which one plays or hears the work.

To be sure, a good live performance can give an impression of the work as an integrated whole. It is conceivable that when the work is played in its complete form, the basic three-variation unit produces a certain large-scale rhythm audible to a sensitive listener. This rhythm is defined in particular by the canons, which tend to be relatively restrained in character, hence constituting regularly occurring points of repose. The work breaks out of this pattern toward the end, where the last half-dozen variations—all extraordinary in one way or another—together serve as the climax.

As in any large work, however, the sheer length of the composition may create the impression that it is of a transcendant character, if only in the simplistic sense of transcending the normal temporal bounds of the style.[14] This alone might explain the special quality that one senses in the return of the aria after the last variation—a moment that will inevitably remind a modern listener of the Da Capo at the end of the variations in Beethoven's piano sonata Op. 109. But there is no retransition leading to the return of the opening theme as there is in the Beethoven work, nor has any material from the aria, other than the bass, been used to any substantial degree in the variations. At best there is an occasional echo of the aria, as in the underlying sarabande rhythms of variations 13 and 25, and again in variation 26, where the dance rhythm serves as one strand in a polymetric texture. Hence, the truly cyclic aspects of the work seem minimal, and it is easy to imagine reordering many of the variations without this having any substantial effect on the whole.[15]

Bach himself would have considered the question of cyclic form somewhat differently from many later composers, as the work was presumably not intended for complete public performance. Few purchasers of the original print of the Goldberg Variations would have regarded it primarily as something to be used for playing through from cover to cover; Goldberg's supposed performances for Keyserlingk would have ended as soon as the latter fell asleep. Thus, the chief principle governing the sequence of the variations, other than the canons, may well have been that of local contrast. Each variation is a self-contained recomposition of the underlying harmonic ground and phrase structure. Successive movements do not add increasingly florid embellishment to a recognizable "theme" or develop its motives in increasingly ingenious ways, and thus, despite the Da Capo of the aria at the end of the series, the variations show little sign of gradually moving away from and then returning to it. At the most, one senses a tendency toward increasing brilliance in the duets and free variations. This trend, however, is countered by several variations of a more restrained or serious nature; these reach their culmination in the somber G-minor arioso of variation 25.

Text and Performance

Anna Magdalena Bach's copy of the aria in the 1725 *Clavier-Büchlein* was once assumed to date from long before the variations themselves and thus to be evidence that the aria, like other pieces in the manuscript, had been borrowed anonymously from another composer, possibly French. But the handwriting is now thought to date from near the time of the work's publication and thus has no bearing on the authorship of the aria (further discussion below).[16] The engraving and publishing were entrusted to Balthasar Schmid of Nuremburg, and as in the first three parts of the *Clavierübung*, some copies of the print itself contain hand-written corrections apparently made in Bach's house. One copy, first recognized by Wolff (1976) as Bach's *Handexemplar*, includes not only corrections but also, neatly written on the last (unprinted) page, Bach's autograph of "various canons upon the first eight fundamental notes of the preceding aria" (BWV 1087).[17]

Alas, while more or less playable on the organ—some of them also on harpsichord—the canons cannot be considered keyboard music. Most make even less satisfactory concert pieces than the canons in the *Musical Offering*. They might have been written as exercises preparatory to composing the Goldberg Variations, but they give the bass in a different rhythmic guise, and two of them are known in slightly revised versions dated 1746 and 1747, respectively; these are listed separately as BWV 1076–77.[18] Kobayashi (1988, 60) dates the autograph of BWV 1087 to 1747–48, but the rest after the first note in the top voice of BWV 1076 avoids an improperly resolved dissonance (c′/d′) in bar 3, indicating that the 1746 version is later.

As for Bach's corrections and additions to the printed text of the Goldberg Variations themselves, these have been incorporated into the edition in NBA V/2. But as in the earlier prints, Bach did not attempt to rectify certain ambiguous ornament signs. This is unfortunate, as the ornament signs present particularly serious problems in the Goldbergs. The imprecision in the original print has been exacerbated by modern editions in which hardly a single sign appears as Schmid engraved it. Schmid's signs for trills and mordents are generally longer than usual (they contain extra "wiggles"), and the vertical or oblique stroke that ought to be drawn at the center or at the beginning of the mordent is instead sometimes placed too far to the right (Example 17.1).

EXAMPLE 17.1.   Goldberg Variations BWV 988, aria, bars 1–2 (upper staff)

Nothing short of a facsimile of the original could present the signs exactly as they appear in Schmid's print. But both BG 3 and NBA V/2 regularize Schmid's mordent signs to a form identical to that for the long trill with suffix (*Nachschlag*).[19] No doubt familiar with Schmid's ambiguous signs, C. P. E. Bach (1753–62, i.2.3.6) later warned of the potential for confusion between a carelessly drawn mordent and a trill with *Nachschlag*. But, in fact, in Schmid's print the vertical stroke is not always as badly misplaced as it is in the modern editions. Anna Magdalena Bach's copy of the aria makes it clear that the ornament sign first encountered in bar 1 of the aria indeed represents a mordent—likewise in bars 2, 5, 8, and so on, and by extension elsewhere in the work.

Unfortunately, a number of other ornament signs must remain ambiguous, as they occur only in the variations, especially the overture. In variation 16 the vague extensions at the beginning of the trill signs in bars 2, 3, 5, and elsewhere might indicate the *tremblement appuyé*, which is how they are interpreted in NBA V/2.[20] Another possibility, however, is the ornament that C. P. E. Bach called the "trill from above" (*Triller von oben*), which he illustrates in a context close to what one finds here (Example 17.2)—a long note following another at the same pitch or one higher (see C. P. E. Bach 1753–62, i.2.3.28). Slight irregularities at the ends of two of these signs (bass, bar 5, and treble, bar 8) have been cited as evidence for a "termination-by-hook" (Schwandt 1990, 68, citing Emery 1953, 64–65). In bar 5, however, the termination or closing turn at the end of the trill possibly would have been played anyway (C. P. E. Bach 1753–62, i.2.3.13), while in bar 8, where the trill is followed by a descending figure, Emanuel Bach counsels against including a termination or suffix (1753–62, i.2.3.16).[21]

EXAMPLE 17.2.   (a) Goldberg Variations BWV 988, variation 16, bar 2; (b) C. P. E. Bach (1753–62), i.2.3.28, *Tab.* 4, *Fig.* 43c

The most celebrated performance elements in the Goldbergs are, of course, the frequent hand-crossings and the use of two manuals. These elements must be considered separately, as variation 1, which employs several hand-crossings (as well as unisons at the end of each half) is designated as being for one manual, while several variations containing only incidental hand-crossings are for two manuals. The use of hand-crossings and other special keyboard techniques was once assumed to have been the result of Domenico Scarlatti's influence. Copies of Scarlatti's *Essercizi* (London, ca. 1739) could indeed have reached Leipzig in time to have inspired the composition of the hand-crossing variations in the Goldbergs, as Marshall notes (1976a, 348).[22] But this can be no more proved or disproved than the suggestion of Rameau's influence on the hand-crossings in Partita No. 1 (see Chapter 15). By 1740, virtuoso hand-crossings were certainly not new to Bach, and the influence of Scarlatti's *Essercizi* on the actual content of the Goldbergs might have been limited to their occasional use of certain etudelike sequences of simple figures, as in a few of the duets.[23]

In any case, to speak merely of "hand-crossings" is to oversimplify. Of the ten variations with significant hand-crossings, five (8, 11, 17, 23, 26) are true duets, virtuoso manifestations of the old *bicinium* or the traditional *pièce croisée* in which the hand-crossings are, at least in principle, incidental products of the free crossing of voices that happen to move in the same register. On the other hand, the five remaining hand-crossing variations (1, 5, 14, 20, 28) include sudden leaps of one hand over the other in order to strike isolated notes in another register. As in the prelude in B♭ (WTC2)—which was probably composed during the same period—the registrally isolated notes imply additional voices, although the sustaining of the notes into lines must be imagined (see Example 12.6). Regardless of the type of hand-crossing, most of the material of a given variation is divided equally between the hands according to some symmetrical pattern. Thus, at the opening of variation 5 the left hand crosses over the right, the pattern being inverted (as is the motivic material itself) after the double bar. In such a manner hand-crossing, potentially the most vulgar of keyboard techniques, is integrated into the type of "architectonic" musical design that had characterized Bach's binary-form pieces since his earliest suites.

The need for two manuals was, as in the second part of the *Clavierübung*, indicated on the title-page. Only here, however, is the use of two uncoupled (independent) keyboards clearly integral to the music.[24] Only in variation 7, where Bach permits the use of either one or two keyboards, and perhaps in the "monodic" variations 13 and 25, where a high treble is accompanied by two lower voices, could the movements designated as being for two keyboards have been conceived apart from double-manual performance. Variation 5, although indicated as being for either one or two manuals, is clearly a duet and is exceedingly awkward to play on one manual. Variation 1, on the other hand, contains hand-crossings but is con- fined to a single manual presumably because the two voices, while sharing some material, are more distinct in character than in the duets; the lower part still bears some resemblance to a traditional instrumental bass line. Bach again offered a choice of one- or two-manual performance in variation 29, whose *batteries* divided between the hands might seem to be best played on one manual. But a passage in the duet variation 23 (bars 27–30), together with the C. P. E. Bach sonata cited below, suggests that Bach would have preferred here the rapid alternation of timbres resulting from performance on two manuals.

The indications for one- or two-manual performance do not specify how each variation is to be registered, but there can be little doubt that Bach expected a player to take full advantage of the capabilities of a given instrument. Organists normally changed registration for each setting in a series of variations. That harpsichordists did the same is clear from C. P. E. Bach's registrations for a *cembalo* sonata (composed in 1747) that ends with a variation movement.[25] As in other German sources of the period (e.g., Adlung 1768), the stops are referred to in the same manner as on an organ (e.g., *Cornet*, *Flöte*), and Emanuel specifies sometimes surprising combinations; for example, for figuration somewhat resembling that of variation 29 he prescribes muted *Cornet* on the upper manual, octave and coupler on the lower.[26] Although most instruments are more limited than the one for which C. P. E. Bach's sonata was intended, the implication is that players need not limit themselves to two plain eight-foot ranks in the duet variations. But surely it is preferable to play the Goldberg Variations on an instrument equipped with more than what has become the normal three stops. A true lute stop and a sixteen-foot would both be welcome, the latter, if not too heavily voiced, being especially useful in those duets where a single eight-foot rank on each manual seems too weak (e.g., variations 23 and 28).

Pianists have dealt with the technical problem posed by the double-manual variations in various ways, some attempting to honor Bach's division of the notes between the two hands, others pragmatically redistributing the notes. Whichever solution is adopted, the musical problem is to maintain the integrity and the distinctness of each of the criss-crossing parts, as in variation 17. There one might attempt to imitate the double-manual harpsichord by giving each voice a distinct sound, by playing one part legato, one staccato, for instance. Yet this would be contrary to the normal manner of articulating Baroque lines (see Chapter 2). Moreover, any suggestion that one part is being subordinated to the other (e.g., through dynamics) would contradict the fact that the voices are of equal importance and based on the same material. It may be better to trust the ear to follow the individual lines rather than attempt to aid the listener through contrived pianistic effects that are liable to distract from the more important business of articulating the lines themselves.

The Aria

Doubts about Bach's authorship of the aria appear to be unfounded (see Neumann 1985 and the reply in Marshall 1989, 54–58). Although clearly a sarabande, it is neither Italian nor French but specifically German galant in style, and certain details point directly to Bach, especially the beautiful broadening out of the rhythm into steadily flowing notes in the last phrase (from bar 27), an idea that also occurs in the sarabandes of French Suites Nos. 3, 4, and 5. The long written-out appoggiaturas (*ports de voix*) on the second beat in bars 1, 5, and 9 also occur in the sarabande of the Fifth Partita and are characteristic of Bach's personal version of galant style; the combination of an intricate melodic surface with a slow harmonic rhythm would become characteristic of Emanuel Bach and other composers brought up in the school of "composition by variation."

The harmonic framework for the aria and the subsequent variations is the bass line with its implied continuo figures—not a series of harmonic progressions in the modern sense (Example 17.3). Actually, neither the aria nor any of the variations

EXAMPLE 17.3.　Goldberg Variations BWV 988, hypothetical *Fundamental-Noten* (with figures)

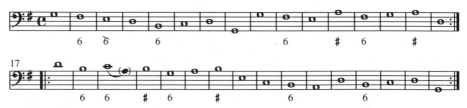

gives the bass in what might be called its hypothetical original form (*"Urform"*). Even in the aria the main tones of the bass—what Bach called the *Fundamental-Noten*—are embellished or altered (cf. Example 17.5). Elsewhere the harmony is further varied by chromatic inflections, above all in the three variations in G minor, one of which (variation 25) substitutes E♭ minor for the expected E♭ major at bar 24 in the middle of the second half. Another alteration occurs in the hand-crossing variations, where the *Fundamental-Noten* may be transferred from the left hand to the right (e.g., variation 5, bars 21–24). Occasionally the *Fundamental-Noten* are also displaced from their usual positions on the downbeats, but displacements by more than a beat, such as occasionally occurred in the old variation-suite, are rare except in the fugal part of the overture (variation 16).

Hence, the harmonic rhythm is consistent throughout the work, one principal harmony appearing in each of the aria's thirty-two bars. The symmetrical layout of the thirty-two bars is especially appropriate for a movement whose scheme was to serve as the foundation for a work containing thirty-two movements in all. Actually, as in earlier binary movements, the symmetry is inexact; the cadence at the end of the first phrase (bar 8) is in the tonic, but the third phrase ends (bar 24) in the relative minor, so that the tonal design is tripartite. The periodic structure, as Marshall (1976, 351–54) noted, is retained in the individual variations; even in the fughetta (variation 10) the subject enters every four bars. The only significant departure from this regular patterning is in the fugal section of the overture (variation 16), and even there the dimensions of the second half as a whole—in effect, sixteen "double measures" of $\frac{3}{8}$—are unaltered. Elsewhere, the elision of phrases prevents the music from appearing to be trapped in a periodic vise, as is the case in many lesser eighteenth-century variation sets. Elided phrasing first occurs in variation 2 (at bar 24) and becomes the norm in the canons, where the periodic structure is further hidden by the overlapping phrases of the individual canonic parts. Nevertheless, the underlying periodicity is less thoroughly disguised than in, say, some of Purcell's grounds.

In addition to the general problem of Schmid's irregular ornament signs (discussed above), the aria raises the question of how to perform the many appoggiaturas indicated as small notes. For these, "pre-beat" performance has often been advocated (e.g., in Neumann 1978, 142). Yet it seems a mistake to disregard the advice that Emanuel Bach published just twelve years later in connection with a musical example showing third-spans (*Tertien-Sprünge*) filled by appoggiaturas, just as in the present passage (Example 17.4a; cf. Example 17.1).[27] Emanuel inveighs

EXAMPLE 17.4.   C. P. E. Bach (1753–62): (a) *Tab*. 3, *Fig*. 9a, with realization; (b) from *Tab*. 4, *Fig*. 20a

against the "odious after-beat [hässlicher Nachschlag]" (1753–62, i.2.2.25; see Example 17b), no doubt because performance off the beat would reduce the series of moderately expressive appoggiaturas to innocuous passing notes. Besides, playing the appoggiatura in bar 4 before the beat creates a stutter, as it immediately follows a sixteenth-note on the same pitch. Since bar 4 merely repeats bar 2 in embellished form, both appoggiaturas must be played on the beat.

At thirty-two bars (sixty-four with repeats), the aria is longer than the average theme of a Baroque variation set, and some of the individual variations are fairly substantial compositions in and of themselves. Hence, it is tempting to omit at least some of the repeats, and in a public performance one can hardly object to this, especially in very long movements such as variations 13 and 25, or those in which the two halves are very similar, such as variation 17.

The Variations

The first variation opens the series with something of a bang. Hand-crossings, which first appear in bar 13, are a development of the leaps in the bass of bar 1. As noted earlier, the hand-crossings do not contradict the direction for single-manual performance, for the texture remains that of a sonata movement, albeit one with unusually athletic violin and continuo parts.

If variation 1 is thus modeled partly on the solo sonata, the three-part texture of variation 2 imitates the trio-sonata. It opens fugally; the initial two-bar interval between entries is reduced to a single bar in the stretto entries of the second half (bars 24ff.), hence pointing toward variation 3, the first of the canons.

All but the last of the canons are also in trio-sonata texture—two canonic voices over a free bass—but they are necessarily somewhat different in style from any of Bach's earlier keyboard works in three voices, such as the Sinfonias. Writing canons is fairly easy; writing canons within the constraints laid down here is not. Bach's abilities were such that even the strictest constructive device did not dictate musical choices to him; nevertheless, the practical requirement that the music must be playable by two hands on one keyboard did lead to writing that would seem rather odd outside of a canonic context. For example, in the first three canons the upper parts cross far more often than would ordinarily be the case in keyboard music, obviously because of the close interval of imitation. Moreover, the individual canonic voices contain occasional odd melodic intervals or form peculiar vertical intervals and are sometimes fragmented into uncommonly short phrases. Especially in the two canons by inversion, unusually rough passing dissonances are allowed. It would be fair to say that the music is a bit contrived. Yet the bass, which is free and not bound by the rules of canon, often shares motivic material with the canonic parts or at least borrows some of their distinctive melodic character. Hence, whatever peculiarities may have been forced upon Bach by the use of canon and by the limitations of ten fingers on one keyboard have been integrated into a distinctive but coherent style.

This style occasionally colors the noncanonic variations as well, suggesting that the peculiar flavor of some of these movements might have been suggested by the types of writing that had to be at least tolerated in the canonic ones. For instance, bar 9 of variation 2 seems very odd; not only do the upper parts momentarily double the third of the harmony, but they do so while forming a bare fourth with the bass (Example 17.5). In fact, the bass note here (f'') is a passing tone, and the underlying harmony is a simple G-major triad or, rather, a routine 5–6 progression over the bass note g—the same as in bar 1.[28]

Variation 4 consists of four-part imitative polpyhony that may suggest a motet and hence a fairly deliberate tempo. Indeed, one can imagine four vocal parts entering in descending order, accompanied by the continuo; the vocal bass enters with the

EXAMPLE 17.5.   Goldberg Variations BWV 988, variation 2:
(a) bars 9–10; (b) analysis

main motive in bar 4. Yet the time-signature ($\frac{3}{8}$) suggests a dance, perhaps a minuet. The leaps in the main motive imply detached articulation; this, together with the normal shortening of tones preceding the suspensions in bars 6, 7, and so on, can make for a transparent texture.[29]

Variation 5, the first of the duets, bears the designation "for 1 or 2 manuals," but this might have been a mistake or a half-hearted attempt to make the work seem more practical for owners of single-manual instruments. In bar 19 Bach added slurs in his own copy (on the eighths e″, c′ and a′, g″); because of the voice-crossing at this point the slurs are realizable only on two manuals.

In Bach's *Handexemplar* variation 7 bears the added heading *al tempo di Giga*. Despite the Italian terminology, this is a French gigue, of the same sort as the one in the French *Ouverture* BWV 831. It need not go too quickly, especially in light of the numerous short trills and appoggiaturas. The option to play the variation on two manuals makes it possible to subordinate the bass to the upper part and, if the keyboards are uncoupled, solves the problem of the unison on e′ in bar 24.[30]

Variation 8 is the first of several movements whose concentrated working out of arpeggios and other virtuoso motives might have been suggested by technical rather than purely musical considerations—as in an etude, although the latter genre did not yet exist. The treatment of the motivic ideas in this variation—especially the symmetrical exchanges of material between the two hands—is in principle the same as in other works, such as the duetti of Bach's previous publication. But the two thematic ideas presented in the first bar by treble and bass, respectively, are developed with such single-minded intensity, and the two parts range up and down each keyboard with such freedom, that the writing must have seemed extraordinary if not slightly deranged by mid-eighteenth century standards of decorum. In this, at least, the music does recall that of Domenico Scarlatti. Yet it is in the variations of this sort that the rationalistic symmetry so characteristic of the early eighteenth century is most in evidence. In the last four bars, for example, the sequential figuration of the right hand makes a downward plunge through almost three octaves, yet this precisely mirrors the writing for the left hand at the end of the first half.

Variation 8 raises a small textual question, since some editors alter a note in bar 3 in order to form a closer parallel with the following bar (Example 17.6). The two bars are not, however, precisely parallel, and the second note in bar 3 (d′) can be

EXAMPLE 17.6.   Goldberg Variation BWV 988, variation 8: (a)
   bars 3–4; (b) analysis

understood as a dissonance that resolves (to c#) on the third beat, the resolution
being transferred to the bass. In modern terms, the dissonant harmony is ii[7]; the
same harmony is involved in two later passages that also are sometimes emended.[31]
But the printed text should probably be allowed to stand, especially as Bach himself
let these "errors" pass while correcting others in each of the three variations in
question.[32]

The fughetta (variation 10) is not very rigorous, all four parts sounding together
only in the last four-bar phrase of each half. In his own copy Bach added a mordent
to the initial note of the subject; the engraver had left out or misdrawn the ornament
in most entries. Presumably, the mordent (as well as the trill on the second note)
can be extended to each statement of the subject.

Variation 11 is in $\frac{12}{16}$ time, which indicates a quick tempo according to Kirnberger
(1771–79, 2/1:124). As in the B♭-major prelude of WTC2, which uses the same
time-signature, one might read a certain delicacy in the material, and the frequent
crossing of the parts can produce a subtle interplay of timbres on a two-manual
instrument if played with a light registration. But delicacy may be out of place here,
for both parts have several long *Doppel-Cadenzen*, which implies brilliance.[33]
Unfortunately, harpsichordists limited to using a single eight-foot stop for each part
will find true brilliance difficult to achieve; perhaps here one would be justified in
sacrificing equality of parts for the sake of brilliance, adding the four-foot rank (if
available) to one voice.

Variation 12, the canon at the fourth, is the first of the two canons by contrary
motion. The canonic voices are composed mostly of long scale fragments; such
material implies a fairly lively tempo. But one rarely hears the variation played that
way, perhaps because the odd chromatic and augmented intervals beginning in bar
24 seem to imply "expressive" performance. In its quasi-ornamental character,
however, the chromaticism somewhat resembles that found in the sarabande of
819a or the Adagio BWV 968. Thus, the individual chromatic tones probably need
not be articulated deliberately, as one would be inclined to do in a chromatic line
moving in larger note-values. The inversional relationship between the canonic
parts is most easily heard when the tempo is quick enough for each bar to be
perceived as a unity; a lively tempo will also help the ear fill in momentarily empty
sonorities like the open fifth on the third beat of bar 24.

If the canon by inversion were exact, the trill in bar 4 would be answered by a mordent in bar 5. But while slurs are added in both bars in the *Handexemplar*, there is no mordent. Perhaps this was an oversight; near the end, a trill in one part is answered by a mordent in the other (see bars 29–30). But ornaments need not always be imitated exactly, even if this might be desirable in principle.[34]

The written-out turns that appear at one point in variation 12 (bars 19–20) become the principal motive in variation 13. The latter, an embellished andante, recalls the dance rhythm of the aria in the emphasis placed on the second beat by both melody and accompaniment. The upper voice is played on a separate manual, as can be done in several sarabandes from the French Suites whose "monodic" texture (also used in chorales) is adopted here. Indeed, the solo line achieves considerable brilliance, ascending in the third phrase to what Bach seems to have regarded by this date as the normal upper limit in keyboard music (d''' in bar 21).

With variation 14 (a duet) the tendency toward increasing brilliance continues, but it is broken off in variation 15, the most lugubrious of the canons, which is also the first of the variations in G minor. The text of both variations is altered slightly in some editions, but the harmony suggests that Bach's text should stand (Example 17.7). In variation 14 the addition of a sharp in bar 25 (right hand) is presumably prompted by the g♯ in the bass just a beat earlier. Yet in this bar the tonality is shifting back toward the tonic G major, and the substitution of g♯' for g' in the treble contradicts the modulation. In variation 15 the slur found in the print in bar 28 points out that the bass note g is an appoggiatura. Thus, it seems unnecessary to suppose (as in NBA V/2) that the slur was a misplaced tie such as occurs in the much less accurate print of the B-Minor *Ouverture*. One might note the recurrence of the appoggiatura (without slur) at the same point in variation 25 (see Example 17.9).

The numerous two-note slurs and the somewhat convoluted chromatic lines of variation 15 invite slow, rhythmically free performance. But the tempo mark *Andante*—the only tempo marking in the original print (unless one counts *Alla breve* in variation 22)—may have been intended to warn against playing the movement as an adagio. *Con moto* would be the modern equivalent. The pulse is on the quarter, not the eighth, and as in the previous canon (variation 12), the larger shape of the lines is likely to be obscured if they become too leisurely. The odd ending, with the upper part ascending quietly to d''', resembles some of the gestures used in Bach's recitatives to set questions (Example 17.8). Hence, while the variation marks the end of the first half of the set, it has an open quality that leads toward the second half.

Variation 16 opens with a tonic chord on the downbeat, like many orchestral overtures (e.g., the one in Bach's B-minor orchestral suite). The chord not only reestablishes the major mode but, together with the scale in the right hand, fills in the middle register, which was left empty at the conclusion of variation 15. The first (dotted) section is, as usual, notated *alla breve*, implying a vigorous tempo. Dots on the sixteenths in bars 8–9 presumably indicate both equal values (as opposed to *notes inégales*) and emphatic articulation. The fugue is ostensibly in four voices, but all sound together only for the value of a single eighth (in bar 23). Nevertheless, this section has (unlike variation 10) the nonperiodic rhythm and elided phrasing of a normal fugue. Only its brevity and the absence of a complete fugal exposition in the

EXAMPLE 17.7. Goldberg Variations BWV 988: (a) variation 14, bars 25–26; (b) variation 15, bars 27–28 (each with analysis)

EXAMPLE 17.8. (a) Goldberg Variations BWV 988, variation 15, bar 32; (b) *Saint Matthew Passion* BWV 244, recitative (NBA No. 7), bars 4b–5a

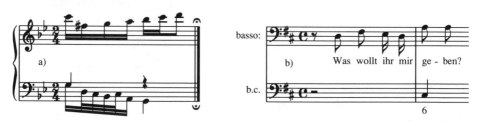

tonic betray the fact that Bach is following a preexistent tonal plan. Within the first exposition the fugue moves from D to E minor, and although the ground bass is treated quite freely, the cadence to E minor arrives on schedule in bar 31, halfway through the section.

Variation 17 is another etudelike duet. Bach's first thought must have been the broken thirds, which climb without a break through two-and-a-half octaves in the first four bars (lower staff); to this he would have added the less regular counterpoint in the right hand.[35] Variation 18 is alone among the canons in its close approach to the *stile antico*. Notated in cut-time, it resembles the *alla breve* (variation 22) not only in its rhythm and notation but in the use of a chain of suspensions as its main motivic idea. The following variation is sometimes regarded as an imitation of lute style and registered accordingly. But variation 19 has little in common with actual lute music. While it employs an arpeggiated motive that might suggest a plucked string instrument, this is only one strand in a three-part contrapuntal texture that is developed permutationally, as in the Sinfonias or some of the preludes of the WTC.

With variation 20 the work resumes the trend toward unabashed virtuosity, taking up the wild leaps, trills, and *batteries* introduced in variation 14. Indeed, from this point onward the duet variations entirely abandon the decorum of ordinary two-part counterpoint. Unlike variation 14, which retained a basic symmetry, variation 20 as well as the next two duet variations moves to new and climactic figuration in its latter stages. The penultimate phrase (bars 25–28) abandons the pretense of two-part counterpoint altogether, dissolving into *batteries* of triplets.

But the following two variations remain relatively restrained. Despite its minor mode and the chromatic embellishment of the *Fundamental-Noten* in the bass, variation 21 does not aim for deep pathos. The motives in sixteenths have few rough edges, flowing relatively smoothly, and the tempo is probably andante, as in an allemande, rather than adagio. The next variation bears the heading *Alla breve*; unlike the somewhat similar variation 18, which seems to represent a canonic duet with bass accompaniment, this is a four-part motet, the bass sharing the main motivic material with the upper parts (bars 9, 17, etc.).

Variation 23 may be the most difficult of the duets, but it is also one of the wittiest. Its material is the G-major scale, treated in close canon (bars 1–7, 13–15) and presented in contrary motion against itself (bars 9–12, 17–20). The idea of introducing climactic figuration in the closing phrase is carried further than in the previous duet, for Bach now doubles the scales in thirds (bar 25) and sixths (bar 31) while again introducing *batteries* (bar 26). A remark by Emanuel Bach suggests that the double scales should be played by repeating the same fingering for each dyad: "With many successive thirds . . . one does better in a quick tempo to continue with the [same] fingers, since crossing them is more difficult."[36] That may be impractical here, since the F♯'s and C♯'s fall rather awkwardly under the fingers, but evidently one can assume a staccato rather than a legato touch.

Variation 24, the canon at the octave, might be a pastorale; the dance is suggested not only by the swaying rhythm but by the brief tonic pedal in the closing bar of each half. The structure differs somewhat from that of the previous canons, since midway through each half the leading voice (*dux*) pauses and exchanges roles with the other canonic part (*comes*). This might be pointed out by a small articulation after the first note of bar 9 and likewise after the third note of bar 24, where the mordent on the next note helps mark the new role of the treble as *dux*.

That Bach paid close attention to the connections between adjacent variations is clear at the start of variation 25, where the dyad g/b heard at the close of the previous variation is repeated with the substitution of b♭. This minimal change announces the last of the minor-mode variations, also the longest and most profound of the "free" settings. While there could hardly be any doubt about the matter, Bach added the tempo mark *adagio* in his own copy, perhaps to emphasize the distinction between this and variation 13, which is similarly scored for a florid treble accompanied by two less active voices on a second keyboard. As always, too slow a tempo may cause the melodic embellishments in the "solo" part to lose urgency and will likely make it impossible to hear the very expressive writing in the two lower parts. These contain simple but impressive counterpoint of their own. For example, the opening of the bass line, already converted into a chromatic descent in the two previous minor-mode variations, is now articulated into a declamatory rhythmic motive (marked by braces in Example 17.9); this consists of an upbeat of three "speaking" notes followed by a "sigh." The motive is later taken up by the tenor (bar 9) and eventually treated in canon by both lower parts (bar 13).

EXAMPLE 17.9.   Goldberg Variations BWV 988, variation 25, bars 27–29a

To be sure, the focus of the movement is on the expressively embellished treble line. The embellishments are thematic, not improvisatory, for the opening bars are recapitulated in the second half; thus, this variation is more a sonata form than any other, even though the recapitulation begins in the subdominant. The most dramatic gesture occurs not at the beginning of the recapitulation (bar 25), as one might expect, but two bars later, where the music modulates back to the tonic. The passage contains an augmented sixth (marked by an asterisk in Example 17.9). This chord, always an extreme harmonic gesture for Bach, had already occurred in bars 3–4, where its appearance so early in the piece was a sign of this variation's special pathos. But the chord has an even greater effect when it is used later, at bar 27, to reverse the modulation into "flat" keys. The subsequent return to the tonic (bars 28–29) coincides with the melody's rapid ascent to d′′′, an extraordinary gesture in a slow movement.

The bright major third at the opening of variation 26 fills the void left by the barren low G at the end of the preceding variation. This is the last of the true duet variations, and it brings the idea of a divided texture to its most extreme development, introducing genuine polymeter as $\frac{3}{4}$ time in one keyboard is juxtaposed against the rare $\frac{18}{16}$ in the other. There is no reason to think that Bach intended any sort of rhythmic "assimilation" of the two lines. Kirnberger, who quoted the upper staff of bar 1 as an example of $\frac{18}{16}$ time (1771–79, 2/1:129–30), does not mention any sort of rhythmic alteration. On the contrary, he tends to support the idea that there are two contrasting meters here, explaining that the sixteenths fall in pairs, not groups of three. Groups of three sixteenths would coincide with the eighth-notes in the other staff, while groups of two create a cross-rhythm (Example 17.10).

EXAMPLE 17.10.   Goldberg Variations BWV 988, variation 26, bars 1–2

It seems less important whether the dotted rhythms are played literally or are adjusted, that is, by making the sixteenth in the dotted figure (lower staff, bars 2ff.) fall with the last sixteenth of the group of six played on the other keyboard. What does matter throughout the movement is that the sarabande rhythm, always present in the lines notated in $\frac{3}{4}$, be clearly heard as such. The variation in effect combines the French dance rhythm with a more or less "Italian" virtuoso line; a similar combination occurs in a piece by Fux that Bach might have known.[37] The dichotomy between the two strands of the texture is strengthened in Bach's *Handexemplar* by the addition of appoggiaturas (presumably short *ports de voix*) to the passages in sarabande rhythm, among them the one shown in the lower staff of Example 17.10, bar 2.

The nearly continual trills in variation 28 recall the closing sections of several late piano works of Beethoven. The resemblance is only superficial, however, and the character of variation 28 should probably not be interpreted as light, feathery, delicate, or however else one might describe the Beethoven pieces. Such trills in a harpsichord piece imply something much more forthright and brilliant, as do the leaps of up to a tenth in the bass and the chords in as many as five voices (bar 9). The piece was perhaps suggested by passages in works by Frescobaldi and later composers in which written-out trills are set against motion in other voices, though none develop the idea so thoroughly or at such length as is the case here.[38]

Written-out trills are also the predominant element in variation 29, where they take the form of parallel $\frac{6}{3}$-chords played by alternating hands. The idea resembles, but does not seem to match exactly, various types of figuration found in the north-

German organ repertory—which is not to say that players did not use it in improvisation. Bach himself frequently used comparable motives in ensemble works,
such as the Third Brandenburg Concerto (first movement). In keyboard playing,
however, the idea must have seemed an extravagant virtuoso gesture, like hand-
crossing. Only here (and briefly, in variation 20) does Bach incorporate it into a
keyboard composition.

Between variation 25 and variation 29 the work has proceeded from its most
introspective to its most extroverted movement. The last variation, the quodlibet,
might have been placed where it is in order to serve as a sort of winding down
preparatory to the closing restatement of the aria. But the evocative title and the
musical quotations contained within inevitably lead one to seek a deeper meaning.
Forkel (1802, 3–4/BR, 301) reported that the Bach family improvised quodlibets at
their annual gatherings, and there survives a fragmentary example for voices and
continuo by the young Bach himself (BWV 524). The one common stylistic element between the latter piece and the quodlibet in the Goldberg Variations is that
both incorporate folk tunes into contrapuntal textures usually associated with more
serious matter. Hence, the somewhat pompous, stolid four-part texture of variation
30 might have represented an affectionate if slightly mocking glance backwards at an
older type of Baroque counterpoint. Each half closes by combining two phrases of
a single tune (*Kraut und Rüben*); the same ingenious device, which is closely
related to stretto, is also used at the end of the Canonic Variations. But the material
reveals its folk origin in the incongruous nature of the melodies—especially the
leaping figures heard after the double bar—and in the heavy-footed rhythms that
articulate each quarter of each bar, even at the cadences.

At least six distinct melodic fragments in the quodlibet are known to be or appear
to be quotations (see Table 17–2; Example 17.11). The most important, those
heard in the top voice at the beginning and end of the first half, have been identified
as coming from two folk-songs (Schulze 1976, 68–69). One of these, *Kraut und
Rüben*, had previously served, under the title *La Capricciosa*, as the basis of Buxtehude's thirty-two *partite* BuxWV 250, a work also in G and forming obvious
parallels to the Goldberg Variations.

Not surprisingly, attempts have been made to discover in variation 30 some

TABLE 17–2. Quotations in the Goldberg Quodlibet

Melodic fragment	Bars in which first used (voice)	Source
A	0–1 (T)	*Ich bin so lang nicht bei dir g'west*
B	3b–4 (T)	quasi-inversion of A; part of same tune?
C	9–10 (S)	continuation of A?
D	13b–15a (A)	part of the same tune?
E	2–3 (A)	*Kraut und Rüben*
F	7–8 (T)	continuation of E

EXAMPLE 17.11.   Goldberg Variations BWV 988, variation 30, chief melodic ideas: (a) bar 1 (tenor); (b) bars 3b–4 (tenor); (c) bars 8b–9 (soprano); (d) bars 13b–15a (alto); (e) bars 2–3 (alto); (f) bars 7–8 (tenor)

programmatic significance. Schulze (1976, 70–72) finds that fragment A belonged to a tune used as a *Kehraus*, that is, a final dance (e.g., for a wedding party). Its use here, especially in conjunction with a sort of wanderer's melody ("Abschieds- oder Wanderlied") might have served as a sort of *envoi* at the end of the set. It seems somewhat silly, however, to suppose that the words associated with fragment A address the aria itself:[39]

Ich bin so lang nicht bei dir g'west	I have for so long a time been away from you

And it is hard to take very seriously the reference to distance or separation in the text associated with fragments E and F:

Kraut und Rüben	Cabbage and beets
haben mich vertrieben,	have driven me away;
hätt' mein' Mutter Fleisch gekocht,	had my mother cooked meat
so wär' ich länger bleiben.	I might have longer stayed.

The direction to repeat the aria after variation 30 suggests that the aria is not really *the* theme of the work but merely one of an infinite number of possible realizations of the *Fundamental-Noten*. The print concludes with the words *e Fine* (and End). But in Bach's *Handexemplar*, at the bottom of the page on which Bach had entered the fourteen canons on the bass notes of the aria (BWV 1087), one finds the word *Etc.* Perhaps this signified that the series could, in principle, continue forever.

18

The Musical Offering
and the Art of Fugue

In his last published keyboard works, Bach continued along the paths followed in Parts 3 and 4 of the *Clavierübung* and in some of the fugues in Part 2 of the *Well-Tempered Clavier*. But despite the dependence on archaic models and the use of *stile antico*, the music is, above all, expressive, occasionally also brilliant. While the writing is difficult—both technically and intellectually—most of it remains music for performance and not merely for contemplation. Yet it is inevitable, due to the unusual format of each work, that studies have tended to treat them as intellectual conundrums or monuments of Bach's contrapuntal skill. Indeed, the superficial devices of canon and fugue embodied in each movement are so closely integrated with the deeper musical content that it is impossible to treat one without also treating the other.

The *Musical Offering* is dated to 1747 with a precision that is unique among Bach's major instrumental works. The *Art of Fugue*, on the other hand, is thought to have grown by accretion through the 1740s. Although the *Art of Fugue* was not published until after Bach's death, an early version was essentially complete by around 1742, and Bach had carried out at least the preliminary stages of its preparation for printing by late 1749. Thus the *Art of Fugue* is not, on the whole, as late as it was once thought to be. A few movements, including the incomplete quadruple fugue, could date from as late as 1749, but it is possible that the two ricercars from the *Musical Offering* were Bach's last entirely new keyboard pieces.

The Musical Offering

Since the final touches on the *Art of Fugue* date from after the completion of the *Musical Offering*, the latter may be considered first. The work grew out of Sebastian's visit in May 1747 to the court of Frederick the Great, where Emanuel Bach was one of the royal harpsichordists. The event was widely reported in the press, and both the King and Bach would have profited from it, at least marginally—the King by the enhancement of his reputation as a patron of the arts and sciences, Bach by the free advertisement of the musical work that, he declared, would soon be engraved. Ironically, a 1748 letter in which Bach mentions the exhaustion of the work's first press-run also refers in passing to the Prussian invasion of Saxony during the 1745 war (BD 1:118 [item 49]/BR, 182).

Although not all the reports give the same details, it appears that Bach, immediately upon his arrival, was asked to improvise on the King's fortepianos, playing among other things a three-part fugue on a theme by the King himself.[1] The King was a capable composer—many of his flute sonatas and several concertos survive—and the chromatic subject might have seemed to Frederick suitably archaic in style for fugal treatment while also expressive and capable of eliciting the sort of contrapuntal complexity for which Bach's music was known.[2] The Berlin newspaper account pointed out that the King himself played the subject for Bach; this might have seemed an extraordinary gesture of respect toward a mere musician, especially one who was titular Capellmeister to Frederick's arch-rival, the Elector of Saxony. It evidently made an impression on Bach, who referred to it in his own dedication in the published work. Within a few months of his visit, Bach had composed the thirteen pieces making up the complete work, had had it engraved and printed, and had sent a specially prepared exemplar to Berlin.[3] The first printing sold out, or, rather, was mostly given away, within a year. A second printing, also of 100 copies, evidently sold out as well, but years later Emanuel Bach could write to Forkel that the work was easily obtainable in manuscript copies from publishers like Breitkopf.[4]

Because of certain peculiarities of the format in which the work was published, most discussions of it have become enmeshed in considerations of the proper ordering of its very diverse parts. The work is composed of two fugues—called ricercars—in three and six voices, respectively; a trio-sonata in four movements; and ten canons in two to six voices. Only the ricercars and two of the canons are readily playable on solo keyboard. The canons, as well as the sonata, might have been envisioned for performance by Frederick and his musicians. But the canons, like other such works, would have served primarily as intellectual amusements, even though a few are somewhat more substantial than most such pieces. The work cannot have been intended for integral public performance, and Bach probably had no "specific order" in mind when he published the work (Wolff 1971, 408). This means, incidentally, that the parallel drawn by Kirkendale (1980) between Bach's purported ordering of this work and an oration in the manner of Quintilian is arbitrary.[5] The two ricercars and the sonata are obviously the main elements, performable as self-contained pieces, and the pragmatic solution adopted in NBA VIII/1 of placing these first, followed by the ten canons, seems eminently reasonable.

While the ricercars are no doubt masterpieces, they probably do not achieve the supreme level reached by parts of the *Art of Fugue* or the Goldberg Variations. The great work in the *Musical Offering* is surely the sonata; the ricercars are too free in form to have concentrated Bach's powers of invention at the highest level. Some of the oddities of both works stem from the nature of Frederick's theme, which is somewhat longer and more homogeneous rhythmically than the average subject in Bach's mature keyboard fugues. Neither ricercar develops the subject in canon or in any of the other types of learned counterpoint that Bach had by that date fully "researched" in the Art of Fugue. Instead, in the expository passages the subject tends to be treated somewhat like a cantus firmus, that is, as a framework for more lively counter-material, while, in the episodes, fragments of the subject are developed imitatively. Neither ricercar does much with its countersubject, although in each case a leaping motive from the countersubject serves as the basis of the final episode.

The Three-Part Ricercar BWV 1079/1 (NBA No. I/1)

The term *ricercar* is most often used today, as in the early Baroque, to refer to an archaic, unusually strict fugue. But it can also refer to a type of improvised prelude, as Wolff (1991a, 330–31) recognized, citing Walther's (1732, 525–26) definition of the term. Hence, it is possible that Bach meant his two ricercars to reflect the two types, the three-part piece corresponding with the initial improvisation on the royal subject that Bach played at Potsdam, the six-part piece with Bach's later working out of the theme in strict counterpoint, away from the keyboard.[6] This would explain why only the six-part ricercar was set out in open score, like the ricercars of Frescobaldi and Froberger, while the three-part ricercar appeared in regular two-staff notation.

It seems unlikely, however, that the three-part piece corresponds exactly with what Bach actually played at Berlin. Bach could hardly have remembered it perfectly, and one would not expect a genuine improvisation on an unfamiliar subject to contain the considerable quantity of nearly verbatim recapitulation found in the three-part ricercar. All the same, improvising a three-part fugue on the long but rhythmically rather simple subject might have been relatively easy for Bach. Particularly where the subject employs long, equal note-values, it would have involved essentially the same much-rehearsed skills involved in playing a chorale fantasia.

If, however, the piece is not a faithful transcription of Bach's improvisation, then it need not be regarded as peculiarly suited to the fortepiano, as Wolff (1987a) has suggested. Had the ricercar been conceived for the piano, one might have expected it to include the dynamic indications already found in Emanuel Bach's Prussian and Württemberg Sonatas, both published in the early 1740s. But the ricercar contains not even an occasional echo, let alone a pianissimo or any of the gradual changes of dynamic level that were indicated in works of the period by closely spaced pianos and fortes. Bach himself, in the dedication, says only that the King set forth the theme on a "clavier"—that is, a keyboard instrument, not the King's own flute—and there is no instrumental designation at all in the score.

A player can, of course, use the dynamic capabilities of the fortepiano to shape the numerous "sigh" motives—which play an important role in the piece beginning at bar 108—and perhaps even to produce what Williams (1983a, 50n) calls "crescendo-decrescendo expressiveness." But introducing dynamic contrasts in, say, bars 38–41 (as envisioned in NBA VIII/1, KB, 116–17), would merely underscore a contrast already articulated by antiphonal exchanges between different voices in different registers. While this might be musically effective, it would be no less arbitrary here than in the numerous other "galant" or "improvisatory" pieces by Bach in which one could introduce the same types of dynamic contrasts.[7]

Not counting the opening exposition (bars 1–30), the piece falls into two halves, the end of the first being marked by an arrival in the dominant minor (bar 109). The two halves are roughly equal in length but formally self-contained and very different in character, reflecting the different character of the two halves of the subject itself. The first half has a symmetrical design in which three expositions alternate with two episodes; the second episode is a recapitulation of the latter part of the first (bars 87–94 || 38–45).[8] Despite this "architectonic" design, the texture is often only pseudo-contrapuntal; the triplets in the episodes are presented in simple antiphonal exchanges between the upper parts, while the bass entries at bars 46 and 95 are accompanied in a sort of *brisé* style.

There is an immediate change of character at the beginning of the second half. The first half is characterized above all by the flowing, sequential character of the triplet episode, which is based on arpeggiation and thus related to the first half of the subject, whose opening notes furnish its bass line. The second half not only introduces "sigh" motives but makes greater use of harsher, more chromatic voice-leading derived from the latter part of the subject. This becomes explicit at bar 115, which introduces a motive consisting of a chromatic scale-fragment in eighth-notes; the motive is a rhythmic diminution of the latter portion of the subject.

Yet, if the first half of the piece is strict in design but free in detail, the reverse is true of the second half, whose intensely chromatic counterpoint is spun out in a more discursive manner. The long, somewhat rambling episode at the beginning comes to a sudden pause at one point (bar 122), only to give way to a little *fuga per diminutionem* that is not pursued further. A few bars later (bar 128) a series of triplets runs in and then immediately disappears. This passage appears to be an improvisatory link to the recapitulatory episode that follows, but it is curious that the triplets should quote the subject of the D-minor fugue of WTC2—another relatively free fugue, with a subject whose two halves are related to one another not unlike those of the royal theme.

Hans David, referring to the long episode as a "fantasia," criticized it as a foreign intrusion, throwing the entire fugue out of "balance" (1945, 107–10). This, however, stemmed from a view of the episode as interrupting a "recapitulation" that begins at bar 87 and continues—after the episode—in bars 129–40. Evidently seeking here the same "monumental conception and impeccable delivery" that he found in the six-part ricercar, David (1945, 134) regarded the absence of a clear geometric symmetry or "balance" as a flaw. Yet the seemingly arbitrary nature of the episode might well have been an intentional reflection of its origin in an improvisation. Moreover, Bach seems to have taken pains to underscore the essentially binary form of the movement. While the second half contains relatively little recapitulation, it concludes with a restatement of the same passage that ended the first half, thus—as in the somewhat comparable F-major fugue of WTC2—ensuring that the piece will give at least the impression of possessing formal closure.

The Six-Part Ricercar BWV 1079/2 (formerly 1079/5; NBA No. I/2)

In the original print the six-part ricercar, together with the puzzle canons, was accompanied by the somewhat contrived acrostic *Regis Iussu Cantio Et Reliqua Canonica Arte Resoluta* (A Composition [literally, Song] by Command of the King, with a Supplement Solved by Canonic Art).[9] This has been explained as a reference to the fact that Bach had used his own theme for the improvisation of a six-part fugue during the Potsdam visit; here Bach makes up for not having used the King's own subject.[10] Bach's autograph has survived for this piece alone (in DSB P 226); it is a fair copy, differing only in a few spots from the print, which invariably gives stronger and presumably later readings.[11] Only once, in bar 62, is the revised version somewhat unsatisfactory; having discovered parallel fifths in the original, Bach was forced to make an awkward passage even harder to play.[12]

The autograph shows that, despite the use of open-score notation in the print, Bach conceived the work as a keyboard piece, writing it on two staves as he also did the *Fuga a 3 soggetti* in the *Art of Fugue*. While the piece is perfectly playable on the harpsichord, other instruments, especially the organ, also come to mind. Indeed, Bach's visit to Potsdam included an organ recital at which he could also have improvised on the royal theme (see BD 2:435 [item 554]/BR, 176). But the six-part ricercar does not require the use of organ pedals, and the clear tone of the harpsichord may actually be preferable in the many dense chords in the lower register (e.g., in bars 29ff. and 79ff.). In addition, the leaping motive in the last episode (bars 90–98) is greatly enlivened by the crisp articulation attainable on a good harpsichord. To be sure, several passages, notably that leading up to the alto entry in bar 86, contain voice-crossings that cannot be conveyed to an audience on *any* keyboard instrument—not even the piano, whose relatively dull attacks might render the thick polyphony especially opaque.

The work is built around twelve statements of the subject, six of which form the opening exposition, the remainder occurring singly, in alternation with episodes. The opening exposition is unavoidably long, constituting more than one-third of the work if one includes as part of the exposition an extension that leads to the first full cadence (bar 39b). As one might expect, this exposition culminates in massive polyphony in six parts, made more impressive by the fact that the last entrance is in the bass (bars 25ff.). But in the course of the next few sections the texture lightens while momentum builds, and something like a trio-sonata texture emerges in the three-part episode over a walking bass at bar 70; it is in this episode that the piece reaches its furthest remove from the tonic (B$^\flat$ minor at bar 73).

Elsewhere, however, this is a more severe work than the three-part ricercar, avoiding the easy-going sequential episodes of the latter. The three largest episodes are fugatos on short themes derived from the subject, using counterpoint that is in some respects even more rigorous than that of the expositions. In the second episode (bars 52–58), three melodic ideas pass permutationally through all six parts, while the last episode (bars 90–98) is a double fugato whose combination of leaping figures (taken from the countersubject) with sustained chromatic lines (from the subject) makes it the climax of the piece.

Inevitably, the six voices do not have the rhythmic independence that they would have in an ensemble work. The extension of the opening exposition (bars 30–39) is the longest passage in which all six voices are present continuously, and it is essentially a ready-made sequential formula in which the texture divides into two sets of three parts, each moving in contrary motion. As Wolff (1968, 127) notes, an earlier and somewhat simpler version of the passage occurs in the *Pièce d'orgue* BWV 572, probably composed at Weimar (Example 18.1). The passage in the

EXAMPLE 18.1.   (a) *Pièce d'orgue* in G, BWV 572, bars 29–32; (b) *Ricercar a 6*, BWV 1079/2, bars 29–30 [*sic*]

ricercar is the piece's one extended sequence, and the one phrase that is recapitulated (bars 79–80 || 29–30, varied and transposed).

The Canons BWV 1079/4a and 1079/4i (formerly 1079/3a and 1079/6; NBA Nos. III/1, III/9)

Only the two *Canones a 2* arc playable on solo harpsichord. One, the first of the *Canones diversi super thema regium* (Various Canons on the Royal Theme), is a crab-canon that can be played on the harpsichord as a *pièce croisée* (as suggested in NBA VIII/1). The other is the first of two puzzle-canons printed on the same sheets as the six-part ricercar, part of the *Reliqua* mentioned in the title of the latter. The canon bears its own title, *Quaerendo invenietis* ("By seeking ye shall find," a paraphrase of Matt. 7:7 or Luke 11:9). The solution printed in the appendix of NBA VIII/1 and other editions is the most graceful, but Bach must have been aware of the existence of at least one other possible solution.[13]

Like most puzzle-canons, this is a perpetual canon, meaning that it repeats endlessly without ever reaching a final cadence. The much longer canons of this type in the *Art of Fugue* are provided with codas that bring them to an end. Perhaps this means that in Bach's day one might have improvised some such coda in a piece like this one, after repeating the main body of the composition as many times as one liked. The fermata customarily added on the downbeat of bar 9 is only a stopgap, and the underlying harmonic progression hardly constitutes a satisfactory cadence.

The Art of Fugue

Alone among Bach's late keyboard works, the *Art of Fugue* was apparently planned from the beginning as a complete and systematic exposition of contrapuntal techniques. While one could find any number of earlier pedagogic collections of fugues and related works, there was no exact precedent for such a monumental collection of self-contained fugal compositions, all using one principal theme. Clearly, Bach intended to make a substantial contribution to the repertory of learned keyboard fugues that extended back to the time of Sweelinck and Frescobaldi. He may also have thought of the *Art of Fugue* as a treatise in the form of concrete examples; at any rate, this is how the work was advertised when it appeared about a year after his death.[14] The *Art of Fugue* would thus have taken its place alongside earlier encyclopedic musical textbooks, such as Fux's *Gradus ad Parnassum*, Rameau's *Traité*, and Mattheson's *Vollkommener Capellmeister*, the last of which even contains what has been seen as a direct challenge to Bach to write such a work.[15] Indeed, Bach has been connected with a "learned tradition" of counterpoint cultivated in north German Baroque circles and preserved in such sources as the "Sweelinck" theory manuscripts.[16] Nevertheless, Bach's own teaching reportedly "omitted all the dry sorts [*trockene Arten*] of counterpoint given by Fux and others"; thus, it is not surprising that his own treatise on fugue eschews elementary examples and consists solely of actual compositions.[17]

In this, Bach had a number of recent models. Fux's *Gradus* (of which Bach owned a copy) had included, beside the numerous illustrations of species counterpoint, several complete pieces, among them Mass movements and other liturgical compositions in *stile antico*. In 1735, Mattheson had published a collection of fugues illustrating various contrapuntal techniques; these have been described as "*galant*" (Stauffer 1983b, 366). In its somewhat ostentatiously archaic notation and style the *Art of Fugue* allied itself with the older and more conservative representatives of the contrapuntal tradition. But it contains too many expressive, galant, even virtuoso elements to represent the pure *stile antico*.

This is not to say that the *Art of Fugue* is free from abstraction. For example, it is not always clear whether the occasionally extreme chromaticism is expressive or is being used for its own sake, as in certain fugal pieces of the early Baroque. The bizarre chromaticism of the Augmentation Canon gives it a peculiar musical flavor not unlike that of several movements in the Goldberg Variations. Moreover, the prevailing style certainly is retrospective. The work was printed in open score, most movements notated *alla breve*. Deeper echoes of older style include the suggestions of modal writing in some movements and the preponderance of designs defined not by tonal considerations but by the introduction of different contrapuntal techniques or new subjects and countersubjects in each section. Many of the fugues lack clearly defined episodes, consisting of a nearly seamless contrapuntal fabric devoid of the clear structural articulations typical of eighteenth-century music. Even the overall form of the work—a series of imitative pieces based on rhythmic and melodic variants of the same subject—might reflect archaic models, although the individual sections of Frescobaldi's and Froberger's capriccios, ricercars, and similar works are not so independent of one another as are Bach's *contrapuncti* and canons, each of which is a distinct composition.

As in the works of Bach's early-Baroque predecessors, however, the theme is subjected to greater variation as the work proceeds.[18] In keeping with the *stile antico*, the theme at first takes simple, unembellished forms. But from the outset it differs from a genuine sixteenth-century subject in its clear tonal implications, alternating between tonic and dominant (tonic and subdominant when inverted). The triadic structure of the subject not only defines it harmonically but makes it readily capable of combination with itself and with other subjects in each of its various forms (inversion, augmentation, etc.). In addition, Bach treats the subject freely and does not insist upon exact, canonic imitation except in the pieces actually designated as canons. Tonal answers as well as more radically altered forms of the subject are used whenever convenient—especially in the more complex fugues— and throughout the work Bach treats fugue as a fluid, sometimes even an improvisational form, never as a mechanical exercise.

In light of its unique character and complexity, it is perhaps inevitable that the *Art of Fugue* has been interpreted as the expression of philosophical and theological abstractions of a sometimes remarkably rarefied nature, most recently by Eggebrecht (1984) and Chafe (1991). Chafe (1991, 54) declares that the "great four-part triple fugue [Contrapunctus 11] . . . gloriously transcends its own figural machinery." But this presupposes that the "machinery"—that is, the musical working out of the thematic material—is incidental to some higher purpose, in this case the introduction of the B-A-C-H motive as "an emblem of his [Bach's] subjective independence" (Chafe 1991, 62). Yet, it is problematical to locate the "tremendously expressive content" of such a work primarily in subjective associations drawn from its thematic material. For the latter can achieve its musical effect only as a result of being integrated into a larger whole, that is, the composition considered in all its musical complexity. The romantically inspired effort to find both cosmic truths and autobiographical references in the work, even when not based on equivocal evidence, tends to devalue Bach's achievement, inasmuch as it focuses attention upon a few rather superficial elements while disregarding the work's immediately practical and expressive qualities.

Other recent scholarship has underscored the practicality of the *Art of Fugue* as a solo keyboard work, and it is no longer uncommon for it to be performed or recorded as such. Thus, it may be necessary to point out that the organization of the work makes it clear that it was intended to serve pedagogic and theoretical, not practical, ends. Unlike the *Well-Tempered Clavier*, which is organized by key, the *Art of Fugue* eschews tonal variety, the order of movements being determined by the contrapuntal technique illustrated in each. The work does not offer lessons in a wide variety of keyboard genres, being restricted to "fugue," broadly defined. While the *Art of Fugue* remains "clavier" music, Bach cannot have expected most purchasers to play it so much as to study it. Nevertheless, that they would have done so at a keyboard instrument was apparently self-evident; Mattheson assumed as much in a brief 1752 report of the work (BD 3:13–14 [item 647]/ BR, 269), and in the twentieth century the case for keyboard use has been made so strongly that it can be considered closed (see below).

Title, Origin, and Ordering of Movements

Whether or not Bach himself gave the work its familiar title is unknown. The title-page of the autograph, though it includes the words *Kunst der Fuga* [*sic*], is in the hand of Bach's son-in-law Altnikol, and the use of the term *Kunst* in the print seems suspiciously modern, though it has a close parallel in Marpurg's *Kunst der Clavierspielen* (Berlin, 1750). It is conceivable that Marpurg himself supplied the title, for Marpurg wrote the preface for the reimpression of 1752.[19] Yet Sebastian is known to have taken care over the titles of the canons, which were revised at his instigation.[20] Thus, it is hard to believe that he did not also decide upon a title for the collection as a whole, on which he worked for eight years or more. In any case, the word *Kunst* ("art") had not yet acquired all of its present connotations; the term probably had more of the sense still seen in the expression "arts and sciences"; that is, it set music on the level of a learned discipline like law or classical philology.[21]

If the first word in the title should probably be understood somewhat archaically, this is certainly the case with the term *Fuge*, which refers here to both the fugues and the canons. As in writings of the sixteenth and seventeenth centuries, "fugue" here means simply "imitation," not a genre of composition. Marpurg (1753–54) used the term in the same way in his *Abhandlung von der Fuge*, distinguishing (1:16) between "periodic" and "canonic" fugues. Here Bach entirely avoids using the term "fugue" as a label for an individual piece, employing instead the term *contrapunctus*. Even that may be less a title than a way of indicating that each piece is an illustration of a particular type of counterpoint (= Lat. *contrapunctus*). Perhaps another reason for using the term was that some of the pieces are not really fugues in the usual sense. The opening bars of Contrapunctus 6, for example, combine different forms of the subject, all in the tonic, no voice entering in direct imitation of any other.

The history of the composition and printing of the *Art of Fugue* has been intensely studied, yet many questions remain unanswered and probably unaswerable. Twelve fugues and two canons are found in the autograph (DSB P 200), which, though largely completed by about 1742, is a fair or revising copy; individual movements could be significantly earlier.[22] Alterations continued to be made in the autograph at least until 1749; some in the hand of the young Johann Christoph Friedrich Bach (Sebastian's second youngest son, then seventeen years old) were presumably made at a time when Sebastian's illness or blindness prevented him from entering them himself. The print reveals further changes, the most obvious ones involving the order of the individual pieces and the addition of several further ones.

Although the work is unlikely to have been completely engraved and printed until after Bach's death, the plates for some of the pieces may have been prepared under his direction. All were engraved—more properly, etched—through a process by which the image of a specially prepared manuscript page could be transferred to a copper printing plate, which therefore preserved most details of the original.[23] This explains the autograph character of many pages in the original print, once thought to have been due to Bach's having carried out the engraving himself. Bach no doubt planned the entire publication in the same detailed manner as he had the *Musical Offering* and the *Clavierübung*, down to the placement of each page turn. But at some point the original plan was altered, probably because of the addition of new pieces, perhaps also because of the expansion of existing ones. It is far from certain that Bach had arrived at a firm conclusion regarding the organization of the print at the time of his death, but the form in which it eventually appeared cannot have been correct.

Despite numerous efforts to discover Bach's intentions, claims to have resolved the "ordering problems" in the *Art of Fugue* have not yet been universally accepted. What is clear is that the print contained several pieces that do not belong, while a portion of one piece, the quadruple fugue, was left out. The mistakes were evidently due to misunderstandings by the editors—presumably Altnikol and C. P. E. Bach—and the engraver Johann Heinrich Schübler.[24] But it may be unfair to accuse the editors of the *Art of Fugue* of "incompetence and carelessness" (Wolff 1975, 75). The elder Bach left a large legacy, both musical and material, which had to be equitably divided between several heirs. At his death there were more pressing matters than the identification and proper ordering of the various portions of the work, including the individual sheets of music paper on which those portions not yet engraved might have been written. Emanuel, who might already have been occupied with the writing and preparation for printing of his own treatise (C. P. E. Bach 1753–62), not to mention his duties at the Berlin court, nevertheless took it upon himself to see the work into print. But it failed to sell even after Marpurg added his preface, and Emanuel was forced to sell the plates a few years later.

The original ordering of the pieces in the autograph, given in Table 18–1, already presented a coherent arrangement, as Wolff (1983c) has shown. The first four pieces (as yet untitled) developed the subject in *rectus* and *inversus* forms, first separately, then in combination. The style, initially quite severe, grew more flexible in the remaining fugues, which came in pairs, the last three pairs alternating with canons. As in the print, the work proceeded toward increasingly learned counterpoint, and the theme underwent greater melodic and rhythmic variation in the more complex pieces.

The relatively pristine scores of the first few pieces in the autograph imply that they had been composed first. Perhaps Bach had originally planned to write the entire work in a fairly pure *stile antico*, only gradually allowing more modern elements of style to enter. In any case, while the autograph was probably begun as a fair copy, by the time Bach was copying the seventh piece (later called Contrapunctus 6) he was revising as he wrote, at least occasionally, and the manuscript took on the character of a revision score.[25] Further revisions—made in some lost manuscript, not the surviving autograph—were carried out for the printed version. These included new endings for the first three fugues and a new opening section for the second double fugue. Bach also rewrote the Augmentation Canon and revised (or authorized the revision of) the rhythmic notation of many pieces.[26]

The movements wholly lacking in the autograph must be relatively late. These

TABLE 18–1.   *Art of Fugue:* Contents of the autograph (DSB P 200)

P 200	SWV*	Description of movement**
1	1	fugue, R
2	3	fugue, I
3	2	fugue, R
4	5	counter fugue, R + I
5	9	double fugue, counterpoint at the 12th
6	10a	double fugue, counterpoint at the 10th
7	6	counter fugue with diminution
8	7	counter fugue with diminution and augmentation
9	15	canon at the octave—twice, first in one-part "puzzle" notation
10	8	3-part triple fugue
11	11	4-part triple fugue
12	(14)	augmentation canon—twice, second time in 1-part "puzzle" notation
13	12	4-part mirror fugue—R version written above I on 8-staff systems
14	13	3-part mirror fugue—I version written above R on 6-staff systems
(15)	(14)	augmentation canon (intermediate version)

*Numbering within BWV 1080; corresponds with the print for Nos. 1–9, 11–13
**R = using *rectus* version of subject
I = using *inversus*

pieces—a new fugue (Contrapunctus 4), the fragmentary quadruple fugue, and a second pair of canons—upset the original plan. Table 18–2 includes a reconstruction of the print as Bach might have intended it to appear; the table follows the controversial suggestion of Butler (1983a) that the work was meant to conclude with the canons rather than with the fragmentary quadruple fugue.[27] All titles are given as they appear in the print, although some of these may be contrary to Bach's plan. The last four entries in the table are for the additional pieces whose inclusion by the editors of the print was also probably contrary to Bach's intentions. Of these, the first three are for alternate versions of other pieces also in the print. The last work, the chorale fantasia *Wenn wir in höchsten Nöthen sein* (BWV 668a), was included solely to compensate for the incompleteness of the last fugue, as the brief prefatory notice in the first edition (1751) explained.[28]

Bach was reported to have dictated the organ chorale shortly before his death, and from this has arisen a good deal of romantic speculation, put to rest in Wolff (1974). The piece is generally traced to the shorter Weimar setting of the same melody in the *Orgelbüchlein* (BWV 641), but it is possible that both pieces go back indepen-

TABLE 18–2. *Art of Fugue:* Hypothetical Order, with Supplementary Pieces

Title (as in print)	Numbering of movement in P 200	*print*	SWV	Remarks
Contrapunctus 1 [R]	1	1	1	Rebarred in $\frac{2}{2}$ (not $\frac{4}{2}$), new ending
Contrapunctus 2 [R]	3	2	2	Revisions as in No. 1
Contrapunctus 3 [I]	2	3	3	Revisions as in No. 1
Contrapunctus 4 [I]	—	4	4	Not in P 200
Contrapunct us 5 [R + I]	4	5	5	P 200: ¢. Print: c
Contrapunctus 6 a 4 in Stylo Francese	7	6	6	Changes in rhythmic notation
Contrapunctus 7 a 4 per Augment et Diminut:	8	7	7	
Contrapunctus 8 a 3	10	8	8	P 200: $\frac{2}{4}$. Print: ¢ values doubled
Contrapunctus 9 a 4 alla Duodecima	5	9	9	Print: values doubled
Contrapunctus 10 a 4 alla Decima	—	10	10	= No. 6 of P 200 with new opening, values doubled
Contrapunctus 11 a 4	11	11	11	P 200: $\frac{2}{4}$. Print: ¢, values doubled, much revised
Contrapunctus inversus a 4	12 (top)	12/2	12/1	P 200: $\frac{3}{4}$. Print: $\frac{3}{2}$, values doubled
Contrapunctus inversus 12 a 4	12 (bottom)	12/1	12/2	Print: alterations as in preceding
Contrapunctus inversus a 3	13 (top)	13/2	13/1	P 200: $\frac{2}{4}$. Print: c, values doubled
Contrapunctus a 3	13 (bottom)	13/1	13/2	P 200: $\frac{2}{4}$. Print: ¢ (error for c?), values doubled
Fuga a 3 Soggetti	—	20	19	Quadruple fugue: autograph in P 200, Beilage 3
Canon alla Ottava	9	16	15	
Canon alla Decima [in] Contrapunto alla Terza	—	17	16	Not in P 200
Canon alla Duodecima in Contrapunto alla Quinta	—	18	17	Not in P 200
Canon per Augmentationem in Contrario Motu	15	15	14	Autograph in P 200, Beilage 1. No. 12 of P 200 is early version

TABLE 18–2.   *Art of Fugue* (continued)

| Title (as in print) | Numbering of movement in | | SWV | Remarks |
	p 200	print		
Contrap: a 4	6	14	10a	Early version of No. 10
Fuga a 2 Clav:	—	19/1	18/1	Arrangement of No. 13/2; autograph in P 200, Beilage 2
Alio modo. Fuga a 2 Clav.	—	19/2	18/2	Arrangement of No. 13/1; autograph in P 200, Beilage 2
Wenn wir in höchsten Nöthen sein	—	21	(BWV 668a)	Early version of BWV 668

dently to a simpler earlier version now lost. Exactly what Bach dictated is, and probably will remain, unclear, but it might have been no more than the small alterations made by Friedrich Bach in several movements surviving in the autograph. The severe yet chromatic style of the fantasia is not inappropriate to the *Art of Fugue*, but it has nothing to do with the subject or tonality of the other pieces and unlike them includes an independent pedal part.

As in most of Bach's other collections, the question of ordering is tangential to the music itself, since the pieces cannot have been meant for cyclic performance. Certainly the work is not a set of variations in the usual sense of the word.[29] There are, however, some indications that the first four fugues in the early version did form a closed, unified group (discussed below).

Performance and Editions

The view that the *Art of Fugue* is best presented by instrumental ensemble seems to have been largely abandoned.[30] The existence of a tradition of keyboard performance dating back at least to the beginning of the nineteenth century has been amply demonstrated.[31] And the ranges of the individual voices, the publication in score (not parts), the absence of continuo figures, and the splitting of some voices into two or even three parts near the ends of several fugues all violate the conventions of eighteenth-century instrumental music. Inner voices sometimes have brief, fragmentary entries solely for the purpose of filling in chords, and occasionally the texture approaches that of the *style brisé*.[32] With the exception of the four-part mirror fugue, the fugues are no less idiomatic than Bach's other keyboard works in learned style while containing little that is particularly suitable to other instruments.

Although the keyboard character of the work becomes self-evident the more one plays it, it is difficult to find unequivocal evidence to support the use of any particular keyboard instrument. Mattheson had mentioned the work as evidence for the superiority of German musicians in organ-playing and fugue-writing, but this does not mean that he took the *Art of Fugue* itself to be primarily an organ work. In any case, the work is entirely *manualiter,* and the style of the bass is unlike that of Bach's pedal parts. Moreover, both the bass and the upper parts extend beyond the ranges employed in Bach's organ music; in particular, the canon at the tenth, which opens with long-sustained notes that might otherwise suggest use of the organ, extends upward to d‴.[33] While the organ—or the modern piano—can of course be used to advantage in many movements, the same considerations that point to the harpsichord as the primary medium in other collections (e.g., the WTC) apply here. As in the six-part ricercar, no one player on one keyboard instrument can render with complete clarity the voice-crossings found in some movements. But the whole idea of somehow conveying to a modern audience the contrapuntal detail of this, or any, Bach keyboard work seems chimerical; the best that can be hoped for is that listeners will glimpse the richness of the texture and the profound expression of most of the movements.

Perhaps more fundamental than the question of the specific keyboard instrument is that of practicality, for the music is supremely difficult to play, especially if taken at the relatively lively tempi implied by the *alla breve* notation of most movements. Much of the *Art of Fugue* seems to abandon entirely the norms of idiomatic Baroque keyboard writing, so that it is virtually impossible to sight-read—a possible explanation for the work's original lack of success in an age when rehearsal in the modern sense was a rare luxury. As in many a twentieth-century piece—and in the six-part ricercar—it is necessary to work out fingerings with great care and to follow them religiously if one is to play without stumbling. The vocal model for many of the fugues may suggest a hyperlegato approach, but through the more articulate manner of performance advocated here for comparable works (e.g., the C-major fugue in WTC1), one can spare oneself many finger substitutions and other unnecessary complications of nineteenth-century fingering.

Only two pieces, the mirror fugues, require abnormally wide stretches of the hand and may have to be divided between two players. The numerous voice-crossings in these pieces make it preferable for the players to use different instruments, as Bach himself directed in his arrangement of the three-part mirror fugue. The arrangement includes an additional free fourth part, and while probably not meant for publication, it appeared in the print under the rubric *a 2 Clav:*—the abbreviation "Clav." (*Claviere*) here obviously meaning separate keyboard instruments. A single player might have been able to manage both mirror fugues more readily on an instrument with the narrow keys that Bach's pupil Agricola evidently favored.[34]

There remains the question of how successful the *Art of Fugue* is in strictly musical terms. Since it is not really a set of variations, it is less a "cycle" than the Goldberg Variations, and each movement must therefore be considered on its own merits. The canons, while no doubt successful as demonstrations of compositional technique, are probably too long, the four-part mirror fugue and some of the other contrapuncti perhaps too contrived to be consistently engaging. Yet individual movements, especially the two triple fugues, must rank among the greatest fugues ever written. In any case the work as a whole must not be judged on the basis of well-meaning but misconceived attempts to perform it in one sitting, which are bound to try the patience of both performer and listener.

The *Art of Fugue* has appeared in many editions, and that in BG 25/1 remains serviceable. More recently it has appeared in editions by Peter Williams, Christoph Wolff, and Davitt Maroney.[35] Williams's edition is in open score, while Wolff and Maroney set out the work in two-staff keyboard score. Wolff's edition, moreover, is in two volumes, the first giving the version of the autograph, thus simplifying performance of the early version. The old Czerny reduction (Leipzig, 1838; many reprints) is inaccurate but remains interesting for the restraint with which Beethoven's most famous student added "expression" markings. Few today will want to use Tovey's edition in score, but his commentary (1931) has not been surpassed.[36]

Contrapuncti 1–5

The print opens with a pair of fugues using the *rectus* version of the subject, followed by a pair using the inversion. In the fifth piece the two forms of the subject are combined. Contrapunctus 4, the second *inversus* fugue, was a late addition lacking in the autograph, as were the codas in each of the first three fugues. Moreover, the places of Contrapuncti 2 and 3 were reversed, and what is now Contrapunctus 3 originally ended with the dominant chord on the downbeat of bar 78. Such an ending might have been intended to form an unbroken connection between this and the following movement (as argued in Bagnall 1975, 60), but it might also have been meant to sound like a modal cadence such as occurs at the end of each of the Kyries in the third part of the *Clavierübung*. The fugue, however, is clearly tonal, and the cadence on the dominant would constitute a rather superficial gesture toward modality.

While Bach eliminated this particular archaism, the original group of four fugues remains unusually old-fashioned even within the *Art of Fugue*. Many passages lack the well-defined harmonic rhythm and strong sense of harmonic directionality that one expects in a late-Baroque work, and the modulatory range is very limited. There are few strong cadences—that is, cadences with root motion in the bass; in Contrapunctus 1 the only full cadence is the one at the end. With the avoidance of full cadences comes an avoidance of sequence and other types of regular harmonic patterning, no doubt in emulation of antique polyphony; this gives at least the impression of an unbroken web of independently flowing voices.

While the "seamless" style obscures the formal outlines of the first three fugues, Bach's tendency toward clarity and logical structure seems to have reasserted itself in Contrapunctus 4, the fugue that was added in the printed version. This piece, though presumably forming the second part of a pair with Contrapunctus 3, is much longer, possessing a relatively clear tonal design articulated by the regular alternation of expositions and episodes, the latter all constructed of sequences employing similar material.[37] The comparatively modern style of Contrapunctus 4 makes the following fugue seem like a stylistic regression when the pieces of the print are played in order. Nevertheless, the "counter fugue" Contrapunctus 5 forms the logical conclusion to the first group, and this perhaps justifies its somewhat grandiose coda in six voices (already present in the version of the autograph).

Of the four original fugues in this group, Contrapunctus 1 is the simplest in style and, for modern audiences, the most accessible, thanks to the surprisingly dramatic pauses and chords just before the ending. Just how to treat these chords and rests (bars 70b–72) is something of a problem for the performer, but the temptation to treat the written values freely should probably be resisted; Bach, as usual, notated the passage very precisely. The reason for the extension of the piece is not entirely clear, but in the earlier version it ended with the long episode (or coda) in bars 63–74; the last five bars, added for the print, contain an additional statement of the subject in the tenor. The abruptness of the original ending (pointed out by Bagnall 1975, 59) was not necessarily to the piece's disadvantage, but most of the other contrapuncti revert to Bach's older practice of concluding shortly after a statement of the subject. The new ending brings the first piece in the collection closer to the pattern that had become established as Bach completed the other pieces. As in several of the other contrapuncti (2, 6), the structure of the first fugue seems free, almost improvisatory; there are no lasting modulations, hence no tonal design, and the order of entries does not follow any obvious pattern. There is a recurring episodic passage, but only the material of two voices is recapitulated, the others adding free counterpoint (bars 16–20 || 35–39 || 66b–70a).

Contrapunctus 2 is marked by its thoroughgoing dotted rhythms, but in both autograph and print these look as if they might have been later additions. The four-note slurs were certainly added; they are present only in the print, and only through bar 21, but are presumably to be extended throughout the piece. The slurs imply that the dotting should be relatively gentle—as in *notes inégales*—and not exaggerated as in an overture. The smoother interpretation would be in keeping with the primarily stepwise voice-leading and would make more understandable the many suspensions consisting of a sixteenth-note tied over the bar-line—a weak enough rhythm without the addition of over-dotting.

For the published version Bach not only eliminated the original quasi-modal ending but also revised one passage (bars 38–42) rather heavily, adding the bass in bars 40–42, where it had been absent. Perhaps Bach felt the passage, which connects the second and third expositions, to be a weak link, but the revisions do not eliminate the rather sudden modulation from A minor to F in the following three measures (bars 42–44). As in Contrapunctus 1 there is a new coda that includes an additional statement of the subject; originally, the last entry was the syncopated one in the tenor at bar 69. Use of the subject in syncopation (*per arsin et thesin*) was one of the rarer (and thus more learned) devices, and it might have been meant to serve as a sort of climax. But it is hidden in the tenor and does not involve any particularly compelling counterpoint; the coda makes for a more decisive ending.

A syncopated form of the subject is used for all three entries in the second exposition of Contrapunctus 3 (bars 23–32). But the technique illustrated in this piece seems to be variation rather than syncopation per se, and the new form of the subject still fits together with the original form of the countersubject. The subject is varied for a second time in the last section (at bar 58), where the countersubject also undergoes variation (e.g., at bar 55). Although Contrapunctus 3 originally came second, the new order makes better sense. Not only does Contrapunctus 3 use more syncopation (or variation) than Contrapunctus 2; it is also the first movement with clearly articulated episodes and the first to maintain a countersubject throughout. Oddly enough, the initial statement of the subject (now inverted) is on the dominant and takes the form that would be appropriate in a tonal answer—that is, with a fourth instead of a fifth as the initial interval. But the "real" form of the subject prevails from the second exposition onward.

The presence of a regular countersubject employed in invertible counterpoint means that Marpurg, and perhaps Bach himself, would have called Contrapunctus 3 a double fugue; if so, the label "simple" fugue sometimes applied here would be a mistake. The countersubject is the source of the material developed in the first two episodes (bars 19–23 and 39–43). Moreover, the chromaticism of the countersubject gives the fugue a special character recalling that of some of the more tortuous ricercars of the early seventeenth century. This seems to point to a slower tempo and, in general, less smooth articulation than would be appropriate in Contrapunctus 2.

The chromaticism helps make this perhaps the most compelling of the four original fugues. Certainly it includes the most remote modulations thus far, passing within a ten-bar span from E minor, at the end of the second episode (bars 42–43), to E^b and C minor at the beginning of the last exposition (bar 51). The climactic moment, however, occurs when the outer voices, moving by contrary motion, pass through an augmented sixth in bar 63. Yet it is characteristic of the elusive style prevailing throughout the *Art of Fugue* that the expected dominant chord never materializes; indeed, it is hard to locate any final V–I cadence. While the augmented sixth resolves normally to a $^6_4$-chord, one must imagine the bass (A) of the latter chord prolonged through bars 64–65 in order to hear a full cadence that is completed in the second half of bar 66.

Contrapunctus 4 opens with the "real" inversion of the subject that was avoided at the beginning of Contrapunctus 3. But the new fugue is more regular in design and less severe in style than the three original ones. Indeed, its design is the most symmetrical in the collection, coming closest to what might be considered a "normal" Bach fugue design. In addition to regular alternations between expositions and episodes, there are complementary cadences to the dominant and the subdominant, respectively, at the middle of each of the two largest episodes (bars 53, 103). In a remarkable exposition at the very center of the piece (bars 61–80), four ascending entries (bass, tenor, alto, soprano) form an ascending sequence (F, g, d, a); the passage carries the piece from the "flat" to the "sharp" side of the tonic (F major to E minor).

Despite the overall symmetry of the movement, Bach saved the climactic contrapuntal device for the return to the tonic at bar 107. This passage, which coincides with the beginning of the last exposition, opens dramatically with a pair of close strettos *per arsin et thesin*, first for the two lower voices, then the two upper. This can be an exciting moment in performance, a good example of how, even in a strict fugue, rhythmic, contrapuntal, and formal elements can combine to create a powerful musical effect.

With Contrapunctus 5 the series turns back toward a purer version of the *stile antico*.[38] The previous fugues having presented the two forms of the subject singly,

Contrapunctus 5 combines them in the opening exposition, where the *rectus* form follows the *inversus* at the distance of three bars. Hence, this is both a "counter" fugue (from German *Gegenfuge*), combining upright and inverted forms of the subject, and a "stretto" fugue, in which imitations begin before the previous statement of the subject has been completed. The strettos in the second exposition (bars 17–32) are again at the distance of three bars, but the time interval changes in each of the remaining three expositions, imitations occurring at the distance of two, six, and four quarter-notes, respectively. One might have expected the smallest time interval to occur in the last exposition, and in a sense this is so, for the time interval diminishes to *zero* in the final phrase: The two forms of the subject are presented simultaneously (as in the close of the D$^\sharp$-minor fugue of WTC2). Otherwise, the closest strettos occur not in the expositions but in the two canonic episodes (at bars 53 and 65). These, while derived from the subject, are really variants of the venerable contrapuntal formula that also served as the basis of the little canon bearing the title *Trias harmonicas* (BWV 1072), published by Marpurg.[39]

The Two Large Counter Fugues: Contrapuncti 6 and 7

With the next pair of fugues the work moves somewhat farther from the pure *stile antico*. Like Contrapunctus 5, both are counter fugues as well as stretto fugues, adding to the previously used forms of the subject diminished and (in Contrapunctus 7) augmented entries. Indeed, combinations of the various forms are so pervasive that there is hardly a moment in either fugue when one is not hearing at least two simultaneous statements of the subject, proceeding at different speeds or in different directions. Yet, despite the use of four different forms of the subject in Contrapunctus 6, and six in Contrapunctus 7, Bach was still able to avoid repeating a given configuration of entries anywhere in Contrapuncti 5, 6, and 7.

Both counter fugues are in common time (not cut-time), and Contrapunctus 6 adopts the dotted style of an overture, bearing the designation *in Stylo Francese* ("in French style"). Despite these "modern" elements, neither Contrapunctus 6 nor 7 has the clear formal articulations of Contrapunctus 5, which otherwise is much closer than they to the *stile antico*. Moreover, while each section of Contrapunctus 5 employs a distinct type of stretto, no particular order seems to govern the combinations of the various forms of the subject in Contrapuncti 6–7. To be sure, the dense imitative fabric of the expositions in Contrapunctus 6 is relieved by several distinct episodes, while Contrapunctus 7 is clearly anchored by the four entries of the subject in augmentation. But neither fugue has a clear modulating design, and the overlapping entrances of the voices tend to prevent phrase-endings or cadences from occurring simultaneously in all four voices. Even the four augmented entries in Contrapunctus 7, while clear enough on paper, do not coincide with cadences or other articulations in the accompanying voices, which move in a nearly unbroken stream of quicker entries and free counterpoint in small note-values. Hence, the augmented entries fail to make the dramatic impact created by, say, the entries of the cantus firmus in a chorale fantasia, and both fugues can seem a bit nebulous in performance.

Yet certain dramatic features in both large counter fugues indicate that Bach's plan in both went beyond a loosely connected series of contrapuntal combinations. Throughout Contrapunctus 6 there is a tension between dotted figures and running sixteenths. In the first half (through bar 38) the running notes never last for more than three consecutive beats in any one voice. But there are a few more extended passages in sixteenths later in the fugue, the longest of which (bars 60b–68a) contains almost continuous running motion in the bass. This serves to drive the music forward into an equally impressive passage (bars 68b–72) in which the dotted rhythm prevails. Contrapunctus 7, with its more homogeneous rhythm, contains nothing so striking, but it does conclude with a short coda (bar 58) reminiscent of those in much earlier works (e.g., the B-minor fugue of WTC1).

In the autograph both pieces were heavily revised—more so than any of the other fugues. Many of the alterations in Contrapunctus 6 involve only the rhythmic notation and were carried out by Friedrich Bach, but most of those in Contrapunctus 7 are compositional and were apparently entered by Sebastian himself. A few late revisions in Contrapunctus 6 were not included in the printed version, perhaps because they were made after the plates had been etched. It is unclear whether or not Bach authorized these changes; Maroney notes that the embellishment of the subject in bar 38 (soprano) would be the only instance of such embellishment in the entire movement, but it is wholly within Bach's style, as are the further changes in bars 46–49.[40]

The greatest number of alterations in Contrapunctus 6 involved the notation of the dotted rhythms, and in this they form a precise parallel with the alterations made for the printed version of the first movement of of the B-Minor *Ouverture* BWV 831 (see Chapter 16). As in BWV 831, only some of the alterations seem to point to real changes in rhythm, others being merely notational. Again, the changes might have been triggered by the use in the same piece of two contrasting types of rhythmic motives: on the one hand, groups consisting of four equal sixteenths, on the other, long notes—either dotted or tied—followed by two or three small note-values. Motives of the latter sort occur in both the subject (bar 3) and in the episodes (e.g., bars 13–14). These motives were rewritten more precisely, giving the small note-values as thirty-seconds, except where the figure occurred in statements of the subject or in passages derived from it (e.g., bars 44–45a). Running sixteenths were also left unaltered (as in bars 54a–57a). It seems clear, then, that Bach meant to keep the two types of figures distinct, with the result, however, that one occasionally hears the gears shifting (as in the middle of bar 54).

The dotted rhythms in the subject pose an additional problem, especially when the normal and diminuted forms of the subject, both of them containing dotted notes, are juxtaposed (as in bars 2–3). Double-dotting only in the normal version would produce a minute inconsistency between it and the diminuted form. Yet, even as notated, the quicker entries alter the rhythm of the last five notes of the subject. Thus, there seems to be no objection to applying the interpretation advocated here for other pieces in overture rhythm: double-dotting on quarters only, not eighths.

The above conclusion applies only in Contrapunctus 6. A more rigorous rhythmic relationship holds between the three forms of the subject employed in Contrapunctus 7, and, perhaps to point this out, only in the latter piece is the contrapuntal device specified in a Latin subtitle (*per Augment[ationem] et Diminut[ionem]*). Literal interpretation of the note-values in Contrapunctus 6 would twice lead to parallel seconds (bars 67, 78) that are awkward both to hear and to play; similar consecutive (not parallel) seconds arise only once in Contrapunctus 7 (bar 39, left hand) and are confined to the two lowest voices. The passage in Contrapunctus 7 shows erasures and revisions in the autograph; Bach did not accept the rough voice-leading without first exploring other possibilities.

The Double Fugues with Invertible Counterpoint: Contrapuncti 9 and 10

In the autograph, although not in the print, the two double fugues are followed by the two triple fugues.[41] All four pieces were originally notated in half the note-values of the print; the notation might have been altered because the smaller note-values seemed to indicate too fast a tempo. When the double fugues were prepared for publication, the original time-signature, c, was retained, but it presumably should have been altered to ¢.[42]

These multiple fugues combine additional subjects with the common subject of the *Art of Fugue*—which from this point on will be termed the *theme*. The new subjects are introduced in expositions of their own; hence, they are not merely countersubjects, as in Contrapunctus 3. Moreover, the use of distinct sections for each subject or combination of subjects gives these pieces the clearly articulated structures typical of Bach's earlier multiple fugues.

The two double fugues were meant to illustrate not only the use of multiple subjects but also double or invertible counterpoint at various intervals. For the print Bach added two canons employing the same varieties of invertible counterpoint. Double counterpoint as explained in textbooks often seems to be entirely a matter of avoiding certain intervals between two voices. But apart from reducing a delightful type of counterpoint to dry, quasi-mathematical rules, such explanations err in being applicable mainly to species counterpoint in two voices, not to the harmonically generated polyphony of a mature Bach fugue. There, certain "forbidden" intervals can become permissible through chromatic alterations of the two inverting parts or through the addition of one or more additional free parts. While even a fugue can get along without it, invertible counterpoint is a necessity in the permutational designs that Bach and his predecessors often adopted. It is also essential in the exchange of material between voices, a device that plays an important role in the recapitulatory schemes of the WTC and other works, though less so here.

Double counterpoint at the octave is essentially a matter of transposing one of two voices an octave (or two) above or below the other. Such writing is so fundamental to fugue that Bach did not bother to devote a contrapunctus to it specifically, although it can be seen in the relationship between, say, theme and countersubject in the opening exposition of Contrapunctus 3 (Example 18.2). The subjects of the double fugues are combined in invertible counterpoint at the twelfth (third) and tenth (fifth), respectively (Examples 18.3, 18.4). In both double fugues the two subjects also invert at the octave, and this makes possible the "paired entries" that

EXAMPLE 18.2.   *Art of Fugue* BWV 1080, Contrapunctus 3:
(a) bars 5–8; (b) bars 15–18 (soprano and bass)

EXAMPLE 18.3.   *Art of Fugue* BWV 1080, Contrapunctus 9:
(a) bars 59–62 (alto and bass); (b) bars 89–92 (soprano and
bass)

serve as climaxes in the last two of the three main sections of Contrapunctus 10
(Example 18.5).[43]

Neither movement was originally a full-fledged double fugue, and Contrapunctus 9 remains one only in Marpurg's sense, since the theme, introduced as the
second subject, lacks an exposition of its own. Yet it is difficult not to regard
Contrapunctus 9 as a true double fugue, inasmuch as the theme enters dramatically, cantus firmus–like, in augmented note values. Bach might have found a
model for this in pieces by Frescobaldi and Froberger in which the final section
similarly combines a new subject with the principal theme in long notes.[44] The first
subject, whose virtuoso character is at once apparent from its initial octave leap and
the running eighths that follow, is one of the longest in any of Bach's mature

EXAMPLE 18.4.   *Art of Fugue* BWV 1080, Contrapunctus 10:
(a) bars 44–47 (alto, tenor); (b) bars 66–69 (soprano and tenor)

EXAMPLE 18.5.   *Art of Fugue* BWV 1080, Contrapunctus 10:
(a) bars 75–78 (soprano, alto, bass); (b) bars 115–18 (alto, tenor, bass)

fugues—but it must be so in order to combine with the long notes of the theme as used in this movement. The new subject includes a prominent "sigh" motive in bar 5, and this is twice involved in chromatic progressions containing an augmented sixth (bars 76–77, 102–3). But these are not moments of great pathos; indeed the piece serves as a demonstration that the art of fugue need not be confined to pieces of a serious or pathetic character.

Contrapunctus 10 is a graver work. Originally, it opened with the exposition of the main theme (bars 23ff.), which was combined only later (bar 44) with the new subject; this early version was included in the print as *Contrap[unctus] a 4* and is designated in some editions (e.g., BG 25/1) as Contrapunctus 14, a title better reserved for the incomplete fugue. In the revised version there is a new opening exposition, but it retains peculiarities traceable to the fact that the subject used was originally conceived as a countersubject to the main theme and is not suitable for a normal fugal exposition of its own. Hence, this is a stretto exposition, and the entries do not follow a normal sequence of pitch-levels, falling instead on I, IV, I, and V (D, G, D, and A), respectively. The last two of these entries are inverted, even though the inversion of the subject is never used in the main body of the fugue. It is not even easy to say where each statement of this subject ends; perhaps the last note of the first entry should be regarded as the f′′ of bar 4.

Possibly in order to make the new opening stretto exposition seem less incongruous, Bach added a partial stretto entry at the first entrance of the main theme as well.[45] But the incongruities are apparent only upon close analysis; in its final form Contrapunctus 10 is as satisfying as any in the *Art of Fugue*.

The Two Triple Fugues: Contrapuncti 8 and 11

In the autograph the two triple fugues appeared together as the climactic conclusion of the series of regular fugues. Each is longer and probably more compelling than any of the other completed contrapuncti; together they form an unparalleled pair of masterpieces. Their separation in the print seems inappropriate, as, more than any other pair, they form *alio modo* illustrations, in three and four parts, respectively, of the same contrapuntal devices. The parallelism extends to the use of the same basic design and the same thematic material, including a version of the B-A-C-H motive that is incorporated into one of the subjects (Example 18.6). Both fugues contain a particularly strong articulation close to the exact midpoint, and each ends with a climactic exposition containing simultaneous entries of all three subjects. These and other complementary relationships between the two contrapuncti are summarized in Table 18–3.

The three-part fugue is divided into two nearly equal halves, even possessing a sort of recurring closing theme in the form of a running figure that appears rather suddenly just before the final cadence of each half.[46] The bipartite division is less clear in the four-part fugue, thanks to its greater number of subdivisions (only the most important of which are shown in Table 18–3). Indeed, it actually contains two strong cadences close to the center: that at bar 71, which is followed by an impressive entrance of the theme (in inversion), and that at bar 89, which is closer to the exact midpoint and immediately precedes the entrance of the third (B-A-C-H) subject. The four-part fugue is clearly the more monumental of the two, and unlike Contrapunctus 8 it uses both upright and inverted forms of two of its subjects, one of which even possesses its own countersubject. Nevertheless, the two fugues are almost precisely equal in length, and the crucial moment at which all three subjects are first combined occurs at virtually the same point in each.

This moment is particularly dramatic in the four-part fugue, since it occurs (bar 146) in the midst of the most chromatic, most rapidly modulating section of the piece. Yet the passage combining the three subjects serves to prepare an even more crucial event, a simultaneous combination of *rectus* and *inversus* forms of the main theme (bar 158). The two forms of the theme had previously entered together in the

EXAMPLE 18.6.   *Art of Fugue* BWV 1080, thematic material
in Contrapuncti 8 and 11 (asterisks indicate sharps absent in
the autograph): (a) Contrapunctus 8, bars 1–5a (alto);
Contrapunctus 11, bars 27b–31a (alto); (b) Contrapunctus 8,
bars 39b–42a (alto); Contrapunctus 11, bars 93b–96
(soprano); (c) Contrapunctus 8, bars 94–98a; Contrapunctus
11, bars 1–5a (alto)

coda of Contrapunctus 5. Here, however, they are presented in double counterpoint at the tenth (compare bars 158–62 and 164–68), and the combination is
integrated into the body of the piece, coinciding with the return to the tonic and
thus marking the beginning of the final section.

This is a splendid moment, perhaps marking the culmination of the whole main
series of eleven contrapuncti. Yet the final section of Contrapunctus 11 maintains
its tension to the very end, in particular through the surprising moves to the
Neapolitan at bar 164 and to the submediant (B♭) just five bars before the end. Only
in the final phrase does the soprano at last restate the theme in the tonic in its *rectus*
form; Bach has so perfectly prepared it that there is no need for a conventional
cadential formula, a final pedal-point, or any other elaboration in order to make the
close completely compelling.[47]

In addition to halving the original note-values of the two triple fugues, Bach
increased the already high degree of chromaticism by inserting accidentals in certain statements of subject b, including its first entry in Contrapunctus 8 (see Example 18.6b). He also rewrote several passages in Contrapunctus 11.[48] But although

TABLE 18–3.   Complementary Structure of Contrapuncti 8 and 11

	Contrapunctus 8			Contrapunctus 11	
bars	*thematic material**	*cadence at end of section*	*bars*	*thematic material**	*cadence at end of section*
1–39a	a	d	1–27a	c	d
39b–93	a + b	d:V	27b–71a	a +cs (both later inverted)	a
94–124	c	a	71b–89a	c inverted	F
125–46	a + b	a	89b–146	a + b, also single entries of c and a (inverted, with cs)	C
147–88	a + b + c	d	146–84	a + b + c; c + its inversion	d

*letters in these columns indicate subjects as shown in Example 18.6.
cs = countersubject

Bach himself was responsible for the engraver's copy of Contrapunctus 11, he did not add a single ornament sign to it, unless one counts the c-appoggiatura on the downbeat of bar 57 (which represents the first note of subject a). On the other hand, the engraver's copy of Contrapunctus 8 was prepared by Friedrich Bach, who was perhaps responsible for extending the ornament in the first statement of subject a (bar 3) to most of the remaining entries. The long trill with closing turn is, however, virtually unplayable in several instances (e.g., bar 83) and can surely be abbreviated or simply omitted.

The Two Mirror Fugues: Contrapuncti 12 and 13

The two mirror fugues, so called because the entire contrapuntal fabric of each can be inverted, are in a sense canons, since they employ a much more rigorous contrapuntal procedure than any of the previous pieces. This may explain why they came last in the autograph as originally constituted and after the main sequence of contrapuncti in the print. As with the triple fugues, Bach chose to write complementary pieces in three (Contrapunctus 13) and four parts (Contrapunctus 12). But the two mirror fugues share no material apart from the theme, which appears in them in very different forms, and the pieces are otherwise as unlike as could be imagined, the four-part Contrapunctus 12 being unusually austere, the three-part fugue one of Bach's liveliest late works.

The two mirror fugues are in some ways the most problematical of all of Bach's late keyboard pieces; their origin, title, ordering, and performance practice all raise interesting questions that can be treated here only summarily. For obvious reasons, mirror pieces have always been rare, but Bach may well have known two settings by

Buxtehude of the chorale *Mit Fried' und Freud'* (BuxWV 76/1–2), published in 1674 at Lübeck. Though not fugues, each is designated a *Contrapunctus* and employs four-part counterpoint invertible at the octave; the second piece is written in mirror counterpoint.[49] Buxtehude's own models were perhaps a collection of hymn settings published in 1669 by Christoph Bernhard (substantial extracts in Snyder 1980, 554–55), and Bach might well have come across these as well, either during his visit to Lübeck or during his student years near Hamburg, where Bernhard was director of music until his death in 1692. Although Butler (1983b, 303) cautions that there is no evidence that Bach "ever encountered the Buxtehude print," it is not inconceivable that the somewhat gloomy and archaic Contrapunctus 12 was directly inspired by the Buxtehude pieces; the similarities in key, meter, and texture are striking.

Still, Bach's mirror fugues are very different from the Bernhard and Buxtehude works. Bernhard's settings are in a quite pure *stile antico*, and both older composers evidently wrote one voice (or rather one pair of voices) at a time. This is clearest at the cadences, which, as in sixteenth-century music, were conceived in terms of motion toward perfect consonances by pairs of voices. Hence, the bass tends to move by step rather than from dominant to tonic, even in final cadences (Example 18.7). In addition, each movement is too short to have contained substantial modulations, which in any case would not have been expected in a quasi-modal seventeenth-century work.

Prior to writing the *Art of Fugue*, however, Bach had already faced the problem of mirror writing within a tonal context, in the gigue of the Sixth English Suite. While the two halves of that work do not form perfect reflections of each other, they illustrate principles that are developed with greater rigor in Contrapuncti 12 and 13. Here the mirror principle extends to the deepest levels of tonal design, and the mirror fugues are, consequently, as much a study in the relations between keys as in invertible counterpoint. Upon inversion an authentic cadence becomes a plagal one, and a modulation from tonic to dominant is pointed toward the subdominant. Thus, in one version of the four-part mirror fugue, the initial imitation is at the dominant; in the other version, the second entry is on the subdominant. In the second episode of the three-part fugue (bars 23–26), one version ascends by sequence through the circle of fifths (D minor, A minor, E minor, B minor) while the other descends (D minor, G minor, C minor, F major). In addition, the three-part fugue illustrates the non-invertibility of the diminished chord: Both versions come to rest on the same harmony at the fermata in bar 59.

Mirror technique is not the only device illustrated here. Like Contrapunctus 3, the four-part mirror fugue twice varies its version of the subject, the second exposition introducing one variation (bar 21), a somewhat different variation appearing in the final entry (bar 50). In addition, each version of the three-part piece employs both *rectus* and *inversus* forms of the subject, though not simultaneously. Moreover, instead of simply inverting the entire texture—which would have meant keeping the same voice in the middle of both versions—Bach employed the more complex system of inversion illustrated in Table 18–4.[50]

Both mirror fugues raise problems of ordering and title. Williams (1986b, xvi) notes that it would be "logical" for the three-part mirror piece (Contrapunctus 13)

EXAMPLE 18.7.   (a) Bernhard, *Prudentia prudentiana, partes* 1
and 2: bars 26–28; (b) Buxtehude, *Mit Fried' und Freud'*
BuxWV 76/1, bars 12b–14; (c) Buxtehude, *Mit Fried' und
Freud'* BuxWV 76/2, bars 12b–15

to come first, just as the triple fugue in three parts precedes the one in four parts.
Yet the four-part mirror (Contrapunctus 12) comes first in both autograph and
print, reflecting the more sophisticated technique of the three-part fugue.

More difficult is the question of which version of each fugue is to be considered
the upright form and which the inversion. In the autograph, Bach wrote the two
versions of each movement simultaneously, on double systems of eight staves (Contrapunctus 12) and six staves (Contrapunctus 13). The print, however, gives the two
versions of each fugue separately, in each case reversing the order vis-à-vis the
autograph; that is, the version placed second is the one placed on top in the

TABLE 18–4.   The Two Versions of Contrapunctus 13

Version	Voice	Form of subject in intial entry	Corresponding voice in other version
Contrapunctus inversus a 3	S	*inversus*	B
BWV 1080/13/1	A	*rectus*	S
top in autograph second in print first note a'	B	*inversus*	A
Contrapunctus a 3	B	*rectus*	S
BWV 1080/13/2	S	*inversus*	A
bottom in autograph first in print first note d"	A	*rectus*	B

autograph. Most editions follow the print; at this point, however, SWV lists the pieces in the order of the autograph (as does Table 18–2). The confusion does not stop here. The print uses the title *Contrapunctus inversus* for both versions of the four-part fugue but only for the second version of the three-part one (see Table 18–4).[51] Further complicating matters is the fact that in Contrapunctus 13 the theme is embellished in such a manner that its upright form *sounds* like an inversion, since it opens with a downard leap from tonic to dominant (d", a') rather than the other way around (see Example 18.8a).

So which version of each fugue is the upright one? The question may not matter very much, and it will not be settled without the discovery of new evidence. But editors and performers do have to decide which piece comes first. The argument to date has focused on the details of the engraving process, especially as it relates to the titles of the pieces as given in the print, which for various reasons appear to be undependable (see especially Wiemer 1977, 32–36). To this might be added the following observations regarding their tonal design. One might suppose the upright version of the four-part fugue to be the one in which the answer occurs at the dominant rather than the subdominant: This is BWV 1080/12/1, the piece placed second in the print. In the three-part fugue one must look to the third entry before either version leaves the tonic; there the dominant again occurs in the version that comes first (on top) in the autograph. It seems reasonable to suppose that this is the upright version of the fugue even though it opens with the *inversus* form of the subject (Example 18.8b).

This is confusing, and it seems to obscure the difference between "original" and "inversion"—which perhaps was Bach's intention. The two versions of both pieces were necessarily composed simultaneously and are virtually equal in musical quality, showing few signs of contrivance. Bach even took care that both versions of each fugue should conclude with something resembling a V–I cadence—not, of course, at the same point in each version, but in any case close to the end. Thus, in the three-part fugue, the bass moves from dominant to tonic two bars before the end in

EXAMPLE 18.8.   *Art of Fugue*: theme as embellished in (a)
BWV 1080/13/2 (theme in upright form); (b) BWV
1080/13/1 (theme in inverted form). Asterisks mark tones of
theme in original (unembellished) form

the "top" version (BWV 1080/13/1) and in the final bar of the "bottom" version
(BWV 1080/13/2). The situation is ambiguous in the more archaic four-part fugue,
whose bass fails to move by direct root motion at the final cadence, as in the
Buxtehude pieces. Here, however, the little flourish in the final bar seems to work
better as a descent to the tonic (BWV 1080/12/1, bass) than as an ascent to the
dominant (BWV 1080/12/2, treble).

Obviously, the order of the pieces is of less importance than their musical effect.
Contrapunctus 13 is by far the more engaging of the two, thanks to its lively gigue
rhythm and clear harmonic directionality; the latter is particularly notable in the
sequences by fifth in the three episodes. The four-part fugue, on the other hand,
lacks episodes, and the voice-crossings at several points make it a bit murky, especially in the "bottom" version (BWV 1080/12/2), which contains perhaps too much
parallel motion low in the bass staff. It comes to life at a brisk tempo, such as is
suggested by the smaller note-values of the autograph version. But few performers
possess hands large enough to accommodate the parallel sixths and occasional
tenths while also playing with the grace, lightness, and evenness demanded by the
flowing figuration. Hence, performance by two players may be as necessary here as
in the three-part mirror fugue, for which Bach prepared a two-keyboard arrangement.[52]

The arrangement (BWV 1080/18) proves somewhat disappointing, since the
added voice is free, that is, not invertible. But an invertible part would necessarily
have been fragmented, musically trivial, or both, defeating the purpose of the
arrangement, which was presumably to give both players something interesting to
do with each hand. Perhaps because it was not completely invertible, Bach appears
not to have prepared the arrangement for printing, and it was published in an early
version that does not reflect revisions made in the solo version. The notes remained
in their original values—half those of the solo version—and bar 4 of the subject and

all parallel passages use equal note-values, without the later dotted rhythm. Evidently, Bach was unhappy with the resulting metrical ambivalence, as he eliminated it almost entirely in the revised solo version.

It is often thought that he did entirely eliminate it. The dotted notation in the subject should certainly be understood as shorthand for triple "skipping" rhythms; the same may also be true of several other examples of duple notation that remained in the solo version as published.[53] But not so in bar 46a, which contains a run of six sixteenth-notes—the only group of more than two sixteenths in the entire piece. The dramatic change in rhythm underscores the structural role of the passage, which is to prepare the return of the theme in the tonic two bars later.[54]

The Incomplete Fugue [Contrapunctus 14]

The famous "unfinished" fugue was apparently one of the four pieces that Bach decided to add to the *Art of Fugue* after completing the early version. While not necessarily Bach's last composition, it is probably very late, composed after some of the other movements had already been prepared for engraving. Whether Bach actually left it unfinished or his heirs simply failed to recognize the sheet or sheets of paper containing its conclusion is unknown. It was included in the print as a *Fuga a 3 Soggetti* (Fugue with Three Subjects). This title is usually taken as meaning the same as "triple fugue," and therefore a mistake, but it is conceivable that the "three subjects" should be understood as distinct from the "theme," which constitutes an additional subject (as in the titles of BWV 574 and 917).

The fugue survives in an incomplete autograph, apparently a revising score. The print gave the fragment up to the half-cadence on the downbeat of bar 233; the autograph contains six more bars and part of a seventh.[55] A remark added in the autograph by Emanuel Bach explains that the score breaks off just after the section in which the subject containing the B-A-C-H motive has been presented. It is still commonly assumed that Sebastian, having finally incorporated his name into the main thematic material of a work, was forced to stop work on it because of illness or blindness. But the assumption is unfounded (see Wolff 1975), and Emanuel's remark might have been intended simply to alert copyists to the fact that the work was incomplete.

That the fragment was even meant to be a part of the *Art of Fugue* was once questioned, since the main theme of the larger work never appears in the extant portion of the fugue. But Gustav Nottebohm (better known as editor of the Beethoven sketchbooks) demonstrated in the late nineteenth century that that theme could, with a few rhythmic alterations, be combined with the fugue's three other subjects.[56] Where Bach would have placed the completed fugue within the work as a whole is uncertain; traditionally it has been placed last, but Butler's (1983a) argument for placing it before the canons cannot be dismissed (see below).

Naturally, speculation has centered on how the fugue might have ended, and many completions have been offered. Most are invalidated by improbable stylistic details, including anachronistic harmonic progressions, faulty voice-leading, or the need for organ pedals (never required in the extant movements). Virtually all reflect the view that the fugue must have been of enormous length, ending with a grand pedal-point or a romantic apotheosis of the main theme—assumptions belied by the relatively unpretentious ending of Contrapunctus 11, which is the real high point of the work, at least as it stands. If Butler is correct, the loss amounts to less than a page of music, or about forty bars (see Table 18–5). This would yield about 280

TABLE 18–5.   Proposed Reconstruction of the Incomplete Fugue

Subject(s) used:	a			b	a+b	c	a+b+c	a+b+c+d
At bar:	1			114	147	193	233	247
Length of				←33→	←46→	←40→	←12→	
section in bars:	←—113—→			←——79——→		←——52——→		←—34—→
Page-breaks in	⋮	⋮	⋮	⋮	⋮		⋮	⋮
original print:	1	2	3	4	5		6	(7)
	⋮	⋮	⋮	⋮	⋮		⋮	⋮
At bar:	1	47	92	139b	186		233	(280)

bars for the complete fugue, which would keep the piece within manageable limits, although forcing certain strictures on its content. What seems clear is that Bach composed the piece in sections, linking them by bridges that perhaps were worked out only during the writing of the surviving autograph. Corrections in the latter show that the closing passages of the first two sections underwent revision,[57] and Wolff (1975, 74) has suggested that the final section was "already written down elsewhere." This final section would have included the introduction of the fourth subject, whose presence in the "last" fugue was indicated in Bach's obituary (BD 3:86 [item 666]/BR, 221).

Nottebohm's combination of the four subjects is not perfect, but a rhythmic alteration of the first subject makes it possible to combine the same four subjects in inversion as well as in *rectus* form (Example 18.9).[58] The last few bars in the autograph (omitted from the print) show that Bach, having introduced the first three subjects, was about to combine them. Presumably, the fourth subject, the theme of the *Art of Fugue*, would have entered soon afterward. The general procedure would not have been unlike that employed in Bach's other fugues with multiple subjects. But the structural proportions would have differed, since the sections would have been of diminishing length, and, if Butler is correct, the theme would not have been heard until very close to the end of the piece, as shown in Table 18–5 (largely after Butler 1983a, 56).

While some will find this design difficult to accept, the fragment is already huge, and the possibility of some unprecedented sort of conclusion cannot be discounted. The opening section, for example, is unusually close to the *stile antico*—so close, in fact, that its nearest relative is not another movement in the *Art of Fugue* but the Confiteor of the B-Minor Mass, a movement that also seems to date from the very end of Bach's life. The Confiteor is a five-part double fugue, in form and proportions not unlike Contrapunctus 10. But in the last section (bar 73) it introduces a

EXAMPLE 18.9.   (a) the four subjects of the incomplete fugue
BWV 1080/19 (three lower voices from bars 233–39a); (b)
same, inverted

Gregorian cantus firmus—in effect a third subject—in long notes (and in stretto).
In other words, what may be Bach's last choral fugue has a structure quite without
precedent but perhaps resembling in some respects the design of his last keyboard
fugue.

Of the three extant sections, the first is practically a self-contained four-part
ricercar in *stile antico*. This section treats its subject with unusual thoroughness,
including *inversus* and stretto expositions, but it has a somewhat rambling character
and lacks the tautness of some otherwise comparable pieces, such as the B♭-minor
fugue of WTC2. With the entry of the second subject (bar 114) the piece virtually
begins anew, the style changing in response to the new subject, which is a long
running theme resembling the first subject of Contrapunctus 9. The style shifts
again with the introduction of the B-A-C-H subject in the third section (bar 193),
the easy diatonic flow of the second subject being replaced by harsh chromatic

motion. Remote keys are hinted at (though not always tonicized) in rapid succession; one remarkable passage contains the rare interval of the diminished sixth (bar 224, last beat). While the exposition of the B-A-C-H subject is much shorter than either of the first two, it is much more concentrated, and there is perhaps a sense of increasing urgency due to the gradual shortening of the sections.

The proposed scheme leaves no room for an exposition of the main theme alone, which must enter as a cantus firmus–like countersubject, as in Contrapunctus 9. If, however, the main theme was to have appeared only briefly and perhaps rather suddenly in the final section, this would have served not only as the piece's climax but also as a sort of explanation for the first three sections, their relevance to the *Art of Fugue* becoming clear in the final summing-up. But it remains possible that Bach, even if he had completed a final quadruple exposition, was undecided about how to connect it with the surviving fragment. The final page of the autograph trails off, the last bar unfinished. The counterpoint a few bars earlier, in the combination of the first three subjects, is not unexceptionable; the third of the chord is doubled on the downbeat of bar 236, and consecutive fifths occur on the downbeats of bars 236 and 237 (soprano and bass). As in the fugue BWV 906/2, Bach might have broken off work after deciding that fundamental changes were necessary; perhaps these were never carried out.

While no completion can pretend to do justice to Bach's plan—whatever it may have been—it seems better to finish the piece in some manner than to break it off exactly where the fragment ends. Breaking off in mid-phrase seems inappropriately dramatic and invites a sentimental response from the listener. The completion suggested in Example 18.10 follows the reconstruction shown in Table 18–5; it includes the inverted combination of subjects from Example 18.9b.[59] Those who find such a reconstruction distasteful might still consider the possibility of bringing the fragment to a quick, provisional cadence, like that shown in Example 18.11, which draws on the original, canceled reading of bars 112–14 (the end of the first section) in the autograph.

Another solution occasionally heard is a return to Contrapunctus 1 after the arrival to the dominant on the downbeat of bar 233—that is, either an immediate, complete repetition of the first fugue or a partial restatement together with a certain amount of newly composed material. But the reference to Romantic cylic form, with its idea of returning to some simple, primeval origin or starting point, seems anachronistic and foreign to Bach's music.

According to Bach's obituary, the *Art of Fugue* was to have included not only a normal quadruple fugue but a mirror fugue with four subjects. This report might have been due to an offhand remark of Bach's or, as Wolff (1975, 74–75) suggests, the discovery of a sketch containing an invertible combination of the four subjects. Such a combination is possible using the forms of the four subjects shown in Example 18.9.

The Canons

It seems anticlimactic to end a study of Bach's keyboard music with the canons of the *Art of Fugue*, but canon is, theoretically, the strictest, most learned type of

EXAMPLE 18.10. The incomplete fugue BWV 1080/19, bars 239ff. (with suggested completion)

EXAMPLE   18.10 (continued)

EXAMPLE 18.10 (continued)

EXAMPLE 18.11.   The incomplete fugue BWV 1080/19:
suggested provisional ending (bars 239ff.)

polyphony. The canons of the *Art of Fugue* are in just two voices, lacking the free
bass line found in the canons of the Goldberg Variations and the Canonic Variations for organ. Thus they are more restricted in their musical possibilities. Yet they
are compositions in the full sense of the word, not epigrammatic puzzles like most
of the canons in the *Musical Offering*. In deciding to write two-part canons that
would also be significant pieces of keyboard music, Bach set for himself a task as
unprecedented as the composition of a full-length three- or four-part mirror fugue.
He carried out this task with characteristic imagination; each canon follows different
structural principles, and each has a distinct musical character, combining galant
melodic formulas in varying proportions with the archaism and abstraction that
color most of the *Art of Fugue*. All four canons operate within a fairly restrained
tonal and harmonic ambitus; the Canon at the Tenth and the Augmentation
Canon, however, both contain a strong dose of local chromaticism.

Only two of the four canons appear in the original autograph, and one of these (the Augmentation Canon) was so completely reworked that the printed version must be regarded as a new piece. Bach may at first have planned to print the canons in the traditional enigmatic notation, since the autograph gives the earliest version of each piece both as a puzzle canon in one voice and in its two-part solution. But in their revised versions, none but the Canon at the Octave could have been adequately represented in puzzle form; the other three depart from a strictly canonic design and therefore had to be written out in two parts. Even so, two of the four remain perpetual canons, with repetitions that could theoretically go on forever, as in the much shorter canons in the *Musical Offering*.

In the print the ordering of the canons appears to have been confused, and while the Augmentation Canon was given first it was probably meant to come last.[60] Hence, the first canon is the one at the octave; this piece not only demonstrates the simplest type of canonic technique but also most clearly follows the design of a traditional perpetual canon. Its giguelike rhythm makes it perhaps the most engaging of the canons; certainly, as the hand-crossing in the final cadence makes clear, it is the most extroverted.

Like each of the remaining canons, the Canon at the Octave is divided into sections somewhat resembling the expositions of a fugue, inasmuch as each section opens with some form of the main theme. The four sections here begin with (1) the inversion, varied (bar 1); (2) the same, in a "tonal" answer (bar 25); (3) the theme in upright form, at the dominant (bar 41); and (4) the same, in the tonic, varied somewhat differently (bar 61). The hand-crossing serves as the climax of what is labeled in several of the other canons as the *finale*, that is, a passage added after the double bar to bring the canon to a satisfactory cadence.[61] Except for the last five bars, the *finale* is essentially identical to the first quarter of the piece (bars 5–23), which therefore falls into a sort of Da Capo form.

The Canon at the Tenth is a demonstration of invertible counterpoint at the same interval as in Contrapunctus 10, and its binary structure reflects this. In the first half, treble imitates bass at the interval of a tenth. The second half (bars 40ff.) consists of the same music with the original bass transposed up an octave and the original treble down a tenth. This has the effect of changing the interval of imitation from a tenth to an octave. The most striking thing about the piece is the very gradual shift in each half from an exceedingly grave *mouvement* in long notes to an almost chaotic flurry of lively figures. Paralleling this is a gradual shift in register from the middle to the top of Bach's keyboard.

Several voice-crossings in the second half make performance on two manuals advisable (as is true also in both versions of the Augmentation Canon). A few puzzling appoggiaturas (bars 37, 76) were perhaps late revisions meant to be played as ordinary sixteenths. Throughout, the original notation combines dotted and triplet rhythms, but triplet "assimilation" as assumed by Czerny and other editors is probably correct. The *finale*, however, clearly shifts to duple rhythm (bar 79). There is no new tempo mark and no new time-signature at this point; each bar presumably remains the same length as before, effectively doubling the speed of the theme (in the bass).

The fermata in the penultimate bar indicates a cadenza over an implied $^6_4$-chord.

While something of a surprise in a canon, the idea of a cadenza in a solo keyboard piece was a familiar one in sonatas of the 1740s. The cadenza should presumably be short and perhaps canonic, like those for two flutes given as models by Quantz (1752, 15.26–30). In Example 18.12 a cadenza by Emanuel Bach for the slow movement of his two-harpsichord concerto of 1740 has been adapted for use here.[62]

EXAMPLE 18.12.   C. P. E. Bach, cadenza H. 264/54 (W. 120/54) for Double Concerto in F, H. 408 (W. 46), second movement, adapted for use in Canon at the Tenth BWV 1080/16

The Canon at the Twelfth is the shortest of the canons but the most intricate in structure, combining elements of binary design with the theoretically infinite form of a perpetual canon. Certain passages, moreover, are constructed so as to sound like a regular fugue, or at least a two-part invention. Although the second voice waits eight bars before entering, statements of the opening motive are then exchanged at half-bar intervals between the two voices in a sort of pseudo-imitation (see bars 9, 17, etc.). As in the Canon at the Tenth, the two halves of the piece are related by invertible counterpoint, the two voices exchanging roles at the center, beginning at bar 34.

The last of the canons has the most complicated title and makes use of what are nominally the most advanced contrapuntal devices. In fact the *Canon per Augmentationem in Contrario Motu* did not necessarily involve any more difficult compositional problems than the others.[63] But it is the most chromatic of the canons and perhaps the most expressive, incorporating both a jagged opening phrase and galant "sighs" in a later passage (bars 23–24). The first voice is imitated in both augmentation and inversion, as the title indicates; in addition, the leading voice (*dux*) contains several varied statements of the theme in diminution (bars 13b–15a, 17b–19a, 30, etc.). But perhaps the most remarkable events are a series of slurred chromatic figures that reach a climax in the dizzying outburst of bar 29.[64] The cadenzalike passage serves to prepare the varied statements of the theme that begin, simultaneously in both voices, in the next bar (bar 30).

The earlier version of the Augmentation Canon is a slighter composition but certainly worthy of Bach, and it might have been included in the original print with greater justification than the early version of Contrapunctus 10.[65] Actually, no fewer than four versions are known: (1) the initial entry in the autograph, probably a fair copy; (2) embellishments added to that, then abandoned; (3) the new composition, entered at the end of the autograph; and (4) the printed version, also preserved in the autograph engraver's copy. Bach's dissatisfaction with the first version is shown by some revisions entered early in the autograph (in bars 3–5). But these led to consecutive fifths and octaves upon imitation (see Baker 1975, 68–69), and, rather than revise it further, Bach abandoned the early version entirely.

Both versions nevertheless follow the same general plan, ending with a restatement of the main theme. In the earlier piece, the restatement is incomplete, and the *finale* (bars 41–44) is actually a lively self-contained mirror canon at the interval of a half-bar—that is, a sort of stretto. In the printed version the *finale* (bars 104–8) restates the entire theme in the upper voice; there is no stretto, but the full statement of the theme gives the piece a more fully rounded design, closer to that of the other canons. This ending is modest yet forceful, expressive and witty at the same time— qualities that we may suppose characterized Bach himself, and which he might well have wished to be present in the conclusion of his last published keyboard work.

Appendix A. Doubtful Works

Although the previous pages have raised questions about Bach's authorship of certain works, there are many more for which these questions remain open. Ideally, perhaps, it would be possible to ignore questions of attribution and judge works strictly on their intrinsic musical merits. But the assignment of a work to Bach inevitably causes us to seek deeper meaning in it, and considerations of authenticity frequently lead to a sharper understanding of style. Even a clearly inauthentic attribution may provide evidence about the influence or posthumous reception of Bach's music. Hence, there is ample justification for a brief discussion of some of the more doubtful keyboard pieces that have been assigned at one time or another to Bach.

Most doubtful and spurious works are listed in the appendix (German *Anhang*) of SWV, where they bear "BWV Anh." numbers. The 1990 edition of SWV places doubtful works in Anhang II, those regarded as clearly spurious in Anhang III; several doubtful pieces continue to bear regular BWV numbers. Some works originally listed in one section have been moved to another, but they retain the numbers assigned to them in the first edition. A listing now given as "BWV 905 / Anh. II 87→" means that the work, once regarded as authentic, has been moved to the "doubtful" category, where it follows the entry for BWV Anh. 87. Many works now regarded as doubtful were edited in BG 36 or BG 42; some of these will appear in a projected volume of the NBA.[1]

Bach himself may have been indirectly responsible for a number of the questionable attributions, since his own collection of music contained anonymous pieces that were later taken to be his own (for examples, see Appendix B). Moreover, in making his own copies of works by other composers, Bach, like any eighteenth-century copyist, often worked from erroneous sources. He may have edited the

377

music being copied, just as he altered his own works when making a revision copy. Sometimes the "editing" may have turned into active composing, as perhaps occurred in the two *partimenti* (BWV 907–8) discussed below or the fugue of the E-Minor Toccata (see Chapter 7).

In general, however, the problem of doubtful and misattributed works is not so great with Bach as with other eighteenth-century composers (e.g., Haydn). The majority of his keyboard works survive in signed autographs, attributed copies by close associates, or well-documented contemporary editions. Nevertheless, distinguishing true from false attributions has occupied Bach scholarship from the beginning of the discipline. Decisions about the authenticity of a work have been based on many factors, but these can be reduced to two main categories: the provenance and reliability of the sources, and the musical style. A work must satisfy criteria in both categories to be judged authentic. Even a work copied by Bach himself or a member of his family must be questioned if it seems stylistically improbable, as in the case of the Telemann suite in CB. On the other hand, something that "sounds like Bach" can hardly be accepted without reservation if the only source is a nineteenth-century edition or a lost manuscript.

But ideas about sources as well as style can change, and studies such as Marshall (1976a) or the discoveries published in Wolff (1985c) have considerably broadened the range of styles and sources associated with Bach. Attributions made on the basis of style are notoriously unreliable, and it is no longer possible to question the authenticity of large numbers of firmly attributed works, as Schreyer (1911–13) did, simply because they appear to violate rules of voice-leading laid down long after Bach's death. The case of BWV 957 (discussed in Chapter 5) shows that even a piece in an apparently uncharacteristic style, moreover one that had been edited from the lost and seemingly unreliable Schelble-Gleichauf manuscript collection, may in fact be a Bach work. On the other hand, when unlikely stylistic details coincide with a shaky attribution, as Williams (1981) recognized was the case in the famous organ "Toccata and Fugue" in D minor BWV 565, there is good reason for doubt.

In many instances, perhaps including BWV 565, it is impossible to reach a clear black-or-white decision about attribution, and various shades of gray must be applied. Even then, much probably depends upon personal temperament and prevailing scholarly fashion—whether it seems more exciting at a given moment to discover new attributions to Bach or to debunk old ones. In general, however, broad skepticism is in order, since one would not wish to reach decisions about any other works or about the nature of Bach's style on the basis of unfounded attributions.

The greatest number of questionable Bach attributions occur in relatively late sources containing pieces whose style or technical quality clearly raises questions. Fugues on the B-A-C-H motive are prominent in this category, one of the best known being a fugue in B♭ (BWV 898) whose pianistic, almost Beethovenian style seems to place it no earlier than the last decade of the eighteenth century. This work, or a clumsy *manualiter* toccata in F minor (BWV Anh. 85), is more likely a pastiche or imitation of Bach by a later composer; indeed, the toccata has an alternate attribution to one Dobenecker.[2]

In other cases the style seems plausible but the nature of the source or attribution makes it unlikely that the work has any connection with Bach or the Bach circle. For example, BWV Anh. 80 is an attractive, technically proficient variation-suite in F. The style is close to that of Buxtehude; passages in the *Allemanda* [sic] and courante also recall Handel's Suite in E, HWV 430, an early work. Conceivably, then, this is a very early Bach work. But the attribution, in lighter ink and in a later hand than the rest of the manuscript, could be nothing more than a nineteenth-century collector's guess.[3]

Similar considerations apply to the *Toccata quasi una fantasia* in A, BWV Anh. 178. While the style is not entirely implausible—among other things, the subject of one fugal section resembles the theme that Bach borrowed for the prelude of the First English Suite—the pattern of transmission would be unique for a Bach work: four English manuscripts, one of them dated 1702, two others attributing the work to Purcell (details in Rose 1968). The one source that apparently mentioned Bach as author (used as the basis of the edition in BG 42) is lost.

Other pieces have a greater chance of being genuine Bach works, despite the absence of completely dependable attributions. A number of these, such as the Suite BWV 821, have already been treated in the main text. Others are treated here in roughly chronological order as determined by style. A few less likely pieces of special historical or musical interest are also included.

Sarabande con partitis BWV 990

Sources: copy from Schelble-Gleichauf collection (lost); copy in Gb. *Edition*: BG 42.

BWV 990 would be a welcome addition to the small list of variation sets by Bach. Although its style has been placed in the mid-seventeenth century (Eichberg 1975, 45–46), the wide-spanning scales and arpeggiation in several of the variations (here called *partite*) would seem unlikely to have been written before the 1690s or so. The same is true of the harmony in some of the more expressive variations (e.g., the Neapolitan in bar 14 of partita 12). The sixteenth and last variation is a little gigue (*L'ultima partita o giguetta*) using the running figuration in $\frac{6}{8}$ found in several of Bach's early gigues (e.g., in BWV 996). While occasionally suggesting north-German organ style, the piece is clearly for harpsichord, above all in its idiomatic use of *style brisé* in several of the variations, especially the last four, which form a self-contained dance suite.

The piece is surely German; the Latinizing title (best translated as "sarabande with variations") is reminiscent of that of BWV 833, and the opening *partita*, that is, the sarabande, seems a specifically German adaptation of the French dance. Its Da Capo form recurs in a number of north-German sarabandes, such as the famous one from Handel's Hamburg opera *Almira* (later arranged as the aria "Lascia ch'io piango" in *Rinaldo*). There is another sarabande of this type in the somewhat doubtful Suite in F Minor BWV 823, whose opening bars contain a descending bass somewhat similar to the one here. Indeed, the present bass line, together with the rhythm, would not be out of place in a chaconne,[4] and the style in some of the variations recalls Handel's early keyboard chaconnes. A few mannerisms, such as the slurred downward leap in bars 6 and 11 of the sarabande, recur in Bach's own early works, and the same motive plays an important role in the first variation (*partita* 2). Hence, if the present order of the variations is original, the composer's first thoughts included the development of an expressive "sigh" figure, not virtuoso showmanship.

The basis of the variations is not primarily the melody of the sarabande but its bass line. Despite the strict maintenance of Da Capo form in all sixteen *partite*, which may grow wearying, BWV 990 remains a very attractive work. The intense concentration on a few simple motivic ideas in *partite* 2, 3, 5, and others—sometimes requiring considerable keyboard dexterity, as in *partite* 6 and 10—points to an intellectually rigorous virtuoso such as Bach. A significant work, BWV 990 would considerably broaden our view of Bach's early style if it could be shown to be his.

Fantasia and Fugue in D Minor BWV 905

Sources: F Ms. 1072; GB DRc E 24 (fantasia, bars 1–15 only); Schelble-Gleichauf collection (lost). *Edition*: BG 42.

Technical and stylistic problems in BWV 905 weaken the case for Bach's authorship, although the brief fantasia appears to have been modeled after the preludes of Corelli's three-part *sonate da camera* (Opera 2 and 4) and in this respect resembles the B-minor prelude of WTC1. A prominent Neapolitan (flattened second degree) in the opening bar of the prelude recurs in bar 19 of the fugue, which, like the prelude, is in three parts. Neither movement modulates very far, and entries of the fugue subject are confined to tonic and dominant. The part-writing is occasionally rough (bars 7–8, 43–44, 52, and 55); several other passages rely on parallel thirds and sixths to a greater extent than one would expect even in one of Bach's early works.

Still, the prelude of the Suite BWV 821 contains similar writing, and, while that work is also somewhat doubtful, Bach's authorship in both seems very possible. The style places BWV 905 in the first decade or two of the eighteenth century; a few "sigh" motives in parallel sixths (prelude, bar 10) probably rule out an earlier date. Hence, the piece could date from Bach's formative years. Despite some technical weaknesses, both movements show some of the audacity expected of him and in any case must be the products of a German composer's emulation of late-Baroque Italian style.

Fugue in E Minor BWV 956

Source: SPK P 804/8 (Leonhart Frischmuth; facsimile in Stinson 1989a, 131). *Edition*: BG 36.

As the sole surviving copy of BWV 956 is by a student of Kellner, it might have been copied from a manuscript in Kellner's possession. Stinson (1989a, 130) suggests that Kellner himself could have been the composer, finding that the piece "betrays nothing of the experimental range of Bach's early efforts." But this is perhaps to overlook the chromatic counter-melody in bars 25–26, the Neapolitan harmonies in bars 48–49, and the well-handled acceleration of surface motion in the final section. There are clumsy moments, including hidden fifths between the two lower parts (bar 21) and a banal lapse into parallel thirds (bar 28). But there is greater variety and more of a sense of drama than in two fugues known to be by Kellner himself,[5] which also lack the vestiges of seventeenth-century style found here, such as the persistent *figure corte*.

The subject, as in BWV 905/2, is of the sequential type that Bach used in some early fugues but largely abandoned after the Weimar period. Moreover, the fugue as a whole resembles those early efforts of Bach in which, after the initial exposition, single entries of the subject alternate with fairly lengthy episodes. The series of modulations suggests some tonal planning, a move to the relative major falling near the exact center (bar 35b). The final entry, in the bass (bar 63), is carefully prepared by an ascending sequence that moves to the tonic swiftly and surely from the fairly remote key of F (bars 57b–60a). In short, BWV 956 remains a "possible" early work of Bach's.

Fugue in E Minor BWV 945

Sources: Hauser collection (lost); SPK P 315. *Edition*: BG 36.

BWV 945 must also be counted as a "possible" work, although both its style and its source situation seem somewhat weaker. The lost copy from the Hauser collection was reportedly an autograph, but it lacked an attribution (Kobayashi 1973, 342, 388). Hence, the assignment to Bach might have depended on an enthusiastic guess by Robert Schumann, who first published the piece in 1839. In P 315—a late Viennese source according to Eichberg (1975, 14)—the fugue occurs anonymously alongside an Allemande and Courante in A (BWV 838) now assigned to Graupner. These have little in common musically with the fugue.[6]

The fugue has a distinctive design not unworthy of Bach: two halves, using different and sharply contrasting countersubjects. The second countersubject, introduced after the cadence at bar 34, is a lively violinistic idea, and in the final phrase a sequence derived from it is used to bring the piece to an impressive conclusion. Yet the more restrained first countersubject is poorly conceived, consistently forming weak passing dissonances—technically, *échapées*—against the other voices. Moreover, the octave leaps in the subject lead to passages that are awkward to play as well as weak contrapuntally, as when the alto leaps over the tenor in bar 22. Yet Bach's own fondness for thematic material containing octaves is clear from BWV 992, 915, and other early works. While this hardly constitutes evidence for his authorship here, it cannot be used to rule it out.

Fugue in D Minor BWV 948

Chief sources: SPK Mus. ms. 10580; LEm Go.S.15; US NHy LM 4941; SPK P 487; copy owned by Forkel (lost). *Editions*: BG 36; Dadelsen and Rönnau (1970).

This is one of the stranger pieces on the fringes of the Bach canon, excluding such obvious pastiches as the *Concerto e Fuga* BWV 909. Its fluent sequences and almost uninterrupted figuration in sixteenths mark it as somewhat later in style than the previous three fugues. Its composer, clearly a virtuoso keyboard player, admired the Italian concerto style but took an individual approach to harmony. The latter is evident in the extended dominant-ninth chord in the subject—prolonged through a whole bar by means of arpeggiated figuration—and in two chromatic sequences (bars 10–11, 54–55), as well as at least one rather surprising sequential modulation (bars 17–19).

Odd things begin to happen toward the end of the piece, where an exposition that seems to mark the return to the tonic (bar 45) is interrupted by a short, unmotivated cadenza (bar 53) in A minor. A fourth voice then enters, seemingly requiring (organ) pedals; yet the new voice does not state the subject until bar 62b. Just before the final cadence there is a second, much more lengthy cadenza passing mechanically through the entire circle of fifths. The BG sets off this passage as an "extended ending" (verlängerter Schluss), since it can be viewed as an interpolation inserted after the diminished chord in bar 66b; it is, however, present in all sources (according to Dadelsen and Rönnau 1970).[7]

Even disregarding the final cadenza, the weak counterpoint (e.g., in bars 13–14, 63–64) and several clumsy modulations (to D minor at bar 12, to F at bar 20) place Bach's authorship in doubt. Bars 65–66 are virtually unplayable even with pedals. Yet the piece has a surprisingly good set of sources, one of which, SPK 10580, was reportedly written in "Bach's immediate circle around 1726–7" (SWV). Perhaps, like the prelude to the Suite BWV 815a, BWV 948 represents an experimental stage of a piece that was never brought to final form; perhaps, like BWV 923a (see below), it was finished by someone other than Bach.

Fugue in A Minor BWV 958

Source: SPK P 291. Edition: BG 42.

BWV 958 somewhat resembles the Italianate fugue BWV 947 (treated in Chapter 5) and the fugue of BWV 905, discussed above. But it occurs only in a late source, and like a number of Bach's earliest fugues it suffers from a distant modulation placed too near the end: G major is reached at bar 50, in a piece only sixty-two bars in length. At least two other passages contain sudden, unmotivated changes of key or material (21–22, 43–46); moreover, the piece fails to maintain the integrity of the three voices, a fourth part entering occasionally but never for more than a few beats.

While the "repercussive" subject seems archaic, the first bar might have been suggested by the opening fugue in Handel's E-Minor Suite HWV 429 (fugue first published 1720). Other passages suggest an acquaintance with the fugue of Bach's E-Minor Toccata.[8] This, together with the free dissonance treatment (bars 17, 19) and some simplistic chordal figuration (bars 44–45, 48), suggests that BWV 958 is likely a derivative work of relatively late date.

Fugue in E Minor BWV 960

Source: ABB (incomplete). Edition: BG 42.

This work also has little chance of being Bach's. It looks more like a weak imitation of one of the preludes from the English Suites, marred by clumsy voice-leading and a simplistic tonal design. Direct octaves and rough passing dissonances occur in bars 9–11 and are restated in bars 72–74; the latter passage is part of a long section (bars 48–91) that modulates several times—that is, redundantly—to G major.[9]

The piece was a late entry, lacking title or attribution, at the very end of the Andreas Bach Book. The copy ends at the bottom of a page, where the indication *Verte* ("turn") suggests that more was to follow. But perhaps only a few bars are lacking; the tonal design (essentially E minor, G, E minor) has been rounded out by bar 115. A conclusion is suggested in Example A.1.

EXAMPLE A.1.   Fugue in E Minor BWV 960: suggested ending (bars 143–47)

Fugue in A Minor BWV 959

Source: Dl Mus. ms. 2405-T-31. *Edition*: BG 42.

Like BWV 960, this piece is mentioned here not because it is likely to be by Sebastian Bach but because it might be the work of one of his younger relatives or students. It seems too eclectic in style to have been written by Sebastian himself at Weimar (as suggested in the NG work-list), despite some possible echoes of the E-Minor Toccata (e.g., in bars 11–12). The figuration is inventive but sometimes more reminiscent of Friedemann than Sebastian Bach. Neither, however, might be expected to have been responsible for the banal episodes in bars 24–29 and 34–36, or the somewhat overdramatic closing gestures in the last four bars.

Sarabande in G Minor BWV 839

Source: "Notenbuch der C. F. Zeumerin" (lost, dated 1735). *Edition*: Kretzschmar (1910).

This graceful and affecting little work is even more suggestive of Friedemann Bach. His authorship would not be ruled out by the title, *Sarrabando del Sig[nore] Bach Lips[ia]*, under which it was given in a lost manuscript collection of short keyboard pieces. Among the contents (according to Kretzschmar 1910, 67) were an aria, vivace, and gigue by "Görner," possibly the J. G. Görner with whom Bach disputed the directorship of music at the university shortly after arriving in Leipzig.

The piece's restless chromaticism is handled well except in the final cadence, where the text might be corrupt.[10] Particularly characteristic of W. F. Bach is a recurring passage built over a bass oscillating between notes a half-step apart (bars 3–4, 9–10, 26–27).[11] The following piece, a *Courante di Bach* in G (BWV 840), is also harmonically adventurous but corresponds with a movement in an *ouverture* by Telemann (TWV 32:13).

Prelude BWV 923a; Scherzo in D Minor BWV 844; Andante in G Minor BWV 969; Presto in D Minor BWV 970

Sources: Schelble-Gleichauf collection (lost); US NHy LM 4813b; SPK P 563 (Michel; BWV 844a, with other short pieces); CH Zz Ms. Car. XV 244, A8b (Nägeli; BWV 844a, with BWV 815a/1); SPK P 804/39 (F. 25/2 [42-bar version of BWV 970]); SPK P 1184 (Homilius? F. 25/2); SPK P 683 (C. P. E. Bach; 44-bar version of BWV 970). *Editions*: by Roitzsch (Leipzig, 1880); BG 42 (BWV 923a, 844, 844a, 969 only).

At least some of these pieces are even more likely than BWV 939 to be by Friedemann Bach, and the set as a whole illustrates how certain later musicians made use of Sebastian's music. In the Yale manuscript the pieces form part of a *Toccatina per il Cembalo* in D minor composed of the following movements: BWV 899/1, BWV 900/2 (transposed to D minor), BWV 923a, BWV 844, BWV 969, and BWV 970.[12] The movements are linked by short transitions to form a continuous cycle, somewhat like the Pastorale BWV 590.

Pastiches formed out of disparate movements are plentiful in manuscripts and prints of the second half of the eighteenth century. The *Toccatina* is a relatively skillful example, but the anachronistic title is sufficient to cast doubt on its authenticity.[13] Although it may be possible to trace each of the individual movements to W. F. Bach, Eichberg's (1975, 25) suggestion that the arranger of the *Toccatina* belonged to the circle of the organist Kittel, one of Bach's last students, remains plausible. A more speculative possibility is that the arrangement has something to do with the Bach student known as Anonymous 5, whose fragmentary copy of BWV 923 (in SPK P 401) breaks off in the same bar (14) in which BWV 923a diverges from its model.[14]

BWV 923a seems to have been adapted from the Prelude BWV 923, an apparently authentic if perhaps unfinished work (see Chapter 10). The new ending provided in BWV 923a includes hand-crossings of a type suggesting that the composer at least knew the C-minor fantasia BWV 906/1. But other figuration ties the hands up in ways that again seem closer to Friedemann than to Sebastian Bach.

A cadence on the dominant serves as bridge to BWV 844. This is evidently a revised version of BWV 844a, also designated a scherzo but in E minor. Both versions are similar in form and proportions to the scherzo of Partita No. 3, the probable "starting point" for the composer, who has been plausibly identified as Friedemann (Eichberg 1975, 26, primarily on the basis of style). The piece has some of his quirky wit and harmonic invention and is perhaps the most successful of the group, especially in the more refined D-minor version.

BWV 969 is an attractive imitation of a fugal trio-sonata movement, with a recurring episodal idea reminiscent of a passage in the opening chorus of Cantata

No. 7.[15] But the form—a sort of modified Da Capo, with the subject entirely absent from the B section—is not found in fugues by J. S. Bach, and details like an unprepared tonic ⁶₄-chord (bar 8) seem to rule out his involvement.

BWV 970 is a revision of a little minuet by W. F. Bach (F. 25/2), one of several hand-crossing pieces apparently inspired by the *Tempo di Menuetto* in Partita No. 5.[16] Actually, F. 25/2 seems to have been revised twice; the first revision led to a forty-four-bar Presto that was subsequently reworked into the forty-eight-bar BWV 970. In all three versions the figuration creates cross-rhythms against the beat (e.g., in bars 7–10), recalling other keyboard works of Friedemann (e.g., the E-Minor Fantasia F. 21, bars 66ff.) and going far beyond the mild hemiolas in the movement from the Partitas.

Despite C. P. E. Bach's clear attribution of the forty-four-bar Presto to his older brother, it is conceivable that the subsequent version (BWV 970) was the work of an anonymous arranger. In any case, BWV 970 shows points in common with both BWV 923a and 844.[17] Certainly, however, there is no reason to suspect J. S. Bach's hand in the revisions of the Presto (as argued in Morana 1990), for BWV 970 retains much of the awkwardness and occasional redundancy of the original; for example, the B section ends with a passage drawn directly from the A section (bars 45–48 || 8–11, and 41–43a || 7–9a).

Fantasia and Fughetta in B♭, BWV 907; Fantasia and Fughetta in D, BWV 908

Chief Sources: SPK P 804/18 (BWV 907), P 804/26 (BWV 908) (both Kellner; title of BWV 907/1: *Prelude*); SPK P 485; SPK AmB 531 (attribution to Bach crossed out); B Br Fétis 7327 (Gerlach); SPK P 1071. *Editions*: by Roitzsch (Leipzig, 1880); BG 42.

These may be the most interesting of the doubtful pieces and the ones most likely to show Bach's hand, as reviser if not as composer. Both are *partimenti*, written on only one staff and, for the most part, in just one voice; the player fills in the harmony according to the figured bass notation, as in Example A.2.[18] Kirnberger

EXAMPLE A.2. Fugue in B♭, BWV 907/2, bars 8b–10 with suggested upper voices: (a) simple; (b) more florid

evidently was responsible for altering the heading of one copy to give the name of the composer as Gottfried Kirchhoff, who had written a series of preludes and fugues of just this sort, according to Marpurg (1753–54, 1:149f.). Since Kirchhoff's work, *L'A B C musical*, has been lost, it is impossible to say whether Kirnberger had actually seen it or was merely relying on Marpurg's description (Schulze 1984a, 125). But the Kirnberger copies are related textually to those by Bach's student Gerlach (see Stinson 1989a, 129; Kobayashi 1978, 51), and thus it is conceivable that Bach himself knew the pieces and employed them in teaching. He could have obtained them directly from Kirchhoff, who had become organist at Halle when Bach declined the city's offer of a job in 1714; two years later Bach examined the organ there.

The keyboard *partimento* was a widely used teaching tool; Kirchhoff might have learned of it from his teacher, Zachow, whose better-known student Handel wrote similar things (for an example, see Mann 1982). Other examples that Bach might have known include a fugue in the first volume of Niedt's *Musicalische Handleitung* (1700) and a set of sixty-two rather simplistic preludes and fugues bearing a very doubtful attribution to Bach himself (in SPK P 296). All of these examples are more or less in *stile antico*; those in BWV 907 and 908, however, are very much in the German keyboard tradition.

Regardless of the composer, if Bach himself made pedagogic use of the pieces he is likely to have revised any material taken from someone else. Marpurg's rather condescending description of Kirchhoff's fugues actually fits the two pieces only approximately. Despite the incompletely realized notation, they are in every other sense finished compositions—distinctive, well-crafted pieces with clear tonal designs. They are longer and more sophisticated than most other *partimenti*, and the initial exposition of each fugue is fully written out through the third statement of the subject. Moreover, a number of episodes contain arpeggiando figuration that, like the passage-work in the middle of the B-major prelude of WTC2 or the praeambulum of Partita No. 5, needs no further filling out.

The bass is so precisely figured that one suspects Bach of having at least revised or supplemented the original figures. Indeed, the overall style hardly rules out Bach, insofar as one can discuss his style in a type of piece of which he left no authenticated examples. Each prelude, although opening with the traditional flourish on the tonic chord, proceeds, like many of the preludes in the *Well-Tempered Clavier*, to sequential repetitions of a single motivic idea. In addition, both the fugue in B$^\flat$ and the prelude in D reveal binary symmetries, with an episode of free figuration near the exact center of each.

Appendix B. The Clavier-Büchlein vor Anna Magdalena Bach

The two little keyboard books for Anna Magdalena Bach are the sources for some of the best-known music associated with the Bach name. In fact, most of the minuets and other small pieces are not by Bach, but they deserve a brief mention here.

Bach presented his second wife with manuscript music books in 1722 and again in 1725; both are now in Berlin (DSB P 224 and SPK P 225). The 1722 book now consists mainly of the early versions of the French Suites, discussed in Chapter 14; the famous minuets and other teaching pieces are in the 1725 book, which has been published in various modern editions. Both manuscripts appear together in NBA V/4; Dadelsen (1988) is a facsimile of the 1725 manuscript.[1] The numbering of pieces here follows the NBA.

Music continued to be entered into both books well after the dates on which Bach presented each to his wife. Bach himself wrote most of the surviving entries in the 1722 volume over the next three or four years. The 1725 book opens with his own copies of Partitas Nos. 3 and 6 (see Chapter 15), but thereafter the pieces in the second book were copied mostly by Anna Magdalena over a long period probably extending into the 1740s. Other members of the family, in particular C. P. E. Bach, also entered individual pieces; Sebastian himself made only a few further contributions. From this, and from the heterogeneous but generally simple musical contents, one gathers that the book was used as teaching material for the younger Bach children.

In addition to the French Suites the 1722 book contains a few short pieces, all discussed elsewhere: the minuets BWV 813/5, 814/5, and 841; the chorale setting BWV 728; and the fragmentary Air with Variations BWV 991. There is also a fragmentary organ fantasia in C, BWV 573.

The 1725 book contains, in addition to the two partitas and two of the French Suites, several vocal works and about two dozen keyboard pieces; the exact number is a matter of definition. Most of the little pieces are anonymous, but a few composers are named, and several pieces once assumed to be by Bach have proved to be by others. All of the anonymous pieces were listed in the appendix of the Schmieder catalogue (SWV) and thus bear "BWV Anh." numbers, although a few might prove to be by Bach.

Most of the little pieces, whether or not bearing an attribution, are simple binary dances in galant style. Bach might have brought back copies of such pieces, intending to use them in teaching, from his trips to Dresden, as Schulze (1979b, 64) suggests was the case with two of the best known of these pieces, the little minuets in G and G minor, Nos. 4–5 (BWV Anh. 114–15). These are from a suite by Christian Pezold, organist at the Sophienkirche in Dresden, where Bach played in 1725. Also perhaps obtained in Dresden was the polonaise in G, No. 28 (BWV Anh. 130), which has been identified as a work of Hasse.[2]

Only a few other pieces have been identified. No. 29 is the C-major prelude from WTC2, and the untitled No. 26 is the aria from the Goldberg Variations. No. 6 (BWV Anh. 183) is a version of *Les bergeries* from Couperin's second book of *Pièces de clavecin* (1717).[3] A minuet copied by Bach with an attribution to "Mons. Böhm" (No. 21) seems too simple and galant in style to be by the well-known composer of that name. But Böhm lived until 1733, serving as Bach's Lüneburg agent for the sale of Partitas Nos. 2 and 3 (see BD 2:169 [item 224]); who else would have been known in the Bach household simply as "Mr." Böhm?[4]

The most extensive of the pieces for solo keyboard (outside of the four suites) is the *Solo per il Cembalo* No. 27 (BWV Anh. 129), which is otherwise known as the first movement of a sonata by C. P. E. Bach.[5] Also possibly by Emanuel Bach is a series of four smaller pieces. Two of these, the marches Nos. 16 and 18 (BWV Anh. 122, 124), have become fairly well known, although only the two polonaises in G minor, Nos. 17 and 19 (BWV Anh. 123, 125), show some inkling of the composer's later *empfindsam* style.[6] The second of these polonaises is also known as a movement of a keyboard sonata that bore an attribution to C. P. E. Bach in a now-lost manuscript copy.[7] On the other hand, the theme of one of the marches (No. 16) recurs in a movement from a flute sonata attributed to Franza Benda (see Dorfmüller 1989). Some of the thematic material of another march in the volume—No. 23 (BWV Anh. 127), one of the most extended and impressive of the marches and dances—resembles that of C. P. E. Bach's *Solo* and, less closely, the opening of Friedemann's Duo for two cembalos, F. 10. Thus, it is possible that these pieces are reworkings, by members of Bach's circle, of familiar melodies that provided ready material for composition exercises (and, presumably, improvisations).[8]

It is conceivable that Anna Magalena Bach herself composed some of the anonymous pieces in the 1725 volume. The likelihood of this is, however, diminished by the fact that some of her unattributed copies have proved to be of works by other composers. Women composers in Germany were few and far between during this period; still, as a former professional musician Anna Magdalena would certainly have possessed the necessary skills (see Marshall 1990, 193).

It is tempting to try to pick from the remaining pieces those that seem likely to be by Sebastian Bach. The long, somewhat asymmetrical phrases of the minuet in F, No. 3 (BWV Anh. 113), indicate a composer of some distinction; also relatively accomplished are the imitative minuet in A minor, No. 14 (BWV Anh. 120), and the chromatic minuet in C minor, No. 15 (BWV Anh. 121). Both, as Dadelsen (NBA V/4, KB, 87) observes, seem likely to be by the same composer, if not Bach himself. Perhaps less likely to be Bach's is the well-known minuet in C, No. 7 (BWV Anh. 116), or the two pieces that follow it, although Bach might have had a hand in their bass lines—particularly in the two versions of the polonaise in F, Nos. 8a–b (BWV Anh. 117). The versions of this polonaise relate to one another much as the two versions of the second courante (with "simple" and varied bass) in the early version of the First English Suite (BWV 806a). The two versions of the aria No. 20 (BWV 515, 515a) are in a similar relationship; here Bach himself wrote out the bass line for the second version (facsimile in NBA V/4, ix). This aria, incidentally, is really a minuet despite the text provided for it ("Erbauliche Gedanken eines Tobakrauchers"), which fits the melody rather poorly.

Bach is known to have composed only one polonaise for keyboard (in the Sixth French Suite), but this manuscript contains six in all—not counting the alternate versions of No. 8—reflecting the popularity of the dance. The polonaise in G minor, No. 10 (BWV Anh. 119), has some of the cocky poise that may originally have been characteristic of the dance but is replaced by fashionable elegance in most of the other examples. This may or may not point to Bach as composer, but it is difficult to rule him out entirely except in the melodically arid polonaise in D minor, No. 24 (BWV Anh. 128).

Also probably not Bach's is the untitled dance No. 32 (BWV Anh. 131), which may be a rigaudon. It could be the composing score of a Bach pupil, though one might question the assumption (in NBA V/4, 104) that this must have been a Bach *son*.[9] A bar appears to be missing in the first strain, which has only seven bars. The well-known musette No. 22 (BWV Anh. 126) also seems uncharacteristic of Bach, due to its Da Capo form and ornamental chromaticism, perhaps meant to evoke a folk idiom. Its title may be mistaken, for it is actually a *murky*, an odd dance of which C. P. E. Bach later wrote several equally eccentric examples.[10]

Chorales like Nos. 12 and 13 (BWV 510–11) or the aria No. 33 (BWV 516) might have served as exercises in continuo realization. But the numbers for soprano and figured bass, like other eighteenth-century *Lieder*, could also have been performed as keyboard solos or as songs in which the vocal line was doubled on the keyboard. The same is true of the settings in the Schemelli *Gesang-Buch* (Leipzig, 1736), for which Bach provided figured basses; how elaborately such basses were meant to be realized is unclear. No. 35 (BWV 514) of the present manuscript is a chorale setting similar to those in the Schemelli book, and here a simple but idiomatic realization, in which a varying number of inner voices is played mainly by the right hand, may be best (Example B.1). It seems unnecessary to turn the graceful little piece into an exercise in strict or elaborate four-part realization.

EXAMPLE B.1.   *Schaff's mit mir, Gott* BWV 514, bars 1–4,
    with suggested inner voices and ornaments

Notes

Chapter 1.

1. An exception was C. P. E. Bach, who was known strictly as a clavier player, even admitting to Burney that he had lost the ability to play on the pedals, through lack of practice. Unlike most of Bach's pupils, he never held an organ position.
2. Bach's Weimar cantatas date mostly from 1714–15, the Leipzig ones from 1723–29. The redating of the Leipzig cantatas is a major feature of the "new" Bach chronology established in the 1950s, which led to major revisions of his biography (see Wolff 1983a, Boyd 1983).
3. See BD 2:10 (item 7)/BR, 49. Citations of this type mean that the entry appearing in *Bach-Dokumente* (BD) is given in translation in *The Bach Reader* (BR).
4. On Bach's use of the harpsichord in the church cantatas, see Dreyfus (1987a, 23–32).
5. See BD 2:175 (item 232)/BR, 113.
6. Bach's contest with Marchand was to have taken place on the harpsichord (see Wolff 1983a, 68); during the 1747 visit to Berlin that led to the *Musical Offering* he played on the King's fortepianos.
7. See Gerber's account in BD 3:476–77 (item 950)/BR, 264–65. For further discussion of the central role of keyboard music in Bach's career, see Siegele (1975, 162–68, especially 167).
8. Professional copying did take place, and some Bach keyboard manuscripts can be traced to publishers such as Breitkopf, who traded in manuscript as well as printed music. Most such copies date from after Bach's death.
9. By "fair copy" I mean an autograph meant to serve as a final, corrected text. "Revision copy," a term introduced by Marshall (1972, 1:5), refers to an "intermediate" score in which Bach made significant compositional alterations while copying from a first draft ("composing score").
10. Recognizing this, Stinson 1989a, a study of the Kellner group of manuscript copies, is subtitled "A Case Study in Reception History."
11. There is no single catalogue of Bach manuscripts, but Kast (1958) lists the holdings of the two main Berlin libraries, and most of the *kritische Berichte* (editors' reports) for the NBA (see below) include indexes of the sources referred to in the respective volumes.
12. Works discovered since 1950 have simply been added at the end of Schmieder's original list, which concluded with BWV 1080 (the *Art of Fugue*).
13. For full bibliographic information regarding these sources, see the list of abbreviations at the head of the Bibliography.
14. At this writing Zietz (1969) remains the only full-length study.
15. The inventories of SPK P 804 in NBA V/5, KB, and of other Kellner manuscripts in Kast (1958) must be updated from the information in Stinson's Tables 1–7 (1989b, 23–42).

16. Among the anonymous pieces are BWV 939–42, 954, and 983; those with only the title by Kellner include BWV 943, 955, 963, and 986–87.

Chapter 2.

1. Those seeking guidance on performance practice in general might start with Brown and Sadie (1990) and the relevant articles in NGDMI. Many introductions, guides, and rule-books on Bach performance exist, and useful information can be gleaned from them, but they must be used with extreme circumspection; this is especially true of a number of works on Bach keyboard music by celebrated performers. Such works tend to be unscholarly and to go out of date or fashion rather quickly, and no attempt has been made to list them in the Bibliography. The one exception that must be singled out for its wisdom and good sense is Kirkpatrick (1984).
2. Among numerous writings, those in Kenyon (1988) are particularly notable. My own initial contribution to the subject (1990) may have underestimated the degree to which some proponents of "authenticity" are motivated by simple antipathy to "modern" culture, as argued by Dreyfus (1983).
3. To retrace the sometimes acrimonious dispute, one might read (in this order): Neumann (1965); Fuller (1977); Donington (1977); Neumann (1977); Neumann (1979); O'Donnell (1979). Also relevant are Neumann (1974) and Fuller (1985).
4. On the generic "clavier" see Marshall (1986, 234); on "demonstration counterpoint" see Williams (1980–84, 3:191–92; 195).
5. Bach owned five *clavecins*, two lute-harpsichords, and a set of clavichords (BD 2:492–39; 504 [items 627 and 628]/BR, 193; 197). Faulkner (1984, 17), among others, has recognized that the "3 *Clavire nebst Pedal* [*sic*]" listed in Bach's estate must have been a composite instrument intended primarily for practicing organ music (cf. Marshall 1986, 220). *Clavecin* might have indicated fortepiano as well as harpsichord.
6. Bach's concern with sonority is evident in the instrumentation of many vocal works and in reports of his views on organ registration; see, for example, the selections from Adlung (1768) in BD 3:191–92 (item 739)/BR, 257–58.
7. The "lute" pieces are discussed in this book as potential keyboard pieces. Another possible exception is the Aria variata BWV 989 (see Chap. 6).
8. Harpsichords could be and perhaps in Bach's day still were sometimes equipped with simple pedalboards; unsustainable bass pedal-points occur in the Third English Suite and the Fifth Brandenburg Concerto as well as in several fugues.
9. See Forkel (1802), 17/BR, 311—the latter with an editorial footnote summarizing the reasons for doubting Forkel's testimony in this case.
10. The idea of dividing Bach's keyboard music between organ and "clavier" seems to be first documented in the list of compositions included in Bach's obituary (BD 3:85–86/BR, 220–21), which was in part the work of C. P. E. Bach.
11. See, e.g., Williams (1980–84, 3:183–91), Blood (1979), and Rasch (1985). The introduction to the topic in Lindley (1990) should be used with caution.
12. For contemporary evidence see BD 2:450 (item 575)/BR, 443; also in Williams (1980–84, 3:188).
13. For example, it appears that the organ prelude and fugue was normally performed on full organ (*organo pleno*); see Williams (1980–84, 3:171–72).
14. Variations in the last movement of a sonata for a four-stop harpsichord composed by C. P. E. Bach in 1747 (H. 53/W. 69) each employ a different registration; see Schulenberg (1987, 111–12).
15. See the discussion of the overture of BWV 831 in Williams (1980–84, 3:180), quoting bars 88–94.
16. This is noted in Rosen (1972, 62–63), perhaps with reference to the misguided prescriptions in Bodky (1960).
17. Williams (1980–84, 3:171), quoting Stauffer (1980, 171).
18. There is no general study of rhythm in Bach's music. Fuchs (1985), Franklin (1987), and Butt (1990) survey Bach's use of articulation signs, i.e., slurs and dots, and give many useful examples. Faulkner (1984) gathers together documentary evidence concerning eighteenth-century fingering and articulation, but the author's assertions and conclusions must be treated with caution.

19. Emanuel Bach (1753–62, i.3.22) prescribes holding single notes for half their written value; this probably was not meant to be taken literally, but it does imply nonlegato as the basic touch.

20. An exceptional series of slurs beginning on the upbeat in Cantata No. 84 (third movement) is suspicious, in part because Rust, who edited the work in BG 20/1 (1872), is known to have altered Bach's notation elsewhere (see Marshall 1983). Similar slurs in some editions of English Suite No. 2 are a misreading; see Chap. 10. Butt (1990, 182) refers to a number of unusually long slurs in the oboe part of BWV 84 as "possibly not in Bach's hand."

21. Thus, analyses of Bach's rhythm that depend on a basic pulsation of small, equal values, as in Cone (1968, 59ff.), seem questionable.

22. For evidence for taking the dot as a rest in Bach's music, see Emanuel Bach (1753–62, i.3.23).

23. Joshua Rifkin has pointed out to me a consistent distinction in the notation of two motives in the overture of the Orchestral Suite BWV 1067 (bars 1–2, etc.), possibly indicating a distinction between "double-dotted" and "single-dotted" rhythms. See also Chap. 16 on BWV 831.

24. O'Donnell (1979) reaches the same conclusion about tempo but supposes further sharpening of certain rhythms as well.

25. A detailed prescription for routine chord-breaking, though possibly applying only in continuo playing, appears in Rameau (1722, 371–72 [Bk. 4, Chap. 3]).

26. Neumann (1978) argues against reliance on C. P. E. Bach (1753–62), often depending on subjective arguments—e.g., that on-beat performance of certain appoggiaturas can "disturb the unity of rhythm" (147)—or on a selective use of the evidence.

27. See Williams (1990, 43) on a passage in the sarabande of Partita No. 6, where he assumes, probably correctly, the use of a "short" appoggiatura. Emanuel Bach is speaking of the long appoggiatura when he objects to appoggiaturas that "corrupt the purity of the voice leading" (1753–62, i.2.2.17).

28. See, for example, the first two *couplets* of Couperin's *Les moissoneurs* (*Second Livre*, Paris, ca. 1717), where the sign for the *unison* dictates "pre-beat" performance of the little note.

29. C. P. E. Bach (1753–62, i.2.2.15); see Figure 79a in the Mitchell translation, and compare bar 2 of the Goldberg aria.

30. Emery (1953, 7) warns against relying on transcriptions when there is some doubt as to the reading of a sign.

31. For example, copies in ABB and MM contain ornaments added by an unknown hand. Even if these were added by Johann Christoph, they are not necessarily representative of Bach's own practice, as is apparently assumed in Neumann (1978, 121) and Hill (1987, 463).

32. The distinction might be traced to the division between *Spielmanieren* and *Setzmanieren* in Marpurg (1755).

33. Vivaldi, for example, did so in several slow movements in the concertos that Bach arranged for keyboard.

Chapter 3.

1. "Die Schöpfung einer Ordnungswelt, die keiner romantischen Beseelung oder gefühlshaften Vermenschlichung noch bedarf" (Gadamer 1946, 15).

2. McClary (1987, 61) too decries excessive "orderliness" in Bach interpretation, apparently associating it with mechanistic ("brain-dead"!) performance styles.

3. On various usages of the word *galant*, see Sheldon (1975; 1989–90).

4. For a contemporary document possibly preserving Bach's own method of harmonic analysis, see Ex. 11.4.

5. The early version, BWV 535a, is given in MM in Bach's own hand.

6. Many works of the type now known as the prelude and fugue appear in the sources under the heading *praeludium*. But the title "prelude and fugue" or its equivalent does occur often in Bach sources and will be retained here for most such pieces.

7. Other composers shared this interest; one of Böhm's suites preserved in ABB is an *ouverture* in D major, and ABB, like other keyboard sources of the period, includes direct transcriptions of orchestral works. On Böhm's influence on Bach, see Zehnder (1988) and Heller (1989).

8. Forkel noted how few musicians of his own time understood the distinction between organ and "clavier" touch; see Forkel (1802, 18/BR, 312).

9. The letter, written January 13, 1775, to Forkel, was the chief basis for the account of Bach's early development in Forkel (1802, 5–6); for the letter, see BD 3:288–90 (item 803)/BR, 278–79.

10. BWV 531 is found in MM. Böhm's C-Major Praeludium occurs in neither ABB or MM, but these manuscripts do contain between them four of Böhm's six surviving free compositions for organ or clavier.

11. Suites in which the relationships between movements are limited to similarities in thematic material are also sometimes considered variation-suites (e.g., in Godt 1990). Here the term will be used only where at least one movement is a full-fledged variation of another.

12. Hill (1987, 21) suggests plausibly that the work is by Reinken; it appears as Suite No. 4 in Wolgast's edition of Böhm's keyboard works (Leipzig: Breitkopf und Härtel, 1927–32). Böhm may never have used this technique; Suite No. 5 in Wolgast's edition, which uses variation technique in the first two movements, is also anonymous in MM, and Howard Schott includes it as Suite No. 29 in his edition of Froberger's keyboard works (Paris: Heugel, 1989).

13. Niedt (1700–17, vol. 1, introduction, paragraph 10) points out the necessity of score notation to good continuo realizations. If, as Schulze (1991) argues (see also Franklin 1991), the "Carnegie manuscript" at Pittsburgh (which uses score notation) is indeed a joint product of Christoph and Sebastian Bach dating from before 1700, then Sebastian must have been familiar with score notation no later than his early teens. Even so, Hill (1990b) maintains that Bach continued to employ tablature for several years in notating his own pieces in certain German genres.

14. See Schulenberg (1982). The evidence for Bach's use of this concept includes statements by C. P. E. Bach (e.g., portions of the letter cited in Note 9) and Kirnberger, the manuscript extracts from Niedt (1700–17, vol. 2) apparently copied by a Bach pupil (see Schulze 1984a, 126–27 and Niedt 1989, xiii), and various musical documents, such as the *partimenti* BWV 907 and 908 discussed in Appendix A.

15. The French word *ouverture* (italicized) will be used here for keyboard suites in orchestral style; see Chap. 4.

16. The autograph of the organ fugue BWV 535, a very accomplished but somewhat archaic piece, is generally dated to the end of the Arnstadt period (see Hill 1987, 4–5; 101; 132), while the concerto transcriptions have been placed in about 1713 (Schulze 1984a, 146–72).

17. The dating of the larger preludes and fugues (e.g., BWV 903 and 904) remains controversial; see Chap. 9.

18. Episodes in the form of short bridges connecting statements of the subject of course occur in earlier works, but in this book the term "episode" will be limited to longer, more distinctly articulated passages.

19. See Schulze (1984a, 18n). The *Pièces de clavecin* of J. C. F. Fischer, published in 1696 and heavily influenced by Lully, also seem to have echoes in Bach's English Suites; two movements were copied near the end of ABB.

20. Friedemann received his *Clavier-Büchlein* at the age of ten in 1720, the date on its title-page. Forkel, however, implies that Bach's students studied for some time prior to receiving any written pieces. See Forkel (1802, 38/BR, 328).

21. But the only mature sonata movement per se for solo keyboard is the third movement (for harpsichord alone) of the Sonata BWV 1019 for violin and obbligato cembalo.

Chapter 4.

1. Individual volumes of the *Neue Bach-Ausgabe* (NBA) are cited here by series and volume numbers (Roman and Arabic, respectively). For editors' names and dates of publication, see Bibliography. "KB" (*kritischer Bericht*) indicates one of the commentary volumes.

2. Ornament tables in both ABB and MM derive indirectly from D'Anglebert's, via tables in other French publications.

3. Material used in the first movement of the Suite HWV 453 was reused in the overture to *Agrippina*, that of the Suite HWV 449 in the overture to *Il pastor fido*. On the dating of Handel's keyboard works, see Best (1983). Williams (1989) compares keyboard overtures by the two composers.

4. The possibility is discussed by Hill (1987, 254–55), who notes that the Telemann pieces, if indeed early transcriptions by Bach, would have served as "significant precedents" for the concerto transcriptions.

5. For what seems to be a different view, see Williams (1980–84, 3:236–37).

6. The closing phrase properly begins after the downbeat of bar 25, not in bar 24. The flat in bar 24 is reported to be an addition to the manuscript, presumably due to a misunderstanding of the phrase structure or harmony.

7. Documentary evidence for this practice is scanty, although it is assumed without comment in modern editions of, e.g., gavotte 2 of the sixth cello suite BWV 1012.

8. Compare, e.g., the toccata in the same key (BWV 915), bars 160–64.

9. Compare bar 15 in the subject of BWV 820 with bars 50ff. in BWV 822.

10. *Aria* is a common title for movements in suites and sonatas by Pachelbel and other seventeenth-century composers; it does not imply imitation of any vocal idiom.

11. E.g., the end of Toccata 11 in *Il secondo libro di toccate* . . . (1627).

12. The repetition of bars 20b–24a, written out in NBA V/10, is indicated by signs in the manuscript and perhaps was meant to occur only after first playing the second half of the piece twice through. The copyist left out the second half of bar 19; the emendation in NBA is plausible, but the tenor in the first half of the bar might have been a misreading by the copyist of tablature letters intended for the treble.

13. The barely hidden octaves at the cadences have parallels in the *Air pour les Trompettes* in the Suite BWV 832.

14. Hill (1987, 418–20) places BWV 833 earlier than BWV 820. While the stylistic differences between the pieces might be due only to their belonging to somewhat different genres, ABB, the source of BWV 820, does appear to be somewhat later than MM.

15. The Italian form of the title in BWV 833 may help explain the stylistically impossible attribution to Bernardo Pasquini offered by several writers and discussed by Hill (1985, 250).

16. Repeated notes also occur, though less prominently, in the allemande of the Suite in G by Reinken.

17. The same notational quirk is found in many lute tablatures and older keyboard suites.

18. Bars 21–22 of the courante correspond to bars 11–13 of the allemande. Similar variation in the durational values of the ground occurs in suites by Niedt, Reinken, and others.

19. Ornaments added in the manuscript but suppressed in the NBA strengthen the movement's French character; these are given in parentheses in Ex. 4.2, although the mordents in bars 11, 13, and 21 seem unidiomatic.

20. BWV 832 appears as item 32/18 in Ruhnke (1984); the attribution to Telemann was suggested by Danckert (1924, 122).

21. A fourth copy once owned by Forkel (later, Spitta) is in PL LZu Ms. Spitta 1752/3.

22. The Brussels source once belonged to Fétis, who believed it autograph; see Dart (1970) and the reply in Dömling and Kohlhase (1971).

23. Triplet rhythms somewhat similar to those found here occur in the trumpet aria of Cantata No. 20, first performed at Leipzig in 1724. It seems unnecessary to "assimilate" the duplets to the triplet rhythm.

24. E.g., in the allemande, the "sighing" fifth in bar 9 and the "obstinate" figure in bars 18–19.

25. Similar difficulties arise in the fugues BWV 946 (bars 36–37) and BWV 954 (bars 28–30, 48) and in BWV 993 (bar 69) when played without pedals.

26. Compare the cadences at the first double bar in the gaillarde in G and in Lully's overture to *Cadmus*, both in D'Anglebert's *Pièces de clavecin*.

27. Much the same harmonic progression occurs near the close of the fugue in the Capriccio BWV 992. Stinson (1989a, 123–24) points out further stylistic parallels in the "Neumeister" chorales.

28. This version cannot be by Bach, as Kohlhase shows (NBA V/10, KB, 119). Gerber's copy was lost until recently; see Wiemer (1987), reporting ornaments in Gerber's copy that suggest that Gerber studied the piece under Bach.

29. Ledbetter (1987) surveys the relationship between music for lute and for harpsichord in seventeenth-century France.

30. Niedt (1700–17, vol. 2) prescribes such a flourish for the beginning of an improvisation, as does C. P. E. Bach more than half a century later (1753–62, ii.41.14).

Chapter 5.

1. Once again, the sole evidence is furnished by the obituary and by Emanuel Bach's letter to Forkel of January 13, 1775 (BD 3:288 [item 803]/BR, 278).
2. Both MM and ABB, which include several of Bach's early clavier fugues, also contain isolated fugues belonging to the north German organ tradition, among them works by Reinken and Heidorn.
3. In addition, Corelli and Legrenzi provided material for the organ fugues BWV 579 and 574. The fugue in the E-Minor Toccata also seems to be based on an Italian work (see Chap. 7).
4. There would be no point in including expositions as "recapitulation," since the subject itself is continually "recapitulated."
5. MM was lost at the time Naumann prepared BG 36 from the copy by Mey (presumed to be a student of Kellner). Wolffheim published the prelude as part of an article (1912) announcing the rediscovery of MM.
6. Suites, for example, are often headed simply *Prelude* or *Allemande* (referring to the first movement).
7. E.g., in the sixteenth-note motive at the end of the subject, which is the basis of the episode at bar 14, and in the treble in bars 60–61. Compare Kuhnau's Biblical Sonata No. 1 (David and Goliath), third movement, bars 8–11, and the opening of the sixth movement (*La gioia degl'Israeliti*).
8. BWV 949 is described as "doubtful" in the work-list in NG, but it bears the explicit attribution *Joh. Seb. Bach* in ABB.
9. The young Bach seems to have had a greater fascination with "sharp" than with "flat" keys; the only deep plunge into flat areas in Bach's early keyboard works seems to be the excursion in the overture of BWV 822.
10. A comparable passage in the allemande of Corelli's Op. 2, No. 3 prompted a famous controversy over the composer's tolerance of barely hidden fifths. Bach writes similarly in BWV 896/2 (bars 38–39), 954 (bar 19), and 951a (bars 20–21).
11. If the pedal part is omitted, perhaps the tenor in the second chord in bar 80 should retain the note a rather than moving to b. Otherwise the harmony on the second beat is V^6_4, which is very rare in Bach's music.
12. Presumably Carlo Francesco Pollarolo (1653–1722). As Silbiger (1987, x) points out, the capricci in ABB are stylistically distinct from the more fluent pieces attributable to this composer in Bologna, Civico Museo Bibliografico Musicale MS DD/53 (facsimile in Silbiger 1987). Pollarolo's operas were, however, known in Hamburg (see Roberts 1986, xi), and Bach might have obtained the pieces there during his student years at Lüneburg.
13. Preller's copy (P 1087) has a pedal marking for the last bass entry, in bar 112. P 409, by an unidentified copyist, has pedal markings in bars 67 and 121; only the last is likely to be authentic.
14. Griepenkerl based his edition on two manuscripts owned by Forkel, one of them supposedly in the hand of Kellner. Even if these sources survived today, the attribution of the work would remain a bit cloudy.
15. Stinson (1989a, 122) notes the "rudimentary style" of BWV 571.
16. In SPK P 247 the additional words *Organist in Freiberg* are a later entry in a foreign hand. SWV lists a fifth source (in Gb); the version is unspecified.
17. The first note in bar 2 was originally a third higher; the last note of the tenor in bar 68 is likewise a third too high (doubling the alto). The weak bass rhythm in bars 10 and 23, in which the final eighth-note is omitted to avoid low AA, is unlikely to be the original reading.
18. Bars 45–47. In P 247 this is part of a passage whose bass is assigned to the pedals (pedal markings appear in bars 27, 40, and 48).
19. The attributions in the Kellner circle copies conceivably stem from a faulty guess on Kellner's part, since only the title of P 804/17 is in his hand.
20. The reference in SWV to a copy of BWV 954 in the "Neumeister" codex at Yale (LM 4708) is erroneous. The P 804 copy of BWV 954 is on different paper from that used for the copies in P 804 of BWV 965 and 966.
21. Through a misunderstanding, the BG gave the source as "Sonata VI." For more on Reinken's originals, see Chap. 6.

22. The subject of BWV 946 is from the last movement of Albinoni's Op. 1, No. 12, in B$^\flat$. Hill (1987, 444–46) argues that BWV 949 is also derived from an Albinoni trio-sonata (Op. 1, No. 7), but the fleeting resemblances cited are not conclusive. Albinoni seems often to have used similar subjects in his fugues; a fugue in another trio-sonata by Albinoni (listed as *So* 21 in Talbot 1990, 280; ed. F. Polnauer [Bryn Mawr, PA: Presser, 1977]) has a subject similar to that of BWV 946. Bach may not have been the only German composer to borrow from Albinoni; the theme in the fugal ritornello of the Concerto BWV 985, Bach's keyboard arrangement of a work by Telemann, has a subject resembling that of the fugue in Albinoni's Op. 1, No. 11.

23. The subject was identified in Michael Talbot's article on Albinoni in NG 1:217.

24. The subject is from the second movement of Op. 1, No. 3, ed. Walter Upmeyer (Nagels Musik-Archiv, 34; 1928).

25. The middle voice in bars 24, 44, etc., comes from bar 8 of Albinoni's first violin part. Also borrowed is the motive in bars 32–33 (treble), heard earlier in bar 5 (middle voice) and in bar 13 of Albinoni's first violin part.

26. Kellner wrote d, e (eighths) in place of d (quarter). Many ornaments in Kellner's copy (some given in the BG within parentheses) are also probably his own additions. See Stinson (1989a, 57–58), for discussion and a facsimile.

27. The model, the second movement of Albinoni's Op. 1, No. 8, is printed in the Supplement to Spitta (1873–80). The complete sonata is edited by Stefan Altner (Hortus musicus, 240; Kassel, 1987).

28. Titles in P 801 and ms. 8 specify *Clavicembalum*. Other relatively early fugues designated as harpsichord pieces in dependable copies include BWV 894, 903, and 944, all discussed in Chap. 9.

29. One of the copies containing both versions, AmB 606, was presumably made for Kirnberger, who was also aware of the existence of different versions of pieces in the *Well-Tempered Clavier*.

30. Hill (1987, 432–33) mentions a copy of BWV 951a at Durham Cathedral that is preceded by a fantasia in the same key; the latter (which Hill reproduces in full) is in the style of a late seventeenth-century violin piece, resembling Bach's early style only superficially.

31. The other work is the very early organ fantasia BWV 563.

32. Corelli's Op. 3, No. 4, was published in 1689, just five years before Albinoni's Op. 1, No. 8.

33. Williams (1980–84, 1:251), however, finds a distinctly " 'German' " quality (original quotation marks) in the episodes.

34. See BWV 951, bars 110–12. Bach apparently reworked the ending several times; one source of BWV 951a (Poel. 9) gives what appears to be an intermediate version.

35. Bars 93–95 correspond with bars 29–31. For the latter, BWV 951a gives a diminished chord, which is less compelling than the Neapolitan of BWV 951.

36. The first thorough argument for the pieces' authenticity was that presented by Wolff (1985c); his findings were initially publicized in Crutchfield (1984).

37. The loss of the source used as the basis for the BG makes it impossible to know if the title is given accurately in the latter. SWV also reports a copy of this version in Gb, described as the "first version with 25 measures."

38. For example, in the fugue the bass wanders between the left hand and the pedals.

39. On Preller's version of the adagio of the Toccata BWV 916 see Schulze (1984a, 85); on his version of BWV 588, see Stauffer (1980, 192, n. 14).

40. Bars 6, 9b–11, 33 of BWV 533a diverge from the corresponding passages in BWV 533.

41. Fingerings in Preller's copy indicate that he took both notes in the left hand.

Chapter 6.

1. Compare Forkel (1802, 23/BR, 317) on those whom Bach (according to Forkel) called " 'clavier hussars'."

2. The alternate title "Fantasia" given in BG 36 is evidently editorial; the copyists of the other sources gave no title or perhaps understood the indication *harpeggiando* over bars 1ff. as a title.

3. The fantasia is included, quite properly as a doubtful work, only in the 1990 revision of SWV,

which lists editions by Max Seiffert, *Anonymi der Norddeutschen Schule: 6 Präludien und Fugen* (Organum, 4/10), and Heinrich Fleischer, *Three Bach Works for Organ* (St. Louis: Concordia, 1960).

4. The opening passage in BWV 922 uses hand-alternations resembling those at the close of BWV 921, and bars 14ff. employ figuration similar to bars 8ff. of BWV 921.

5. Compare bars 96ff. with BWV 533a/1, bars 20ff.

6. The titles of both BWV 917 and 574 are quoted here from Johann Christoph Bach's copies; BWV 574 appears in ABB.

7. Williams (1980–84, 3:92) notes resemblances between this work and a Kuhnau sonata.

8. Williams (1980–84, 3:101) finds stylistic parallels in the opening chorus of the Weimar cantata BWV 61.

9. Compare the choral entrance "Ich harre des Herrn" on an Eᵇ-major chord following a chord of G at the end of the preceding duet in the early cantata BWV 131. Kuhnau, in his preface to a set of cantata libretti published in 1710, seems to refer to such an effect when he suggests the use of "a new key [*tonus*]" when the text introduces a *conjunctio adversativa* such as "but" (*sondern*; see Richter 1902, 152).

10. Frescobaldi had already used the indication *adasio* (i.e., adagio) to indicate similar nuances in his *Fiori musicali.*

11. The title was omitted in the BG.

12. Federhofer (1958, 267) describes a treatise attributed to Poglietti containing a collection of short fugues based on various bird-calls and other extra-musical references.

13. For example, MM indicates bars 18–20 by repeat signs and contains a number of altered readings. Hill (1987, 689–91) lists variants but concludes (364–67) that the MM text was not copied from an autograph.

14. The *Ursprung der musicalisch-Bachischen Familie* (BD 1:255–61 [item 184]/BR, 202–8) describes Jacob as an oboist. But he also studied flute with Buffardin, according to a later entry by C. P. E. Bach, and Protz (1957, 407n) explains that the term *Hautboist* was used for all military musicians. One wonders if the Swedish connection has anything to do with the presence in ABB of several pieces by Christian Ritter, identified in the manuscript as Swedish Capellmeister although living in Hamburg from 1700.

15. Some of the symbols or "figures" of the lament recur, apparently with similar expressive meaning, in Bach's early organ chorales; see Breig (1990b, 171).

16. The additional heading *Arioso* is a later addition in MM, according to NBA V/10, KB.

17. See the trio-sonata Op. 1, No. 12, first movement, bar 18; this is the same sonata whose fourth movement supplied the subject for BWV 946.

18. The indication *adagio poco* in the BG derives from late sources and is erroneous.

19. One might also recall the posthorn motive in the *Aire pour les Trompettes* in BWV 832; Albinoni's Op. 1, No. 12, also opens with a downward octave leap.

20. The title, given wrongly in the BG, is correctly *Fuga all'imitazione di posta.* If the subject is indeed based on a trumpet call, it is not one of those recorded in an eighteenth-century Swedish document (see Walter 1976, 30).

21. Ed. J. C. M. van Riemsdijk (Amsterdam: Den Algemeenen Muziekhandel, 1886). The first five pieces (the basis of BWV 965) can also be consulted in the Supplement to Spitta (1873–80). Spitta himself owned the copy now in PL LZu, which had previously belonged to Forkel (partial facsimile in Wolff 1989, 321, labeled as BWV 832). I am grateful to Christoph Wolff for making his microfilm copy of this source available to me.

22. Walker (1989, 23) distinguishes between the true "permutation fugue" and the "strict double fugue" found in Reinken's *Hortus musicus.* Both types depend upon a systematic cycling of material through all parts, without episodes or lasting modulations.

23. In modern editions the six-beat bars of the courante are divided in two; the original notation is restored in Ex. 6.2 (a superfluous sharp in the bass figuration for the first note of the example is omitted).

24. The gamba part, while notated separately from the continuo, only rarely functions as an independent fourth voice.

25. Compare bars 64–65 of the fugue with bars 41–42 in the third movement of BWV 1043. An even

closer parallel occurs in the "Dorian" toccata for organ, BWV 538/1 (bars 21–22), which contains an important parallel with BWV 966 as well (see below).

26. The courante in this particular set is a new piece, not a variation of the allemande.

27. The term *figura corta* is used here for stepwise motives consisting of two sixteenths and an eighth (or similar rhythms). The pervasive use of such figures for a section or for an entire piece is characteristic of some seventeenth-century composers.

28. Hill (1987, 368–71) argues that the Krebs/Kellner version is earlier. Krebs omits variation 9, and Kellner omits both variations 8 and 9, placing variation 10 after variation 4, but his text is otherwise close to that of Krebs.

29. The NBA gives two versions for the theme, based on the copies by Krebs and J. C. Bach, respectively. Kellner's copy is closer to the NBA's main text (Krebs) than it is to the variant version (J. C. Bach).

30. NBA V/10, KB, 49. The word *manuale* is masculine; hence, *Man. italiana* in this sense would be ungrammatical. But Christoph Bach's faulty Italian is evident elsewhere as well (e.g., in his title for BWV 992).

31. The first ending of the second half of variation 9 is one such point; the first ending as given in the editions is a conjecture, and perhaps the repetition should be omitted altogether.

32. Similar notation occurs, in a somewhat similar context, in the ABB copy (No. 22) of a toccata by Pachelbel. See also the discussion of BWV 806a in Chap. 13.

Chapter 7.

1. B Br 4093 contains all but the Toccata in D Major. LEm ms. 8 contains four toccatas, but only two of these, BWV 910 and 913, are in the same hand and on the same paper.

2. One pair consists of the multimovement *manualiter* Toccata in F♯ Minor and the one-movement *pedaliter* toccata in F, BWV 540/1; another contains the *manualiter* work in D and the famous "Toccata and Fugue" in D Minor BWV 565, whose authenticity is questioned in Williams (1981).

3. The toccatas have been edited more recently in volume 3 of Lohmann (1968–79) together with other *manualiter* works; regarding the selection, see Marshall (1986, 215).

4. Hill (1987, 624) places all three toccatas within the last of three "phases" in the compilation of ABB.

5. While Bach did not know Keiser personally (according to C. P. E. Bach, BD 3:289 [item 803]/BR, 279), he might have heard such pieces during his Lüneburg years. Cf. the overtures to Keiser's *Adonis* and *Janus*, both in *Handel Sources*, vol. 1 (New York: Garland, 1986).

6. Some apparent errors in the printed text (in BG 30) may be due to poor transmission, but faulty counterpoint in the string parts (e.g., bars 15–18) and clumsy vocal writing (bar 45) in the first chorus raise questions about Bach's authorship. See Glöckner (1988).

7. Compare bars 138b–39 with bars 13–15 of the cantata chorus. Bach later used essentially the same bass in the opening movement of Cantata No. 78, in which the ostinato line is treated much as a fugue subject, migrating into the upper parts and even undergoing inversion.

8. Compare bars 12–15 of BWV 532/1 with bars 78–80 in BWV 912. The fugue of BWV 532 includes at its center entries in F♯ minor and C♯ minor (bars 64b, 80).

9. The marking is absent in some sources. Froberger, Kuhnau, and other German writers use the word *discrezione* and its cognates to refer to rhythmically free performance.

10. In this, BWV 912 differs from the organ fugue in D (BWV 532/2), whose later version includes substantial interpolations affecting the basic design.

11. Steglich's suggestion (p. 91 of his edition) is repeated in Lohmann (1968–79, 3:x).

12. Similar ornaments are also written out in three of the four movements of a D-minor suite (No. 20 in MM), serving there as in BWV 912 as a unifying motif. The suite is anonymous in the source but is included in Wolgast's edition of Böhm's keyboard works (see Chap. 3, Note 12).

13. The early version is included in later reprints by C. F. Peters. Not all variants in the early print can be authentic; for example, some B♭'s may be editorial additions, reflecting the fact that even the later version appears to have been notated without a key signature.

14. The title, *In honorem delectissimi fratris Christ. B. Ohrdruffiensis*, appears in the catalogue of the collection of the nineteenth-century collector Franz Hauser (see Kobayashi 1973, 341).

15. Compare bars 13–14 with BWV 989, variation 9, bar 7.
16. Compare bars 291–93 (Ex. 7.2) with BWV 965, allemande, bars 24b–26. In revising the toccata Bach varied the original bass in much the same way as he had embellished Reinken's, converting stepwise eighths to arpeggiation in sixteenths (cf. Ex. 6.3).
17. Compare bars 63–68 with BWV 922, bars 14–30.
18. Pestelli (1981) gives a legible facsimile of the fugue as it appears in Naples, Biblioteca del Conservatorio, Ms. 5327, fols. 46v–49r. Selfridge-Field (1990) assigns it the number Z722 and notes the presence in the manuscript (whose shelf-mark is given as Oc.2.4) of works by Durante and Platti.
19. Bars 111b–114 and 125–128a of BWV 914 correspond to bars 43b–46a and 47–50a, respectively, of the Italian piece.
20. To judge from the variants listed in BG 36, P 213 also gave readings that are occasionally somewhat closer to those of the Naples fugue, especially in bars 87–89. The remaining movements of the toccata were reportedly added in P 213 by the Hamburg organist J. C. Westphal, who also altered the text of the fugue to agree with that given by Gerber (on Westphal's identity, see Terry 1969). Evidence for an intermediate version occurs in other manuscripts, including SPK P 508 and PL LZu Ms. Spitta 1658; these contain nineteenth-century copies of the fugue (alone) with a shorter version of the coda.
21. Probably inauthentic is the version of the "Rust'sche" manuscript reported in BG 36, which gives minor-chord endings (avoiding the "Picardy third") for movements 2 and 4. Much the same anachronistic formula occurs in the D-minor toccata BWV 565/1 (see Williams 1981).
22. The dotted notation of the subject is presumably to be "assimilated" to the triplets of the countersubject.
23. Compare bars 158–60 with 91–93. For an attempt to analyze the fugue as a musical equivalent of the "rhetoric of persuasion," see Harrison (1990).
24. A copy in US NHy LM 5052 has pedal indications in the "tutti" sections despite the presence of the word *manualiter* on the title-page.
25. For further examples of such endings, see the discussion in Williams (1980–84, 3:236–41).

Chapter 8.

1. A distinction is sometimes drawn between the terms "arrangement" and "transcription," the latter implying something closer to a verbatim copy or reduction of the original. No such distinction will be made here, since the lines are too hard to draw; for example, some of the works in question would have to be considered arrangements in one movement, transcriptions in another.
2. Forkel says that Bach transcribed "all" of Vivaldi's concertos, perhaps meaning only those "which were then just published," i.e., Vivaldi's Op. 3 (Forkel 1802, 24/BR, 317). Forkel apparently did not know that Bach had arranged works by composers other than Vivaldi, nor does he seem to have had access to the transcriptions themselves; otherwise he would not have regarded the solo part of one of Bach's harpsichord concertos as one of the transcriptions (see Schulze 1984a, 146–47). For an interpretation of Forkel's phrase "lehrte ihn [Bach] musikalisch denken," see Wolff (1988c).
3. The duchy of Weimar was shared during this period by two co-reigning dukes, Wilhelm Ernst and his nephew Ernst August; Johann Ernst was the younger half-brother of the latter.
4. BD 1:20 (item 1).
5. Hill (1987, 255), noting the existence of other transcriptions in ABB, questions the need for invoking an Amsterdam practice as an influence on Bach. The keyboard suites by Dieupart copied by Bach are also playable as ensemble works, and Dieupart himself was known for his keyboard performances of works by Corelli.
6. On the transcription of Vivaldi's Op. 3, No. 5 (R. 519) by J. A. Scheibe (Bach's critic), see Stinson (1990), which includes a legible facsimile of the complete transcription. The latter is edited in Stinson (1992) together with transcriptions by others of works by Telemann and Tartini.
7. Particularly problematic are BWV 983, which is anonymous in its only early source (SPK P 804/35), and BWV 592a, found only in one late source. No fewer than nine of the *manualiter* transcriptions are *unica*.

8. SPK P 280, Bernhard Bach's copy, includes as a twelfth piece the organ transcription BWV 592. The title-page (facsimile in Schulze 1984a, 197), declaring all twelve originals to be Vivaldi's, is in the hand of Bernhard's son Johann Ernst, who studied with Sebastian beginning in 1737.

9. Some of the figuration in the concerto arrangements, e.g., that shown in Ex. 8.6b, is without precedent in Bach's earlier works. Hence, one may question the view that Bach's transcriptions are "artificial works which have more in common with the solid traditions of German keyboard music than with the colourful vivacity of the orchestral concerto" (Drummond 1980, 17).

10. For Walther, see the editions by Max Seiffert (DDT, 26–27 [Leipzig, 1906]) and Tamás Zászkal-iczky (Budapest: Editio musica, 1976). One reason for supposing that his arrangements preceded Bach's are the relatively early dates of the composers whose works Walther transcribed.

11. Bach did rewrite a solo passage employing repeated notes in Concerto No. 7 (third movement, bars 56–59) and a short phrase for the tutti in Concerto No. 14 (third movement, bars 15–16a).

12. The device was sometimes used by strings in conjunction with or in imitation of the organ tremulant (see Carter 1991). It involves no cessation of sound and is thus distinct from portato (or, as it is often called, portamento).

13. E.g., in Concerto No. 1/movement 1/bars 42ff., and in 5/1/50ff., 10/3/37ff., and 10/4/41ff.

14. See, e.g., 4/1/23–30; 5/2/9, 15, etc.; 10/3/10. The examples from Concertos Nos. 5 and 10 are the results of verbatim copying from the originals.

15. E.g., the flying octaves of 11/1/76–78, or the rapid arpeggiation (taken unaltered from the original) in 9/2/13ff.

16. The note d''' occurs in 3/3/49 (later altered in SPK P 804, as Schulze 1984a, 171, observes) and 4/1/50. The latter also includes the note c''''', so the d''' cannot be considered "isolated" (Marshall 1986, 231–32). Low BB occurs in Concerto No. 8 (several times), low BB♭ in Concerto No. 11.

17. In 2/1/25 and 9/1/31 the transcription fails to ascend to d''', which would correspond with the original. See previous Note on the alteration for Concerto No. 3 in P 804. In Concerto No. 4, the note d''' is not really "avoided" (Marshall 1986, 231–32); it simply happens to occur only once. On the other hand, d''' clearly is avoided in the prelude (bar 72) of English Suite No. 3—surely a harpsichord piece—as Peter Watchorn kindly reminds me.

18. The organ concerto BWV 595 also uses manual alternations within the opening ritornello; since the original has not been found, it is impossible to say whether or not these corresponded with solo/tutti alternations.

19. See, e.g., Concerto No. 1, third movement, bars 57–58 and 73–74. Here and elsewhere the breaking of sixteenth-note beams in BG 42 is editorial, although Bach later used this notation at points where changes of manual occur (e.g., in the *Clavierübung*).

20. A comparable passage in the B-Minor Sinfonia BWV 801 was surely intended for a single keyboard; see Chap. 10.

21. Compare bars 35–37a here with bars 65ff. in the first movement of BWV 809.

22. The BG omits a "solo" indication at bar 23, perhaps because the passage is a solo *within* a ritornello.

23. In Concerto No. 7 a double bar dictates the repetition of the opening ritornello of the last movement (piano, according to the print), but the movement is otherwise through-composed.

24. Written-out reprises are especially associated with C. P. E. Bach, but they also occur in the Triple Concerto BWV 1044 and in the *Jigg* of an early Handel suite (HWV 438). On the movements in the English Suites that are provided with *doubles* and *agrémens*, see Chap. 13.

25. Compare first movement, bars 45b–51a, and third movement, bars 88–111.

26. The title in P 280 is *la Stravaganza Op. IV, Concerto I. transposto da B♭ in G*.

27. Ryom (1986, 473) reports that the theme recurs in an aria in Vivaldi's opera *Orlando finto pazzo* (1714).

28. Mey may have been a student of Kellner; see Stinson (1989a, 31).

29. A transposition downward by a third (as in Concerto No. 5) is not impossible but would place the original adagio in C♯ minor, which seems unlikely.

30. A similar melodic line occurs in the *fantasia* movement of Bonporti's Invention Op. 10, No. 5, published in 1712. A copy annotated by Bach dates from around 1723 (NBA IX/2, 214).

31. Ex. 8.5 follows P 804 except as follows: treble, bars 30b through first beat of 32, P 804 reads a third

higher; tenor, bar 32, P 804 reads c', f', f', f', c'. The apparently defective text in BG 42 is that of P 280 with the addition of a flat on tenor e' in bar 31.

32. The composer is indicated in SWl Mus. ms. 3530 only as "Marcello"; errors in the manuscript suggest that the transposition to C was the copyist's work, as Manfred Fechner argues in his edition (Leipzig: Peters, 1977). The C-minor version is item Z799 in Selfridge-Field's (1990) catalogue of the works of the Marcello family; the published version in D minor is D935. Selfridge-Field seems to hold out the possibility that Benedetto was after all the composer, describing the attribution to Alessandro only as "reasonably secure" (365). The concerto, incidentally, is cited not in a 1976 novel by Alberto Berti but in *Anonimo veneziano* (Milan: Rizzoli, 1971), a "testo drammatico" by Giuseppe Berto that served, according to a prefatory note, as the basis of a film by Enrico Maria Salerno planned for release in 1973.

33. BWV Anh. 81, ed. in BG 38:l; facsimile in Stinson (1989a, 133–34).

34. The reconstruction by Ettore Bonelli (Padua: Zanibon, 1964) appears to disregard Bach's version while adding numerous anachronistic performance markings and, according to the English mis-translation of the preface, a "realization of the double bass and Cymbals."

35. Although Walther's copy (not seen here) is reportedly in the original key (see Selfridge-Field 1990, item C788), Schulze (1984a, 164) calls it a "copy of the arrangement BWV 981." On Scheibe's copy (which assigns the original to Vivaldi), see Stinson (1990, 263).

36. The work was previously attributed to Vivaldi (listed in Ryom 1979 as Anh. 10). The presumed model, known from a manuscript in Lund (Sweden), was not seen here. The Lund manuscript attributes the work to Vivaldi, but a manuscript from the Este collection (now in A Wn, according to Ryom 1969, 82) assigns it to Torelli (see Haas 1927, entry 143a, which gives the instrumentation as *violino principale*, two violins, two *violette*, violone, and continuo). The identification was made by Albert vander Linden (Ryom 1969, 88) and is mentioned in Schulze 1984a, 167.

37. The sentence quoted in BR, 64, under the title "Bach Instructs the Duke," actually refers to the teaching of one Jagemann; see BD 2:44 (item 53). Walther began teaching the Prince in 1707 and continued when the latter returned from his university studies in 1713.

38. ". . . ein verschwiegener Gruss in die Ewigkeit" (Schering 1902–3, 241).

39. See the edition by Siegfried Kross in *Georg Philipp Telemann: Musikalische Werke*, vol. 23 (Kassel: Bärenreiter, 1973).

40. See Albinoni, Op. 1, No. 11, second movement, ed. Walter Kolneder (Mainz: Schott, 1959).

41. Williams (1984) argues that BWV 1029 originated as a concerto.

42. Bach also omits most of the slurs and of course the figures over the bass, but these might have been absent from the early version of Telemann's score.

43. For a substantial quotation from the allegro as published in the Prince's Op. 1, see Schering 1903–4, 567. I am grateful to Joshua Rifkin for making available copies of the print and of the manuscript parts for the B♭-major concerto (in ROu Mus. ms. saec. xvii.18 51.39a); the manuscript version includes a second solo violin part.

44. Bach transcribed R. 208a for organ as BWV 594. Similar themes occur in the third movement of a concerto that Walther wrongly attributed to Meck and in the first movement of a *Concerto e Fuga* (BWV 909) bearing a clearly spurious attribution to Bach (ed. in BG 42).

45. Compare the cadential formula in bars 50–51 (also found in Concerto No. 12 [BWV 983], second movement, bars 7–9), with BWV 808, first movement, bars 31–33; the texture and material in bars 52–54 and elsewhere are also reminiscent of the suite movement.

46. BWV 595 repeats, perhaps unnecessarily, the statements of the ritornello theme in C (bars 1, 7b), G (9b, 16), E minor (25, 31b), and D minor (33b, 50). The modulation between the two last keys includes a jarring juxtaposition of the chords of B major (e:V) and G minor (d:iv).

47. There is, however, an *Ecco* movement composed of continuous forte/piano alterations in Bonporti's Op. 10, No. 10 (not one of the pieces copied in SPK P 270).

Chapter 9.

1. On the Marchand affair, see the accounts of Birnbaum (BR, 444) and Forkel (1802, 7–8/BR, 303–4). The apparent conflicts between the two (see Wolff 1983a, 68) might be due to Birnbaum's

reflecting Bach's own modesty in recounting the event (cf. BD 3: 443 [item 927]/BR, 287). Forkel uses the incident to illustrate the superiority of Germanic "ideas" over French elegance, but this, like everything else in Forkel, should be read in light of a remark in Bernal (1987, 215): "While exclusive professionalism was the distinctive form of Göttingen scholarship, the chief unifying principle of its content was ethnicity and racism." This may be an overstatement, but Forkel did teach at Göttingen, and his Bach biography contains an unattractive chauvinistic element.

2. On the doubtful fantasias and fugues BWV 905, 907, and 908, see App. A.

3. Another such piece is BWV 539/1, a short *manualiter* prelude paired in a few sources with the organ arrangement of the fugue of the violin sonata BWV 1001. The pairing may not stem from Bach (Stauffer 1980, 121–22), but there is no *manualiter* fugue in D minor to go with the prelude.

4. See fantasia, bars 87–88, 92–94; fugue, bars 16, 26–32.

5. E.g., the outer movements of BWV 1046a (the early version of the First Brandenburg Concerto) and the preludes of English Suites Nos. 3 and 5. Stinson (1989b, 457–58) finds parallels between the fantasia and the organ preludes BWV 544/1, 548/1, and 552/1, whose style indeed seems later.

6. At bar 53, in the middle section, the treble has the inversion of the opening motive of the principal subject. But this leads to nothing and seems to have no significance in the overall design.

7. The second subject also has its own sharply contrasting countersubject, an arpeggiated idea; the combination of the two at bar 41 is reminiscent of the third episode of the fantasia (bars 81ff.).

8. There is an interesting realization of the prelude of BWV 944 by Liszt in a Romantic sort of neo-Baroque style, available in various modern reprints.

9. The subject also resembles that of the first allegro of the Torelli work transcribed as Concerto No. 8 (BWV 979), as Keller (1950, 82) observed.

10. BWV 1044 adds new ritornellos at the beginning and end of each movement and inserts other ritornellos as well. While in harmony with mid-eighteenth-century views on concerto form (see Stevens 1971, 89), the structure of the arrangement ignores the ritornello structure already built into the prelude. This would necessarily raise some question about the extent of Bach's involvement in BWV 1044 even if the concerto did not possess other oddities, such as the extended keyboard range (to f'''). For arguments on both sides, see NBA VII/3, KB, 47–48.

11. See bar 53b in BWV 894/1, bar 109 in the first movement of BWV 1052.

12. The arranger of BWV 1044 must have been conscious of the underlying progression, and the new ritornello composed for the last movement is based on a sort of harmonic reduction of the original fugue subject.

13. See bar 90. The concerto at this point (third movement, bar 120) inserts a ritornello—the only substantial ritornello in this movement apart from those added at beginning and end.

14. Compare bars 84–85 of the fugue with bar 22 of the prelude, and the bass in bar 133 of the fugue with bar 10 of the prelude.

15. C. P. E. Bach's fantasias are primarily for the clavichord, and the dynamic markings adopted in the BG from the late copy P 577 presuppose a clavichord or fortepiano.

16. This version is characterized by added embellishments in the recitative, given as "variants" in the old Bischoff edition. These and other variants seem stylistically foreign to W. F. Bach.

17. Stauffer (1989) lists no fewer than thirty-seven sources, twenty more than were known to Hans David (1926).

18. Dreyfus (1987a, 149) argues that the early version BWV 1050a employed a small violone (sounding at written pitch) that was used at Weimar.

19. The bars from BWV 903a that were later replaced are given in BG 36:219–20. The other early version (that of P 803) differs from the familiar one in giving a shorter form of the cadenza in bars 21–24 (readings in BG 36:xliii).

20. As Schenker (1984, 28) appears to do.

21. None of Schenker's analyses of the passage is entirely satisfactory; see Schenker (1984), which includes a previously unpublished sketch (editor's notes, Example G). My own analytic sketches are intended only to illustrate the melodic shape of the bass and upper voices; they should not be understood as "Schenkerian" reductions.

22. Bar 37 evidently appears in various ways in the sources. The startling chord ($g^{\flat}$/$b^{\flat}$/c'/$e^{\flat}$'/$b^{\flat}$'/$d^{\flat}$'') given on the second beat in Dadelsen's edition (which is based on P 651) is a passing sonority prolonging the diminished chord on the downbeat.

23. E.g., Friedemann's Fantasia in E minor, F. 21; Emanuel's first "Prussian" Sonata, H. 24 (W. 48/1); and a flute sonata in D by Johann Christoph Friedrich.

24. The relationship, noted by Schleuning (1969, 78), was taken up by Tagliavini (1986). Bach used the version of the concerto found in Vivaldi's autograph, R. 208 (M. 314), not the version published as Op. 7, No. 11 (R. 208a = M. 452). There is also a recitative movement in Bonporti's Op. 10, No. 1, but this is not one of the movements copied by Anonymous 5.

25. See Dreyfus (1987a, 72–107, especially 89–91). Dreyfus does not mention the additional evidence furnished by the concerto arrangement BWV 594, but it was independently noted in Tagliavini (1986, 248 and 250).

26. Because the bass notes are never sustained beyond what can be managed by manuals alone, the suggestion in BG 36:xlii that the work was conceived for an instrument equipped with an actual pedalboard seems unlikely.

27. Forkel, perhaps misunderstanding an old notational convention, misread $b^{\flat}{}'$ for $b^{\flat\flat}{}'$ in bar 60; many subsequent editors followed him, including Schenker, who presents a polemical analysis justifying this reading (Schenker 1984, 38–39).

28. The sequential nature of bars 49ff. seems to have been first noticed by Schenker, but his analytical sketches (in Schenker 1984, 37 and 83) continue to insist on the faulty reading in bar 50.

29. See the fantasias in $E^{\flat}$ and in A, H. 277–78 (W. 58/6–7), published in 1785.

30. See Heinse (1903, 59), quoted in Schleuning (1973, 279).

31. Schenker (1984) contains a chart showing all the variants of the subject.

32. Dates for both autographs are from Schulze (1984b). Marshall (1976b; 1989, 315n. 13) points out several aspects of the source that might link it with the partita.

33. Rameau's rondeau *Les Cyclopes* was published in 1724, fourteen years before Scarlatti's *Essercizi*. Sheveloff (1986, 112) finds little evidence of Scarlatti's music having reached Germany before the latter part of the century.

34. Emanuel's earliest keyboard sonata was composed in 1731, according to a list of works that he himself probably prepared (see Berg 1979). No such list exists for W. F. Bach.

35. Interruptions also occur at the repeats in the Dresden autograph, but the Bethlehem autograph gives first endings that maintain the motion in triplets. It is unclear why these are absent in the Dresden autograph.

36. A similar notational convention seems to be assumed in Altnikol's copies (SPK P 402 and 430) of the prelude in $F^{\sharp}$ minor of WTC2 (bars 7–8); see Chap. 12.

37. The convention of adding an accidental to an ornament sign to indicate the precise notes of the ornament already occurs with Couperin, but it seems to have been unknown in the Bach circle prior to Emanuel Bach. See C. P. E. Bach (1753–62, i.2.3.19, especially the additions of 1787).

38. E.g., the "Wedge" for organ BWV 548/2, the fugue in the C-major solo violin sonata BWV 1005, and the fugues in the lute works BWV 997 and 998 (discussed in Chap. 16).

39. Thus Dadelsen and Rönnau (1970), following a suggestion in Schreyer (1911–13, 2:34–36).

40. The completion in Ex. 9.6 derives almost all of its material from the extant fragment; its length is based on the assumption that the fugue would have filled the bottom of fol. 3v in the Dresden autograph as well as one face of a now missing folio originally attached to fol. 1 (see Schulze 1984b).

41. See the excerpt from P 551 in BG 36:xliv.

42. As in an example taken from a relatively late source, in Hogwood (1988, 152). Stauffer (1989, 161) gives an illustration from a Salzburg copy of BWV 903 implying that each chord in the arpeggio passage is to be rolled twice. C. P. E. Bach (1753–62) at one point (i.3.26) clearly calls for a single upward and a single downward arpeggio on unspecified "long" note-values, but in reference to half-note chords in his own D-Major Fantasia H. 160 (W. 117/14) he directs that each chord be "twice broken" (*im Harpeggio zweymahl vorgetragen*, ii.40.14), without specifying the direction of the arpeggiations.

Chapter 10.

1. The CB is now kept in the Yale University library at New Haven. Herz (1984) contains a detailed description of CB, supplementing and correcting that in NBA V/5, KB; most of the dates and

identifications of handwriting given below are taken from these two sources. The only true critical edition is NBA V/5; there is also a facsimile edition by Ralph Kirkpatrick (New Haven: Yale University Press, 1959). A popular edition by Herrmann Keller (Kassel: Bärenreiter, 1927; available in various reprints) attempts completions of the fragmentary pieces but is riddled with errors.

2. The full title of the organ book (DSB P 283) makes its pedagogic purpose clear; it begins: *Orgel-Büchlein worinnen einem anfahrenden Organisten Anleitung gegeben wird, auf allerhand Art einen Choral durchzuführen...* (see BD 1:214 [item 148]/BR, 75).

3. CB numbers correspond with the numeration of the pieces in NBA V/5. The pieces are not actually numbered in the manuscript.

4. Indepdendent texts for BWV 924, 924a, 925–26, 928, and 930–32 are apparently found only in CB; of these only BWV 926 and 928 appear in composition or revision autographs. BWV 927 exists anonymously in both CB and SPK P 804/53, and in later sources; BWV 939–42 are evidently preserved only in anonymous copies in SPK P 804/53.

5. The table in D'Anglebert's *Pièces de clavecin* (Paris, 1689) appears to have been the model for that in Dieupart's *Six Suittes de Clavessin* (Amsterdam, 1701), from which Bach copied several suites (see Schulze 1984a, 18).

6. One nineteenth-century editor was badly confused by this notation; see the discussion of English Suite No. 2 in Chap. 13.

7. Neumann (1978, especially 127–32) presents an unnecessarily polemical argument to prove the same point. His argument for "pre-beat" performance (132–49) is less solid and depends on questionable assumptions about "harmonic logic," "rhythmic logic," etc.

8. The more usual interpretation, which stems from an overly literal reading of D'Anglebert's table, is that D'Anglebert's *cadence* is a trill preceded by a turn (see, e.g., Neumann 1978, 392).

9. *Triller von unten* and *Triller von oben*; see C. P. E. Bach (1753–62, i.2.3.22–28).

10. The same is true of the prelude BWV 930 = CB 9; these are the only two pieces with fingering assuredly by Bach.

11. LeHuray (1981) makes a similar observation about Byrd's music.

12. See bars 22–23 and 39 (right hand), 34–35 and 38–39 (left hand).

13. Edition in BG 40:151. The source, SPK P 285, also contains the similarly reworked chorale setting BWV 683a (given in NBA IV/4, KB, 51).

14. Another source (SPK P 1149) attributes BWV Anh. 73 merely to "Bach"; the independent pedal part is not typical of C. P. E. Bach's fully authenticated organ works, but the style of the added portions does not rule out his authorship. For a facsimile from R 25, see NBA IV/1, KB, 122–24. The work derives from BWV 639 (in the *Orgelbüchlein*).

15. BWV 1044 is based in part on BWV 894 (see Chap. 9). BWV 668 is derived from the prelude *Wenn wir in höchsten Nöthen sein* BWV 641 in the *Orgelbüchlein*.

16. Dates are from Herz (1984) and Stinson (1989a).

17. The same movement appears in BWV 814a (a version of the Third French Suite); see Chap. 14. Bach's entry in CB looks like a rough draft, implying that BWV 929 is the original version.

18. At this writing the NBA has not yet issued the preludes, apart from those preserved in the CB. Dehnhard (1973) is a good edition.

19. In the source the lower staff of bar 9 repeats the reading of bar 8. The simpler emendation found in many editions (a, b, c') is that of BG 36.

20. Plath (NBA V/5, KB, 54) dates the first entry to 1722–23, the completion to 1725–26.

21. In CB the piece is labeled *Praeludium 2*, but the digit is a later addition.

22. It is not entirely clear whether or not the final revision is in Bach's own hand; the omission of necessary accidentals implies that whoever made the entry was composing, not copying from another source.

23. The piece following BWV 931 in CB (after a blank page) is an untitled bass line resembling the ritornello for a continuo aria. While conceivably another exercise in improvisation or composition over a bass line, corrections by the unidentified copyist imply that it is a first draft. BWV 931 is often taken to be the work of an unidentified "French composer" (as in Herz 1984, 93).

24. The most important sources containing all six preludes are SPK P 885 (Kittel) and SPK P 540

(Forkel). Individual preludes also occur in manuscripts by the copyist known as Michel, who was employed by Emanuel Bach.

25. Siegele (1975, 119) takes the high note as a sign that the piece was originally in C and was transposed up a step to fit into the ascending sequence of keys used for the set.

26. Kellner's copy indicates lute as the medium; the suggestion that the piece is "for lute or keyboard" was made by Spitta (1873–80, 2: 646, quoted by Kohlhase, NBA V/10, KB, 156).

27. Bach continued to use "Dorian" signatures until around 1723. In CB he still uses the two-flat signature for both the Invention and the Sinfonia in C minor, but these are notated with three flats in the revised version of 1723.

28. BWV 872a/1 occurs as an independent piece (without the Fughetta BWV 872a/2) in SPK P 226; see Chap. 12.

29. Dadelsen (1975, 133) speaks of BWV 841–42 as "composition exercises of the young Wilhelm Friedemann that J. S. Bach corrected [verbessert]."

30. None is by an identified copyist: SPK P 648 and P 1094; LEm ms. 2a; and DK Kk Weyse C, I, 105. BWV 952 is edited in BG 36:184 and by Dehnhard.

31. Reported by Hans-Joachim Schulze in a program note in Bach-Fest Buch (1975, 171; subsequently in Schulze 1984a, 81). Griepenkerl's edition, which was the sole source for the BG, was based on a manuscript said to be in Kellner's hand.

32. Bach's son, born in 1715, died in Jena in 1739, more than a decade before Preller's arrival; see Schulze (1984a, 80–88).

33. See, e.g., the second part of the overture in A by Dieupart, from one of the two suites copied by Bach.

34. Bach employs a comparable technique in the central section (bars 33–58) of the opening movement in the B-minor flute sonata BWV 1030.

35. The source containing the most complete selection from the group is SPK ms. 10490 (see Brokaw 1985, 24–25).

36. Stinson (1989a, 127) points out the unusual order of the first three entries (I, V, V) but finds this insufficient reason for doubting the work's authenticity (questioned in the NG work-list).

37. Compare the subjects of the "Erselius" Fugue BWV 955 and of the chorus "Himmelskönig, sei willkommen" in Cantata No. 182; also the chorus "And with his stripes" in Messiah (where the same motive appears in the minor mode).

38. Reports that the Yale copy is incomplete are erroneous; a fragment on page 53 is followed by a complete copy on the next two pages. The handwriting was identified in Kobayashi (1983).

39. Herz (1984, 209–10) traces the tuning instructions to the first edition of Werckmeister's Orgel-Probe (Frankfurt and Leipzig, 1681), which was not seen here. Neither the tuning instructions nor the stringing charts in the Yale manuscript match other printed works of Werckmeister.

40. Compare bars 6–7 with BWV 903/1, bars 33–34; bars 24–25 (or 27–28 et al.) with BWV 903/1, bars 36–37; also bars 42–43 with BWV 903/1, bar 34. Bar 20 also recalls solo figuration from the D-Minor Concerto BWV 1052 (first movement, bars 46ff.). These parallels eliminate most of the doubts about Bach's authorship raised by an early edition of BWV 923 (Berlin: T. Trautwein, 1826; cited in SWV) that attributes the work to W. H. Pachelbel. This attribution is not found in any extant source, and nothing in the works attributed to W. H. Pachelbel in the edition by Hans Joachim Moser and Traugott Fedtke (W. H. Pachelbel: Gesamtausgabe der erhaltenen Werke für Orgel und Clavier [Kassel: Bärenreiter, 1957]) approaches BWV 923 in the ingenuity of its harmonic progressions or figuration.

41. This aspect of the work anticipates some of the sonatas of C. P. E. Bach, in particular the curious four-movement sonata in D minor composed in 1749, H. 60 (W. 65/24).

42. Copied by Friedemann: Inventions in E minor, F, A minor, and B♭, and most of the Invention in G. Fair-copy autographs: Inventions in C, D minor, E♭, and D. The systematic order of the keys of the pieces suggests that Bach planned both sets ahead of time.

43. What may be an intermediate arrangement, in which each invention is immediately followed by the sinfonia in the same key, occurs in DSB P 219, a copy by Anonymous 5.

44. See BD 3:476 (item 950)/BR, 264. Gerber's account does not mention the Sinfonias, but these are perhaps to be understood among the Inventions.

45. See, for example, the first movement of Emanuel's First Prussian Sonata H. 24 (W. 48/1), the

second movement of Friedemann's Sonata in D, F. 3, and the final movement of Emanuel's Sixth Württemberg Sonata H. 36 (W. 49/6).

46. The initial word is *Auffrichtige*, not *aufrecht* ("upright") as one might guess from BR, 86, which gives a translation of the complete title (original in BD 1:220–21 [item 153]).

47. On the meaning of *durchführen*, see Sachs (1980, 138–40), who points out the close line-by-line parallelism of the extended titles of both collections.

48. Cf. Walther's (1732, 178) definition of *Composition*: "die Wissenschaft, Con- und *Dissonanzen* also zusammen zu setzen."

49. Flindell (1984, 9–12) suggests that the change from *Praeambulum* to *Inventio* was related to Werckmeister's usage of the latter term.

50. SPK P 270 contains copies by Anonymous 5 of four of Bonporti's inventions, to which Bach added some basso continuo figures. The copy dates from 1723 according to Kobayashi (NBA IX/2, 214). These versions of the sonatas were edited in BG 45 as possible works of Bach. Facsimiles of the copies in P 270 appear in the edition of Bonporti's Op. 10 by Roger Elmiger and Micheline Mitrani (Biblioteca Musicale Trentina, 6/1–2, 2d ed., 1984).

51. See, for example, the two-part pieces among Pachelbel's Magnificat fugues, ed. Hugo Botsiber and Max Seiffert in DTÖ 17 (1901).

52. But the continuolike bass line in bars 1–2 is embellished by the treble in bars 3–4, hence conforming to the principle in the other inventions by which the bass, if present at the opening, presents a countersubject to the treble theme.

53. Forkel refers to the Sinfonias as inventions in the title that he added to his own copy, SPK P 220; cf. Forkel (1802, 55/BR, 341).

54. *Johann Sebastian Bach: Inventionen und Sinfonien*, ed. Erwin Ratz and Karl Heinz Füssl (Vienna: Wiener Urtext Edition, 1973). Less adequate is the edition by Rudolf Steglich (new edition, Munich: Henle, 1979) with a cursory editorial commentary, whose English translation contains errors that will baffle students—e.g., the reference to "triplets" (for *Triospiel*, i.e., playing in three voices) in Sinfonia No. 5. Among other elementary analytical studies are J. N. David (1957) and, on the sinfonias, Johnson (1986).

55. The alterations begin with the bass at bar 21b and lead to an extended closing phrase, which reaches the final cadence on the third beat rather than the downbeat of the last bar.

56. The fifth note of the subject was originally c", with parallel readings in each subsequent statement. In Ex. 10.11, in addition to the change indicated, bass f was originally g.

57. The treble of bar 5 shows alterations in both CB and P 610 to correspond with the revised version of the subject, but neither is assuredly by Bach. The original reading for the second note of bar 5 is d", not b♭'.

58. For a survey of twentieth-century opinions on the problem in this particular piece and elsewhere, see Schleuning (1979, 33–60, especially 59–60).

59. See, e.g., the cadential formula at the end of the four-part chorale *Jesu, meines Herzens Freud'* BWV 361 or in bar 2 of "Freuet euch, ihr Christen alle" (BWV 40/8).

60. See C. P. E. Bach (1753–62, i.2.3.18). The passage explains the substitution in some sources of appoggiaturas for short trills in the subject of the Fughetta BWV 961.

61. The staccato dots in some editions of the D-Major Invention are all erroneous, stemming from a "chance ink-spot" in bar 5 according to Dadelsen, in the preface to the offprint from NBA V/3 (Kassel: Bärenreiter, 1971), vii.

62. The copies of Sinfonia No. 5 by Gerber and Anonymous 5 differ in interesting ways from both the original version in CB and the final state of P 610. Bach himself entered the ornaments and embellishments into Gerber's copy, perhaps relying on memory, since these differ somewhat from the readings of P 219, where the ornaments are also a later addition.

63. The C-Minor Fantasia (i.e., Sinfonia) would have occupied two missing pages at the end of CB; its text, as well as the missing second half of the Fantasia in D, is reconstructed in NBA V/5 from SPK P 220.

64. As Plath notes in NBA V/5, 126. If Plath's reading is correct, the bass of bars 1–2 would have had to be composed before the treble, which fits only with the revised bass line.

65. In P 610 Bach writes the note as d♭', probably to avoid misunderstandings created by the notation

in CB, which uses a single flat. Oddly enough, in P 610 Bach used a single large flat for the b♭♭′ in the same bar.

66. G♭ and C♭, given in bars 13 and 26, respectively, in BG 3, are absent from both CB and P 610.

67. See C. P. E. Bach (1753–62, i.3.18); the relevant discussion at the end of the paragraph was added only in the 1787 edition.

Chapter 11.

1. The editions were by Forkel (Leipzig, ca. 1801), Schwenke (Bonn, 1801 or 1802), and Nägeli (Zürich, 1801).

2. Exemplars are reported from the 1713 Vienna edition and the 1715 Augsburg editions; Walther (1732, 246) mentions a 1702 edition. Modern edition in Ernst von Werra, *Johann Kaspar Ferdinand Fischer: Sämtliche Werke für Klavier und Orgel* (Leipzig: Breitkopf und Härtel, 1901).

3. The subject of Fischer's fugue in E, also used by Bach, resembles a traditional Gregorian motive, while the subject of the E-minor fugue also occurs in Buxtehude's Praeludium BuxWV 142 in the same key.

4. SPK P 401, copied by Anonymous 5. The copies of the preludes in CB show traces of a similar ordering, and changes in the numbering of a few pieces in the autograph of WTC2 suggest that there, too, some minor-key pairs might have once preceded the corresponding ones in the major.

5. Fischer also published a volume of such pieces, the *Blumen Strauss aus dem anmuthigsten musicalischen Kunst Garten* (Augsburg, 1732); another example available in modern reprint is Gottlieb Muffat's 72 *Versetln sammt 12 Toccaten . . .* (Vienna, 1726).

6. Reprint in *Faksimile-Reihe Bachscher Werke und Schriftstücke*, vol. 5 (Leipzig, n.d.).

7. For the German text, see BD 1:219 (item 152).

8. One exception, the trio for the closing minuet of the Suite BWV 819, is in E♭ minor.

9. For example, the quasi-scientific study by Barnes (1979) assigns "prominence" values to individual major thirds on a largely subjective basis; Barnes asserts that because the prelude in C♯ of WTC1 is "a fast-moving piece in two parts . . . the ear has no chance to judge whether the major thirds are good or bad" (49, 51).

10. Forkel's assertion that Bach favored the clavichord in his own playing (Forkel 1802, 17/BR, 311) may represent a confusion between the preferences of the older Bach sons (his principal informants) and those of Sebastian himself.

11. Agricola's copy in D, in SPK P 595, reportedly contains pedal indications.

12. One of the most thoroughgoing examples of recapitulation, however, occurs in the fugue in F♯ of Part 2. The term "recapitulation," it will be recalled, is used here for any episodic passage that is restated, including restatements that are transposed or in inverted counterpoint.

13. Bischoff's edition, still available in modern reprints, is somewhat more arbitrary than the BG and often fails to distinguish between authentic and inauthentic variants.

14. Older literature refers to a "Fischof autograph," actually the copy by Anonymous 5 (DSB P 401); a "Zürich autograph" (now in NL DHgm), in fact a copy by Bach's student Meissner; and a "Müller autograph" (DSB P 202) predominantly in the hand of Anna Magdalena Bach. The actual autograph (DSB P 415) was referred to as the "Volkmann-Wagener autograph."

15. The pages bearing the fugue in F♯ and the beginning of the prelude in F♯ minor are missing from P 415, but the text can be reconstructed from copies.

16. See NBA V/6.1, Appendix 1. This version, designated α1, is known from the "Konwitschny" manuscript, preserved on film in LEb (see Stauffer 1989, xxviiin. 18). Its readings are usually close to those of Forkel's edition (the "Forkel version" of the older Bach literature).

17. The first seven preludes in CB represent Dürr's version α2, and their divergencies from α1 are listed in NBA V/6.1, KB, 134. The four remaining preludes represent stage α3; Bach had evidently carried out further revisions on WTC1 while the CB was being copied.

18. The chief source for the information in Table 11–1 is NBA V/6.1, KB.

19. All the preludes were expanded or significantly revised in some way save for those in E, F, F♯ minor, G♯ minor, B♭ minor, B, and B minor. The fugues in G and B♭ minor were also slightly expanded, and the ending of the fugue in B♭ was rewritten.

20. For this reason the score in NBA V/5 bears a footnote indicating that its text, transcribed literally from the CB, may be "nicht authentisch." Riedel (1969, 93–96) refers to the text of NBA V/5 as a "conflated version."

21. Bars 28–34 are absent in the earlier versions.

22. The early edition by Schwenke gave an additional bar prior to bar 23; this reading recurs in some later editions. The insertion was not necessarily Schwenke's own invention; see NBA V/6.1, KB, 181.

23. Schenker (1969, 37), among others, opts for the diminished chord, since the alternate interpretation would have the suspension (c′) ornamented by its own resolution (b).

24. In the earlier versions Bach was less careful about voice-leading, allowing a number of octave doublings (e.g., in bar 12) as he did in other arpeggiando passages, e.g., in the Chromatic Fantasia.

25. Bach later made an additional rhythmic change to improve the voice-leading in bar 15; this, as well as a late alteration in bar 12, is omitted in most editions prior to NBA V/6.1.

26. Marpurg (1753–54, vol. 1, *Tab. X, Fig.* 1).

27. The early version skips bars 26–35 and has just two bars in place of bars 35–38. In an intermediate version (given in Appendix 2 of NBA V/6.1) the figuration of bars 34–35 is somewhat simpler, and there are three bars in place of the last four of the familiar version.

28. This was probably the normal meaning of the word in the Baroque. In Frescobaldi's *Fiori musicali* (Venice, 1635), which Bach knew, the preface already directs the use of "adasio" (= adagio) playing at *trilli* (i.e., at cadences?) and *passi affetuosi*.

29. The alteration is visible in the copy in P 401, reproduced in Dürr (1986).

30. See Helms (1981). Dürr (1986) gives facsimiles of the relevant pages from P 401.

31. Kirnberger (1771–79) reduces the texture of the prelude in A minor and the fugue in B minor to a figured bass.

32. Example 11.4 is transcribed from the facsimile in Dürr (1986, 164–65); not all figures are clearly legible, and a few notes appear not to bear any figures.

33. See "Der Organische von der Fugue," in Schenker (1925–30); Schenker criticizes Riemann and Busoni for seeing a division at bar 15.

34. P 415 contains a few subsequent revisions, notably the exchange of the first and fourth notes in the opening bar, as well as a later revision of the bass in bar 8 and of parallel passages. Editions in which the prelude opens on g♯‴ give the earlier reading.

35. The same would be true in bar 29, if the slash visible in the facsimile of the autograph indeed represents an acciaccatura between the notes b♯ and d″; it is absent from the NBA and most other editions.

36. No. 6 in Froberger's autograph collection of 1658, No. 6 in the edition by Guido Adler (in DTÖ 4/1, 6/2).

37. Marpurg (1753–54) used the term *Doppel-Fuge* for any fugue with a regular countersubject, but the term is misleading in cases such as this, where the second subject is never passed systematically through all five voices.

38. Some editors clarify the voice-leading by altering the f‴ in bar 96 from a whole-note to a half-note, but this has little justification in the sources. The other five-part fugue also contains some ambiguous voice-leading (fugue in B♭ minor, bar 37); see the discussion in BG 14:237–38.

39. Mozart's arrangements of certain Bach fugues are only the best known of many. One of the sources containing the "correction" in bar 96 is by Schwenke (SPK P 204), who arranged some of the pieces in WTC2 for string quartet; these are in SPK St 455. The NG work-list for Mozart lists an arrangement of the present fugue for string quintet as a doubtful work.

40. Reported in NBA V/6.1, KB, 428. One of the copies also contains the ornamented version of the D-minor fugue, discussed below; in bars 42–43 of the present fugue this copy includes an attractive embellished reading for the treble, adopted in some of the early editions and possibly authentic.

41. The Weimar organ compass is uncertain; see Williams (1980–84, 3:125). Bach's Leipzig organ parts avoid low C♯ (see Marshall 1986, Table 4).

42. Facsimile in Dürr (1986). I do not know the meaning of the indication *c.e.* in bar 11, but it cannot be an abbreviation for *con espressione*, since the contemporary term would have been *con affetto* or the like.

43. See NBA V/6.1, KB, 170. The source, the copy in NL DHgm, is actually a composite manuscript,

one portion of which was copied by Meissner. The D-minor fugue is in the portion (which Dürr designates B2.12) by an unidentified copyist.

44. Virtually unplayable ornaments were also added to Bach's original text in the printed version of the three-part triple Contrapunctus 8 in the *Art of Fugue*; this might have been authorized by Bach, but the *Abklatschvorlage* (see Chap. 18) for this piece was not in his hand.

45. This version was unknown to Forkel, and, since the prelude is not in the CB, its first publication appears to be that in Appendix 1 of NBA V/6.1. Also little known is the late revision in bar 34 (the substitution of g for e in the tenor) to avoid a cross-relation.

46. The bass anticipates the full form of the second subject in bars 18b–20. The combination of this archaic subject with a vivid running idea has a fortuitous parallel in the chorus "Wretched Lovers" in Handel's *Acis and Galatea* (HWV 49a), composed around 1717.

47. The pencil entry (illegible in facsimiles) reportedly reads "nicht Allabrevemässig sondern wie der 1ste Tact gewesen, fortgespielt." The remark was included in an eighteenth-century copy and hence could have been added to the autograph by a member of the Bach circle; see Dürr (1988b, 97).

48. Following the dotted eighth, P 415 has four thirty-seconds followed by a sixteenth; the first two thirty-seconds were later altered (not necessarily by Bach) to sixty-fourths. Only P 401 among the early sources is reported to give a grammatically correct reading, which most editions follow.

49. For arguments for and against a D-minor original, see NBA V/6.1, KB, 188. Marpurg (1753–54, vol. 1, *Tab.* XI, *Fig.* 2) quotes the opening of the fugue in D minor, but most of his quotations from pieces in "difficult" keys are transposed up or down a half-step.

50. Marpurg 1753–54, 1:8. Walther (1732) uses the same term for an *inversus* answer.

51. Forkel, in one of the passages that led contemporaries to doubt his musicality, argued for what is in fact a completely erroneous reading of bars 25–26, eliminating the suspension while creating parallel octaves with the treble (see Forkel 1802, 27/BR, 320).

52. The Gounod parallel was noted by Riedel (1969, 337).

53. A number of Bach's ensemble movements with arioso melodies include a similar element in the accompaniment, assigning it either to the string or woodwind chorus (First Brandenburg Concerto, adagio) or to continuo alone (Cantata No. 202, opening aria).

54. For other views on how to articulate the subject, see Williams (1983a, 338–39).

55. Some editions place a slash through the end of the trill sign, signifying a terminating turn (suffix). While the suffix should presumably be played (see C. P. E. Bach 1753–62, i.2.3.13 and i.2.3.23), the sign for it is not in the autograph.

56. Salzer (1929–30) argues for the motivic nature of virtually all ornaments in the music of J. S. and C. P. E. Bach, but this depends upon the Schenkerian doctrine of "parallel structure."

57. The sign is present in the Konwitschny manuscript (the source of the early version) and as a later addition in P 202.

58. Bars 17–18 are absent in the early version. In bar 1 the autograph lacks the trill, but the trill is present in P 401 and other copies. The autograph does have it in bars 7 and 12 (left hand).

59. Although the relevant pages of the autograph are lost, the dotted figure is already present in the version of the Konwitschny manuscript. The latter lacks the *tr*, but this would have been understood.

60. Bach slightly expanded the fugue as well, turning the final bar into two.

61. Compare, for example, Cantata No. 127 (*Herr Jesu Christ, wahr'r Mensch und Gott*), third movement, bars 31ff.

62. As in the G-major fugue, one suspects the thirty-seconds to have arisen as embellishments of figures in simple sixteenths. But the Konwitschny manuscript preserves only a few such readings here, e.g., in bars 16b–17a.

63. The prelude preceding Fischer's E♭-major fugue opens somewhat like the Praeludium in the same key, BWV Anh. 177 (ed. in BG 36:88). This fine piece is now regarded as the work of Johann Christoph Bach (1642–1703), but if so it is probably earlier than the Fischer work.

64. Compare the subject of Canzona I in Frescobaldi's *Secondo libro di toccate* . . . (Rome, 1627).

65. Rosen (1972, 128) notes the somewhat similar thematic use of a cadential formula in the first movement of Haydn's D-Major Quartet Op. 50, No. 6.

66. As Marpurg (1753–54, 1:46) puts it, the answer is "borrowed" (*entlehnet*) from the subdominant (*der Quarte*).

67. See Recercar 8 in the *Recercari et Canzoni* (Rome, 1615). The material and rhythm of the opening section in Bach's fugue suggest a more recent model: the closing fugue in the last sonata (also in A) of Corelli's Op. 3, from which Bach had borrowed the subjects of the organ fugue in B minor BWV 579.

68. Bars 46–48 || 17–19 transposed; 49–50 || 29–30 transposed; treble of 51–54 || alto of 17–20.

69. See NBA V/6.1, KB, 190. The First Brandenburg Concerto has been dated to 1716; see Dreyfus (1987a, 253n. 38). Dürr (1984, 63) argues against assuming an "allzu frühe Entstehung."

70. See bars 16, 43, 48, 69, etc. One hand must stretch a ninth even if the final bass note is sustained by pedal (bar 86).

71. Bars 30–36 are derived from bars 19–21 (repeated); bars 37–44 || 9–16, with transposition and voice-exchange. The first two bars of the coda (45–46) originally repeated bars 15–16, transposed by a fifth, but Bach later exchanged the two upper parts.

72. Both movements lack tempo markings in the Konwitschny manuscript.

73. For example, the fourth note of the tenor entry in bar 4 was originally c$''$, not d$'$; this is confirmed by the earlier copy P 401.

74. One might compare the final allegro of Corelli's Op. 3, No. 7. Both the texture and the opening thematic material of Bach's prelude also have a close parallel in the *bizzaria* movement of Bonporti's Op. 10, No. 7 (not one of the movements in SPK P 270).

75. Keller (1965, 127) sees here an analogy to the *Devisen-Arie* (motto aria) of Italian Baroque opera.

76. Ties could be introduced between tenor and bass f$'$ on the fourth beat of bar 13 and between alto and soprano g$'$ in bar 44. Compare bar 3 in the Sinfonia in B$^\flat$.

Chapter 12.

1. At first Bach may have intended to form a set of only fifteen pieces in "primary" keys; see Franklin (1989b, 259).

2. Actually, Bach seems to have kept at least two distinct copies of each prelude and fugue, only one of which survives in most cases; see below.

3. Emanuel's earliest sonatas can be securely dated back to 1731 (see Berg 1979); those of Friedemann are not so easily datable, but two mature works were published in the 1740s.

4. Franklin (1989b) and Jones (see Note 7) provide detailed discussions of the sources. The older discussions in Breckoff (1965) and Brokaw (1985) also contain still-useful information (see also Brokaw 1989); Kobayashi (1988) and Herz (1990) provide dates for the autographs.

5. For a facsimile of the London autograph (GB Lbl, Add. ms. 35021), see Franklin and Daw (1980) and the review by Wolff (1983b).

6. Aspects of handwriting and paper-type, discussed in detail in Kobayashi (1988) and Franklin (1989b, 244–54), furnish another index for the threefold division.

7. Franklin (1989b) distinguishes two distinct "stages" of revision (these are distinct from the three stages of copying in the London autograph). Richard D. P. Jones has further refined the chronology of Bach's revisions in the London autograph (see *MT* 132 [1991]:441–46, 607–9). In addition, he suggests that Bach may indeed have produced a fair copy (since lost), and reassesses Altnikol's first copy P 430, granting it greater authority than most previous editors have done. In the absence of a complete critical report (promised in Jones's forthcoming edition), Table 12–1 and the discussions here of individual movements refer only to "early" and "later" versions.

8. An attempt to see the piece as a Frescobaldian *toccata di durreze e ligature* (in Keller 1965, 136–37, repeated in Brokaw 1989, 228) overlooks important distinctions in rhythm and tonal design.

9. For the early version (BWV 870a), see No. 8 in BG 36, Appendix. Lindley (1989a) lists errors in two more recent editions, and both Lindley (1989a) and Brokaw (1989) include facsimiles from SPK P 1089 showing the prelude and the beginning of the fugue.

10. It is unclear whether or not Bach had planned the expansion of the C-major prelude before commencing the fair copy in the London autograph. Franklin and Daw (1980, vi) point to some evidence against this, but see Brokaw (1989, 233) and Jones (*MT* 132:442).

11. For a more conventional sequence using similar motivic material, see the Concerto for two harpsichords BWV 1061, first movement, bars 5–6.

12. See bar 27b, corresponding with bar 13 in the first section. It is perhaps necessary to emphasize that G minor is never the dominant of C major; in the present context it must be understood as ii of IV, just as D minor at bar 13 is ii of I.

13. Bar 30 corresponds with bar 15 in BWV 870a.

14. Brokaw (1989, 236–37) sets forth the opposite view that the revisions of the bridge "seem intended to obscure . . . the crucial medial cadence" (i.e., at bar 20). But in fact the revisions increase the amount of contrast between the bridge and the recapitulation.

15. Other sources show later refinements, e.g., a rewritten right-hand part in bars 67–70.

16. See Lindley (1989a). One must question what Lindley calls the "remarkable 1-1-1 fingering" for the alto in the final cadence of the prelude, which makes it impossible to hold the quarter-note d', or the cramped 5-3 fingering for the right hand in bars 21–2 of the fugue (Lindley's Ex. 11). Lindley seems to agree with Faulkner (1984, 23), who supposes that the fingerings in Vogler's copy "probably transmit Bach's intentions"; LeHuray (1990) gives a judicious evaluation of Vogler's fingerings.

17. Some editors see a new (tenor) voice entering in bar 14, but there remains only one middle part through bar 18. The eighths in bar 16 (e$^{b\prime}$, c″, b$^{b\prime}$, c″) are beamed together in the London autograph, not divided between tenor and alto as in some editions.

18. On BWV 547, see Stinson (1989a, 115).

19. For the earliest version of the prelude (BWV 872a/1), see BG 14:243.

20. The voice-leading is further revised in the Altnikol copies, although Franklin (1989b, 269n) holds out the possibility that the latter might give an intermediate version.

21. The ornament, already present in the early version, is notated as a c-appoggiatura (not a small eighth-note) in the early sources, which seems to imply fairly short performance. The word *allegro* (uncapitalized) occurs over the second beat of bar 25 in the autograph.

22. For the nineteen-bar early version, see BG 36:225. The intermediate version apparently has never been published.

23. It is not entirely clear which are the earlier and which the later readings, although the Altnikol group gives what seem to be a few distinctly earlier variants in the prelude (bars 49, 61). In the past, a C-minor version of the fugue in a copy from the Kellner circle (SPK P 804/11) has been assumed to be an early version, but this is uncertain, especially in light of Kellner's unauthorized transposition of the "Albinoni" Fugue BWV 950.

24. Kirnberger (1771–79, 2/1:124) quotes the subject of the present fugue alongside that of BWV 961 (in $\frac{12}{8}$) in order to demonstrate that the latter is slower.

25. The first four (chromatic) notes of the second subject are foreshadowed in bar 20 and by the repeated chromatic figures used as counterpoint to the first subject in the *inversus* exposition.

26. Franklin (1989b, 269–70) considers all ten preludes of group 2 (to which the D-major belongs) as employing a "reprise" and five as having a "large three-part structure." But the late appearance of the reprise in some of these (e.g., F minor) distinguishes them from full-fledged sonata forms.

27. Friedemann still avoids the literal return in the first movement of F. 3.

28. That is, a dotted eighth followed by a sixteenth is to be executed as a triplet quarter followed by a triplet eighth.

29. For the earliest version, BWV 875a, see BG 36:226. The London autograph, which gives an intermediate version, is in the hand of Anna Magdalena Bach, as is a copy in SPK P 226 giving a slightly earlier intermediate version. Sebastian himself entered a first group of revisions in the London copy. Later revisions, among them the thirty-seconds in bars 22 and 24, were added in the London copy, but in an unidentified hand (see Franklin 1989b, 273–74n).

30. The source, SPK P 595/5, gives the fugue in D under the title "Fugetta" (see Brokaw 1985, 30); Breckoff (1965, 73) reports the presence of pedal markings.

31. Thus, one might add the prelude to the list of pieces from WTC2 regarded by Franklin (1987, 459) as possibly meant for the lute-harpsichord. The traditional late dating of the lute suite BWV 998, accepted by Franklin, is challenged by Kobayashi (1988, 65).

32. This reading could be an error or a late revision; some copies apparently have b″, not b$^{b\prime}$, on the last eighth of bar 45.

33. The London reading b, a, g$^{\sharp}$ is clearly wrong; the later reading g$^{\sharp}$, f$^{\sharp}$, e creates hidden octaves with

the treble (A, G$^\sharp$). Altnikol's reading b, g$^\sharp$, e makes little sense motivically; Kirnberger's text (c$^{\prime\prime}$, b, a) seems strongest but was later altered to g$^\sharp$, f$^\sharp$, e.

34. Marpurg (1753–54, vol. 1, *Tab.* 20, *Fig.* 4) quotes a subject and a countersubject—both similar to the present themes except for mode (Phrygian)—from Froberger's Fantasia 2 (I am grateful to Howard Schott for the identification). Froberger, like Bach, introduces the subject in diminution shortly after the halfway point.

35. This interpretation is bolstered by the ornament signs in the autograph. The prefixed trills in bars 29 and 86 (*Triller von unten* and *von oben*, respectively) sound odd with a sharp upper note, less so the ordinary trills in bars 33 and 89.

36. Nevertheless, Williams (1983a, 337) counsels against playing the opening of the prelude "smoothly," and indeed the slurs imply some articulation of each half-note beat. In bar 11 the first two beats are slurred together, but here the bass has a dotted half on the downbeat.

37. The subject of the last movement of the Fifth Brandenburg Concerto has a similar metrical shape and is equally subject to misunderstanding.

38. A fourth appearance of the episode, in bars 66–71, is cut off prematurely, and the section continues with two further entries of the subject.

39. In place of appoggiaturas on the second beat in bars 44 and 67, the autograph has here the sign for a *tremblement appuyé*.

40. The second countersubject cannot be used in the bass, as this would produce parallel fifths.

41. See, e.g., the *brisé* writing in bar 15 and the somewhat spurious exchange of material between bass and tenor in bars 23 and 25, where the notated imitation is hardly audible as such. Bars 15 and 25 are notated somewhat differently in the earlier (?) version transmitted in the Altnikol copies.

42. The most convincing case is in the three-part mirror fugue in the *Art of Fugue* (see Chap. 18). The evidence gathered by Collins (1966, 311–12) for the pervasive "resolution" of triplets to duplets in Bach's music is scanty, but some such convention might apply in a few special rhythmic figures.

43. The first subject enters twice toward the end of the second section (bars 29, 34b), but neither entry is combined with a full statement of the second subject.

44. The interpolation, essentially a dominant pedal, resembles the dominant pedal in the F-minor fugue (bars 50ff.) in both structural function and rhythm (repeated eighth-note chords).

45. Altnikol's copy in P 402 lacks the tempo mark. Among other readings in the Altnikol group of sources are rhythmic variants for the last two bars; these variants suggest that the dotting on the sixteenths might not originally have been present throughout the prelude.

46. See Snyder (1980, 549–53), who includes a quotation from Werckmeister's *Harmonologia musica* of 1702 that draws a connection between canon and "gedoppelt *Contrapunctus*."

47. The close of the prelude seems to have made an impression on Friedemann Bach, for he appears to quote it in his Fantasia in C Minor F. 16 (bar 54).

48. The Altnikol copies give what are probably later readings, notably in bars 14, 18, and 32. The status of Bach's other autograph, P 274, is unclear; while closer to BWV 901/1 in bar 6 it appears to give revised readings in bars 8, 16, and 23.

49. See bar 8, where the two autographs find different ways of maintaining the appearance of four parts.

50. E.g., in bars 23–32; the technique is used with particular intensity in the incomplete fugue in C minor BWV 906/2.

51. If one cannot engage the coupler while playing, the first section can be played on the coupled eight-foot ranks, the second section on the upper keyboard, and the third section on the lower keyboard with the addition of the four-foot rank (drawn by the left hand while it rests in bar 96).

52. The low notes are found in the London autograph, the eighth-rest in the Altnikol copies.

53. As Jones points out (*MT* 132:609), altered readings in Altnikol's copy P 430 produce a more regular sequence in bars 23–24 and make bar 30 consistent with parallel passages in bars 1, 17, and 26. Nevertheless, the reading of the London autograph (later, according to Franklin 1989b, 265) may be superior in bar 24, where the dominant chord on the third beat seems stronger than Altnikol's ii^7.

54. Larsen (1972, 143) refers to Seiffert (1899, 206–7) for comparable themes by Pachelbel, Buxtehude, and others. These are actually closer to the subject of the F-minor fugue of WTC1 than to Handel's.

55. Marshall (1976b, 6) points out formal similarities as well as the use of the same sort of notation to indicate hand-crossing in the autographs of the two pieces.
56. E.g., those in the Sonata in G for two flutes and continuo BWV 1039 (= the gamba sonata BWV 1027).
57. This formula may be related to a type of cadence kindly pointed out to me by Russell Stinson in certain early pieces, e.g., BWV 1097 (one of the "Neumeister" chorales). These place a particularly harsh clash between tonic pedal and dominant harmony in the penultimate bar.
58. Cf. *Recercar ottavo, obligo di non uscir mai di grado* in Frescobaldi's *Il primo libro di capricci . . .* (Rome, 1626). Butler also sees Bach's countersubject as an example of *contrapunto alla zoppa*, a "rhythmic obligo."
59. While the combination of the two subjects in the B-major fugue is invertible at the octave, Bach never actually inverts the counterpoint of bars 27–30 at the octave.
60. The fugue, though hardly a sonata form, does have a sonatalike tonal design. Cadences in the dominant (bar 27) and subdominant (bar 60) mark the ends of the "exposition" and "development," respectively.
61. See H. 36 (W. 49/6), first movement, bar 64.

Chapter 13.

1. For the original titles of the Partitas, see Chap. 15. Bach's own title for the English Suites is unknown; a copy by C. F. C. Fasch has a title resembling that of the Partitas, but as it mentions Bach's Leipzig post it cannot date from before 1723 (see NBA V/7, KB, 39–40).
2. On the date and for a facsimile of Bach's Dieupart copies, see Kobayashi (1989, 38); also Schulze, (1984a, 42n). A piece by Couperin appears in the second Little Keyboard Book for Anna Magdalena Bach; see also the discussion below of the *agrémens* for the sarabande in the Second English Suite.
3. In the sources of Bach's suites the term *gigue* is sometimes spelled *gique*, no doubt reflecting the local pronunciation. Walther (1732, 281) gives the alternative spelling *Gicque*. *Gigue* will be used here throughout.
4. Kuhnau had used the word *partie*, evidently an exact equivalent for *partita*. The word *suite* went undefined in Walther (1732), even though he used it in the definition of the word *Ouverture*.
5. The familiar order was recognized as normal by the late seventeenth century; Mortier's posthumous print of Froberger's suites (Amsterdam, ca. 1697) disregarded the composer's original disposition of the movements in favor of what was called on the title-page a *meilleur ordre*.
6. Dürr's commentaries (NBA V/7–8, KB) are the source for most of the information given here regarding the sources of the English and French Suites.
7. Dieupart himself allowed the possibility of performing his suites as ensemble works; it is unclear whether or not Bach was aware of this when he made his copies of two of the works.
8. In DSB P 1072, begun by the Bach student Anonymous 5 around 1719, the words *1re Suite* in the title for BWV 806 are a later addition. The numbering of the suites still differs from that of the final version in Gerber's copies, which date from 1725 (NBA V/7, KB, 16ff.).
9. P 1072, in its final state, is entitled *Six Suittes avec leurs Preludes* [sic] *pour le Clavecin*. Walther gave a similar title in his copy of BWV 806a.
10. Forkel (1802, 56/BR, 343). The words "Fait pour les Anglois" in one eighteenth-century source are a later addition in an unidentified hand, possibly but not necessarily J. C. Bach (NBA V/7, KB, 29; see facsimile in NBA V/7).
11. Dieupart's suites (Amsterdam, 1701; modern edition by Paul Brunold [Monaco: Editions de L'Oiseau-Lyre, 1934]) bear a dedication to the Countess of Sandwich, and the composer reportedly spent much of his career in England, although Walther (1732) does not mention this.
12. The copy of the revised version made by Anonymous 5 in P 1072 was completed before the title was changed (see Note 8 above).
13. BWV 806a is edited in NBA V/7. An adequate dating for Walther's copy (DSB P 803) is not available at this writing; it cannot be assumed to have been made while Bach was still in Weimar.
14. The suite BWV 818a contains another instance of Bach's composing a new movement as a variation of an existing one (see Chap. 14).

15. I am grateful to David Fuller for confirming that Walther's copy in DSB P 801 does not include the gigue in A. It does include Dieupart's A-major suite, according to Zietz (1969), who also states that both are in Walther's hand.

16. Jaccottet (1986, 198–99) points out several additional thematic parallelisms between BWV 806 and the Dieupart suite. Some less convincing parallels are drawn in Dannreuther (1893–95, 1:138).

17. P 1072 is the principal source for both editions. A facsimile in NBA V/7 shows the first page of music in P 1072, containing the passage in question; this served as the basis for the reading in Ex. 13.1. Yet the text of NBA V/7 repeats the sign found in BG 13 and 45, in which the vertical stroke is displaced to the left, as in the sign for a mordent. The same apparently inauthentic sign recurs through both BG and NBA editions of the English Suites; no mention of the discrepancy can be found in NBA V/7, KB.

18. See bars 1, 6, 13, and 16. In some editions these signs are replaced by undulating vertical lines, indicating a broken chord; BG 45 has both indications.

19. See Walther (1708, 37, paragraph 87), where the sign is used to indicate the breaking of pairs of eighth-notes moving in parallel thirds. In the next paragraph, however, the same sign on a chord consisting of two quarters, also a third apart, indicates an acciaccatura.

20. Walther's title for courante 2 is *courante précedent* [sic] *avec la Basse Simple*; although this movement corresponds with double 2 of the revised version, there are substantial differences between the two. Courante 2 was omitted in the copy by Mempell (LEm ms. 8), which suggests that there was some ambiguity in Bach's own material as to which movements were to be copied.

21. Several copies preserve what may be an intermediate version for bar 24 (see NBA V/7, KB). In Ex. 13.4a, NBA V/7 gives alto e' as a dotted half, but the notehead was possibly filled in, to judge from the film of P 803 seen here. The sharp on bass d suggested by the NBA in the same bar has no basis in the source.

22. The editor of BG 13 added staccato dots under the slurs, perhaps under the impression this was an example of *Bebung*. But this effect is achievable only on the clavichord and involves an alteration of pitch.

23. Concertos: first movement of First and Fourth Brandenburg Concertos; fugues: "Wedge" in E minor for organ BWV 548/2, second movement of Sonata in C for violin BWV 1005, second movement of lute suites BWV 997, 998.

24. Possible piano passages: from bar 55/note 2 through bar 59/1 (left hand: to 60/1); 62/2 to 66/1; 70/2 to 78/1; 80/2 to 82/1.

25. There is a type of concerto movement in which the first solo entrance is quiet or lyrical, but Bach imitates this type only in later, more galant works, e.g., the fragmentary opening allegro of the A-major flute sonata BWV 1032 (see Marissen 1988).

26. P 1072 and several other early sources give the *agrémens* in this form. The version on two staves, which includes alterations in the inner voices in bars 15–16, 19, etc., apparently derives from the lost copy by Gerber (see NBA V/7, KB, 77).

27. It may be significant for dating that the prelude employs a cadence formula rare in later works but used in the same key in the second movement of Concerto No. 12 (BWV 983), bars 8–9. The third movement of the same concerto (bars 41–44) is practically quoted in the gigue of Suite No. 4.

28. For Dürr's reconstruction of the earlier reading (originally present but erased in AmB 489, a copy owned by Agricola and Kirnberger), see NBA V/7, KB, 138. NBA V/7 contains a facsimile of the page in P 1072 bearing Bach's autograph entry of the later version.

29. The dissonances in bars 9 and 11 were overlooked by most copyists as well as the editors of BG 13 and 45.

30. Frescobaldi: preface (*Al lettore*) to the first book of toccatas (Rome, 1615). Bach: see the title of P 1072, quoted in Note 9.

31. Cf. prelude, bars 46, 50, etc., and the musette.

32. There are two distinct versions of the ornamentation. Gerber and Anonymous 5 give mordents on the upbeats in bars 18, 20, and 21. The Agricola/Kirnberger copy (AmB 498) places mordents on the downbeats of bars 19, 21, and 22, marking the downbeats but weakening the effect of the passage.

33. Echoes of the same idea occur in the prelude BWV 894/1 and in the opening sinfonia of Cantata

No. 169, probably based on a lost concerto (in the later version for harpsichord, BWV 1053, the opening gesture is accompanied by the lower string parts).

34. The motive is perhaps what led Dannreuther (1893–95, 1:138) to claim this piece as further proof of Dieupart's influence on Bach.

35. Staccato strokes appear in AmB 489 and related copies. A few late copies, e.g., that by Fasch, omit the tempo mark and have common time in place of cut-time.

36. The late source AmB 489 contains a few additional ornaments—not found in most editions prior to the NBA—as well as some signs that may represent further "diminutions" (as Dürr suggests, NBA V/7, KB, 153).

37. The variations are described and transcribed by Dürr in NBA V/7, KB, 156. For Kirnberger's "method," see Chap. 14 on the gigue of the E-Major French Suite.

38. The figuration resembles that in the little prelude BWV 900/1, also in E minor, which might be a contemporary work.

39. This would have been indicated by a slur in addition to the dots; see C. P. E. Bach (1753–62, i.3.19).

40. Bach uses rondeau form in the gavottes of the early Suite BWV 822, the violin partita BWV 1006, and the flute suite BWV 1067.

41. The mordent in the theme, placed editorially on bass g in Ex. 13.10b, actually appears on the alto or tenor note in the sources, according to NBA V/7, KB, 172.

42. Cf. the gavotta in Corelli's Concerto Grosso in F, Op. 6, No. 9.

43. A copy by Penzel, a student at the Thomasschule (LEm Poel. mus. Ms. 26).

44. In the *Art of Fugue*, both *rectus* and *inversus* versions of the four-part mirror fugue have trills in bars 11 and 23. There, and in the two-harpsichord arrangement of the three-part mirror fugue, a few other ornaments are present only in the *rectus* or the *inversus*, not in both.

45. Siegele (1960) is a detailed description of the present gigue.

Chapter 14.

1. NBA V/8, KB, 77–78; see BD, 3:173 (item 715).

2. These are the organ fantasia BWV 573 and the Air with Variations BWV 991 (see Chap. 10). There might once have been many more sketches or drafts; about forty leaves were removed, probably in the eighteenth century (see NBA V/4, KB, 26).

3. The 1725 volume contains two of the French Suites as well as two of the Partitas, but otherwise it is of relatively little importance as a source of Bach's own music. See Appendix B.

4. See, for example, the revisions in: Suite No. 3, allemande, bar 10; sarabande, bars 21–22. Suite No. 4, allemande, bars 7, 9, 14; gavotte, bar 5. Suite No. 5, allemande, bars 7, 21. The changes are most easily studied by comparing versions "A" and "B" in NBA V/8 (discussed below).

5. Because Jones and Müller both give each suite in only one version (corresponding more or less with NBA version "B"), these editions are not mentioned in the lists of editions preceding the discussions of the individual suites.

6. Anna Magdalena's copies of two suites in the 1725 *Clavier-Büchlein* (also in NBA V/4) give texts essentially identical to Dürr's version "B."

7. In bar 14—see the facsimile from P 224 in NBA V/4.

8. Dürr in effect indicates (NBA V/8, KB, 58) that the readings for version "B" are indeed a collation, at least as far as performance signs are concerned.

9. La Couperin appeared in the *Quatrième Livre* of 1730. A copy of Couperin's rondeau *Les bergeries* in P 225 is distinct from the version in Couperin's *Second Livre* (1717), but it is unclear whether the version in P 225 derives from the print or from a prepublication manuscript.

10. Partita No. 1 was published in 1726, and Partita No. 6 occupies some of the early pages in the 1725 *Clavier-Büchlein*.

11. The BWV number 819a originally applied only to the new allemande; it has now been extended to the entire suite as given by Vogler.

12. Compare BWV 819, bars 2–3 and 9–10, with BWV 817, bars 1 and 9. The two movements also share a syncopated motive, used in the second half of each (BWV 819, bar 20; BWV 817, bar 22b), and both turn to the relative minor just after a cadence to the tonic (in BWV 819, see bar 7).

13. Dürr criticizes the chromaticism of the new allemande as "somewhat artificial" (NBA V/8, KB, 76).
14. Anonymous 5 is thus the only copyist to give both allemandes, and his entry of the new allemande has been dated to "after 1731" (Helms 1981, 193–94). Dürr places Vogler's copy no later than 1729.
15. It is conceivable, however, that there ought to be a tie between the first two notes of the bass in both versions of bar 10.
16. Compare bars 25–28 with English Suite No. 2, bourrée 2, bars 17–20.
17. E.g., the dotted rhythms in the bass in allemande, bars 7, 15, where the Altnikol copy gives apparently earlier readings.
18. Compare bar 20b in the allemande of English Suite No. 6.
19. The bass also takes the melody after the double bar in the sarabande of the Sixth English Suite, but only for two bars.
20. See the discussion of such repeats in BWV 820 and 822 (Chap. 4). As no copyist is reported to have written out the Da Capo, the fermata in the last measure (as shown in modern editions) is presumably a *fine* indication and does not imply any particular lengthening of the last note.
21. The note-values in the gigue of the partita were doubled when it was published; hence, both gigues originally used the same principal note-values: dotted quarters and eighths.
22. Similar rhythmic notation occurs in sections of Froberger's canzoni and capricci. There is also an example in the *manualiter* setting of *Wir glauben all' an einen Gott* BWV 681 in Part 3 of the *Clavierübung.*
23. See also the discussion of Partita No. 6 in Chap. 15. Starke (1972, 34–36) argues for literal interpretation of the notation in the triple-time versions of Froberger's gigues. The MM gigues include those belonging to Suites Nos. 5 and 7 in Wolgast's edition of Böhm's keyboard music; on Wolgast's Suite No. 5, see Chap. 3, Note 12.
24. Cut-time appears to have been the norm in seventeenth-century duple-time gigues. The NBA's version "B" has common time, but Jones reports in his edition that P 418, P 420, and Gerber all give cut-time.
25. Related types of courantes and gigues appear in the suites for cello and violin; at least the cello suites are probably earlier (see Eppstein 1976, 47).
26. The dissonance in bar 1 (a'/g″) is resolved by transfer, that is, treble g″ resolves to bass f on the second half of the fourth beat. This simply does not work when the upper line is moved to the bass.
27. Anna Magdalena's hasty writing of slurs is evident in the facsimile in NBA V/4, viii. Slurs in her copy of the gigue from the first cello suite (in SPK P 269) are equally careless.
28. Except for the alternate minuet and an important variant in the sarabande (see Ex. 14.5), the text of BWV 814a differs only in small details from that of NBA version "B."
29. That BWV 814a stands between versions "A" and "B" may also be implied by its readings in bar 23 of the anglaise, where Anonymous 5 first changed and then restored the original reading; BWV 814a retains the rejected note d' in place of bass a'.
30. The loss of the autograph page that presumably gave the title of the movement makes it uncertain what Bach originally called it (see NBA V/4, KB, 32).
31. Curiously, the low note is avoided in the first ending (bar 16A), and one must emend the d in bar 9 to D upon repetition.
32. The NBA gives the minuet only as part of version "B"; in the copy by Anonymous 5 it is a late insertion of the same date as that of the allemande of BWV 819a (facsimile in NBA V/8).
33. At least some of the mordents in CB appear to be later additions. Those in the subject of the gigue in French Suite No. 4 appear only in the copies by Anonymous 5 and Gerber.
34. See bass of allemande, bars 17–18; courante, 11–12 and 32; gavotte 1, 13–15.
35. See below on the prelude. In gavotte 2, bars 26–28 recall the prelude in F minor and the fugue in F♯ of WTC2.
36. Michel also copied BWV 872a/1; see Chap. 12.
37. See the facsimile in Dadelsen (1958, plate 8), transcribed in Marshall (1972, sketch 167).
38. In bar 19, a copy from the second half of the eighteenth century (DSB AmB 76) reportedly gives the second note in each of the top two voices as a sixteenth (without double-dotting on the downbeat). This source also has a plausible variant in the allemande, bar 7 (bass).
39. E.g., "Mein gläubiges Herze" in BWV 68, or the duet "Wir eilen mit schwachen doch emsigen Schritten" in BWV 78.

40. As Jones suggests (page 81 of his edition).

41. Walther (1732, 372), citing Mattheson (1713); the citation suggests that Walther knew few examples firsthand.

42. In the autograph (see the facsimile in NBA V/4 or that attached to the separate edition of BWV 816 by Hans-Christian Müller [Vienna: Wiener Urtext, 1983]) some of the sixteenths are clearly insertions, the products of revisions made either while copying or shortly thereafter.

43. Gerber already had the revised version available for his copy, made in 1725 or soon afterward. The only revisions involving changes in notes appear to be those in the bass of the courante, bar 29, and of the polonaise, bar 2.

44. Cf. Forkel (1802, 38/BR, 328) on Bach's habit of playing a piece for a student prior to the latter's studying it.

45. See the *polacca* in the First Brandenburg Concerto and the polonaise in the suite with flute BWV 1067.

46. There is apparently no manuscript authority for placing the minuet immediately before the gigue, as in some editions. Altnikol, Gerber, and Vogler all place it after the gigue, which is where it is printed in the NBA.

47. On Kirnberger's *Methode Sonaten aus'm Ermel zu schüddeln* (Berlin: Birnstiel, 1783), see Newman (1961), who includes the first half of Kirnberger's derived sonata.

Chapter 15.

1. For the announcement of Partita No. 1 in the November 1, 1726, issue of the Leipzig *Post-Zeitungen*, see NBA V/1, KB, 9.

2. The cantatas in question include BWV 35, 47, 169, 49, and 188; see Dreyfus (1987a, 63).

3. Partita No. 3 was likewise restricted to a relatively narrow range in the version of the *Clavier-Büchlein*, reaching d''' only in the scherzo, added for the print. The low AA in the allemande was also a later addition. For more on the dating of works through keyboard range, see Dürr (1978).

4. See Marshall (1976a, 347–48) on the possibility of Scarlatti's influence on Bach, which might be seen not only in the hand-crossings in Partitas Nos. 1 and 5 but in the wild leaps of the capriccio in Partita No. 2 and the acciaccatura in the scherzo of Partita No. 3 (bar 28).

5. The full title, repeated in essentially the same form in each installment of the Partitas, begins: *Clavier Ubung* [sic] *bestehend in Praeludien, Allemanden, Couranten . . . und anderen Galanterien; Denen Liebhabern zur Gemüths-Ergoezung verfertiget von Johann Sebastian Bach . . . .*

6. For details of the work's publishing history, see NBA V/1, KB, 9ff. There were two subsequent issues of uncertain date, each containing a small number of musically insignificant changes.

7. The *Handexemplar*, GB Lbl Hirsch III.37, is referred to in NBA V/1, KB, as exemplar G 23.

8. Wolff (1991b, 218, translation of 1979, 68). The previous quote is from Wolff (1991b, 215, translation of 1979, 67). The exemplar in question is the NBA's G 25 (in US Wc); the three others showing alterations are G 24 (in SPK), G 26 (US U), and G 28 (A Wn-h).

9. Questionable emendations occur in Partita No. 1/mvt. 7/bars 16, 48; 2/1/28, 6/6; 3/1/13, 4/8; 4/3/15; 5/2/10, 5/5; 6/1/90, 4/30. While some of these may be justifiable on musical grounds, all are open to question, as the printed text was left to stand in the *Handexemplar*.

10. The early forms of the minuets are edited in NBA V/1, KB, 72–73, from SPK P 672 (Michel). A copy of Partitas Nos. 2, 3, and 5 by Penzel (LEm Go.S.307) contains what Jones allowed to be possible early readings (NBA V/1, KB, 43), but this seems unlikely, especially in light of Marissen's (1990) refutation of the idea that Penzel's copies of certain other works stem directly from a lost early version.

11. Williams (1986–87, 32), assuming that the right hand should cross the left, concludes that the piece calls for emphatic staccato playing.

12. These entries are in the exemplar in US Wc (= G 25).

13. NBA V/1 follows the undependable manuscript copy by Penzel (= H 58). In addition, the altered rhythm in the exemplar in US Wc (= G 25) is reported apparently incorrectly in NBA V/1, KB, 31, which omits the dot following soprano b♭' (second beat, last note). The same apparent error is repeated in the example in Wolff (1979, 69; Ex. 16.1 in Wolff 1991b, 219), but the dot is clearly

visible in the facsimile from G 25 on the facing page and correctly reported in the list of readings (Wolff 1979, 73; 1991b, 216).

14. I.e., a *Pralltriller;* see C. P. E. Bach (1753–62, i.2.3.36).

15. Readings are as reported in Wolff (1979, 73), although the mordent indicated for e$^{b''}$ in bar 2 would be better replaced by a trill.

16. The sign in the autograph is no clearer. To judge from the facsimile (Dadelsen 1988), neither NBA V/4, KB, 74, nor NBA V/1, KB, 60, reproduces it exactly.

17. See the facsimiles in Dadelsen (1988—autograph) and Wolff (1984—print, also in NBA V/1).

18. In order to avoid an awkward page-turn, the gigue starts at the beginning of the next page. This left three systems free after the conclusion of the burlesca.

19. The scherzos from the Bonporti *Inventioni da Camera* (Bologna, 1712) edited in BG 45 bear no particular resemblance to this one, nor to the one attributed to Bach as BWV 844 (see App. A).

20. The exemplars are those in US Wc (G 25), US U (G 26), and A Wn-h (G 28). Their variant readings were omitted from NBA V/1, KB, and were first published in Wolff (1979, 74).

21. These alterations occur in G 25 and G 28, according to Wolff (1979, 74). The open fifths in bars 39–41 could have been avoided by altering the bass, as was done in bar 27.

22. The list of readings in Wolff (1979, 74) omitted the bar number "46" for the last three entries; there seem to be further omissions in Wolff (1991b, 217).

23. I owe this insight, gained in the course of an audition, to Ralph Kirkpatrick, who made me sing the middle part.

24. Ambiguities in the original print led to misreadings for the slur and ornament in bars 1, 13, and 29 of the sarabande in BG 3 and other editions prior to NBA V/1.

25. E.g., Löhlein (1765, 2:129–31); further discussion in Schulenberg (1984, 78–79).

26. The second half of the gigue also includes (in bars 70–73) a quasi-inversion of a passage from the first half (bars 21–24).

27. The delay might have been related to Bach's assuming the directorship of the Leipzig Collegium Musicum in April 1729; another possibility is that the engraver, Bach's student J. Gotthilf Ziegler, had been unavailable (see Butler 1986, 15–16).

28. Cf.: overture, bars 41–43, and praeambulum, bars 37–38; gigue of Partita No. 4, bars 33–36, and praeambulum, bars 32–36. There is also a resemblance between the main theme of the praeambulum and that of the opening movement of the sixth sonata (also in G) from the ca. 1726 set by J. G. Graun.

29. For evidence elsewhere that may favor assimilation, see the discussions of the F$^\sharp$-minor prelude in WTC2 (Chap. 12) and the three-part mirror fugue in the *Art of Fugue* (Chap. 18).

30. The note d''' occurs also once in the praeambulum (bar 87).

31. The passage in C. P. E. Bach (1753–62, i.2.2.11) arguing for meaningful distinctions in the written values of appoggiaturas was added only in the third (1787) edition; Emanuel's own early works make no such distinctions.

32. The c-appoggiaturas are absent from NBA V/1 but appear correctly in BG 3. In bar 20 the sign in the print is distinctly beneath the main note (see Ex. 15.6b), at least in the exemplar (from LEm) of the 1731 print reproduced in Wolff (1984).

33. The quarters in bars 24, 26, etc., are followed by sixteenth-rests, the latter being effectively equivalent to a second dot. In the print, single eighths and sixteenths following dots (e.g., in bar 9, third beat) are consistently aligned vertically with one another.

34. There exist similar pieces by C. P. E. Bach (H 1 5 = W. 111), engraved in 1731 (see Butler 1986, 12–15; facsimile in Berg 1985, 5:103), and by W. F. Bach (F. 25/1–2), as well as a movement in an anonymous suite in G (listed in Kast 1958 as Incerta 68) in SPK P 368 whose style owes something to Bach's Partitas. There is no reason to think that any of these movements were transcribed from violin pieces, as suggested by Morana (1990) for F. 25/2, although the transcriptions BWV 964 and 1006a do contain somewhat similar figuration.

35. Williams (1986–87, 34) dismisses the use of two manuals while admitting it to be "charming" and "Rameauesque."

36. The E-Minor Partita was first printed separately, like the others in the set, but no exemplars survive of the first edition, whose existence is inferred from manuscript copies, contemporary references to it and from corrections in the 1731 print.

37. There had been a slight hint of such integration in the Toccata in G Minor; see Chap. 7.
38. In revising the work for publication, Bach extended the episode by two bars (bars 74–75), lengthening the C-major "plateau."
39. See Harnoncourt (1970, 8) and Chafe (1991, 355–57) on the singular style of the aria. The early version of the aria in BWV 244b (probably dating from 1727) uses lute rather than viola da gamba; Bach might have written it with the possibility of keyboard performance in mind, as he apparently did the lute part in the Saint John Passion.
40. Schulze (1984a, 115–16) dates the autograph entries in DSB St 162 (sole source of BWV 1019a) to 1725. Eppstein (1964) argues that the original *Violino solo* movement was accompanied by viola da gamba, without harpsichord.
41. Thus, the air would seem redundant if transferred to a position beside the *Tempo di Gavotta*, as suggested in Louwenaar (1982–83).
42. NBA V/1 emends bar 30 "by analogy to bars 10 and 26" (KB), changing treble e' to d" and bass e' to d'. But the *Handexemplar* retains the printed text without alteration, and the departure from the pattern established in bar 26 is not necessarily a problem.
43. In both versions the trill sign in bar 29 extends to the third beat (contrary to BG 3 and NBA V/1), suggesting that the figure on the third beat should be played as a continuation or termination of the trill.
44. The ornament in bar 17 is not on the eighth-note a' (as it appears in NBA V/1) but on c" in both the print and in the autograph; the latter also places a mordent on g' at the corresponding point in bar 19.
45. Corrections in P 225 (e.g., in bar 7) show that the version in BWV 1019a is indeed earlier, though not necessarily the earliest. Further revisions were made for the print.
46. Eppstein (1964) reconstructs the entire movement, giving a different solution for these bars.
47. See Collins (1966, 311–12) for an argument in favor of more extensive rhythmic alteration.
48. Louwenaar (1983–84, 12–13) makes a similar observation.
49. The passing notes and the beams signifying sixteenths (originally, thirty-seconds) were insertions in bars 9 and elsewhere (see the facsimile in Dadelsen 1988). A similar process may have occurred in the B-minor prelude of WTC2.
50. See, for instance, the subject of Canzon 1.

Chapter 16.

1. The date is based on an autograph entry in Walther's personal copy of the *Lexicon* (Walther 1732); see NBA V/2, KB, 15–16.
2. Glöckner (1981) aims at reconstructing the repertory of the Collegium Musicum from surviving sources; Wolff (1985a) discusses which of Bach's own works might have been performed by the Collegium.
3. The copy by Oley of the early version (in US Bp, source A in NBA V/2, KB) differs from the print in the unbroken beaming of eighth-notes at certain points where changes of manual occur (e.g., first movement, bars 67, 69), a sign that the dynamic markings were additions in the lost autograph.
4. A. M. Bach's copy: in DSB P 226. The announcement of Partita No. 5 in 1730 indicated that two more would follow; see BD 2:202 (item 276).
5. The *Handexemplar* is GB Lbl K.8.g.7, designated source G in NBA V/2, KB. The engravers of the print are identified in Butler (1980).
6. Debatable readings include some slurs in the overture (bars 47–48, 77–78); the addition of an appoggiatura in the second passepied (downbeat of bar 17) and a trill in the gigue (bar 22); and the placement of dynamic markings in the last movement of the concerto (bars 33 and 53).
7. Quantz and the Graun brothers probably visited Bach at Leipzig; C. P. E. Bach (1773, 201) reported that most of the leading musicians of Germany visited the Bach house in Leipzig during his own youth, that is, the 1720s and early 1730s (BD 3:289 [item 803]/BR, 279).
8. Scheibe's review appeared in late 1739, following his criticism of Bach's vocal works. See BD 2:373–74 (item 463). The translation in BR, 234, is from the expanded version published in 1745.
9. On written-out embellishment in string works by Pisendel and J. G. Graun and other Germans, see Fechner (1980).

10. Schering (1902–3, 243) noted the resemblance to the theme of the final section of the *symphonie* that opens the ballet *Impatientia* in Muffat's *Florilegium primum* (Passau, 1696; ed. in DTÖ 2 by Heinrich Rietsch [1894]).

11. The "Dekolierung" given by Landowska (1924, 131, reproduced in Schleuning 1979 and elsewhere) eliminates only the most superficial layer of melodic embellishment.

12. The return, following almost immediately upon a cadence to A minor at the end of the middle section (bar 150), sounds like the Da Capo of an aria and has parallels in sonata and concerto movements from the same period, e.g., C. P. E. Bach, Concerto H. 411 (W. 8); see Davis (1988, 74).

13. NBA V/2 adds a forte marking for the right hand on the authority of one manuscript copy of the print containing additions from an unidentified source (source L; see NBA V/2, KB, 34). The print has only the word *piano* and a bracket between the staves, its usual way of indicating that the dynamic applies to both staves.

14. As pointed out in NBA V/2, KB, 61, the *piano* cannot apply to the a″ on the downbeat and must have been misplaced a half-beat to the left. The second edition adds an eighth-rest in the inner voice at this point; *forte* could also have been added if it were intended.

15. The most relevant article here is Neumann (1974); see also Neumann (1965; 1977; and 1979) and Fuller (1977; 1985).

16. BWV 831a is edited separately in NBA V/2. It lacks many of the ornaments of the printed version, but the only substantial difference in the notes occurs where the printed version would have otherwise descended to FF♯ (bourrée 2, bar 12). There is a second copy of BWV 831a in LEm ms. 8 (Preller).

17. Both Neumann (1974) and NBA V/2, KB, 50–51, cite against the view adopted here the many additional ornaments in the Preller copy of BWV 831a (partly transcribed in NBA V/2, KB, 87–88). As in other heavily ornamented Preller copies, the ornaments, which are probably Preller's own (see Schulze 1984a, 85), indeed require a slow tempo, but this does not necessarily reflect Bach's own practice around 1730. Neumann supposes that Preller's copy was "written probably in the 1730s," but it can hardly have been copied much before 1750, since Preller was born in 1727 (Schulze 1984a, 76–77).

18. Thirty-seconds also appear in the early version in bars 8, 11, and 12 (left hand); 153 (first beat); and 160–61.

19. In the earlier version some of the dotted rhythms were already notated in this manner, e.g., in bar 4.

20. See C. P. E. Bach (1753–62, i.2.3.6) on the normal long trill with suffix or turn; also on leaving space (*Raum*) after a trill on a dotted note (i.2.3.14, Ex. h) and on omitting the turn when, as in this case, it is already written out (i.2.3.16, Example d).

21. The first entry is that of the soprano in bar 89; cf. the rising sequence near the end of the fugue in the toccata of Partita No. 6 (bars 78–81).

22. The first courante in the *Pièces de clavessin* (Paris, 1687) of Elizabeth Jacquet de La Guerre opens in a vaguely similar way; there is no reason to think that Bach knew the piece.

23. The first edition likewise placed an erroneous slur on the tenor in passepied 2, bars 1–2, by false analogy to the tie in the bass. The errors in the passepied and sarabande were perpetuated in BG 3 and other modern editions.

24. This is a point in favor of the authenticity of BWV 821, since the latter is clearly *not* an imitation of the echo in BWV 831.

25. Compare the aria "Flösst, mein Heiland" (bars 43b–45) in Part 4 of the Christmas Oratorio (BWV 248/4); also bars 1–2 in the first movement of the Concerto in C minor for two harpsichords and strings BWV 1060, also known in modern arrangements for oboe and violin.

26. Dreyfus (1987b, 182 and 185); see also Dreyfus (1985a, 351–56).

27. Brahms's *Fünf Klavierstücke* (Anh. 1a, No. 1, in McCorkle 1984) include two arrangements of the last movement from the G-Minor Sonata BWV 1001 and one (for the left hand) of the famous chaconne from the D-Minor Partita BWV 1004.

28. ". . . lassen sich aber auf dem Clavier sehr wohl spielen" (BD 3:124 [item 695]).

29. "Ihr Verfasser spielte sie selbst oft auf der Clavichorde" (BD 3:292–93 [item 808]).

30. Chromatic decoration of half-cadences occurs in both the Sonata BWV 964 (first movement,

penultimate bar) and the harpsichord concerto in F, BWV 1057 (second movement, bar 69, first recorder).

31. The same countersubject is found in the fugue of the Third Violin Sonata BWV 1005.

32. The subject is quoted in Mattheson (1737; see BR, 230); as Mattheson does not mention the remarkable scoring for solo violin, he may have known the work from a transcription or an impromptu keyboard performance.

33. This according to Agricola's note in Adlung (1768, 2:139, = BD 3:195 [item 744]/BR, 259).

34. Documented in the letter by Johann Elias Bach in BD 2:366 (item 448)/BR, 163.

35. "Das ungedämpfte Register des Fortepiano" (C. P. E. Bach 1753–62, ii.41.4). Adlung (1768, 2:137) seems to describe the sympathetic vibrations (*Nachsingen*) that arose when playing on the undamped lute-harpsichord.

36. The problems are evident in the errors and corrections in the copy of the original (SPK P 804/40) by Kellner, who attempted to resolve the *scordatura* into normal notation (see Stinson 1989a, 60).

37. See the facsimile of the autograph with introduction by Godelieve Spiessens (Fontes musicae bibliothecae regiae belgicae, I/1 (Brussels: Bibliotheca Regia Belgica, 1981). Schulze's identification of "Monsieur Schouster" as the Leipzig book dealer Jacob Schuster (in Rehm 1983, 247) supersedes an earlier identification with the bass singer and chamber musician Joseph Schuster the Elder, documented at Dresden from 1744 (possibly 1741) to 1784 (Schulze 1966, 33).

38. Radke (1964) compares the two versions. The tablature is reproduced in full in NBA V/10, KB.

39. See Dreyfus (1985b) for an account of the organ version as a sort of pseudo-concerto with "metaphorical soloist." Swanton (1985) also discusses the organ part of BWV 29, reproducing the first page of the autograph (SPK St 106); there are no explicit pedal indications, but use of the pedals appears to be implied by the notation in bars 13ff.

40. The octave notation of the first four movements, retained in BG 45, led to unfounded suggestions that the work was actually for flute (or violin) and continuo (see NBA V/10, KB, 143). The notation might have stemmed from an indication in the lost autograph for octave transposition in case of keyboard performance, as in the aria "Betrachte, meine Seele" in the Saint John Passion.

41. The note also occurs in the Triple Concerto BWV 1044.

42. The earliest source of the "Wedge," according to Stinson (1989a, 24), is a joint copy by Bach and Kellner (SPK P 274) dated "after 1727."

43. Naturals must be added on A in bar 13 (bass) and a″ in bar 18. The tablature is reproduced in full in NBA V/10, KB.

44. A natural might be added on e in bar 44 of the double to agree with the same bar in the gigue.

Chapter 17.

1. Wolff (1988b) is a general discussion of Bach's "late" works, emphasizing the composer's continuing use of galant idioms while singling out the B-Minor Mass and Art of Fugue as "aid[ing] a definition of the last phase of Bach's activity" (translation from Wolff 1991b, 364).

2. Butler (1990, 43–44) argues that the title-page was engraved before Bach had decided to include any "free" works, i.e., ones not based on chorales.

3. ". . . einige *Clavier* Sachen, die hauptsächlich vor die Herrn *Organist*en gehöre . . ." (BD, 2:335 [item 434]/BR, 162).

4. Wolff (1984, 30) points out Grigny's possible influence on the structure of Bach's volume; Bach had copied out the Grigny work at Weimar between 1708 and 1713.

5. Butler's dating depends upon some fairly vague parallels to the insecurely dated lute works BWV 997–98. The tonalities ascend in a symmetrical pattern (E minor, F, G, A minor), but the last two pieces could have been transposed.

6. A similar procedure is often used at the recapitulation in allegro movements in galant trio-sonatas (e.g., in works by J. G. Graun and C. P. E. Bach), where alternate phrases of the theme may be divided between the upper parts. J. S. Bach does something similar in the first movement of the B-minor flute sonata BWV 1030 (see bars 35ff.).

7. *Clavier Ubung bestehend in einer ARIA mit verschiedenen Verænderungen vors Clavicimbal mit 2 Manualen . . . .* For the date 1741, rather than 1742, see NBA V/2, KB, 94, and Butler (1988).

8. Another explanation, offered by Wolff (NBA V/2, KB, 109), is that the engraver Schmid, not Bach himself, was the publisher.

9. See NBA V/2, KB, 113. Forkel's story presumably came via W. F. Bach, who was working in Dresden during the period in question.

10. It is impossible to say how many such works Bach knew or knew of; composers include Byrd, Bull, Sweelinck, Frescobaldi, Poglietti, and Buxtehude. The fragmentary Air with Variations BWV 991 in the 1722 *Clavier-Büchlein* apparently would have been an example of the pedagogic type.

11. The sarabande (in NBA V/2, KB, 110) consists of two repeated eight-bar phrases, the second subdivided by an additional double bar (thus in the source, SPK P 4/2)—perhaps a copyist's way of indicating a *petite reprise*. A somewhat similar bass line occurs in the first three movements of Reinken's C-Major Suite (in MM, No. 15).

12. One might compare Bach's demonstration of the universal applicabilty of "composition by varia-tion" with the application of twelve-tone technique to a wide variety of vocal and instrumental forms in Berg's *Wozzeck*.

13. Butler (1990, 103–4) argues that the first three settings in BWV 769 were composed in late 1745; Wolff (1976, 240–41) had suggested that BWV 769 followed the fourteen canons BWV 1087, now dated "ca. 1742–46" by Butler (1990, 104).

14. Cf. the remarks on the length of the *Art of Fugue*, as compared with Quantz's ideal proportions for a concerto of sonata, in Breig (1982, 115).

15. Bach indeed reordered the Canonic Variations BWV 769 in their printed version, and the copies of the early chorale *partite* give the individual variations in differing orders.

16. Small differences in the ornaments and especially in the rhythm of bar 24 show that the copy probably stems from a prepublication autograph; see NBA V/2, KB, 101–2.

17. "Verschiedene *Canones* über die ersteren acht Fundamental-Noten vorheriger Aria. von J. S. Bach." Facsimile (from Bach's *Handexemplar* in F Pn) in NBA V/2, which also includes Wolff's edition of and solutions to the canons.

18. See the discussion and facsimiles in Wolff (1991b, 168–71). One of the canons, BWV 1076, is held by Bach in Haussmann's well-known 1746 portrait, reproduced on the cover of BR and elsewhere.

19. The regularized ornament signs are explained in NBA V/2, KB, 114, as corresponding with the main version (*Hauptform*) of the sign as found in the print; no attempt was made to draw a "hypothetical distinction" between Schmid's long and short trill (and mordent) signs.

20. The term *tremblement appuyé* is D'Anglebert's; presumably it can be applied to the sign shown in NBA/2 (a long trill sign with straight initial vertical extension), although the sign is not shown or named in either of the main Bach sources on ornaments, CB and C. P. E. Bach (1753–62).

21. Schwandt (1990, 65–67) lists further "errata" in NBA V/2, including ornament signs, but many of the readings cited represent legitimate editorial intervention.

22. Marshall (1976a, 347–48) suggests various other "possible intermediaries" for the transmission of the Scarlatti style to Bach.

23. For example, compare variation 17 with *Essercizi*, No. 18 (K. 18), bars 28–29.

24. The keyboards must be uncoupled in order to permit the sounding of unisons.

25. On changing registrations between individual variations on a chorale tune, see Williams (1980–84, 3:157). The contract offered to Bach in 1713 by Halle also required him to "change the stops at each verse" (BD 2: 50 [item 63]/BR, 65). For the C. P. E. Bach sonata (H. 53 = W. 69), see the facsimile of a manuscript copy with autograph additions in Berg (1985, 3:319). The copy is the work of Schlichting, who was working for Emanuel around 1750 (see Rifkin 1985, 160n), although the autograph entries dictating the registrations may be later.

26. This registration occurs in variation 3 of the sonata finale.

27. C. P. E. Bach does not illustrate the "realization" shown in Ex. 17.4a, which is based on the description in his verbal text (1753–62, i.2.2.14).

28. As printed, the slur on the alto in bar 9 appears to be on notes 1–3, not 1–4 as in BG 3. Either reading is possible, however, as the middle voice in this bar has an embellished version of the ascending fourth that appears in plain form in bar 1. In bar 9 the motive is embellished in a manner corresponding to Kirnberger's *accentuirte Brechung* ("broken chord with acciaccatura"; see Kirn-berger 1771–79, 1:217).

29. As Schwandt (1990) points out, the sharp in bar 32A is editorial; it seems unnecessary.

30. An error in BG 3 and other editions is worth noting: read b' for a' on the downbeat of bar 25.
31. See variation 16, bar 21, where the last note in the alto is sometimes changed from e" to f'"; and variation 26, bar 14, where the second note of the alto is usually changed from d" to e". Four exemplars of the original print—but not Bach's—contain a hand-written correction of the reading in variation 16 (according to NBA V/2, KB, where bar numbers for the variants in bars 21 and 22 are apparently incorrect). On transferred resolution, see Arnold (1931, 840–55), especially his Ex. 7, taken from C. P. E. Bach (1753–62, ii.13.2.4—Ex. 358c in Mitchell's translation). There is another example of transferred resolution in variation 9, last bar, where the tied b' in the alto resolves as a" in the soprano.
32. Two errors were, however, left to stand in the Handexemplar in variation 25; both involve missing accidentals, which are supplied by other exemplars (bar 2: flat on a; bar 13: sharp on f).
33. The ornament in bar 13, read as a normal trill in NBA V/2, is a "doppelt-cadence" according to Schwandt (1990, 67). Actually, the sign in the print may be a tremblement appuyé, but a Doppel-Cadenz (trill from above) would be in keeping with the trills from below in bars 6–7 and 14–15.
34. Compare the discussion of the trills in the gigue of English Suite No. 6 (Chap. 14).
35. NBA V/2 reads g on the downbeat of bar 29, following a custos in the print; this is stronger than the printed b and corresponds with the bass of the aria.
36. "Bey vielen hinter einander vorkommenden Tertien . . . setzt man bey geschwindem Zeitmasse lieber mit den Fingern fort, indem alsdenn das Abwechseln schwerer fällt" (1753–62, i.1.69).
37. See the seventh partita in Fux's Concentus musico-instrumentalis (Nuremberg, 1701), edited in DTÖ 47 (1916) and as "Nürnberger Partita" by Adolf Hoffmann (Wolfenbüttel: Möseler, 1939).
38. Among Bach's possible sources for the idea are several pieces in the Aggiunta added to the 1637 edition of Frescobaldi's Toccate d'intavolatura (Bk. 1) and the chaconne that closes Fischer's Pièces de clavecin (ABB No. 47).
39. The suggestion was made by Baensch (1934), cited by Schulze (1976, 67). The words of both tunes were entered into one copy of the print by an unidentified writer perhaps belonging to the Kittel circle; see Schulze (1976, 66).

Chapter 18.

1. The chief sources, listed in NBA VIII/1, KB, 102, are the contemporary newspaper reports (see BD 2:434–35 [item 554]/BR, 176); Bach's printed dedication to Frederick, dated two months later (BD 1:241–42 [item 173]/BR, 179); Bach's obituary (BD 3:85 [item 666]/BR, 220), written by Agricola and Emanuel Bach—neither of whom was assuredly present; van Swieten's 1774 letter describing a conversation with the King (BD 3:276 [item 790; facsimile opposite page 224]/BR, 260); and Forkel's account (1802, 9–10/BR, 305–6), evidently based on a vivid retelling of the story by Friedemann Bach (who Forkel says had been present).
2. See (Wolff 1991a, 326–28) for further discussion of the possible origin of the theme.
3. Wolff (1971) refutes earlier theories that the work was composed and printed piecemeal over a longer period. The music was engraved by Schübler, who a year or two later published the six organ chorales known by his name.
4. Letter of Sept. 15, 1774; No. 189 in Suchalla (1985).
5. Each of the following gives the movements in different orders: the original print, the edition in BG 31/2, the edition in NBA VIII/1, the 1950 edition of SWV (SWV now follows the NBA), and the study by Hans David (1945). For replies to Kirkendale (1980), see Williams (1985b) and Wolff (1991b, 421–22).
6. C. P. E. Bach, in his letter to Forkel of Jan. 13, 1775 (BD 3:289 [item 803]/BR, 278), noted that Sebastian composed "everything" (alles) not based on an improvisation "without instrument" (ohne Instrument).
7. Wolff (1987a, 208) notes that Bach is unlikely to have intended any of his other music for the fortepiano prior to Silbermann's creation of an "improved model" around 1745–46, although Badura-Skoda (1991) presents evidence for the presence of fortepianos in Leipzig as early as 1731.
8. Substantial portions of the second and third expositions are also taken with little change from previously heard material (bars 80–86 || 65–71 and 95–101 || 41–52).

9. In the specially prepared dedication copy sent to Berlin (DSB AmB 73) this acrostic accompanies the *three*-part ricercar, which is where it appears in NBA VIII/1.
10. See Hans David (1945, 42) and Wolff (1971, 394); the original account in the obituary (BD 3:85 [item 666]/BR, 220) is confirmed by Forkel (1802, 10/BR, 305–6).
11. This is true even in bar 79, where the autograph version is slightly more complex. NBA VIII/1, KB, 91–94, discusses all ten revised passages, presenting the two versions of each on parallel staves.
12. A note (f) is missing in bar 61 of the later version as given in NBA VIII/1; see NBA VIII/1, KB, 92, Ex. 3.
13. Four further solutions from early sources are given as *Beispielen* 11–14 in NBA VIII/1, KB, 141–43. The first, however, incorporates a misplaced repeat sign, while the second and fourth are ruled out by the improper dissonance treatment in bars 19 and 5–6, respectively.
14. " . . . Kunst der *Fuga* in 24. Exempeln," from the notice of June 1, 1751, in the *Leipziger Zeitungen*, reprinted in BD, 3:8–9 (item 639).
15. See Mattheson (1739, 441), cited in Butler (1983b, 295) and Stauffer (1983b, 366–67).
16. For the text of the treatises, see *Werken van Jan Pieterszn. Sweelinck*, 10 (ed. H. Gehrmann, 1901); for a critical discussion, see Walker (1985–86).
17. C. P. E. Bach's letter of Jan. 13, 1775 (BD 3:289 [item 803]/BR, 279). BR misleadingly renders the word *Arten* as "species."
18. See the illustration of "rhythmic metamorphoses of the principal theme" in Wolff (1983c, 141; translation from Wolff 1991b, 276).
19. This preface replaced a short notice in the 1751 edition concerning the unfinished fugue; the music itself was unchanged.
20. This is clear from a remark entered by Friedrich Bach into the autograph *Abklatschvorlage* of the Augmentation Canon.
21. Cf. a 1725 citation from Gottsched in Grimm and Grimm (1854–1960, 5:2,669: " . . . man zankte sich zum Exempel, ob die Vernunftlehre eine Kunst oder eine Wissenschaft sei. . . ."
22. Hoke (1979) contains facsimiles of both the autograph (P 200) and the print; the latter includes hand-written corrections corresponding to the errata list (in C. P. E. Bach's hand) on the back of page 4 of Beilage 3 of P 200.
23. The manuscript, which was written on one side only and soaked in oil to render it transparent, was then traced in reverse onto the prepared plate. Such a manuscript is called an *Abklatschvorlage*; one autograph example, that for the Augmentation Canon, survives (facsimile in Hoke 1979). The process is described in Koprowski (1975).
24. J. H. Schübler, identified as the engraver of the *Art of Fugue* by Wiemer (1977, 40ff.), was the brother of the Johann Georg who engraved and published the "Schübler" organ chorales.
25. For example, corrections made while copying appear to have taken place in bar 62 in the alto and possibly also in the tenor.
26. For example, Contrapuncti 1–3, originally barred in "double measures" of $\frac{4}{2}$ (like the six-part ricercar), were altered to normal cut-time; the note-values of Contrapuncti 8 and 11–13 were doubled.
27. Butler's order is based in part on what he takes to be traces of altered page numbers in the print. While this aspect of his hypothesis is debatable, the logic of his ordering remains impressive. It represents a revision of that proposed by Wiemer (1977), who placed the incomplete fugue last.
28. Even this work was presented imperfectly, since at least the first twenty-five bars evidently existed in a later version, the fragmentary BWV 668, preserved (under the title *Vor deinen Thron tret' ich*) at the end of the manuscript of the "Eighteen" organ chorales (DSB P 271).
29. The description of the *Art of Fugue* as a variation work was first given by Forkel (1802, 53; see BR, 340).
30. The most influential of many arrangements was that of Wolfgang Graeser, who not only orchestrated the work for a celebrated performance conducted by the Thomaskantor Karl Straube in 1927 but also wrote an influential study (Graeser 1924).
31. See the lists of editions in Dedel (1975, 53–54) and of performances in Kolneder (1977, vol. 5).
32. See, for example, Contrapunctus 1, bars 36–47, and the tenor in bars 60–63.
33. The treble rises to e''' in the three-part mirror fugue, and the bass consistently extends upward to d'—to e' in the four-part mirror fugue.

34. See Adlung (1768, 2:23–24; also in BD 3:193 [item 742]/BR, 258).
35. Williams (1986b), Wolff (1987b), Maroney (1989). Users of Maroney's edition should beware several unsubstantiated assertions in the commentary, e.g., that Bach "must . . . have had the harpsichord predominantly in mind."
36. Heinrich (1983) gives a more detailed analysis of the fugues.
37. The episodes follow cadences to D minor (bar 23), A minor (43 and 53), C (87), and G minor (103).
38. The print gives the time-signature as **C**, but this is surely an error for **¢**, found in the autograph.
39. For a facsimile from Marpurg (1753–54) and a solution, see BR, 175 and 403.
40. See Maroney (1989, 115). Wolff (1987b) gives the embellished reading in his text for the earlier version, i.e., that of the autograph.
41. The seemingly irrational order of the print (see Table 18–2) was probably due to considerations growing out of a desire for conveniently placed page turns; see Wiemer (1977, 50ff.) and Butler (1983a, 52–53).
42. An entry in Friedrich's hand in the autograph indicates how Contrapunctus 9 was to appear in the print.
43. On "paired entries," see the discussion of the fugue in G minor from WTC2 in Chap. 12.
44. See, e.g., the canzona *La bergamesca* in Frescobaldi's *Fiori musicali*.
45. The earlier version opened with the soprano entry in bar 23; all of the voices accompanying this entry, including the partial stretto entry in bar 24, were added later. The soprano line in bars 26b–30a serves as a second countersubject to the theme, but its role in the piece is very minor.
46. Bars 178–80 constitute a quasi-inversion of bars 91–93.
47. Even the trill sign placed over the penultimate chord in the Czerny edition is inauthentic and quite unnecessary.
48. Especially bars 22b–24a, 81b–83a, and 144–46a. The reduction of values in Contrapunctus 8 was authorized by a note in Bach's hand (see Wolff 1975, 77).
49. Snyder (1980, 558–59) suggests that, despite their texts, these pieces might be examples of learned keyboard music. Neither, however, is idiomatic, and one source points to ensemble performance. See Snyder (1987, 216–18, also 508n. 3).
50. Bach permitted himself a few departures from strict mirror inversion in order to avoid a series of unprepared $\frac{6}{4}$-chords in bars 14–16.
51. Wiemer (1977, 33–35) suggests that the term *inversus* in the titles actually indicates the use of mirror technique itself, not the upright or inverted status of the individual versions.
52. Maroney (1989, 118) suggests transposing the alto of bars 24–25 up an octave in BWV 1080/12/2 to accommodate players with "smaller hands"; this eliminates the parallel tenths but not the other difficulties. The one truly unmanageable stretch in the three-part fugue, on the fermata in bar 59 of the "top" version, could be finessed by a cadenza or a freely arpeggiated chord at this point.
53. See bars 19, 21, and 49. Discrepancies between the print and the duo version in bar 21, and between the autograph and the print of the three-part version in bar 49, suggest triple interpretation; cf. the F♯-minor prelude in WTC2.
54. No source for any version has dots in bar 46a (contrary to what is implied by Maroney 1989, 119). The facsimile of the autograph (Hoke 1979) shows a smear possibly indicating that Bach blotted out a dot after the first note in the alto (b♭′) in the "bottom" version. The print seems to call here for skipping triplet rhythms in the bass, but these occur only in the "top" version, where they are notated without dots and without the note-values of the treble adding up properly. The thirty-seconds in the treble might have arisen when Bach, in preparing the *Abklatschvorlage*, erroneously copied the unreduced original values. Any correction that Bach then made might have been invisible to the engraver (tracing through the back of the sheet), who then compounded the error in an attempt to correct it.
55. The autograph (Beilage 3 of P 200) is on the same type of paper used for the engraver's *Abklatschvorlagen*; the significance of this was pointed out by Wolff (1975, 73).
56. Nottebohm's solution, published in *Musik-Welt* 20 (1881): 232–36, is quoted in the preface of Williams (1986b) and in Wolff (1975, 73).

57. Bar 111 was inserted and the next three bars reworked; the lower staff at the end of the second section (bars 190–92) also shows corrections.
58. Bach already alters the rhythm of the first subject once (bar 158) in order to make for a smoother combination with subject 2.
59. For another completion along similar lines, though without the inversion, see Maroney (1989, 69).
60. See Wiemer (1977, 52–53) and Butler (1983a, 51–54).
61. The term *finale* occurs in the autograph of the first version of the Augmentation Canon and in the print of the Canon at the Twelfth.
62. Example 18.12 is based on a cadenza in B Br Ms. U5871 (page 18, number 52) for the Concerto H. 408 (W. 46) in F. The cadenza probably dates from well after 1740.
63. The title, like the piece itself, underwent changes; the title given here is that of the print.
64. All but the first accidental in bar 29 appears to have been a later addition in the earlier of the two autograph scores (P 200, page 38). Even later are the slurs in bars 15–16, 22, 28–29, etc., added only in the autograph *Abklatschvorlage* (Beilage 1 of DSB P 200).
65. For the earlier version of the Augmentation Canon, see BGA 25/1:111–13, Wolff (1987b, vol. 1), or Williams (1986b).

Appendix A.

1. Important recent discussions of doubtful keyboard works are to be found in Eichberg (1975), Hill (1987), and Stinson (1989a). The work-list in NG appears to depend on Eichberg (1975) in many instances, and some of the remarks concerning attribution can no longer be upheld.
2. BWV Anh. 85 was seen here only in the apparently corrupt text attributed to Dobenecker in the nineteenth-century edition by Franz Commer, Musica Sacra, 1 (Berlin: Bote und Boke, n.d.).
3. The source is claimed as a Bach autograph in van Patten (1950, 9). The attribution, on the first page, is not visible in van Patten's facsimile.
4. See, for example, the Passacaille in the same key by Louis Couperin.
5. BWV Anh. 180 in D minor, ed. in BG 36 as a work of Bach; and Fk. n. v. 39 in C minor, available in several editions as a work of W. F. Bach. See Stinson (1989a, 172n. 26).
6. BWV 838 appears in BG 42. For the complete suite, see Lothar Hoffmann-Erbrecht, ed., *Johann Christoph Graupner: Acht Partiten* (Mitteldeutsches Musikarchiv, I/2. Leipzig: VEB Brietkopf und Härtel, 1953).
7. The one source seen here (US NHy LM 4941) proceeds directly to the cadenza without the intervening, shorter ending shown in BG 36. Curiously, the next piece in the manuscript (a fugue in C by "J. Krieger") does have two alternate endings, although neither is a cadenza.
8. Compare bars 43 and 57 here with the subject and bars 68–69 of the fugue in the E-Minor Toccata.
9. Presumably, the bass note on the downbeat of bar 68 should be G, not E as given in BG 42.
10. Four bars from the end, the upper staff might have been copied a third too high; for treble d″, d″, read b♮′, b♮′, and for alto b♮′, c″, b♮′, a′, read g′, a♭′, g′, e♭′. Perhaps the alto in the penultimate bar should also read a third lower.
11. Compare the polonaise in C minor (F. 12/2), bars 21–22, or the polonaise in D minor (F. 12/4), bars 9–12 (= Sonata in G [F. 7], second movement, bars 17–20; I am grateful to Peter Wollny for pointing out the concordance).
12. Naumann, editor of BG 42, was unaware of the Yale manuscript and thus failed to reproduce BWV 970. All four pieces appear in the supplement to the old Peters edition of Bach's keyboard works; some passages of BWV 970 appear as examples in Morana (1990).
13. Another possible pastiche is the Fantasia in G Minor BWV 920, also edited in BG 42 from the lost Schelble-Gleichauf collection. It is clumsy in many passages, and there is little reason to think that it contains any material from the Bach circle.
14. I am grateful to Peter Wollny for furnishing me with much information about BWV 844 and 970 as well as a copy of P 683.
15. Compare bars 12–13 with BWV 7, first movement, bars 3–4. Eichberg (1975, 29) suggests that BWV 969 might be the arrangement of an ensemble work.

16. In SPK P 804/39, F. 25/2 follows a similar minuet in G minor (F. 25/1, reused as a movement in the Suite F. 24). See Morana (1990, 23–25) for a facsimile of both minuets.
17. Compare the somewhat awkward hand-crossings in BWV 923a, bars 22–23, with those in BWV 970, bars 26, 28; and the syncopated lines of BWV 844 (and 844a), bars 2–3, with BWV 970, bars 11–12. The opening themes of BWV 844 and 970 (and F. 25/2) are both built over similar bass lines.
18. BG 42 renotated both pieces on two staves, with modernized clefs. The supplement to the old Peters edition includes both the original notation and a pianistic realization by Czerny; another realization, equally pianistic in style, occurs in PL LZu Spitta Ms. 1658 (for BWV 908 only).

Appendix B.

1. The old edition by Richard Batkas (Callwey: Kunstwart-Verlag, 1906, many reprints), based on BG 43/2, is reliable, but Schering's preface, added for the eighth impression (1935), is outdated.
2. The pieces by Richter in Friedemann's keyboard book may also stem from Dresden; see Chap. 10.
3. The simplified left-hand part and other alterations in the Couperin work seem unlikely to stem either from an authentic early version or from Bach; see the discussion in NBA V/4, KB, 81.
4. One candidate is the oboist Johann Michael Böhm, Telemann's brother-in-law and possibly a friend of J. F. Fasch (this information kindly furnished by Bruce Haynes).
5. On Emanuel's Sonata H. 16 (W. 65/7), see Schulenberg (1984, 122–25), a few errors in which are corrected in Horn (1988, 85n). Later versions of the sonata are published complete in Berg (1985, 3:196–204).
6. Glöckner (1981, 53) dates C. P. E. Bach's handwriting in the four pieces to 1732. Dadelsen assigns all four pieces to C. P. E. Bach (NBA V/4, KB, 37–38), but they are anonymous in the manuscript and the attribution cannot be regarded as certain.
7. The sonata, not listed by Wotquenne (1905), is mentioned in the entry for H. 1 in Helm (1989, 3) and edited in NBA V/4, *Anhang* 1.
8. See the entry in SWV for Anh. 40, a song from Sperontes' *Singende Muse an der Pleisse* (Leipzig, 1736), whose incipit is similar to that of H. 16, F. 10, etc. BWV Anh. 40 is accepted (on somewhat slender grounds) as a work of J. S. Bach in BC (entry H 3).
9. Schulze (1975, 48) identifies the hand as that of J. C. Bach, "hardly before 1745," but Joshua Rifkin has kindly indicated to me the possibility of a Bach daughter being involved here.
10. See the character piece entitled L'Aly Rupalich (H. 95 = W. 117/27) in Berg (1985, 5:196).

Bibliography

Abbreviations

Acta	*Acta musicologica*
AMw	*Archiv für Musikwissenschaft*
BACH	*Bach: The Quarterly Journal of the Riemenschneider Institute*
BC	*Bach-Compendium* (full citation below)
BD 1	*Bach-Dokumente I* (full citation below)
BD 2	*Bach-Dokumente II* (full citation below)
BD 3	*Bach-Dokumente III* (full citation below)
BG	*Bachgesamtausgabe* (full citation below under Bach, Johann Sebastian, 1851–1900; volumes cited are listed below)
BJ	*Bach-Jahrbuch*
BJHM	*Basler Jahrbuch für historische Musikpraxis*
BMw	*Beiträge zur Musikwissenschaft*
BR	*Bach Reader* (full citation below)
BWV	catalogue number of work listed in SWV (see below)
CB	*Clavier-Büchlein vor Wilhelm Friedemann Bach* (see Chapter 10)
CM	*Current Musicology*
CMS	*College Music Symposium*
DDT	Denkmäler deutscher Tonkunst
DTÖ	Denkmäler der Tonkunst in Österreich
EKJ	*Early Keyboard Journal*

For library and manuscript sigla, see p. 432.

EKSN	*Early Keyboard Studies Newsletter* (Westfield, Massachusetts)
EM	*Early Music*
F.	catalogue number of work by W. F. Bach, listed in Falck (1913—see below)
Fk. n. v.	catalogue number of work attributed to W. F. Bach, listed in Kast (1958—see below), not in Falck (1913)
H.	catalogue number of work by C. P. E. Bach, listed in Helm (1989—see below)
JAMS	*Journal of the American Musicological Society*
JM	*Journal of Musicology*
JMR	*Journal of Musicological Research*
JMT	*Journal of Music Theory*
Mf	*Die Musikforschung*
ML	*Music and Letters*
MQ	*The Musical Quarterly*
MT	*The Musical Times*
MTS	*Music Theory Spectrum*
NBA	*Neue Bach-Ausgabe, Notenband* (full citation below under Bach, Johann Sebastian, 1954– ; list of volumes cited below)
NBA, KB	*Neue Bach-Ausgabe, Kritischer Bericht* (full citation below under Bach, Johann Sebastian, 1954– ; list of volumes cited below)
NG	*The New Grove Dictionary of Music and Musicians* (full citation below)
NGDMI	*The New Grove Dictionary of Musical Instruments* (full citation below)
RIM	*Rivista italiana di musicologia*
SIMG	*Sammelbände der Internationalen Musik-Gesellschaft*
SJ	*Schütz-Jahrbuch*
SWV	Wolfgang Schmieder, *Bach Werke-Verzeichnis* (full citation below under Schmieder 1990)
TWV	catalogue number of work by Telemann in Ruhnke (1984—see below)
W.	catalogue number of work by C. P. E. Bach in Wotquenne (1905—see below)
WTC	The *Well-Tempered Clavier* (see Chapters 11–12)

BG and NBA: Volumes Cited

BG vol.	Date	Editor	Contents
3	1853	C. F. Becker	BWV 772–801, 910–11, 944, *Clavierübung*
13/2	1863	Franz Espagne	BWV 806–17
14	1866	Franz Kroll	WTC
20/1	1872	Wilhlem Rust	BWV 81–89
25/1	1878	Wilhlem Rust	BWV 1080
30	1884	Paul Graf Waldersee	BWV 141–50
31/2	1885	Alfred Dörffel	BWV 1079
36	1890	Ernst Naumann	individual keyboard works
38	1891	Ernst Naumann	free organ works
40	1893	Ernst Naumann	organ chorales
42	1894	Ernst Naumann	keyboard arrangements, etc.
43/2	1884	Paul Graf Waldersee	Little Keyboard Books for A. M. Bach
45/1	1895	Ernst Naumann	BWV 806–17 (rev. ed.)
45/2	1897	Alfred Dörffel	BWV 996–98, CB, etc.

NBA vol.	Date	KB	Editor	Contents
IV/1	1983	1987	Heinz-Harald Löhlein	organ chorales, partitas
IV/4	1969	1974	Manfred Tessmer	*Clavierübung*, Pt. 3
IV/5–6	1972, 1964	1978–79	Dietrich Kilian	organ preludes and fugues
IV/7	1984	1988	Dietrich Kilian	miscellaneous organ works
V/1	1976	1978	Richard Douglas Jones	*Clavierübung*, Pt. 1
V/2	1977	1981	Walter Emery / Christoph Wolff	*Clavierübung*, Pt. 2 / BWV 988, 1087
V/3	1970	—	Georg von Dadelsen	BWV 772–801
V/4	1957	1957	Georg von Dadelsen	DSB P 224, P 225
V/5	1962, rev. 1973	1963	Wolfgang Plath	CB
V/6.1	1989	1989	Alfred Dürr	WTC1
V/7	1979	1981	Alfred Dürr	BWV 806–11
V/8	1980	1982	Alfred Dürr	BWV 812–19
V/10	1976	1982	Hartwig Eichberg	BWV 820, 822–23, 832–33, 963, 989, 992–93
			Thomas Kohlhase	BWV 995–1000, 1006a
VII/3	1986	1989	Dietrich Kilian	BWV 1041–44
VIII/1	1974	1976	Christoph Wolff	BWV 1079, 1072–78, etc.
IX/2	1989	—	Yoshitake Kobayashi	*Die Notenschrift Bachs*

Library and Manuscript Sigla

Note: Library names and collection locations are subject to change. Names and sigla given here are those used in recent literature. The "country" element has been omitted from sigla for German libraries; other library sigla include the country abbreviation.

A Sd	Salzburg, Dom-Musikarchiv
A Wn	Vienna, Österreichischer Nationalbibliothek
A Wn-h	Vienna, Österreichischer Nationalbibliothek, Sammlung Anthony van Hoboken
ABB	Andreas Bach Book (LEm III.8.4; see Chapter 1, "Some Major Manuscript Sources for the Early Works")
AmB	Amalienbibliothek (the library of Princess Anna Amalie of Prussia, now divided between DSB and SPK)
B Bc	Brussels, Conservatoire Royal de Musique
B Br	Brussels, Brussels, Bibliothèque Royale Albert 1er
CH Zz	Zürich, Zentralbibliothek
DK Kk	Copenhagen, Det Kongelige Bibliotek
Dl	Dresden, Landesbibliothek
DS	Darmstadt, Hessische Landes- und Hochschulbibliothek
DSB	Berlin, Deutsche Staatsbibliothek
DSB P	Berlin, Deutsche Staatsbibliothek, Mus. ms. Bach P (followed by shelf mark; used for scores, including keyboard works)
F	Frankfurt-am-Main, Universitäts-Bibliothek
F Pn	Paris, Bibliothèque National
Gb	Göttingen, Johann-Sebastian-Bach-Institut
GB DRc	Durham, Cathedral Library
GB Lbl	London, The British Library
HAu	Halle, Universitäts- und Landesbibliothek
Hs	Hamburg, Staats- und Universitätsbibliothek
LEb	Leipzig, Bach-Archiv
LEm	Leipzig, Musikbibliothek
LEu	Leipzig, Universitätsbibliothek
MM	Möller Manuscript (SPK Mus. ms. 40644; see Chap. 1, "Some Major Manuscript Sources for the Early Works")
NL DHgm	The Hague, Gemeente Museum
P	= DSB P or SPK P
PL LZu	Łodz, Biblioteka Universytecka
ROu	Rostock, Universitätsbibliothek
SPK	Berlin, Staatsbiliothek Preussischer Kulturbesitz
SPK P	Berlin, Staatsbiliothek Preussischer Kulturbesitz, Mus. ms. Bach P (followed by shelf mark; used for scores, including keyboard works)

SWl	Schwerin, Wissenschaftliche Allgemeinbibliothek
US BER	Berea, Ohio, Baldwin-Wallace College, Riemenschneider Memorial Bach Library
US Bp	Boston Public Library
US NHy	New Haven, Yale University
US U	Urbana, Illinois, University of Illinois
US Wc	Washington, D.C., Library of Congress (used in Chap. 14 for the manuscript US Wc ML 96.B186)

Literature

ADLUNG, JACOB. 1768. *Musica mechanica organoedi*. Ed. Johann Lorenz Albrecht, with additional material by J. F. Agricola. Berlin: Friedrich Wilhelm Birnstiel. Facsimile ed. Christhard Mahrenholz, Documenta Musicologica, 1/18. Kassel: Bärenreiter, 1961.

ANSEHL, PETER, KARL HELLER, and HANS-JOACHIM SCHULZE, eds. 1981. *Beiträge zum Konzertschaffen Johann Sebastian Bachs*. Bach-Studien, 6. Leipzig: Breitkopf und Härtel.

APEL, WILLI. 1967. *Geschichte der Orgel- und Klaviermusik*. Kassel: Bärenreiter. Translated and revised by Hans Tischler as *The History of Keyboard Music to 1700*. Bloomington: Indiana University Press.

ARNOLD, F. T. 1931. *The Art of Accompaniment from a Thorough-Bass as Practised in the XVIIth and XVIIIth Centuries*. Oxford: Oxford University Press.

BACH, CARL PHILIPP EMANUEL. 1753–62. *Versuch über die wahre Art das Clavier zu spielen*. 2 vols. Berlin: Christian Friedrich Henning (vol. 1), Georg Ludwig Winter (vol. 2). Facsimile, with a *Nachwort* by Lothar Hoffmann-Erbrecht and a supplement containing the additions from the edition of 1787–97. Leipzig: VEB Breitkopf und Härtel, 1981. Translated by William J. Mitchell as *Essay on the True Art of Playing Keyboard Instruments*. New York: Norton, 1949. Most citations to this work take the form i.2.3.4, referring to volume, chapter, subchapter, and paragraph number, respectively, in the first edition. Mitchell's translation groups the forty-one short chapters of vol. 2 into seven.

———. 1773. [Autobiography]. In Burney 1772–73, vol. 3. Translation in Newman (1965); facsimile in Newman (1967).

BACH, JOHANN SEBASTIAN. 1851–1900. *Werke*. 46 vols. Edited by the Bach-Gesellschaft. Leipzig: Breitkopf und Härtel. Numerous reprints. For editors and dates of individual volumes, see the list of volumes cited (above).

———. 1954– . *Neue Ausgabe sämtlicher Werke*. Edited by the Johann-Sebastian-Bach-Institut, Göttingen, and the Bach-Archiv, Leipzig. Kassel: Bärenreiter. *Kritische Berichte* (Editorial Reports) in separate volumes. For editors and dates of individual volumes, see list of volumes cited (above).

Bach-Compendium: Analytisch-bibliographisches Repertorium der Werke Johann Sebastian Bachs. 1985– . Ed. Hans-Joachim Schulze and Christoph Wolff. Leipzig and Dresden: Edition Peters.

Bach-Dokumente I: Schriftstücke von der Hand Johann Sebastian Bachs. 1963. Ed. Werner Neumann and Hans-Joachim Schulze. Kassel: Bärenreiter.

Bach-Dokumente II: Fremdschriftliche und gedruckte Dokumente zur Lebensgeschichte Johann Sebastian Bachs. 1969. Ed. Werner Neumann and Hans-Joachim Schulze. Kassel: Bärenreiter.

Bach-Dokumente III: Dokumente zum Nachwirken Johann Sebastian Bachs. 1972. Ed. Hans-Joachim Schulze. Kassel: Bärenreiter.

Bach-Fest Buch. 1975. Program book for III. Internationales Bachfest der DDR Leipzig 16.–23.9.75.

Bach Reader, The. 1966. Ed. Hans T. David and Arthur Mendel. Rev. ed. New York: Norton.

BADURA-SKODA, EVA. 1991. "Komponierte J. S. Bach 'Hammerklavier-Konzerte'?" *BJ* 77:159–71.

BAENSCH, OTTO. 1934. "Nochmals das Quodlibet der Goldbergvariationen." *Zeitschrift für Musik* 101:322–23.

BAGNALL, ANNE. 1975. "The Simple Fugues." In "Seminar Report" (see Wolff 1975), *CM* 19:59–61.

BAKER, THOMAS. 1975. "Bach's Revisions in the Augmentation Canon." In "Seminar Report" (see Wolff 1975), *CM* 19:67–71.

BARNES, JOHN. 1979. "Bach's Keyboard Temperament: Internal Evidence from the *Well-Tempered Clavier.*" *EM* 7:236–49.

BECKER, HEINZ. 1953. "Ein unbekannter Herausgeber der Bach-Gesamtausgabe." *Mf* 6:356–57.

BENSTOCK, SEYMOUR, ed. N.d. *Johann Sebastian Bach: A Tercentenary Celebration.* Westport, CT: Greenwood Press. Forthcoming.

BERG, DARRELL. 1979. "Toward a Catalog of the Keyboard Sonatas of C. P. E. Bach." *JAMS* 32:276–303.

———, ed. 1985. *The Collected Works for Solo Keyboard by Carl Philipp Emanuel Bach 1714–1788.* New York and London: Garland. Facsimiles of eighteenth-century sources. Reviewed in Schulenberg (1987).

BERKE, DIETRICH, and DOROTHEE HANEMANN, eds. 1987. *Alte Musik als ästhetische Gegenwart: Kongressbericht Stuttgart 1985.* 2 vols. Kassel: Bärenreiter.

BERNAL, MARTIN. 1987. *Black Athena: The Afroasiatic Roots of Classical Civilization.* Vol. 1: *The Fabrication of Ancient Greece, 1785–1985.* London: Free Association Books.

BEST, TERRENCE. 1983. "Handel's Harpsichord Music: A Checklist." In Hogwood and Luckett (1983, 171–87).

BINGMANN, ANKE, KLAUS HORTSCHANSKY, and WINFRIED KIRSCH, eds. 1988. *Studien zur Instrumentalmusik: Lothar Hoffmann-Erbrecht zum 60. Geburtstag.* Frankfurter Beiträge zur Musikwissenschaft, 20. Tutzing: Hans Schneider.

BIRTEL, WOLFGANG, and CHRISTOPH-HELLMUT MAHLING, eds. 1986. *Aufklärung: Studien zur deutsch-französischen Musikgeschichte im 18. Jahrhundert—Einflüsse und Wirkungen,* Band 2. Annales Universitatis Saraviensis: Reihe Philosophische Fakultät, 20. Heidelberg: Carl Winter Universitätsverlag.

BLOOD, WILLIAM. 1979. " 'Well-Tempering' the Clavier: Five Methods." *EM* 7:491–97.

BLUME, FRIEDRICH. 1963. "Outlines of a New Picture of Bach." *ML* 44:214–27.

BODKY, ERWIN. 1960. *The Interpretation of Bach's Keyboard Works.* Cambridge, MA: Harvard University Press.

BOYD, MALCOLM. 1983. *Bach.* The Master Musicians Series. London: J. M. Dent.

BRECKOFF, WERNER. 1965. *Zur Entstehungsgeschichte des zweiten Wohltemperierten Klaviers von Johann Sebastian Bach.* Tübingen: n.p.

BREIG, WERNER. 1975. "Bachs Goldberg-Variationen als zyklisches Werk." *AMw* 32:243–71.

———. 1976. "Bachs Violinkonzert d-Moll. Studien zu seiner Gestalt und seiner Entstehungsgeschichte." *BJ* 62:7–34.

————. 1982. "Bachs 'Kunst der Fuge': Zur instrumentalen Bestimmung und zum Zyklus-Charakter." *BJ* 68:103–23.

————. 1990a. "Die geschichtliche Stellung von Buxtehudes monodischen Orgelchoral." In Edler and Krummacher (1990, 260–74).

————. 1990b. "Textbezug und Werkidee in Johann Sebastian Bachs frühen Orgelchorälen." In Petersen (1990, 167–82).

BROKAW, JAMES A. II. 1985. "Recent Research on the Sources and Genesis of Bach's Well-Tempered Clavier, Book II." *BACH* 16/3 (July):17–34.

————. 1989. "The Genesis of the Prelude in C Major, BWV 870." In Franklin (1989a, 225–39).

BROWN, HOWARD MAYER, and STANLEY SADIE, eds. 1990. *Performance Practice: Music after 1600*. The New Grove Handbooks in Music. New York: Norton.

BRUSNIAK, FRIEDHELM, and HORST LEUCHTMANN, eds. 1989. *Quaestiones in musica: Festschrift für Franz Krautwurst zum 65. Geburtstag*. Tutzing: Hans Schneider.

BUCH, DAVID J. 1985. "Style brisé, Style luthé, and the Choses luthées." *MQ* 71:52–53.

BUELOW, GEORGE. 1983. "Johann Mattheson and the Invention of the *Affektenlehre*." In Buelow and Marx (1983, 393–407).

————. 1989. "Expressivity in the Accompanied Recitatives of Bach's Cantatas." In Franklin (1989a, 18–35).

————. 1991. "A Bach Borrowing by Gluck: Another Frontier." *BACH* 22/1 (Spring/Summer):43–61.

BUELOW, GEORGE J., and HANS JOACHIM MARX, eds. 1983. *New Mattheson Studies*. Cambridge: Cambridge University Press.

BUKOFZER, MANFRED. 1939–40. "Allegory in Baroque Music." *Journal of the Warburg and Courtauld Institutes* 3:1–22.

BURNEY, CHARLES. 1772–73. *Carl Burney's der Musik Doctors Tagebuch seiner musikalischen Reisen*. Translated by C. D. Ebeling (I–II) and J. C. Bode (III). Hamburg: Bode. Facsimile ed. Richard Schaale, Documenta Musicologica, 1/19. Kassel: Bärenreiter, 1959.

BUTLER, GREGORY. 1977. "Fugue and Rhetoric." *JMT* 21:49–109.

————. 1980. "Leipziger Stecher in Bachs Originaldrucken." *BJ* 66:9–26.

————. 1983a. "Ordering Problems in J. S. Bach's *Art of Fugue* Resolved." *MQ* 69:44–61.

————. 1983b. "*Der vollkommene Capellmeister* as a Stimulus to J. S. Bach's Late Fugal Writing." In Buelow and Marx (1983, 293–305).

————. 1986. "The Engraving of J. S. Bach's *Six Partitas*." *JMR* 7:3–27.

————. 1988. "Neues zur Datierung der Goldberg-Variationen." *BJ* 74:219–21.

————. 1990. *Bach's Clavier-Übung III: The Making of a Print. With a Companion Study of the Canonic Variations on "Vom Himmel Hoch," BWV 769*. Durham, NC, and London: Duke University Press.

BUTT, JOHN. 1990. *Bach Interpretation: Articulation Marks in Primary Sources of J. S. Bach*. Cambridge: Cambridge University Press.

CANNON, BEEKMAN C. 1947. *Johann Mattheson: Spectator in Music*. Yale Studies in the History of Music, 1. With preface by Leo Schrade. New Haven, CT: Yale University Press. Reprint, n.p.: Archon Books, 1968.

CARTER, STEWART. 1991. "The String Tremolo in the 17th Century." *EM* 19:42–59.

CHAFE, ERIC. 1981. "Key Structure and Tonal Allegory in the Passions of J. S. Bach: An Introduction." *CM* 31:39–54.

————. 1982. "J. S. Bach's *St. Matthew Passion*: Aspects of Planning, Structure, and Chronology." *JAMS* 35:49–114.

————. 1991. *Tonal Allegory in the Vocal Music of J.S. Bach*. Berkeley: University of California Press.

CLARK, STEPHEN L., ed. 1988. *C. P. E. Bach Studies*. Oxford: Oxford University Press.

COLLINS, MICHAEL. 1966. "The Performance of Triplets in the Seventeenth and Eighteenth Centuries." *JAMS* 19:281–323.

CONE, EDWARD T. 1968. *Musical Form and Musical Performance*. New York: Norton.

————. 1974. "Bach's Unfinished Fugue in C Minor." In Marshall (1974, 149–55).

COOPER, BARRY. 1972. "An Unknown Bach Source." *MT* 113:1,167–69.

COUPERIN, FRANÇOIS. 1717. *L'Art de toucher le clavecin*. Paris: Author. With German translation by Anna Linde and English translation by Mevanwy Roberts. Wiesbaden: Breitkopf und Härtel, 1933.

CRUTCHFIELD, WILL. 1984. "33 Bach Organ Preludes Are Discovered at Yale." *New York Times* (Dec. 19):C-19.

DADELSEN, GEORG VON. 1957. *Bemerkungen zur Handschrift Johann Sebastian Bachs, seiner Familie und seines Kreises*. Tübinger Bach-Studien, 1. Trossingen: Hohner.

————. 1958. *Beiträge zur Chronologie der Werke Johann Sebastian Bachs*. Tübinger Bach-Studien, 4–5. Trossingen: Hohner.

————, ed. 1975. *Joh. Seb. Bach: Suiten, Sonaten, Capriccios und Variationen*. Munich: Henle.

————, ed. 1988. *Johann Sebastian Bach: Klavierbüchlein für Anna Magdalena Bach 1725*. Documenta Musicologica, 2/25. Kassel: Bärenreiter. Facsimile of SPK P 225, with commentary.

DADELSEN, GEORG VON, and KLAUS RÖNNAU, eds. 1970. *Joh. Seb. Bach: Fantasien, Präludien und Fugen*. Munich: Henle.

DAHLHAUS, CARL. 1967. *Musikästhetik*. Cologne: Musikverlag Hans Gerig. Translated by William W. Austin as *Esthetics of Music*, with new author's preface. Cambridge: Cambridge University Press, 1982.

DAMMANN, ROLF. 1986. *Johann Sebastian Bachs "Goldberg-Variationen."* Mainz: Schott.

DANCKERT, WERNER. 1924. *Geschichte der Gigue*. Leipzig: Kistner and Siegel.

DANNREUTHER, EDWARD. 1893–95. *Musical Ornamentation*. London: Novello.

DART, THURSTON. 1970. "Bach's Early Keyboard Music: A Neglected Source (Brussels, B.R., Fétis 2960)." *Acta* 42:236–38. Reply in Dömling and Kohlhase (1971).

DAVERIO, JOHN. N.d. "The 'Unraveling' of Schoenberg's Bach." In Benstock (n.d.).

DAVID, HANS. 1926. "Die Gestalt von Bachs Chromatischer Fantasie." *BJ* 23:23–67. With twenty-four-page *Anhang* containing musical examples and textual notes, bound separately.

————. 1945. *J. S. Bach's Musical Offering: History, Interpretation, and Analysis*. New York: G. Schirmer. Reprint, New York: Dover, 1972.

DAVID, JOHANN NEPOMUK. 1957. *Die zweistimmigen Inventionen von Johann Sebastian Bach*. Göttingen: Vandenhoeck und Ruprecht.

————. 1962. *Das Wohltemperierte Klavier: Versuch einer Synopsis*. Göttingen: Vandenhoeck und Ruprecht.

DAVIS, SHELLEY G. 1988. "C. P. E. Bach and the Early History of the Recapitulatory Tutti in North Germany." In Clark (1988, 65–82).

DEDEL, PETER. 1975. "Dissemination and Dispute." In "Seminar Report" (see Wolff 1975), *CM* 19:50–54. On the *Art of Fugue*.

DEHNHARD, WALTER, ed. 1973. *Johann Sebastian Bach: Kleine Präeludien und Fughetten*. Vienna: Wiener Urtext.

————, ed. 1977–83. *Johann Sebastian Bach: Das wohltemperierte Clavier*. 2 vols. Vienna: Wiener Urtext.

DERR, ELLWOOD. 1981. "The Two-Part Inventions: Bach's Composer's *Vademecum*." *MTS* 3:26–48.

DÖMLING, WOLFGANG, and THOMAS KOHLHASE. 1976. "Kein Bach-Autograph: Die Handschrift Brüssel, Bibliothèque Royale, II. 4093 (Fétis 2960)." *Acta* 43:108–9.

DONINGTON, ROBERT. 1973. *A Performer's Guide to Baroque Music*. New York: Scribner's.

———. 1977. "What *Is* Rhythmic Alteration?" *EM* 5:543–44.

———. 1982. *Baroque Music: Style and Performance: A Handbook*. New York: Norton.

DORFMÜLLER, KURT. 1989. "Eine Themenverwandtschaft im Umkreis Bach-Benda." In Brusniak and Leuchtmann (1989, 71–77).

DOUGLASS, FENNER, OWEN JANDER, and BARBARA OWEN, eds. 1986. *Charles Brenton Fisk, Organ Builder*. Vol. 1, *Essays in His Honor*. Easthampton, MA: The Westfield Center for Early Keyboard Studies.

DREYFUS, LAURENCE. 1980. "Basso Continuo Practice in the Vocal Works of J. S. Bach: A Study of the Original Performance Parts." Ph.D. diss., Columbia University.

———. 1983. "Early Music Defended against Its Devotees: A Theory of Historical Performance in the Twentieth Century." *MQ* 69:297–322.

———. 1985a. "J. S. Bach's Concerto Ritornellos." *MQ* 71:327–58.

———. 1985b. "The Metaphorical Soloist: Concerted Organ Parts in Bach's Cantatas." *EM* 13:237–47.

———. 1987. *Bach's Continuo Group*. Cambridge, MA: Harvard University Press.

———. 1987b. "The Capellmeister and His Audience: Observations on 'Enlightened' Receptions of Bach." In Berke and Hanemann (1987, 1:180–89).

DRUMMOND, PIPPA. 1980. *The German Concerto*. Oxford: Clarendon Press.

DÜRR, ALFRED. 1953. "Johann Gottlieb Goldberg und die Triosonate BWV 1037." *BJ* 40:51–80. Reprinted in Dürr (1988a).

———. 1978. "Tastenumfang und Chronologie in Bachs Klavierwerken." In Kohlhase and Scherliess (1978, 73–88). Reprinted in Dürr (1988a).

———. 1981. "Zur Form der Präludien in Bachs Englischen Suites." In Ansehl, Heller, and Schulze (1981, 101–8). Reprinted in Dürr (1988a).

———. 1984. *Zur Frühgeschichte des Wohltemperierten Klaviers I von Johann Sebastian Bach*. Nachrichten der Akademie der Wissenschaften in Göttingen, I. Philologisch-Historische Klasse, Jahrgang 1984, Nr. 1. Göttingen: Vandenhoek und Ruprecht.

———. 1985. "The Historical Background of the Composition of Johann Sebastian Bach's *Clavier* Suite [*sic*]." *BACH* 16/1 (January):53–68.

———. 1986. "Ein Dokument aus dem Unterricht Bachs." *Musiktheorie* 1:163–70.

———. 1988a. *Im Mittelpunkt Bach: Ausgewählte Aufsätze und Vorträge*. Edited by the Board of the Johann-Sebastian-Bach-Institut, Göttingen. Kassel: Bärenreiter. Reprints of articles; references are to the original publications.

———. 1988b. "Das Präludium Es-Dur BWV 852 aus dem *Wohltemperierten Klavier*." In Bingmann, Hortschansky, and Kirsch (1988, 93–101).

EDLER, ARNFRIED, and FRIEDHELM KRUMMACHER, eds. 1990. *Dietrich Buxtehude und die europäische Musik seiner Zeit. Bericht über das Lübecker Symposion 1987*. Kieler Schriften zur Musikwissenschaft, 35. Kassel: Bärenreiter.

EGGEBRECHT, HANS HEINRICH. 1957. "Arten des Generalbasses im frühen und mittleren 17. Jahrhundert." *AMw* 14:61–82.

———. 1984. *Bachs Kunst der Fuge: Erscheinung und Deutung*. Munich: R. Piper.

EICHBERG, HARTWIG. 1975. "Unechtes unter Bachs Klavierwerke." *BJ*, 61:7–49.

EMERY, WALTER. 1953. *Bach's Ornaments*. London: Novello.

EPPSTEIN, HANS. 1964. "Zur Problematik von J. S. Bachs Sonate für Violine und Cembalo G-dur (BWV 1019)." *AMw* 21:217–42.

————. 1970. "Zur Vor- und Entstehungsgeschichte von J. S. Bachs Tripelkonzert a-moll (BWV 1044)." *Jahrbuch des Staatlichen Instituts für Musikforschung Preussischer Kulturbesitz* 3:44.

————. 1976. "Chronologieprobleme in Johann Sebastian Bachs Suiten für Soloinstrument." *BJ* 62:35–57.

————. 1986. "Johann Sebastian Bach und der galante Stil." In Birtel and Mahling (1986, 209–18).

FALCK, MARTIN. 1913. *Wilhelm Friedemann Bach: Sein Leben und seine Werke.* Leipzig: Kahnt. 2d ed., 1919.

FANNA, ANTONIO, and GIOVANNI MORELLI, eds. 1988. *Nuovi studi vivaldiani: edizione e cronologia critica delle opere.* Studi di Musica Veneta/Quaderni Vivaldiana, 4. 2 vols. Florence: Olschki.

FAULKNER, QUENTIN. 1984. *J. S. Bach's Keyboard Technique: A Historical Introduction.* St. Louis: Concordia.

FECHNER, MANFRED. 1980. "Improvisationsskizzen und ausnotierte Diminutionen von Johann Georg Pisendel, dargestellt an in Dresden handschriftlich überlieferten Konzerten von Johann Friedrich Fasch und Johann Gottlieb Graun." In *Zu Fragen der Verzierungskunst in der Instrumentalmusik der ersten Hälfte des 18. Jahrhunderts,* 35–55. Studien zur Aufführungspraxis und Interpretation von Instrumentalmusik des 18. Jahrhunderts, 11. Blankenburg/Harz: n.p.

FEDERHOFER, HELLMUT. 1958. "Zur handschriftlichen Überlieferung der Musiktheorie in Österreich in der zweiten Hälfte des 17. Jahrhunderts." *Mf* 11:264–79.

FERGUSON, HOWARD. 1975. *Keyboard Interpretation from the 14th to the 19th Century: An Introduction.* London: Oxford University Press.

FLADE, ERNST. 1953. *Gottfried Silbermann: Ein Beitrag zur Geschichte des deutschen Orgel- und Klavierbaus im Zeitalter Bachs.* 2d ed. Leipzig: Breitkopf und Härtel.

FLINDELL, E. FREDERICK. 1984. "Apropos Bach's Inventions, Part III." *BACH* 15/2 (April):3–17.

FORCHERT, ARNO. 1985–86. "Musik und Rhetorik im Barock." *SJ* 7–8: 5–21.

————. 1987. "Bach und die Tradition der Rhetorik." In Berke and Hanemann (1987, 1:169–78).

FORKEL, JOHANN NICOLAUS. 1802. *Ueber Johann Sebastian Bachs Leben, Kunst und Kunstwerke.* Leipzig: Hoffmeister und Kühnel. Facsimile, Frankfurt am Main: H. L. Grahl, 1950. Translation in BR, 295–356. Ed. Walther Vetter. Kassel: Bärenreiter, 1968.

FRANCK, WOLF. 1949. "Musicology and Its Founder, Johann Nicolaus Forkel (1749–1818)." *MQ* 35:588–609.

FRANKLIN, DON O. 1987. "Articulation in the Cembalo Works of J. S. Bach: A Notational Study." In Berke and Hanemann (1987, 2: 452–66).

————, ed. 1989a. *Bach Studies.* Cambridge: Cambridge University Press.

————. 1989b. "Reconstructing the *Urpartitur* for WTC II: A Study of the 'London autograph' (BL Add. MS 35021)." In Franklin (1989a, 240–78).

————. 1991. "The Carnegie Manuscript and J. S. Bach." *BACH* 22/1 (Spring/Summer): 5–15.

FRANKLIN, DON, and STEPHEN DAW, eds. 1980. *Johann Sebastian Bach: Das Wohltemperierte Clavier II: Facsimile of the Autograph Manuscript in the British Library, Add. MS 35021.* London: The British Library.

FUCHS, JOSEF RAINERIUS. 1985. *Studien zu Artikulationsangaben in Orgel- und Clavierwerken von Joh. Seb. Bach.* Tübinger Beiträge zur Musikwissenschaft, 10. Neuhausen-Stuttgart: Hänssler.

FULLER, DAVID. 1977. "Dotting, the 'French Style,' and Frederick Neumann's Counter-Reformation." *EM* 5:517–43.

————. 1985. "The 'Dotted Style' in Bach, Handel and Scarlatti." In Williams (1985a, 99–117).

————. 1990. "The Performer as Composer." In Brown and Sadie (1990, 117–46).

FULLER MAITLAND, J. A. 1925. *The "48": Bach's Wohltemperiertes Clavier.* 2 vols. London: Oxford University Press.

GADAMER, HANS-GEORG. 1946. *Bach und Weimar.* Weimar: Hermann Böhlaus Nachfolger.

GECK, MARTIN, ed. 1960. *Bach-Interpretation.* Göttingen: Vandenhoeck und Ruprecht.

GERMANN, SHERIDAN. 1985. "The Mietkes, the Margrave and Bach." In Williams (1985a, 119–48).

GERSTENBERG, WALTER. 1954. "Generalbasslehre und Kompositionstechnik in Niedts 'Musikalischer Handleitung'." In *Bericht über den Internationalen Musikwissenschaftlichen Kongress Bamberg 1953,* ed. Wilfried Brennecke, Willi Kahl, and Rudolf Steglich, 152–55. Kassel: Bärenreiter.

GLÖCKNER, ANDREAS. 1981. "Neuerkenntnisse zu Johann Sebastian Bachs Aufführungskalender zu 1729 und 1735." *BJ* 67:43–75.

————. 1988. "Zur Echtheit und Datierung der Kantate BWV 150 'Nach dir, Herr, verlanget mich'." *BJ* 74:195–203.

GODT, IRVING. 1990. "Politics, Patriotism, and a Polonaise: A Possible Revision in Bach's *Suite in B Minor.*" *MQ* 74:610–22.

GRAESER, WOLFGANG. 1924. "Bachs 'Kunst der Fuge'." *BJ* 21:1–104.

GRIMM, JACOB, and WILHELM GRIMM. 1854–1960. *Deutsches Wörterbuch.* 16 vols. Leipzig: S. Hirzel.

GUSTAFSON, BRUCE. 1979. *French Harpsichord Music of the 17th Century.* Studies in Musicology, 11. Ann Arbor, MI: UMI Research Press.

HAAS, ROBERT. 1927. *Die estensischen Musikalien: Thematisches Verzeichnis.* Regensburg: Gustav Bosse.

HANKS, SARAH ELIZA. 1972. "The German Unaccompanied Keyboard Concerto in the Early Eighteenth Century, Including Works of Walther, Bach and Their Contemporaries." Ph.D. diss., University of Iowa.

HARNONCOURT, NIKOLAUS. 1970. "The Origin of the St. Matthew Passion." Program booklet accompanying his recording: *J. S. Bach: Matthäuspassion.* Telefunken SAWT 9572/75-A. Pp. 4–14.

HARRISON, DANIEL. 1990. "Rhetoric and Fugue: An Analytical Approach." *MTS* 12:1–42.

HASE, HERMANN VON. 1911. "Carl Philipp Emanuel Bach und Joh. Gottl. Im. Breitkopf." *BJ* 8:86–104.

HAYS, ELIZABETH LORETTA. 1976. "F.W. Marpurg's *Anleitung zum Clavierspielen* (Berlin, 1755) and *Principes du clavecin* (Berlin, 1756): Translation and Commentary." Ph.D. diss., Stanford University, 1976.

HEIMANN, WALTER. 1973. *Der Generalbass-Satz und seine Rolle in Bachs Choral-Satz.* Freiburger Schriften zur Musikwissenschaft, 5. Munich: Musikverlag Emil Katzbichler.

HEINRICH, ADEL. 1983. *Bach's "Kunst der Fuge": A Living Compendium of Fugal Procedures. With a Motivic Analysis of All the Fugues.* Washington, DC: Catholic University of America Press.

HEINSE, WILHELM. 1903. *Hildegard von Hohenthal: Erster und zweiter Theil.* Sämmtliche Werke, 5. Ed. Carl Schüddekopf. Leipzig: Insel-Verlag.

HELLER, KARL. 1989. "Norddeutsche Musikkultur als Traditionsraum des jungen Bach." *BJ* 75:7–19.

HELM, E. EUGENE. 1972. "The 'Hamlet' Fantasy and the Literary Element in C. P. E. Bach's Music." *MQ* 58:277–96.

———. 1989. *Thematic Catalogue of the Works of Carl Philipp Emanuel Bach.* New Haven, CT: Yale University Press.

HELMS, MARIANNE. 1981. "Zur Chronologie der Handschrift des Anonymus 5." Anhang 1 to NBA V/8, KB:183–95.

HENNING, UTA. 1982. "The Most Beautiful among the Claviers." *EM*, 10:477–86. On a reconstructed lute-harpsichord.

HERZ, GERHARD. 1984. *Bach-Quellen in Amerika/Bach Sources in America.* Bärenreiter: Kassel. German and English versions in parallel columns.

———. 1990. "Yoshitake Kobayashi's Article 'On the Chronology of the Last Phase of Bach's Work—Compositions and Performances: 1736 to 1750'—An Analysis with Translated Portions of the Original Text." *BACH* 21/1 (Spring):3–25.

HEUSSNER, HORST, ed. 1964. *Festschrift Hans Engel zum siebzigsten Geburtstag.* Kassel: Bärenreiter.

HILL, JOHN WALTER. 1979. *The Life and Works of Francesco Maria Veracini.* Studies in Musicology, 3. Ann Arbor, MI: UMI Research Press.

HILL, ROBERT S. 1985. *"Echtheit angezweifelt*: Style and Authenticity in Two Suites Attributed to Bach." *EM* 13:248–55.

———. 1986. "Die Herkunft von Bachs 'Thema Legrenzianum'." *BJ* 72:105–7.

———. 1987. "The Möller Manuscript and the Andreas Bach Book: Two Keyboard Anthologies from the Circle of the Young Johann Sebastian Bach." Ph.D. diss., Harvard University.

———. 1990a. "Stilanalyse und Überlieferungsproblematik: Das Variationssuiten-Repertoire J. A. Reinckens." In Edler and Krummacher (1990, 204–14).

———. 1990b. "Tablature versus Staff Notation: Or, Why Did the Young J. S. Bach Compose in Tablature?" In Walker (1990, 349–59).

HIRSCHMANN, WOLFGANG. 1988. "Zur konzertanten Struktur der Ecksätze von Johann Sebastian Bachs Concerto BWV 971." *AMw* 45:148–62.

HOFFMANN-ERBRECHT, LOTHAR. 1983. "Von der Urentsprechung zum Symbol: Versuch einer Systematisierung musikalischer Sinnbilder." In Rehm (1983, 116–25).

HOFMANN, KLAUS. 1988. "Über Themenbildung und thematische Arbeit in einigen zweiteiligen Präludien des Wohltemperierten Klaviers II." In Wolff (1988b, 48–57).

HOGWOOD, CHRISTOPHER. 1988. "A Supplement to C. P. E. Bach's *Versuch*: E. W. Wolf's *Anleitung* of 1785." In Clark (1988, 133–57).

HOGWOOD, CHRISTOPHER, and RICHARD LUCKETT, eds. 1983. *Music in Eighteenth-Century England: Essays in Memory of Charles Cudworth.* Cambridge: Cambridge University Press.

HOKE, HANS GUNTER, ed. 1979. *Johann Sebastian Bach: Die Kunst der Fugue, BWV 1080: Autograph; Originaldruck.* Faksimile-Reihe Bachscher Werke, 14. Edited, with a study, by Hans Gunter Hoke. Mainz: Schott.

HORN, WOLFGANG. 1988. *Carl Philipp Emanuel Bach: Frühe Klaviersonaten.* Hamburg: Karl Dieter Wagner.

HOSLER, BELLAMY. 1981. *Changing Aesthetic Views of Instrumental Music in 18th-Century Germany.* Studies in Musicology, 42. Ann Arbor, MI: UMI Research Press.

JACCOTTET, CHRISTIANE. 1986. "L'influence de la musique française pour clavecin dans les *Suites Anglaises* de Johann Sebastian Bach et, plus spécialement, la première en La Majeur BWV 806." In Birtel and Mahling (1986, 195–99).

JOHNSON, THEODORE O. 1986. *An Analytical Survey of the Fifteen Sinfonias (Three-Part Inventions) by J. S. Bach.* Lanham, MD: University Press of America.

KAST, PAUL. 1958. *Die Bach-Handschriften der Berliner Staatsbibliothek.* Tübinger Bach-Studien, 2–3. Trossingen: Hohner-Verlag.

KAUSSLER, INGRID, and HELMUT KAUSSLER. 1985. *Die Goldberg-Variationen von J. S. Bach.* Stuttgart: Freies Geistesleben.

KELLER, HERMANN. 1948. *Die Orgelwerke Bachs.* Leipzig: C. F. Peters.

———. 1949. "Über Bachs Bearbeitungen aus dem 'Hortus musicus' von Reinken." In *Société internationale de musicologie: Quatrième Congrès Bâle . . . Compte rendu*, 161. Kassel: Bärenreiter.

———. 1950. *Die Klavierwerke Bachs.* Leipzig: C. F. Peters.

———. 1965. *Das Wohltemperierte Klavier.* Kassel: Bärenreiter. Translated by Leigh Gerdine. New York: Norton, 1976.

KENYON, NICHOLAS, ed. 1988. *Authenticity and Early Music.* Oxford: Oxford University Press. Reviewed in Rosen (1990).

KIRKENDALE, URSULA. 1980. "The Source for Bach's *Musical Offering*: The *Institutio oratoria* of Quintilian." *JAMS* 33:88–141.

KIRKPATRICK, RALPH. 1984. *Interpreting Bach's Well-Tempered Clavier: A Performer's Discourse of Method.* New Haven, CT: Yale University Press.

KIRNBERGER, JOHANN PHILIPP. 1771–79. *Die Kunst des reinen Satzes in der Musik.* 4 pts. in 2 vols. Berlin and Königsberg: Christian Friedrich Voss in Commission (vol. 1), G. J. Decker and G. L. Hartung (vol. 2). Facsimile, Hildesheim, Germany: Olms, 1968. Translation by Jurgen Thym and David Beach of vol. 1 and of vol. 2, pt. 1, as *The Art of Strict Musical Composition.* New Haven, CT: Yale University Press, 1982.

———. 1773. *Die wahren Grundsätze zum Gebrauch der Harmonie. . . .* Berlin: G. J. Decker and G. L. Hartung. Facsimile, Hildesheim, Germany: Olms, 1970.

KITTEL, JOHANN CHRISTIAN. 1808. *Der angehende praktische Organist.* Erfurt: Beyer und Maring.

KLEIN, HANS-GÜNTER. 1970. *Der Einfluss der vivaldischen Konzertform im Instrumentalwerk Johann Sebastian Bachs.* Collection d'Études Musicologiques, 54. Strasbourg: P. H. Heitz.

KOBAYASHI, YOSHITAKE. 1973. *Franz Hauser und seine Bach-Handschriftensammlung.* Göttingen: n.p.

———. 1978. "Neuerkenntnisse zu einigen Bach-Quellen an Hand schriftkundlicher Untersuchungen." *BJ* 64:43–60.

———. 1983. "Der Gehrener Kantor Johann Christoph Bach (1673–1727) und seine Sammelbände mit Musik für Tasteninstrumente." In Rehm (1983, 356–62).

———. 1988. "Zur Chronologie der Spätwerke Johann Sebastian Bachs: Kompositions- und Aufführungstätigkeit von 1736 bis 1750." *BJ* 74:7–72. Partial English translation in Herz (1990).

———. 1989. *Die Notenschrift Johann Sebastian Bachs: Dokumentation ihrer Entwicklung.* NBA, IX/2. Kassel: Bärenreiter.

KOCH, HEINRICH CHRISTOPH. 1782–1793. *Versuch einer Anleitung zur Composition.* 3 vols. Leipzig: Adam Friedrich Böhme, and Rudolstadt: Löwe Erben und Schirach. Facsimile, Hildesheim, Germany: Olms, 1969.

KOHLHASE, THOMAS, and VOLKER SCHERLIESS, eds. 1978. *Festschrift Georg von Dadelsen zum 60. Geburtstag.* Neuhausen-Stuttgart: Hänssler.

KOLNEDER, WALTER. 1977. *Die Kunst der Fuge: Mythen des 20. Jahrhunderts.* 5 vols. Wiesbaden: Breitkopf und Härtel.

KOPROWSKI, RICHARD. 1975. "Bach 'Fingerprints' in the Engraving of the Original Edition [of the *Art of Fugue*]." In "Seminar Report" (see Wolff 1975), *CM* 19:61–67.

KRETZSCHMAR, HERRMANN. 1910. "Das Notenbuch der Zeumerin." In *Jahrbuch der Musikbibliothek Peters für 1919*, 52–72. Leipzig: C. F. Peters.

Kross, Siegfried. 1969. *Das Instrumentalkonzert bei Georg Philipp Telemann*. Tutzing: Hans Schneider.

Kunze, Stefan. 1969. "Gattungen der Fuge in Bach's Wohltemperiertem Klavier." In Geck (1969, 74–93).

Ladewig, James. 1991. "Bach and the *Prima prattica*: The Influence of Frescobaldi on a Fugue from the *Well-Tempered Clavier*." *JM* 9:358–74.

Landowskwa, Wanda. 1924. *Music of the Past*. Translated from the French by William Aspenwall Bradley. New York: Knopf.

Landshoff, Ludwig. 1933. *Revisions-Bericht zur Urtextausgabe von Joh. Seb. Bach: Inventionen und Sinfonien*. Leipzig: C. F. Peters.

Larsen, Jens Peter. 1972. *Handel's Messiah*. New York: Norton.

Ledbetter, David. 1987. *Harpsichord and Lute Music in Seventeenth-Century France*. Bloomington: Indiana University Press.

Lee, Douglas A. 1988. "C. P. E. Bach and the Free Fantasia for Keyboard: Deutsche Staatsbibliothek Mus. ms. Nichelmann 1N." In Clark (1988, 177–84).

LeHuray Peter. 1981. "English Keyboard Fingering in the 16th and Early 17th Centuries." In Ian Bent, ed., *Source Materials and the Interpretation of Music: A Memorial Volume to Thurston Dart*. London: Stainer and Bell.

———. 1990. *Authenticity in Performance: Eighteenth-Century Case Studies*. Cambridge: Cambridge University Press.

Leppert, Richard, and Susan McClary, eds. 1987. *Music and Society: The Politics of Composition, Performance and Reception*. Cambridge: Cambridge University Press.

Lindley, Mark. 1982. "An Introduction to Alessandro Scarlatti's *Toccata prima*." *EM* 10:333–39.

———. 1985. "Keyboard Technique and Articulation: Evidence for the Performing Practices of Bach, Handel and Scarlatti." In Williams (1985a, 207–43).

———. 1989a. "Early Fingering: Some Editing Problems and Some New Readings for J. S. Bach and John Bull." *EM* 17:60–69.

———. 1989b. *Lutes, Viols and Temperament*. London: Cambridge University Press.

———. 1990. "Tuning and Intonation" and "Keyboard Fingerings and Articulation." In Brown and Sadie (1990, 169–85; 186–203).

Lockwood, Lewis, and Edward Roesner, eds. 1990. *Essays in Musicology: A Tribute to Alvin Johnson*. Philadelphia: American Musicological Society.

Löhlein, Georg Simon. 1765. *Clavier-Schule oder kurze und gründliche Anweisung zur Melodie und Harmonie*. Leipzig and Züllichau: Waisenhaus- und Fromannische Buchhandlung.

Lohmann, Heinz, ed. 1968–79. *J. S. Bach: Sämtliche Orgelwerke*. 10 vols. Wiesbaden: Breitkopf und Härtel.

Louwenaar, Karyl. 1982–83. "Which Comes First: Sarabande or Air? A Study of the Order of the Movements in Bach's Keyboard Partitas." *EKJ* 1:7–15.

———. 1983–84. "A Reconsideration of the Rhythmic Interpretation of the Gigue from Bach's Sixth Partita, BWV 830." *EKJ* 2:1–20.

McClary, Susan. 1987. "The Blasphemy of Talking Politics during Bach Year [1985]." In Leppert and McClary (1987, 13–62).

McCorkle, Margit L. 1984. *Johannes Brahms: Thematisch-bibliographisches Werkverzeichnis*. Munich: Henle.

McIntyre, Ray. 1965. "On the Interpretation of Bach's Gigues." *MQ* 51:478–92.

Mann, Alfred, ed. 1982. *G. F. Händel: Aufzeichnungen zur Kompositionslehre*. Hallische Händel-Ausgabe, Supplement, Band I. Kassel: Bärenreiter.

MARISSEN, MICHAEL. 1988. "A Critical Reappraisal of J. S. Bach's A-Major Flute Sonata." *JM* 6:367–86.

———. 1990. "Form and Scoring in J. S. Bach's Brandenburg Concertos." Ph.D. diss., Brandeis University.

MARONEY, DAVITT, ed. 1989. *Joh. Seb. Bach: Die Kunst der Fuge für Cembalo (Klavier) BWV 1080*. Munich: G. Henle.

MARPURG, FRIEDRICH WILHELM. 1750. *Kunst der Clavierspielen*. Berlin: Henning. Revised edition, 1762. Facsimile of the revised edition, Hildesheim, Germany: Olms, 1969.

———. 1753–54. *Abhandlung von der Fuge*. 2 vols. Berlin: A. Haude and J. C. Spener. Facsimile, Hildesheim, Germany: Olms, 1970.

———. 1755. *Anleitung zum Clavierspielen*. Berlin: A. Haude and J. C. Spener. Facsimile of the second edition (Berlin, 1765), New York: Broude, 1969. Translation in Hays (1976).

———. 1756. *Principes du clavecin*. Berlin: A. Haude and J. C. Spener. Facsimile, Geneva: Minkoff Reprint, 1974. French language edition, with additions, of Marpurg (1755). Translation in Hays (1976).

MARSHALL, ROBERT L. 1972. *The Compositional Process of J. S. Bach: A Study of the Autograph Scores of the Vocal Works*. 2 vols. Princeton, NJ: Princeton University Press.

———, ed. 1974. *Studies in Baroque Music in Honor of Arthur Mendel*. Kassel: Bärenreiter.

———. 1976a. "Bach the Progressive: Observations on His Later Works." *MQ* 62:313–57. Reprinted in Marshall (1989, 23–58).

———, ed. 1976b. *Johann Sebastian Bach: Fantasia per il Cembalo, BWV 906/1*. Leipzig: Neue Bach-Gesellschaft. Facsimile edition with introduction. Translation as "The Autograph Fair Copies of the *Fantasia per il cembalo*, BWV 906" in Marshall (1989, 193–200).

———. 1983. "*Editore traditore*: Ein weiterer 'Fall Rust'?" In Rehm (1983, 183–91). Translated as " 'Editore traditore': Suspicious Performance Indications in the Bach Sources" in Marshall (1989, 241–54).

———. 1986. "Organ or 'Klavier'? Instrumental Prescriptions in the Sources of Bach's Keyboard Works." In Stauffer and May (1986, 212–39). Reprinted as "Organ or 'Klavier'? Instrumental Prescriptions in the Sources of the Keyboard Works" in Marshall (1989, 271–93).

———. 1989. *The Music of Johann Sebastian Bach: The Sources, the Style, the Significance*. New York: Schirmer Books. Reprints of sixteen articles, those originally in German translated into English. References are to the original publications except where this volume contains new material.

———. 1990. "The Notebooks for Wilhelm Friedemann and Anna Magdalena Bach: Some Biographical Lessons." In Lockwood and Roesner (1990, 192–200).

MATTHESON, JOHANN. 1713. *Das Neu-Eröffnete Orchestre*. . . . Hamburg: Author and Benjamin Schillers Witwe.

———. 1731. *Grosse General-Bass-Schule*. Hamburg: Johann Christoph Lissner. Facsimile, Hildesheim, Germany: Olms, 1968.

———. 1737. *Kern melodischer Wissenschaft . . . als ein Vorläuffer des Vollkommenen Capellmeisters*. . . . Hamburg: Christian Herold.

———. 1739. *Der vollkommene Capellmeister*. Hamburg: Christian Herold. Facsimile ed. Margarethe Riemann. Kassel: Bärenreiter, 1954. Translated by Ernest C. Harriss as *Johann Mattheson's* Der vollkommene Capellmeister: *A Revised Translation with Critical Commentary*. Studies in Musicology, 21. Ann Arbor, MI: UMI Research Press, 1981.

MORANA, FRANK. 1990. "The Presto in D Minor, BWV 970: Its Authenticity Reconsidered." *BACH* 21/3 (Winter):9–29.

MOZART, LEOPOLD. 1756. *Versuch einer gründlichen Violinschule*. Augsburg: Verlag des Verfassers (Johann Jacob Lotter). Translation, from the first and third (1787) editions, by Edith Knocker as *A Treatise on the Fundamental Principles of Violin Playing*, 2d ed. Oxford: Oxford University Press, 1949.

NEUMANN, FREDERICK. 1965. "La note pointée et la soi-disant 'manière française'." *Revue de musicologie* 51:61–92. Translated by Raymond Harris and Edmund Shay as "The Dotted Note and the So-called French Style." *EM* 5 (1977):310–24.

———. 1974. "The Question of Rhythm in the Two Versions of Bach's French Overture, BWV 831." In Marshall (1974, 183–94).

———. 1977. "Facts and Fiction about Overdotting." *MQ* 63:155–85.

———. 1978. *Ornamentation in Baroque and Post-Baroque Music, With Special Emphasis on J. S. Bach*. Princeton, NJ: Princeton University Press.

———. 1979. "Once More: the 'French Overture Style'." *EM* 7:39–115.

———. 1985. "Bach: Progressive or Conservative and the Authorship of the Goldberg Aria." *MQ* 71:281–94.

The New Grove Dictionary of Music and Musicians. 1980. Ed. Stanley Sadie. 20 vols. London: Macmillan.

The New Grove Dictionary of Musical Instruments. 1984. Ed. Stanley Sadie. 3 vols. London: Macmillan.

NEWMAN, WILLIAM S. 1961. "Kirnberger's *Method for Tossing Off Sonatas*." *MQ* 47:517–25.

———. 1965. "Emanuel Bach's Autobiography." *MQ* 51:363–72.

———, ed. 1967. *Carl Philipp Emanuel Bach's Autobiography—1773*. Hilversum, The Netherlands: Knuf. Facsimile edition from Burney (1773).

NIEDT, FRIEDRICH ERHARDT. 1700–17. *Musicalische Handleitung*. 3 vols. Hamburg: Nicolaus Spieringk, 1700 (vol. 1); Benjamin Schiller, 1706 (vol. 2); Benjamin Schillers Erben, 1717 (vol. 3). Revised edition, ed. Johann Mattheson, Hamburg: Benjamin Schillers Witwe and Johann Christoph Kissner, 1721. Facsimile of the revised edition (Biblioteca Organologica, 32), Buren, The Netherlands: Knuf, 1976. Extracts from vol. 1 translated in Arnold (1931) and in BR; complete translation in Niedt (1989).

———. 1989. *The Musical Guide*. Trans. Pamela L. Poulin and Irmgard C. Taylor, with introduction and notes by Pamela L. Poulin. Oxford: Clarendon Press.

O'DONNELL, JOHN. 1979. "The French Style and the Overtures of Bach." *EM* 7:190–96, 336–45.

OSTHOFF, WOLFGANG, and REINHARD WIESEND, eds. 1987. *Bach und die italienische Musik*. Venice: Centro Tedesco di Studi Veneziani.

PATTEN, NATHAN VAN. 1950. *A Memorial Library of Music at Stanford University*. Stanford, n.p. Catalogue of rare music books, scores, and manuscripts.

PETERSEN, PETER, ed. 1990. *Musikkulturgeschichte: Festschrift für Constantin Floros zum 60. Geburtstag*. Wiesbaden: Breitkopf und Härtel.

PESTELLI, GIORGIO. 1981. "Un'altra rielaborazione bachiana: la fuga della toccata BWV 914." *RIM* 16:40–44.

———. 1985. "Bach, Handel, D. Scarlatti and the Toccata of the Late Baroque." In Williams (1985a, 277–91).

PROTZ, ALBERT. 1957. "Zu Johann Sebastian Bachs 'Capriccio sopra la lontananza del suo fratello dilettissmo'." *Mf* 10: 407.

QUANTZ, JOHANN JOACHIM. 1752. *Versuch einer Anweisung die Flöte traversiere zu spielen*. Berlin: Johann Friedrich Voss. Facsimile of the third edition (Breslau: Johann Friedrich

Korn der Ältere). Kassel: Bärenreiter, 1953. Translated by Edward J. Reilly as *An Essay on Playing the Flute*. London: Faber, 1966.

RADKE, HANS. 1964. "War Johann Sebastian Bach Lautenspieler?" In Heussner (1964, 281–89).

RAMEAU, JEAN-PHILIPPE. 1722. *Traité de l'harmonie*. Paris: Jean-Baptiste-Christophe Ballard. Facsimile, New York: Broude, 1965. Translated by Philipp Gossett as *Treatise on Harmony*. New York: Dover, 1971.

RASCH, RUDOLF. 1986. "Does 'Well-Tempered' Mean 'Equal-Tempered'?" In Stauffer and May (1986, 293–310).

REHM, WOLFGANG, ed. 1983. *Bachiana et alia musicologica: Festschrift Alfred Dürr zum 65. Geburtstag am 3. März 1983*. Kassel: Bärenreiter.

REIDEMEISTER, PETER, and VERONIKA GUTMANN, eds. 1983. *Alte Musik: Praxis und Reflexion*. Winderthur, Germany: Amadeus.

RICHTER, BERNHARD FRIEDRICH. 1902. "Eine Abhandlung Joh. Kuhnaus." *Monatshefte für Musik-Geschichte* 34:147–54.

RIEDEL, HERBOT HUGO. 1969. "Recognition and Re-Cognition: Bach and *The Well-Tempered Clavier I*." Ph.D. diss., University of California, Berkeley.

RIEMANN, HUGO, ed. 1912. *Musikgeschichte in Beispielen; eine Auswahl von 150 Tonsätzen. . . .* Leipzig: E. A. Semmann. With commentary by Arnold Schering.

RIFKIN, JOSHUA. 1985. " '. . . Wobey aber die Singstimmen hinlänglich besetzt seyn müssen . . .': Zum Credo der h-Moll-Messe in der Aufführung Carl Philipp Emanuel Bachs." *BJHM* 9:157–72.

ROBERTS, JOHN H., ed. 1986. *Reinhard Keiser: La forza della virtù*. Handel Sources, 2. New York: Garland.

ROSE, GLORIA. 1968. "Purcell, Michelangelo Rossi and J. S. Bach: Problems of Authorship." *Acta* 40:203–19.

ROSEN, CHARLES. 1972. *The Classical Style: Haydn, Mozart, Beethoven*. New York: Norton.

———. 1988. *Sonata Forms*. Rev. ed. New York: Norton.

———. 1990. "The Shock of the Old." *The New York Review of Books* 37/12 (July 19):46–52.

RUHNKE, MARTIN, ed. 1984. *Georg Philipp Telemann: Thematisch-Systematisches Verzeichnis seiner Werke. Instrumentalwerke*. Band 1. Kassel: Bärenreiter.

RYOM, PETER. 1966–67. "La comparaison entre les versions différentes d'un concerto d'Antonio Vivaldi transcrit par J. S. Bach." *Dansk Aarbog for Musik Forskning* 1966–67:91–111.

———. 1969. "A propos de l'inventaire des oeuvres de l'Antonio Vivaldi: Etude critique des catalogues et nouvelles découvertes." *Vivaldiana* 1:69–114.

———. 1979. *Verzeichnis der Werke Antonio Vivaldis. Kleine Ausgabe*. 2d ed. Leipzig: VEB Deutscher Verlag für Musik.

———. 1986. *Répertoire des Oeuvres d'Antonio Vivaldi: Les compositions instrumentales*. Copenhagen: Engstrøm & Sødring.

SACHS, KLAUS-JÜRGEN. 1980. "Die 'Anleitung . . . , auff allerhand Arth einen Choral durchzuführen', als Paradigma der Lehre und der Satzkunst Johann Sebastian Bachs." *AMw* 37:135–54.

SALZER, FELIX. 1929–30. "Über die Bedeutung der Ornamentik in Philipp Emanuel Bachs Klavierwerken." *Zeitschrift für Musikwissenschaft* 12:398–418.

SCHEIBE, JOHANN ADOLPH. 1738–40. *Der critische Musicus herausgegeben von Johann Adolph Scheibe*. 2 vols. Hamburg: Thomas von Wierings Erben (vol. 1), Rudolph Beneke (vol. 2).

———. 1745. *Johann Adolph Scheibens, Königl. Dänis. Capellmeisters, Critischer Musicus. Neue, vermehrte und verbesserte Auflage*. Leipzig: Bernhard Christoph Breitkopf.

SCHEIDE, WILLIAM H. 1982. " 'Nun ist das Heil und die Kraft' BWV 50: Doppelchörigkeit, Datierung und Bestimmung." *BJ* 68:81–102.

SCHENKER, HEINRICH. 1925–30. *Das Meisterwerke in der Musik: Ein Jahrbuch.* 3 vols. Munich, Vienna, and Berlin: Drei Masken. Facsimile in one volume, Hildesheim, Germany: Olms, 1974.

———. 1984. *Five Graphic Music Analyses.* With a new introduction and glossary by Felix Salzer. New York: Dover.

———, ed. 1984. *J. S. Bach's Chromatic Fantasy and Fugue.* Trans. and ed., with a commentary, by Hedi Siegel. New York: Longman. Originally published Vienna: Universal, 1910.

SCHERING, ARNOLD. 1902–3. "Zur Bach-Forschung." *SIMG* 4: 234–43.

———. 1903–4. "Zur Bach-Forschung II." *SIMG* 5: 565–70.

SCHLEUNING, PETER. 1969. " 'Diese Fantasie ist einzig . . .': Das *Recitativ* in Bachs Chromatischer Fantasie und seine Bedeutung für die Ausbildung der Freien Fantasie." In Geck (1969, 57–73).

———. 1973. *Die Freie Fantasie: Ein Beitrag zur Erforschung der klassischen Klaviermusik.* Göppinger Akademische Beiträge, 76. Göppingen: Kümmerle.

———. 1979. "Verzierungsforschung und Aufführungspraxis: Zum Verhältnis von Notation und Interpretation in der Musik des 18. Jahrhunderts." *BJHM* 3:11–114.

SCHMIEDER, WOLFGANG. 1990. *Thematisch-systematisches Verzeichnis der musikalischen Werke Johann Sebastian Bachs: Bach-Werke-Verzeichnis.* 2d, überarbeitete und erweiterte Ausgabe. Wiesbaden: Breitkopf und Härtel. Originally published Leipzig: Breitkopf und Härtel, 1950.

SCHREYER, JOHANNES. 1911–13. *Beiträge zur Bach-Kritik.* 2 vols. Leipzig: Merseburger.

SCHULENBERG, DAVID. 1982. "Composition as Variation: Inquiries into the Compositional Procedures of the Bach Circle of Composers." *CM* 33:57–87.

———. 1984. *The Instrumental Music of Carl Philipp Emanuel Bach.* Studies in Musicology, 77. Ann Arbor, MI: UMI Research Press.

———. 1987. Review of Berg (1985). *JAMS* 40: 105–12.

———. 1988. "Performing C. P. E. Bach: Some Open Questions." *EM* 16:542–51.

———. 1990. "Authenticity and Expression in the Harpsichord Works of J. S. Bach." *JM* 8:449–76.

———. 1991. Review of Kenyon (1988). *CM* 48:78–87.

———. N.d. "Musical Expression and Musical Rhetoric in the Keyboard Works of J. S. Bach." In Benstock (n.d.).

SCHULZE, HANS-JOACHIM. 1966. "Wer intavolierte Johann Sebastian Bachs Lautenkompositionen?" *Mf* 19:32–39.

———. 1975. "Die Bach-Überlieferung: Plädoyer für ein notwendiges Buch." *BMw* 17:45–58.

———. 1976. "Melodiezitate und Mehrtextigkeit in der Bauernkantate und in den Goldbergvariationen." *BJ* 62:58–72.

———. 1978. "Das Stück in Goldpapier." *BJ* 64:19–42.

———. 1979a. "Cembaloimprovisation bei Johann Sebastian Bach: Versuch einer Übersicht." In *Zu Fragen der Improvisation in der Instrumentalmusik der ersten Hälfte des 18. Jahrhunderts,* 50–57. Studien zur Aufführungspraxis und Interpretation von Instrumentalmusik des 18. Jahrhunderts, 10. Blankenburg/Harz: n.p.

———. 1979b. "Ein 'Dresdner Menuett' im zweiten Klavierbüchlein der Anna Magdalena Bach. Nebst Hinweisen zur Überlieferung einiger Kammermusikwerke Bachs." *BJ* 65:45–64.

————, ed. 1979c. *Johann Sebastian Bach: Drei Lautenkompositionen in zeitgenössischer Tabulatur.* Leipzig: Zentralantiquäriat der DDR.

————. 1984a. *Studien zur Bach-Überlieferung im 18. Jahrhundert.* Leipzig: Edition Peters.

————, ed. 1984b. *J. S. Bach: Fantasie und Fuge C-moll für Cembalo.* Facsimile of Dl Mus. 2405 T 52, Aut. 3 (autograph of BWV 906). Leipzig: Zentralantiquäriat der DDR.

————. 1991. "Bach und Buxtehude. Eine wenig beachtete Quelle in der Carnegie Library zu Pittsburgh/PA." *BJ* 77:177–81.

SCHWANDT, ERICH. 1990. "Questions concerning the Edition of the 'Goldberg Variations' in the *Neue Bach Ausgabe* [*sic*]." *Performance Practice Review* 3/1 (Spring):58–69.

SCHWEITZER, ALBERT. 1934. *J. S. Bach.* 10th ed. Leipzig: Breitkopf und Härtel. Enlarged from the original *J. S. Bach le musicien-poète.* Leipzig: Breitkopf und Härtel, 1905.

SEATON, DOUGLAS. 1975. "The Autograph: An Early Version of the 'Art of Fugue'." In "Seminar Report" (see Wolff 1975), *CM* 19:54–59.

SEIDEL, ELMAR. 1985. "Die harmonische Grossform der Fuge von Bachs Toccata in C-dur (BWV 564) und die Tonartenlehre deutscher Theoretiker der Bachzeit." In Wolff (1985d, 25–40).

SEIFFERT, MAX. 1899. *Geschichte der Klaviermusik.* Leipzig: Breitkopf und Härtel. Facsimile, Hildesheim, Germany: Olms, 1966.

SELFRIDGE-FIELD, ELEANOR. 1990. *The Music of Benedetto and Alessandro Marcello: A Thematic Catalogue with Commentary on the Composers, Repertory, and Sources.* Oxford: Clarendon Press.

SHELDON, DAVID A. 1975. "The Galant Style Revisited and Re-evaluated." *Acta* 4:240–70.

————. 1989–90. "The Concept *galant* in the 18th [*sic*] Century." *JMR* 9:89–108.

SHEVELOFF, JOEL. 1986. "Domenico Scarlatti: Tercentenary Frustrations (Part II)." *MQ* 72:90–118.

SIEGELE, ULRICH. 1960. "Die musiktheoretische Lehre einer Bachschen Gigue." *AMw* 17:152–67.

————. 1975. *Kompositionsweise und Bearbeitungstechnik in der Instrumentalmusik Johann Sebastian Bachs.* [2d ed.] Tübinger Beiträge zur Musikwissenschaft, 3. Neuhausen-Stuttgart: Hänssler.

————. 1983. "Bachs Stellung in der Leipziger Kulturpolitik seiner Zeit." *BJ* 69:7–50.

————. 1989. "The Four Conceptual Stages of the Fugue in C Minor, *WTC* I." In Franklin (1989a, 197–224).

SILBIGER, ALEXANDER, ed. 1987. *Bologna, Civico museo bibliografico musicale, MS DD/53; Florence, Biblioteca del Conservatorio de musica Luigi Cherubini, MS D 2534.* Seventeenth-Century Keyboard Music, 10. New York: Garland.

SNYDER, KERALA J. 1980. "Dietrich Buxtehude's Studies in Learned Counterpoint." *JAMS* 33:544–64.

————. 1987. *Dieterich Buxtehude: Organist in Lübeck.* New York: Schirmer Books.

SPITTA, PHILIPP. 1873–80. *Johann Sebastian Bach.* 3 vols. Leipzig: Breitkopf und Härtel. Trans. Clara Bell and J. A. Fuller Maitland. London: Novello, 1889. Reprint, New York: Dover, 1952.

STARKE, DAVID. 1972. *Frobergers Suitentänze.* Darmstadt: Edition Tonos.

STAUFFER, GEORGE. 1980. *The Organ Preludes of Johann Sebastian Bach.* Studies in Musicology, 27. Ann Arbor, MI: UMI Research Press.

————. 1983a. "Bach's Pastorale in F: A Closer Look at a Maligned Work." *Organ Yearbook* 14:44–60.

——. 1983b. "Johann Mattheson and J. S. Bach: The Hamburg Connection." In Buelow and Marx (1983, 353–68).

——. 1987. "Forkel's Letters to Hoffmeister & Kühnel: A Bach Biographical Source Recovered." *JM* 5:549–61.

——. 1989. " 'This fantasia . . . never had its like': On the Enigma and Chronology of Bach's Chromatic Fantasia and Fugue in D Minor, BWV 903." In Franklin (1989a, 160–82).

——, ed. 1990. *The Forkel–Hoffmeister & Kühnel Correspondence: A Document of the Early 19th-Century Bach Revival*. New York: C. F. Peters.

STAUFFER, GEORGE, and ERNEST MAY, eds. 1986. *J. S. Bach as Organist: His Instruments, Music, and Performance Practices*. Bloomington: Indiana University Press.

STEVENS, JANE. 1971. "An Eighteenth-Century Description of Concerto First-Movement Form." *JAMS* 24:89–95.

STINSON, RUSSELL. 1989a. *The Bach Manuscripts of Johann Peter Kellner and His Circle: A Case Study in Reception History*. Durham, NC, and London: Duke University Press.

——. 1989b. "Toward a Chronology of Bach's Instrumental Music: Observations on Three Keyboard Works." *JM* 7:440–70.

——. 1990. "The 'critischer Musikus' as Keyboard Transcriber? Scheibe, Bach, and Vivaldi." *JMR* 9:255–71.

——, ed. 1992. *Keyboard Transcirptions from the Bach Circle*. Recent Researches in the Music of the Baroque Era, 69. Madison, WI: A-R Editions.

SUCHALLA ERNST, ed. 1985. *Briefe von Carl Philipp Emanuel Bach an Johann Gottlob Immanuel Breitkopf und Johann Nikolaus Forkel*. Mainzer Studien zur Musikwissenschaft, 19. Tutzing: Hans Schneider.

SWANTON, PHILIP. 1985. "Der Generalbass in J. S. Bachs Kantaten mit obligater Orgel." *BJHM* 9:89–155.

TAGLIAVINI, LUIGI FERDINANDO. 1986. "Bach's Organ Transcription of Vivaldi's 'Grosso Mogul' Concerto." In Stauffer and May (1986, 240–55).

TALBOT, MICHAEL. 1990. *Tomaso Albinoni: The Venetian Composer and His World*. Oxford: Clarendon Press.

TERRY, MIRIAM. 1969. "C. P. E. Bach and J. J. H. Westphal—A Clarification." *JAMS* 22:106–15.

TOVEY, DONALD FRANCIS, ed. 1924. *Johann Sebastian Bach: Forty-Eight Preludes and Fugues*. 2 vols. (analytical commentary and musical text). London: Oxford University Press.

——. 1931. *A Companion to "The Art of Fugue."* London: Oxford University Press.

VENDRIX, PHILIPPE. 1989. "Zum Lamento aus J. S. Bachs Capriccio BWV 992 und seinen Vorläufern." *BJ* 75:197–201.

WADE, RACHEL. 1981. *The Keyboard Concertos of Carl Philipp Emanuel Bach*. Studies in Musicology, 48. Ann Arbor, MI: UMI Research Press.

WAGNER, GÜNTHER. 1979. "Concerto-Elemente in Bachs zweistimmigen Inventionen." *BJ* 65:37–44.

WALKER, PAUL. 1985–86. "From Renaissance 'Fuga' to Baroque Fugue: The Role of the 'Sweelinck Theory Manuscripts'." *SJ* 7–8:93–104.

——. 1989. "Die Entstehung der Permutationsfuge." *BJ* 75:21–41.

——, ed. 1990. *Church, Stage, and Studio: Music and Its Contexts in Seventeenth-Century Germany*. Studies in Musicology, 107. Ann Arbor, MI: UMI Research Press.

WALTER, HORST. 1976. "Das Posthornsignal bei Haydn und anderen Komponisten des 18. Jahrhunderts." *Haydn-Studien* 4/1 (May):21–34.

WALTHER, JOHANN. 1708. *Praecepta der musicalischen Composition* [Ms.]. Ed. Peter Benary. Leipzig: VEB Breitkopf und Härtel, 1955.

———. 1732. *Musicalisches Lexicon oder Musicalische Bibliothec.* . . . Leipzig: Wolffgang Deer. Facsimile ed. Richard Schaal, Dokumenta Musicologica 1/3. Kassel: Bärenreiter, 1953.

WIEMER, WOLFGANG. 1977. *Die wiederhergestellte Ordnung in Johann Sebastian Bachs Kunst der Fuge.* Wiesbaden: Breitkopf und Härtel.

———. 1987. "Ein Bach-Doppelfund: Verschollene Gerber-Abschrift (BWV 914 und 996) und unbekannte Choralsammlung Christian Friedrich Penzels." *BJ* 73:29–73.

———. 1988. "Carl Philipp Emanuel Bachs Fantasie in c-Moll—ein Lamento auf den Tod des Vaters?" *BJ* 74:163–77.

WILLIAMS, PETER. 1980–84. *The Organ Music of J. S. Bach.* 3 vols. Cambridge: Cambridge University Press.

———. 1981. "BWV 565: A Toccata in D Minor for Organ by J. S. Bach?" *EM* 9:330–37.

———. 1983a. "J. S. Bach's *Well-tempered Clavier*: A New Approach." *EM* 11:46–52, 332–39.

———. 1983b. "The Snares and Delusions of Musical Rhetoric: Some Examples from Recent Writings on J. S. Bach." In Reidemeister and Gutmann (1983, 230–40).

———. 1984. "Bach's G Minor Sonata for Viola da Gamba and Harpsichord BWV 1029." *EM* 12:345–54.

———, ed. 1985a. *Bach, Handel, Scarlatti: Tercentenary Essays.* Cambridge: Cambridge University Press.

———. 1985b. "Encounters with the Chromatic Fourth; or, More on Figurenlehre, 1 [and 2]." *MT* 126:276–78, 339–43.

———. 1985c. "*Figurae* in the Keyboard Works of Scarlatti, Handel and Bach: An Introduction." In Williams (1985a, 327–46).

———. 1986a. "The Acquisitive Minds of Handel & Bach: Some Reflections on the Nature of 'Influences'." In Douglass, Jander, and Owen (1986, 267–81).

———, ed. 1986b. *J. S. Bach: Kunst der Fuge.* London: Eulenburg.

———. 1986–87. "Hints for Performance in J. S. Bach's *Clavierübung* Prints." *EKJ* 5:29–44.

———. 1989. "French Overture Conventions in the Hands of the Young Bach and Handel." In Franklin (1989a, 183–93).

———. 1990. "Keyboards." In Brown and Sadie (1990, 20–43).

WOLFF, CHRISTOPH. 1968. *Der stile antico in der Musik Johann Sebastian Bachs: Studien zu Bach's Spätwerk.* Wiesbaden: Franz Steiner.

———. 1971. "New Research on Bach's *Musical Offering*." *MQ*, 57:379–408. Also in Wolff (1991b, 239–58).

———. 1974. "Johann Sebastian Bach's 'Sterbechoral': Kritische Fragen zu einem Mythos." In Marshall (1974, 283–97). Translated as "The Deathbed Chorale: Exposing a Myth" in Wolff (1991b, 282–94).

———. 1975. "The Last Fugue: Unfinished?" Contribution to "Seminar Report: Bach's 'Art of Fugue': An Examination of the Sources." *CM* 19:71–77. Also as "Bach's Last Fugue: Unfinished?" in Wolff (1991b, 259–64).

———. 1976. "Bach's Handexemplar of the Goldberg Variations." *JAMS* 29:224–41. Also as "The Handexemplar of the Goldberg Variations," in Wolff (1991b, 162–77).

———. 1979. "Textkritische Bemerkungen zum Originaldruck der Bachschen Partiten." *BJ* 65:65–74. Translated as "Text-Critical Comments on the Original Print of the Partitas," in Wolff (1991b, 214–22).

———. 1982. "Das Hamburger Buxtehude-Bild: Ein Beitrag zur musikalischen Ikonographie und zum Umkreis von Johann Adam Reinken." In A. Grassmann and W. Neuge-bauer, eds., *800 Jahre Musik in Lübeck*, 64–79. Lübeck: Der Senat der Hansestadt Lübeck—Amt für Kultur. Translated by Thomson Moore as "The Hamburg Group Portrait with Reinken and Buxtehude: An Essay in Musical Iconography." In *Boston Early Music Festival and Exhibition 8–14 June 1987* (program book), 102–12.

———. 1983a. Article on Johann Sebastian Bach in *The New Grove Bach Family*. The Composer Biography Series. New York: Norton. Revision of the article in NG.

———. 1983b. Review of Franklin and Dow (1980). *BJ* 69:123–4.

———. 1983c. "Zur Chronologie und Kompositionsgeschichte von Bachs Kunst der Fuge." *BMw* 25:130–42. Translated as "The Compositional History of the Art of Fugue," in Wolff (1991b, 265–81).

———, ed. 1984. *Johann Sebastian Bach: Clavier-Übung Teil I–IV. Faksimile-Ausgabe nach Exemplaren der Musikbibliothek der Stadt Leipzig*. Leipzig: Peters. Four volumes plus commentary volume. Page references are to the latter, which is reprinted as "The Clavier-Übung Series" in Wolff (1991b, 189–213).

———. 1985a. "Bach's Leipzig Chamber Music." *EM* 13:65–75. Also in Wolff (1991b, 223–38).

———, ed. 1985b. *Johann Sebastian Bach: Orgelchoräle der Neumeister-Sammlung*. New Haven, CT: Yale University Press, and Kassel: Bärenreiter.

———, ed. 1985c. *The Neumeister Collection of Chorale Preludes from the Bach Circle: Facsimile Edition of the Yale Manuscript LM 4708*. New Haven, CT: Yale University Press. "Introduction" reprinted as "The Neumeister Collection of Chorale Preludes from the Bach Circle," in Wolff (1991b, 107–27).

———, ed. 1985d. *Orgel, Orgelmusik und Orgelspiel: Festschrift Michael Schneider zum 75. Geburtstag*. Kassel: Bärenreiter.

———. 1986a. "Johann Adam Reinken und Johann Sebastian Bach: Zum Kontext des Bachschen Frühwerkes." *BJ* 71:99–117. Translated as "Johann Adam Reinken and Johann Sebastian Bach: On the Context of Bach's Early Works" in Stauffer and May (1986, 57–80). Translation reprinted in Wolff (1991b, 56–71).

———. 1986b. "Johann Sebastian Bach's Third Part of the *Clavier-Übung*." In Douglass, Jander, and Owen (1986, 283–91).

———. 1987a. "Bach und das Fortepiano." In Osthoff and Wiesend (1987, 197–209).

———, ed. 1987b. *Johann Sebastian Bach: Die Kunst der Fuge*. 2 vols. Frankfurt: C. F. Peters.

———. 1988a. "Bachs Spätwerk: Versuch einer Definition." In Wolff (1988b, 15–22). Translated as "Toward a Definition of the Last Period of Bach's Work" in Wolff (1991b, 359–76).

———, ed. 1988b. *Johann Sebastian Bachs Spätwerk und dessen Umfeld: Perspektiven und Probleme. Bericht über das wissenschaftliche Symposion anlässlich des 61. Bachfestes der Neuen Bachgesellschaft Duisburg, 28–30. Mai 1986*. Kassel: Bärenreiter.

———. 1988c. "Vivaldi's Compositional Art and the Process of 'Musical Thinking'." In Fanna and Morelli (1988, 1–17). Reprinted as "Vivaldi's Compositional Art, Bach, and the Process of 'Musical Thinking' " in Wolff (1991b, 72–83).

———. 1989. "From Berlin to Lodz: The Spitta Collection Resurfaces." *Music Library Association Notes* 46:311–27.

———. 1991a. "Apropos the Musical Offering: The Thema Regium and the Term *Ricercar*." In Wolff (1991b, 324–39). A revised translation of: (1) "Überlegungen zum 'Thema Regium'," *BJ* 59 (1973): 33–38, and (2) "Der Terminus 'Ricercar' in Bachs Musikalischem Opfer," *BJ* 53 (1967):70–81.

———. 1991b. *Johann Sebastian Bach: Essays on His Life and Music*. Cambridge, MA:

Harvard University Press. Reprints of thirty-two articles, those originally in German translated into English. References are to the original publications except where this volume contains new material.

WOTQUENNE, ALFRED. 1905. *Catalogue thématique des oeuvres de Charles Philippe Emmanuel Bach (1714–1788)*. Leipzig: Breitkopf und Härtel. Reprints, 1964, 1972, as *Thematisches Verzeichnis der Werke von Carl Philipp Emanuel Bach*.

ZASLAW, NEAL. 1989. *Mozart's Symphonies: Context, Performance Practice, Reception*. Oxford: Clarendon Press.

ZEHNDER, JEAN-CLAUDE. 1988. "Georg Böhm und Johann Sebastian Bach: Zur Chronologie der Bachschen Stilentwicklung." *BJ* 74:73–110.

———. 1991. "Giuseppe Torelli und Johann Sebastian Bach: Zu Bachs Weimarer Konzertform." *BJ* 77:33–95.

ZIETZ, HERMANN. 1969. *Quellenkritische Untersuchungen an den Bach-Handschriften P 801, P 802 und P 803. . . .* Hamburg: Wagner.

NOTE ON THE INDEXES: This is a selective index. Authors and editors cited in the text are indexed only where they are of historical significance. In general, the content of tables and bibliographic references is not indexed, nor are most musical sources (manuscripts). The Index of Works includes doubtful and spurious works that have been attributed to J. S. Bach.

The principal discussion of a work or topic is in **boldface**; discussions accompanied by musical examples are in *italic*; principal discussions illustrated by examples are in ***boldface italic***.

Index of Works

Collections and Groups of Works

Individual Works by BWV Number

General Index

461

O